www.wadsworth.com

www.wadsworth.com is the World Wide Web site for Thomson Wadsworth and is your direct source to dozens of online resources.

At *www.wadsworth.com* you can find out about supplements, demonstration software, and student resources. You can also send email to many of our authors and preview new publications and exciting new technologies.

www.wadsworth.com
Changing the way the world learns®

American Foreign Policy
and Process

American Foreign Policy and Process

Fourth Edition

JAMES M. McCORMICK
Iowa State University

THOMSON
WADSWORTH

Australia • Canada • Mexico • Singapore • Spain
United Kingdom • United States

THOMSON
WADSWORTH

Publisher: Clark Baxter
Executive Editor: David Tatom
Senior Development Editor: Stacey Sims
Assistant Editor: Rebecca Green
Editorial Assistant: Reena Thomas
Senior Marketing Manager: Janise Fry
Marketing Assistant: Tara Pierson
Project Manager, Editorial Production: Jennifer Klos

Print Buyer: Lisa Claudeanos
Permissions Editor: Joohee Lee
Production Service: Stratford Publishing Services
Copy Editor: Cathy Jewell
Cover Designer: Brian Salisbury
Cover Image: David Frazier/Getty Images;
    Marcus Lyon/Getty Images
Text and Cover Printer: Webcom
Compositor: Stratford Publishing Services

Printed in Canada
1 2 3 4 5 6 7 08 07 06 05 04

For more information about our products, contact us at:
Thomson Learning Academic Resource Center
1-800-423-0563

For permission to use material from this text or product, submit a request online at
http://www.thomsonrights.com.
Any additional questions about permissions can be submitted by email to
thomsonrights@thomson.com.

Library of Congress Control Number: 2004102432

ISBN 0-534-61853-7

Thomson Wadsworth
10 Davis Drive
Belmont, CA 94002-3098
USA

Asia
Thomson Learning
5 Shenton Way #01-01
UIC Building
Singapore 068808

Australia/New Zealand
Thomson Learning
102 Dodds Street
Southbank, Victoria 3006
Australia

Canada
Nelson
1120 Birchmount Road
Toronto, Ontario M1K 5G4
Canada

Europe/Middle East/Africa
Thomson Learning
High Holborn House
50/51 Bedford Row
London WC1R 4LR
United Kingdom

Latin America
Thomson Learning
Seneca, 53
Colonia Polanco
11560 Mexico D.F.
Mexico

Spain/Portugal
Paraninfo
Calle Magallanes, 25
28015 Madrid, Spain

In memory of my parents

Contents

Documents and Document Summaries, Figures, Tables, and Maps

DOCUMENTS AND DOCUMENT SUMMARIES

FIGURES

MAPS

TABLES

Preface

The fourth edition of *American Foreign Policy and Process* is revised and updated, covering policy and process developments through the George W. Bush administration and assessing how the tragic events of September 11, 2001 affected U.S. foreign policy. The book is intended to serve as a comprehensive text for the first course in U.S. foreign policy and as a supplemental text in a global politics or comparative foreign policy course where American actions are analyzed. In addition, it remains appropriate as a ready reference for the first graduate course in the study of American foreign policy or the foreign policy process.

Values and beliefs continue as the basic organizing theme for the text because policy actions are always taken within a value context. Yet, this emphasis on values and beliefs is not necessarily presented in a way to promote a particular point of view. Instead, the intent is to portray how values and beliefs toward foreign affairs have changed over the course of the history of the republic and how U.S. foreign policy has thus changed from its earliest years and since September 11.

To accomplish this end, the text is once again divided into three parts. Part I, which consists of six chapters, focuses upon the values and beliefs that have shaped policy historically (Chapter 1), during the height of American globalism and the Cold War years (Chapters 2 and 3), during the post-Vietnam years of the Nixon, Ford, Carter, and Reagan administrations (Chapter 4), during the immediate post-Cold War years of the Bush and Clinton administrations years (Chapter 5) and before and after 9/11 during the George W. Bush administration (Chapter 6). In each of these chapters, I discuss a wide variety of foreign policy actions that illustrate the values and beliefs of the particular period and administration. Part II, which also consists of six chapters, examines in some detail the policy-making process and how various institutions and groups—the president (Chapter 7), the Congress (Chapter 8), the key bureaucracies (Chapters 9 and 10), political parties and interest groups (Chapter 11), and the media and public opinion (Chapter 12)—compete to promote their own values and beliefs in American policy abroad. At this juncture, too, I provide essential information on how foreign policy decisions are made, and I assess the relative importance of these institutions and groups in that process. Part III, a concluding chapter, discusses alternate views of what values and beliefs may shape American foreign policy in the post–9/11 world.

Those familiar with the third edition will immediately recognize both continuity and change from that edition. First, each chapter has been revised and updated to reflect important changes in both U.S. policy and in the policy-making process, especially in light of September 11. Second, while the total number of chapters has remained the same at thirteen, several chapters have been restructured and a new separate chapter on the George W. Bush administration has been added. While the first three chapters largely remain the same, each has been trimmed to place a greater focus on key themes in each one. Chapter 4 consolidates the fourth chapter and part of the fifth from the third edition, and it now contrasts the foreign policy approaches adopted by the Nixon administration through the Reagan administration from the Vietnam War years to the end of the Cold War. Chapter 5 now compares the two administrations directing American foreign policy immediately after the end of the Cold War (George H.W. Bush and Bill Clinton) and contrasts their differing approaches to U.S. actions abroad. Chapter 6 is entirely new and focuses on the foreign policy of the George W. Bush administration, both prior to and after 9/11. Chapters 7 and 8 update and include the latest research on the role of the president and the role of Congress through the George W. Bush presidency and illustrate how the executive/congressional relations have changed in light of September 11. Chapters 9 and 10 once again discuss the bureaucracies across two chapters. These chapters now include a greater discussion of the economic bureaucracies, especially the Office of the United States Trade Representatives, and the new security bureaucracy, the Department of Homeland Security. Chapters 11 and 12 continue to provide separate treatments of political parties and interest groups on the one hand and media and public opinion on the other. The most significant additions are the coverage of new interest groups involved in the foreign policy process, an assessment of the news media after 9/11 and the war in Iraq, and the latest public opinion analyses after 9/11 and the Iraq War.

Third, the fourth edition continued to incorporate a number of tables, figures, and maps to portray more fully the story of American foreign policy and the process of policy formulation. Similarly, I continue to provide summaries of key foreign policy documents (e.g., NSC-68, NAFTA or GATT accords) to enable students to gain a greater understanding of these important foreign policy actions. In both instances, though, I have trimmed the number of each to give greater focus to the critical entries. Finally, and importantly, I give considerable attention to making the discussion more accessible and more "reader friendly" by providing the most up-to-date policy examples and utilizing numerous headings throughout the text.

In the course of developing the fourth edition, I have incurred a number of debts to individuals and institutions. I am now happy to have the opportunity to acknowledge my thanks to them publicly. First of all, colleagues at several institutions offered their comments and suggestions for improving the book from the third edition: Eric Einhorn of University of Massachusetts at Amherst, Yale Ferguson of Rutgers, and Pat Regan of Binghamton University undertook comprehensive and careful reviews; Dick Weisfelder of the University of Toledo and Bob Wendzel of the Air War University showed continued interest in a new edition and encouraged me to complete one—soon; and other colleagues who have used the text informally also made suggestions for improvement. I am particularly indebted once again to my friend and colleague, Eugene R. Wittkopf of Louisiana State University, for allowing me to use some data on U.S. foreign policy and for sharing some results of his latest public opinion analyses with me. I also want to thank James Meernik of the University of North Texas for allowing me to use some data that he had previously collected on the use of American force abroad. A substantial part of Chapter 6 is drawn from a chapter that I contributed to Steven E. Schier's *High Risk and Big Ambition: The Presidency of George W. Bush*, published by the University of Pittsburgh Press. I am grateful to the University of Pittsburgh Press for allowing me to use that material in this volume. Despite the many useful comments from colleagues and friends, an author's stubbornness often stood in the way of incorporating all of these suggestions; nonetheless, I am most grateful for the time and energy provided on my behalf by these good colleagues.

Second, colleagues and staff in the Department of Political Science at Iowa State University and elsewhere provided moral support from time to time, especially as I sought to balance my administrative and research duties to complete this revision. I particularly want to thank Christopher Ball, Young Kihl, Richard Mansbach, Neil Mitchell, and Clive Thomas for their suggestions and encouragement while I was undertaking these revisions. Barb Marvick, Joyce Wray, and Darlene Brace generously afforded me various forms of assistance during the course of doing these revisions, for which I am most thankful. I particularly want to acknowledge the excellent work of Barb Marvick in creating several tables and figures for various chapters. Several student assistants—John Chiodo, Andrea Rheinhart, Christopher Roberts, Kim Saak, and Brandi Scott—were also helpful to me in commenting on previous chapters, collecting some specific pieces of data, and assisting with the development of tables and the bibliography. I am also grateful to officials at various executive branch agencies, congressional offices, and the Library of Congress's Congressional Research Service who answered my peculiar and numerous inquiries over the years. Finally, I am delighted to thank the staff of the William Robert Parks and Ellen Sorge Parks Library at Iowa State University. They were generous with their time in helping me obtain numerous idiosyncratic pieces of information on American foreign policy.

Third, students in my U.S. Foreign Policy and Current Issues in American Foreign Policy courses have often unwittingly inspired my work on many of the topics in this volume. They have endured virtually all of the arguments presented here, and they often questioned them. By doing so, they have encouraged me to rethink my views and to pursue several important new lines of research. From that process, they have unwittingly contributed to making this a better text, and they deserve my heartfelt thanks.

Fourth, this revision started when I was still under contract with F. E. Peacock Publishers, Inc., and I would be remiss if I did not thank Ted Peacock and Dick Welna for their support and friendship over the years and for their encouragement of this new edition. As I noted in each of the earlier editions, from my first association with Peacock Publishers, I sensed the commitment to its authors and to quality publishing. I can report that such a commitment continued through Peacock Publishers's incorporation into Thomson Wadsworth. Happily, too, I can sense the same kind of commitment from David Tatom, Executive Editor, Political Science, at Thomson Wadsworth, and I look forward to a long association with him and Thomson Wadsworth. I have also benefited from the good and able work by my development editor at Thomson Wadsworth for this fourth edition, Stacey Sims, and I want to thank her for such generous efforts on my behalf. At the production stage, Dennis Troutman of Stratford Publishing Services was most helpful and also deserves my thanks for his assistance.

Finally, let me thank three other important people in my life. Thanks to Carol for listening so patiently—and continuously—to my travails over trying to complete the fourth edition and for serving as such a model of scholarly commitment with her own writing. Thanks, too, to my parents, Joseph A. and Helen M. McCormick, to whose memory I lovingly dedicate this edition.

All of these individuals and institutions (and others whom I may have inadvertently omitted) deserve my sincere thanks. As always, though, final responsibility for the book rests with me, and any errors of fact and interpretation are mine alone.

PART I

Values and Policies
in American
Foreign Affairs

In Part I of *American Foreign Policy and Process,* we survey the beliefs and values that have been the basis of America's foreign policy actions. While we provide the reader with an overview of the beliefs that have shaped American foreign policy throughout its history, we place special emphasis on the post–World War II period—the era of greatest American global involvement. Values and beliefs have been chosen as the basic organizing scheme because policy actions are always taken within such a value context. The beginning analyst who can appreciate how belief systems influence policy choices will be in a good position to understand the foreign policy actions of a nation.

Values and beliefs, however, cannot be understood in isolation; their importance is useful only within the context of actual foreign policy behavior. Thus, as an aid in appreciating how beliefs and attitudes have shaped American policy, we provide a narrative of foreign policy actions that reflect the underlying belief system during various periods of U.S. diplomatic history. It is our hope that through illustrations of both beliefs and actions, the reader will come away better able to interpret the foreign policy of the United States.

To accomplish these ends, Part I is divided into six chapters. In Chapter 1, we begin our analysis by discussing the effects of two important traditions in American foreign policy: the commitment to isolationism and the reliance on moral principle as important foreign policy guides. These traditions are reviewed to illustrate how they affected American international behavior throughout the first 150 years of the nation and how they continue to influence American policy to the present day. In Chapter 2, we focus on the development of American globalism in the immediate post–World War II years and how America's beliefs about the world changed sharply. We discuss in detail the emergence of the Cold War and the military, economic, and political dimensions of the new U.S. foreign policy doctrine—the global containment of communism. This doctrine both represented a dramatic departure from America's isolationist past, because it called for universal action on the part of the United States, and reflected substantial continuity as well, because it sought to be grounded in moral principle. In Chapter 3, we describe the new set of values and beliefs—the Cold War consensus—that came to dominate America's thinking about its role in the world from the late 1940s to the mid-1960s. This consensus produced a discernible set of foreign policy responses by the United States. In this chapter, too, we analyze how these Cold War beliefs came under attack from abroad (through the weakening of the Eastern and Western blocs, the emergence of the Sino-Soviet split, the development of the nonaligned movement) and at home (principally over the Vietnam War) and how commitment to them within the American leadership and the public changed.

With the breakdown of the Cold War consensus, finalized by the Vietnam War, succeeding administrations attempted to bring forth new foreign policy perspectives to replace this shattered worldview. From the late 1960s to the present, the dominant foreign policy beliefs of U.S. policy makers have shown a considerable degree of fluctuation from one administration to the next. We have witnessed movement from the realist approach adopted by the Nixon–Ford administrations to the idealist approach of the Carter administration, then back to elements of the Cold War in the Reagan administration, especially in its first term. In turn, the Bush administration adopted a more realist approach as it sought to deal with the ending of the Cold War. The Clinton administration sought to retard the isolationist impulse in the post–Cold War era and attempted to follow some familiar democratic principles as a guide to America's future foreign policy. The George W. Bush administration initially sought to introduce a "distinctly American internationalism," but the events of September 11, 2001, propelled the administration to expand its unilateralist approach and to pursue a new globalism known as the "war on terrorism."

The second half of Part I focuses on the differing value emphases within these administrations and how they have produced differing U.S. foreign policy behavior. In Chapter 4, we first compare the "realist" approach that President Richard Nixon brought to foreign policy in the late 1960s and early 1970s with the "idealist" approach that President Jimmy Carter adopted in the late 1970s and illustrate the sharp differences between them. The former administration sought to introduce a "power politics" approach; the latter sought to reintroduce a stronger moral content to U.S. actions abroad, especially with regard to global human rights. Neither approach, however, succeeded in maintaining the support of the American people for very long, and both came under attack from critics at home and abroad.

In turn, the Carter administration was replaced by the Reagan administration. That administration initially adopted a bipolar view of the world—one closely reminiscent of the containment and Cold War policies of three decades earlier. While this approach enjoyed some initial success, it, too, encountered substantial resistance. By the end of the first term and the beginning of the second term of the Reagan presidency, a discernible change in course had taken place. Reagan's earlier approach was replaced by one that sought to be more accommodative in bilateral relations with the Soviet Union, even as it continued to challenge that nation for influence in other areas of the world.

In Chapter 5, we evaluate the approaches adopted by the George H. W. Bush administration and the William J. Clinton administration as the Cold War between the United States and the Soviet Union ended. The Bush administration adopted many of the values and beliefs of the second term of the Reagan administration, but it also sought to put its own stamp on foreign policy. Most notably, the Bush administration tried to adopt foreign policy values that would allow it to address the significant transformations that had taken place in the international Communist movement. In reality, the approach largely resembled a combination of realist and idealist beliefs without setting a clear course for the post–Cold War era. Like the Bush administration, the Clinton administration initially had great difficulty developing a coherent set of policies to follow from the principles that it thought important to promote. Over the course of its eight years in office, the Clinton administration moved from an idealist approach toward a more realist one. During the early years, the Clinton administration emphasized economic engagement and the "strategy of enlargement" of market democracies. Faced with a variety of global challenges that did not easily fit within that framework, the Clinton administration moved in the direction of a more realist approach during its second term in office. In many ways, the foreign policy approaches of Bush and Clinton also failed to capture the imagination of the American public, and, with an exception or two in both administrations, neither succeeded in placing a permanent stamp on the direction of American foreign policy.

In Chapter 6, we survey the initial values and beliefs that the George W. Bush administration brought to policy and the initial policies that it pursued from those values. In particular, we focus on the impact of the events of September 11, 2001, and how that set of events appeared to change the scope and direction of administration policy. We also consider whether the new American "war on terrorism" will have the effect of producing a new foreign policy consensus.

1

America's Traditions in Foreign Policy

Wherever the standard of freedom and Independence has been
or shall be unfurled, there will her heart, her benedictions
and her prayers be. But she goes not abroad, in search of monsters
to destroy. She is the well-wisher to the freedom and independence
of all. She is the champion and vindicator only of her own.

SECRETARY OF STATE JOHN QUINCY ADAMS
JULY 4, 1821

Do not think . . . that the questions of the day are mere questions
of policy and diplomacy. They are shot through with the principles of life.
We dare not turn from the principle that morality and not expediency
is the thing that must guide us and that we will never condone
iniquity because it is most convenient to do so.

PRESIDENT WOODROW WILSON
OCTOBER 1913

Politics, at its roots, deals with values and value differences among individuals, groups, and nations. Various definitions of the term *politics* attest to the central place that values play in political life. Political scientist Harold Lasswell has written, for example, that politics "is the study of influence and the influential. . . . The influentials are those who get the most of what there is to get."[1] What there is to get, Lasswell continued, is values, such as "*deference, income, and safety*."[2] Drawing upon Aristotle and Max Weber, Robert Dahl notes that what seems to be common across different definitions of politics is that they deal with values such as power, rule, and authority.[3] David Easton's famous definition of politics is even more explicit in its assessment of the relationship between politics and values: "Politics is the authoritative allocation of *values*."[4] According to this definition, authority structures (e.g., governments) distribute something, and that something is values.

Values refer to "modes of conduct and end-states of existence" that guide people's lives. They are "abstract ideals" that serve as an "imperative" for action.[5] Further, values are viewed as "goods" (not in a material, but in an ethical sense) that ought to be obtained or maintained by a person or a society. In the Declaration of Independence, for instance, the values of life, liberty, and the pursuit of happiness were explicitly stated as reasons for creating the United States. These values, moreover, came to serve as guides to political action in the earliest days of the nation. Indeed, such values have remained important to this day. Liberty, or freedom, is emphasized again and again by American political leaders as one value that differentiates this nation from so many others.

VALUES, BELIEFS, AND FOREIGN POLICY

Because the essence of politics is so closely related to achieving and maintaining particular values, the analysis of values and beliefs is a deliberate choice as the organizing theme for studying the foreign policy of the United States.[6] Further, because values and beliefs are the motivating forces for individual action—and because we shall make the assumption that foreign policy is ultimately the result of individual decisions—their importance for foreign policy analysis becomes readily apparent. Thus, by identifying the values and beliefs that American society fosters, we ought to be in a good position to understand how they have shaped our actions toward the rest of the world.

Social psychologists have provided an important analysis of the relationships among values, beliefs, and the behavior of individuals. Milton Rokeach defines beliefs as propositions "inferred from what a person says or does" and whose content "may *describe* an object or situation as true or false; *evaluate* it as good or bad; or *advocate* a certain course of action as desirable or undesirable." Individuals thus may have numerous beliefs, but some are more central than others in accounting for their behavior. These core beliefs are values. As Rokeach notes, "A value is a type of belief, centrally located within one's total belief system, about how one ought, or ought not, to behave, or about some end state of existence worth, or not worth, attaining." Although these values are likely to be few in number, they are crucial in understanding the attitudes and behaviors that an individual expresses.[7] By extension, then, nation-states would operate in the same way, since ultimately individuals comprise them.

The use of values and beliefs (or "ideas," as Judith Goldstein and Robert Keohane called them[8]) as our organizing scheme and focusing on nations and individuals contrasts with other principal models of analysis offered in recent years: the rational actor model, the organizational process model, and the governmental or bureaucratic politics model.[9] While each of these models has something to offer in helping us analyze foreign policy, none of them focuses sufficiently on the role of values and beliefs.

The rational actor model, for example, begins with the assumption that nations (like individuals) are self-interested and seek to maximize their payoffs (or outcomes) when making foreign policy decisions. In this model, the key to understanding foreign policy is to identify the policy preferences and their rank ordering for a state. From a values perspective, however, the source of individual preferences and the relative ordering of those preferences have not been well explored. The organizational process model focuses more on identifying the decision-making routines by policy makers. As a result, foreign policy behavior is less the result of clear choices and more a function of organizations following standing operating procedures. In large measure, the values and beliefs of the policy makers are assumed and not fully analyzed. The bureaucratic politics model gives some attention to the role of values and beliefs (since each bureaucracy has institutional beliefs that it is seeking to maximize). Still, the primary explanatory focus is on the competition among the bureaucracies, based upon relative power and influence, and the roles of values and beliefs within the bureaucracies are not brought into sharp focus. In this sense, while these foreign policy models have much to offer (and careful readers will note that we will use them in various ways throughout the book), an initial focus upon values and beliefs will enable us to provide a fuller picture in understanding America's foreign policy decisions.

Some Cautions with This Approach

There are some potential difficulties in focusing on values and beliefs and in assuming a direct analogy between individuals and nation-state behavior in analyzing American foreign policy. First, other factors such as the idiosyncratic personality traits of some leaders, the dynamics of the bureaucratic environment, and the restraints of the governmental process will intrude on any complete identification of a nation's values and beliefs.[10] While recognizing these factors and the wealth of research that has gone into their analysis by others, we contend that the role of underlying values and beliefs remains critically important and should not be overlooked in foreign policy analysis. Second, the very definition of national values is likely to be problematic. Whose values are we to identify? Should they be the values of political leaders or the public at large? With both the public and the elite, the array of values in a pluralist society is considerable, ranging from religiously based to more secularly driven values. While our analysis will focus primarily on particular values held by the political elites, the values and beliefs of the public, by necessity, will also be considered and examined. Third, by focusing on values and beliefs, and using them as the basis for explaining U.S. foreign policy, we are close to relying on the national character (or, more generally, the political culture) explanation of behavior.[11] As A. F. K. Organski has asserted, the national character approach makes several key assumptions:

> (1) that the individual citizens of a nation share a common psychological make-up or personality or value system that distinguishes them from the citizens of other nations, (2) that this national character persists without major changes over a relatively long period of time, and (3) that there is a traceable relationship between individual character and national goals.[12]

Such assumptions are very difficult to make. Thus, there are limitations to the national character approach as a meaningful explanation of foreign policy, and it cannot be relied on completely. Its use in a more limited sense to identify the "basic attitudes, beliefs, values, and value orientations" of a society as a beginning point for analysis is appropriate, however, since individuals (and hence, nations) make decisions within the context of a particular array of values and beliefs.[13]

Some Rationales for This Approach

Although we acknowledge and recognize these limitations, we believe that this values approach is a sufficiently useful first step to warrant more coverage than it has received. Moreover, our analysis does not contend that certain values and beliefs are unchangeable, although surely some principles are less changeable than others. Rather, we shall assess the changes in value emphasis and their consistency, especially in the past six decades, when the United States has been an active and continuing participant in the global arena.

Beyond the utility of the values approach to analyzing the foreign policy of any nation, it is especially germane to the study of American foreign policy for at least three additional reasons. First, the nation was explicitly founded on particular sets of values, and these values made the United States view itself as "different" (or "exceptional") from the nations of the Old World from which it originated. In this view, politics was not to be conducted upon the principles of power politics, but it was to be conducted on the basis of democratic principles. In the view of many, then, America should act in the world only on the basis of moral principles or in defense of such principles. Domestic values, at all times, were to be the guide to political behavior. Whether the United States lived up to these standards is debatable, but the inevitable desire to justify actions within a value context emphasizes the role of such principles as guides to U.S. foreign policy.

Second, since some American values toward international affairs have changed in recent years, an understanding of these changes is especially important for U.S. foreign policy analysis. As we shall discuss, America has moved from its isolationist past to an active globalism in the post–World War II years. Indeed, a particular set of values, often labeled the Cold War consensus, came to dominate the motivations of American policy actions from the late 1940s to at least the middle 1960s. In the post-Vietnam period (roughly 1973–1990), the value orientation of the various American administrations toward the world has changed a number of times—from the realism of the Nixon years, to the idealism of the Carter term, and back to the Cold War realist values of the Reagan and Bush administrations. With the emergence of the post–Cold War era, the Clinton administration initially introduced a greater emphasis on greater global and economic engagement and the promotion of democracy and then moved back to a focus on global political-military concerns. The George W. Bush administration reflects similar shifts in its foreign policy values and emphases, propelled most dramatically by the terrorist attacks upon the United States in the fall of 2001. While the administration started with a unilateralist emphasis, it was compelled to move in the direction of greater multilateralism (at least for a time) as it sought to implement its war on terrorism. With such discernible shifts throughout the recent history of U.S. foreign policy and the current search for a definitive set of foreign policy values, a knowledge of both past value approaches and their policy implications is important as the United States looks toward the twenty-first century.

Third, the lack of a foreign policy consensus at either the elite or mass levels in American society today further invites the use of a values approach. According to several national surveys, none of the foreign policy approaches of the post-Vietnam and the post–Cold War era has been fully embraced by the American public or its leaders. Both the public at large and the American leadership are divided as to the appropriate set of values to guide American policy for the future. While we shall discuss these divisions fully in Chapters 12 and 13, suffice it to say that values and beliefs will remain a useful way of understanding American foreign policy, especially as the United States seek to combat global terrorism.

Finally, and on a normative level, there have been efforts lately by analysts to reincorporate the role of values into the study of foreign policy and foreign policy decision making. In recent years, prominent political scientists have sought to keep ethical values more fully as part of the discussion and have argued strongly for their incorporation into international politics, in general, and into foreign policy calculations, in particular.[14]

In this first chapter, then, we begin our analysis by sketching the historical values and beliefs of American society and then suggest how they have influenced our foreign policy toward the rest of the world, especially in the first century and a half of the nation.

THE UNITED STATES: A NEW DEMOCRATIC STATE

Numerous scholars have noted that the United States was founded upon values that were different from those of the rest of the world.[15] It was to be a democratic nation in a world governed primarily by monarchies and autocracies. Indeed, according to one historian, America's founders "didn't just want to believe that they were involved in a sordid little revolt on the fringes of the British Empire or of European civilization. They wanted to believe they were coming up with a better model, . . . a better way for human beings to form a government that would be responsive to them."[16] Thomas Jefferson stated this view best when he described the new American state as "the solitary republic of the world, the only monument of human rights . . . the sole depositary of the sacred fire of freedom and self-government, from hence it is to be lighted up in other regions of the earth, if other regions shall ever become susceptible to its benign influence."[17] Because of its democratic value emphasis, moreover, America developed with the belief that its society was unique and possessed a set of values worthy of emulation by others. In this sense, the country emerged as a deeply ideological society (although Americans do not readily admit it), and as one not always tolerant of those who hold contrary views.[18]

A Free Society

In 1776 the United States was explicitly conceived in liberty and equality in contrast to other nations, where ascription and privilege were so important.[19] It emerged as an essentially free society in a world that stressed authority and order. This new American state, to a large measure, was dynamic, classless, and free, in contrast to Europe, which was largely classbound and restrictive.[20] (Revolutionary France does not fit this description, but "classbound and restrictive" certainly describes politics under the Concert of Europe, the European power arrangement dominated by the conservative regimes of Prussia, Russia, and Austria after the defeat of Napoleon.[21]) Thus, the American Revolution was fought in defiance of the very principles by which Europe was governed. In this sense, there developed a natural aversion to European values—and foreign policies—which further reinforced America's beliefs in its own uniqueness.

The fundamental American beliefs that were perceived to be so different from European values of the time can be summarized in the notion of classical liberalism, especially as espoused by John Locke.[22] In this liberal tradition the individual is paramount, and the role of government is limited. Government's task is to do only what is necessary to protect the life and liberty of its citizens and to provide for their happiness. Citizens are generally left alone, free to pursue their own goals and to seek rewards based solely on their abilities.

Equality before the Law

From such a concern for the individual, personal freedom and personal achievement naturally emerged as cherished values in American society. Yet equality before the law was also necessary to ensure that all individuals could maximize their potential on the sole basis of their talents. In a society that placed so much emphasis on the freedom of the individual, however, equality was viewed in a particular way. What was guaranteed was not equality of outcomes (substantive equality) but equality of opportunity (procedural equality) for all.[23] Although all citizens were not guaranteed the same ultimate station in life, all should (theoretically) be able to advance as far as their individual capabilities would take them. While equality of opportunity is thus important to American society, the freedom to determine one's own level of achievement remained the dominant characteristic of this new society. In his inaugural address in January 2001, President Bush captured this view of the importance of the individual and of the importance of freedom and equality in this way: "The grandest of these ideals is an unfolding American promise that everyone belongs, that everyone deserves a chance, that no insignificant person was ever born."[24]

One prominent visitor to the United States quickly recognized the distinctive values of America in 1831 and 1832. The French nobleman Alexis de Tocqueville was struck by the extraordinary amount of social and political democracy existing within the United States. In *Democracy in America,* his book cataloguing this visit, de Tocqueville was amazed at the level of social democracy ("The social condition of the Americans is eminently democratic; this was its character at the foundation of the colonies, and it is still more strongly marked at the present day"); its extent of equality ("Men are there seen on a greater equality in point of fortune and intellect, or, in other words, more equal in their strength, than in any other country of the world, or in any age of which history has preserved the remembrance"); and the degree of popular sovereignty ("If there is a country in the world where the doctrine of the sovereignty of the people can be fairly appreciated, where it can be studied in its application to the affairs of society, and where its dangers and its advantages may be judged, that country is assuredly America").[25] To be sure, de Tocqueville raised some concerns about this equality and its implication for governance on domestic and foreign policy matters, but his admiration for America as a different kind of nation was indeed profound.[26]

Importance of Domestic Values

The early leaders of the new American state differed from their European counterparts in a third important way: the relationship between domestic values and foreign policy. Unlike the European states of the time, most of the new American leaders did not view foreign policy as having primacy over domestic policy or as a philosophy whereby the power and standing of the state must be preserved and enhanced at the expense of domestic well-being. Nor did these new leaders view foreign policy values and domestic policy values as distinct from one another, where one moral value system guided domestic action and another, by necessity, guided action between states. Instead, most early American leaders saw foreign policy as subservient to the interests of domestic policy and domestic values. One recent analysis of Thomas Jefferson's beliefs on the relationship between the domestic and foreign policy arenas best captures the predominant view at the outset of the American republic: "The objectives of foreign policy were but a means to the ends of posterity and promoting the goals of domestic society, that is, the individual's freedom and society's well-being."[27]

Dual Emphases on Isolationism and Moral Principle

Such values and beliefs came to have important consequences for foreign policy action by this new nation. Because the United States adopted a democratic political system, developed strong libertarian and egalitarian values domestically, and believed in the primacy of domestic over foreign policy, two important foreign policy traditions quickly emerged: an emphasis on isolationism in affecting whether to be involved abroad and an emphasis on moral principle in shaping that involvement.[28] Both traditions, moreover, were surely viewed as complementary to one another and were intended to assist in perpetuating unique American values: the former by reducing U.S. involvement in world affairs, and particularly those of Europe; the latter by justifying U.S. involvement abroad only for sufficient ethical reasons. At times, these two traditions pulled in different directions (one based on the impulse to stay out of world affairs, the other based on the impulse to reform world affairs through unilateral action), but both came to dominate the foreign policy action of the new state.

THE ROLE OF ISOLATIONISM
IN AMERICAN FOREIGN POLICY

Both philosophical and practical reasons led the United States in an isolationist direction. Philosophically, since democratic values were so much at variance with those of the rest of the world, many early Americans came to view foreign nations, and especially European states, with suspicion.[29] They feared that the nation's values would be compromised by other states and that international ties would only entangle the United States in alien conflicts. From the beginning, therefore, there was a natural inclination in American society to move away from global involvement and toward isolationism. Throughout the greatest part of the history of this nation, in fact, isolationism best describes America's foreign policy approach.[30]

Although philosophical concepts influenced the isolationist orientation, it was also guided by some important practical considerations. First, the United States was separated geographically from Europe—the main arena of international politics in the eighteenth and nineteenth centuries—and from the rest of the world. Staying out of the affairs of other nations, therefore, seemed a practical course. Second, the United States was a young, weak country with a small army and a relatively large land mass, so seeking adversaries and potential conflicts abroad would hardly be prudent. Third, domestic unity—a sense of nationalism—was still limited and merited more attention than foreign policy. Finally, the overriding task of settling and modernizing the American continent provided reason enough to adopt an isolationist posture.[31]

Two Statements on Isolationism

Early in the history of the country, two statements—Washington's Farewell Address and the Monroe Doctrine—effectively portrayed isolationism and set limits on its application. The first president's Farewell Address of September 1796 was originally meant to thank the American people for their confidence in his leadership, but it also contained a series of warnings about problems that could arise and threaten the continuance of the republic. Washington admonished American citizens not to become involved in factional groups (i.e., political parties), sectional divisions (e.g., East vs. West or North vs. South), or international entanglements. His comments on international involvements are instructive in explaining what isolationism was to mean in determining American foreign policy for a century and a half.

America's attitude toward the world, Washington said, should be a simple one:

> Observe good faith and justice toward all nations. Cultivate peace and harmony with all. In the execution of such a plan nothing is more essential than that permanent, inveterate antipathies against particular nations and passionate attachments for others should be excluded, and that in place of them just and amicable feeling toward all should be cultivated.[32]

He warned against the danger of forming close ties with other states:

> a passionate attachment of one nation for another produces a variety of evils. Sympathy for the favorite nations, facilitating the illusion of an imaginary interest in cases where no real common interest exists, and infusing into one the enmities of the other, betrays the former into a participation in the quarrels and wars of the latter without adequate inducement or justifications.[33]

And Washington provided a "rule of conduct" for the United States and admonished that any involvement in the Byzantine politics of Europe would not be in this country's best interest:

> The great rule of conduct for us in regard to foreign nations is, in extending our commercial relations to have with them as little political connection as possible. So far as we have already formed engagements let them be fulfilled with perfect good faith. Here let us stop. Europe has a set of primary interests which to us have none or a very remote relation. Hence she must be engaged in frequent controversies, the causes of which are essentially foreign to our concerns. Hence, therefore, it must be unwise in us to implicate ourselves by artificial ties in the ordinary vicissitudes of her politics or the ordinary combinations and collisions of her friendship or enmities.[34]

In sum, Washington suggested that while the foreign policy of the United States should not be totally noninvolved (because economic ties with some states were good and useful, and amicable diplomatic ties with others were commendable), he strongly opposed the establishment of any permanent political bonds to other countries. Importantly, he directly warned against any involvement in the affairs of Europe.

While Washington's Farewell Address outlined a general isolationist orientation to the world, the Monroe Doctrine set forth specific guidelines for U.S. involvement or noninvolvement in international affairs. This doctrine—named after President James Monroe's seventh annual message to the Congress, on December 2, 1823—was promulgated in part as a response to the possibility of increased activities by the European powers in the affairs of the American continents, especially when some South American states were moving toward independence or had just achieved it.[35] Monroe's message contained several distinct and identifiable themes: a call for future noncolonization in Latin America by the European powers and a "maintenance of the *status quo*" there, a declaration about the differences in the political systems of Europe and America, and a statement indicating that the United States would not interfere in the affairs of Europe.[36]

Monroe stated the first of these themes by declaring that the American continents "are henceforth not to be considered as subjects for future colonization by any European power." Such involvement in the affairs of the Americas would affect the "rights and interests" of the United States. Near the end of the message, he highlighted the differences in policies between the United States and Europe toward each other and toward Latin America:

> Of events in that quarter of the globe [Europe] with which we have so much intercourse and from which we derive our origin, we have always been anxious and interested *spectators*. . . . In the wars of the European powers in matters relating to themselves we have never taken any part, nor does it comport with our policy so to do. . . . With the movements in this hemisphere we are of necessity more immediately connected and by causes which must be obvious to all enlightened and impartial observers. The political system of the allied powers is essentially different in this respect from that of America. These differences proceed from that which exists in their respective Governments. . . . We owe it, therefore, to candor and to the amicable relations existing between the United States and those powers to declare that we should consider any attempt on their part to extend their system to any portion of this hemisphere as dangerous to our peace and safety. With the existing colonies or dependencies of any European power we have not interfered and shall not interfere. But with the Governments who have declared their independence and maintained it, and whose independence we have, on great consideration and on just principles, acknowledged, we could not view any interposition . . . by any European powers in any other light than as the manifestation of an unfriendly disposition toward the United States.[37]

The Monroe Doctrine thus gave rise to the "two spheres" concept in American foreign policy by emphasizing the differences between the Western and Eastern Hemispheres—the New World versus the Old World.[38] As Washington had done earlier, Monroe's statement called for political noninvolvement in the affairs of Europe. But Monroe's message did more than Washington's; it specified that the U.S. policy of political noninvolvement in European affairs did not apply equally to Latin American affairs. By asserting that the "rights and interests" of the United States would be affected by European involvements in the Western Hemisphere, it stipulated that the United States did, indeed, have political interests beyond its borders—particularly in Latin America. In this sense, U.S. political isolationism did not wholly apply to the Western Hemisphere. Instead, U.S. political interests in Latin America became widespread, and they had their origins in the Monroe Doctrine.

Viewed together, these two messages can be a valuable guide in understanding this country's isolationist orientation toward global affairs. The principles enunci-

Table 1.1 Content of International Agreements by the United States

Content	Years 1778–1899	Years 1947–1960
Alliance	1	1,024
Amity and Commerce	272	3,088
Boundary	32	4
Claims	167	105
Consular Activities	47	212
Extradition	47	12
Multilateral	37	469
Territorial Concessions	18	4
Total	621	4,918

SOURCES: Calculated from Igor I. Kavass and Mark A. Michael, *United States Treaties and Other International Agreements, Cumulative Index 1776–1949,* Vol. 2 (Buffalo, NY: Wm. S. Hein & Co., Inc., 1975); and from Igor I. Kavass and Adolf Sprudzs, *United States Treaties Cumulative Index 1950–1970,* Vol. 2 (Buffao, NY: Wm. S. Hein & Co., Inc., 1973). For a discussion of how the table was constructed, see the text and note 41.

ated in them generally reflected the diplomatic practices of the United States throughout much of the nineteenth century and into the twentieth, and their words became the basis of the nation's continuing foreign policy.

The Isolationist Tradition in the Nineteenth Century

As a result of the isolationist nature of foreign policy during the nineteenth century, there was a severe restriction on treaty commitments that would bind the United States politically to other states. In fact, one prominent historian has pointed out that the United States made no treaties of alliance between the treaty with France in 1778 and the Declaration of the United Nations in 1942.[39] A survey of American treaties, however, would show that the United States did in fact enter into a number of agreements on political matters with other states.[40] For example, the United States enacted agreements on extradition, navigation of the seas, treatment of nationals, and amity and friendship. None of these "political" treaties could be construed as "entangling" alliances, however; instead they served primarily to facilitate amicable trade relations with other states.

A summary of the kind of agreements made by the United States from its founding to the twentieth century and, for comparison, from 1947 to 1960 is displayed in Table 1.1.[41] The first column of data for the 1778–1899 period confirms the large emphasis upon economic ties and the limited political ties in the early history of the nation. Amity and commerce and claims (largely economic) constitute about 70 percent of the agreements. Even the agreements with more direct political elements, such as those dealing with consular activities and extradition, are largely routine matters for fostering good relations with other states, rather than highly controversial political issues. Only those pacts that deal with boundary issues and with territorial concessions (e.g., the Louisiana Purchase, the purchase of Alaska, the Oregon Treaty, or the Gadsden Treaty) might be placed in the more controversial category. Even those, however, still comprise less than 10 percent of all commitments. The single alliance was the treaty with France, which was ultimately left to lapse in 1800.[42]

By contrast, the data for 1947–1960—the initial period of America's active entry into global affairs—show a strikingly different pattern of commitments. First, the sheer number of agreements is markedly different from one period to the next—from just over 600 in a 120-year period to over 4,900 in a fourteen-year period. While economic agreements (amity and commerce) still constituted the largest single type (about 63 percent), alliances and multilateral commitments now constituted over 30 percent of all agreements. To be sure, these alliances ties were broadly defined—such as setting up military bases, establishing defense pacts and mutual security agreements, and sending military missions to particular nations—but they nevertheless demonstrated a much different level and scope of involvement than what occurred in the country's early years. Similarly, the number and kind of multilateral pacts are also distinctive in the two periods. For the more recent period, the number of such pacts was now over 10 times greater, and their content reflected a new dimension to such ties. At least 15 percent of the multilateral pacts in the immediate postwar years were now defense commitments; no such level was registered in the earlier period.

In short, then, the comparative data bring into sharp relief the fact that America's global involvement in the late eighteenth century and the entire nineteenth century was very different than today. The first 120 years of the republic produced relatively few international agreements, and even these were largely restricted to fostering amicable relations and sound commercial ties between the new American states and the rest of the world.

A brief survey of the diplomatic history of the United States during the nineteenth century gives further evidence of a commitment to the principles of Washington and Monroe. For example, President James K. Polk, in his first annual Address to the Congress on December 2, 1845, reemphasized the tenets Monroe had set down twenty-two years earlier: "It should be distinctly announced to the world as our settled policy, that no future European colony or dominion shall, with our consent, be planted or established on any part of the North American continent."[43] While Polk did not explicitly allude to the ongoing dispute with the British over the Oregon Territory in his reaffirmation of Monroe's policy, the implication (in the view of at least one noted diplomatic historian) was quite clear.[44] Similarly, Polk expressed concern over rumors that the British were about to obtain land in the Yucatan. In a message to Congress (April 29, 1848), Polk said that the "United States would not permit such a deal, even with the consent of the inhabitants."[45]

During this same period the United States concluded the Clayton-Bulwer Treaty, which stipulated that neither Britain nor the United States would ever "obtain or maintain for itself any exclusive control" over a canal across the isthmus at Panama and that "neither will ever exert or maintain fortification commanding the same, or in the vicinity thereof, or fortify, or colonize, or assume, or exercise any dominion over Nicaragua, Costa Rica, the Mosquito Coast, or any part of Central America."[46] While this pact was later viewed as a mistake by some because it gave some standing to the British in the hemisphere, it did allow continued involvement by the United States in the political affairs of Latin America. Consistent with the prescriptions of the Monroe Doctrine, it also tried to regulate European affairs in the area.[47]

Late in the nineteenth century, during the presidency of Grover Cleveland, American policy makers again invoked the principles of the Monroe Doctrine to support Venezuela's claim against the British over a boundary dispute between British Guiana and Venezuela. On July 29, 1895, Secretary of State Richard Olney sent a note to the British stating that they were violating the Monroe Doctrine and that the United States could not permit any weakening of this policy. The British, with good reason, rejected this interpretation. President Cleveland responded angrily, asked Congress for funds to establish a boundary commission to investigate the dispute; he got them quickly, thus fueling war fever over this relatively minor issue.[48] The incident thus illustrates the continuing influence of the Monroe Doctrine on American foreign policy throughout much of the nineteenth century.[49]

The Isolationist Tradition in the Early Twentieth Century

Despite the appeal of imperial expansion for some American leaders, global isolationism and noninvolvement continued to be the guiding principle toward much of European interaction. Only when moral principle justified interventionist policy into European affairs, as the case of World War I surely illustrates and as we discuss shortly, was isolationism abandoned temporarily. Even then, though, interventionism was largely a last resort and was justified in strong moral tones by the Wilson administration. By contrast, several social, economic, and political actions, largely directed toward Europe, illustrate the preferred isolationist sentiment that continued to dominate American thinking and policy in the early decades of the twentieth century.

In social policy, perhaps the most notable development in the early twentieth century was the passage of the National Origins Act of 1924. This legislation restricted further immigration from Southern and Eastern Europe and forbid immigration from the Orient. It was largely a reaction to the fear of the development of communism within the country (the so-called red scare) and the fear of aliens that had also shaken the country. Importantly, it represented an attempt to control foreign influences within the United States through more stringent regulation of immigration. In economic policy, the Smoot-Hawley tariff of 1930 was passed, imposing high tariff barriers for selling foreign products in the United States. Such protectionist legislation was yet a further attempt to isolate the United States from the effects of global economic influences. Further, in the words of one analyst, "the belief . . . that the Depression stemmed from forces abroad against which the United States had to insulate itself . . . also gave a 'protective' tariff an irresistible symbolic appeal."[50] In the political arena, the isolationist impulse was equally pronounced. After American involvement in World War I, a "return to normalcy" was the dominant theme. This theme implied a more isolationist and pacifist approach toward world affairs and was manifested in American rejection of membership in the League of Nations, established after World War I, its refusal to recognize the Soviet Union (until 1933) and other regimes of which it disapproved, its attempt to outlaw international war with the signing of the Kellogg-Briand Pact in 1928, and its effort to limit global armament through a series of conferences in the 1920s and again in the early 1930s. In addition, a strong pacifist movement emerged with more than 50 peace societies developing across the country in the 1920s. The efforts to eliminate international war were viewed as partial reparation for involvement in World War I and as an effort to prevent such involvement in the future. Thus, international reform was wholly consistent with domestic reform in the minds of many Americans.[51]

Involvement in Latin America in the Twentieth Century

Unlike the rest of the world, isolationism and noninvolvement were not the guiding principles toward Latin America in the new century. Instead, the 1904 Roosevelt Corollary to the Monroe Doctrine refined the meaning of that doctrine and expanded U.S. involvement in the Western Hemisphere. As a means of blunting possible European intervention into the affairs of some Western Hemisphere states that had not paid their debts, President Theodore Roosevelt extended the meaning of the Monroe Doctrine to include American intervention, if necessary, to protect the region.

In a letter to the Congress on December 6, 1904, Roosevelt outlined his rationale for this addition to the Monroe Doctrine:

> Chronic wrongdoing, or an impotence which results in a general loosening of the ties of civilized society, may in America, as elsewhere, ultimately require intervention by some civilized nation, and in the Western Hemisphere the adherence of the United States to the Monroe Doctrine may force the United States, however reluctantly, in flagrant cases of such wrongdoing or impotence, to the exercise of an international police power. Our interests and those of our southern neighbors are in reality identical. They have great natural riches, and if within their borders the reign of law and justice obtains, prosperity is sure to come to them. While they thus obey the primary laws of civilized society they may rest assured that they will be treated by us in a spirit of cordial and helpful sympathy. We would interfere with them only in the last resort and then only if it became evident that their inability or unwillingness to do justice at home and abroad had violated the rights of the United States or had invited foreign aggression to the detriment of the entire body of American nations.[52]

Ironically, the Monroe Doctrine, which had been initiated to prevent intervention from abroad, was now used to justify American intervention in the Western Hemisphere.

This policy was quickly implemented in 1905 by American intervention into the Dominican Republic to manage its economic affairs and to prevent any other

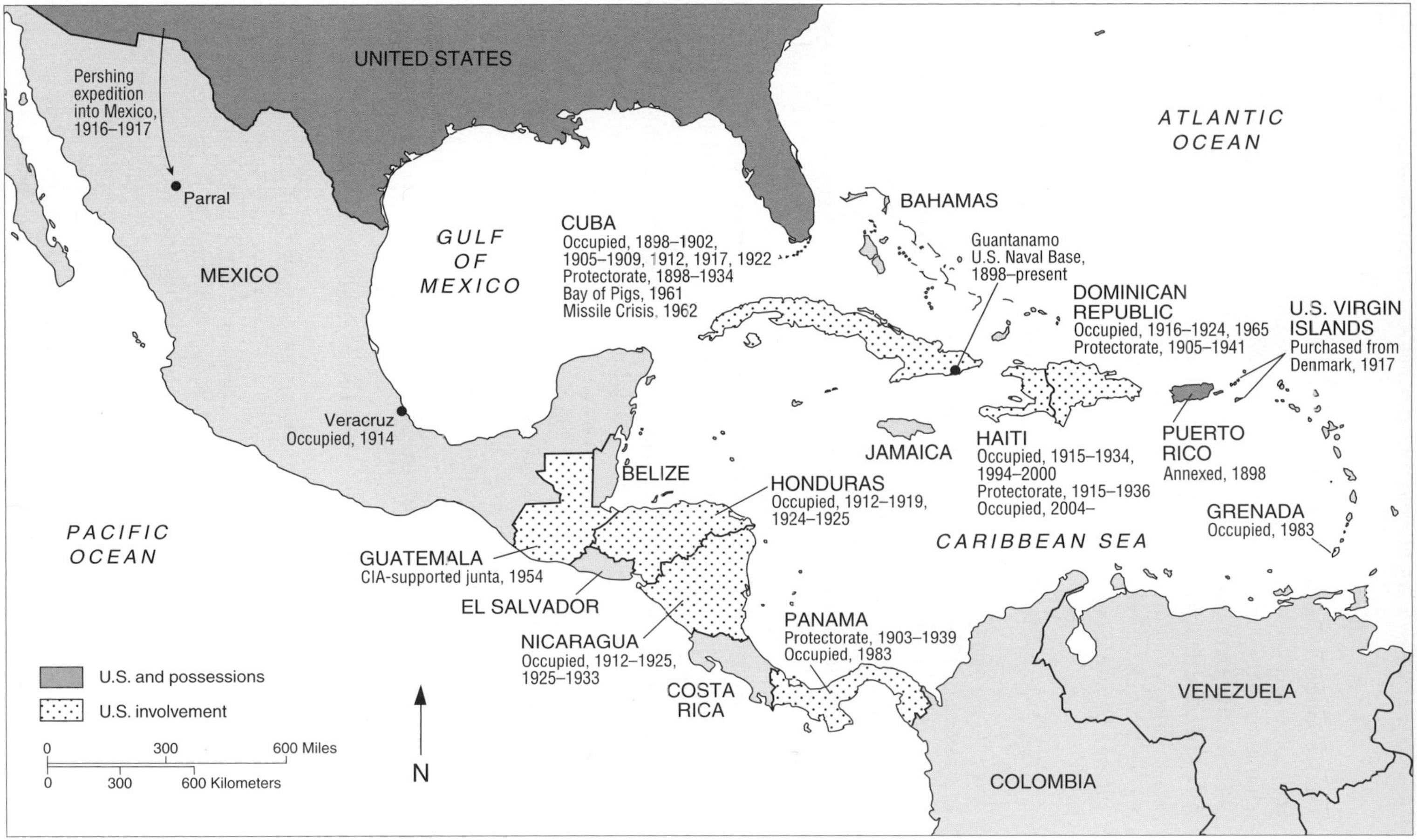
UNITED STATES
Pershing expedition into Mexico, 1916–1917
Parral
MEXICO
GULF OF MEXICO
ATLANTIC OCEAN
BAHAMAS
CUBA
Occupied, 1898–1902, 1905–1909, 1912, 1917, 1922
Protectorate, 1898–1934
Bay of Pigs, 1961
Missile Crisis, 1962
Guantanamo U.S. Naval Base, 1898–present
DOMINICAN REPUBLIC
Occupied, 1916–1924, 1965
Protectorate, 1905–1941
U.S. VIRGIN ISLANDS
Purchased from Denmark, 1917
Veracruz
Occupied, 1914
JAMAICA
HAITI
Occupied, 1915–1934, 1994–2000
Protectorate, 1915–1936
Occupied, 2004–
PUERTO RICO
Annexed, 1898
BELIZE
HONDURAS
Occupied, 1912–1919, 1924–1925
GRENADA
Occupied, 1983
PACIFIC OCEAN
GUATEMALA
CIA-supported junta, 1954
CARIBBEAN SEA
EL SALVADOR
PANAMA
Protectorate, 1903–1939
Occupied, 1983
NICARAGUA
Occupied, 1912–1925, 1925–1933
COSTA RICA
VENEZUELA
COLOMBIA
U.S. and possessions
U.S. involvement
0 300 600 Miles
0 300 600 Kilometers
N

MAP 1.1 U.S. Involvements in Central America and the Caribbean, 1898–2004

SOURCE: The involvement data for 1898–1939 are taken from the map in Walter LeFeber's *The American Age* (New York: W. W. Norton and Company, 1989), p. 233. The subsequent American involvements have been added by the author.

outside interference. Similar financial and military interventions followed on the basis of this experience. The United States became involved in the affairs of the Dominican Republic, Haiti, Nicaragua, and Mexico, with intervention in each of these countries throughout the early years of the twentieth century. American forces occupied the Dominican Republic from 1916 to 1924, Haiti from 1915 to 1934, Nicaragua from 1912 to 1925 and 1926 to 1933, and Mexico for a time in 1914. In addition, the United States established a protectorate over Panama from 1903 to 1939 and over Cuba from 1898 to 1934.[53]

The Monroe Doctrine in the Present Era

Since World War II, the Monroe Doctrine has hardly lost its relevance for American policy. In 1954, the United States supported a coup that overthrew the government of the Jacobo Arbenz Guzman regime in Guatemala, after Arbenz had initiated domestic reform programs and had received arms shipments from the Soviet bloc. Both the fear of communism in the Western Hemisphere and the tradition of the Monroe Doctrine figured prominently in American support for the coup.[54] After Fidel Castro had seized power in Cuba in 1959, a U.S.-backed force of Cuban exiles was organized and trained to topple the Castro regime. In April 1961, the abortive Bay of Pigs invasion ended in disaster, but it was defended as an attempt to stop the spread of communism in the Western Hemisphere. In 1962, the Monroe Doctrine again justified the American blockade against Cuba after the discovery of Soviet missiles in that country. In his address to the nation during the Cuban Missile Crisis, President John Kennedy noted how these missiles violated "the traditions of this nation and the Hemisphere."[55] In April 1965, when Communists were allegedly seizing power in the Dominican Republic, President Lyndon Johnson sent in some 23,000 U.S. and Organization of American States (OAS) forces to protect American citizens and to restore a government more favorable to the United States.

The tenets of the Monroe Doctrine continued to shape American foreign policy in the Western Hemisphere over the past three decades. In September 1979, when the presence of 2,000 to 3,000 Soviet combat troops was revealed in Cuba, Senator Richard Stone of Florida cited the Monroe Doctrine as one reason the troops had to be removed. When successful political revolutions occurred in El Salvador and Nicaragua in 1979, the United States immediately became concerned that these revolutions would produce "Soviet beachheads" at America's backdoor in the Western Hemisphere. Moreover, the Reagan administration challenged the new Marxist-led Sandinista government in Nicaragua and, by late 1981, had initiated a covert operation to support the Contras, a counterrevolutionary force committed to the overthrow of that new Nicaraguan government. When the funding for the Contras was stopped by the U.S. Congress from late 1984 to late 1986, Reagan administration officials devised a scheme to continue supporting the rebel Contra forces by secretly selling arms to Iran and transferring part of the proceeds to the Nicaragua rebels. This operation became known as the Iran–Contra affair.

During the 1980s, too, the Reagan and Bush administrations were heavily involved in Panama. The United States worried about the corrupt regime of

Manuel Antonio Noriega in Panama and its implication for American influence in that country. General Noriega, who had ruled Panama since the violent death of General Omar Torrigos in 1981, reportedly made huge profits from the drug trade that traversed Panama, and in turn became increasingly repressive in the treatment of his citizens. The Reagan administration sought and obtained his indictment on drug smuggling in Miami and undertook various efforts to oust Noriega from power through American economic and diplomatic actions. After a military coup covertly supported and encouraged by the Bush administration failed in October 1989, the United States employed a military force totaling about 25,000 to overthrow the Noriega regime two months later. Noriega was captured, brought to the United States, and convicted on drug trafficking charges.

As the Clinton administration sought to remove General Raoul Cedras and restore democratically elected President Jean-Bertrand Aristide to power in Haiti in 1994, the Monroe Doctrine hovered in the background as an important policy justification. While the administration was initially much more reluctant to intervene or remain in other trouble spots around the world (e.g., Bosnia, Somalia, or Rwanda), the proximity of Haiti to the United States and its location in the Western Hemisphere (as well as the promotion of democracy) became part of the rationale for American occupation of that country in September 1994. The George W. Bush administration has equally taken a keen interest in the Western Hemisphere with its support for legislation to aid Colombia in its fight against drug trafficking, including the continuing use of American military advisors, and its interest in promoting a free trade zone among the states in the region. In late February 2004, the pattern continued. President Bush directed U.S. Marines into Haiti to restore and maintain order after President Jean-Bertrand Aristide fled the country, apparently with American encouragement.

In short, the imperative to keep the Western Hemisphere free of outside powers and to keep the Monroe Doctrine alive continues largely unabated. Similarly, the American view, since at least Theodore Roosevelt, that it could use its power to establish order in this region also is alive and well.

THE ROLE OF MORAL PRINCIPLE
IN AMERICAN FOREIGN POLICY

The founding of the United States with a unique set of values, as well as the nation's development in the context of political isolationism, yielded another important dimension of America's foreign policy: a reliance on moral principle as a guide to world affairs.[56] Americans never felt very comfortable with international politics (especially power politics as practiced in the Old World), and they had largely honored the imperative to stay away from foreign entanglements. This policy of political noninvolvement generated a distinct approach to the world when the country occasionally did become involved in international politics. As political scientist John Spanier and others have argued, discernible American attitudes developed toward such important political concepts as the balance of power, war and peace, and force and diplomacy.[57] More generally, the role of moral values (as opposed to political interests) became an important feature of American policy making. On occasion, this moral fervor produced policies that had the quality of crusades seeking to right a perceived wrong as the United States did become involved in global affairs.

Before we proceed, we ought to add a note here about moral principles and their relationship to policies followed by all nations. Our discussions are not intended to convey that moral principle is absent in the action of other nations and that only the actions of the United States are based upon such principles. To be sure, all nations are governed by particular value codes, although they are clearly different (or at least have different emphases) as we move from one state to another. What we do mean to communicate, however, is that the United States, as a nation, has been particularly sensitive to reconciling its actions with moral principle, perhaps more so than many other nations. Indeed, the religious traditions that undergirded the founding of the nation and the continued impact of those traditions to this day account in perhaps large part for this reliance on moral principle in foreign affairs. As we shall subsequently discuss, the fidelity to those principles in action has not always been sustained; yet, the very concern for moral principle is an important characteristic of U.S. foreign policy, especially when compared to other national traditions at the beginning of the American Republic.

Moral Principle and the Balance of Power

The balance of power concept, which has dominated policy making in Europe since the inception of the nation-state system there, is predicated on several key assumptions. First, it assumes that all states are interested in preventing large-scale war and in preserving the existence of at least the major states in the international system. Second, it is based on the view that all states are fundamentally motivated in their foreign policy behavior by power considerations and national interests. Third, it assumes that states are willing and able to join alliances (and to change alliances) to prevent the dominance of any one state. Fourth, it assumes that there will be few domestic political constraints preventing states from acting in the political arena.[58] The essence of the balance of power concept is the adroit use of diplomacy and bargaining, but it maintains that force and violence can—and should—be used to perpetuate the system.

Until recently, the United States has tended to reject philosophically virtually all the key assumptions of balance of power politics.[59] American society has maintained that foreign policy should be motivated not by interests and power considerations but by moral principles; domestic values have been seen as the sole basis for foreign policy behavior. As Henry Kissinger, a critic of American antipathy toward power politics, has observed: "It is part of American folklore that, while other nations have interests, we have responsibilities; while other nations are concerned with equilibrium, we are concerned with the legal requirements of peace."[60]

The views of war and peace and force and diplomacy in American society follow from its views of power politics. Because Americans have rejected the balance of power concept, most would find little comfort in Karl von Clausewitz's dictum that war is "the continuation of political activity by other means."[61] Instead, Americans have generally perceived war and peace as dichotomous: Either war or peace exists. Intermediate conditions in which limited force is used (e.g., uses of military force to settle border disputes or short-term interventions to achieve some limited objectives, such as the use of American forces in Bosnia in 1995 or Kosovo in 1999) are not always understandable or tolerable to many Americans. When war does break out, and the country does have to get involved, an all-out effort should be made to win the war. If the cause is sufficiently important in the first place, should not the effort be complete and total? Alternatively, if the cause is not important, why should U.S. forces be committed at all?

The continued impact of this view of war and peace to the present is illustrated by public reaction to "limited wars" engaged in by the United States over the past five decades. For many Americans, the conduct of the Korean and Vietnam wars was perceived as extraordinarily frustrating because an all-out military effort was not undertaken. Instead, a mixture of military might and diplomacy was employed. As a result, the outcomes were not wholly satisfactory—prolonged stalemate in the first, defeat in the second. Even the highly successful effort of the United States in the Persian Gulf War of 1991 did not end satisfactorily for some because political restraints entered the process once again. In particular, segments of the public (including the American general in charge of coalition forces against Iraq) were unhappy that the United States did not "finish the job" at the end of that war. More generally, American involvements in peace building, peacemaking, or humanitarian interventions (e.g., in Somalia in 1992–1993, Bosnia in 1995 and after, and in Kosovo in 1999) have received mixed levels of support from the public and explain in part the initial impulse of the George W. Bush administration to seek to reduce American actions abroad in 2001.

By contrast to this attitude on limited war, note the American public's response to the "war on terrorism" after 9/11. When the Bush administration initially issued a clarion call for an all-out war on terrorism, including taking all actions necessary, the public responded with the highest levels of support ever received for an American presidency. While George W. Bush had averaged in the mid-50 percent approval rating prior to September 11, 2001, his support averaged in the mid-80 percent in the months immediately following this tragedy.[62] The American public supports all-out efforts on war and peace issues, and they tend to be more skeptical of in-between measures.

The public's view of force and diplomacy parallels the attitudes toward peace and war. Americans generally believe that when a nation resorts to force, its use should be sufficient to meet the task at hand. There should be no constraints of "politics" once the decision to use force has been made. As a consequence, combining force and diplomacy (as in the balance of power approach) is not understandable to large segments of the American people because it appears to compromise the country's moral position. Again, the Korean and Vietnam wars illustrate this point. In both instances, "talking and fighting" were not well understood or well received by many Americans. The efforts by Richard Nixon and

Henry Kissinger to combine force and diplomacy (a policy of "coercive diplomacy") were criticized by both the political right and the political left because they suggested a certain amoralism in American foreign policy efforts.

American diplomacy, too, has historically been heavily infused with this moral tradition. Historian Dexter Perkins has noted that this kind of reliance on moral principle has produced a certain "rigidity" in dealing with other nations. Diplomacy, by its very nature, requires some compromise on competing points, he argues. However, when "every question is to be invested with the aura of principle, how is adjustment to take place?"[63] Similarly, Spanier has noted that, given that moral principle is so prevalent in American policy making, it has traditionally been difficult for Americans to understand how compromise is possible or necessary on some questions in global politics.[64] When to compromise, and over what principles, remains a source of debate for many Americans.

Moral Principle and International Involvement

Prior to 1947, when the United States finally committed itself to global involvement, American engagement in global affairs was generally tied to explicit violations of international ethical standards by other states. Four prominent instances—the War of 1812, the Spanish–American War, World War I, and World War II—illustrate the importance of moral principle as a justification for U.S. involvement and foreign policy actions.[65]

War of 1812 The first instance when isolationism was abandoned in the name of moral principle was the War of 1812. When the U.S. Congress finally voted a declaration of war against Great Britain in June 1812, it did so only after various efforts to avoid involvements with the dominant European powers of the time— France and England—and only after what it perceived as continuous violations of an important principle of international law: freedom of the seas for neutral states.[66] Under a series of policy directives to limit Napoleon's power and enhance its own, the British government barred American commerce from France or any continental ports that barred the British. Further, it barred any neutral American vessel that had not passed through a British port or paid British customs duties from carrying on commerce. U.S. ships violating such standards were subject to seizure. (France, under Napoleon, enacted similar restrictions on American shipping, but, for a variety of reasons, the United States responded with greater hostility to the British strictures.[67]) Such British actions infuriated the United States, and American leaders characterized them as blatant violations of freedom of the seas. In addition to the seizure of American vessels, the British went further in their effort to control the seas through the practice of impressment, which involved seizing sailors from American vessels and forcing them into the British navy (because they were alleged to be deserters from the Royal Navy). Impressment, too, further challenged America's freedom of commerce and the seas and was seen as besmirching U.S. national honor. While America's involvement in this war proved costly and ultimately unpopular and the final results largely confirmed the status quo, it does suggest the potency of moral principle in guiding early American action.[68]

Spanish–American War In the Spanish-American War (1898), a variety of arguments based on moral principle was advanced to justify American actions: the harsh Spanish treatment of the Cubans, the sinking of the American battleship Maine, and the personal affront to President William McKinley by the Spanish ambassador in a private letter. (The ambassador portrayed McKinley as a "bidder for the admiration of the crowd" and as a "common politician."[69]) Fewer arguments for American participation were cast on the basis of how it might affect the national interest; instead, in one view, moral arguments provided the dominant rationale.[70]

World War I American participation in World War I in 1917 and 1918 was also cast in terms of the same kind of moral imperative, rather than in response to the demands of the balance of power in Europe. Only for sufficient ethical cause did the United States feel compelled to enter this European conflict. In this case, the ethical justification was provided by Germany's violation of the principle of freedom of the seas and the rights of neutrals through its unrestricted warfare campaign on the open seas.[71]

The outrage that developed in 1915 with the sinking of the British passenger ship the *Lusitania* (and later, the *Sussex*), with the accompanying loss of American lives, provided sufficient reason to abandon isolationism temporarily. The proximate events that precipitated United States entry into the war, however, were the German announcement of its unrestricted submarine warfare in February 1917 and Germany's Zimmermann Telegram to Mexico that sought to prod that country into war with the United States.[72] Even as the United States embarked on this course, continued moral justification was reflected in the slogans devised to boost American participation: World War I was to be a "war to end all wars" and a campaign to "make the world safe for democracy."

World War II Finally, U.S. participation in World War II from 1941 to 1945 also reflected the ethical roots of the country's foreign policy behavior. Although the United States was assisting the allies before its formal involvement, U.S. reentry into world conflict could be justified only in terms of some moral violation. The Neutrality Act of 1939, for example, had reduced the restrictions on arms sales and allowed the United States to supply its allies, France and Britain. The Destroyers for Bases deal with Great Britain—in which the United States gained naval and air bases in Newfoundland and some Caribbean islands in exchange for fifty destroyers—occurred in September 1940.[73] In March 1941, moreover, the Congress passed the Lend-Lease Act as another way to help the allies.[74] Nevertheless, it was not until the Japanese bombing of Pearl Harbor, Hawaii, on December 7, 1941, "a date which will live in infamy" as President Franklin Delano Roosevelt described it, that the United States was accorded a wholly satisfactory reason for plunging the country into the conflict.[75] Then the United States, consistent with its attitude, felt compelled to seek "absolute victory," as Roosevelt said. A total war effort was mounted that ultimately led to the unconditional surrender of the Japanese in September 1945, only a few months after the victory in Europe had been secured.

Implications for U.S. Involvement

In general, these instances demonstrate that the United States has been reluctant to give up its isolationism and did so only for identifiable moral reasons. That is, the United States traditionally agreed to international involvement only in response to perceived violations of clearly established principles of international law and not to respond to the requirements of power politics, as many other states have done. As a consequence, sustained American activities in the world of power politics have been decidedly few in the past and have been entered into only in special circumstances.

After each of the first three involvements discussed here, the United States generally moved back to its favored position of isolationism, and none brought about a basic change in American foreign policy orientation. (The significance of World War II is considerably different, and Chapter 2 discusses its impact on U.S. foreign policy.) After the War of 1812, for example, the immediate reaction was the reaffirmation of the policy of noninvolvement in European affairs by the Americans and the call for no European involvement in Western Hemispheric affairs via the Monroe Doctrine of 1823.

The strong American affinity toward isolationism was vividly demonstrated at the end of World War I with the rejection of the idealistic foreign policy proposed by President Woodrow Wilson. "Wilsonian idealism," as it came to be called, attempted to shake the United States from its isolationist moorings and encourage America to be a continuing participant in global affairs. This idealism, largely borne out of President Wilson's personal beliefs, consisted of several key tenets. First, moral principle should be the guide to U.S. actions abroad. Second, the Anglo-American values of liberty and liberal democratic institutions are worthy of emulation and promotion worldwide. Indeed, they are necessary if world peace is to be realized. Third, the old order, based upon balance of power and interest politics, must be replaced by an order based upon moral principles and cooperation by all states against international aggression. And fourth, the United States must continue to take an active role in bringing about these global reforms.[76] For Wilson, then, moral principle would serve as a continuing guide to global involvement, but the interests of humankind and global reform would take precedence over any narrowly defined national or state interest.

The most complete statement of the new world that Wilson envisioned was probably summarized in his Fourteen Points, which he offered to a joint session of the U.S. Congress in January 1918 and which became the basis for the Paris Peace Conference at the end of World War I.[77] This new order would ban secret diplomacy and foster international trade among nations. It also emphasized self-determination and democracy for nations and set forth several specific requirements for resolving nationality and territorial issues in Central Europe at

Document 1.1   Wilson's Fourteen Points

I. Open covenants of peace, openly arrived at. . . .

II. Absolute freedom of navigation upon the seas. . . .

III. The removal, so far as possible, of all economic barriers and the establishment of an equality of trade conditions among all the nations. . . .

IV. Adequate guarantees given and taken that national armaments will be reduced to the lowest point consistent with domestic safety.

V. A free open-minded, and absolutely impartial adjustment of all colonial claims. . . .

VI. The evacuation of all Russian territory and such a settlement of all questions affecting Russia . . . [and] an unhampered and unembarrassed opportunity for the independent determination of her own political development and national policy. . . .

VII. Belgium . . . must be evacuated and restored without any attempt to limit the sovereignty which she enjoys in common with all other free nations.

VIII. All French territory should be freed and the invaded portions restored, and the wrong done to France by Prussia in 1871 in the matter of Alsace-Lorraine, which has unsettled the peace of the world for nearly fifty years, should be righted. . . .

IX. A readjustment of the frontiers of Italy should be effected along clearly recognizable lines of nationality.

X. The peoples of Austria-Hungary . . . should be accorded the freest opportunity of autonomous development.

XI. Rumania, Serbia, and Montenegro should be evacuated; occupied territories restored; Serbia accorded free and secure access to the sea; and the relations of the several Balkan states to one another determined by friendly counsel along historically established lines of allegiance and nationality. . . .

XII. The Turkish portions of the present Ottoman Empire should be assured a secure sovereignty, but the other nationalities . . . under Turkish rule should be assured . . . [an] opportunity of autonomous development, and the Dardanelles should be permanently opened as a free passage to the ships and commerce of all nations. . . .

XIII. An independent Polish state should be erected . . . [with] political and economic independence and territorial integrity . . . guaranteed by international covenant.

XIV. A general association of nations must be formed under specific covenants for the purpose of affording mutual guarantees of political independence and territorial integrity to great and small states alike.

SOURCE: Taken from a speech by President Woodrow Wilson to a joint session of the U.S. Congress as reported in *Congressional Record*, January 8, 1918, 691.

---

the time. (A summary of Wilson's Fourteen Points is presented in Document 1.1.) Point 14 of this plan, however, was particularly notable—and ultimately troubling to many Americans—because of its explicit rejection of isolationism. This point called for the establishment of a collective security organization—a League of Nations—that would rid the world of balance of power politics and create a world order based on universal principles. The League was to be an organization that would exploit the cooperative potential among states and emphasize the role of collective (i.e., universal) action to stop warfare and regulate conflict. As such, it would require each participant to be involved in the affairs of the international system. If the United States were to join such an organization, it would be permanently involved in global politics and would be an active participant in this global reform effort. In essence, Wilson's collective security proposal would have moved the United States away from isolationism, and it would have produced a strong moral cast to American involvement and to global politics generally.

Wilson's plan for a League of Nations became a reality for a time, but without the participation of the United States; the U.S. Senate failed to pass the Versailles peace treaty by the necessary two-thirds vote. Indeed, on two of three different roll calls, the treaty failed even to obtain majority support in that body.[78] Despite America's long-standing rejection of balance of power politics, it remained unwilling to increase its global involvement in order to destroy this system. Instead, the United States reaffirmed its isolationist beliefs and reverted to "normalcy" in the 1920s and remained in that posture throughout the 1930s as well.

The return to isolationism was also manifested in another way in the interwar years. As the situation in Europe began to polarize, and conflict seemed once again imminent, the United States passed a series of neutrality acts in 1935, 1936, and 1937. These acts sought to prevent the export of arms and ammunition to belligerent countries and to restrict travel by American citizens on the vessels of nations involved in war.[79] The ultimate aim was to reaffirm U.S. noninvolvement and to reduce the prospects of the United States being drawn into war through these means. Although President Roosevelt had by 1939 asked for and received some alterations in the neutrality acts of the past,[80] it was not until the Japanese attack that the United States was again fully shaken from its isolationist stance.

CONCLUDING COMMENTS

The reliance on isolationism and moral principle largely forms the essence of America's past in foreign policy,[81] and these values and beliefs continue to affect the country's orientation to the world to this day. To be sure, the American approach to the world, however, would be altered in response to the shock of World War II, the substantial destruction of the major European powers of France, Britain, and Germany, the emergence of the Soviet challenge, and the onset of the Cold War. Noninvolvement in global affairs was rejected, even as a commitment to the pursuit of moral principles served as a guide to policy.

With the collapse of the Soviet Union, the end of the Cold War, and the emergence of terrorism on American soil, the appeal of these traditional values has reemerged, as the United States struggles to shape a new foreign policy for the twenty-first century. The Bush administration initially moved in the direction of a more unilateralist (and isolationist) approach to the world. Since September, 2001, however, the administration has lurched in the other direction with a commitment to a new globalism, animated by the moral outrage from the attacks on the Pentagon and the World Trade Center. The exact shape and magnitude of this new globalism continue to evolve, but the approach continues to be informed by the principles of America's past—the promotion of freedom and democracy in a world now fraught with terrorism and new kinds of conflicts.

In the next five chapters, we will highlight the changes in America's values and beliefs in the foreign policy area during the post–World War II years and in the post–Cold War period as well. We seek not only to demonstrate how these historical traditions have changed in emphasis or application from administration to administration, but also to illustrate how these traditions have continued to influence the various administrations and their policies. In Chapter 2 we specifically examine the global political and economic factors that shook the United States from its isolationist moorings and propelled it into global politics. At the same time, we shall see how moral principle as a guide to policy remained largely intact.

NOTES

1. Harold D. Lasswell, *Politics: Who Gets What, When, How* (New York: Whittlesey House, 1936), p. 3.

2. Ibid. Emphasis in original.

3. Robert A. Dahl, *Modern Political Analysis,* 2nd ed. (Englewood Cliffs, NJ: Prentice-Hall, Inc., 1970), pp. 4–6. Also see Christian Bay, *The Structure of Freedom* (New York: Atheneum Publishers, 1965), pp. 20–21, for another discussion of the definition of politics.

4. David Easton, *The Political System* (New York: Alfred A. Knopf, Inc., 1953), p. 90. Emphasis added.

5. Milton Rokeach, *Beliefs, Attitudes and Values* (San Francisco: Jossey-Bass, Inc., 1968), pp. 124, 159–160.

6. We shall use the terms *values* and *beliefs* interchangeably throughout this book. These concepts (along with attitudes), while distinct, are very closely related to one another, as discussed in Rokeach, *Beliefs,* pp. 113 and 159–160.

7. See Milton Rokeach's discussion under "Attitudes" in the *International Encyclopedia of the Social Sciences* (New York: The Macmillan Company and The Free Press, 1968), pp. 449–457. The quotations are from pp. 450 and 454, respectively. Emphasis in original.

8. Judith Goldstein and Robert O. Keohane, "Ideas and Foreign Policy: An Analytic Framework," in Judith Goldstein and Robert O. Keohane, eds., *Ideas and Foreign Policy: Beliefs, Institutions, and Political Change* (Ithaca, NY, and London: Cornell University Press, 1993), pp. 3–30. Some of the discussion of the models following in the next paragraph draws upon Goldstein and Keohane.

9. Graham Allison, *Essence of Decision* (Boston: Little, Brown and Co., 1971).

10. A book that surveys the research done within the context of these various factors to explain foreign policy is Lloyd Jensen, *Explaining Foreign Policy* (Englewood Cliffs, NJ: Prentice-Hall, Inc., 1982).

11. For a discussion of how the political culture concept can be used to explain a nation's behavior, see Gabriel Almond and Sidney Verba, *The Civic Culture* (Boston: Little, Brown & Co., 1963).

12. A. F. K. Organski, *World Politics* (New York: Alfred A. Knopf, Inc., 1968), p. 87.

13. Kenneth W. Terhune, "From National Character to National Behavior: A Reformulation," *Journal of Conflict Resolution* 14 (June 1970): 259. For more discussion of Terhune and others on national character, see Howard Bliss and M. Glen Johnson, *Beyond the Water's Edge: America's Foreign Policies* (Philadelphia: J. B. Lippincott Co., 1975), pp. 93–98.

14. See Joseph S. Nye, *Nuclear Ethics* (New York: The Free Press, 1986); Stanley Hoffmann, *Duties Beyond Borders: On the Limits and Possibilities of Ethical International Politics* (Syracuse: Syracuse University Press, 1981); and Robert W. McElroy, *Morality and American Foreign Policy: The Role of Ethics in International Affairs* (Princeton, NJ: Princeton University Press, 1992). The McElroy volume brought the Nye and Hoffmann books

to my attention at p. 3, for which I am grateful.

15. See, for example, Seymour Martin Lipset, *The First New Nation* (Garden City, NY: Anchor Books, 1967); Russel B. Nye, *This Almost Chosen People* (East Lansing: Michigan State University Press, 1966); John G. Stoessinger, *Crusaders and Pragmatists* (New York: W. W. Norton and Company, 1979), pp. 3–7; Edmund Stillman and William Pfaff, *Power and Impotence: The Failure of America's Foreign Policy* (New York: Vintage Books, 1966), pp. 15–59; Paul A. Varg, *Foreign Policies of the Founding Fathers* (East Lansing: Michigan State University Press, 1963), pp. 1–10; and John Spanier, *American Foreign Policy Since World War II,* 9th ed. (New York: Holt, Rinehart and Winston, 1982), pp. 1–14. Spanier's essay is perhaps the best brief treatment of this and related topics discussed here. Its utility here will be readily apparent.

16. Professor Frank A. Cassell (chairman, Department of History, University of Wisconsin–Milwaukee) made this characterization in a 1989 Independence Day interview. See Jerry Resler, "Living On: U.S. as Model Would Please Founder," *Milwaukee Sentinel,* July 4, 1989, part 4, p. 1.

17. Quoted in Robert W. Tucker and David C. Hendrickson, "Thomas Jefferson and Foreign Policy," *Foreign Affairs* 69 (Spring 1990): 136.

18. George F. Kennan made this point about the ideological roots of American society by noting the isolated development of the United States and the Soviet Union. This development in relative isolation from the rest of the world produced a strong sense of righteousness. See his "Is Detente Worth Saving?" *Saturday Review,* March 6, 1976, 12–17.

19. Lipset, in *The First New Nation,* uses the values of equality and achievement as the basis of his analysis.

20. This description, as noted in Spanier, *American Foreign Policy,* p. 7, was true for most Americans, but not all. Some were clearly excluded from the political process—notably blacks, women, Indians, and many who were propertyless.

21. Gordon A. Craig and Alexander L. George, *Force and Statecraft,* 3rd ed. (New York and Oxford: Oxford University Press, 1995), pp. 27–31.

22. On his view of the goals and limits of government, see John Locke, *Two Treatises of Government,* portions of which are reprinted in William Ebenstein, *Great Political Thinkers: Plato to the Present,* 3rd ed. (New York: Holt, Rinehart and Winston, 1965), pp. 404–408, in particular. Also see the discussion of classical liberalism in Everett C. Ladd, Jr., "Traditional Values Regnant," *Public Opinion* 1 (March/April 1978): 45–49; and Charles W. Kegley and Eugene R. Wittkopf, *American Foreign Policy: Pattern and Process,* 4th ed. (New York: St. Martin's Press, 1991), pp. 249–250.

23. These values are discussed in Ladd, "Traditional Values and Regnant," and some evidence is presented on the American commitment to these values and beliefs at the time.

24. "President George W. Bush's Inaugural Address," January 20, 2001 at http://www.whitehouse.gov/news/ inaugural-address.html, accessed on April 16, 2002.

25. Alexis de Tocqueville, *Democracy in America,* edited and abridged by Richard D. Heffner (New York: New American Library, 1956), pp. 49, 54, and 56 for the quoted passages.

26. See ibid. and David Clinton, "Tocqueville's Challenge," *The Washington Quarterly* 11 (Winter 1988): 173–189.

27. Tucker and Hendrickson, "Thomas Jefferson and Foreign Policy," p. 139. For a discussion of how Jefferson's views were shared by other early leaders, see pp. 143–146. On the difficulty of Jefferson's actually making this distinction work, see pp. 146–156.

28. See Spanier, *American Foreign Policy,* pp. 6 and 12. Previously, *isolationism* and *moralism* were used as summary terms. The use of "moralism," however, may have a pejorative connotation for some (and it has surely been used that way). That is not the intent here. Rather, it is to convey the important role that values have played in the way America has thought about its involvement in the global arena. Hence, moral principle as a guiding tradition will be used here.

29. Dexter Perkins, *Hands Off: A History of the Monroe Doctrine* (Boston: Little, Brown & Co., 1941), pp. 3–26.

30. See Cecil V. Crabb, Jr., *Policy-Makers and Critics: Conflicting Theories of American Foreign Policy* (New York: Frederick A. Praeger, Inc., 1976), pp. 1–33, for an extended discussion of this isolationist tradition.

31. See ibid., pp. 7–15, for a discussion of several different dimensions of isolationism in America's past.

32. "Washington's Farewell Address," *Annals of the Congress of the United States,* 4th Cong., 2nd sess., 1786–1797, 2877.

33. Ibid.

34. Ibid., p. 2878.

35. Albert Bushnell Hart, *The Monroe Doctrine: An Interpretation* (Boston: Little, Brown & Co., 1916), pp. 20–68.

36. These themes are succinctly discussed in Evarts Seelye Scudder, *The Monroe Doctrine and World Peace* (Port Washington, NY: Kennikat Press, 1972), pp. 15–20. The quote is at p. 19. Emphasis in original.

37. "President's Message," *Annual of the Congress of the United States,* 18th Cong., 1st sess., 1823–1824, 22–23. Emphasis added.

38. Several scholars have emphasized how the Monroe Doctrine, more than any other policy statement, formalized and solidified the U.S. isolationist tradition in world affairs—at least toward Europe. See, for instance, Perkins, *The Evolution of American Foreign Policy,* 2nd ed. (New York: Oxford University Press, 1966), pp. 33–38; Nye, *This Almost Chosen People,* p. 184; and Spanier, *American Foreign Policy,* p. 6.

39. Thomas A. Bailey, *The Man on the Street: The Impact of American Public Opinion on Foreign Policy* (New York: MacMillan, Inc., 1948), p. 251.

40. A survey of all international agreements during the early history was undertaken using the listing compiled by Igor I. Kavass and Mark A. Michael, *United States Treaties and Other International Agreements Cumulative Index 1776–1949* (Buffalo, NY: William S. Hein and Company, Inc., 1975), pp. 3–130. For the latter period, the data source was Igor I. Kavass and Adolf Sprudzs, *United States Treaties Cumulative Index 1950–1970,* vol. 2 (Buffalo, NY: William S. Hein and Company, Inc., 1973), pp. 11–444, and some additional agreements from the first source for the years 1947–1949 at pp. 526–615.

41. The table was constructed using the sources listed in note 40. The category labels were derived largely from the descriptions of the agreements given in the first source. For manageability and convenience, agreements in different years in the 1778–1899 period were segmentally categorized (e.g., 1778–1799, 1800–1850, etc.), and the overall results were collapsed and categorized. For the second part of the table (1947–1960), the same categories were used. While the content of the categories is relatively self-evident, the alliance, amity and commerce, and multilateral categories deserve some comment. The alliance category consisted primarily of formal military commitments, but it also included establishing military bases, signing mutual security agreements, and sending military missions to other countries. The amity and commerce category included a wide array of commercial, health and sanitation, technical cooperation, educational, aviation, and postal agreements, among others, and commitments for friendly relations with other states. The multilateral category included all agreements that were designated as such by the source. The actual content of those pacts covered a wide array of issues, but the multilateral designation was retained to show the degree to which the United States committed itself to groups of other states during this period. Finally, some agreements overlapped the categories, and some judgments were made to place them into one category rather than another. Others categorizing the pacts might come up with a different classification and slightly different results. It is unlikely, however, that the general pattern of the results would be changed.

42. Perkins, *The Evolution of American Foreign Policy,* p. 30, reports that the French alliance was not renewed in that year.

43. Thomas A. Bailey, *A Diplomatic History of the American People* (New York: F. S. Crofts & Co., 1942), p. 238.

44. Ibid.

45. Hart, *Monroe Doctrine,* p. 115.

46. Robert H. Ferrell, *American Diplomacy: A History* 3rd ed. (New York: W. W. Norton and Company, Inc., 1975), p. 231.

47. Ibid., pp. 231–232.

48. For a discussion of the various challenges to the Monroe Doctrine in the latter half of the nineteenth century, see Scudder, *Monroe Doctrine;* and Hart, *Monroe Doctrine.*

49. See Perkins, *The Evolution of American Foreign Policy,* pp. 35–36, on this point and on the general applicability of the Monroe Doctrine and its declining influence as well (pp. 32–36).

50. Robert Dallek, *The American Style of Foreign Policy* (New York: Alfred A. Knopf, 1983), p. 110. The discussion here is based upon pp. 92–122.

51. Ibid., p. 96–97, in which Dallek discusses the various implications of the pacifist movements in this time period.

52. *Congressional Record,* December 6, 1904, 19.

53. Ferrell, *American Diplomacy,* pp. 395–415. The American occupations and protectorates in the Caribbean are outlined by Walter LaFeber, *The American Age: United States Foreign Policy at Home and Abroad Since 1750* (New York: W. W. Norton and Company, 1989), p. 233.

54. Walter Lefeber, *Inevitable Revolutions: The United States in Central America* (New York: W. W. Norton and Company, 1984), pp. 111–126, especially pp. 118–123.

55. President Kennedy's address to the nation can be found in Robert F. Kennedy, *Thirteen Days* (New York: Signet, 1969), pp. 131–139. The quoted passage is at p. 132.

56. See Dexter Perkins, *The American Approach to Foreign Policy* (Cambridge, MA: Harvard University Press, 1962), pp. 72–97, for a cogent discussion of moral principles as a guide in American foreign policy.

57. See Spanier, *American Foreign Policy,* pp. 9–11; and Stoessinger, *Crusaders and Pragmatists,* pp. 5–7.

58. A discussion of the assumptions, aims, and means of the balance of power can be found in Edward V. Gulick, *Europe's Classical Balance of Power* (Ithaca, NY: Cornell University Press, 1955), pp. 3–91.

59. Changes in American policy makers' attitudes and beliefs toward a balance of power system occurred dramatically during the years in which Henry Kissinger was responsible for formulating American policy. This will be discussed in Chapter 4.

60. Henry A. Kissinger, *American Foreign Policy,* expanded ed. (New York: W. W. Norton and Company, 1974), pp. 91–92.

61. Carl von Clausewitz, *On War,* ed. and trans. Michael Howard and Peter Paret (Princeton: Princeton University Press, 1976), p. 87. Spanier, *American Foreign Policy,* p. 10, also raises this point and discusses the dichotomous view of war and peace upon which we draw.

62. See the job approval chart in David W. Moore, "Bush Approval at 50%, Tied for Lowest of Presidency," The Gallup Organization at http://www.gallup.com/content/default.asp?ci=9742, accessed on March 11, 2004.

63. Perkins, *American Approach,* p. 77.

64. Spanier, *American Foreign Policy,* p. 11.

65. These instances are discussed in George F. Kennan, *American Diplomacy 1900–1950* (New York: Mentor Books, 1951); Robert Endicott Osgood, *Ideals and Self-Interest in America's Foreign Relations* (Chicago: The University of Chicago Press, 1953); and Farrell, *American Diplomacy,* pp. 123–153.

66. Harry L. Coles, *The War of 1812* (Chicago: The University of Chicago Press, 1965), pp. 1–37; and Farrell, *American Diplomacy,* pp. 136–141.

67. Coles, *The War of 1812,* pp. 1–37; and Farrell, *American Diplomacy,* pp. 136–141.

68. Ibid., p. 142.

69. Kennan, *American Diplomacy 1900–1950,* p. 14; and Farrell, *American Diplomacy,* p. 353.

70. For a critical assessment of the impact of popular sentiment on this conflict, see Kennan, *American Diplomacy 1900–1950,* pp. 15–16.

71. Ferrell, *American Diplomacy,* pp. 456–462; and Kennan, *American Diplomacy 1900–1950,* pp. 50–65.

72. Ferrell, *American Diplomacy,* pp. 468–469.

73. Ibid., pp. 556–558.

74. P.L. 77–11, March 11, 1941. 55 Stat 31.

75. Speech by President Franklin D. Roosevelt to a joint session of Congress. The quotation can be found in the *Congressional Record,* 77th Cong., 1st sess., Vol. 87, December 8, 1941, 9519.

76. On Wilson's beliefs, see John G. Stoessinger, *Crusaders and Pragmatists: Movers of Modern American Foreign Policy,* 2nd ed. (New York: W. W. Norton and Company, 1985), pp. 8–27; and Michael H. Hunt, *Ideology and U.S. Foreign Policy* (New Haven, CT: Yale University Press, 1987), pp. 125–136, especially at pp. 129–135.

77. For a listing of the Fourteen Points and a discussion of the Paris Conference, see Ferrell, *American Diplomacy,* pp. 482–492. The depiction of the new order draws upon Hunt, *Ideology and U.S. Foreign Policy,* p. 134.

78. Robert Farrell, *American Diplomacy: The Twentieth Century* (New York: W. W. Norton and Company, 1988), p. 153.

79. See the text of the Neutrality Act of 1935 (August 31, 1935) or the Neutrality Act of 1936 (February 29, 1936) for a full treatment of the restrictions on arms exports and travel by Americans. Both are reprinted in Nicholas O. Berry, ed., *U.S. Foreign Policy Documents, 1933–1945: From Withdrawal to World Leadership* (Brunswick, OH: King's Court Communications, Inc., 1978), pp. 25–27, 32.

80. See the Neutrality Act of 1939 (November 4, 1939), reprinted in ibid., pp. 58–60.

81. See Howard Bliss and M. Glen Johnson, *Beyond the Water's Edge: America's Foreign Policies,* chap. 4, for a discussion of other values that have shaped the American style. Also see Hoffmann, *Gulliver's Troubles, or the Setting of American Foreign Policy* (New York: McGraw-Hill, 1968), chaps. 5 and 6.

2

America's Global Involvement and the Emergence of the Cold War

It is logical that the United States should do whatever it is able to do
to assist in the return of normal economic health in the world. . . .
Our policy is directed not against any country or doctrine but against
hunger, poverty, desperation and chaos. Its purpose should be the revival
of a working economy in the world so as to permit the emergence
of political and social conditions in which free institutions can exist.

SECRETARY OF STATE GEORGE C. MARSHALL
ADDRESS AT HARVARD UNIVERSITY, JUNE 5, 1947

It is clear that the main element of any United States policy
toward the Soviet Union must be that of a long-term, patient
but firm and vigilant containment of Russian expansive tendencies.

MR. X [GEORGE F. KENNAN]
"THE SOURCES OF SOVIET CONDUCT," *FOREIGN AFFAIRS,* JULY 1947

World War II plunged the United States into global affairs. By the end of 1941, the country had fully committed itself to total victory, and its involvement was to prove crucial to the war effort. Because of its central importance to allied success, and its substantive involvement in international affairs, the United States found it difficult to change course in 1945 and revert to the isolationism of the past. To be sure, the first impulse was in this direction. Calls were heard for massive demobilization of the armed forces, cutbacks in the New Deal legislation of President Franklin Roosevelt, and other efforts toward political and economic isolationism.[1] However, at least three sets of factors militated against such a course and propelled the United States in the direction of global power: (1) the global political and economic conditions of 1945 to 1947; (2) the decision of leading political figures within the United States to abandon isolationism after World War II; and, most important, (3) the rise of an ideological challenge from the Soviet Union.

In this chapter, we first examine these factors and how they led to the abandonment of isolationism and the adoption of globalism by the United States. In turn, we set forth the military, economic, and political dimensions of this new globalist involvement—summarized under the rubric of the containment doctrine—and discuss how this involvement became both universal in scope and remained moral in content. As will be shown in Chapter 3, moreover, the containment doctrine produced a distinct set of foreign policy values, beliefs, and actions on the part of the United States.

THE POSTWAR WORLD
AND AMERICAN INVOLVEMENT

The international system that the United States faced after the defeat of Germany and Japan was considerably different from any that it had faced in its history: The traditional powers of Europe were defeated or had been ruined by the ravages of war; the global economy had been significantly weakened by that war; and a relatively new power, the Soviet Union, equipped with a threatening ideology, had survived the war—arguably in better shape than any other European power. Yet, the United States was in a relatively strong political, economic, and military position. Such conditions seemed to imply the need for sustained U.S. involvement, despite its isolationist past.

Yet, such a decision for involvement was made neither quickly or automatically; rather, it seemed to come about over the course of several years and largely through the confluence of several complementary factors. We begin our discussion, therefore, with a brief description of three of these factors and suggest how they interacted with one another to move the United States toward sustained global involvement.

The Global Vacuum: A Challenge
to American Isolationism

The first important factor that contributed to America's decision to move away from isolationism was the political and economic conditions of the international system immediately after World War II. The land, the cities, and the homes, along with the economies, of most European nations had been devastated by the war. Sizeable portions of the land had been either flooded, scorched from battle, or confiscated for military operations. Even the land that remained for cultivation was in poor condition. Hunger was widespread, and a black market in food flourished. The industrial sectors of these nations, along with the major cities, were badly damaged or in total ruins. London, Vienna, Trieste, Warsaw, Berlin, Rotterdam, and Cologne, among others, bore the scars of war. Millions of people were homeless, too. By one estimate, 5 million homes had been destroyed, with many more millions badly damaged. In a word, Europe was a "wasteland."[2]

European economies were weak, in debt, and driven by inflation. Britain, for example, had to use up much of its wealth to win the war and, with a debt of about $6 billion at war's end, had to rely upon American assistance to remain solvent.[3] France, the Netherlands, Belgium, and other European states were in no better shape. Each had to rely, in varying degrees, upon American assistance to meet its financial needs. Foreign and domestic political problems also faced these states. Several British and French colonies were demanding freedom and independence. In Syria, Lebanon, Indochina, and later Tunisia, Morocco, and Algeria, for instance, indigenous movements were seeking independence from France. The British were confronted by independence efforts in India, Burma, Ceylon, and Palestine, among others. Britain faced domestic austerity, while the French struggled at home with governmental instability and worker discontent. With such problems at home and abroad, neither of these states was in a position to assert a very prominent role in postwar international politics.

The conditions in Germany and Italy further contributed to the political and economic vacuum in Europe. Both of these powers had been defeated, and Germany was divided and occupied. Italy had a huge budget deficit in 1945–1946 (300 billion lire by one estimate) as well as an extraordinarily high rate of inflation. Germany, too, was in debt, owing nearly nine times more than at the beginning of World War II.[4] Overall, then, Europe, which for so long had been at the center of international politics and for so long had shaped global order, was ominously weak, both politically and economically. None of the traditional European powers seemed able to exert its traditional dominance in global politics.

In contrast to the postwar portrait of Europe, the United States was healthy and prosperous. Its industrial capacity was intact, and its economy was still booming. In the mid-1940s, the United States had growing balance of trade surpluses and huge economic reserves. For example, while Europe had trade deficits of $5.8 billion and $7.6 billion in 1946 and 1947, the United States in those same years had trade surpluses of $6.7 billion and $10.1 billion. Furthermore, American reserve assets—about $26 billion—were substantial and growing.[5]

The military might of the United States, too, seemed preeminent at that time. American troops occupied Europe and Japan. The nation had the world's largest navy ("The Pacific and the Mediterranean had become American lakes," in the words of one historian[6]). And, of course, the United States alone had the atomic bomb. In this sense, the United States possessed the capacity to assume a global role. Moreover, the international environment seemed highly conducive to both the possibility, and the necessity, for America to play a dominant role in global affairs.

American Leadership and Global Involvement

A second factor that encouraged the United States to abandon its isolationist strategy was the change in worldview among American leaders during and immediately after World War II. Most important, President Franklin Roosevelt had long concluded that America's response to global affairs after World War I had been ill-advised and that such a response should not guide American policy after World War II.[7] Instead, Roosevelt had decided that continued American involvement in global affairs was necessary and, early on in the war, had revealed his vision of world order in the postwar period.

Roosevelt's Plan The first necessity in Roosevelt's plan was the total defeat and disarming of the adversaries, with no leniency shown toward aggressor states. Second, there must be a renewed commitment on the part of the United States and others to prevent future global economic depressions and to foster self-determination for all states. Third, there must be the establishment of a global collective security organization with active American involvement. Finally, above and beyond these efforts, the allies in war must remain allies in peace in order to maintain global order.[8]

This last element of the plan was the core of Roosevelt's global blueprint.[9] American involvement in world affairs and its cooperation with the other great powers were essential. Indeed, Roosevelt's design envisaged a world in which this postwar cooperation among the four principal powers (United States, Great Britain, USSR, and China) would yield a system in which they acted as the "Four Policemen" to enforce global order. In other words, unlike Wilson's League of Nations, where all states would act to stop warfare and regulate conflict, only the great powers would have this responsibility. Such a vision bore a striking and unmistakable resemblance to traditional balance of power politics, although Roosevelt was unwilling to describe it in such terms.

Strategy: Building Wartime Cooperation To make this global design a reality, two major tasks confronted Roosevelt's diplomatic efforts during the war. One was directed toward building wartime cooperation, which would continue after the war. The other was directed toward jarring the United States from its isolationist moorings and positioning the country in such a way that it would retain a role in postwar international politics. To realize the first goal, the building of cooperation with the Soviet Union was deemed essential. Roosevelt, unlike some of his advisors and some State Department officials, believed that cooperation with the Soviet Union was possible after the end of World War II. He believed that the Soviet Union was motivated, in the shorthand of Daniel Yergin, more by the "Yalta Axioms" (the name is taken from the 1945 wartime conference in which political bargains were struck between East and West) than by the "Riga Axioms" (the name is taken from the Latvian capital city where a U.S. mission was located which "issued constant warning against the [Soviet] international menace" in the 1920s and 1930s).[10]

In the Yalta view, the Soviet Union was much like other nations in terms of defining its interests and fostering its goals based on power realities (the Yalta Axioms) rather than being driven primarily by ideological considerations (the Riga Axioms). As Yergin contends, "Roosevelt thought of the Soviet Union less as a revolutionary vanguard than as a conventional imperialist power, with ambitions rather like those of the Czarist regime."[11] Because of this perceived source of Soviet policy, Roosevelt judged that the Grand Alliance would be able to continue on a "businesslike" level as long as each recognized the interests of the other. Moreover, since the Soviet Union would be concerned about the reconstruction of its economy and society after the devastation of the war, it would have even further incentives to seek postwar stability and peace.

According to one well-known political analyst, there was another reason why Roosevelt thought that this cooperation could continue: the power of personal diplomacy.[12] Because Roosevelt had steered American policy toward the recognition of the Soviet Union, shared Stalin's anxiety over British imperialism, and seemed to recognize Soviet interest in the Baltics and Poland, cooperation would be possible.

To facilitate postwar cooperation with the Soviets, Roosevelt made a concerted effort throughout the war to foster good relations with them. The United States extended Lend-Lease assistance to the Soviet Union (albeit not as rapidly as the Soviet Union wished) and agreed to open up a second front against the Germans to relieve the battlefield pressure placed on them (albeit not as soon as the Soviet Union wanted). Through the several wartime conferences—Teheran, Cairo, Moscow, and Yalta—Roosevelt gained an understanding of the degree of Soviet insecurity regarding its exposed western borders and the need to take this factor into account in dealing with them. At the same time, though, he became increasingly convinced that he could work with "Uncle Joe" Stalin and that political bargains and accommodations with the Soviets were possible.

Strategy: A Role in Postwar International Politics Among the wartime conferences, the one that bears most directly upon postwar arrangements was the Yalta Conference, held in that Crimean resort during February 1945. Not only did this conference achieve agreement on a strategy for the completion of the war effort, but also it appeared to achieve commitments on the division and operation of postwar Europe. Such understandings were important because they signaled continued American interest and involvement in global affairs—specifically Europe's—but they also signaled that the competing interests of states were subject to negotiation and accommodation. Spheres of influence and balance of power politics were expressly incorporated in these agreements, and the major powers were to possess the greatest amount of importance in fulfilling them.[13]

Specifically, Roosevelt, Stalin, and British Prime Minister Winston Churchill agreed to zones of occupation of Germany by the Americans, British, French, and Russians. Second, they provided some territorial concessions to the Soviets at the expense of Poland. (In turn, Poland was to receive some territory from Germany.) Third, the wartime leaders allowed an expansion of the Lublin Committee, which was governing Poland, to include some Polish government officials who were in exile in London as a way of dealing with the postwar government question in Poland. Fourth, they proclaimed the Declaration of Liberated Europe, which specified free elections and constitutional safeguards of individual freedom in the liberated nations. And, finally, the conferees produced an agreement on the Soviet Union's joining the war against Japan and the veto mechanism within the Security Council of the United Nations.[14]

In light of subsequent events, Roosevelt has been highly criticized for the bargains that were struck at Yalta. The Soviets got several territorial concessions and, in the space of a few short years, were able to gain control of the Polish government as well as other Eastern European governments. Roosevelt's rationale was that only by taking into account the interests of the various parties (including the Soviets) was a stable postwar world possible. Moreover, he also appeared to consider the Soviet sense of insecurity along its western border in making some of these arrangements. Finally, and perhaps most important, Soviet troops already occupied these Eastern European states.[15] Any prospects of a more favorable outcome for the Western states appeared to be more in the realm of hope than a real possibility. Despite these criticisms, the Yalta agreements do mark the beginning of an American commitment to global involvement beyond the wartime period. In addition, with the agreement on the operation of the Security Council and the subsequent conference on the United Nations Charter in San Francisco during April 1945, the United States was rather quickly moving itself toward global involvement.[16]

The Rise of the Soviet Challenge

This commitment to international involvement was no less true for President Roosevelt's successor, Harry S Truman, and his principal foreign policy advisors. But this commitment was expanded and solidified by the rise of the Soviet ideological challenge that developed by late 1946 and early 1947.

Although Truman's foreign policy approach was not nearly as well developed as that outlined by Roosevelt's postwar plan, there was no inclination on the part of President Truman to reject continued American involvement in the world. Three sets of factors seem to have shaped his commitment to involvement: (1) his Wilsonian idealism, (2) the wartime situation existing when he assumed office, and (3) the views of his principal foreign policy advisors.

Wilsonian Idealism Truman, prior to assuming the presidency, had displayed a commitment to an international role for the United States. In particular, he agreed

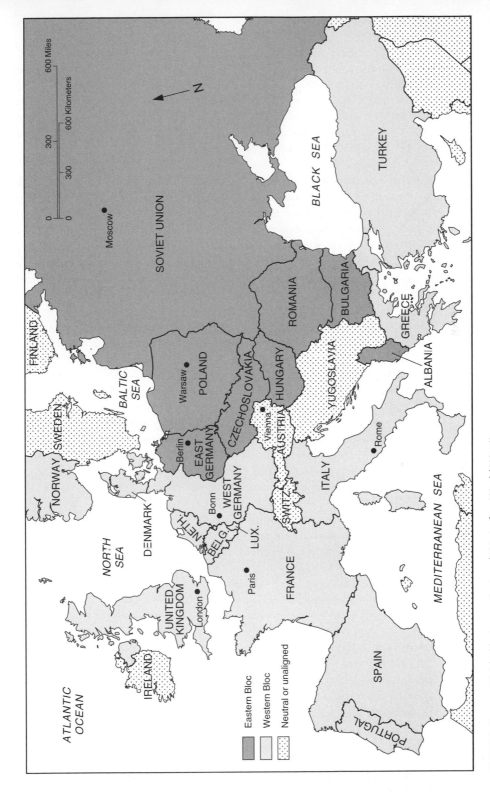

MAP 2.1 Europe Divided between East and West after World War II

with Woodrow Wilson that America should participate in world affairs, particularly through a global organization. As a consequence, Truman worked in the Senate to gain support for the emergent United Nations. At the same time, like Wilson, he tended to see the United States as a moral force in the world and was somewhat suspicious of the postwar design epitomized by the Four Policemen plan.[17] Nonetheless, he supported and worked to put Roosevelt's plan into practice.

Wartime Situation   Truman's commitment to global involvement was aided by the circumstances at the time he became president. President Roosevelt had died just after the Yalta agreements on postwar Europe had been concluded, just prior to the United Nations Conference in San Francisco, and just before the Allies had been ultimately successful in World War II. As a result, Truman felt the Yalta agreements had to be implemented, the United Nations needed to become a reality, and the war had to be won. In all of these areas, President Truman followed his predecessor.

Views of Truman's Advisors   Truman's closest advisors were also influential in reinforcing the commitment to a global role for the United States. In particular, such key advisors as Admiral William D. Leahy, Ambassador Averell Harriman, Secretary of State Edward R. Stettinius, and Secretary of War Henry Stimson all counseled for a continuance of a leading role for the United States.[18] Later, such men as Secretary of State James Byrnes, Undersecretary of State (and later Secretary of State) Dean Acheson, and Navy Secretary James V. Forrestal became Truman's key policy advisors. These new advisors also tended to favor an active global involvement, especially with their less favorable view of the Soviet Union, although, according to historian Ernest May, "their prejudices and predispositions can serve as only one small element" in the change of American policy toward the Soviet Union.[19]

Nevertheless, the issue soon became less one of whether there should be American global involvement and more a question of the degree of that involvement. Fueled by negative assessments of the Soviet Union by seasoned diplomatic observers, Truman's advisors increasingly focused upon the threat posed by international communism generally and by the Soviet Union specifically.[20] In time, the shape of America's postwar global role became largely a consequence of the perceived intentions of Soviet ideology.

Truman's Early Position   In the first months after assuming office, President Truman followed Roosevelt's strategy for peace and American involvement by trying to maintain great-power unity. As he said: "I want peace and I am willing to work hard for it: . . . to have a reasonably lasting peace, the three great powers must be able to trust each other." Likewise, he remained faithful to the requirements of the Yalta agreements and tried to cajole Stalin to do the same by telling Soviet Foreign Minister Molotov to "carry out your agreements."[21]

A Changing Environment   By the time of the Potsdam Conference (July 1945), President Truman was increasingly urged to be tough with the Soviets, while still seeking postwar cooperation. Although the accommodation that came out of Potsdam over German reparations and German boundaries, as well as other agreements, were deemed tolerable, American officials ultimately came away uneasy over the future prospects of Soviet-American relations.[22] Subsequent meetings in London (September 1945), over peace treaties for Finland, Hungary, Romania, and Bulgaria, and in Moscow (December 1945), over adherence to the Yalta accords, reinforced this uneasiness and continued to highlight the growing suspicion between the United States and the Soviet Union.[23]

The end of the 1945 and early months of 1946 seemed to mark a watershed in Soviet-American relations.[24] By this time, the American public, Congress, and the president's chief advisors were increasingly lobbying for tougher action against Soviet noncompliance with the Yalta agreements and with its efforts to undermine governments in Eastern Europe. Coupled with these domestic pressures were ominous statements by Stalin and Churchill about American and Soviet intentions toward the world.

Stalin Attacks Capitalism In a speech on February 9, 1946, Soviet leader Joseph Stalin alarmed American policy makers by attacking capitalism, suggesting the inevitability of war among capitalist states, and calling for significant economic strides to meet the capitalist challenge. At the outset of the speech, Stalin noted the dangers from capitalist states: "Marxists have repeatedly declared that the capitalist world economic system conceals in itself the elements of general crisis and military clashes. . . ." Near the end, Stalin asserted that "the party intends to organize a new powerful advance in the national economy. . . . Only under these circumstances is it possible to consider that our country will be guaranteed against any eventuality."[25]

While the meaning and intent of Stalin's remarks inevitably fostered some debate (one analysis suggested that Stalin really did not want a "new war" and said so through 1947), and these comments "constituted about one-tenth of the address,"[26] the ultimate effect was quite profound on American policy makers. Indeed, in the assessment of two prominent diplomatic historians of this period, the meaning of these passages was clear. Stalin was suggesting that "war was inevitable as long as capitalism existed," and "that future wars were inevitable until the world economic system was reformed, that is, until communism supplanted capitalism. . . ."[27]

Churchill's Response On March 5, 1946, Winston Churchill reciprocated by articulating the West's fear of the East. In his famous "iron curtain" speech at Westminster College in Fulton, Missouri, Churchill called for "a fraternal association of the English-speaking peoples . . . a special relationship between the British Commonwealth and Empire and the United States" to provide global order since "from Stettin in the Baltic to Trieste in the Adriatic, an iron curtain has descended across the Continent. Behind that line lie all the capitals of the ancient states of Central and Eastern Europe." Moreover, these states and many ancient cities "lie in what I must call the Soviet sphere," Churchill continued, "and all are subject in one form or another, not only to Soviet influence but to a very high and, in many cases, increasing measure of control from Moscow."[28] This speech marked a frontal attack on the Soviet Union, and, like Stalin's February speech, suggested the impossibility of continued Soviet-American cooperation in the postwar world because of the differing worldview held by each nation. Importantly, President Truman seemed to be giving some legitimacy to such a view, since he accompanied Churchill to Missouri.[29]

Kennan's Perception from Moscow At about the same time as these two important speeches were delivered, George Kennan, an American diplomat serving in Moscow at the time, sent his famous "long telegram" to Washington. (The actual date of the message is February 22, 1946.) In this lengthy message, Kennan outlined his view of the basic premises of the Soviet world outlook, the "Kremlin's neurotic view of world affairs," the "instinctive Russian sense of insecurity," and its "official" and "subterranean" actions against free societies. Its policies, Kennan argued, will work vigorously to advance Soviet interests worldwide and to undermine Western powers. "In general," Kennan noted near the end of the message, "all Soviet efforts on [an] unofficial international plane will be negative and destructive in character, designed to tear down sources of strength beyond reach of Soviet control."

Kennan, however, put it even more succinctly in the concluding section of the telegram:

> [W]e have here a political force committed fanatically to the belief that with US there can be no permanent modus vivendi, that it is desirable and necessary that the internal harmony of our society be disrupted, our traditional way of life be destroyed, the international authority of our state be broken, if Soviet power is to be secure. Finally, it is seemingly inaccessible to considerations of reality in its basic reactions. For it, the vast fund of objective facts about human society is not, as with us, the measure against which outlook is constantly tested and reformed, but a grab bag from which individual items are selected arbitrarily and tendentiously to bolster an outlook already preconceived.[30]

In essence, this view of the Soviet Union has come to be summarized as the Riga Axioms (in contrast to the Yalta Axioms, which President Roosevelt had adopted). Ideology, and not the realities of power politics, was the important determinant of Soviet conduct. These statements by Stalin and Churchill and the circulation of Kennan's "long telegram" within the Washington bureaucracy increased the clamor for a changed policy toward the Soviet Union.[31] They produced a "get tough" policy on the part of the United States. And they permanently changed the role of the United States in global affairs.

AMERICA'S GLOBALISM:
THE TRUMAN DOCTRINE AND BEYOND

The immediate response to these calls for a "get tough" policy was reflected in American policy over Soviet troops remaining in Iran in March 1946. Under the Tripartite Treaty of Alliance signed by Iran, the Soviet Union, and Great Britain in January 1942, Allied forces were to be withdrawn from Iranian territory within six months after hostilities had ended between the Allies and the Axis powers. By March 2, 1946—six months after the surrender of Japan—all British and American forces had indeed withdrawn from Iran, but Soviet forces had not. Instead, the Soviets were sending additional troops into Iran, were continuing to meddle in Iranian politics, and apparently had designs on Turkey and Iraq from their Iranian base.[32]

With such circumstances, the American leadership decided to stand firm on the withdrawal of Soviet forces. Secretary of State James Byrnes and British Foreign Minister Ernest Bevin gave important speeches that made the West's position clear. In a late February 1946 speech, Secretary Byrnes had asserted:

> We have joined our allies in the United Nations to put an end to war. We have covenanted not to use force except in the defense of law as embodied in the purposes and principles of the [U.N.] Charter. We intend to live up to that covenant.
>
>   But as a great power and as a permanent member of the Security Council *we have a responsibility to use our influence to see that other powers live up to their covenant.* . . .
>
>   We will not and we cannot stand aloof if force or threat of force is used contrary to the purposes and principles of the Charter. We have no right to hold our troops in the territories of other sovereign states without their approval and consent freely given.[33]

Later, on March 16, Secretary of State Byrnes reiterated American resolve in another speech by repeating some of the themes from the earlier address. Faced with British and American resolve and with an imminent UN Security Council session on the Iranian issue, the Soviet Union began to seek a negotiated solution. In early April 1946, an agreement was reached that called for the withdrawal of all Soviet forces from Iran by the middle of May 1946.[34] Thus, when America adopted a tougher policy line toward the Soviet Union, it was able to achieve results.

Despite the initial success of this firmer course in early 1946, the real change in America's policy toward the Soviets (and ultimately toward the rest of the world) was not fully manifested until a year later. The occasion was over the question of aid to two strategically important countries, Greece and Turkey.

The Greek government was under pressure from a Communist-supported national liberation movement, while Turkey was under political pressure from the Soviet Union and its allies over control of the Dardanelles (the straits that provide access to the Mediterranean from the Soviet Union's Black Sea ports) and over territorial concessions to the Soviets in Turkish–Soviet border areas.[35] Because the British, in February 1947, had indicated to the Americans that they could no longer aid these countries, the burden apparently now fell to the Americans if these states were to remain stable. Accordingly, President Truman decided to seek $400 million in aid for these Mediterranean states.

The granting of aid itself was not a sharp break from the past, since the United States had provided assistance in 1946.[36] What was dramatic about the aid request was its *form, rationale,* and *purpose*. The form of the request was a formal speech by President Truman to a joint session of Congress on March 12, 1947. The rationale for the request was even more dramatic: a need to stop the expansion of global communism. And the purpose was startling: to commit the United States to a global strategy against this Communist threat.

In his speech, in which he announced what has come to be known as the Truman Doctrine, the president first set out the conditions within Greece and Turkey that necessitated this assistance. Then he more fully outlined the justification for his policy and identified the global struggle that the United States faced. The United States, he said, must *"help free peoples to maintain their free institutions and their national identity against aggressive movements that seek to impose upon them totalitarian regimes."* Moreover, such threats to freedom affect the security of the United States: *"totalitarian regimes imposed upon free peoples, by direct or indirect aggression, undermine the foundations of international peace and hence the security of the United States."* At this juncture in history, President Truman continued, the nations of the world faced a decision between two ways of life: one free, the other unfree; one based *"upon the will of the majority,"* the other based upon *"the will of a minority,"* one based upon *"free institutions,"* the other based upon *"terror and oppression."* The task for the United States, therefore, was a clear one, he concluded: *"we must assist free peoples to work out their own destinies in their own way."* The challenge to the Soviet Union was now clearly drawn; the Cold War had begun.[37]

The specific policy that the United States was to adopt in this struggle with the Soviet Union was the *containment* strategy. This term was first used in an anonymously authored article in *Foreign Affairs* magazine in July 1947. (Its author was quickly identified, though, as George Kennan, by then the head of the Policy Planning Staff at the Department of State in Washington, and the article actually grew out of his original "Long Telegram" sent to the State Department a year earlier.) According to Kennan, the appropriate policy to adopt against the Soviet challenge was "a long-term patient but firm and vigilant containment of Russian expansive tendencies." Specifically, he called for the application of "counter-force at a series of constantly shifting geographical and political points," against Soviet action. By following such a policy, the United States may, over time, force "a far greater degree of moderation and circumspection . . . and in this way . . . promote . . . tendencies which must eventually find their outlet in either the break-up or the gradual mellowing of Soviet power."[38]

Kennan identified a number of conditions within the Soviet system that would aid this containment policy in achieving the prescribed goal. The population "in Russia today," he noted, "is physically and spiritually tired." The impact of the Soviet system on the young remains unclear. The performance of the Soviet economy "has been precariously spotty and uneven."[39] And the issue of succession was surely incomplete:

> the future of Soviet power may not be by any means as secure as Russian capacity for self-delusion would make it appear to the men in the Kremlin. That they can keep power themselves, they have demonstrated. That they can quietly and easily turn it over to others remains to be proved.[40]

Although Kennan was confident that a steady course by the United States would be successful, he was not precise in stating what the actual substance of the counterforce or containment toward the Soviet Union should be. As a result, the response by American policy makers was to embark upon a series of sweeping military, economic, and political initiatives from 1947 through the mid-1950s to control international communism, a direction that Kennan later criticized.[41]

ELEMENTS OF CONTAINMENT:
REGIONAL SECURITY PACTS

The first, and probably principal, containment initiative was the establishment of several regional politico-military alliances. In Latin America, the *Rio Pact* (formally known as the Inter-American Treaty of Reciprocal Assistance) was signed in September 1947 by the United States and twenty-one other American republics. In Western Europe, the *North Atlantic Treaty Organization* (NATO) was set up in April 1949 by the United States, Canada, and ten (later thirteen in the 1950s, fourteen by 1982) Western European nations. In Asia, two important pacts were established: the *ANZUS Treaty* of September 1951,[42] and the Southeast Asia Collective Defense Treaty of September 1954. The former treaty involved the United States, Australia, and New Zealand, while the latter included the United States, the United Kingdom, France, Australia, New Zealand, Pakistan, the Philippines, and Thailand and formed what became known as the *Southeast Asia Treaty Organization* (SEATO). For the SEATO treaty, a protocol was added to provide security protection for South Vietnam, Cambodia, and Laos. (This protocol would become most important in light of America's subsequent involvement in the Vietnam War.[43]) Map 2.2 portrays these organizations and the areas covered by each and also summarizes the principal goals of each organization and the nations that comprise the membership.

One other collective security organization, the *Central Treaty Organization* (CENTO), was also established during this time period, although the United States was not a direct member. This organization evolved out of a bilateral pact of mutual cooperation between Iraq and Turkey (the so-called Baghdad Pact of February 1955) and was formally constituted in 1959 with the inclusion of the United Kingdom, Pakistan, and Iran. However, through an executive agreement with Turkey, the United States pledged to support the security needs of CENTO members and to provide various kinds of assistance. In addition, the United States

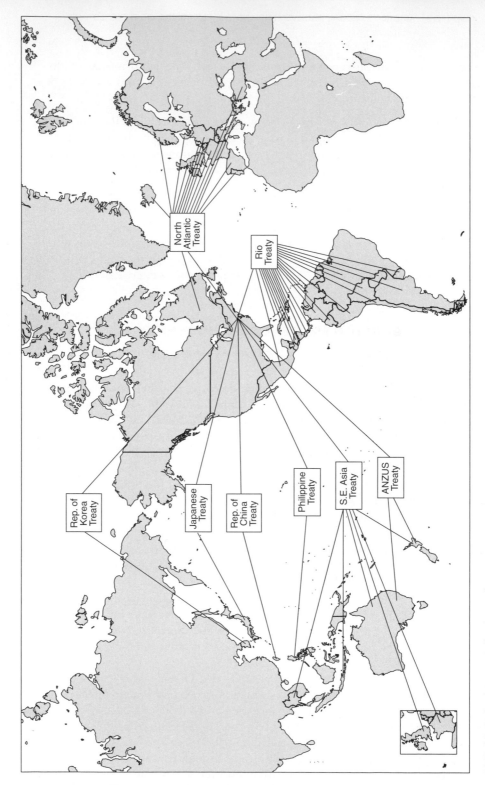

MAP 2.2 United States Collective Defense Arrangements

MAP 2.2 Continued

Multilateral Pacts

Rio Treaty, or the Inter-American Treaty of Reciprocal Assistance (22 Nations)

A treaty signed September 2, 1947, which provides that an armed attack against any American state, "shall be considered as an attack against all the American States and . . . each one . . . undertakes to assist in meeting the attack. . . ."

Membership: United States, Mexico, Cuba, Haiti, Dominican Republic, Honduras, Guatemala, El Salvador, Nicaragua, Costa Rica, Panama, Colombia, Venezuela, Ecuador, Peru, Brazil, Bolivia, Paraguay, Chile, Argentina, Uruguay, and Trinidad and Tobago.

North Atlantic Treaty (16 Nations)

A treaty signed April 4, 1949, by which "the Parties agree that an armed attack against one or more of them in Europe or North America shall be considered an attack against them all; and . . . each of them . . . will assist the . . . attacked by taking forthwith, individually and in concert with the other Parties, such action as it deems necessary, including the use of armed force. . . ."

Membership: United States, Canada, Iceland, Norway, United Kingdom, Netherlands, Denmark, Belgium, Luxembourg, Portugal, France, Italy, Greece (joined in 1952), Turkey (1952), Federal Republic of Germany (1955), and Spain (1982)

ANZUS Treaty (3 Nations)

A treaty signed September 1, 1951, whereby each of the parties "recognizes that an armed attack in the Pacific Area on any of the Parties would be dangerous to its own peace and safety and declares that it would act to meet the common danger in accordance with its constitutional processes."

Membership: United States, New Zealand, and Australia

Southeast Asia Treaty (7 Nations)

A treaty signed September 8, 1954, whereby each party "recognizes that aggression by means of armed attack in the treaty area against any of the Parties . . . would endanger its own peace and safety" and each will "in that event act to meet the common danger in accordance with its constitutional processes."

Membership: United States, United Kingdom, France, New Zealand, Australia, Philippines, and Thailand

Bilateral Pacts

Philippine Treaty

A treaty signed August 30, 1951, whereby each of the parties recognizes "that an armed attack in the Pacific Area on either of the Parties would be dangerous to its own peace and safety" and each party agrees that it will act "to meet the common danger in accordance with its constitutional processes."

Membership: United States and the Philippines

Japanese Treaty

A treaty signed January 19, 1960 (replacing the original security treaty of September 8, 1951), whereby each part "recognizes that an armed attack against either Party in the territories under the administration of Japan would be dangerous to its own peace and safety and declares that it would act to meet the common danger in accordance with its constitutional provisions and processes."

Membership: United States and Japan

Republic of Korea Treaty

A treaty signed October 1, 1953, whereby each party "recognizes that an armed attack in the Pacific area on either of the Parties . . . would be dangerous to its own peace and safety" and that each party "would act to meet the common danger in accordance with its constitutional processes."

Membership: United States and the Republic of Korea

Republic of China Treaty

A treaty signed December 2, 1954, whereby each of the parties "recognizes that an armed attack in the West Pacific Area directed against the territories of either of the Parties would be dangerous to its own peace and safety . . ." and that each "would act to meet the common danger in accordance with its constitutional processes." The territory of the Republic of China is defined as "Taiwan (Formosa) and the Pescadores."

Membership: United States and the Republic of China

actively participated in CENTO meetings and assisted with the pact's joint undertakings. Because of the active involvement in the operation of the organization by
the United States and because of its indirect pledge of support, CENTO was
actually another link in the global security arrangements the United States initiated in the immediate postwar years. All of these defense agreements had provisions for assistance when confronted by armed attacks, threats of aggression, or
even internal subversion in the case of SEATO. For the ANZUS, SEATO, Rio,
and CENTO pacts, however, the response was not automatic. Instead, in the main,
each of the signatories agreed "to meet the common danger in accordance with
its constitutional processes."[44] NATO is usually identified as an exception among
these pacts for at least two reasons: (1) the commitment by the parties to respond
to an attack appears to be more automatic than the other pacts; and (2) the organizational structure within NATO developed much more fully than in the other
pacts.

First, Article 5 of the NATO agreement seemed to call for an automatic
armed response on the part of the signatories to an attack:

> The Parties agree that an armed attack against one or more of them in
> Europe or North America shall be considered an attack against them all,
> and consequently they agree that, if such an armed attack occurs, each of
> them . . . with assist the Parties so attacked forthwith, individually, and in
> concert with the other Parties, such action as it deems necessary, including
> the use of armed force, to restore and maintain the security of the North
> Atlantic area.[45]

Yet constitutional scholar Michael Glennon has cautioned against too facile
an interpretation of this article. As he noted, a party to the pact could take actions it "deems necessary," but troops are not necessarily required automatically.
Indeed, at the time, Secretary of State Dean Acheson, in commenting on this
treaty provision, downplayed the automaticity of troop commitments, since, he
acknowledged, only Congress had that authority. However, both Acheson and
congressional allies of the Truman administration vigorously opposed a reserva-
tion to the NATO treaty that would have spelled out the limited nature of the
commitment more fully. The Truman administration apparently wanted to maintain some ambiguity over the meaning of this article, both to accommodate critics
at home and to reassure allies abroad.[46] In this sense, the commitment in the
NATO treaty does appear to be a bit different than in the other pacts during this
time.

Second, the members of the NATO pact also established an integrated military command structure and called for the commitment of forces to NATO
(although the forces remained under ultimate national command) by each of the
member states. In both of these ways, then, NATO proved the most important of
the regional security pacts, since it involved the area of greatest concern for American interests and because Europe was regarded as the primary area of potential
Soviet aggression.

In addition to the regional military organizations that were set up, a series of
bilateral defense pacts were established in Asia to combat Soviet and Chinese

aggression. Bilateral pacts were completed with the Philippines (1951), Japan (1951), the Republic of Korea (1953), and the Republic of China (Taiwan 1954). These pacts resulted from two major political events in Asia in the late 1940s and early 1950s: the Communist triumph in China under Mao Tse-tung in 1949 and the war that broke out in Korea in 1950 (see below).[47] With these bilateral treaties in the early 1950s, the mosaic of global security was largely completed. Moreover, a quick look at Map 2.2 indicates that the United States was quite successful in forming alliances in most areas that were not directly under Soviet control.

Nevertheless, two prominent regions, Africa and the Middle East, were still not directly covered by these security arrangements. Here too, however, some elements of containment were evident. In Africa, for instance, the European colonial powers still held sway, and thus the region was largely under the containment shield through these allied states.[48] The security efforts in the Middle East region were more complex. Although the regimes in this area at this time were mainly traditional monarchies, stirrings of nationalism and pan–Arabism within Egypt under Gamal Abdel Nasser and the spread of these sentiments throughout the region made treaty commitments difficult. Added to these factors were America's close ties to Israel over the festering Arab-Israeli conflict. Despite these hindrances, the United States did initiate one important security proposal to the nations in this volatile area: the so-called Eisenhower Doctrine.

This doctrine arose from a speech given by President Dwight D. Eisenhower to a joint session of Congress over perceived trouble in the Middle East and the need for the United States to combat it. "If power-hungry Communists should either falsely or correctly estimate that the Middle East is inadequately defended, they might be tempted to use open measures of armed attack," President Eisenhower declared. To combat this eventuality, he asked Congress for authority to extend economic and military assistance as needed and "to use armed forces to assist any such nation or group of such nations requesting assistance against armed aggression from any country controlled by international communism."[49] U.S. security commitments were now truly global in scope.

ELEMENTS OF CONTAINMENT:
ECONOMIC AND MILITARY ASSISTANCE

The second set of initiatives to implement the containment strategy focused upon economic and military assistance to friendly nations. From the late 1940s and through the mid- and late 1950s, substantial aid (reaching over $10 billion in 1953) was provided to an ever-expanding set of nations throughout the world. While the initial goal of these assistance efforts was to foster the economic well-being of the recipient societies, the ultimate rationale, especially after 1950, became *strategic* and *political* in content: to ensure the stability of those states threatened by international communism and to build support for anticommunism on a global scale. Three important programs reflect the kinds of assistance initiated by the United States during this period as well as its change in orientation over time:

1. The Marshall Plan
2. The Point Four program
3. The mutual security concept[50]

The Marshall Plan

Proposed in a speech by Secretary of State George Marshall at the Harvard commencement exercises in June 1947, the Marshall Plan is the best-known U.S. assistance effort. Marshall called for the Europeans to draw up a plan for economic recovery and pledged American economic support to implement such an effort. As a consequence of this speech and subsequent European-American consultations, President Truman asked Congress for $17 billion over a four-year period from 1948 to 1952 to revitalize Western Europe. The enormity of such an aid commitment becomes apparent when compared to the approximately $1 billion of assistance offered to Eastern Europe after the collapse of the Iron Curtain in 1989 and 1990. Its size is also reflected in the fact that the Marshall Plan aid program constituted about 1.2 percent of the GNP of the United States at the time. Over recent years, the amount of U.S. development assistance has constituted well under 0.5 percent of the GNP. In 2000, it constituted only 0.10 percent of the GNP.[51]

The rationale for the Marshall Plan was to rebuild the economic system of Western Europe. As a key trading partner for the United States, a healthy Europe was important to the economic health of America. Beyond these economic concerns, though, there were political concerns. If Europe did not recover, the region might well be subject to political instability and perhaps Communist penetration and subversion. According to one analysis of the decision making over the Marshall Plan, this "threat" dimension became particularly important in the late stages of deliberations (February through April 1948, just prior to the enactment of the plan).[52] In this sense, by the time of its formal passage by Congress, the European Recovery Program, or Marshall Plan, had clear elements of the containment strategy.

Point Four

While the Marshall Plan proved remarkably successful in fostering European recovery, President Truman also envisioned a larger plan of assistance for the rest of the world. His Point Four program was announced in his inaugural address of January 20, 1949. (The name was derived from the fact that this was the fourth major point in his suggested courses of action for American policy.) The aim of this program was to develop on a global scale the essentials of the Marshall Plan, which was then under way in Western Europe. Unlike the Marshall Plan, though, Point Four was less a cooperative venture with participating states and more a unilateral effort on the part of the United States, although America's allies might also become involved. In essence, the program was to provide industrial, technological, and economic assistance to the underdeveloped nations of the world.[53] In this sense, the Point Four program was an imaginative and substantial commitment to global economic development by the United States.

The Mutual Security Concept

While Point Four had some of the same ambitious economic—and undoubtedly political—motivations as the Marshall Plan, the program never really received sufficient funding authorization from the Congress.[54] Instead, this strategy of global assistance was rather quickly replaced by a new approach that was more explicitly political in content, the mutual security concept. The mutual security approach emphasized aiding nations to combat communism and to strengthen the security of the United States and the "free world." In addition to the change in rationale for aid, the kind of assistance also changed from primarily economic and humanitarian aid to military assistance by the early and mid-1950s. While economic aid was not halted during this period, its purpose changed. Now economic assistance was more likely given to bolster the overall security capability of friendly countries.

These changes in aid policy can be explained by the deepening global crisis that the United States perceived in the world. Tensions between the Soviet Union and the United States were rising over Soviet actions in Eastern Europe and its potential actions toward Western Europe. The Korean War had broken out, apparently with Soviet compliance. The Chinese Communists later entered this conflict, again evoking concern over Communist intentions. Domestically, too, there was an increased sense of Communist threat, led by the verbal assaults of Senator Joseph McCarthy of Wisconsin on various individuals and groups for being "soft on communism." All in all, America's national security was perceived to be under attack, and this required some response.

The first manifestation of this new aid strategy was the Mutual Defense Assistance Act of 1949.[55] This act, signed after the completion of the NATO pact and after the Soviets had tested an atomic bomb, provided for military aid to Western Europe, Greece, Turkey, Iran, South Korea, the Philippines, and the "China area." The strategic location of these countries is quite apparent; most bordered the Soviet Union or mainland China. Although the amount of aid called for in this act was relatively small, its significance lay in the fact that it was the initial effort in military aid by the United States.

A later act, the Mutual Security Act of 1951, marked the real beginning of growth in military assistance funding. Equally important, the language of the act dramatically illustrated the linkage between this new aid policy and American security. The aim of this act was

> to maintain the security and to promote the foreign policy of the United States by authorizing military, economic, and technical assistance to friendly countries to strengthen the mutual security and individual and collective

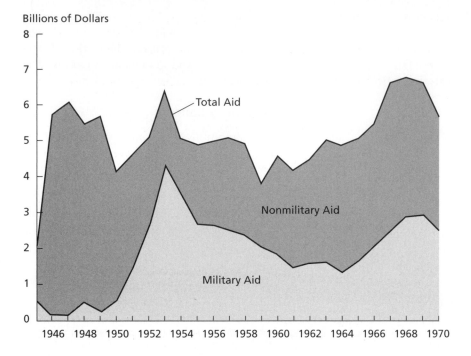

FIGURE 2.1 Patterns in Foreign Aid, 1945–1970 (Net Grants and Credits)

SOURCE: *The Statistical History of the United States from Colonial Times to the Present* (New York: Basic Books, Inc., 1976), pp. 274, 872.

defenses of the free world, [and] to develop their resources in the interest of their security and independence and the national interest of the United States.[56]

With successive mutual security acts like these, American global assistance, and particularly military assistance, increased sharply. Furthermore, the number of recipient countries also began to grow. As Figure 2.1 shows, military assistance came to dominate the total assistance effort. Even with the addition of food aid under Public Law 480 in 1954 and with the inclusion of some technical and developmental assistance to particular countries (e.g., Yugoslavia and Poland),[57] the proportion of military assistance was often greater than nonmilitary assistance until about 1960. By that time, a new approach to aid, one motivated more explicitly by development considerations, was already being contemplated and was finally implemented under the Kennedy administration in 1961, with the establishment of the Agency for International Development (AID). Still, the political rationale for economic aid continued. Aid was intended to save America's friends from Soviet (and Chinese) communism.

ELEMENTS OF CONTAINMENT:
THE DOMESTIC COLD WAR

The third element in the containment strategy was primarily domestic. Its aim was to make the American people aware of the Soviet threat and to change American domestic priorities to meet it. In essence, this aspect of containment might be labeled the *domestication* of the Cold War. One important document, completed by the National Security Council in April 1950 and entitled NSC-68, summarized the goals of this effort and provided a good guide to the subsequent domestic and international changes that occurred to meet the perceived Communist threat. Along with the Korean War, discussed in the next section, NSC-68 solidified America's commitment to the containment policy course.

NSC-68: Defense

NSC-68 was the result of a review of American foreign and domestic defense policies by State and Defense Department officials under the leadership of Paul Nitze. (Since the report remained classified until 1975, it also gives us a unique picture of the thinking of American officials without the restraint that might characterize documents written for public disclosure.) The document itself is a rather lengthy statement that begins by outlining the nature of the current international crisis between the Soviet Union and the United States and then goes on to contrast the foreign policy goals of Washington and Moscow in much the same vein as the Truman Doctrine, albeit in much harsher language. Document 2.1 excerpts portions of NSC-68 that depict these alternate views of the world.[58] Note the way that Soviet and American goals are characterized in the document and the nature of the conflict that the United States now faced.

NSC-68 analyzed four different policy options for the United States in responding to the Soviet challenge: (1) continuing the current policies; (2) returning to isolationism; (3) resorting to war against the Soviet Union; or (4) "a rapid build-up of political, economic and military strength in the Free World." After careful analysis of each one along military, economic, political, and social aspects, the study recommends that a rapid buildup of American and allied strength "is the only course which is consistent with progress toward achieving our fundamental purpose. The frustration of the Kremlin design requires the free world to develop a successfully functioning political and economic system and a vigorous political offensive against the Soviet Union."[59]

What makes NSC-68 particularly distinct from the other elements of containment is its emphasis upon a domestic response to the Soviet Union. While the report calls for aiding allies and promoting anticommunism around the world, it offers substantial commentary on the need for building up America's military capacity and eliciting greater support against the Soviet challenges at home.

The U.S. military, NSC-68 contended, was inferior to that of the Soviets in number of "forces in being and in total manpower." The amount of U.S. defense

Document 2.1   Excerpts from NSC-68, April 14, 1950

FUNDAMENTAL DESIGN OF THE UNITED STATES

The fundamental purpose of the United States is laid down in the Preamble of the Constitution. . . . In essence, [it] is to assure the integrity and vitality of our free society, which is founded upon the dignity and worth of the individual.

FUNDAMENTAL DESIGN OF THE KREMLIN

The fundamental design of those who control the Soviet Union and the international communist movement is to retain and solidify their absolute power, first in the Soviet Union and second in the areas now under their control. In the minds of the Soviet leaders, however, achievement of this design requires the dynamic extension of their authority and the ultimate elimination of any effective opposition to their authority. . . . The United States, as the principal center of power in the non-Soviet world and the bulwark of opposition to Soviet expansion, is the principal enemy whose integrity and vitality must be subverted or destroyed by one means or another if the Kremlin is to achieve its fundamental design.

NATURE OF THE CONFLICT

The Kremlin regards the United States as the only major threat to the achievement of its fundamental design. There is a basic conflict between the idea of freedom under a government of law, and the idea of slavery under the grim oligarchy of the Kremlin. . . . The idea of freedom, moreover, is peculiarly and intolerably subversive of the idea of slavery. But the converse is not true. The implacable purpose of the slave state to eliminate the challenge of freedom has placed the two great powers at opposite poles. It is this fact which gives the present polarization of power the quality of crisis.

The assault on free institutions is world-wide now, and in the context of the present polarization of power a defeat of free institutions anywhere is a defeat everywhere. . . .

In a shrinking world, which now faces the threat of atomic warfare, it is not an adequate objective merely to seek to check the Kremlin design, for the absence of order among nations is becoming less and less tolerable. This fact imposes on us, in our own interests, the responsibility of world leadership. It demands that we make the attempt, and accept the risks inherent in it, to bring about order and justice by means consistent with the principles of freedom and democracy. . . . Coupled with the probable fission bomb capability and possible thermonuclear bomb capability of the Soviet Union, the intensifying struggle requires us to face the fact that we can expect no lasting abatement of the crisis unless and until a change occurs in the nature of the Soviet system.

SOURCE: *A Report to the National Security Council, April 14, 1950*, pp. 5–9. Declassified on February 27, 1975, by Henry A. Kissinger, Assistant to the President for National Security Affairs.

spending was also relatively low, about 6 to 7 percent of the GNP as compared to more than 13 percent of GNP by the Soviet Union. In response, NSC-68 called for a rapid buildup of the American military establishment to counteract the Soviet challenge. Indeed, it went beyond this important general demand by proposing a new policy on military budgeting approach: In the future, it may be necessary to meet defense and foreign assistance needs by the reduction of federal expenditures in other areas—and by tax increases.[60] In effect, this policy was to place defense spending as the number one priority in the budgeting process of the U.S. government. Instead of defense being a residual category of the budget, it was to become the focal point of future allocation decisions. The rest of the budgetary items would become residual categories.

NSC-68 had at least one other significant statement on military planning. In the body of the report (and not specifically in its conclusions), the document calls for the United States to "produce and stockpile thermonuclear weapons in the event they prove feasible and would add significantly to our net capability."[61] Although this reference is relatively oblique in the context of the entire report, it was significant in terms of timing. During this period, the Truman administration was embroiled in a policy debate on whether to go forward with the building of the H-bomb.

NSC-68: Internal Security

A second important domestic issue discussed in the report was the moral capabilities of the United States. This area was also vulnerable, since the Soviets might well seek to undermine America's social and cultural institutions by infiltration and intimidation:

> Those that touch most closely our material and moral strength are obviously the prime targets, labor unions, civic enterprises, schools, churches, and all media for influencing opinion. The effort is not so much to make them serve obvious Soviet ends as to prevent them from serving our ends, and thus to make them sources of confusion in our economy, our culture and our body politic.[62]

Hence, the development of internal security and civilian defense programs was necessary. The government must "assure the internal security of the United States against dangers of sabotage, subversion, and espionage," the report noted. And the government must also "keep the U.S. public fully informed and cognizant of the threats to our national security so that it will be prepared to support the measures which we must accordingly adopt."[63] In essence, there should be efforts to protect the American people against subversion and to gain their support for Cold War policies.

To a considerable degree, these recommendations became American policy in the early 1950s, sparked by American involvement in the Korean War. Defense expenditures escalated to a level of more than 10 percent of the GNP in the early 1950s and generally stayed above 8 percent throughout the 1960s. Similarly, defense spending as a percentage of the federal budget rose sharply in the fifties to more than 50 percent and remained over 40 percent for all the years of the Johnson administration. A parallel growth pattern occurred in the size of the United States armed forces, with the number of people under arms reaching over 22 per 1,000 population in the early fifties and remaining about 14 per 1,000 population throughout the heart of the Vietnam War years. Figure 2.2 provides a summary view of these trends during the 1946–1968 period.[64] Additionally, the H-bomb program was given the go-ahead, and nuclear weapons became a part of defense strategy.

Efforts to ensure internal security were undertaken, too. As we have already noted, Senator Joseph McCarthy initiated his campaign against "Communists"

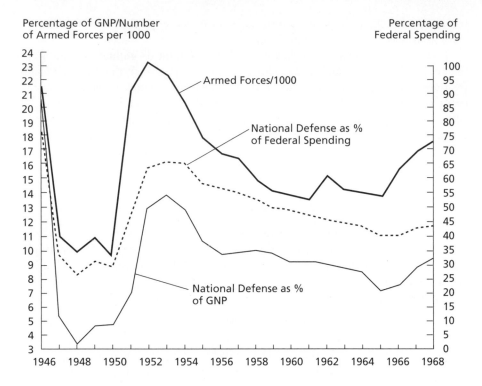

FIGURE 2.2 National Defense Expenditures
and U.S. Armed Forces per 1,000 Population, 1946–1968

SOURCES: The data for national defense as a percentage of federal spending and GNP are
taken from Alice C. Moroni, *The Fiscal Year 1984 Defense Budget Request: Data Summary*
(Washington, DC: Congressional Research Service, 1983), p. 13. Total National Defense data,
rather than only Department of Defense data, are used here. The two totals are usually very
close (p. 14). The armed forces percentages were calculated from total population (Part 1, p. 8)
and armed forces (Part 2, p. 1141) data in U.S. Bureau of the Census, *Historical Statistics of the
United States, Colonial Times to 1970,* Bicentennial Edition, Parts 1 and 2 (Washington, DC: U.S.
Government Printing Office, 1975).

within the government. In addition to his unswerving attacks, the public raised
questions about Communist subversion within America. The various investigations by the House Un-American Activities Committee of the 1950s and 1960s
reflect this growing concern with possible Soviet penetration. FBI and CIA surveillance activities in this area were also prevalent, as the Church Committee
investigations of intelligence activities were to reveal in the mid-1970s. Furthermore, efforts to employ loyalty oaths reflected this trend toward national security
consciousness. In short, political attacks, from the schoolroom to the boardroom,
produced a sense of widespread fear about veering too far from the mainstream on
foreign policy issues. To a remarkable degree, a foreign policy consensus was the
result of the political and psychological effects of the Cold War, and foreign policy debate suffered. When debate did occur, it was more often on foreign policy
tactics than on fundamental strategy.[65]

THE KOREAN WAR: THE FIRST
MAJOR TEST OF CONTAINMENT

Although the events in Greece and Turkey stimulated the emergence of containment policy in 1947, the first major test of this policy, and what brought the Cold War fully into existence, occurred in Korea in 1950. On June 25, 1950, North Korea attacked South Korea, which quickly engaged the Soviet Union, China, and the United States in a confrontation on the Korean peninsula. For the United States, too, it provided the raison d'être for fully implementing the various elements of the containment strategy outlined above.

American Involvement in Korea

A brief description of the situation on the Korean peninsula, the origins of the conflict, and the extent of U.S. involvement illustrates that conflict's significance for American postwar policy. Korea had been annexed by the Japanese in 1910 and was finally freed by American and Soviet forces at the end of World War II. By agreement between the two countries, Korea was then temporarily divided along the 38th parallel, with Soviet forces occupying the North and U.S. forces occupying the South (see Map 2.3). Despite several maneuvers by both sides, this division assumed a more permanent cast when a UN-supervised election in the South resulted in the establishment of the Republic of Korea on August 15, 1948, and when the adoption of a constitution in the North resulted in the creation of the Democratic People's Republic of Korea on September 9, 1948.[66] Each regime claimed to be the government of Korea, and neither would recognize or accept the legitimacy of the other. While Soviet and American occupying forces left in 1948 and 1949, respectively, the struggle between the two regimes (with the support of their powerful allies) was not finished.

This struggle soon erupted into sustained violence in mid-1950. When the North Koreans attacked South Korea, their powerful allies were quickly brought back into this conflict. Indeed, the United States viewed this attack on the South as Soviet-inspired and Soviet-directed.[67] While a great deal of scholarship has been directed at whether this view was accurate,[68] a former undersecretary of state at the time, U. Alexis Johnson, has made the essential point over this debate: "Whatever prompted Kim [Il-Sung, the North Korean leader] to order the attack, this is certain: At the time no responsible official in the United States or among our allies seriously questioned that the aggression was Soviet-inspired and aimed principally at testing our resolve."[69] With this overriding perception, the United States had little recourse but to respond and to make the containment doctrine a reality.

Within days, President Harry Truman ordered American air and naval support for the beleaguered South Korean troops and dispatched the Seventh Fleet to patrol the Formosa Strait to prevent Communist Chinese actions against the nationalist government on Taiwan. In addition, Truman sought and quickly obtained both United Nations Security Council condemnation of the attack and

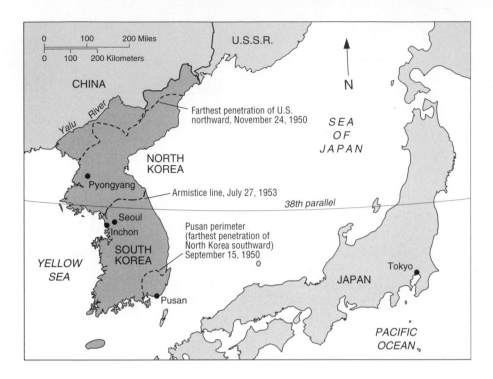

MAP 2.3 The Korean War, 1950–1953

support for a collective security force to be sent to aid the South Korean forces under U.S. direction. (The UN action was made possible by the Soviet Union's boycott of UN Security Council sessions because the China seat had not been given to the Communist government led by Mao Tse-tung. As a result, the Soviet Union was unable to exercise its veto.) Although some fourteen other nations ultimately sent forces to aid the South Koreans, the bulk of the war effort was carried by the Americans.[70] Indeed, the commander of all UN and U.S. forces in Korea was General Douglas MacArthur.

Initially, the American-led effort in Korea fared badly. Allied troops were driven to a small enclave around Pusan in Southeast Korea, and the North Koreans were on the verge of overrunning the entire peninsula. In September 15, 1950, however, General MacArthur executed his Inchon landing near Seoul behind North Korean lines, and, within a matter of weeks, proceeded across the 38th parallel into North Korea. While this invasion was brilliant as a strategic move, the Chinese became alarmed as MacArthur's forces moved ever northward, coming within miles of the Chinese border.[71]

While the Chinese had warned the West indirectly, through India in September 1950, that they would not "sit back with folded hands and let the Americans come to the border,"[72] the warning was not believed by U.S. policy makers. Beginning as early as mid-October 1950, Chinese People's Volunteers began crossing into North Korea to aid that government's forces. By late November 1950, the total Chinese forces totaled more than 300,000 fighting alongside the North Koreans against the UN and U.S. forces. The massive Chinese intervention drove allied forces back across the 38th parallel, the "temporary" dividing line between North and South Korea. Stalemate ensued.

General MacArthur proposed that U.S. forces carry the war into China as a way to resolve the conflict. Because President Truman had ordered him not to make public statements without administration approval and because administration policy was to limit the conflict, Truman fired General MacArthur for insubordination. This action caused an outpouring of support for MacArthur and the vilification of President Truman.[73] By and large, the American people continued to support the proposition that, once a war was undertaken, it should be fought to be won; it should not be limited by political constraints. The Truman administration felt otherwise; as General Omar Bradley, chairman of the Joint Chiefs of Staff, put it: "So long as we regarded the Soviet Union as the main antagonist and Western Europe as the main prize" a massive invasion of China "would involve us in the wrong war at the wrong place at the wrong time and with the wrong enemy." In other words, involvement in the land war in Asia would lead "to a larger deadlock at greater expense" and would do little to contain Soviet designs on Western Europe.[74]

By July 1951, truce talks were arranged and fighting ceased for the most part by the end of the year. An armistice, however, did not come about for another year and a half, as a prolonged controversy developed over the repatriation of prisoners of war, and as an American election occurred with Korea as an important issue. An uneasy peace eventually did result with the establishment of a demilitarized zone between North and South Korea. The first test of containment, however, brought numerous lessons for American policy makers for the future course of the Cold War.[75]

Korea and Implications for the Cold War

Political scientist Robert Jervis argues that American involvement in Korea "shaped the course of the Cold War by both resolving the incoherence which characterized U.S. foreign and defense efforts in the period 1946–1950 and establishing important new lines of policy."[76] American involvement resolved that incoherence by moving the United States to match its perceived sense of threat from the Soviet Union and international communism with policies consistent with that threat. New actions were undertaken in at least three different areas, and the political rhetoric of the late 1940s became policy during the 1950s.

The first policy effect of the Korean war was a sharp increase in the American defense budget and the militarization of NATO. While NSC-68 had called for such military increases, they did not result until U.S. involvement in Korea and were largely sustained after it. Note from Figure 2.2 how high military spending (either as a percentage of the GNP or as a percentage of the budget) remained throughout much of the 1950s. Similarly, the establishment of an integrated military structure of NATO and the eventual effort to rearm West Germany followed directly on the heels of American involvement in Korea. The threat of Soviet expansionism had been made real with the actions in Asia.

A second effect of the Korean War was that it brought home to American policy makers the need to maintain large armies and to take action against aggression, wherever it appeared. Limited wars, too, may be necessary, however unpopular at home.[77] In this view, if the United States did not confront aggression in one dispute, American resolve in others would be questioned. Indeed, the Korean experience had already raised this doubt. After all, Secretary of State Dean Acheson had seemed to indicate, in a speech in January 1950, that the Korean peninsula was not within the American "defense perimeter" in Asia.[78]

A third effect of the Korean War was to solidify the American view that a Sino-Soviet bloc promoting communist expansion was a reality and that there was a need to combat it. The Chinese intervention on the side of the North Koreans illustrated the extent to which the Soviet Union controlled China. Indeed, the views that "China and Russia were inseparable were products of the war."[79] Moreover, the various bilateral pacts in Asia were established after the Korean War was under way. In sum, then, the outbreak of the Korean War and American involvement were to bring about a most dramatic correspondence between U.S. policy beliefs and its actions.

Yet a fourth impact, beyond Jervis's discussion, seems reasonable, especially if we keep in mind the date on which NSC-68 was issued (April 1950) and when the Korean War began (June 1950). In many ways, the actions in Korea gave further credence to the global portrait outlined in NSC-68, as well as the need to make rapid changes in the security arrangements of America and the free world. Moreover, in relatively short order, that is exactly what happened.

Finally, a preeminent American diplomatic historian of this generation, John Lewis Gaddis, has summarized the principal importance of the Korean War in this way: "the real commitment to contain communism everywhere originated in the events surrounding the Korean War, not the crisis in Greece and Turkey [in 1947]."[80]

CONCLUDING COMMENTS

In Chapter 1, we noted that isolationism and moralism were America's twin pillars from the past. The Cold War period and the containment policy appear to represent a sharp break from this heritage, at least with respect to isolationism. On one level, of course, the United States did abandon isolationism for a policy of globalism.[81] On another level, globalism was largely a unilateralist approach on the part of the United States, a strategy of going it alone in the world, or at least attempting to lead other nations of the world in a particular direction. In other words, much as the original isolationism was unilateralist; so, too, was the containment policy. It was a strategy by the United States to reshape global order through its own design and largely through its own efforts.

The heritage of moral principle is more readily evident in the Cold War period and the containment policy. The universal campaign that the United States initiated was highly consistent with its past. Moral accommodation with the values of Russian communism, and all communism, was simply not acceptable. In fact, some even sought to "roll back" communism rather than just contain it. Like the efforts in America's past (the War of 1812, the Spanish-American War, World War I, and World War II), then, the containment strategy represented an all-out attempt, in this case, to confront the moral challenge from the Soviet Union and all it represented. Moral values, moreover, served as a primary justification for American policy once again.

In the next chapter, we examine more fully the values and beliefs that shaped the U.S. approach to the world during the height of the Cold War. A Cold War consensus among American leaders and the public was developing in the late 1940s and the early 1950s, and the Korean War only served to solidify it. This consensus provided the rationale for the complete implementation of the containment policy during the rest of the 1950s and 1960s and guided U.S. policy during the several decades until it was challenged by the emergence of the Sino-Soviet split, the nonaligned movement, the Cuban Missile Crisis, and the Vietnam War.

NOTES

1. Joseph M. Jones, *The Fifteen Weeks* (New York: The Viking Press, 1955), pp. 89–99.

2. The term is from Richard Mayne's Chapter 2 title in his *The Recovery of Europe 1945–1973* (Garden City, NY: Anchor, 1973), pp. 27–52. The discussion here draws upon this chapter as well as p. 14 on the extent of decolonization.

3. Ibid., pp. 39–40.

4. Ibid.

5. Stephen E. Ambrose, *Rise to Globalism: American Foreign Policy 1938–1976* (New York: Penguin Books, 1976), p. 16. A good discussion of the economic strength of the United States in the immediate postwar period can be found in Joan Edelman Spero, *The Politics of International Economic Relations,* 2nd ed. (New York: St. Martin's Press, 1981), pp. 23–30, and 33–41. The economic data cited are at p. 36.

6. Ambrose, *Rise to Globalism,* p. 16.

7. John Lewis Gaddis, *The United States and the Origins of the Cold War 1941–1947* (New York and London: Columbia University Press, 1972), p. 1. See also Daniel Yergin, *Shattered Peace: The Origins of the Cold War and the National Security State* (Boston: Houghton Mifflin Company, 1977), pp. 42–68.

8. Gaddis, *Origins of the Cold War,* p. 2.

9. Yergin, *Shattered Peace,* pp. 43–46.

10. Ibid., pp. 17–68. The quote about Riga is at p. 19.

11. Ibid., p. 55.

12. Michael McGwire, "National Security and Soviet Foreign Policy," in Melvyn P. Leffler and David S. Painter, eds., *Origins of the Cold War: An International History* (London and New York: Routledge, 1994), p. 61.

13. See the discussion of the Yalta agreements in Robert H. Ferrell, *American Diplomacy: A History* 3rd ed. (New York: W. W. Norton and Company, 1975), pp. 594–603.

14. Ibid.

15. James Lee Ray, *Global Politics,* 2nd ed. (Boston: Houghton Mifflin Company, 1983), p. 30.

16. For some evidence that the United States was already planning a sustained global involvement during World War II, see Melvyn P. Leffler, "National Security and U.S. Foreign Policy," in Melvyn P. Leffler and David S. Painter, eds., *Origins of the Cold War: An International History* (London and New York: Routledge, 1994), pp. 18–19.

17. Yergin, *Shattered Peace,* pp. 71–73.

18. Ibid. Also see Gaddis, *Origins of the Cold War,* pp. 200–206.

19. Ernest R. May, *"Lessons" of the Past* (New York: Oxford University Press, 1973), pp. 20–22. The quotation is from p. 22.

20. See ibid., pp. 22–32, for a discussion of the views of these diplomatic assessments and their impact on Truman and his advisors.

21. Harry S Truman, *Year of Decision* (New York: Doubleday & Co., Inc., 1955), p. 99. The earlier passage is quoted in Gaddis, *Origins of the Cold War,* p. 232.

22. For a recent description and assessment of the Potsdam Conference, see Charles L. Mee, Jr., *Meeting at Potsdam* (New York: M. Evans & Co., Inc., 1975).

23. Gaddis, *Origins of the Cold War,* pp. 263–281.

24. Ibid., pp. 282–312.

25. Both passages were originally from *Pravda,* the Communist party newspaper, and were quoted in B. Thomas Trout, "Rhetoric Revisited: Political Legitimation and the Cold War," *International Studies Quarterly* 19 (September 1975): 264 and 266.

26. The "new war" remark is quoted from *Pravda* and is from ibid., p. 265, as is this assessment. The second quotation is from ibid at p. 269.

27. The first quote is from Walter Lafeber, *America, Russia, and the Cold War 1945–1975* (New York: John Wiley and Sons, 1976), p. 39, and the second is from Gaddis, in *Origins of the Cold War,* p. 299.

28. The text of the speech can be found in Robert Rhodes James, ed., *Winston S. Churchill, His Complete Speeches 1897–1963,* vol. VII: 1943–1949 (New York: Chelsea House Publishers, 1974), pp. 7285–7293. The quoted passages are at pp. 7289 and 7290, respectively.

29. Yergin, *Shattered Peace,* p. 176.

30. The complete text of the "long telegram" can be found in Kenneth M. Jensen, ed., *Origins of the Cold War: The Novikov, Kennan, and Roberts' "Long Telegrams" of 1946* (Washington, DC: United States Institute of Peace, 1991), pp. 17–31. The quoted phrases are at pp. 20, 23, 28 and 29. The last passage can also be found in George F. Ken-

nan, *Memoirs 1925–1950* (Boston: Little, Brown & Co., 1967), p. 557.

31. Interestingly, a few months after Kennan's "long telegram" was sent from Moscow to Washington, the Soviet Ambassador to the United States, Nikolai Novikov, sent a telegram to Moscow in September 1947. That telegram, dubbed the "Novikov Telegram," and only made public in the summer of 1990, "mirrored" the Kennan "long telegram" in that it depicts the inherent designs of the United States for world domination and for challenging the Soviet Union. In essence, the Soviets, too, seemed to be having increasing misgivings about continuing U.S.–Soviet cooperation in the postwar years. The complete text of the telegram can be found in Jensen, *Origins of the Cold War: The Novikov, Kennan, and Roberts' "Long Telegrams" of 1946,* pp. 3–16.

32. The discussion draws upon Jones, *The Fifteen Weeks,* pp. 48–58, especially at pp. 48–49 here.

33. Quoted in ibid., p. 54. Emphasis in original.

34. Ibid., p. 56. Jones does point out that the Soviets apparently got some concessions for their withdrawal.

35. Lafeber, *America, Russia, and the Cold War,* pp. 50–59, provides a useful description of the situation in Greece at this time, while Jones, *The Fifteen Weeks,* pp. 59–77, describes the situations in Greece and Turkey during 1946 and 1947.

36. These characteristics of the Truman Doctrine are from Lafeber, *America, Russia, and the Cold War,* p. 53.

37. The "Truman Doctrine" speech can be found in *House Documents, Miscellaneous,* 80th Cong., 1st sess., Vol. 1 (Washington, DC: Government Printing Office, 1947), Document 171. Emphasis added here. John Lewis Gaddis, in his book *Strategies of Containment* (New York: Oxford University Press, 1982), pp. 65–66, asserts that the Truman Doctrine was not so much meant as a call to attack "communism" as it was to attack "totalitarianism" in general. Truman's reference to two ways of life referred to totalitarianism vs. democracy. Only later did the commitment to contain communism really develop. See his "Was the Truman Doctrine a Real Turn-

ing Point?" *Foreign Affairs* 52 (January 1974): 386–402.

38. George Kennan has reprinted his July 1947 article from *Foreign Affairs* entitled "The Sources of Soviet Conduct" in his *American Diplomacy 1900–1950* (New York: Mentor Books, 1951). The quoted passages are at pp. 99 and 105.

39. Mr. X [George Kennan], "The Sources of Soviet Conduct," in James M. Mc-Cormick, ed., *A Reader in American Foreign Policy* (Itasca, IL: F. E. Peacock Publishers, Inc., 1986), pp. 68–69.

40. Ibid., pp. 70–71.

41. George Kennan, in his *Memoirs 1925–1950,* pp. 354–367, contends that the implementation of containment by such sweeping actions was not what he had intended. He envisioned a more limited, more measured response than what resulted. Also see his views on the Truman Doctrine at pp. 313–324. A more recent summary of Kennan's views on containment are available in "Containment Then and Now," *Foreign Affairs* 65 (Spring 1987): 885–890.

42. ANZUS was seen as protection against Japanese expansion into the South Pacific in light of the experience of World War II, as well as an anti-Communist alliance in the face of the Korean War. For an extended discussion of ANZUS from the perspective of one of the partners, see Malcom McKinnon, *Independence and Foreign Policy: New Zealand in the World Since 1935* (Auckland: Auckland University Press, 1993).

43. A brief description of the development of these organizations, and the charter of each one, can be found in Ruth C. Lawson, *International Regional Organizations: Constitutional Foundations* (New York: Praeger, 1962). The subsequent discussion of CENTO is also based upon this source.

44. The Rio Pact did not have this language, but it did state that the "Contracting Parties may determine the immediate measures which it may individually take in fulfillment of the obligation." Quoted in Michael Glennon, *Constitutional Diplomacy* (Princeton, NJ: Princeton University Press, 1990), p. 207.

45. *NATO Handbook* (Brussels: NATO Information Service, 1980), p. 14.

46. This discussion draws upon the analysis and documentation by Glennon, *Constitutional Diplomacy,* pp. 209–214. The statements from Acheson are at pp. 210–211.

47. On the evolution of American strategy policy toward China and Asia in the late 1940s and early 1950s, see Thomas H. Etzold, "The Far East in American Strategy, 1948–1951," in Thomas H. Etzold, ed., *Aspects of Sino-American Relations Since 1784* (New York: New Viewpoints, 1978), pp. 102–126. On the Korean War, see Allen S. Whiting, *China Crosses the Yalu* (Stanford: Stanford University Press, 1960); and John W. Spanier, *The Truman-MacArthur Controversy and the Korean War* (New York: W. W. Norton and Company, 1965). On the importance of the Korean War in actually instigating the containment policy and producing the Cold War, see Gaddis, "Was the Truman Doctrine a Real Turning Point?" and Robert Jervis, "The Impact of the Korean War on the Cold War," *The Journal of Conflict Resolution* 24 (December 1980): 563–592.

48. In fact, the original NATO pact (subsequently altered in January 1963) covered "the Algerian Departments of France" in its security network. In this limited sense, a small part of Africa was originally included in NATO. See Article 6 of the NATO charter in *NATO Handbook,* p. 14 on this point.

49. The speech by President Eisenhower can be found in *House Documents, Miscellaneous,* 85th Cong. 1st sess., Vol. 1 (Washington, DC: U.S. Government Printing Office, 1957–1958), Document 46. The first quote is from this document. The latter quote is from Public Law 85–7, which was passed on March 9, 1957, to put the Eisenhower Doctrine into effect.

50. This section draws largely upon the fine summary of American foreign aid policy between 1945 and 1964 presented in *Congress and the Nation 1945–1964* (Washington, DC: Congressional Quarterly Service, 1965), pp. 160–186.

51. The text of Secretary of State Marshall's address can be found in *New York Times,* June 6, 1947, 2. The Soviet Union and Eastern European states were invited to participate in the Marshall Plan under the original formulation. While Poland and Czechoslovakia showed some initial interest, the Soviet

Union quickly vetoed their efforts. See Ferrell, *American Diplomacy,* pp. 634–635. The percentage of GNP for the Marshall Plan was calculated from data presented in U.S. Bureau of Census, *Historical Statistics of the United States, Colonial Times to 1970,* Bicentennial Edition. Parts 1 and 2 (Washington, DC: U.S. Government Printing Office, 1970). Aid effort over time by the United States can be found in the yearly reports by Development Co-Operation (Paris: Organization for Economic Cooperation and Development). The datum for 2000 is from the OECD Web site at http://www.oecd.org/jpg/M00001000/M00001390.jpg, accessed on April 28, 2002.

52. Gilbert Winham, "Developing Theories of Foreign Policy Making: A Case Study of Foreign Aid," *The Journal of Politics* 32 (February 1970): 41–70.

53. President Truman's 1949 inaugural address with the Point Four provision can be found in *Senate Documents, Miscellaneous,* 81st Cong., 1st sess., Vol. 1 (Washington, DC: Government Printing Office, 1949), Document 5.

54. See Robert A. Pastor, *Congress and the Politics of U.S. Foreign Economic Policy 1929–1976* (Berkeley: University of California Press, 1980), p. 269.

55. *Congress and the Nation 1945–1964,* p. 166.

56. The Mutual Security Act of 1951 can be found as Public Law 82–165, passed on October 10, 1951.

57. Aid was given to some countries in order to bolster their economies and their political will to retain some independence from Moscow. See *Congress and the Nation 1945–1964,* pp. 161–162.

58. *A Report to the National Security Council, NSC-68,* Washington, DC, April 14, 1950, p. 13.

59. Ibid., p. 54.

60. Ibid., p. 57. The quoted phrase on military strength is at p. 31, and the information on spending is at p. 25 in NSC-68. On these points and others on NSC-68, see John C. Donovan, *The Cold Warriors: A Policy-Making Elite* (Lexington, MA: D. C. Heath and Company, 1974), pp. 81–96.

61. *A Report to the National Security Council, NSC-68,* p. 39.

62. Ibid., p. 34.

63. Ibid., p. 63.

64. Similar data are reported in James L. Payne, *The American Threat* (College Station, TX: Lytton Publishing Company, 1981), p. 291.

65. See Howard Bliss and M. Glen Johnson, *Beyond the Water's Edge: America's Foreign Policies* (Philadelphia: J. B. Lippincott Co., 1975), pp. 3–10, for a discussion of the "costs of consensus" and for another set of assumptions comprising the postwar consensus.

66. For various accounts of the Korean War, upon which we relied for this summary, see John G. Stoessinger, *Why Nations Go To War,* 5th ed. (New York: St. Martin's Press, 1990), pp. 55–83, especially at p. 61; Spanier, *The Truman-MacArthur Controversy and the Korean War,* especially pp. 23–26; Young W. Kihl, *Politics and Policies in Divided Korea: Regimes in Contest* (Boulder, CO: Westview Press, 1984), pp. 27–42; and Whiting, *China Crosses the Yalu.*

67. See, for example, Stoessinger, *Why Nations Go to War,* p. 61; and Spanier, *The Truman-MacArthur Controversy,* pp. 23–26.

68. John Merrill in his *Korea: The Peninsular Origins of the War* (Newark: University of Delaware Press, 1989) has catalogued five different kinds of explanations for the outbreak of the war: (1) Moscow ordered the North Koreans to invade the South; (2) the South Koreans provoked the North into an attack; (3) the South Koreans, in conjunction with the United States, initiated the war; (4) the deeply divided North Koreans "sprang the war on their unsuspecting Soviet allies"; and (5) the war was the result of regional politics initiated by the Soviet Union "to bring the independently minded Chinese leadership back into line and to frustrate American plans to establish a permanent military presence in Japan." The quoted passages are at pp. 19 and 48, respectively. Another recent study, quoting a North Korean official, argues that Stalin "reluctantly consented" to the surprise attack on the South. The author writes: "Stalin was giving a nod to the general idea of an inva-

sion but had made consultations with Mao a condition for his unequivocal assent to any future detailed plan of action." See Sergei N. Goncharov, John W. Lewis, and Xue Litai, *Uncertain Partners: Stalin, Mao, and the Korean War* (Stanford: Stanford University Press, 1993), p. 144. The first quotation is a quote from Goncharov et al. of the North Korean official, while the second is the judgment of these authors. In July 1994, South Korean officials announced that Soviet documents provided to them by Russian President Boris Yeltsin a month ealier "showed that Soviet dictator Josef Stalin and Chinese leader Mao Tse-tung approved Kim Il-Sung's attack on South Korea in June 1950." See Sam Jameson, "Kim Plotted Korean War, South Claims," *Des Moines Register,* July 21, 1994, 10A.

69. Quoted in Frederick H. Hartmann and Robert L. Wendzel, *America's Foreign Policy in a Changing World* (New York: Harper-Collins College Publishers, 1994), p. 222. The original source is U. Alexis Johnson, *The Right Hand of Power* (Englewood Cliffs, NJ: Prentice-Hall, 1984), p. 99.

70. Stoessinger, *Why Nations Go to War,* p. 67.

71. See the chronology of events in Whiting, *China Crosses the Yalu,* and in John E. Mueller, *War, Presidents, and Public Opinion* (New York: John Wiley and Sons, 1973), among others, upon whom we rely.

72. As quoted in Whiting, *China Crosses the Yalu,* p. 93.

73. On the firing and its implications for American foreign policy, see Spanier, *The Truman-MacArthur Controversy and the Korean War.*

74. Bradley is quoted in Robert H. Ferrell, *American Diplomacy: The Twentieth Century* (New York: W. W. Norton and Company, 1988), pp. 284–285.

75. Mueller, *War, Presidents, and Public Opinion,* pp. 25–27.

76. Jervis, "The Impact of the Korean War on the Cold War," p. 563.

77. These effects are derived from ibid.

78. In a speech to the Press Club on January 12, 1950, Secretary of State Dean Acheson had indicated that the U.S. "defensive perimeter runs along the Aleutians to Japan and then goes to the Ryukyus. We hold important defense positions in the Ryukyu Islands, and these we will continue to hold. . . . The defensive perimeter runs from the Ryukyu to the Philippine Islands." Korea thus was outside this defense line. See Dean Acheson, *Present at the Creation* (New York: W. W. Norton and Company, 1969), p. 357.

79. Jervis, "The Impact of the Korean War on the Cold War," p. 584.

80. Gaddis, "Was the Truman Doctrine a Real Turning Point?" p. 386.

81. For an extended discussion of the following argument in a similar vein, and from which we draw, see Edmund Stillman and William Pfaff, *Power and Impotence* (New York: Vintage Books, 1966), especially at pp. 15 and 58–59.

3

The Cold War Consensus and Challenges to It

Let every nation know, whether it wishes us well or ill, that we shall pay any price, bear any burden, meet any hardship, support any friend, oppose any foe to assure the survival and the success of liberty.

PRESIDENT JOHN F. KENNEDY
INAUGURAL ADDRESS, JANUARY 1961

In honor of the men and women of the armed forces of the United States who served in the Vietnam War. The names of those who gave their lives and of those who remain missing are inscribed in the order they were taken from us.

INSCRIPTION ON THE VIETNAM VETERANS MEMORIAL
WASHINGTON, D.C.

From the Cold War environment, and the initial encounter of the Korean War, an identifiable foreign policy consensus developed among the American leadership and the public at large. This consensus was composed of a set of beliefs, values, and premises about America's role in the world and served as an important guide for U.S. behavior during the heart of the Cold War period (the late 1940s to the late 1960s). In the first part of this chapter, we shall undertake (1) to identify the principal components of the Cold War consensus, (2) to illustrate how strongly the key values of this consensus were held within American society, and (3) to provide a brief description of how the Cold War evolved in the first three decades after the end of World War II. In particular, we will show how the Cold War consensus largely prevailed in shaping American policy making during this period, but that the Cold War interactions between the United States and the Soviet Union also reflected both periods of hostility and periods of accommodation.

In the second half of the chapter, we will discuss how the Cold War consensus came under challenge during the 1960s from a variety of sources: (1) a changing international environment, particularly in the Third World, Eastern Europe, and Western Europe, which made implementing the containment policy more difficult; (2) the American domestic environment, particularly as a result of the Cuban Missile Crisis and the Vietnam War, which made policy making more difficult; and (3) the emergence of new political leadership in the late 1960s and 1970s with alternate views for achieving global order even in the face of Soviet and Communist challenge. In sum, both anticommunism and containment, as the cornerstones of American foreign policy, would be modified but not abandoned as the United States entered the 1970s. And some of the chill of the Cold War would be removed.

KEY COMPONENTS
OF THE COLD WAR CONSENSUS

Lincoln P. Bloomfield has compiled an extensive list of U.S. foreign policy values in his book *In Search of American Foreign Policy*.[1] Table 3.1 reproduces a portion of his list, and it will serve as a starting point for our discussion of the Cold War consensus.

America's Dichotomous View of the World

Bloomfield reminds us of the dichotomous view most Americans held of the world: one group of nations led by the United States and standing for democracy and capitalism, another group led by the Soviet Union and standing for totalitarianism and socialism. Even this dichotomy is not wholly accurate because the United States came to define the "free world" not in a positive way—by adherence to democratic principles of individual liberty and equality—but in a negative way—by adherence to the principles of anticommunism. Thus the "free world" could equally include the nations of Western Europe (including the dictatorships

Table 3.1 The American Postwar Consensus in Foreign Policy

1. Communism is bad; capitalism is good.

2. Stability is desirable; in general, instability threatens U.S. interests.

3. Democracy (our kind, that is) is desirable, but if a choice has to be made, stability serves U.S. interests better than democracy.

4. Any area of the world that "goes socialist" or neutralist is a net loss to us and probably a victory for the Soviets.

5. Every country, and particularly the poor ones, would benefit from American "know-how."

6. Nazi aggression in the 1930s and democracy's failure to respond provides the appropriate model for dealing with postwar security problems.

7. Allies and clients of the United States, regardless of their political structure, are members of the Free World.

8. The United States must provide leadership because it (reluctantly) has the responsibility.

9. "Modernization" and "development" are good for poor, primitive, or traditional societies, and they will probably develop into democracies by these means.

10. In international negotiations the United States has a virtual monopoly on "sincerity."

11. Violence is an unacceptable way to secure economic, social, and political justice— except when vital U.S. interests are at stake.

12. However egregious a mistake, the government must never admit having been wrong.

SOURCE: *In Search of American Foreign Policy: The Humane Use of Power* by Lincoln P. Bloomfield. Copyright 1974 by Oxford University Press, Inc. Reprinted by permission of the author.

of Spain and Portugal through the mid–1970s) and the military regimes of Central and South America because they embraced anticommunism. Such an "alliance" provided a ready bulwark against Soviet expansion.

U.S. Attitudes toward Change

While a substantial part of such a "free world" structure was grounded in this abiding concern over Soviet expansion, a second concern also permeated this thinking: U.S. attitudes toward stability and change. During this period, change in the world was viewed suspiciously. It tended to be seen as Communist-inspired and, therefore, something to be opposed. Stability was generally the preferred global condition.

Change was feared because it might lead to enhanced influence (and control) for the Soviet Union. This gain in influence could occur directly (by a nation's formal incorporation into the Soviet bloc) or indirectly (by a state's adopting a "neutral" or "nonaligned" stance in global affairs). As a consequence, Americans also tended to be skeptical of new states following the "nonaligned" movement initiated by Prime Minister Nehru of India and President Tito of Yugoslavia, among others. At this time, such a movement represented a "loss " for America's effort to rally the world against revolutionary communism.

Change was even more troublesome for the United States when it appeared in a nationalist and revolutionary environment. While the United States tended to have philosophical sympathy for such nationalist and anticolonialist efforts, the global realities, as viewed by American policy makers, often led them to follow a different course. J. William Fulbright, senator from Arkansas and former chairman of the Senate Foreign Relations Committee, described this dilemma for America when dealing with forces of nationalism and communism in a revolutionary setting:

> we are simultaneously hostile to communism and sympathetic to nationalism, and when the two become closely associated, we become agitated, frustrated, angry, precipitate, and inconstant. Or, to make the point by simple metaphor: loving corn and hating lima beans, we simply cannot make up our minds about succotash.[2]

The resultant American policy, as Fulbright goes on to state, was often to oppose communism rather than to support nationalism.

American Intervention to Stall Communism

This fear of change was manifested in yet a more dramatic way: the several American military interventions (either directly or through surrogates) in the 1950s and 1960s to prevent Communist gains. A few instances will make this point. In 1950, of course, U.S. military forces were sent to South Korea to assist that government's defense from the attack by the North Koreans. In 1953, the United States was involved in the toppling of Prime Minister Mohammed Mossadegh of Iran and the restoration of the Shah. In 1954, the CIA assisted in the overthrow of the Jacobo Arbenz Guzman government in Guatemala because of the fear of growing Communist influence there. In 1958, President Eisenhower ordered 14,000 marines to land in Lebanon to support a pro-Western government from possible subversion by Iraq, Syria, and Egypt.

The early 1960s saw the occurrence of three more interventions for a similar reason. In April 1961, the Bay of Pigs invasion of Cuba by Cuban exiles was attempted without success. This effort was designed to topple the Communist regime of Fidel Castro, who had seized power in 1959, and was planned and organized by the CIA. In 1965, President Lyndon Johnson ordered the marines to land in Santo Domingo, Dominican Republic, to protect American lives and property from a possible change in regimes there. Communist involvement in this unrest was the rationale. Finally, of course, the prolonged involvement in Vietnam, beginning in a substantial way in the early 1960s (although having a history back to at least 1946), was justified by the desire to prevent the fall of South Vietnam, and subsequently all of Southeast Asia, to the Communists.[3]

Beyond these direct interventions, the military was used in another way as an important instrument of American policy during the heart of the Cold War period. Two foreign policy analysts, Barry M. Blechman and Stephen S. Kaplan, provide some useful data on this topic in their examination of the "armed forces as a political instrument." According to these analysts, "[a] political use of the armed forces occurs when physical actions are taken by one or more components of the uniformed military services as part of a deliberate attempt by the national authorities to influence, or to be prepared to influence, specific behavior of individuals in another nation without engaging in a continuing contest of violence."[4] Thus, a naval task force that is moved to a particular region of the world, troops put on alert, a nonroutine military exercise begun, and the initiation of reconnaissance patrols can all be illustrations of this use of armed forces when they are characterized by specific political goals directed at another country.

Using these criteria, then, Bechman and Kaplan identified some 215 incidents from 1946 to 1975. For the period that marked the height of the Cold War (1946–1968), some 181 incidents occurred. The top half of Table 3.2 shows the breakdown of these incidents from the administrations of Truman through Johnson. President Eisenhower used these military instruments most frequently (although he was in office longer than the other presidents), but presidents Kennedy and Johnson had the highest average use of these types of military instruments during their tenures. Further, Latin America and Asia were the most frequent areas of these incidents for all the presidents from Truman through Johnson. For President Truman, as one might suspect, Europe commanded the greatest attention in the use of this kind of military force.

Overall, then, even though the number of direct military interventions is relatively limited, the use of military armed forces as a political instrument was quite frequent during the period of the Cold War consensus. Moreover, Blechman and Kaplan conclude that "when the United States engaged in these political-military activities, the outcomes of the situations at which the activity was directed were often favorable from the perspective of U.S. decision makers—at least in the short term."[5] In the long term though, Blechman and Kaplan were less optimistic; nevertheless, this consequence of the Cold War consensus appeared to be popular among policy makers.

The bottom half of Table 3.2 shows the American use of force for the last two decades of the Cold War—from President Nixon through President Reagan.[6] During this period, the use of American force waned somewhat, with a decline from 181 incidents during the first two decades to 133 incidents during the last two decades of the Cold War. This decline in the use of force occurred across all areas of the world when compared with the two earlier decades, except for the Middle East and North Africa region. In this region, the incidents of the use of American force rose dramatically, from thirty incidents through 1968 to fifty-two incidents during the 1969 through 1988 period—a 60 percent increase from the first two decades of the Cold War. With the dramatic events in this region for all American administrations—from the Yom Kippur War of 1973 during the Nixon administration and the Egyptian-Israeli and Syrian-Israeli disengagement agreements during the Ford administration to the Camp David Accords for President Carter and the Lebanon involvement during the Reagan administration—this increase becomes more understandable, but the rise is still quite remarkable.

When the use of force in this latter part of the Cold War years is analyzed by administration, all presidents—except President Reagan—relied less on the use of military force than did their predecessors during the first two decades of the Cold

Table 3.2 Use of American Military Force during Eight Administrations, 1946–1988 (Categorized by Regions)

Administration	Latin America	Europe	Middle East and North Africa	Rest of Africa	Asia	Total
Truman	5	16	7	1	6	35
Eisenhower	18	6	13	2	19	58
Kennedy	17	6	4	2	11	40
Johnson	13	11	6	5	13	48
Nixon	6	2	9	—	12	29
Ford	—	1	4	1	6	12
Carter	3	2	4	4	5	18
Reagan	25	1	35	4	9	74
Regional Totals	87	45	82	19	81	

SOURCES: Calculated by the author from Barry M. Blechman and Stephen S. Kaplan, *Force Without War: U.S. Armed Forces as a Political Instrument* (Washington, DC: The Brookings Institution, 1978), pp. 547–553, for the years 1946–1975; Philip D. Zelikow, "The United States and the Use of Force: A Historical Summary," in George K. Osborn, Asa A. Clark IV, Daniel J. Kaufman, and Douglas E. Lute, eds., *Democracy, Strategy, and Vietnam* (Lexington, MA: D. C. Heath and Company, 1987), pp. 34–36, for the years 1975–1984; and for 1985–1988 from data generously supplied by James Meernik of the University of North Texas. See the text and these sources for a definition of what constitutes an incident in which military force is used.

War. By contrast, President Reagan accounted for more than 55 percent of all the use of American forces during these two decades. Further, his administration was the most frequent initiator of the use of American force among any postwar American president. This conclusion holds even when we take into account that Reagan served longer than any of the other presidents surveyed here, except for President Eisenhower. Yet, comparing the eight years of the Reagan administration with the eight years of the Eisenhower administration, the Reagan administration's usage of force was still slightly more than a quarter larger (74 incidents versus 58 incidents).

Thus, displays of force and occasional violence came to be justified to defend American interests. Challenges to national security (increasingly defined as global security) were not to go unmet. Instead, confronting potential aggressors was essential to world peace. The so-called Munich syndrome, the fear of appeasing an aggressor as Chamberlain had done with Hitler, became another theme of American Cold War thinking. In short, drawing upon historical analogies as a guide to present policy was an important source of this kind of response to aggression.[7]

The United States as Model

Given the nature of the perceived global struggle, a final important theme emerged from this postwar consensus. The United States came to believe that it alone could "solve" the problems of the poor and emerging nations through the application of its technological skills.[8] Additionally, the United States tended to offer itself as the model for the achievement of development and democracy. Such a policy came to be viewed as a markedly paternalistic one and one that some states viewed warily. Thus large-scale development efforts were initiated, particularly in the 1960s, to pursue this ideal. This policy, however, led to frustration for Americans when development did not occur as rapidly as envisioned or when democracy did not result. Nonetheless, this belief during the 1950s and 1960s, seems to summarize nicely the general value orientation that the United States employed to achieve its view of global order and to oppose the strategy of the Soviet Union.

THE PUBLIC AND THE
COLD WAR CONSENSUS

Bloomfield's list provides an excellent summary of Cold War consensus, but it does not convey how deeply held these views were among the American public during the late 1940s and 1950s. Fortunately, some limited public opinion survey data are available and provide additional support for Bloomfield's generalizations.[9] In particular, these survey results depict prevailing American attitudes toward the perceived threat from international communism, the use of American troops to combat it abroad, and, more generally, how the public thought relations should be conducted with the Soviet Union.

Table 3.3 summarizes the results to a survey question asked on three different occasions in 1950 and 1951: "In general, how important do you think it is for the United States to try to stop the spread of communism in the world?" On average, 80 percent of the American public identified stopping communism as a "very important" goal of the United States, and another 8 percent said that this goal was a "fairly important" goal. Only 5 percent of the American public saw stopping communism as "not important." When the public had been asked a similar question two years earlier about the threat of communism spreading to specific regions and countries, the results were virtually the same (Table 3.4). Between 70 and 80 percent of the public agreed with the statement that if Western Europe, South America, China, or Mexico were to go Communist it would make a difference to the United States.

The public also was quite willing to use American force to stop the spread of communism, even if it meant going to war. In two surveys, one in 1951 and another in 1952, the public was asked the following: "If you had to choose, which would you say is more important—to keep communism from spreading, or to stay out of another war?" Less than 30 percent of the public chose to stay out of war, and about two-thirds of the public was quite willing to take action to stop the spread of communism. Further, when the public was asked about the use of American forces to stop Communist attacks against particular countries or regions, the response was usually overwhelmingly favorable. For Communist attacks against the Philippines, the American-occupied zone in Germany at the time (and what eventually became West Germany), or Formosa, the public

**Table 3.3 Attitudes toward Stopping
the Spread of Communism, 1950–1951**

In general, how important do you think it is for the United
States to try to stop the spread of communism in the world—
very important, only fairly important, or not important at all?

Survey Date	Very Important	Fairly Important	Not Important	Don't Know
January 1950	77%	10%	5%	8%
April 1950	83	6	4	7
June 1951	82	7	4	7

SOURCE: Eugene R. Wittkopf, *Faces of Internationalism: Public Opinion and
American Foreign Policy,* Table 6.1 (p. 169). Copyright 1990, Duke University Press.
Reprinted with permission.

favored going to war with the Soviet Union if these attacks happened. Similarly, the public favored using force if Central or South America were attacked by another country. Indeed, the public appeared willing to sustain a worldwide effort to stop communism, including the use of armed forces.[10]

Short of force, the American public also expressed support for efforts to stop communism. It was generally quite willing to provide economic and military assistance to countries threatened by international communism. As political scientists Benjamin Page and Robert Shapiro report: "By March 1949, for example, NORC [National Opinion Research Center] found solid support for military aid to Europe (60% approving), for continuing the Marshall Plan (79%), and for maintaining or increasing the level of [European] recovery spending (60%)."[11] Further, in surveys by NORC between January 1955 and January 1956, the average level of support for using economic aid to help countries opposing Communist aggression was about 81 percent. Similarly, support for use of military assistance in six surveys in 1950 and 1951 averaged 57 percent among the American public.[12]

Finally, by the end of World War II, the public was highly suspicious of dealing with the Soviet Union. As Page and Shapiro also report, a large majority of the American people felt as early as March 1946 that the United States was "too soft" in dealing with the Soviet Union. Moreover, by March 1948, that percentage increased even more, to 84 percent of the public.[13] Further, they report that the percentage of the American public expecting cooperation with the Soviet Union dropped precipitously from mid-1945 through mid-1949 to roughly 20 percent and that this drop occurred across all educational levels in American society.[14] This wariness of the Soviet Union, moreover, was to continue throughout the Cold War years.

In short, after summarizing a wealth of American survey data on the early Cold War period, Page and Shapiro conclude: "The U.S. public accepted the logic of the Cold War and favored appropriate policies to carry it out."[15]

Table 3.4 Attitudes toward the Threat of Communism, 1948

Question Wording A: Do you think it makes much difference to the United States whether the countries in Western Europe go Communist or not?

Question Wording B: Do you think it makes much difference to the United States whether Germany goes Communist or not?

Question Wording C: How about China? [Do you think it makes much difference to the United States whether China goes Communist or not?]

Question Wording D: And how about the small countries in South America? [Do you think it makes much difference to the United States whether they go Communist or not?]

Question Wording E: Do you think it makes much difference to our country whether China goes Communist or not?

Question Wording F: How about Mexico—Do you think it would make much difference to our country whether or not Mexico were to go Communist?

Questions Wording G: And how about the countries in South America? [Do you think it makes much difference to our country whether they go Communist or not?]

Region/ Country	Survey Date	Question Wording	Yes	No	Don't Know
Western Europe	July 1948	A	80%	10%	10%
Germany	July 1948	B	80	9	11
China	July 1948	C	73	14	13
South America	July 1948	D	70	15	15
China	November 1948	E	71	17	12
Mexico	November 1948	F	82	8	10
South America	November 1948	G	80	8	12

SOURCE: Eugene R. Wittkopf and James M. McCormick, "The Cold War Consensus: Did It Exist?" *Polity* 22 (Summer 1990): 633. Reprinted with permission.

PATTERNS OF INTERACTIONS
DURING THE COLD WAR, 1946–1972

Even with these deeply held views that constituted the Cold War consensus and the evident hostility between the United States and the Soviet Union, the Cold War interactions between these two states were not played out in a straight-line fashion of either increasing or decreasing levels of hostility. Instead, the Cold War was largely a series of ebbs and flows, from periods of greater to those of lesser hostilities and from periods of greater to those of lesser advantage by one power over the other. Neither party obtained all the goals that had motivated this conflict, but neither party was able to vanquish the other. As these nations changed in their capabilities and as the international system changed, the nature of the Cold War changed and the first major attempt at accommodation occurred by the early 1970s.

Foreign policy analyst and later national security advisor to President Carter Zbigniew Brzezinski has nicely captured these ebbs and flows in U.S.-Soviet relations over the height of the Cold War and has categorized them into six different phases through 1972.[16]

The early phases of the Cold War were marked by uncertainty in the relationship between the two powers. By the 1948–1952 period, however, the Soviet Union was in a more assertive policy pattern, and the United States was largely relegated to respond to the Soviet challenge, whether that challenge occurred in Eastern Europe, with the fall of Czechoslovakia, Hungary, and Poland and the Berlin blockade of 1948–1949, or in Asia, with the establishment of communism in China and the outbreak of the Korean War. Hostility and conflict were sharp and intense.

During the 1953–1957 phase, by contrast, the United States was in a better position to respond to this challenge. Indeed, in Brzezinski's estimation, the United States was preeminent on numerous fronts—politically, militarily, economically, and domestically—during these years. U.S. military capability was enhanced with a large increase in its long-range nuclear bomber fleet, its adoption of a nuclear strategy of massive retaliation, and the conventional arms buildup in Western Europe. The American economy was expanding, and the gap in the strengths of the two economies was widening. The United States was also in a strong position politically, and was largely able to work its political will in international affairs through the several alliance structures that it had created globally.

Even during this period of American ascendancy and intense rivalries between the two emerging superpowers, though, there were some nascent efforts at accommodation. After Stalin's death in 1953, President Dwight Eisenhower made a conciliatory speech to the Soviet Union, which responded with some informal contacts. In 1955, an Austrian State Treaty was agreed upon in which Soviet and American troops would be withdrawn from that country.[17] In July of that same year, the "spirit of Geneva" blossomed with a summit conference among the leaders of the United States, the Soviet Union, France, and Great Britain.[18] Similarly, Soviet Premier Nikita Khrushchev, at the Twentieth Party Congress, renounced the inevitability of war among the capitalist states—an important Stalinist tenet—and raised the prospect that some longer-term accommodation with the West might be possible.[19] "Peaceful coexistence" had entered the lexicon of American-Soviet diplomacy, but rivalries were still intense.

In the next phase of the Cold War, roughly 1958 and beyond, hostilities heated up once again. The Soviets attempted to engage in a truly global policy and expanded their activities in Europe, the Middle East, Africa, Asia, and even in the Western Hemisphere. Soviet Premier and Communist Party Secretary Nikita Khrushchev proclaimed his nation's support for "national liberation struggles" around the world and attempted to place the United States on the defensive in numerous trouble spots.

In Europe, for example, the United States and the Soviet Union faced off over the future of Berlin in 1958–1959 and 1961.[20] In November 1958, the Soviet Union proposed to sign a separate peace treaty with the East German government, ending its control over the Soviet sector of Berlin and allowing the East Germans to control access to the British, French, and American sectors. (Since Berlin was located about 100 miles inside East Germany, it was particularly vulnerable to such action.) The Soviet Union did not act immediately, however. Instead, it served notice that Moscow would give the West six months to solve this problem before it effected this change in status for Berlin. The United States viewed this declaration as an ultimatum and stood firm to resist it. The Soviet deadline passed without incident, however, and no immediate change in the status of Berlin occurred.

In 1961, the Berlin issue was raised anew by Khrushchev with a newly elected American president, John F. Kennedy. The Soviet demands were essentially the same: a peace treaty that would include giving East Germany control over access to Berlin, an end to all access rights by the Western allied powers, and the establishment of West Berlin as a "free city" within East German territory. President Kennedy responded by indicating U.S. determination to defend West Berlin, and he took several actions to demonstrate that resolve.[21] In a matter of days, on August 13, 1961, the Soviet Union and the East German government began to seal East Berlin from the West by building a wall of wire and eventually of mortar. The Berlin Wall was both a response to the actions of the U.S. and its allies in Berlin and to the extraordinary flow of East German refugees to West Berlin. Moreover, the Berlin Wall—which stood until November 9, 1989—came to serve as a prominent symbol of the Cold War and the deep ideological and political gulf that existed between East and West.

In the developing world, similar confrontations occurred, reflecting how the East versus West dimension dominated global politics during this period. In the central African republic of Congo (later called Zaire), the United States and the USSR found themselves supporting opposite sides in a civil war that erupted after that nation gained independence from Belgium in June 1960. Both powers sent considerable resources to bolster their allies as the Cold War was played out in an arena far from either power's territory. In the Western Hemisphere, a similar phenomenon took place. With Fidel Castro's successful revolution in Cuba and his eventual declaration that he was a Marxist-Leninist, a second confrontation between East and West was played out with the Bay of Pigs in April 1961. In Asia, too, the United States and the Soviet Union were deeply involved in the civil war in Laos, resulting in another East versus West conflict.[22]

The Cold War reached its climax with the Cuban Missile Crisis of October 1962 and its aftermath and with the escalation of the Vietnam War. During this period, the United States once again asserted its globalist posture and challenged the Soviet Union and its allies. Changes in governments from Brazil to Algeria and from Ghana to Indonesia produced a global environment more favorable to U.S. interests. Yet, as Brzezinski contends, this "new phase did not involve a return to the mutual hostility of the fifties."[23] Instead, further efforts at accommodation persisted. The negotiation of the Limited Test Ban Treaty in 1963 and the Nuclear Non-Proliferation Treaty in 1968, the opening of a "hotline" between Washington and Moscow, the beginning of a more differentiated strategy toward Eastern Europe on the part of the United States, and the continuance of super-power summitry all suggested that the tenor of the Cold War was changing. These events, and several international shifts in power, had a profound impact on the stability of the Cold War consensus, as we discuss shortly.

The final phase in Brzezinski's description of the Cold War dates from 1969, with Richard Nixon's assumption of the presidency, and ends roughly with the Moscow Summit of 1972. At that summit, the Strategic Arms Limitation Talks (SALT I) produced two important nuclear arms pacts: an agreement limiting offensive arms and an agreement limiting defensive arms (the Anti-Ballistic Missile Treaty). The significance of these agreements lay in the mutual recognition by each superpower of the destructive capacity of its nuclear arsenal and the need to address this common dilemma. Equally significant, this summit recognized the essential equivalence of the United States and the USSR in international affairs. As a result, agreements for greater political, economic, and social agreements were struck, in addition to the military accords. The intense chill of the Cold War appeared to be replaced by the spirit of detente ("relaxation of tensions") between the superpowers.

This period of detente proved to be somewhat short-lived, lasting at most until December 1979, when the Soviets invaded Afghanistan. Detente, however, was frayed and unraveling earlier, from the mid-1970s onward, as disputes between the two superpowers arose over the lack of fidelity to political, military, and economic agreements struck in 1972. Similarly, elements of the Cold War were resurrected during the Reagan years, especially during his first term. Only toward the end of the Reagan administration and with the ascendancy of Mikhail Gorbachev in the Soviet Union was the Cold War thaw under way once again.

CHALLENGES TO THE COLD WAR CONSENSUS

Despite these ebbs and flows in the Soviet-American relationship and the resurgence of the Cold War in the early 1980s, the values and beliefs of the Cold War consensus were beginning to be challenged as early as the mid- to late 1960s. The predominant challenge came from the changing world environment—a world that was increasingly multipolar rather than bipolar. New power centers began to appear within the Communist world, among the Western allies, and between the developed world and the Third World.[24] Other serious challenges to the postwar consensus were over the limits of American power as exercised in the Cuban Missile Crisis in October 1962, but even more so over America's Vietnam policy, particularly from 1965 to the early 1970s. While these latter two challenges were initiated abroad, their impact was profoundly manifested at home. In particular, Vietnam policy produced a full-blown domestic debate over the conduct of American foreign policy and is often cited as having signaled the death knell of the Cold War consensus.

Sino-Soviet Split

The policy split between the People's Republic of China and the Soviet Union, the two largest Communist powers, challenged the Cold War assumption about the basic unity of international communism and the degree to which communism was directed from Moscow. Throughout the height of the Cold War, the United

States had treated communism as a monolithic movement that everywhere took its orders from the Soviet Union. When China and the Soviet Union became increasingly antagonistic toward one another in the late 1950s and early 1960s, the West, and the United States in particular, was challenged to rethink their assumption about Communist unity.

In many ways, the Sino–Soviet split should not have been surprising to U.S. policy makers. Both *historical rivalries* and *social-cultural differences* had long characterized Soviet-Chinese relations. Historically, the Soviet Union had always wanted to gain access to and control over Asia, and, in turn, had always feared the growth of Chinese influence. Likewise, the Chinese had always perceived the Russians as an "imperialist" power and as a threat to their sovereignty and territorial integrity. Territorial disputes date back at least to the signing of the Treaty of Nerchinsk in 1659 and continued into the nineteenth and twentieth centuries as the disintegration of China took place at the hands of outside powers—including the Russians.[25]

On a cultural level, too, deep suspicions have always permeated Soviet and Chinese views of one another. The Soviets viewed the "Mongols" from the East with grave concern, while the Chinese regarded the Soviet commissars with similar apprehension. To the Chinese, the Soviets were "foreigners" and "barbarians," intent upon destroying the glories of Chinese culture and society. Although the other "imperialist" powers were driven from China with Mao's successful revolution of 1949, the Soviets never left. Their continued presence reinforced Chinese hostility toward the Soviets.

Despite these profound suspicions of one another, a formal alliance was still forged between the Soviet Union and the People's Republic of China in 1950. This pact raised the belief in official Washington that past differences were resolved, rather than temporarily shelved. In fact, mutual self-interest apparently dictated this formal tie. The China of Mao Tse-tung, although successful in its domestic revolution, was still weak and hardly independent. The Soviets, badly in need of global partners in a world of capitalist powers, had much to gain by allying with their new ideological partner.[26] But new differences between the two Communist giants quickly began to arise and were superimposed on the disputes of the past. The new difficulties were mainly *economic* and *ideological*. Although the Soviet Union provided economic and technological assistance to China, neither was sufficient. Such low aid levels frustrated the Chinese aim of self-sufficiency, a goal that the Soviet Union did not share. Furthermore, the Soviet Union refused to help the Chinese build an independent nuclear force. This singular technological failure has been identified by some as the catalyst for the reemergence of the Sino-Soviet split.[27]

On an ideological level, Mao's brand of communism, unlike what Soviet Premier Nikita Khrushchev was enunciating, did not call for a policy of "peaceful coexistence" with the West.[28] Nor did it call for emulating the Soviet model of heavy industrialization as the road to modernization and socialism. Further, the Soviets and the Chinese disagreed over the de-Stalinization movement, engaged in a rather continuous debate over the degree of diversity allowable among Communist states and parties, and adopted differing views on the nature of the worldwide revolutionary movement.[29] In short, Mao's proclamations on the "correct" interpretation of Marxism–Leninism were increasingly perceived as direct challenges to Soviet leadership of the Communist world.

By the late 1950s and into the early 1960s, the traditional Sino-Soviet split emerged full blown once again. American officials slowly began to recognize this global reality and the need for a policy that did not homogenize the Communist powers.

Disunity in the East and West

A second fissure in America's view of the Communist world as wholly unified occurred in Eastern Europe. While the differences that emerged within the Warsaw Pact—the military alliance between the Soviet Union and its Eastern European neighbors—were nowhere as severe as the Sino-Soviet split, they again suggested that some change was needed in the unidimensional way in which the United States viewed and approached the Communist world during the Cold War.

Uprisings in East Germany in 1953 and Poland in 1956, outright revolt in Hungary later in the same year, and the call for communism "with a human face" in Czechoslovakia by 1968 all signaled a changed Eastern Europe. Considering also Yugoslavia's long-standing independent Communist route, Albania's departure from the Warsaw Pact in 1968, and Romania's break with Eastern Europe over the recognition of West Germany in 1967, Eastern Europe was hardly the model of alliance unity. It soon became apparent to American observers that exploiting the internal differences within the Eastern bloc was yet another way of moving these nations away from Soviet control. Furthermore, Eastern European nations themselves sought to expand economic advantage through diplomatic contact and recognition.[30] Failure to seize available economic and political opportunities could prove highly dysfunctional for the long-term American policy of combating international communism. Yet such opportunities would be lost if the world were conceptualized and treated only through strict bloc-to-bloc relations.

But fissures in this unified East versus unified West definition of global politics were not confined to disharmony among the Communist states. If the Soviet Union faced challenges from the People's Republic of China and Eastern Europe, America faced several challenges within its own NATO alliance. By the early 1960s, the United States could no longer automatically expect the Western European states to follow its foreign policy lead. More accurately, the United States could no longer dictate Western policy. With the economic recovery of France and West Germany and the emergence of the European Common Market, a number of European states wanted to exercise a more independent role in world affairs—or at least not be so subservient to American policy prescriptions.

The best example of this fissure within the Western bloc was the foreign policy pursued by France under President Charles de Gaulle (1958–1969), the undisputed leader of this challenge to U.S. leadership. Under de Gaulle's guidance, France sought to restore some of its lost glory by reducing its strong linkage with the United States, weakening overall American influence over Western European affairs, and improving ties with the Soviet Union and Eastern Europe. De Gaulle's ultimate goal, in fact, was to break the "hegemonic" hold of both the Soviet

Union and the United States on Europe and to establish a "community of European states" from the "Atlantic to the Urals."[31] In this global design, France would be able to reassert its central role in European politics.

To accomplish this, de Gaulle undertook a series of initiatives to reduce American influence on the continent and to weaken Soviet control as well. First, in 1958, shortly after gaining the French presidency, de Gaulle reportedly proposed a three-power directorate for the NATO alliance. Under this proposal, policy decisions within the Western alliance could result only with the unanimous consent of the United States, Great Britain, and France. In effect, such a proposal would give France a veto over NATO policy. Second, de Gaulle, despite American objections, announced his plan to develop an independent French nuclear force, the *force de frappe,* and refused to join American and British (and later, German) plans for an integrated nuclear force. Third, and perhaps most dramatically, de Gaulle announced in 1965 that France was withdrawing from the military structure of NATO the next year. This last act was probably the single most potent challenge to Western unity. The appearance of political divisions within the NATO structure became a reality with de Gaulle's military withdrawal.

Both the Kennedy and Johnson administrations favored a strong, unified Europe, closely allied to the United States. De Gaulle did not favor such close American involvement in European affairs. Instead, President de Gaulle took a series of actions to reshape Western European politics more in accord with his views and as a further means of frustrating American dominance. Thus he sought to reshape the European Common Market, increase French-German ties (at the expense of American-German relations), and isolate Great Britain from European affairs. First, de Gaulle attempted to reduce the supranational components of the Common Market—the power of the European commission, for example—and to increase the emphasis on intergovernmental components within the organization. To accomplish this, he proposed the Fouchet Plan, which was both a broadening of coverage of the Common Market concept to include political, cultural, and defense activities within a European union and a lessening of centralized control. Although this plan was ultimately rejected, it caused considerable controversy and division within the European Community. Second, de Gaulle, on two different occasions (1963 and 1967), vetoed British entry into the Common Market, fundamentally because Britain was too close to the United States. Third, de Gaulle sought, largely unsuccessfully, to forge a strong alliance between France and West Germany. His strategy, once again, was to break the close ties between the United States and the Federal Republic. In the main, he was rebuffed by successive German chancellors, although he did manage to put into effect a German-French Treaty of Friendship in January 1963.[32]

Bridges across East and West

Although de Gaulle's actions were not the only source of dissension within the Western alliance, they did represent the most consistent pattern of moving away from the bipolar world of the Cold War. De Gaulle's challenge to a bipolar world did not stop with these actions toward America and Western Europe. He also opened up a series of contacts with Eastern Europe and took policy steps clearly at odds with the bloc-to-bloc relations of the previous decade. Such actions alarmed the Americans because de Gaulle was operating unilaterally and outside the policy of the Western Alliance; they undoubtedly pleased the Eastern Europeans because they granted these nations some legitimacy in the eyes of the West; and they probably caused a mixed reaction among the Soviets because, while granting recognition to Eastern Europe, they had the potential effect of undermining Warsaw Pact unity.

De Gaulle's strategy toward Eastern Europe was first to increase social, cultural, and economic ties and then to proceed toward political accommodation. For instance, educational exchanges, tourism, and trade between France and Eastern Europe were increased dramatically. More important, perhaps, France initiated political contacts at the highest levels of government with the Eastern Europeans.

In the first part of his political campaign to "build bridges" to the East, de Gaulle sent his foreign affairs minister to several Eastern European countries. This action was dramatic in itself and was in response to the visits to France by numerous political officials from Eastern Europe. But even more dramatic was de Gaulle's decision to visit Eastern Europe himself. He subsequently made official visits to the Soviet Union in June 1966, Poland in September 1967, and Romania in May 1968. Additionally, he had accepted invitations to visit Czechoslovakia, Hungary, and Bulgaria, although these trips were not made before he left office.[33] The significance of these visits cannot be overstated, since Western policy was not to yield any official diplomatic recognition to the Eastern European governments because of their failure to recognize West Germany.

Throughout these visits, and despite acknowledged differences between East and West, mutual calls for reconciliation were made. De Gaulle's characterization of Europe's division into blocs as "artificial" and "sterile" epitomizes his continuing effort to break the political divisions of the Cold War.[34] His effort gave impetus to greater contact between Eastern and Western Europe. For instance, West Germany's policy toward Eastern Europe (*Ostpolitik*) was slowly nurtured during the 1966 to 1969 period and came to fruition after 1969. French initiatives were important harbingers of changes in the politics of the European continent. For Americans, these initiatives once again demonstrated the difficulties of conducting policy based on *biopolarity* in a world that was increasingly *multipolar*.

The Nonaligned Movement

In the post–World War II years, another major political force was unleashed: the desire for independence by colonial territories, especially throughout Asia and Africa. In fact, more than ninety nations were granted or achieved political independence from the colonial powers from 1945 through 1980. Fourteen states became independent in the years from 1945 to 1949, nine states in the 1950–1959 period, forty-three states from 1960 to 1969, twenty-six states from 1970 through 1979, eight states from 1980 to 1989, and twenty-four states from 1990 to 2000 (see Table 3.5).[35] This surge of independence began in Asia and northern Africa. Pakistan, India, and the Philippines, among others, gained independence in the

Table 3.5 The Growth of New Nations, 1945–2000

Nations Gaining Independence 1945–1949

Bhutan	Jordan	Lebanon	Sri Lanka
India	Korea, North	Myanmar	Taiwan
Indonesia	Korea, South	Pakistan	
Israel	Laos	Philippines	

Nations Gaining Independence 1950–1959

Cambodia	Libya	Morocco	Tunisia
Ghana	Malaysia	Sudan	Vietnam
Guinea			

Nations Gaining Independence 1960–1969

Algeria	Cyprus	Malawi	Senegal
Barbados	Equatorial Guinea	Maldives	Sierra Leone
Benin	Gabon	Mali	Singapore
Botswana	Gambia	Malta	Somalia
Burkina Faso	Guyana	Mauritania	Swaziland
Burundi	Ivory Coast	Mauritius	Tanzania
Cameroon	Jamaica	Nauru	Togo
Central African Republic	Kenya	Niger	Trinidad and Tobago
Chad	Kuwait	Nigeria	Uganda
Congo	Lesotho	Rwanda	Zambia
Congo, Dem. Republic	Madagascar	Samoa	

Nations Gaining Independence 1970–1979

Angola	Fiji	Qatar	Tonga
Bahamas	Grenada	St. Lucia	Tuvalu
Bahrain	Guinea-Bissau	St. Vincent and the Grenadines	United Arab Emirates
Bangladesh	Kiribati	Sao Tome and Principe	
Cape Verde	Mozambique	Seychelles	
Comoros	Niue	Solomon Islands	
Djibouti	Oman	Suriname	
Dominica	Papua New Guinea		

Nations Gaining Independence 1980–1989

Antigua and Barbuda	Brunei	Micronesia, Fed. States	Vanuata
Belize	Marshall Islands	St. Kitts and Nevis	Zimbabwe

Nations Gaining Independence 1990–1999

Armenia	Georgia	Namibia	Ukraine
Azerbaijan	Kazakhstan	Palau	Uzbekistan
Belarus	Kyrgyzstan	Russia	Yemen
Bosnia and Herzegovina	Latvia	Slovak, Rep.	
Croatia	Lithuania	Slovenia	
Eritrea	Macedonia	Tajikistan	
Estonia	Moldova	Turkmenistan	

SOURCE: The dates of independence for the new nations from 1945 to 2000 were taken from Bruce Russett, Harvey Starr, and David Kinsella, *World Politics: The Menu for Choice,* 6th ed. (Boston: Bedford/St. Martin's Press, 2000), pp. 492–498.

late 1940s, while Tunisia, Cambodia (Kampuchea), Morocco, Libya, and Malaysia, among others, gained their sovereignty by the mid-1950s. The decolonization of Africa mainly occurred in the early 1960s, although Ghana and Guinea led the way by gaining independence in the late 1950s. By the end of the 1960s, in fact, some 66 new nations were part of the international system, and this process continued into the 1970s, albeit at a slower pace.

This decolonization movement proved to be a third major challenge to the bipolar approach that was at the base of American foreign policy during the Cold War years. These new states generally refused to tie themselves into the formal bloc structures of the Cold War and, instead, preferred to follow an independent, nonaligned foreign policy course. Moreover, these new states actually started a nonaligned movement to demonstrate their independence.

The founder of this nonaligned movement was Jawaharlal Nehru of India, who as early as 1946 had stated that India "will follow an independent policy, keeping away from the power politics of groups aligned one against another."[36] He continued his efforts on behalf of this movement once he reached power in India, and he then proceeded to help organize the Conference of Afro-Asian States held at Bandung, Indonesia, in 1955. This conference is sometimes cited as the initial effort toward the development of a nonaligned movement, since it was the first time that former colonial territories met without the presence of European powers. However, the tone of the debate and the principles adopted later were criticized as not fully reflecting the principles of nonalignment.[37]

The more formal institutionalization of this movement was the Belgrade Conference in September 1961. Spurred on by the organizational efforts of leaders such as Tito of Yugoslavia, Nasser of Egypt, Nkrumah of Ghana, and Sukarno of Indonesia, as well as Nehru, this conference of twenty-five nations produced a statement of principles for those nations seeking a "third way" in world politics.[38]

In effect, these states not only wanted to reject bloc politics, they also wanted to expand the areas of the world that were part of the nonaligned movement. They saw their contribution to world peace as directly opposite to the way world politics had been conducted up to that time—that is, taking an active part in world affairs through their own initiatives and in their own way without going through coordinated actions of a bloc of states. More specifically, these states rejected military alliances with, or military bases for, the superpowers so that the politics of the Cold War could be extended through such intermediary states. In this sense, nonalignment did not mean noninvolvement or total rejection of global politics, but it did mean the rejection of the way international politics had been played during the Cold War.[39]

This movement proved highly successful, and adherents to its beliefs rapidly increased in number. In the space of less than a decade, the membership had doubled, with fifty-three nations attending the Third Summit Meeting in Lusaka, Zambia, in September 1970.[40] These new members came primarily from colonial territories as they gained their independence in the early to middle 1960s. Essentially, then, the new participants in world politics were joining the ranks of the nonaligned.

The United States, however, was always a bit skeptical of the nonaligned movement and its degree of independence in world politics. Indeed, a continuous debate existed from the movement's inception over how "nonaligned" the movement was. The organization's policy pronouncements have often been more critical of the actions of the West than of the East, and it was typically more critical of capitalism than socialism. Further, several prominent nations within the organizations had close ties with the Soviet Union. Cuba, Vietnam, and Afghanistan, among others, could hardly be viewed as "nonaligned" in global politics during much of the history of this movement. Despite this anomaly within the nonaligned movement, the movement itself provided yet another reason for American policy makers to conclude that global politics would not conform to their image of East versus West.

The Missiles of October: The First Crisis of Confidence

The last important challenge to America's Cold War consensus—prior to the Vietnam War—was the Cuban Missile Crisis. Although both of these episodes were foreign policy events, their impact was as much domestic as it was foreign, and they profoundly affected America's thinking about its role in the world. These episodes brought home to American leaders and to the American people—in most dramatic fashion—the limits of the United States in influencing the Soviet Union and Third World areas. Both also illustrate the limited extent to which American beliefs and values were able to create the global design envisioned by the Cold War consensus.

The Cuban Missile Crisis of October 16–28, 1962, was the closest that the United States and the Soviet Union had come to nuclear confrontation since the advent of atomic power. Cuba, under the leadership of Fidel Castro since 1959, had by this time declared itself a "Marxist-Leninist" state and had sought assistance from the Soviet Union against alleged American intrigues. The crisis centered on the introduction of "offensive" intermediate range ballistic missiles into Cuba by the Soviet Union during the fall of 1962. Such Soviet actions were in violation of its stated commitment to introduce only "defensive" weapons into Cuba.

Upon the discovery of the missiles on October 16, 1962, President John Kennedy set out to devise an appropriate strategy to remove these missiles from territory only 90 miles from American shores. After a week of highly secret deliberations through his Executive Committee of the National Security Council, President Kennedy finally announced on October 22, 1962, that a naval quarantine would be set up 800 miles around Cuba to interdict the further shipment of missiles. Furthermore, President Kennedy threatened the Soviet Union with a nuclear response if the missiles in Cuba were used against the United States. In addition, a series of other measures, ranging from actions through the Organization of American States and the United Nations to bilateral contacts with the Soviet Union, were undertaken to remove the missiles already in place.

After another week of tense confrontation and exchanges of diplomatic notes, the Soviet Union agreed to remove the missiles under United Nations supervision.

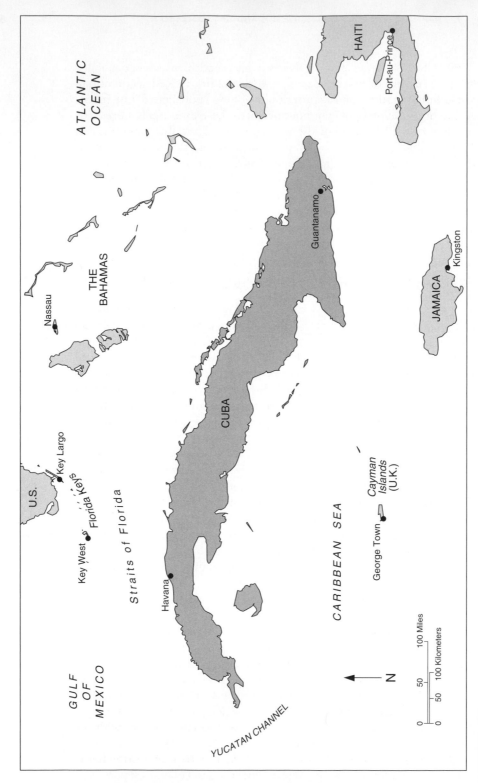

MAP 3.1 Cuba

The United States also pledged that it would not attempt to overthrow the Castro regime in Cuba. Subsequent revelations about the crises through a series of conferences in the late 1980s and early 1990s among American, Soviet, and Cuban participants now reveal that an informal exchange was struck between the United States and the Soviet Union. The Soviet Union would remove its threatening missiles from Cuba, and the United States would remove its threatening missiles from Turkey.[41]

The Missile Crisis has long been subject to analysis and reanalysis, and various lessons have been gleaned from it for Soviet-American relations during the Cold War and for nuclear relations generally.[42]

Lesson 1: Risk of Nuclear Annihilation First, the crisis fully brought home to both Soviet and American leaders (and their populaces) that nuclear annihilation was a real possibility. Mutual assured destruction, or MAD, was no longer an abstract theory. While the United States may have been relatively safe from Soviet nuclear attacks in the 1950s, the development of intercontinental missiles—and even intermediate range missiles that had been placed in Cuba—demonstrated that this condition no longer existed. Americans were now vulnerable to Soviet nuclear power, just as the Soviets were to the U.S. nuclear arsenal.

More recently, political analysts Len Scott and Steve Smith concluded that, with the new data available on the crisis, this lesson is even clearer today. "Recent sources," they report, "seem to show absolutely clearly that U.S. decision-makers were extremely worried about the prospect of any Soviet nuclear response, so much so that the result was to nullify the enormous nuclear superiority that the United States enjoyed at the time."[43] Two other analysts, James Blight and David Welch, writing from new material and from the review conference discussions, identify the "perceptions of risks" as the first "meta-lesson" to be drawn from the Cuban Missile Crisis.[44]

Put differently, mutual survival proved more important than the unilateral interests of either country during this episode. Despite their avowed antipathy toward one another, then, neither the Soviet Union nor the United States wanted to back the other into a corner where all-out war (and nuclear holocaust) or surrender were the only options. This caution was also reflected in the various personal accounts of the decision making during the crisis and in the importance that was attached to "placing ourselves in the other country's shoes."[45]

Lesson 2: Possibility of Rational Policy Making Such caution also yielded a second lesson. Both the United States and the Soviet Union were capable of evaluating in a rational way their national interests and global consequences—a lesson that was especially important for American policy makers. Because of the Cold War consensus, Americans had tended to view skeptically the decision making of the Soviet Union. Being so consumed by Marxist-Leninist ideology, would the Soviets be able to assess the costs and the consequences of their actions and respond prudently? The answer was clearly yes, as reflected in the outcome of the crisis, and in the subsequent scholarly research on this event.[46] Rational policy making with the Soviet Union might just be possible.

Yet, some recent assessments also make clear the need to go beyond the rational policy-making assumption in drawing any lessons from this dramatic crisis episode. First, reliance on the "rational actor" assumption alone fails to account "for the values and priorities of the president. For that, cognitive models are required."[47] That is, an understanding of the values, beliefs, and perceptions of the leaders and the roles these factors played is important for understanding the successful resolution of the crisis and is a useful lesson to take away from this confrontation. Second, organizational and bureaucratic factors in policy making (see Chapters 9 and 10) actually produced more nuclear risks during the crisis than previously thought. Policy managers were, in fact, less successful in controlling the details of their subordinates in the field than many might want to believe.[48] One recent analysis that focuses on the crisis, for example, makes this point dramatically by noting that, during this period, "the U.S. nuclear command system clearly did not provide the certainty in safety that senior American leaders wanted and believed existed at the time."[49]

Lesson 3: Likelihood of Mutual Accommodation Finally, and perhaps most important, the episode suggested that the Soviet Union and the United States were going to be major participants in international relations for a long time and that each state might just as well devise policies that would acknowledge the interests and rights of the other. Neither superpower would be able to dislodge the other from its place in world politics quickly or easily. For the Americans, any vision of "rolling back communism" then was illusory at best; for the Soviets, any vision of capitalist collapse was similarly myopic. Thus the Americans and the Soviets each learned that accommodation with their major adversary was possible—and necessary—for mutual survival. In this sense, and somewhat ironically, the nuclear showdown over the missiles in Cuba has been cited as the beginnings of detente between the Soviet Union and the United States.

In sum, then, the Cuban Missile Crisis—even with the Soviet humiliation over the removal of its missiles from Cuba—challenged the Cold War view that the Soviet Union or communism could be quickly and easily dislodged from global politics. A foreign policy based solely upon this assumption was therefore likely to remain frustrating and self-defeating. (Although this point is difficult to demonstrate, the Soviet Union probably learned similar lessons about the United States.) At the same time, and equally important, the Cuban Missile Crisis illustrated the possibility of negotiating with an implacable foe—even over the most fundamental of questions—and accommodating a world of different political and social systems.

THE VIETNAM DEBACLE

American involvement in Vietnam began at the end of World War II and lasted for almost thirty years, until the evacuation of American embassy personnel from Saigon at the end of April 1975. That involvement spanned six administrations, from President Truman to President Ford, and it was guided largely by the values

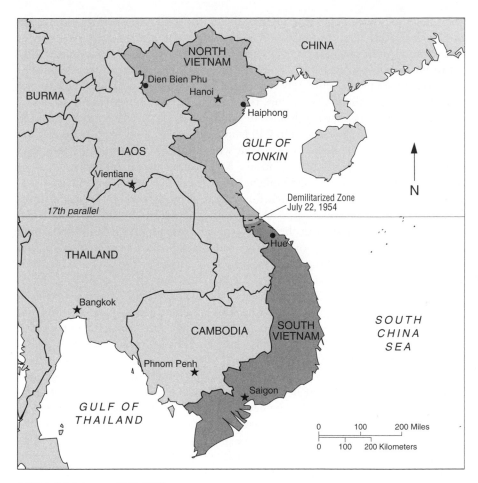

MAP 3.2 Vietnam, 1954–1975

and beliefs of the Cold War consensus. This involvement, however, produced the most divisive foreign policy debate in the history of the republic, and it ultimately produced a major foreign policy defeat for the United States as well. At home, the most important outcome of the Vietnam War was that it signaled a change in the Cold War foreign policy approach—at least until the emergence of the Reagan administration in the 1980s. Before we assess the overall impact of Vietnam, let us present a brief sketch of American involvement there.

The Origins of Involvement, 1945–1963

Although President Roosevelt gave the first hints of American interest in Indochina when he indicated a preference for an international trusteeship arrangement over countries that today are Cambodia, Laos, and Vietnam near the end of World War II, the events of the immediate postwar years and the rise of the Cold War propelled the United States in a different direction. While the Truman administration had serious reservations about identifying itself with colonialism, Soviet actions toward Eastern Europe, Communist success in China, and uncertainty about the political leanings of Ho Chi Minh—the leader of the Vietnamese independence movement—ultimately moved the United States to assume "a distinctly pro-French 'neutrality.'" As a result, the United States began providing clandestine economic and military assistance to France in the late 1940s in its war against the Vietminh (the followers of Ho Chi Minh).[50]

After the outbreak of the Korean War, which seemed to confirm Washington's suspicions about Soviet global intentions, American involvement deepened as did the war in Indochina against the French. More than $133 million of military hardware was committed to the French for Indochina, and another $50 million was sent in economic and technical assistance to the governments that the French had established there. Throughout the rest of the Truman administration, the United States provided more and more military and economic assistance. American aid constituted 40 percent of the total costs of the ongoing war for the French against the insurgents in Indochina.[51]

The Eisenhower administration took the rationale for American involvement in Vietnam one step further by invoking much of the language of the Cold War over the conflict there and by continuing to increase assistance to the non-Communist and French-backed Vietnamese government. In a 1954 news conference, President Eisenhower referred to the "falling dominoes" in Southeast Asia, and Secretary of State John Foster Dulles hinted at the role of the Chinese Communists in causing the unrest in Indochina.[52] Yet, the Eisenhower administration did not go much beyond providing economic and military assistance throughout its years in office. In fact, it explicitly ruled out the use of American force to rescue the French from defeat at the decisive battle of Dien Bien Phu with the Vietminh in 1954, and instead sought to achieve a negotiated outcome between the French and the Vietminh at a 1954 Geneva conference on Indochina.[53] That conference called for an armistice between the parties, a temporary division of the country at the 17th parallel, and elections in 1956 to unify the country. The United States neither signed these accords nor endorsed them, and the all-Vietnam election scheduled for 1956 was never held.

Instead, the United States quickly became the principal supporter of the non-Communist government of Premier (later President) Ngo Dinh Diem in South Vietnam. Diem came to be identified as "America's Mandarin," as he sought to replace French influence with close American ties.[54] Moreover, President Eisenhower and Secretary of State Dulles believed Diem represented the best prospect for developing a non-Communist Vietnam. Between 1955 and 1961 the United States provided $1 billion in aid to Diem, and by 1961, South Vietnam was the fifth largest recipient of U.S. foreign assistance.[55] Even with this massive assistance, the stability of the Diem government was still precarious throughout the late 1950s.

Upon taking office in 1961, President Kennedy expanded military and economic assistance to South Vietnam and contemplated sending in American military forces to prevent the fall of South Vietnam to communism. Yet, he did not quite take that step. Instead, he incrementally enlarged the number of American military "advisors" in South Vietnam from 685 when he took office to about 16,000 by the time of his assassination.[56] Even so, President Kennedy appeared to commit the United States to the defense of South Vietnam, although, by one account, he did not give an "unqualified commitment to the goal of saving South Vietnam from Communism."[57] Nonetheless, President Kennedy's actions had taken the United States further down the path to military involvement and may well have continued in that direction had he remained in office.[58]

American Military Involvement in Vietnam, 1964–1975

It was, however, President Lyndon Johnson who fully changed the U.S. involvement in South Vietnam from a political to a military one. He both broadened and deepened America's commitment to preserve a non-Communist South Vietnam and was ultimately the one who decided to send in American combat forces.

As the stability of the South Vietnamese government worsened (some nine changes of government occurred from the time of the coup against President Diem in November 1963 until February 1965) and as North Vietnamese and Vietcong successes increased, the Johnson administration sought a new strategy to hold on to South Vietnam.[59] At least as early as February 1964, American clandestine operations were under way against North Vietnam. Ultimately, these actions led to attacks by the North Vietnamese upon two American destroyers, the *Maddox* and the *C. Turner Joy* in the Gulf of Tonkin, off the North Vietnamese coast, in August 1964. These attacks were quickly used by the Johnson administration to seek congressional approval of the presence of American military in Southeast Asia.[60] In a matter of hours, Congress approved the Gulf of Tonkin resolution, which authorized the president to take "all necessary measures" in Southeast Asia (see Chapter 7).

For the Johnson administration, this resolution became the equivalent of a declaration of war, and U.S. retaliatory airstrikes were quickly ordered. By December 1964, air attacks against North Vietnamese infiltration routes through Laos had begun. By February 1965, "Operation Rolling Thunder," a bombing strategy to weaken North Vietnam resistance and bring it to the negotiating table, was initiated. By March 1965, the first American ground troops landed, and a rapid buildup in these forces was ordered in July of that year.[61] Indeed, the number of forces continued to escalate until they ultimately reached over a half million American soldiers by late 1968.

Despite this vast commitment of personnel and materiel, the war continued to go badly for the South Vietnamese and the United States. The Tet offensive (named after the occurrence of the lunar new year) perhaps more than any other event brought this home to Americans. This offensive consisted of widespread attacks by the North Vietnamese and the Viet Cong (or the National Liberation Front of South Vietnam) over a six-month period beginning at the end of January 1968. While the offensive was ultimately a military failure for the North Vietnam, costing it tens of thousands of lives, it was a political success in that it demonstrated the vulnerability of South Vietnam, despite years of war. Moreover, the impact of this offensive within the United States was immediate—a sharp drop in the American public's optimism about the war.[62] Additionally, the political pressure on President Johnson became so severe that, in March 1968, he voluntarily withdrew from considering a reelection campaign.

President Richard Nixon, elected as Johnson's successor in part on a commitment to change Vietnam policy, did adopt a different strategy. He began to decrease American military involvement through a policy of "Vietnamization" of the war—a policy whereby the South Vietnamese military would replace American soldiers—and also pursued peace negotiations (begun originally in mid-1968 in Paris) through both open and secret channels.

With Vietnamization, American forces in Vietnam were reduced from about 543,000 shortly after President Nixon took office to about 25,000 by the end of his first term.[63] As part of this Vietnamization strategy, the Nixon administration invaded Cambodia in April 1970, with the expressed purpose of wiping out the North Vietnamese sanctuaries or safe havens in that country. To many Americans, though, this action appeared to be a widening of the war. Protests erupted across the United States, and tragedy struck on two college campuses (Kent State University and Jackson State University) where student protesters were killed. Further opposition to the war resulted.

After one final North Vietnamese offensive in the spring of 1972 had been repulsed and after further American bombing of the North near the end of the negotiations, a settlement was finally arranged. After continuous involvement by the United States since 1965 and the loss of more than 58,000 American lives and countless Vietnamese, a cease-fire agreement, formally called "The Agreement on Ending the War and Restoring the Peace," was signed on January 27, 1973.[64] The agreement called for the withdrawal of all Americans and the return of prisoners of war. In addition, it allowed the North Vietnamese to keep their military forces in South Vietnam, and it left open the question of the future of South Vietnam. On balance, the agreement was less a "peace with honor," as it was portrayed at the time, and more a mechanism for enabling the United States to leave Vietnam.[65]

Although the cease-fire reduced the level of fighting and provided a way for the United States to extricate itself from Vietnam, it did not totally end the war or end American involvement. The end of American involvement really came two years later, during the Ford administration. With the fall of Saigon and the final evacuation of all American personnel, American involvement ceased on April 30, 1975. The fall of Saigon represented a humiliating defeat for a policy based on preventing Communist success in that Southeast Asian country. This defeat produced searching policy reflection at that point, but not before the basic premises of America's Vietnam involvement had come under scrutiny and intense debate.

Some Lessons from Vietnam

Several political and military explanations have been offered for the American defeat. Some have focused, for example, on the military tactics that the United States used in responding in Vietnam and the very nature of "limited war."[66] The use of a policy of "graduated response" did not allow the United States to take maximum advantage of its military capabilities. Others point to the failure to adjust the military strategy to the nature of the unconventional war in Vietnam and the futility of the "search-and-destroy" (i.e., forces sent to find the enemy and destroy them) approaches against the adversary.[67] Still others point to the political problems associated with the war. The "legitimacy" of the South Vietnamese government remained a problem, and its shaky domestic support weakened its efforts.[68] By contrast, the determination and will of the North Vietnamese were much greater than many had suggested. Even under the pressure of intensive bombing and high causalities, they continued to fight. Yet other explanations focus on the loss of support for the war back home and the nature of American leadership.[69] Both the American public and the Congress ultimately were unwilling to sustain support for the war. Some no longer supported the war because they believed that it was not being prosecuted fully, while others no longer believed that it was moral or ethical to engage in this conflict. Hence this foreign policy defeat, and various explanations for it, produced a significant reexamination of the Cold War consensus and contributed substantially to undermining (or at least revising) it.

Indeed, several domestic consequences for foreign policy emanated from the Vietnam War experience and had a profound effect on the direction of American actions abroad.

Consequence One: The U.S. Role The first general consequence of the domestic turmoil over the Vietnam War was the questioning of the U.S. role in the world. Should the United States be responsible for political activity everywhere in the world—especially in a country half a world away with only the most tangential relationship to American national security? Was the American public willing to support and legitimize such actions? Was the public willing to support a policy that had only the most lofty goals in international affairs? The American public's response to these questions by the early 1970s was generally a resounding "No." There were limits to American power; there were limits to America's responsibility; and there were limits to how much globalism the American public would tolerate. The role of the United States would need to be much more limited in scope.

Consequence Two: Questions of Strategy A second general lesson learned from the Vietnam case was a greater hesitancy in fighting limited war, and a belief that a different strategy would need to be pursued in doing so. By the late 1970s and early 1980s, the U.S. military leadership became increasingly uneasy about suggestions to quickly deploy American forces abroad and came to demand from their political leaders clearer missions, adequate resources, and a reasonable "exit" strategy. This "Vietnam Syndrome" was most poignantly played out during the Persian Gulf War of 1991, when General Colin Powell, Chairman of the Joint Chiefs of Staff, and General Norman Schwartzkopf, commander of American forces in the Middle East region, sought and obtained an overwhelming force level to displace the Iraqis from Kuwait. More recently, too, this syndrome was in the minds of policy makers as they contemplated actions in the Balkans in the mid-1990s, in Afghanistan after September 11, 2001, and in Iraq in 2003.

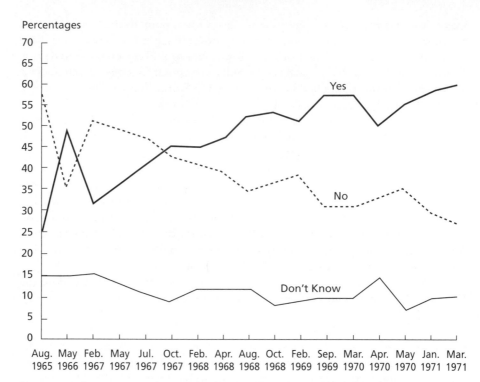

Percentage of responses to the question: "In view of the developments since we entered the fighting in Vietnam, do you think the U.S. made a mistake sending troops to fight in Vietnam?" (Gallup Organization data)

FIGURE 3.1 The "Mistake" Question on Vietnam

SOURCE: Adapted from a portion of Table 3.3 in John E. Meuller, *War, Presidents and Public Opinion* (New York: John Wiley and Sons, Inc., 1973), pp. 54–55.

Consequence Three: Open Public Debate The Vietnam experience also had a third consequence for American foreign policy at home. Foreign policy goals now became a ready source of public debate. Public opinion challenged the leadership policy on Vietnam. By 1968 and early 1969, a majority of the American public viewed Vietnam as a "mistake."[70] (See the public opinion data in Figure 3.1.) Moreover, after the Tet offensive of 1968, the number of "hawks" declined, although the public still did not favor immediate withdrawal. By late 1969, however, the support for withdrawal rose to almost the 70 percent level.[71] In the Congress, too, divisions were apparent between "liberals" and "conservatives" and between "hawks" and "doves" on foreign policy matters.[72] Such divisions stand in sharp contrast to the philosophies of just a few years earlier when "liberals" and "conservatives," despite their differences on domestic matters, often stood together on foreign policy issues. After the Vietnam experience, no such harmony was evident. Foreign policy matters had now become a subject for domestic debate.

Consequence Four: The Collapse of the Cold War Consensus The fourth general consequence followed from these earlier ones and is directly germane to our discussion of the Cold War consensus. The value and belief consensus that had guided the conduct of foreign policy since the end of World War II was shattered. No longer could the American foreign policy elite depend on general support for their foreign policy goals and actions. And America's foreign policy elite were equally divided among themselves about the relative role of the United States in world affairs.

CONCLUDING COMMENTS

More than any other action, the Vietnam War appears responsible for ultimately shattering the Cold War consensus and producing a reassessment of America's approach to international affairs. Moreover, the public, as well, had seemingly changed views from what it had embraced in the 1950s. In the post–Vietnam era, the threat of communism remained real to most Americans, but they were no longer as enthusiastic about using economic and military aid or American soldiers to combat it. Furthermore, the public was much more favorable to greater accommodation with the Soviet Union and less inclined to confrontation with that nation.[73]

Thus, Vietnam, coupled with the other Cold War challenges that we have discussed, produced a foreign policy vacuum at home. The nation was ready for new ideas for dealing with the rest of the world. A unique opportunity existed for succeeding presidents to develop a new foreign policy approach. Each new administration for the next two decades attempted to initiate this new change of direction. In the following chapters, we survey the realist and idealist approaches of the Nixon and Carter administrations, a modified Cold War approach by the Reagan administration, and a pragmatic approach by the Bush administration, and we evaluate their relative success in shaping a new direction in U.S. foreign policy for the remaining Cold War years.

NOTES

1. Lincoln P. Bloomfield, *In Search of American Foreign Policy: The Humane Use of Power* (New York: Oxford University Press, 1974).

2. J. William Fulbright, *The Arrogance of Power* (New York: Vintage Books, 1966), p. 77. His conclusion on American policy choice in this dilemma is on p. 78.

3. See the Rusk-McNamara Report to President Kennedy in Neil Sheehan, Hedrick Smith, E. W. Kenworthy, and Fox Butterfield, *The Pentagon Papers as Published by New York Times* (New York: Bantam Books, Inc., 1971), p. 150, for a statement of American objectives in Southeast Asia.

4. Barry M. Blechman and Stephen S. Kaplan, *Force Without War* (Washington, DC: The Brookings Institution, 1978), p. 12. The examples are from p. 13. Emphasis in original.

5. Ibid., p. 517. Their skepticism over the long term is at p. 532.

6. The use of force data for mid-1975 through late 1984 were taken from Philip D. Zelkow, "The United States and the Use of Force: A Historical Summary," in George K. Osborn, Asa A. Clark IV, Daniel J. Kaufman, and Douglas E. Lute, eds., *Democracy, Strategy,*

and Vietnam (Lexington, MA: D. C. Heath and Company, 1987), pp. 34–36, while the data for 1985–1988 were generously supplied by James Meernik of the University of North Texas from his research on this topic.

7. As Ernest May points out, however, American policy makers have often used historical analogies badly by preparing for the last war. See his *"Lessons" of the Past: The Use and Misuse of History in American Foreign Policy* (New York: Oxford University Press, 1973), especially his discussion of the Korean War and Truman's use of the 1930s as the analogue for U.S. policy, pp. 81–86.

8. On this "skills thinking" in the American approach to foreign policy, see Stanley Hoffmann, *Gulliver's Troubles, or the Setting of American Foreign Policy* (New York: McGraw-Hill, 1968), pp. 148–161.

9. See, for example, the discussion of polling results from the early Cold War period in Benjamin I. Page and Robert Y. Shapiro, *The Rational Public: Fifty Years of Trends in Americans' Policy Preferences* (Chicago: University of Chicago Press, 1992). I am also indebted to Eugene Wittkopf for sharing some public opinion poll results with me and allowing their inclusion here. A more complete analysis of some of the public opinion data from the Cold War years discussed here is presented in Eugene R. Wittkopf and James M. McCormick, "The Cold War Consensus: Did It Exist?" *Polity* 22 (Summer 1990): 627–653.

10. See Ibid., p. 633, and Eugene R. Wittkopf, *Faces of Internationalism: Public Opinion and American Foreign Policy* (Durham: Duke University Press, 1990), p. 178.

11. Page and Shapiro, *The Rational Public,* p. 201.

12. Wittkopf and McCormick, "The Cold War Consensus: Did It Exist?" p. 635.

13. Page and Shapiro, *The Rational Public,* p. 200.

14. Ibid., pp. 203–204.

15. Ibid., p. 202.

16. Zbigniew Brzezinski, "How the Cold War Was Played," *Foreign Affairs* 51 (October 1972): 181–204. Our subsequent discussion of these phases is drawn from his work and from the others cited below (see notes 17 and 19).

17. See John Lewis Gaddis, *The Soviet Union and the United States: An Interpretative History* (New York: John Wiley and Sons, 1978), pp. 214–215; and Seyom Brown, *The Faces of Power* (New York: Columbia University Press, 1983), p. 92.

18. Gaddis, *The Soviet Union and the United States: An Interpretative History,* p. 215.

19. Paul Marantz, "Prelude to Detente: Doctrinal Change Under Khrushchev," *International Studies Quarterly* 19 (December 1975): 510.

20. Brown, *The Faces of Power,* pp. 138–145.

21. Ibid., p. 222–233.

22. Ibid., p. 214.

23. Brzezinski, "How the Cold War Was Played," p. 194.

24. In his review and critique of Henry Kissinger's approach to international politics, Richard Falk identifies some of these characteristics as the basis for the growth of multipolarity and shows how they fit into Kissinger's foreign policy design. See Richard Falk, "What's Wrong with Henry Kissinger's Foreign Policy," *Alternatives* 1 (March 1975): 86. An earlier analysis of the "challenge to consensus" can be found in Howard Bliss and M. Glen Johnson, *Beyond the Water's Edge: America's Foreign Policies* (Philadelphia: J. B. Lippincott, 1975), pp. 1–26. Their analysis focuses primarily on the impact of Vietnam.

25. For an informative discussion of these historical antipathies, see Harrison E. Salisbury, *War Between China and Russia* (New York: W. W. Norton and Company, 1969), pp. 13–52. Also see John G. Stoessinger, *Nations in Darkness: China, Russia, and America,* 3rd ed. (New York: Random House, 1978), pp. 212–218; and Robert C. North, *The Foreign Relations of China,* 2nd ed. (Encino and Belmont, CA: Dickenson Publishing Company, Inc., 1974), pp. 112–122, for two other lucid discussions of this dispute.

26. Stoessinger, *Nations in Darkness,* pp. 214–215.

27. For an examination of the centrality of military issues in the Sino-Soviet split, see North, *The Foreign Relations of China,* pp. 41–46, 121.

28. Ibid., pp. 116–120.

29. These issues and others are discussed in Donald S. Zagoria, *The Sino-Soviet Conflict 1956–1961* (Princeton, NJ: Princeton University Press, 1962).

30. The extent of these East–West contacts is analyzed in Josef Korbel, *Detente in Europe: Real or Imaginary?* (Princeton, NJ: Princeton University Press, 1972).

31. For a summary of de Gaulle's vision of European and global politics upon which we reply, see ibid., pp. 40–60; Alfred Grosser, *French Foreign Policy Under de Gaulle* (Boston: Little, Brown, 1965), especially pp. 13–28; Edward A. Kolodziej, *French International Policy under de Gaulle and Pompidou* (Ithaca, NY: Cornell University Press, 1974); Edward A. Kolodziej, "Revolt and Revisionism in the Gaullist Global Vision: An Analysis of French Strategic Policy," *The Journal of Politics* 33 (May 1971): 448–477; Roy C. Macridis, "The French Force de Frappe," and William G. Andrews, "de Gaulle and NATO," in Roy C. Macridis, ed., *Modern European Governments: Cases in Comparative Policy Making* (Englewood Cliffs, NJ: Prentice-Hall, 1976), pp. 75–116.

32. On this point, see Josef Joffe, "The Foreign Policy of the German Federal Republic," in Roy C. Macridis, ed., *Foreign Policy in World Politics,* 5th ed. (Englewood Cliffs, NJ: Prentice-Hall, Inc., 1976), p. 141.

33. This discussion draws upon Korbel, *Detente in Europe,* pp. 40–60.

34. Ibid., p. 58.

35. The dates of independence for the new nations from 1945 to 2000 were taken from Bruce Russett, Harvey Starr, and David Kinsella, *World Politics: The Menu for Choice,* 6th ed. (Boston: Bedford/St. Martin's Press, 2000), pp. 492–498.

36. Richard L. Park, "India's Foreign Policy," in Roy C. Macridis, ed., *Foreign Policy in World Politics,* 5th ed. (Englewood Cliffs, NJ: Prentice-Hall, Inc., 1976), p. 326.

37. On this point, see the discussion in Peter Willetts, *The Non-Aligned Movement: The Origins of a Third World Alliance* (London: Frances Pinter Ltd., 1978), p. 3.

38. See Roderick Ogley, ed., *The Theory and Practice of Neutrality in the Twentieth Century* (New York: Barnes and Noble, Inc., 1970), pp. 189–194.

39. For two important discussions of the notion of nonalignment, see Cecil V. Crabb, Jr., *The Elephants and the Grass: A Study of Nonalignment* (New York: Frederick A. Praeger, 1965); and Willets, *The Non-Aligned Movement,* especially pp. 17–31.

40. See Table 1.1 in ibid. for a summary of the various nonaligned conferences and their membership.

41. Theodore Sorensen, one of President Kennedy's advisors and who edited Robert Kennedy's book on the missile crisis, now acknowledges "that the missile trade had been portrayed as an explicit deal in the diaries on which the book was based, and that he [Kennedy] had seen fit to revise that account in view of the fact that the trade was still a secret at the time, known to only six members of the ExComm." This quote is from James G. Blight and David A. Welch, *On the Brink: Americans and Soviets Reexamine the Cuban Missile Crisis,* 2nd. ed. (New York: The Noonday Press, 1990), p. 341. This admission was made by Sorensen at the 1989 Moscow Conference on the Cuban Missile Crisis.

42. See ibid., but also see Len Scott and Steve Smith, "Political Scientists, Policy-makers, and the Cuban Missile Crisis," *International Affairs* 70 (October 1994): 659–684, which seeks to summarize and analyze various old and new interpretations of events and lessons from the crisis by incorporating the findings from the various academic analyses and the review conferences held on this topic.

43. Ibid., p. 681.

44. Blight and Welch, *On the Brink,* p. 347.

45. Robert F. Kennedy, *Thirteen Days* (New York: Signet Books, 1969), p. 124.

46. See, for example, the study of Ole R. Holsti, Richard A. Brody, and Robert C. North, "The Management of International Crisis: Affect and Action in American-Soviet Relations," in Dean G. Pruitt and Richard C. Snyder, eds., *Theory and Research on the Causes of War* (Englewood Cliffs, NJ: Prentice-Hall, Inc., 1969), pp. 62–79.

47. Scott and Smith, "Political Scientists, Policy-makers, and the Cuban Missile Crisis," p. 680.

48. See ibid. throughout, but especially at pp. 682–683.

49. Scott Sagan, *The Limits of Safety: Organizations, Accidents, and Nuclear Weapons* (Princeton, NJ: Princeton University Press, 1993), p. 151, as quoted in Scott and Smith, "Political Scientists, Policy-makers, and the Cuban Missile Crisis," p. 682.

50. George C. Herring, *America's Longest War: The United States and Vietnam* (New York: Alfred A. Knopf, 1986), pp. 7–10. The quote is at p. 10.

51. These data are primarily from Leslie H. Gelb with Richard K. Betts, *The Irony of Vietnam: The System Worked* (Washington, DC: The Brookings Institution, 1979), p. 46. But also see Herring, *America's Longest War: The United States and Vietnam,* pp. 18 and 19, for the first two pieces of data.

52. Gelb with Betts, *The Irony of Vietnam: The System Worked,* pp. 50, 51.

53. See the chapter on "The Decision Not to Intervene in Indochina 1954," in Morton Berkowitz, P. G. Bock, and Vincent J. Fuccillo, *The Politics of American Foreign Policy* (Englewood Cliffs, NJ: Prentice Hall, Inc., 1977), pp. 54–74. Also see Sheehan et al., *The Pentagon Papers, New York Times* edition, pp. 13–22; Herring, *America's Longest War: The United States and Vietnam,* pp. 41–42; and Timothy J. Lomperis, *The War Everyone Lost—and Won* (Washington, DC: CQ Press, 1984), p. 48, on the Geneva Accords.

54. On the role of the United States in backing Diem and the "America's Mandarin" label, see Stanley Karnow, *Vietnam: A History* (New York: Viking Press, 1983), pp. 206–239.

55. On the level of support, see Herring, *America's Longest War: The United States and Vietnam,* p. 57.

56. The information in this paragraph and earlier is from Sheehan et al., *The Pentagon Papers,* pp. 76, 78 and 83.

57. Ibid., p. 107.

58. See Richard K. Betts, "Misadventure Revisited," in James M. McCormick, ed., *A Reader in American Foreign Policy,* (Itasca, IL: F. E. Peacock Publishers, Inc., 1986), p. 100, for this assessment.

59. On the changes in Vietnamese governments, see Lomperis, *The War Everyone Lost—and Won,* p. 62.

60. See Sheehan et al., *The Pentagon Papers* at pp. 236–237 for the chronology of events in 1964. For the controversy of what really happened in the Gulf of Tonkin, see Herring, *America's Longest War: The United States and Vietnam,* pp. 119–123.

61. Sheehan et al., *The Pentagon Papers,* pp. 308–309, 459–461.

62. Lomperis, *The War Everyone Lost—and Won,* pp. 76–79. On the Tet offensive, also see Karnow, *Vietnam: A History,* pp. 515–566.

63. Ibid., p. 82. On the Cambodian invasion, see pp. 83–85.

64. According to the fact sheet issued by the Vietnam Veterans Leadership Program of Houston, Inc., 57,704 deaths occurred in the Vietnam War. The number of names inscribed on the Vietnam Veterans War Memorial in Washington, DC, however, is 58,132. On the last "Easter Invasion," see Lomperis, *The War Everyone Lost—and Won,* pp. 87–90.

65. Ibid., p. 94, for terms of the negotiated settlement and Herring, *America's Longest War: The United States and Vietnam,* pp. 255–256, for this assessment of it.

66. One recent assessment of this view is George C. Herring, *LBJ and Vietnam: A Different Kind of War* (Austin: University of Texas Press, 1994) at pp. 178–186, although he also focuses significantly on the role of President Johnson and his leadership style.

67. On these explanations, ibid., pp. 276–278.

68. See Lomperis, *The War Everyone Lost—and Won,* for a thorough examination of the national legitimacy question. For many lessons of Vietnam, see Gelb with Betts, *The Irony of Vietnam: The System Worked,* pp. 347–369.

69. See ibid. and Herring, *LBJ and Vietnam: A Different Kind of War.*

70. See Table 3.3 on public opinion survey results regarding support and opposition to the Vietnam War in John E. Mueller, *War, Presidents and Public Opinion* (New York: John Wiley and Sons, 1973), pp. 54–55.

71. Page and Shapiro, *The Rational Public,* pp. 232–235.

72. For one summary of the literature on domestic policy/foreign policy divisions among liberals and conservatives, see Bruce Russett, "The Americans' Retreat from World Power," *Political Science Quarterly* 90 (Spring 1975): 1–21, especially pp. 14 and 15.

73. Wittkopf and McCormick, "The Cold War Consensus: Did It Exist?" discusses the public's view in the post-Vietnam period.

4

American Foreign Policy after Vietnam: From Realism to Idealism and Back Again

[T]he United States will participate in the defense and development
of allies and friends, but . . . America cannot—and will not—conceive
all plans, design *all* programs, execute *all* the decisions and
undertake *all* the defense of the free nations of the world.

PRESIDENT RICHARD NIXON
"U.S. FOREIGN POLICY FOR THE 1970S"
FEBRUARY 18, 1970 (EMPHASIS IN ORIGINAL)

[W]e are now free of that inordinate fear of communism which once
led us to embrace any dictator who joined us in that fear. . . . It is a new world
that calls for a new American foreign policy—a policy based on constant
decency in its values and on optimism in our historical vision.

PRESIDENT JIMMY CARTER
COMMENCEMENT ADDRESS AT THE
UNIVERSITY OF NOTRE DAME, MAY 1977

General Secretary Gorbachev, if you seek peace, if you seek prosperity for the
Soviet Union and Eastern Europe, if you seek liberalization: Come here to this
gate! Mr. Gorbachev, open this gate! Mr. Gorbachev, tear down this wall!

PRESIDENT RONALD REAGAN
BRANDENBURG GATE, BERLIN
JUNE 12, 1987

With the breakdown of the Cold War consensus seemingly finalized by America's agonizing defeat in the Vietnam War, succeeding administrations attempted to offer new foreign policy approaches to replace this shattered world-view. In this chapter, we discuss the values and beliefs that the Nixon, Carter, and Reagan administrations brought to U.S. foreign policy. Each relied upon considerably different value perspectives to inform foreign policy making. The Nixon administration sought to employ a "power politics" or "realist" approach to U.S. policy; the Carter administration tried to employ a "global politics" or "idealist" approach; and the Reagan administration tried to combine these approaches by resurrecting the values of the Cold War.[1] While none of these administration succeeded in producing a new foreign policy consensus (and each met with substantial criticism and resistance), each approach brought a distinct and identifiable worldview to U.S. foreign policy after the height of the Cold War.

REALISM AND IDEALISM
AS FOREIGN POLICY CONCEPTS

Realism and *idealism* are two concepts that require some discussion before we proceed.[2] Each has been widely used to describe the behavior of individuals and states in the study of foreign policy. Each is an ideal type, a phenomenon in which individuals and states are closer to one approach than the other, but do not match either perfectly. Earlier postwar presidents (e.g., Truman or Eisenhower) may have combined elements of realism and idealism, but none matched these characteristics as well as Nixon, Carter, and Reagan in their foreign policy behavior. In this sense, realism and idealism serve as important ways to think about foreign policy actions of these administrations even if these concepts do not fully describe them.

The realist approach is based upon several key assumptions about world politics: (1) the nation-state is the primary actor in world politics; (2) interest, defined as power, is the primary motivating force for the action of states; (3) the distribution or balance of power (predominantly military power) at any given time is the key concern that states must address; and (4) the quality of state-to-state relations (and not the character of domestic politics within another state) is the primary consideration that should shape how one nation responds to another. For the realist, since human nature is ultimately flawed, efforts at universal perfection in global politics are myopic, shortsighted, and ultimately dangerous. Instead, moral considerations in foreign policy are largely derived from what is good for the state and for its place in international politics.

In this view, foreign policy is a highly conflictual process between states, with each seeking to further its interests and with each warily monitoring the activities of others. Balance of power politics predominates because all states are concerned about the relative distribution of power at any one time, and all states are trying to maximize their own power and standing in international affairs.

The idealist approach starts with a different set of assumptions: (1) the nation-state is only one among many participants in foreign policy; (2) values, rather than interests, are predominant in shaping foreign policy responses; (3) the distribution of power is only one of many values of concern to the idealist, with social and economic issues equally as important as military ones; and (4) overall global conditions, not state-to-state relations, dominate foreign policy considerations. For the idealist, human nature can be changed, improving humankind is a laudable goal, and universal values should be the basis of action.

In this view, foreign policy should be a cooperative process between states and groups. Joint efforts ought to be undertaken to address the problems facing humankind, whether they be political, military, economic, or social. International institutions (e.g., international and regional organizations) are crucial to shaping global politics, and balance of power politics are largely to be eschewed.

REALISM AND THE NIXON ADMINISTRATION

The Nixon administration adopted a foreign policy approach more closely approaching the realist tradition than did earlier post–World War II presidents. Its approach was based upon the principles of the "balance of power" and was to be anchored in a global equilibrium among the United States, the Soviet Union, and the People's Republic of China (and later, Japan and Europe). This realist perspective was to enable the United States to play a more limited global role and to utilize substantial amounts of regional power (and power centers) to foster American interests worldwide. At the same time, it would allow the United States to remain an important, even dominant, participant in global affairs. One should keep in mind that this new realism in foreign policy was precipitated by the events surrounding the Vietnam War (see Chapter 3). Indeed, the Nixon administration was as much consumed by the events in Vietnam as it was in reordering superpower relations. Both factors pointed the United States in the direction of a different approach to foreign policy, however.

The Nixon Approach to Foreign Policy

Several dimensions of this policy design were foreshadowed in a *Foreign Affairs* article written by Nixon almost two years before he took office.[3] Nixon emphasized two main points: (1) the importance of bringing the People's Republic of China back into the world community; and (2) the more limited role for the United States in regional disputes in the future. The United States, Nixon wrote, "cannot afford to leave China forever outside the family of nations. There is no place on this small planet for a billion of its potentially most able people to live in angry isolation." At the same time, Nixon argued that a "policy of firm restraint" must be employed to persuade Beijing to accept the "basic rules of international civility."

Nixon also foreshadowed a change in American policy toward regional conflict: "Other nations must recognize that the role of the United States as world policeman is likely to be limited in the future." If U.S. assistance is requested, it must come only after a regional collective effort has been attempted and failed and only when a collective request is made to the United States. Unlike the Vietnam experience, direct intervention by the United States must be reduced or limited.

Other essential elements of President Richard Nixon's approach to the world, however, were described more fully in his State of the World Report to the Congress in early 1970.[4] In the statement, he outlined his conception of how to build a new "structure of peace" in the world. Three principles shaped the "Nixon Doctrine" and were driven in no small measure by his desire to shape a role for the United States after America's departure from Vietnam:

1. Peace would require a partnership with the rest of the world.
2. Peace would require strength to protect U.S. national interests.
3. Peace would require a willingness to negotiate with all states to resolve differences.

What these principles meant was that the role of the United States was to be diminished and its power was to be shared with others in terms of preserving world order. Such a design also meant that the United States would act to protect its interests and would do so primarily through the use of military might. Furthermore, the United States would welcome the opportunity to negotiate with other states to resolve outstanding differences.

Such a conception was some distance from the postwar consensus that had put so much stock in the ability of the United States to carry the burden of the responsibilities in the "free world." In addition, President Nixon made two other important observations in this speech. First, he recognized that the world was multipolar: "Today, the nature of that world has changed—the power of individual Communist nations has grown, but international Communist unity has been shattered." Second, he acknowledged the power of nationalism in the developing world. Moreover, he implied that this nationalism should not be equated with the increase in Communist penetration: "Once, many feared that they [the new nations] would become simply a battleground of cold-war rivalry and fertile ground for Communist penetration. But this fear misjudged their pride in their national identities and their determination to preserve their newly won sovereignty."

In all, then, this design pointed to a different foreign policy approach for the United States and represented a sharp break with the postwar consensus.[5]

Henry Kissinger and World Order

While President Nixon's statements outlined the key components of a new policy approach, his national security advisor, and later secretary of state, Henry Kissinger, provided a more complete exposition of what the policy design would look like in practice. To appreciate Kissinger's approach, we must begin with his basic philosophy of international politics, which was developed from a number of years of academic writing and from practical foreign policy experience in previous administrations.

For Henry Kissinger, the essential problem in the postwar world was a structural one: the lack of a *legitimate international order*.[6] Both the United States and the

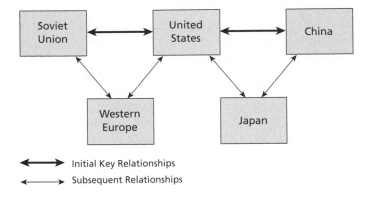

Initial Key Relationships

Subsequent Relationships

FIGURE 4.1 The Principal Participants in the Balance
of Power System Conceptualized by Nixon and Kissinger

Soviet Union had tended to think of the world in terms of absolutes and had tried to impose their own views of world order in international politics. Neither had succeeded. As a result, a "revolutionary" and multipolar international system appeared, characterized by (1) the emergence of many states and new centers of power, (2) the growth of vast new technologies that has created great disparities in power, and (3) the appearance of a diversity of political purposes by these states. All these forces made it difficult to establish or maintain any legitimate order. Thus, according to Kissinger, the most important challenge confronting the United States was "to develop some concept of order in a world which is bipolar militarily but multipolar politically."

To create such order, Kissinger argued, the United States must think more along the lines of balance of power politics. While America's idealism of the past should not be abandoned, the requirements of global equilibrium should give some "perspective" to such idealism. The United States should not be afraid to pursue its interests; it should not be afraid to pursue equilibrium; and it should not be afraid to think in terms of power.[7]

What Kissinger proposed was an international order in which stability was a fundamental goal—in contrast to absolute peace, a goal so essential in America's past. Only by achieving a stable international system would international peace really become possible.[8] When stability was the goal and was achieved, competing powers would recognize the rights of one another, and this situation would hold the best prospect for achieving international peace because no state would attempt to impose its views on the international system.

To achieve stability and an equilibrium of forces, the legitimacy of states and of the international system had to be recognized. A prerequisite for such legitimacy was for states to accept the rights and interests of other nations and contain their revolutionary fervor. Henry Kissinger (and President Nixon) therefore proposed a "structure of peace" that would be composed of a "pentagonal" balance of power among the United States, the Soviet Union, the People's Republic of China, Western Europe, and Japan.[9] The emphasis would be to gain some accommodation among the first three, with Western Europe and Japan added later to this global design.

An important requirement of this design was that deviations from respecting the rights and interests of other states would not go unpunished. If, for example, a state took actions outside its "traditional area of interest," other states should take action to demonstrate that violations of the required "norms of international conduct" would not be tolerated. For instance, if the Soviet Union provided economic or military support to revolutionary forces in Angola—an area where it had no historical tie—as it did in 1975, some response must be made. The response could take the form of reducing the quality of the bilateral relationship between the United States and the Soviet Union (e.g., reducing trade or the prospects of future arms negotiations) or in the multilateral relationship in the third area itself (e.g., giving direct assistance to the factions opposing the Soviet-backed group in Angola). Whichever strategy is employed, some action must be taken. The intent of such action is to bring home to the offending state the limitations of acceptable international behavior and demonstrate that attempts at expansion (and upsetting international stability) would not go unpunished. In this way, conflict itself would contribute to stabilizing the international order.

This approach to violations of acceptable norms of international behavior came to be known as *linkage* in the operation of the Nixon–Kissinger system. Put differently, this concept meant that the character of behavior in one foreign policy arena (e.g., completing bilateral trade agreements) was inevitably linked to the character of behavior in another foreign policy arena (e.g., aiding insurgents in a Third World nation). It is significant to note that the Nixon–Kissinger approach did not link foreign and domestic arenas. For Nixon and Kissinger, linkage did not mean, for example, predicating the completion of arms agreements on changes in domestic conditions within the Soviet Union. Nonetheless, the importance of this concept to the Nixon–Kissinger approach should not be minimized; it was indeed at the heart of their foreign policy strategy.

By getting all states to accept the legitimacy of the rights and interests of one another and by employing the notion of linkage, Kissinger believed that the United States would go a long way to achieving global stability. In the short run, the success of this strategy meant the abandonment by the United States, the Soviet Union, and the People's Republic of China of their universal goals of transforming international politics to their own ends. Furthermore, it meant that a policy of cooperation would be mixed with a policy of competition in the relationship among these states. This approach, which became to be labeled *detente,* or relaxation of tension between the superpowers, was an attempt to build some predictability into international politics. In the long run, if this approach could be institutionalized, a global order based upon balance of power principles would be a reality.

Domestic Values and Foreign Policy

Aside from bringing a policy of accommodation with adversaries to American foreign policy, Henry Kissinger also challenged four other precepts of past American approaches to the world. First, he believed that diplomacy (or the "statesman" as he labeled it in his essay on the subject[10]) was the key to the resolution of disputes and to the operation of international politics. As he said, "negotiation is the mechanism of stability because it presupposes that maintenance of the existing order is more important than any dispute within it." Moreover, he was willing to negotiate outstanding differences between states as the principal means of achieving stability. Second, Kissinger adopted a different attitude toward the use of force and the combining of force with diplomacy. His view may best be summarized as, "Negotiate when possible, use force when necessary." Furthermore, Kissinger believed in the use of relative levels of force in efforts to achieve foreign policy goals. Such an attitude toward force and the use of degrees of force was again wholly at odds with America's past. Third, Kissinger challenged the postwar consensus in yet another way. His view was that domestic values should not dominate American foreign policy. Policy should not become excessively moralistic; when it does, he argued, policy becomes dangerous, especially in a pluralistic world.[11] The United States should be guided by its historical values, but it should seek to evoke them in the world rather than try to impose them on it. Finally, Kissinger wanted a clear demarcation between the operation of domestic politics and foreign policy. In particular, he did not want the U.S. Congress imposing conditions on the ability of a nation's "statesman" to operate in the international system. Thus, he vigorously opposed the imposition of restraints on trade with the Soviet Union because of its treatment of Jews who sought to emigrate. While human rights standards were perfectly acceptable in domestic politics, these standards were, he believed, unacceptable in the conduct of foreign policy. Put differently, the domestic policies of a nation mattered less to Kissinger than the way that nation treated the United States in foreign affairs. The principal guide to American foreign policy should be the condition of relations *between* nations, not the domestic conditions *within* another nation.[12]

THE NIXON–KISSINGER WORLDVIEW IN OPERATION

Many of Richard Nixon and Henry Kissinger's views on world order, the use of force and diplomacy, and the role of domestic values were manifest in American foreign policy actions from 1969 through 1976.[13] Yet these views and actions also stimulated some important criticisms from their attempt to impose this realist approach to American foreign policy.

Developing Sino-Soviet-American Detente

Almost immediately upon assuming office, National Security Advisor (and later Secretary of State) Henry Kissinger and President Nixon set out to establish the model of world order that they proposed. By November 1969, the first discussions with the Soviet Union over nuclear accommodation were under way. The Strategic Arms Limitation Talks (SALT) were initiated in Geneva and proceeded through several sessions before agreement was reached in 1972. At the Moscow

Summit in May 1972, President Nixon and Soviet President Leonid Brezhnev signed the SALT I accords, which consisted of two agreements. One, the Interim Agreement on Offensive Strategic Arms, called for limitations on the offensive nuclear weapons that the Soviet Union and the United States were allowed; the other, the Anti-Ballistic Missile Treaty, limited the development of defensive nuclear weapons systems by the two superpowers. These pacts signaled the first agreements to stabilize a structure of world order between the two superpowers and to institute a stable "balance of terror" between them. They became synonymous with the notion of detente.

The Moscow Summit meetings produced more than military accommodation between the United States and the USSR; they also produced a series of political, economic, and social/cultural arrangements. A political agreement ("Basic Principles of Relations Between the United States and the Union of Soviet Socialist Republics") was reached, in which the principle of linkage was presumably institutionalized because each country pledged not to take advantage of the other, either "directly" or "indirectly." An economic commitment was made to improve trade relations between the two countries, and a Joint Commission was established for that purpose. Four social/cultural agreements were also signed in Moscow. These agreements called for U.S./Soviet cooperation on protecting the environment, enhancing medical science and public health cooperation, undertaking joint space activities (including the 1975 Apollo–Soyuz flight), and furthering science and technology.[14] The essence of detente with the Soviet Union was in place with these 1972 agreements because broad avenues of cooperation were opened in the context of a relationship that was still competitive. An important part of the three-pronged global order seemed to be operating.

Similar efforts at achieving global stability were initiated with the other major player in the Nixon–Kissinger design: the People's Republic of China. In late 1970, Premier Zhou Enlai gave the first hints of an interest in establishing contact with the United States.[15] The United States responded quickly and positively. By mid-1971, Henry Kissinger made a secret trip to Beijing in order to pave the way for a visit by an American president to that long-isolated country. On July 15, 1971, President Nixon appeared on American radio and television with the shock announcement: He had been invited to the People's Republic of China, had accepted the invitation, and would go there as soon as arrangements could be worked out. Nixon visited China in February 1972 and, by any analysis, enjoyed a huge success.

The Shanghai Communique resulted from this meeting and was issued from that Chinese city on February 28, 1972.[16] While the communique reflected the differing worldviews of the two nations, it did provide areas of global and bilateral commonalties. For instance, it reflected some movement on the question of Taiwan through confirmation by both sides that there was only "one China"; it opposed "hegemony" in the world (a not-so-subtle strategy by the United States to use the "China card" to influence Soviet behavior); and it called for efforts at normalization of relations (although full diplomatic relations would not be achieved until the Carter administration); and it opened up trade and other contacts between the American and Chinese peoples. Overall, the content of the communique did not provide the areas of cooperation that the Moscow meeting would, but it had the seeds of such cooperation. Nonetheless, it was remarkable in a more profound sense: After more than thirty years, formal contact between harsh adversaries was begun. The Asian component of the Kissinger–Nixon global design seemed to be falling into place as well.

The last component of this detente strategy was the Final Act of the Conference on Security and Cooperation in Europe signed in Helsinki, Finland, on August 1, 1975.[17] It was signed after President Nixon had left office, but while Henry Kissinger still dominated policy, and it signaled efforts at expanding detente from involving only the superpowers to including all European states.

The conference itself was composed of thirty-five countries from Eastern and Western Europe and the United States and Canada from North America. The Final Act (or the Helsinki Accords as they are sometimes called) was a "political statement," rather than a legally binding treaty of international law. It was composed of three "baskets" of issues, with each basket containing provisions for enhancing cooperation among the signatory nations. The first basket dealt with principles of conduct toward one another and ways to reduce military tension among them; the second dealt with efforts to enlarge cooperation in economic, technological, and environmental arenas; and the third dealt with a series of measures for fostering closer social/cultural interaction among participants. The Final Act, however, was not viewed as an end in itself; instead, it was seen as the beginning point of an evolving cooperative process in Central Europe, much as the Moscow and Shanghai agreements of 1972 were viewed. In this sense, with the Helsinki Accords, the "relaxation of tensions" and the stability of the international order that Nixon and Kissinger had envisioned expanded to all of Central Europe.

Force and Diplomacy in the Third World

Two events illustrate the importance of combining force and diplomacy for implementing the Nixon–Kissinger approach. The first involved negotiations over ending the Vietnam War, the second entailed the use of "shuttle diplomacy" in the Middle East. From the outset of Kissinger's tenure as national security advisor, he saw negotiations as the key to the resolution of the Vietnam War.[18] A two-track system of secret and open negotiations was put into effect immediately. These negotiations, however, did not produce quick results. In an attempt to get the negotiations back on track, force—and in this case the escalation of force—needed to be added to the diplomatic track. For Nixon and Kissinger, force could be used to demonstrate resolve concerning their bargaining position and to prod their adversary to serious negotiations.

As a consequence, the use of escalating force was combined with the ongoing Vietnam negotiations in an effort to produce diplomatic results. In April 1970, Kissinger and Nixon agreed to an American "incursion" into Cambodia—a neutral country—essentially escalating the war (although secret bombing attacks had previously occurred). This action was undertaken to demonstrate U.S. resolve on the issue and as a way to move the North Vietnamese toward serious negotiations.

About two years later (May 1972), when negotiations were again stalled, the bombing and blockading of Hanoi and Haiphong were used for the same expressed goal.[19] Third, after Kissinger had so solemnly announced that "peace is at hand" in late October 1972, and that only a few details were left to negotiate, the final negotiations abruptly hit a snag. As a consequence, President Nixon intensified the bombing of North Vietnam in December 1972 as a way to reopen negotiations and to bring about the successful completion of an agreement.[20] By late January 1973, a Vietnam disengagement was signed in Paris.

The other major illustration of combining force and diplomacy occurred in the Middle East. After the Arab initiation of force in the Yom Kippur War of October 1973, and the imposition of the oil embargo by the Arab oil states, the United States first used American military assistance to reinforce Israel, but then Kissinger used his considerable diplomatic skills to negotiate a series of disengagement pacts among Egypt, Syria, and Israel. These agreements began to untangle the Middle East conflict, but they had, perhaps, more importance in turning the oil spigot back on for the United States. Intermittently, over a period of months from 1973 through 1975, Henry Kissinger shuttled between Cairo, Tel Aviv, and Damascus to hammer out two disengagement agreements over the Sinai Peninsula, between Egypt and Israel, and one over the Golan Heights, between Syria and Israel. Such diplomatic actions brought into sharp relief the central role that negotiations placed upon the "statesman." Although Kissinger's further efforts were ultimately stalled by intransigence on both sides, even his efforts to that point illustrated how diplomacy could be a powerful tool in moving toward international order.

Human Rights and Foreign Policy Action

Finally, Kissinger and Nixon brought a separation between American domestic values and American foreign policy actions during its time in office. This separation was perhaps best illustrated in policy toward authoritarian and totalitarian regimes. For instance, Nixon and Kissinger were reluctant to bring to the attention of the Chilean and Greek juntas publically their concerns about violations of human rights because of the overriding importance of such states to establishing global order. Similarly, U.S. policy toward South Africa continued tacit support for that regime, despite its apartheid policy of legally separating races in social and political life. Once again, strategic considerations became an important motivating force for the Nixon administration.

Toward totalitarian regimes, Nixon and Kissinger seemed to operate on a similar dichotomy. For instance, Kissinger opposed giving any official Washington recognition to Alexsandr Solzhenitsyn when he was expelled from the Soviet Union, just as he opposed the Jackson–Vanik Amendment to the Trade Act of 1974. This amendment essentially made free emigration policy a requirement for any U.S. trading partner seeking most-favored-nation status. Because the Soviet Union enforced a restrictive emigration policy, most-favored-nation trading status was denied them. Domestic politics in any state were to be subordinated to the requirements of international politics. To the extent that domestic situations within another state were to be addressed, these were to be done through "quiet diplomacy"—secret representations to the offending regime.

Criticisms of the Nixon–Kissinger Approach

Despite the policy successes that Nixon and Kissinger brought to U.S. foreign policy in the 1970s, their foreign policy approach was subject to criticism both for the content of its policy and for the style of policy making. These criticisms came from analysts across the political spectrum.

From the left, the most telling critique was offered by political scientist Richard Falk in an essay aptly entitled "What's Wrong with Henry Kissinger's Foreign Policy?"[21] His criticisms focused upon the lack of moral content in Kissinger's policy and its irrelevance to the last quarter of the twentieth century. Kissinger's concern with order and stability in international politics ignored the more important questions of peace and justice in global affairs. In Falk's view, the most pressing issues of international politics were not power and domination, as Kissinger emphasized, but hunger, poverty, and global inequity. Yet, his policy approach had no direct way to deal with these important concerns; rather, Kissinger's global order was predicated upon preserving the nation-state system and attempting to manage that system by moderating conflict among a few, strong Northern Hemisphere states. Such a view represents the "underlying conceptual flaw in Kissinger's approach."[22] This "cooperative directorate among great powers" that Kissinger envisioned was shortsighted in more fundamental ways as well: It accepted as inevitable the persistence of large-scale misery and repression. It enabled the disfavored many to be kept under control by the favored few.[23]

From the right, the Kissinger approach was also criticized in terms of moral relativity. In particular, political conservatives viewed the policy of detente as morally bankrupt because it gave international status and recognition to regimes that the United States had largely rejected as totalitarian and illegitimate previously. Indeed, the opening to the People's Republic of China was particularly troubling, since the United States had never recognized or interacted very much with the regime of Mao Tse-tung. Suddenly, this situation changed almost overnight. While the change was not as abrupt with the Soviet Union, the effect was largely the same.

William Buckley, a leading conservative spokesperson, put this criticism in a slightly different way. He argued that the detente policy was based upon an "ideological egalitarianism" that implied that there were no fundamental differences between the American, Soviet, and Chinese societies. As he noted in a televised interview with Henry Kissinger, the Chinese had been most often described as "warlike," "ignorant," "sly," and "treacherous" in a 1966 American poll in the United States. One month after President Nixon's return from China in 1972, however, the description had changed dramatically. Now, the Chinese were most often described as "progressive," "hard-working," "intelligent," "artistic," and "practical."[24] Yet, the regime in Beijing (at that time) had hardly changed its policy at all; only American policy had changed. Detente, therefore, had the effect of reducing the ideological distinction between the United States and these Communist states almost overnight.

Yet a third criticism from the right, and hardly divorced from the other two, is that detente was a strategy that connoted a "no win" strategy against communism. By accepting the legitimacy of these other key states and by working with them, these states were perpetuated, not undermined, which presumably had been the U.S. aim for three decades.

The detente approach was criticized from yet another quarter. One former Kennedy and Johnson administration official did not see the policy as particularly new or as necessarily advantageous to the United States both in terms of policy abroad and in terms of decision making at home.[25] On a policy level, detente was not really a new policy toward the Soviet Union, the policy had produced few benefits for the West, and Soviet political cooperation had not significantly improved. On a decision-making level, the Nixon–Kissinger style was inappropriate for a great power and a democratic society. Kissinger's "lonely cowboy" approach to policy making limited the foreign policy agenda that could be pursued. The result was "a policy that ignore[d] relations with nations that happen . . . to be outside the spotlight, and . . . encourage[d] a practice of haphazard improvisation."[26] Further, this "policy of maneuver," by the "Master Player," was built on secrecy and personalism that were hardly consistent with a democratic society. By tradition, policies must be fully explained to the American public—something that Nixon and Kissinger were not wont to do.

A Break with Tradition

In short, opponents (and even admirers) appeared on both the political right and the political left to charge that the Nixon–Kissinger "power politics" strategy was fundamentally amoral and inconsistent with America's past, and that its style of decision making challenged democratic traditions at home. Despite these fundamental criticisms, America's approach to the world had come a considerable distance from its traditional past. American policy had moved away from an emphasis on both moral principle and isolationism; instead it had embraced the basic elements of realism. From an initial postwar moral crusade, driven largely by fervent anticommunism, the United States had now adopted an approach driven by the principles of pragmatism and "power politics." However, support for this approach was to wane rather quickly, and the 1976 presidential election was fought, at least in part, on the morality of American foreign policy. That election produced a new president—one committed to a foreign policy based on moral standards.

IDEALISM AND THE
CARTER ADMINISTRATION

Jimmy Carter ran for president in 1976 on the theme of making American foreign policy compatible with the basic goodness of the American people; he came to office pledged to restore integrity and morality to American diplomacy. With those fundamental concerns, President Carter introduced a policy approach that was closer to the idealist approach than that of earlier presidents after World War II. His approach sought to reorient the focus of America's foreign policy away from a singular emphasis on adversaries, and especially the Soviet Union (as had characterized Nixon–Ford–Kissinger) toward a policy with a truly global emphasis. Four major policy areas would be highlighted: (1) emphasizing domestic values in foreign policy, (2) improving relations with allies and resolving regional conflict, (3) de-emphasizing the Soviet Union as the focus of U.S. policy, and (4) promoting global human rights.[27] Despite his initial idealism, however, by the last year of his term, Carter had reverted to a policy much more consistent with the realist policies of previous postwar presidents.

The Carter Approach to Foreign Policy

From the outset, President Jimmy Carter highlighted the importance of domestic values as a guide to American foreign policy. In this sense, his approach was consistent with a reliance on moral principle so evident in America's historical past and in sharp contrast with the previous two administrations. For his presidency, domestic values were to be preeminent in the shaping of America's foreign policy; the United States must "stand for something" in the world. Even more, America should serve as a model for other nations.

In his inaugural address, President Carter stated these beliefs forcefully. He said: "Our Nation can be strong abroad only if it is strong at home. And we know that the best way to enhance freedom in other lands is to demonstrate here that our democratic system is worthy of emulation."[28] He went on to say that the United States would not act abroad in ways that would violate domestic standards. In a similar vein, during his 1977 Notre Dame commencement address, President Carter again emphasized the moral basis of American policy: "I believe we can have a foreign policy that is democratic, that is based on fundamental values, and that uses power and influence which we have for humane purposes."[29]

In addition to emphasizing this moral basis of policy, President Carter also called for a different style of foreign policy—one that would be "open and candid," and not one that was a "policy by manipulation" or based on "secret deals." Such references were apparently to what he saw as the style adopted during the years that Henry Kissinger was at the helm of American foreign policy.

Finally, while the president recognized that moral principle must guide foreign policy, he acknowledged that foreign policy cannot be "by moral maxims." The United States would have to try to produce change rather than impose it. In this sense, Carter believed that there were limits to what the United States could do in the world. Although these limits would need to be recognized, America could not stand idly by. The United States should try to play a constructive and positive role in shaping a new world order. This role should be through an American policy "based on constant decency in its values and on optimism in our historical vision."[30]

Carter and Global Order: New States and Old Friends

The focus of the Carter administration also reflected its view of the world. Its policy would not be simply one of anticommunism inherited from the past. (President Carter said, "We are now free of that inordinate fear of communism which once led us to embrace any dictator who joined us in that fear.") Instead, the

Carter administration proposed a policy of global cooperation, especially with the newly influential countries in Latin America, Africa, and Asia, but also with the industrial democracies of the world. The aim of such an effort would be "to create a wider framework of international cooperation suited to the new and rapidly changing historical circumstances."[31] Moreover, this policy sought to move beyond one seeking global stability among the strong to a policy that recognized the reality of the new states and their place in the world order.

Within this same global context, crucial regional trouble spots of the world were to be important areas of American foreign policy concentration. Efforts at resolving the seemingly intractable problems of the Middle East were to have a high priority in the Carter administration. The festering problems of southern Africa—Rhodesia, Namibia, and South Africa, for example—would need solutions if a more just and peaceful global order were to evolve. Similarly, the problems with Panama and the Canal, and the potential of this issue for generating hostility toward the United States in the Western Hemisphere, also formed part of this strategy of addressing regional conflicts as a stepping-stone to a more stable international order.

A second major focal point within this global approach was the improvement of relations with Western Europe and Japan. This emphasis upon better trilateral relations was again in part a response to the previous administration's emphasis on improving relations with adversaries. For instance, Kissinger's much heralded "Year of Europe" for 1973 was essentially stillborn as pressing Middle East problems arose. As a result, fissures began to appear in ties with America's traditional friends. Economic, political, and military differences with its principal postwar allies therefore were to be focal points of policy development for the Carter administration.

Carter and the Soviet Union

With such a global emphasis, the centrality of the Soviet-American relationship was downgraded. To be sure, detente policy with the Soviet Union would not be abandoned, but it would be placed in a larger context of global issues. In particular, President Carter was committed to joint efforts at strategic arms control; thus, this aspect of the Soviet-American tie would be the continuing and central part of the relationship. The broad comprehensive detente approach of the previous administrations, however, would not be the aim of the Carter administration. Economic, sociocultural, and political cooperation could continue, but only on the basis of mutual advantage. What was crucial here was that such cooperation would not be linked to the overall quality of the relationship. In this sense, the "linkage" notion of the past would be jettisoned.[32]

In essence, Carter's approach to the Soviet Union assumed that the world order of the late 1970s and early 1980s would not be achieved merely by harnessing the Soviet-American relationship. Detente had neither produced stability in U.S.–Soviet relations nor had it addressed the crucial global and regional issues. Instead, it had encouraged a variety of critics at home and abroad and had diverted attention from important global concerns. In short, the heart of international politics in this period had moved beyond this bilateral relationship, and any vision of an improved world along the Kissinger design was not politically feasible.

Carter's initial approach toward the Soviet Union deeply offended and confused the Soviets. This approach was offensive because the Soviet Union had commanded the bulk of America's attention since 1945 and because it had gained superpower status only five years before in the series of Moscow agreements of May 1972. Now this status was apparently being denied. This confused the Soviets because they saw themselves as the critical nation that could affect conflict in the world, especially in the nuclear age. Despite their centrality to questions of war and peace, the Carter administration seemed to be shoving them aside. The Soviets did not quite know how to react to America's emphasis on moral principle and on globalism as espoused by Jimmy Carter, nor to the emphasis on human rights.

Carter and Human Rights

Indeed, the pivotal new focus of the Carter administration was the emphasis on human rights.[33] The role of this policy in the Carter administration can be gleaned from his inaugural address:

> Our commitment to human rights must be absolute. . . . Because we are free, we can never be indifferent to the fate of freedom everywhere. Our moral sense dictates a clear-cut preference for those societies that share with us an abiding respect for individual human rights. We do not seek to intimidate, but it is clear that a world which others can dominate with impunity would be inhospitable to decency and a threat to the well-being of all people.[34]

Such a human rights philosophy was to provide the key moral principle for guiding American foreign policy. The United States would not conduct "business as usual" with nations that grossly and consistently violated the basic rights of its citizens. Instead, America would require states to change their domestic human rights behavior if they wished amicable relations with the United States. While President Carter made it clear that the human rights criterion would not be the only consideration, he also believed "that a significant element in our relationships with other governments would be their performance in providing basic freedoms to their people."[35]

The human rights issue appealed to Jimmy Carter because of his strong personal and religious beliefs about individual dignity, but also because of the issue's strong domestic appeal, especially after Vietnam, Watergate, and revelations about CIA abuses. The "something" that the United States would stand for in the world would now be something that it had historically embraced, the freedom of the individual. At the same time, the human rights issue appealed across the political spectrum and thus would be domestically attractive. Conservatives would like this policy because it would presumably condemn Communist nations for their totalitarian practices, while liberals would like it because the United States would now reexamine its policy toward authoritarian states.

THE CARTER WORLDVIEW
IN OPERATION

In the main, Carter's initial foreign policy strategy was well received by the American public. His approach represented a reemergence of American idealism with a clear emphasis on traditional American values and beliefs. Coupled with the idealism of the Carter approach, however, was the realization of the limits of American power. While the United States could assist in the shaping of global order, it did not have the power to direct the international system of the 1970s—a system so diverse and complex that no nation or set of nations could impose its views of international order. In this sense, the Carter approach was partly compatible with the previous Kissinger approach: The United States must evoke a global order through its actions. However, the focal point of this new order was considerably different from the past. Yet the Carter approach met with criticism and challenge in two areas (improving human rights and dealing with the Soviet Union), but with some success in a third (resolving Third World conflicts).

Improving Human Rights

Definition and Policy Almost immediately, the Carter administration faced the problem of clearly defining human rights and establishing a consistent application of this policy on a global basis. Although President Carter originally sought to focus his human rights policy on the humane treatment of all individuals—and their freedom from torture and arbitrary punishment for expressing political beliefs—the administration initially defined it broadly to include the promotion of political, economic, and social rights of all individuals.[36] Such a broad definition left the United States open to criticism in this area, especially in meeting the economic rights of all. As a result, the United States might well have been espousing a policy that it did not adhere to itself.

Furthermore, the Carter administration was not always clear as to how human rights were to fit into policy decision in dealing with other states. That is, should the human rights condition be the defining criterion for dealing with another nation, or should it be only one of several criteria? After some review and discussion, the administration seemed to settle on the latter. For example, Secretary of State Cyrus Vance cautioned against "mechanistic formulas" for the human rights campaign, and President Carter recognized the limitation of "rigid moral maxims" in his Notre Dame speech.[37] As a result, though, the administration seemed to lose some of its enthusiasm for human rights promotion, and a detectable pullback in this policy occurred over its first year in office.

Implementation A second problem also arose. How was the human rights campaign going to be put into effect? How far was the United States willing to go to produce human rights change? Was it willing to stop all contact with the nations allegedly pursuing human rights violations? Was the United States going to cut all diplomatic, economic, or military ties to offending states? Or, alternatively, was the United States going to continue these ties or modify them in line with more responsive behavior by the other nations? After all, was not this a better way to exercise influence over another nation than by stopping all contact, and thus all means of influence? In short, what were the best tactics for encouraging human rights improvements in target nations?

Indeed, aid—and particularly military aid—was cut off to principal offender nations such as Chile, Argentina, Uruguay, Guatemala, Nicaragua, Vietnam, Cambodia, Uganda, and Mozambique.[38] Economic aid was used to encourage continued human rights improvements for another group of states. But the primary instrument used toward states with poor human rights records was diplomatic "jawboning"—publicly and privately bringing to the attention of the foreign governments American dissatisfaction with their human rights practices. Clearly, there were limits as to how much the United States could or wanted to do in the human rights area.

Applicability   A third major problem was: To whom should the human rights policy apply? The paradox of the Carter policy was evident when nations saw, on the one hand, the United States calling for the free exercise of human rights, particularly in the Soviet Union and in Latin America, but, on the other hand, the United States providing economic and military assistance to nations often cited as having serious human rights violations—such as South Korea, the Philippines, and Iran, among others. Juxtaposing the human rights policy against the demands of realpolitik became a central dilemma for the Carter administration and a constant target of attack by its critics.

The apparent problem of selective application was criticized from two different directions. From one perspective, neoconservative critics argued that the human rights standards as practiced by the United States against "moderately repressive" but friendly regimes was, in effect, undermining these states and American global influence. The unintended result of this action might well be the replacement of these imperfect regimes by ones opposed to U.S. interests—for example in Iran and Nicaragua. Whatever the merits of human rights, the requirements of global balance of power politics could not be wholly jettisoned.[39] In this sense, quiet efforts as well as intergovernmental, semigovernmental, and nongovernmental efforts were necessary to pursue human rights in the international system.[40] From another perspective, critics argued that the U.S. human rights policy was yet another way to impose American values on the international system. Moreover, it reflected both the lack of political realism and the importance of American moral principle in shaping foreign policy. In this respect, it was another of America's attempts to shape global politics. As well-intentioned as was the human rights goal, it was inappropriate for the diverse international system and would ultimately be dysfunctional for global order. Such a refrain was heard from Third World leaders and even from some American allies, notably France and Germany.

Positive Effects   In this context, the human rights campaign by the Carter administration produced both negative and positive effects. While the number of countries with an improved human rights record did increase slightly during the Carter years, much greater gains were necessary if global human rights conditions were to be changed substantially. To be sure, some tangible instances of improved global human rights were registered by the Carter administration. The Dominican Republic made a turn toward democracy; elections were announced for 1978 in Peru, Ecuador, and Bolivia; improved conditions were evidenced in Colombia, Malaysia, Honduras, Morocco, and Portugal, among others; political prisoners were released in Sudan, Nepal, Indonesia, Haiti, and Paraguay in the first year of the policy; and instances of torture apparently did show a decline.[41]

More significantly, perhaps, American prestige in various areas of the world was enhanced. The United States began to stand for particular political values in world affairs. As a result, a more receptive attitude toward American initiatives was forthcoming throughout the world, and especially within the developing world. Perhaps the greatest demonstration of this human rights impact was in Africa. The black nations of southern Africa, in particular, began to have confidence in the Carter administration and American policy toward that region. Through the vigorous efforts of Andrew Young, President Carter's ambassador to the United Nations, the frontline states around white-ruled Rhodesia (Angola, Botswana, Mozambique, Tanzania, Zambia) began to believe that the Carter administration was willing to seek a just solution to the problems of that nation (now Zimbabwe), Namibia, and South Africa itself. Moreover, the pivotal African state of Nigeria also began to express confidence in the American administration by receiving President Carter for an official visit.[42]

Finally, President Jimmy Carter seemed to place the greatest benefit of his human rights policy on the intangible change of atmosphere and attitude toward individual liberties on a worldwide scale during his years in office. As he notes, "The lifting of the human spirit, the revival of hope, the absence of fear, the release from prison, the end of torture, the reunion of a family, the newfound sense of dignity" were the ultimate measure of the worth of the human rights policy.[43]

Negative Effects   On the negative side, the human rights campaign caused friction with friendly but human rights–deficient nations. Relations with Nicaragua, Argentina, Brazil, Iran, and South Korea, among others, were strained by these calls for human rights efforts. Further, the human rights policy contributed to problems in Soviet-American relations. The policy was particularly challenging to detente because it implied an "intervention" into the internal affairs of other states. Nonintervention in internal affairs, by contrast, had been the benchmark of the detente approach that evolved under the Nixon–Ford–Kissinger administration.[44]

Beyond the apparent violation of national sovereignty, the human rights policy threatened the Soviet Union for a more fundamental reason: Fostering individual freedom of expression and tolerating diversity directly affronted totalitarian control at home and foreshadowed a weakening of Soviet control over Eastern Europe. As a result, the Soviet Union attacked Carter's human rights policy and contended that the United States itself was guilty of human rights violations because of the lack of economic rights for its citizens—insufficient employment, inadequate health care, and unsatisfactory social welfare benefits. Furthermore, the atmosphere for conducting relations between the United States and the Soviet

Union was affected by the human rights campaign, as Foreign Minister Andrei Gromyko implied in April 1977, after initial arms control discussions had broken down.[45]

Dealing with the Soviet Union

The essential aim of the Carter administration was to downgrade the dominance of the Soviet-American relationship in the foreign policy of the United States and to concentrate efforts primarily on the other areas of the world. As one analyst has aptly put it, the goal was to contain the Soviet Union, not by directly confronting it as in the past, but "by drying out the pond of possible Soviet mischief" through resolving global issues.[46] If global problems were addressed, global intrusions by the Soviets would be much less likely, and the Soviet Union would be contained.

Despite this initial intention to downgrade the relationship, it never really was possible to do so. Carter's failure to establish a clear and consistent policy toward the Soviet Union was probably the greatest shortcoming of his initial foreign policy plan. At least three different reasons may be cited for the overall inconsistency of Carter's policy toward the Soviet Union.

Soviet Centrality First, the Soviets would not allow the United States to downgrade their centrality to global politics. The Soviet Union's prestige was damaged by the Carter policy. Since the Soviet Union had placed a great effort on achieving superpower military and political parity and had finally achieved it with the 1972 agreements, it was unwilling to yield to playing "second fiddle" on global issues. Thus, the Soviets challenged Carter on human rights, but they also attacked him on arms control, despite their desire for it. More important, the Soviets challenged Carter's attempt to focus on Third World issues. The Soviets sought to make inroads into the Western Hemisphere, especially in Central America through Cuba (or so the United States believed). The Soviets, too, were not restraining the Vietnamese in Asia and were continuing their military deployments there. Finally, the Soviet Union continued its pressure on Western Europe through an increase in its own military capabilities.[47]

Competing Perspectives in the Administration Second, officials within the Carter administration were divided over how best to deal with the Soviet Union. Carter's two top advisors, Secretary of State Cyrus Vance and National Security Advisor Zbigniew Brzezinski took differing views on dealing with Moscow. Secretary Vance appeared to be committed to Carter's globalist perspective and wanted to deal with the Soviets on a piecemeal basis without linkage. Brzezinski appeared to be of two minds in dealing with the Soviets.[48] That is, Brzezinski had formally rejected the notion of linkage as the guide to American policy in dealing with the Soviets, yet he adopted a policy stance that seemed markedly close to it. In fact, the first time that the Soviets took significant actions in a "third area"—by supporting the sending of Cuban troops to Ethiopia—Brzezinski resurrected aspects of the original Kissinger formula for dealing with the Soviet-American relationship. He wanted to confront the Soviets directly and to downgrade any remaining elements of the detente relationship. To Brzezinski, these activities in the Horn of Africa should affect the SALT negotiations, and he said so directly.[49] Others within the Carter administration—Secretary of State Cyrus Vance and Secretary of Defense Harold Brown, as well as the president himself—were not willing to go as far as Brzezinski on this issue. While Brzezinski eventually lost out in this debate, it was this kind of dispute over how to deal with the Soviets, and especially how multilateral events were to affect bilateral relations between the two superpowers, that dominated the Carter administration agenda during its first three years.

American Domestic Attitudes A third factor that made it difficult for the United States to move away from a perception of the Soviets as dominant in foreign policy matters was the nature of American domestic beliefs. A real dualism existed in the minds of the American public. While most Americans supported detente efforts by a wide margin, they were also increasingly wary of growing Soviet power vis-à-vis the United States. Additionally, the American public continued to see the Soviet Union as central to U.S. foreign policy.[50]

Accompanying this dual attitude was a shift away from support for cuts in defense spending, which had been so strong in the immediate post-Vietnam years. By 1977, and especially by 1978, support for more defense spending was increasing, and the public's willingness to favor military force against Soviet incursions was also becoming more evident.[51] Thus, from the viewpoint of domestic politics, the Soviet-American relationship still seemed very crucial, and the Carter administration was no doubt aware of these changing beliefs and the need to accommodate them in the foreign policy arena.

For various reasons, then, the Soviet-American relationship could not be removed from its dominant role in American foreign policy despite the Carter administration's initial hopes. Moreover, the inability of the administration to integrate fully the primacy of this relationship into its foreign policy design and its "strategic incoherence" when it tried to do so plagued the administration throughout its four years.[52]

Resolving Third World Conflicts

The area of greatest success for the Carter administration in implementing its global design was in addressing particular Third World conflicts. During his administration, President Carter was able to alleviate, if not resolve, conflict in Central America over the Panama Canal, in the Middle East between Egypt and Israel, and in southern Africa over Rhodesia and Namibia. Finally, although Carter's establishment of formal diplomatic relations between the People's Republic of China and the United States can hardly be characterized as dealing with a Third World conflict, it was important for lessening regional conflict in Asia.

The Panama Canal Perhaps the greatest arena of success was the resolution of the Panama Canal dispute. For more than two decades, the United States had negotiated the transfer of the Canal and the Canal Zone to sole Panamanian sovereignty. The failure to resolve this dispute was one of those regional issues undermining American influence in Central and South America, and was one of the issues that President Carter was determined to address during his presidency.

Indicative of the importance of this issue was the fact that the first Presidential Review Memorandum emanating from the Carter administration dealt with the Panama Canal.[53] With such a central priority, the American and Panamanian negotiators set out to reach an agreement. In a few short months, they succeeded. By September 1977, moreover, the two treaties that constituted the agreement were ready for an elaborate signing ceremony in Washington. All Latin American countries were invited to witness the signing of these two pacts, and it was a triumphant occasion for the Carter administration.

One of the pacts, the Panama Canal Treaty, called for the total transfer of Canal control to Panama by the year 2000, with intermediate stages of transfer during the 22 years of the pact. The second agreement, the Neutrality Treaty, would become effective in the year 2000 and was of unlimited duration. This pact states that the Canal would be permanently neutral, secure, and open to the vessels of all nations in time of peace and war. Moreover, the United States and Panama agreed to maintain and defend this neutrality principle. President Carter viewed these pacts as clearly compatible with his goals of reducing regional conflicts and fostering global justice. Both of those goals would minimize anti-American feelings and enhance American prestige and influence abroad.[54]

The Middle East   In the Middle East, a constant regional trouble spot, the initial strategy of the Carter administration was to seek a comprehensive settlement through a Geneva conference, cosponsored with the Soviet Union. This approach did not get very far because the Israelis were reluctant to participate and the Arabs demanded maximum Palestinian participation.[55] The Israeli fear was that it would be outvoted in such a conference by the larger number of Arab states and the Soviet Union. Hence the outcome of such a meeting would be far from their liking.

In November 1977, however, President Anwar Sadat of Egypt took a dramatic step to move the peace process along. He announced that he was willing to go to Jerusalem to seek peace. Prime Minister Menachem Begin of Israel quickly issued an invitation for President Sadat to speak to the Israeli Parliament. On November 19, 1977, President Sadat landed in Jerusalem for three days of discussions with the Israelis.[56] The importance of this visit cannot be overstated. It broke the impasse that had set into the Middle East peace process since the shuttle diplomacy of Henry Kissinger; it established the precedent of face-to-face negotiations between Arabs and Israelis; and it raised hopes for real progress.

Such hopes were soon dashed. Both sides still held strong positions on the fundamental questions of the return of Arab lands and Israeli security. By the summer of 1978, an impasse had set in, despite mediation efforts by President Carter. At this juncture, President Carter himself took a bold gamble by inviting President Sadat and Prime Minister Begin to Camp David, Maryland—the presidential retreat—for in-depth discussions on the Middle East. As a result of thirteen days of

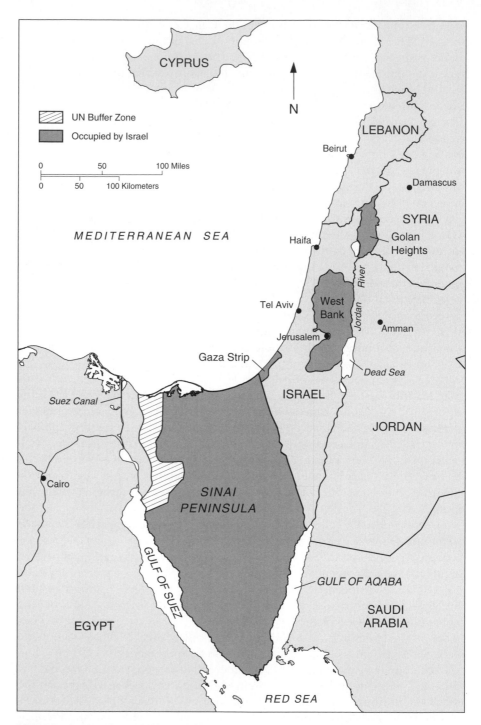

MAP 4.1 Israel and Its Neighbors, 1977

SOURCE: Boundaries taken from http://www.dartmouth.edu/~gov46/israel-egypt-1975.gif.

Document Summary 4.1   The Camp David Accords between Egypt and Israel, September 1978

FRAMEWORK FOR PEACE
IN THE MIDDLE EAST

This framework called for a "just, comprehensive, and durable settlement of the Middle East conflict through the conclusion of peace treaties based upon Security Council Resolutions 242 and 338 in all their parts." (The resolutions called for an exchange of land by Israel—the territories seized in the June 1967 war—for peace with their Arab neighbors— an end to the state of war with Israel.) It consisted of two parts.

The first part of the framework dealt with resolving the conflict over the West Bank of the Jordan and the Gaza Strip, which Israel had seized. This portion called for the establishment of a self-governing authority within these territories "for a period not exceeding five years." By at least the third year of that self-governing authority, "negotiations will take place to determine the final status of

the West Bank and Gaza and its relationship to its neighbors and to conclude a peace treaty between Israel and Jordan. . . ." These negotiations will involve representatives from Egypt, Israel, Jordan, and "representatives of the inhabitants of the West Bank and Gaza. . . ."

The second part of the framework called for Egypt and Israel "to negotiate in good faith with a goal of concluding within three months from the signing of this Framework a peace treaty between them." [This treaty was ultimately signed in March 1979 in Washington, DC. Under this treaty, Israel returned the Sinai Peninsula to Egypt, and Israel and Egypt ended their state of war, recognized one another, and established diplomatic relations.]

SOURCE: This description is drawn from the framework, which was printed in Department of State Publication 8954, *The Camp David Summit* (Washington, DC: Office of Public Communications, Bureau of Public Affairs, September 1978).

---

intense negotiations, "A Framework for Peace in the Middle East" was agreed to by the two competing parties and witnessed by President Carter.[57]

The signing of the Camp David Accords on September 17, 1978, was another highlight of the Carter foreign policy. See Document Summary 4.1. Some real progress had been made in addressing the Middle East conflict. Furthermore, in March 1979, a peace treaty based on the Camp David framework was signed between Egypt and Israel. A comprehensive peace settlement, however, ultimately eluded the Carter administration, as all the Arab states except Egypt refused to accept and participate in the Camp David framework.

Rhodesia, Namibia, and South Africa The third region of the world where the Carter administration achieved some success was in southern Africa over the questions of Rhodesia and Namibia. The role of the United States was not as direct as in the Panama Canal and the Middle East, but it was nonetheless important. Specifically, the Carter administration adopted a strong stand for black majority rule in these areas and assisted the British in achieving a successful outcome for Rhodesia, now Zimbabwe. The United States, with the assistance of other Western states, maneuvered the South African government to accept a UN resolution on the transfer of power in Namibia.[58]

In the case of Rhodesia, the Carter administration ceased trade with the white-dominated government and imposed economic sanctions on it in the first

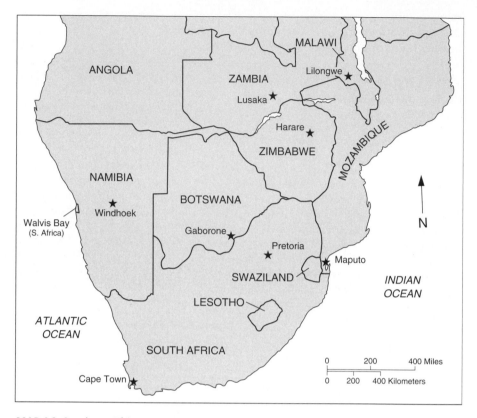

MAP 4.2 Southern Africa

year of its term, bringing U.S. policy in line with long-standing UN sanctions. Even when the white-minority government and some black leaders had reached an "internal settlement" in 1978, the administration refused to lift sanctions because dissident factions in exile outside the country had not participated in the settlement. By adopting such a stance, despite considerable opposition within Congress, the United States gave impetus to the British efforts toward a comprehensive settlement involving all parties. Such a settlement was ultimately worked out in the Lancaster House negotiations in London during the fall of 1979, and the agreement was put into effect in 1980.[59] Majority rule was obtained in former Rhodesia, and the Carter administration rightly claimed credit for its role.

The same policy posture was adopted toward South Africa: a firm stance against apartheid and a call for the transfer of control of Namibia to majority rule. Under U.S. policy pressure and that of other states, South Africa did agree to UN Resolution 435 on this transfer. The transfer of power met numerous snags and was not implemented during the Carter years. (In fact, it was not fully implemented until 1990.) Nonetheless, the decision to promote the American domestic values of respecting human rights and fostering majority rule won praise for the United States throughout Africa.

People's Republic of China Finally, the Carter administration's decision to establish formal diplomatic relations with the People's Republic of China on January 1, 1979, was another major foreign policy success. Although this decision caused some initial difficulties with Taiwan (since relations were broken with this government), it was generally hailed as an important milestone in American foreign policy. Opening relations with Beijing reduced hostilities between two important states and had the potential of easing conflicts in East Asia. At the same time, though, this step created another uncertainty in America's approach to its traditional adversary, the Soviet Union, and reinforced the Soviet view that the Carter administration was more interested in dealing with other states than with it.

REALISM IN THE LAST YEAR: A RESPONSE TO CRITICS

By 1979, the Carter foreign policy was already subject to considerable criticism on the grounds that it was inconsistent, incoherent, and a failure. According to one critic, it was leading to a decline in America's standing abroad.[60] While some successes in Carter's global approach might be identified, too many problems were evident, without a clear strategy for dealing with them. A revolution occurred in Iran, replacing the Shah (whom the Carter administration had supported) with a markedly anti-American regime; a revolution succeeded in Nicaragua, with the United States adopting a policy that pleased neither the Somozistas nor the Sandinistas; the Middle East peace effort was in a holding pattern with Arab rejection of the Camp David framework; and Soviet power continued to grow without an American response. On all these fronts, a certain malaise seemed to have set into the Carter foreign policy, marked by indecision and inability to act, and for such reasons, a change in policy direction might well have been anticipated. Yet two international events ultimately proved critical to the Carter foreign policy change.

The seizure of American hostages in Iran in November 1979, and the Soviet invasion of Afghanistan a month later were the watershed events in the global approach of the Carter administration.[61] Despite the administration's effort to move away from concentrating on the Soviet Union, these two events brought that nation back into focus for America—the former indirectly, because it raised the prospect of Soviet inroads into the Middle East and Southwest Asia; the latter directly, because it projected the Soviet Union into the center of global affairs once again.

American Hostages in Iran

The November 1979 seizure and holding of sixty-three Americans in the U.S. Embassy in Tehran, Iran, produced perhaps the Carter administration's greatest foreign policy challenge. It also produced a clear change in policy orientation and direction by the Carter administration, with a new national self-interest now dominating its agenda. Rather than trying to accommodate Third World demands, as had been attempted in previous years, the United States now took a variety of steps, from breaking diplomatic relations, to seizing Iranian assets, to imposing sanctions, and ultimately attempting a military rescue of the hostages as a means of demonstrating resolve. Such actions also connoted a return to a realist perspective in foreign policy and away from the idealism that President Carter had initially tried to pursue. Unfortunately, this strategy failed to yield quick results, and the American hostages were not freed for 444 days—immediately after President Carter left office on January 20, 1981.

Soviet Invasion of Afghanistan

The Soviet invasion of Afghanistan also had a pronounced effect on President Carter's view of the Soviet Union and on his foreign policy approach as well. Regarding Carter's new view of the Soviet Union after this invasion, it was poignantly summarized by the president himself in an ABC television interview at the time: "My opinion of the Russians has changed most drastically in the last week [more] than even in the previous 2½ years before that."[62] The invasion also had an immediate impact on his approach to foreign policy. President Carter promptly moved away from his global approach, with the Soviet Union only one among many countries. Instead he now adopted the bilateral approach of the past, with the Soviet-American relationship at the center of his policy making. New policy actions quickly followed from this new orientation. While not all the earlier initiatives were jettisoned, the issue areas that the Carter administration had emphasized early on in its term were given a secondary role.

The Carter administration adopted a series of responses to the Soviet Union over the invasion of Afghanistan. The ratification of the SALT II treaty was shelved in the U.S. Senate; high technology sales to the Soviet Union were halted; Soviet fishing privileges in American waters were restricted; and a grain embargo was imposed upon the Soviet Union.[63] A little later, an American boycott of the 1980 Summer Olympics in Moscow was announced.

Global Events and Soviet-American Relations

Global events now were increasingly interpreted through lenses that focused on their effect on Soviet-American relations. The principal U.S. efforts during 1980 were to rally its friends to contain the Soviet Union. Moreover, it was during this time that such global goals as arms transfer controls were downplayed as a signal to the Soviets of American resolve. For instance, discussions were held with the Chinese about providing them with arms. Furthermore, the United States began an effort to shore up its ties in the Persian Gulf and in Southwest Asia. Military aid was quickly offered to Pakistan, and National Security Chief Zbigniew Brzezinski made a highly publicized trip to the Khyber Pass to illustrate American determination over Afghanistan. Contacts were also made with friendly regimes in the Middle East to gain base and access rights for the United States in case of an emergency. Finally, the development of the U.S. Rapid Deployment Force—an elite military force that could respond quickly to an emergency anywhere in the world—was given a top priority.

As a further signal to the Soviet Union, President Carter in his 1980 State of the Union Address warned the Soviets that "an attempt by any outside force to gain control of the Persian Gulf region will be regarded as an assault on the vital interests of the United States. It will be repelled by use of any means necessary, including military force."[64] Quickly labeled the Carter Doctrine, this statement was highly reminiscent of an earlier era, with its Cold War rhetoric and its reliance on the essential elements of containment. Nonetheless, it accurately set the tone for the final year of the Carter administration and the policy shift that had occurred in the administration.

Foreign Policy and the 1980 Campaign

Despite President Carter's attempt to change foreign policy direction, the perception of ineffectiveness continued to haunt his administration. As a consequence, foreign policy, with particular emphasis on the Iranian and Afghan experiences, became an important campaign issue in the 1980 presidential election.[65] Now, however, instead of focusing on a foreign policy that was "good and decent," as in 1976, the Republican challenger to President Carter, Ronald Reagan, called for a policy to "make America great again." Such a policy was surely a call to move away from the idealism of the early Carter years. Yet it was a call to pursue the kind of foreign policy that President Carter himself had tried to initiate in his last year in office.

REALISM AND THE REAGAN ADMINISTRATION

Just as Jimmy Carter shifted away from the foreign policies of the Nixon–Ford–Kissinger years, Ronald Reagan sought to chart a different course than Carter. Ronald Reagan campaigned for the presidency on the principle of restoring American power at home and abroad, and his foreign policy was aimed at reflecting such power. Whereas Jimmy Carter attempted to move away from the power politics of the Kissinger era and away from a foreign policy that focused directly on adversaries—and particularly the Soviet Union—Ronald Reagan embraced the need for power—especially military power—and the need to focus on the Soviet Union and its expansionist policy. During its second term, however, the Reagan administration sought and successfully obtained some accommodation with the Soviet Union, although without altering its anti-Soviet approach in Third World areas.

Values and Beliefs of the Reagan Administration

Ronald Reagan did not bring to the presidency a fully developed foreign policy design, but he did bring to the office a strongly held worldview. For him, the prime obstacle to peace and stability in the world was the Soviet Union, and particularly Soviet expansionism. The principal foreign policy goal of the United

States, therefore, was to be the revival of the national will to contain the Soviet Union and the restoration of confidence among friends that America was determined to stop communism. Furthermore, the United States had to make other nations aware of the dangers of Soviet expansionism.

The ideological suspicion with which President Reagan viewed the Soviet Union was stated rather dramatically at his first news conference in January 1981 in which he noted that the Soviet leadership was committed to "world revolution" and that "they reserved unto themselves the right to commit any crime; to lie; to cheat," as a means of obtaining what they wanted.[66] In 1983, echoing this first news conference, President Reagan assailed the morality of the Soviet Union once again and denounced it as an "evil empire" and the United States, in his judgment, remained in a moral struggle with that nation.[67]

Such a consistently hostile view of the Soviet Union brought to mind comparisons with the U.S. foreign policy orientation of the 1950s, when the Cold War consensus was dominant. It surely stood in contrast to Jimmy Carter's view only four years earlier that "we are now free of that inordinate fear of communism."[68] Instead, President Reagan's view implied the centrality of the Soviet Union and its foreign policy objectives to American actions abroad. Indeed, to many observers, such a posture suggested the emergence of a new Cold War.[69]

The Policy Approach of the Reagan Administration

Despite the ideological cohesion that seemed to permeate the Reagan administration, the translation of that perspective into a working foreign policy was not readily apparent to outside observers. In fact, charges were immediately made by policy analysts that the Reagan administration really had no foreign policy because it appeared to have no coherent strategy for reaching its goals. Critics complained that rhetoric served as policy. Such a failing was particularly accented since the Reagan administration had come into office determined to bring coherence and consistency to foreign affairs, which they charged the Carter administration had failed to do.[70]

Yet this criticism is a bit overstated, since Secretary of State Alexander Haig provided a statement of principles and the underlying rationale for dealing with the world early in his tenure. Describing his approach as a "strategic" one, Secretary Haig asserted that American foreign policy behavior was based upon four important pillars:

1. The restoration of our economic and military strength;
2. The reinvigoration of alliances and friendships;
3. The promotion of progress in the developing countries through peaceable changes;
4. A relationship with the Soviet Union characterized by restraint and reciprocity.[71]

None of these pillars should be pursued independently, and policy initiatives in any one of these areas must support the others. The glue that would hold these "pillars" together was the Soviet-American relationship because, as Secretary Haig indicated, "Soviet-American relations must be at the center of our efforts to promote a more peaceful world."[72]

Rebuilding American Strength

The Reagan administration quickly called for an increase in military spending. It proposed a $1.6 trillion defense buildup over a six-year period (1981–1986). While the buildup was across the entire military—from a larger navy to a modernized army and air force and from the development of a new rapid deployment force to better pay for military personnel—the strategic modernization plan attracted much of the attention in the early part of the Reagan presidency.[73]

Under this plan, each component of America's nuclear triad—the array of land-based missiles, sea-based nuclear missiles, and intercontinental nuclear-armed bombers—would be modernized, and the strategic command and control structures, the technical communication facilities that provide direction for U.S. nuclear forces,[74] would be upgraded to guard against any possible first strike from the Soviet Union. The Reagan administration also pursued two other actions to improve America's nuclear capability—one regional, the other global. On a regional level, the Reagan administration proposed to carry out the NATO alliance's Dual Track decision of 1979. According to that decision, new intermediate-range or theater nuclear weapons would be deployed in Western Europe if negotiations on theater nuclear arms control failed. On a global level, President Reagan called for the United States to "embark on a program to counter the awesome Soviet missile threat with measures that are defensive." Such a defensive missile system against the Soviet threat "could pave the way for arms control measures to eliminate . . . [nuclear] weapons themselves."[75] Formally called the Strategic Defense Initiative (SDI) but more commonly known as "Star Wars"—after the popular motion picture—this proposal was viewed by critics as a further escalation of the arms race.

Reinvigorating Allies

The reinvigoration of the allies meant basically to upgrade the military strength of the West and to have the allies support the political leadership of the United States globally. In the military area, as noted, the United States succeeded in having the Western Europeans go forward with the rearmament component of the Dual Track decision: the deployment of the 572 Pershing II and cruise missiles began by late 1983, after arms negotiations stalled.[76] In addition, the United States wanted the Europeans to accept a greater defense burden as a means of counteracting growing Soviet power in their region and wanted the Japanese to assume greater military responsibility in East Asia. Appeals were made for the Europeans to follow the American lead in enacting sanctions against the Soviet Union and Poland after the imposition of martial law in the latter nation in late 1981, although the success was limited. The United States also tried to stop the Europeans from completing the natural gas pipeline arrangement with the Soviet

Union at about the same time and, later, the Reagan administration sought (without success) to impose sanctions on the Europeans themselves over their failure to follow American wishes.[77]

Bolstering Friends in the Developing World

The meaning of the third pillar—a commitment to progress in the Third World—was to reflect a sharp shift in strategy toward American friends in the developing states. As compared to the Carter years, the Reagan administration changed policy in three distinct ways. First, unlike President Carter, who expressed a sympathy for Third World aspirations, the Reagan administration challenged those nations to pull themselves up by their own bootstraps and to seek improvement through the efforts of private enterprise. The administration soon developed the Caribbean Basin Initiative as a model for utilizing the private sector to stimulate development. While economic assistance to the Caribbean would be increased by $350 million under this plan, preferential trade access to the American market for the Caribbean states and increased American investments in the region were the key development components of this initiative.[78] Second, the administration increased reliance on military assistance as an "essential" element of American policy. To implement this policy, the Reagan administration scrapped the arms transfer policy of the Carter administration and, following a plan more attuned to its philosophical orientation, announced that it would provide military assistance to "its major alliance partners and to those nations with whom it has friendly and cooperative security relationships."[79] Third, American policy would now focus on how regional conflicts would be analyzed and acted upon by the United States. Regional conflicts would not be assessed on the basis of regional concerns only. Conflicts in the developing world had to be recast into the underlying global conflict that the Reagan administration saw in the world. In turn, U.S. actions in these regional disputes must recognize that global reality. Therefore the emphasis was on how regional conflicts affected U.S.-Soviet relations. The aim was to build a "strategic consensus" against the Soviet Union and its proxies.[80] Only after the danger posed by the Soviet Union in these conflicts was addressed could regional concerns be brought into the resolution of the conflicts.

Restraint and Reciprocity with the Soviet Union

The fourth pillar of the Reagan administration's approach to foreign policy focused directly on the Soviet Union. Only if the Soviet Union demonstrated restraint in its global actions would the United States carry on normal and reciprocal relations with it. In this sense, the familiar linkage notion of the Kissinger years was at the heart of any relationship with the Soviet Union. Specifically, Secretary Haig stated that the United States would "want greater Soviet restraint on the use of force. We want greater Soviet respect for the independence of others. And we want the Soviets to abide by their reciprocal obligations, such as those undertaken in the Helsinki Accords." No area of international relations could be left out of this restraint requirement. "We have learned that Soviet-American agreements, even in strategic arms control, will not survive Soviet threats to the overall military balance or Soviet encroachments . . . in critical regions of the world. *Linkage is not a theory; it is a fact of life that we overlook at our peril.*"[81]

THE REAGAN WORLDVIEW
IN OPERATION

With these four pillars as the primary guide to U.S. foreign policy, the Reagan administration took actions toward the Soviet Union, Central America, southern Africa, and the Middle East to reshape the direction of American foreign policy.

Policy Actions toward the Soviet Union

Because the Soviet Union had exercised neither policy restraint nor reciprocity in the past, the Reagan administration did not seek to improve relations immediately. Instead, the United States sought to rally other states against the Soviet Union and adopted several initial measures to prod it to exercise international restraint. First, administration officials publicly criticized the Soviet Union. President Reagan and Secretary Haig attacked the Soviet system as bankrupt and on the verge of collapse, charging the Soviets with fomenting international disorder.[82] Second, the administration took direct steps to demonstrate American resolve. In addition to its strategic modernization plan, the administration called for producing and stockpiling the neutron bomb, a new kind of weapon (originally proposed during the Carter years) that killed people but did not destroy property. Most significant, perhaps, the United States promptly imposed sanctions upon the Soviet Union and Poland in 1981 to show its dissatisfaction with the imposition of martial law by Poland's Communist government and Soviet support for that action.[83]

Third, some actions were *not* taken to demonstrate that normal relations could not occur until the Soviet Union showed restraint. In this connection, the two most important omissions were the failure to move rapidly on arms control and the failure to engage in summit meetings. In fact, arms control discussions were initially put on the back burner until the United States completed the arms buildup. Additionally, questions of a summit meeting between the Soviet and American presidents were put off with the comment that the conditions were not appropriate and that little valuable discussion would result.

Despite a relationship that was marked primarily by harsh rhetoric and strong action, some initial cooperative elements were still evident. In the economic area, the Reagan administration lifted the grain embargo in April 1981—an embargo President Carter had put into effect after the Afghanistan invasion—despite its commitment to isolating and punishing the Soviet Union. Within a year, the administration sought to expand grain sales to the Soviet Union and eventually agreed to a new five-year grain deal.[84] In the military area, the administration also stated that it would continue to adhere to the SALT I and SALT II limitations if the Soviets would.[85]

In the diplomatic area, Secretary of State Haig met with Soviet Foreign Minister Andrei Gromyko during his visit to the UN General Assembly in the fall of 1981, despite the chilly political atmosphere. Finally, the intermediate nuclear force (INF) talks—talks on nuclear missiles with ranges only within Europe—reluctantly were begun by the Reagan administration during November 1981—much earlier than expected given the overall political climate. Seven months later, President Reagan also initiated the Strategic Arms Reduction Talks (START)—talks on intercontinental nuclear weapons—despite the seemingly confrontational environment.[86] By November 1983, however, neither of these talks had reached any agreement, and the United States went ahead with its deployment of intermediate missiles in Europe.[87] The Soviet Union walked out of the INF negotiations and, within one month, declared that it would not proceed with the Strategic Arms Reduction Talks either. Further, the Soviets resumed and expanded the deployment of their intermediate range nuclear missiles in Central Europe, announced the deployment of more nuclear submarines off the American coasts in retaliation for the new American weapons in Western Europe, and withdrew from the 1984 Olympic Games in Los Angeles, claiming that Soviet athletes would not be safe there.[88]

The consequence of this barrage of various charges and actions by both superpowers was that Soviet-American relations by mid-1984 were "at the lowest level for the entire postwar period."[89] The "restraint and reciprocity" that the Reagan administration had initially set out to achieve had not been accomplished, but the plan of restoring the Soviet Union to the center of American foreign policy and building up U.S. defenses was well under way.

Policy Action toward the Third World

Central America   In Central America, the response of the Reagan administration toward the unrest in El Salvador reflected its basic foreign policy approach. The administration quickly moved to interpret the ongoing civil war in El Salvador as Soviet and Cuban directed. Calling El Salvador a "textbook case" of Communist aggression, the Reagan administration issued a white paper outlining the danger there.[90] Furthermore, testifying at a House Foreign Affairs Committee hearing in March 1981, Secretary of State Haig charged that the Communist attack on El Salvador was part of a "four-phased operation" aimed at the ultimate Communist control of Central America.[91]

Military assistance and the threat of military action were the principal instruments used by the Reagan administration to respond to the situation. Military aid totaling $25 million was immediately proposed for the government of El Salvador in its struggle with rebel forces, with more to come. The number of military advisors was increased from 20 to 55 by the spring of 1981.[92] Over the next several years, El Salvador and its neighbor Honduras became leading recipients of U.S. foreign assistance.

A similar policy approach, and some of the administration's harshest rhetoric, was directed toward El Salvador's neighbor Nicaragua. President Reagan described the Sandinista-led government of Nicaragua as "a Communist reign of terror," and Nicaraguans themselves as "Cuba's Cubans" for their assumed involvement in

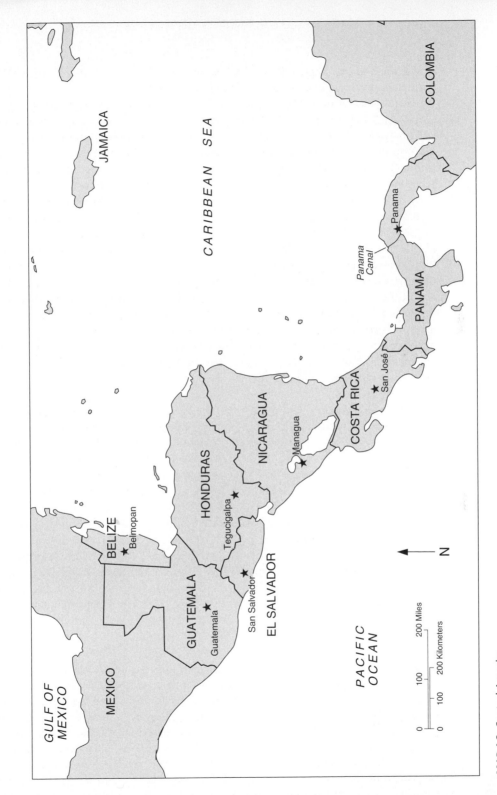

MAP 4.3 Central America

aiding the Salvadoran guerrillas.[93] He also quoted directly from the Truman Doctrine of four decades earlier to justify the need for American action in the region ("I believe that it must be the policy of the United States to support free peoples . . .").[94] Charging that the Nicaraguan government was arming the guerrillas in El Salvador, the Reagan administration, upon taking office, cut off $15 million of economic aid to that country.[95] By early 1982, in fact, the Reagan administration had a clandestine operation under way in Honduras—supporting Nicaraguan rebels, or Contras, who were opposed to the Sandinista government.[96]

The hardline policy of containing communism in Latin America was perhaps manifested most dramatically with the American invasion of the Caribbean island of Grenada in October 1983. After Marxist Prime Minister Maurice Bishop was killed on October 19, 1983, and after a more radical group seized control, the United States agreed to join forces with the five members of the Organization of Eastern Caribbean States "to restore order and democracy" in Grenada. This action was officially taken to ensure the safety of between 800 and 1,000 Americans—mostly medical students—and to "forestall further chaos."[97] Within a few days, the American control of the island was achieved, the Marxist regime had been replaced, and the return to a Western-style democracy was under way. The intervention, moreover, demonstrated that the Reagan administration would confront Marxist regimes and use military force, if necessary.

Southern Africa   In southern Africa, the Reagan administration's actions followed a similar pattern against potential Communist gains. The administration adopted a policy of "constructive engagement" toward South Africa and linked any settlement in Namibia (or Southwest Africa) to the removal of Soviet-backed Cuban forces from Angola. These policies were predicated upon several key beliefs. First, South Africa was staunchly anti-Communist, and, as a result, the United States should not seek a confrontational approach toward it. Second, the conflict in the region had East-West overtones that could not be overlooked. After all, South Africa was confronted by a Marxist regime in Angola, which was backed by Cuban soldiers and Soviet arms.[98] Third, only when the South Africans felt more confident of American support could the United States try to exert influence upon them to change their apartheid policy and to seek a solution to the question of Namibia. In this region, the strategic concern of controlling communism produced a markedly different approach than the Carter administration had adopted.

The Middle East   In the Middle East, the administration's primary strategy was also aimed at stopping any potential Communist gains. No new initiatives were proposed, nor was there much effort to proceed with the Camp David framework inherited from the Carter administration. Instead, as elsewhere, the Reagan administration attempted to rally the Arab states against the Soviet Union and to engage the Israelis in a strategic understanding. A new Persian Gulf command, with the Rapid Deployment Force as part of that structure, was announced. Negotiations were held with several Middle East states regarding American base and access rights in the region. Egypt, Sudan, Somalia, and Oman, for example, agreed to joint military exercises with the United States,[99] and the United States also obtained military cooperation from the Israelis.[100] The most dramatic examples of using military assistance to bolster American influence against the Soviet Union also occurred in this region. The United States agreed to sell technologically advanced aircraft equipment and the Airborne Warning and Control System (AWACS) aircraft to Saudi Arabia in October 1981 and agreed to supply forty F-16 fighter aircraft to Pakistan (an arms deal worth more than $3 billion) as part of its strategy for Southwest Asia.[101]

The Reagan administration's emphasis on global concerns over local concerns ultimately proved short-lived in this volatile region. By the summer of 1982—and wholly as a result of Israel's invasion of Lebanon and its advance all the way to Beirut—the Reagan administration was fully immersed in local issues in the Middle East. As a result, the Reagan administration had to respond to local issues, not global ones. The administration sought to negotiate a cease-fire between the Israelis and the surrounded Palestinian forces in West Beirut and a withdrawal of Syrian and Israeli forces from Lebanon itself. Moreover, even President Reagan moved into a mediator posture with a new policy initiative (labeled the Reagan Initiative) to serve as a follow-up to the Camp David framework. The initiative called for a Palestinian homeland federated with Jordan, an end to Israeli settlements in the West Bank, and security for Israel.[102]

The depth of American involvement in the area even reached the point of deploying American military personnel on two different occasions. The administration sent a contingent of American Marines into Lebanon in August 1982, as part of an effort to evacuate the Palestine Liberation Organization (PLO) members from Beirut, where the Israelis had surrounded them. This mission was successfully completed without major incident. In September 1982, however, the Marines were again dispatched to Lebanon as part of a Multinational Force (MNF) composed of military personnel from several Western nations. While the MNF was to serve as a "peacekeeping" force between the various Lebanese factions and to facilitate a negotiated settlement among them, the task proved elusive and ultimately disastrous.[103] As factional feuding continued, the role of the MNF became increasingly unclear. In time, the U.S. Marines, encamped at the Beirut airport, became identified with the central government and became the target for snipers from the other Lebanese factions. Moreover, the Marines became the target of a terrorist bombing on October 23, 1983, that killed some 241 Americans in an attack on their barracks. Although the Reagan administration originally intended to deal with regional issues in a global context, it became deeply involved in "local issues" in the Middle East without a well-conceived policy.

CHALLENGES TO THE REAGAN APPROACH

Despite the efforts of the Reagan administration to redirect the focus and content of American policy to the Soviet danger, the rest of the world would not easily follow its lead. Concern—and at times rejection—over the ideological tone and substance of the Reagan foreign policy came from both international and domestic sources. Such challenges both made it difficult for the Reagan administration to continue the ideological consistency that it originally intended and contributed to some modification in it over time.

International Differences

The Western European states, for example, were reluctant to follow the Reagan administration's political lead in dealing with the Soviet Union. Whether it was over martial law in Poland or the building of a natural gas pipeline from the Soviet Union to Western Europe, the Europeans were concerned with preserving contacts with Eastern Europe, not disrupting them.[104] Similarly, while the Europeans were committed to the Dual Track decision of 1979, they were unsure (and uneasy) about President Reagan's commitment to pursuing negotiations seriously. With his harsh rhetoric, his strategic modernization plan, and his reluctance to proceed very quickly with arms control talks, President Reagan did not seem to be following a policy of arms restraint. Further, the hundreds of thousands of demonstrators in London, Rome, Berlin, and Bonn protesting the Reagan arms policy created further political difficulties for European leaders.[105] Finally, some European and Latin American states failed to support either the American approach to the situation in El Salvador or its policy toward Nicaragua.[106]

Domestic Differences

Domestic challenges arose, too. In particular, American public opinion was increasingly skeptical of continued defense spending and indicated support for the nuclear freeze movement. Although the public was willing to support some increase in defense spending when the Reagan administration took office, the situation had changed considerably by 1983. By then, 45 percent of the American public indicated that the United States was spending too much on the military, and only 14 percent indicated that the United States was spending too little.[107] Similarly, public opinion polls consistently showed that more than 60 percent of the American public supported a "mutual and verifiable freeze" of nuclear weapons between the Soviet Union and the United States.[108] This nuclear freeze movement was able to turn out more than 700,000 people to demonstrate in New York City in June 1982—one of the largest single demonstrations in American political history. The composition of the demonstration—individuals from a wide variety of political and social backgrounds—reflected the diversity of support for this movement.[109]

Similarly, domestic challenges arose over Central American policy. In particular, the public expressed concern over potential American involvement in the region, especially as more American advisors were being sent there. Would American combat forces be sent to the region? Was this involvement the beginning of another Vietnam-like quagmire in which American involvement would slowly escalate? This kind of fear caused Secretary of State Haig to rule out the use of American troops in Central America.[110] In addition, others argued that local conditions in Central America, such as poverty and inequality, ought to be given greater credibility in explaining the political unrest in the region than the Reagan administration had allowed.

POLICY CHANGE: ACCOMMODATION WITH THE SOVIET UNION

After President Reagan won a resounding election to a second term in November 1984, he immediately announced that his administration would continue to do "what we've been doing."[111] In reality, the administration made some significant changes in its foreign policy. While President Reagan did not abandon his hard-line position on Soviet expansionism in Third World areas, he did make a significant change in the bilateral relationship with the Soviet Union by adopting a much more accommodationist approach to that adversary and setting the stage for the ending of the Cold War.

Sources of Change

At least three factors contributed to the movement away from the previous hard-line approach of the Reagan administration toward the Soviet Union and toward seeking agreements with that adversary: (1) a change in the policy stance of the American leadership; (2) the emergence of new leadership and "new thinking" in the Soviet Union; and (3) the domestic realities of the arms race between the superpowers. Although it is difficult to specify which of these factors (and presumably others as well) weighed most heavily in this policy change—or to show fully how they interacted with one another—a brief discussion of each will portray the change in approach.

Policy Shifts Secretary of State George Shultz initially signaled a change in emphasis by the Reagan administration as early as October 1984. At that time, Shultz declared that linkage between Soviet behavior around the world and the quality of relations between the two superpowers was

> not merely a 'fact of life' but a complex question of policy. There will be times when we must make progress in one dimension of the relationship contingent on progress in others. . . . At the same time, linkage as an instrument of policy has limitations; if applied rigidly, it could yield the initiative to the Soviets, letting them set the pace and the character of the relationship. . . . In the final analysis, linkage is a tactical question; the strategic reality of leverage comes from creating facts in support of our overall design.[112]

In other words, policy must be more flexible than before.

In his second inaugural address, President Reagan, too, suggested a new flexibility by committing his administration to better relations with the Soviet Union, especially in the area of nuclear arms control. Specifically, he indicated that the United States would seek to reduce the cost of national security "in negotiations with the Soviet Union." These negotiations, however, would not focus just on limiting an increase in nuclear weapons, but they would "reduce their numbers."[113] To appreciate how significant a change had occurred, recall how the Reagan administration initially rejected arms control negotiations.

"New Thinking" A second factor that contributed to the possibility of accommodation between the two superpowers was the 1985 selection of Mikhail Gorbachev as the general secretary of the Communist party of the Soviet Union, and eventually as president of the Soviet Union. Gorbachev's rise to power was critical, because he brought with him several important conceptual changes to Soviet foreign policy thinking and a commitment to improving relations with the United States. In fact, he added two major concepts to the political lexicon of the 1980s and 1990s, *perestroika* and *glasnost*. Perestroika referred to the "restructuring" of Soviet society in an effort to improve the economy, while glasnost referred to a new "openness" and movement toward greater democratization within the Soviet system.

Such "new thinking" by the Soviet leadership, as Gorbachev himself called it, came to have important implications for Soviet-American relations. In contrast to earlier desires for "nuclear superiority," the Soviet leadership began to embrace the concepts of "reasonable sufficiency" as a nuclear weapons strategy in dealing with the West and to recognize the need for greater "strategic stability" in the nuclear balance as well. In such an environment, nuclear arms accommodation between the two superpowers became a viable option. Furthermore, the Soviet leadership indicated that the struggle between capitalism and socialism had changed, and political solutions, rather than military ones, ought to be pursued.[114]

The Sustained Arms Race Yet a third factor may well have been the most pivotal for both nations: the increasing domestic burden of sustained military spending. In both societies, the military burden of continued confrontation was distorting and undermining the domestic health of their economies. In the Soviet Union, the basic needs of its people could not be met, as more and more resources were spent on the military. Gorbachev's hope of restructuring the Soviet system could not be realistically undertaken as long as military spending consumed so much of the wealth of the society. In the United States, with military budgets approaching $300 billion per year and federal budget deficits increasing, the health of the economy remained in question. Further, no longer could the Reagan administration count on public support for increased military spending.[115]

The Return of Soviet-American Summitry

The first significant manifestation of a changed policy was the reemergence of summitry between American and Soviet leaders. Surprisingly, considering his initial reluctance to talk with the Soviet, President Reagan ultimately held more summits with Soviet leaders than any other American president. In the space of about three and a half years, he held five summits with President Gorbachev.[116] Each of these summits proved to be important building blocks for improving Soviet-American ties.

The first summit between President Reagan and General Secretary Mikhail Gorbachev was held in Geneva, Switzerland, on November 19–21, 1985, and it was called the "Fireside Summit" for the backdrop in which the talks were held. No important agreements emerged; rather, it was an opportunity for both leaders to get to know each other better and to exchange views on numerous issues, including arms control, human rights, and regional conflicts. In effect, this summit was really a prelude to the next one.[117]

The second and third summits were arguably the most important ones of the Reagan presidency. The October 1986 summit, held in Reykjavik, Iceland, focused largely on seeking progress in the nuclear arms talks under way between the Soviet Union and the United States. The most significant products of this summit were agreements in principle to reduce all strategic nuclear weapons 50 percent over a five-year period and to limit intermediate-range nuclear forces to 100 warheads for each side.[118] These commitments were significant for advancing work on a strategic arms reduction (START) agreement and on an intermediate nuclear forces (INF) agreement. Disagreement remained, however, over negotiations on space-based missiles (the "Star Wars" defense systems), threatening to undermine the work in the other two areas. Still, the INF discussions were eventually separated from the other talks and that action quickly led to the completion of the Intermediate Nuclear Forces (INF) Treaty (discussed below), which was signed at the third summit in Washington in December 1987.

The fourth summit, held in Moscow in late May and early June 1988, was primarily to exchange instruments of ratification of the new INF Treaty, seek further progress in strategic arms negotiations, and discuss other key global issues.[119] The fifth and final Soviet–American summit of the Reagan administration was a brief one-day meeting in New York City in December 1988 in conjunction with President Gorbachev's visit and speech to the United Nations.[120] It was an opportunity for a final exchange of views before Reagan left office and for the new president-elect, George Bush, to meet the Soviet leader.

The INF Treaty

The most important manifestation of progress in Soviet–American relationship in Reagan's second term was the completion of the Intermediate Nuclear Forces (INF) Treaty. This treaty culminated a long series of negotiations that had originally begun in November 1981, broke off in November 1983, and resumed again after a joint Soviet–American agreement to link all nuclear arms negotiations—one track on intermediate nuclear forces, a second on strategic nuclear forces, and a third on defense and space arms—in a set of "New Negotiations" in January 1985.[121] After the 1986 Reykjavik summit, however, the INF talks were selected for accelerated action and were eventually completed and signed in December 1987.

The treaty called for the elimination of all intermediate-range nuclear weapons within three years and all medium-range nuclear weapons within eighteen months.[122] It also prohibited the United States and Soviet Union from ever again possessing such weapons. In addition, it provided a series of on-site inspections for each party and set out exacting procedures on how these nuclear weapons should be destroyed. Finally, it established a Special Verification Commission, which would be continuously in session to deal with any issues that might arise.

The military significance of the INF Treaty has sometimes been questioned. It required relatively few nuclear missiles to be destroyed, and each superpower retained a formidable arsenal with which to destroy one another and the world at large. The political significance of the pact, however, is less debatable. The INF Treaty represented the first nuclear arms reduction pact in human history, and it gave real momentum to arms control and arms reduction for the future. With the incorporation of on-site inspection into the pact, it initiated a new departure in the verification of arms control agreements between the superpowers.

POLICY CONTINUITY: REAGAN DOCTRINE AND THE THIRD WORLD

If actions toward the Soviet Union represented an important source of change, policy toward the Third World—and the perceived role of the Soviet Union in causing unrest there—represented an area of continuity for the Reagan administration during its second term. This continuity was reflected in the formal emergence of the "Reagan Doctrine," a policy supporting anti-Communist movements in various locations around the world that was demonstrated most dramatically by support of the Nicaraguan Contras, even as Congress cut off military support for that operation from 1984 to 1986. This latter episode, known as the "Iran–Contra affair" (discussed below) reflected the administration's determination to "stand tall" against perceived Communist penetration in Central America. At the same time, the episode produced a major inconsistency in policy: The Reagan administration secretly abandoned its official policy of an arms embargo toward Iran in an attempt to free American hostages in the region.

The Reagan Doctrine

By 1985, the administration's support for anti-Communist forces in the Third World had gained such prominence and permanency that it took on a name of its own: the "Reagan Doctrine." Unlike U.S. policy that focused on containing the expansion of communism, the Reagan Doctrine espoused "providing assistance to groups fighting governments that have aligned themselves with the Soviet Union."[123] Despite the thaw in relations with the Soviet Union during Reagan's second term, the strategy was still pursued vigorously and proved to be the main thread of continuity with the hard-line policy of anticommunism that was so prominent in 1981.

What this policy meant in reality was that several anti-Communist movements across three continents received both covert and overt American economic and military assistance and political encouragement in their fights against the Communist governments in power. In Asia, for example, the United States continued to support the Afghan rebels in their battle with the Soviet troops and the Soviet-backed Kabul government. In Kampuchea (present-day Cambodia), the United States also clandestinely funneled aid to groups opposing the government supported by the occupying Vietnamese troops. In Africa, the Reagan administration persuaded Congress to repeal its prohibition on aid to forces opposing the Angolan government, and it continued to support rebel leader Jonas Savimbi and his National Union for the Total Independence of Angola (UNITA) in its fight against the Marxist-supported government there. In Central America, of course, the Reagan administration continued to support the Nicaraguan Contras against the Sandinista government, even as Congress diligently attempted to end such aid.

A useful indicator of how institutionalized the Reagan Doctrine became was the 1985 foreign aid authorization bill. While that bill not only included some nonmilitary humanitarian aid for the Nicaraguan rebels, support for other anti-Communist rebel groups was publicly acknowledged with a $5 million allocation to the Cambodian rebels and a $15 million "humanitarian" allocation to the Afghan people.[124] As alluded to above, the congressional prohibition on aid to rebel forces in Angola was formally rescinded in this legislation.

The Iran–Contra Affair, 1984–1986

The episode that best illustrates the extent to which the administration embraced the Reagan Doctrine was the Iran–Contra affair from 1984 through 1986. This affair brought together two vexing foreign policy problems for the Reagan administration.[125] The first was the question of dealing with the Sandinista government in Nicaragua. The Reagan administration viewed the Sandinistas as avowed Marxists intent upon spreading revolution throughout Central America. The second was the question of dealing with Iran and its government led by Ayatollah Khomeini. That government had seized 63 Americans in November 1979, held most of them hostage for 444 days, and released the remaining 52 hostages on the day of President Reagan's inauguration. To deal with these two policy questions, the Reagan administration supported the Nicaraguan Contras fighting against the Sandinistas in various ways, including the use of U.S. clandestine assistance, and continued observance of President Carter's trade sanctions against Iran, including a prohibition on U.S. arms sales to that country.

Beginning in 1984, however, policies toward Nicaragua and Iran faltered, and eventually unraveled by mid-1985. Iran's actions in support of terrorism caused the first challenge to the Reagan administration's policy. As a result of the U.S. presence in a multinational peacekeeping force in Lebanon in 1982 and 1983, anti-American sentiment and terrorism against the United States rose significantly. In October 1983, terrorists bombed U.S. Marine barracks in Lebanon. In early 1984, three Americans were seized in Beirut. The next year, four more Americans were taken hostage. Both the American public and President Reagan became increasingly impatient over the hostage situation. Indeed, by mid-1985, President Reagan decided to reverse the long-standing policy of an arms embargo against Iran in an attempt to free U.S. hostages.

Yet the Reagan administration's policy reversal toward Iran was not done in isolation; it quickly became tied to an attempt to save its policy of aiding the Nicaraguan Contras. In October 1984, Congress had cut off all American military assistance to the Nicaraguan Contras with the passage of the most restrictive

version of the Boland Amendments. (These amendments, named after Congressman Edward Boland of Massachusetts, were a series of measures attached to
defense appropriations bills and continuing resolution from 1982 to 1986 aimed at
shaping policy toward Nicaragua [see Chapter 8].) In light of this congressional
action, high administration officials almost immediately undertook efforts to keep
the Contras together in "body and soul," as President Reagan had instructed.
What ultimately emerged from these efforts was a covert operation by private
operatives to raise money and provide support for the Nicaraguan rebels. There
were at least two means of raising money to support the Contras: contributions by
private individuals and other governments, and the clandestine sale of arms to the
Iranian government and the transfer of profits to the Nicaraguan rebels. The latter
effort, largely directed by Lt. Col. Oliver North of the National Security Council
staff, provided for several shipments of arms to Iran and profits from those sales
transferred to the Contras in 1985 and 1986. Importantly, throughout the entire
episode and during the investigations afterward, President Reagan consistently
denied both that he knew that the arms sales profits were being transferred to the
Contras and that the arms sales to Iran were tied solely to the freeing of American
hostages held in Lebanon.

The Iran–Contra affair affected both procedural and policy aspects of American foreign policy during the latter years of the Reagan administration. It damaged both the clarity and credibility of the administration's policy and challenged
the way the Reagan Doctrine was being carried out. It had a profound effect upon
congressional-executive relations and upon public support for foreign policy. Yet,
it also demonstrated the extent to which the administration was willing to go to
try to enforce the Reagan Doctrine.

POLICY CHANGE
TOWARD THE THIRD WORLD:
PHILIPPINES, PLO, AND SOUTH AFRICA

Although policy adherence to the Reagan Doctrine marked the administration's
approach to the Third World, three important policy changes did occur in different regions of the world. One was in Southeast Asia, a second in the Middle East,
and the third in Africa.

The Aquino Victory

The first change was over the Philippines and the movement toward democracy
under Corazon Aquino in 1985 and 1986. The United States had long supported
the government of Ferdinand Marcos, principally because of his anti-Communist
credentials and because of the need to maintain two strategic U.S. bases on Philippine soil (a naval base at Subic Bay and an air base at Clark Field). Yet Marcos's
dismal human rights record and authoritarian rule had long been a source of embarrassment and concern to U.S. policy makers. With the assassination of Senator

Benigno Aquino, Jr., the leading opposition politician to Marcos, and the rise in strength of the New People's Army—a Marxist opposition group—and other nationalist opposition groups, the Reagan administration came under increasing pressure to reevaluate its policy. By 1984, the reevaluation had begun, and a National Security Council directive anticipated a post-Marcos period.[126]

When President Marcos suddenly agreed to hold a "snap election" in early 1986 to demonstrate his popularity, Corazon Aquino, wife of the assassinated senator and a political novice, agreed to run against him. Although Marcos was declared the election winner, accusations of voter fraud were rampant. Opposition groups surrounded the presidential palace and called for Marcos to give up power. At that juncture, the Reagan administration threw its full support behind the opposition candidate, Corazon Aquino, and informed Marcos that he should resign. Within a matter of days, he left the country and took up exile in Hawaii.

The significance of this action for the Reagan administration was that it represented a clear departure from previous policy, away from maintaining stability through support for authoritarian rule and toward the promotion of human rights and democracy. This action seemed to be particularly at odds with an administration that had previously supported Third World stability as the less dangerous way to thwart potential Communist expansion.

U.S.-PLO Dialogue

A second illustration concerned the question of talking with the Palestine Liberation Organization (PLO) in any Middle East peace negotiations. Since 1975, as part of the commitments associated with second disengagement agreement between Israel and Egypt, the United States had pledged to Israel that it would have no contact with the PLO until at least two conditions were met: (1) the PLO recognized the right of the state of Israel to exist; and (2) the PLO accepted UN resolutions 242 and 338 as the basis for negotiations in the Middle East.[127] Over the years, a third condition for any contact between the PLO and the United States was added: (3) the PLO would have to renounce the use of terrorism.[128] Although a variety of efforts was undertaken by Secretary of State George Shultz in the mid-1980s, no real accommodation occurred among the parties to the ongoing dispute.

In November 1988, however, the Palestine National Council, the political assembly of the PLO, took a dramatic step to change the situation. First, it declared an independent Palestinian state in the area occupied by Israel and sought recognition from abroad. Second, and most important for U.S. policy, it moved to accept the first American condition for discussion between the parties and accepted in part the second condition. On the third condition, however, it "condemned" terrorism but did not renounce it. By mid-December 1988, however, Yasir Arafat, head of the PLO, sensing the political value of discussions with the United States, announced his full acceptance of the three explicit conditions for U.S.-PLO dialogue and his renunciation of terrorism. Within a matter of hours, President Reagan determined that Arafat's statement met American conditions and announced a shift in American policy.[129]

Opposition to Apartheid

The third arena of change was South Africa. Although all American administrations, including Reagan's, had long opposed South Africa's policy of apartheid—segregation of the races—the Reagan administration had followed a policy of "constructive engagement" in which "quiet diplomacy" was seen as the best way to elicit change in that strategically important country. By August 1985, however, Congress had become impatient with such a strategy and was on the verge of passing a compromise bill that would have imposed economic sanctions on South Africa as a more tangible way to effect change. In a clear reversal of policy, and undoubtedly as an attempt to rescue the initiative from Congress, President Reagan issued an executive order imposing virtually the same set of sanctions that Congress had proposed.[130]

In 1986, however, the Reagan administration failed to take any further action against South Africa. At the same time, Congress pressed ahead and passed a new, tough sanctions bill, the Anti-Apartheid Act of 1986, over President Reagan's veto. The policy change that President Reagan had originally put into place after congressional prodding in 1985 was now made permanent by an act of Congress in 1986. In this sense, the policy change on the part of the Reagan administration was less its own and more the result of congressional action.

CONCLUDING COMMENTS

The Nixon, Carter, and Reagan administrations offered different approaches to American foreign policy as the Cold War was changing and winding down. The Nixon and Carter approaches sought, albeit in different ways, to change the emphasis from the globalism of the Cold War and its basic tenets, while the Reagan approach sought to restore those values. The greatest value change that the Nixon years brought to U.S. policy was a movement away from the emphasis on moral principle and greater acceptance of traditional realism as the basis of actions toward the rest of the world. At least until the last year of its time in office, the Carter administration sought to continue the limited globalism of the Nixon years (defined more with an emphasis upon trilateral and Third World relations than upon superpower ties) but to change from the largely singular moral emphasis on anti-Communism to a more comprehensive, morally based approach, best exemplified by its human rights campaign. The Reagan administration sought less to impose a new value approach and more to restore an earlier one, best epitomized by the Cold War consensus. That is, while the Reagan administration continued the moral emphasis of the Carter administration (although now the target was once again global communism, not global human rights violations), it sought to restore an American globalism more reminiscent of an earlier era.

The Reagan administration largely succeeded in that effort by again placing the Soviet Union at the center of American foreign policy, challenging the Soviets worldwide, and attempting to rally the nations of the non-Communist world against the Soviet Union. During its second term, however, the Reagan administration moved from confrontation to accommodation with the Soviet Union, notably completing the first nuclear arms reduction treaty (the INF Treaty) in history. Toward the rest of the world, however, the Reagan administration continued to pursue a staunch anti-Communist policy with a more mixed result. Still, the global conditions were changing and within a year of the end of the Reagan administration, the Cold War began to unravel, posing new challenges to the values and direction of American foreign policy. In the next chapter, we examine the effort of the Bush and Clinton administrations to deal with a world without the Soviet Union as the center of American foreign policy.

NOTES

1. The approach of the Ford administration (1974–1976) is not treated separately here because Henry Kissinger continued to serve as national security advisor (through 1975) and as secretary of state (through 1976).

2. For a detailed listing of the assumptions of realism and idealism, see Charles W. Kegley, Jr., "The Neoliberal Challenge to Realist Theories of World Politics: An Introduction," in Charles W. Kegley, Jr., *Controversies in International Relations Theory* (New York: St. Martin's Press, 1995), pp. 4–5. For another statement of the idealism/liberalism tradition in international politics, see Robert O. Keohane and Joseph S. Nye, Jr., *Power and Interdependence,* 2nd ed. (Glenview, IL: Scott, Foresman/Little Brown, 1989).

3. Richard M. Nixon, "Asia After Viet Nam," *Foreign Affairs* 46 (October 1967): 111–125. The quoted passages are at pp. 121, 123, and 114.

4. Richard M. Nixon, *U.S. Policy for the 1970s, A New Strategy for Peace. A Report to the Congress* (Washington, DC: Government Printing Office, February 18, 1970). The quoted passages are at pp. 2 and 3. For the earlier statements on some of these principles, see Richard M. Nixon, "Informal Remarks in Guam with Newsmen, July 25, 1969," and "Address to the Nation on the War in Vietnam, November 3, 1969," in *Public Papers of the Presidents of the United States, Richard Nixon 1969* (Washington, DC: U.S. Government Printing Office, 1971), pp. 544–556 and pp. 901–909, respectively. Indeed, the "Nixon Doctrine" is sometimes referred to as the "Guam Doctrine."

5. For a more detailed and recent treatment of the Nixon approach to foreign policy, including some more comparisons with earlier post–World War II approaches and America's historical traditions, see Henry Kissinger, *Diplomacy* (New York: Simon & Schuster, 1994), pp. 703–718.

6. This section draws upon Kissinger's important essay "Contemporary Issues of American Foreign Policy." It is printed as Chapter 2 in Henry A. Kissinger, *American Foreign Policy,* 3rd ed. (New York: W. W. Norton and Company, 1977), pp. 51–97. The quoted passage is at p. 79.

7. Ibid., pp. 91–97.

8. See Henry A. Kissinger, *A World Restored: Metternich, Castlereagh and the Problems of Peace 1812–1822* (Boston: Houghton Mifflin Company, 1957) on the importance of stability, especially at p. 1.

9. President Nixon's commitment to the balance of power and to this pentagonal world can be found in *Time,* January 3, 1972, and quoted in Kissinger, *Diplomacy,* p. 705: "I think it will be a safer world and a better world if we have a strong, healthy United States, Europe, Soviet Union, China, Japan, each balancing the other, not playing one against the other, an even balance."

10. For a description of the characteristics of the "statesman," see Kissinger's essay "Domestic Structure and Foreign Policy," in James N. Rosenau, ed., *International Politics and Foreign Policy,* rev. ed. (New York: Free Press, 1969), pp. 261–275. The quoted passage on the importance of negotiations to stability is at p. 274.

11. Kissinger, *American Foreign Policy,* pp. 120–121.

12. For a further analysis of the dimensions of Kissinger's approach described here, and a strong critique of it, see Falk, "What's Wrong with Henry Kissinger's Foreign Policy?" *Alternatives* I (1975): 79–100.

13. Once again, the analysis includes the years extends through 1976 (although President Ford came to office in August 1974) because Henry Kissinger continued to direct American foreign policy.

14. "U.S.-U.S.S.R. Exchanges Programs," *GIST* (Washington, DC: Department of State, April 1976).

15. See the excerpts from Henry Kissinger's *White House Years* (Boston: Little, Brown, 1979) on China in *Time,* October 1, 1979, 53–58.

16. The Shanghai Communique is reprinted in Gene T. Hsiao, ed., *Sino-American Detente and Its Policy Implications* (New York: Praeger Publishers, Inc., 1974), pp. 298–301.

17. This discussion draws upon "Conference on Security and Cooperation in Europe," *Department of State Bulletin* 77 (September 26, 1977): 404–410. The notion of "baskets" to summarize their work came from the conference itself (p. 405).

18. See his essay in *American Foreign Policy,* expanded ed. (New York: W. W. Norton and Company, 1974), pp. 99–135.

19. See John G. Stoessinger in his *Henry Kissinger: The Anguish of Power* (New York: W. W. Norton and Company, 1976), pp. 62–63.

20. Ibid., p. 73.

21. Falk, "What's Wrong with Henry Kissinger's Foreign Policy?" pp. 79–100.

22. Ibid., p. 98.

23. Ibid., p. 99.

24. William F. Buckley, Jr., "Politics of Henry Kissinger," transcript of *Firing Line* program, originally telecast on the Public Broadcasting System, September 13, 1975, p. 5. Mr. Buckley was quoting from Gallup Polls.

25. George W. Ball, *Diplomacy for a Crowded World* (Boston: Atlantic Monthly/Little Brown, 1976), pp. 108–129.

26. Ibid., p. 15. The other quotes are from pp. 13 and 14.

27. This global perspective (and changes in it) is discussed in part in Leonard Silk's brief analysis of an address by Zbigniew Brzezinski, "Economic Scene: New U.S. View of the World," *New York Times,* May 1, 1979, D2; and in an address by Cyrus Vance, "Meeting the Challenges of a Changing World" (Washington, DC: Bureau of Public Affairs, Department of State, May 1, 1979).

28. Jimmy Carter, "Inaugural Address of President Jimmy Carter: The Ever-Expanding American Dream," *Vital Speeches* 43 (February 15, 1977): 258.

29. Jimmy Carter, "Humane Purposes in Foreign Policy," Department of State News Release, May 22, 1977, p. 1 (Commencement Address at the University of Notre Dame).

30. Ibid., p. 2.

31. Ibid., pp. 1, 5.

32. See the discussion in Elizabeth Drew, "A Reporter at Large: Brzezinski," *The New Yorker* (May 1, 1978): 90–130, over the extent to which linkage was applied, especially pp. 117–121.

33. Although the Carter administration is usually identified with human rights, congressional action on this issue began at least in 1973 with hearings by the International Organizations and Movements Subcommittee, headed by Donald Fraser. On this point, see the discussion in Harold Molineu, "Human Rights: Administrative Impact of a Symbolic Policy," in John C. Grumm and Stephen L. Wasby, eds., *The Analysis of Policy Impact* (Lexington, MA: Lexington Books, D. C. Heath and Company, 1981), pp. 24–25.

34. "Inaugural Address of President Jimmy Carter: The Ever-Expanding American Dream," p. 259.

35. Jimmy Carter, *Keeping Faith* (New York: Bantam Books, 1982), p. 145.

36. See the comprehensive description of human rights categories in *Human Rights and U.S. Foreign Policy* (Department of State Publication 8959, Washington, DC: Bureau of Public Affairs, 1978), pp. 7–8, that the Carter administration issued. Secretary of

State Cyrus Vance had outlined these same categories in a speech to the University of Georgia School of Law on April 30, 1977 (*Department of State Bulletin* 76 [May 23, 1977]: 505–508).

37. See Lincoln P. Bloomfield, "From Ideology to Program to Policy," *Journal of Policy Analysis and Management* 2 (Fall 1982): 6.

38. In reality, some nations (Argentina, Brazil, and Guatemala, for example) simply rejected American military assistance after attacks on their human rights records by the United States. See Charles W. Kegley, Jr., and Eugene R. Wittkopf, *American Foreign Policy: Pattern and Process,* 2nd ed. (New York: St. Martin's Press, 1982), p. 595.

39. These arguments are developed in Jeane J. Kirkpatrick, "Dictatorships and Double Standards," *Commentary* 68 (November 1979): 34–45; and "Human Rights and American Foreign Policy: A Symposium," *Commentary* 79 (November 1981): 42–45.

40. See, for example, the proposal by William F. Buckley, Jr., in his "Human Rights and Foreign Policy," *Foreign Affairs* 58 (Spring 1980): 775–796. Also, see Arthur Schlesinger, Jr., "Human Rights and the American Tradition," *Foreign Affairs* 57 (Winter 1978/1979): 503–526, for his view on intergovernmental and nongovernmental organizations.

41. See Department of State, *Report on Human Rights Practices in Countries Receiving U.S. Aid. Submitted to the Committee on Foreign Relations,* U.S. Senate and Committee on Foreign Affairs, U.S. House of Representatives (Washington, DC: Government Printing Office, 1979), pp. 4–5; Bloomfield, "From Ideology to Program to Policy," p. 9; and Warren Christopher, "The Diplomacy of Human Rights: The First Year," Speech to the American Bar Association, February 13, 1978 (Washington, DC: Department of State, 1978).

42. See Colin Legum, "The African Crisis," in William P. Bundy, ed., *America and the World 1978* (New York: Pergamon Press, 1979), pp. 633–651.

43. Carter, *Keeping Faith,* p. 150.

44. See, for example, the Helsinki Accords discussed above.

45. Christopher S. Wren, "After a Rebuff in Moscow, Detente Is Put to the Test," *New York Times,* April 1, 1977, IA, 8A.

46. Stanley Hoffmann, "Carter's Soviet Problem," *The New Republic* 79 (July 29, 1978): 21. On this point and for a discussion of other Carter difficulties discussed here, see Stanley Hoffmann, "A View from at Home: The Perils of Incoherence," in William P. Bundy, ed., *America and the World 1978* (New York: Pergamon Press, 1979), pp. 463–491.

47. Most significant, perhaps, the Soviet Union began the deployment of the SS-20s, its intermediate-range ballistic missiles, in the late 1970s.

48. Such a dualism in Brzezinski's thinking about the Soviets probably should not have been unexpected. His academic career had been largely made on the basis of a strong anti-Soviet view. Thus, his concern with global issues was a more recent phenomenon in his thinking.

49. Drew, "A Reporter at Large: Brzezinski," p. 117.

50. John E. Rielly, ed., *American Public Opinion and U.S. Foreign Policy 1979* (Chicago: The Chicago Council on Foreign Relations, 1979), pp. 5 and 15.

51. Bruce Russett and Donald R. Deluca, "'Don't Tread on Me': Public Opinion and Foreign Policy in the Eighties," *Political Science Quarterly* 96 (Fall 1981): 381–399.

52. Stanley Hoffmann, "Requiem," *Foreign Policy* 42 (Spring 1981): 11.

53. Carter, *Keeping Faith,* p. 157.

54. Ibid., p. 184.

55. Ibid., p. 292.

56. Ibid., pp. 296–297.

57. Department of State Publication 8954, *The Camp David Summit* (Washington, DC: Office of Public Communications, Bureau of Public Affairs, September 1978).

58. See UN Security Council Resolution 435 in *Resolutions and Decisions of the Security Council, Security Council Official Records: Thirty-Third Year* (New York: United Nations, 1979), p. 13, for the resolution that South Africa eventually said that it would work to put into effect.

59. See Henry Wiseman and Alastair M. Taylor, *From Rhodesia to Zimbabwe: The Politics of Transition* (New York: Pergamon Press, 1981).

60. For an analysis of the Carter foreign policy from this perspective, see Robert W. Tucker, "America in Decline: The Foreign Policy of 'Maturity,'" in William P. Bundy, ed., *America and the World 1979* (New York: Pergamon Press, 1980), pp. 449–488.

61. The impact of these events on Carter foreign policy is discussed in Richard Burt, "Carter, Under Pressure of Crises, Tests New Foreign Policy Goals," *New York Times,* January 9, 1980, A1 and A8, upon which we rely.

62. "My Opinion of the Russians Has Changed Most Drastically," *Time,* January 14, 1980, 10.

63. These actions are outlined in a speech that President Jimmy Carter gave to the nation on January 4, 1980. The speech can be found in *Vital Speeches of the Day* 46 (January 15, 1980): 194–195.

64. Jimmy Carter, "State of the Union 1980," *Vital Speeches of the Day* 46 (February 1, 1980): 227.

65. Poll results suggested that the failure to secure the quick release of the American hostages contributed significantly to the electoral defeat of Jimmy Carter in 1980.

66. "Transcript of President's First News Conference on Foreign and Domestic Topics," *New York Times,* January 30, 1981, A10.

67. "Excerpts from President's Speech to National Association of Evangelicals," *New York Times,* March 9, 1983, A18.

68. Jimmy Carter, "Humane Purposes in Foreign Policy," p. 1.

69. See, for example, Robert E. Osgood, "The Revitalization of Containment," William P. Bundy, ed., *America and the World 1981* (New York: Pergamon Press, 1982), pp. 465–502.

70. One American diplomat was quoted as saying, "Aside from opposing the Soviets, we don't really have a foreign policy." See Hedrick Smith in "Discordant Voices," *New York Times,* March 20, 1981, A2.

71. See, for example, the following statements by Alexander Haig and issued by the Department of State, "A New Direction in U.S. Foreign Policy" (April 14, 1981); "Relationship of Foreign and Defense Policies" (July 30, 1981); and "A Strategic Approach to American Foreign Policy" (August 11, 1981). The four items here are quoted from the last one at p. 2. We rely upon this last one for our subsequent analysis.

72. Ibid. Later section subtitles are from these points.

73. On these plans, see, for example, *Congressional Quarterly Almanac 1981* (Washington, DC: Congressional Quarterly, Inc., 1982), pp. 240–241; and Stephen Webbe, "Defense: Reagan Plans Largest U.S. Military Buildup Since Vietnam. . . ." *Christian Science Monitor,* May 1, 1981, 8–9. The latter article puts the buildup at $1.5 trillion.

74. Alexander Haig, "Arms Control and Strategic Nuclear Forces" (Washington, DC: Bureau of Public Affairs, Department of State, November 4, 1981). The elements of strategic modernization are drawn from that statement.

75. "Peace and Security," President Reagan Televised Address to the Nation, March 23, 1983, reprinted in *Realism, Strength, Negotiation: Key Foreign Policy Statements of the Reagan Administration* (Washington, DC: Department of State, May 1984), p. 43.

76. See William P. Bundy, "A Portentous Year," in William P. Bundy, ed., *Foreign Affairs: America and the World 1983* 62 (1984): 499, on the centrality of the deployment issue in Soviet-American relations.

77. On June 18, 1982, President Reagan imposed sanctions on American subsidiaries or their licensees from continuing to supply the Soviets over the gas pipeline. See Josef Joffe, "Europe and America: The Politics of Resentment (Cont'd)," in William P. Bundy, ed., *America and the World 1981* (New York: Pergamon Press, 1982), pp. 573–574.

78. "Caribbean Basin Initiative," *GIST* (Washington, DC: Department of State, February, 1982).

79. The White House Office of the Press Secretary, press release on arms transfer policy, July 9, 1981.

80. See the survey of Reagan's foreign policy in the November 9, 1981, issue of

Newsweek, in which there is "A Tour of Reagan's Horizon," pp. 34–43. The mention of "strategic consensus" for the Middle East is at p. 41, but the concept can be applied to all areas of the world during the Reagan administration.

81. Haig, "A Strategic Approach to American Foreign Policy," p. 3. Emphasis added.

82. See, for example, the "Text of Haig's Speech on American Foreign Policy," *New York Times,* April 25, 1981, 4, and his characterization of the Soviet Union. Also see the chronology in Bundy, ed., *America and the World 1981,* p. 728, for President Reagan's comment at his June 16, 1981, press conference in which he says that the Soviet Union "shows signs of collapse." (The quote is from Bundy.) The text of President Reagan's remarks can be found in "The President's News Conference of June 16, 1981," *Weekly Compilation of Presidential Documents* 17 (June 22, 1981): 633.

83. On the neutron bomb, see Leslie H. Gelb, "Reagan Orders Production of 2 Types of Neutron Arms for Stockpiling in the U.S.," *New York Times,* August 9, 1981, 1. On sanctioning the Soviet Union over Poland, see the president's statement in *Weekly Compilation of Presidential Documents* 17 (January 4, 1982): 1429–1430.

84. Steven Weisman's "Reagan Ends Curbs on Export of Grain to the Soviet Union," *New York Times,* April 25, 1981, 1 and 6, discusses the lifting of the embargo. The expansion of grain sales is reported in John F. Burns, "U.S. Will Permit Russians to Triple Imports of Grain," *New York Times,* October 2, 1981, A1 and D14. A five-year grain deal was eventually agreed to in July 1983: Steven R. Weisman, "A New Pact Raises Soviet Purchases of American Grain," *New York Times,* July 29, 1983, A1 and D9. Also see William G. Hyland, "U.S. Relations: The Long Way Back," in William P. Bundy, ed., *America and the World 1981,* pp. 542–543.

85. Bernard Gwertzman, "U.S. Says It Is Not Bound by 2 Arms Pacts With Soviet," *New York Times,* May 20, 1981, A11.

86. On the Haig-Gromyko meeting and for prospects on arms control talks, see Bernard Gwertzman, "U.S. and Soviet Agree to Renew Weapons Talk," *New York Times,* September 24, 1981, A1 and A10.

87. A discussion of the INF negotiations can be found in Strobe Talbott, "Buildup and Breakdown," in William P. Bundy, ed., *America and the World 1983,* pp. 587–615. On the first deployment, see James M. Markham, "First U.S. Pershing Missiles Delivered in West Germany," *New York Times,* November 24, 1983, A14.

88. The cataloguing of these events and other Soviet actions can be found in the "Cooling Trend in Soviet Policy," *Christian Science Monitor,* May 25, 1984, 1. On the explanation for the withdrawal from the Olympics, see "U.S.-Soviet Ties Termed 'Worst Ever,'" *Des Moines Sunday Register,* May 27, 1984, 1.

89. The comment was by a Soviet official and is quoted in ibid.

90. "Communist Interference in El Salvador" (Washington, DC: Bureau of Public Affairs, Department of State, February 1981), p. 1. Special Report No. 80.

91. See the testimony of Secretary of State Alexander Haig in *Foreign Assistance Legislation for Fiscal Year 1982,* Hearing before the Committee on Foreign Affairs, the House of Representatives, 97th Cong., 1st sess. (Washington, DC: U.S. Government Printing Office, 1981), p. 194.

92. See the chronology in Bundy, ed., *America and the World 1981,* p. 749.

93. Ibid.

94. "Reagan Says Security of U.S. Is at Stake in Central America," *Des Moines Register,* April 28, 1983, 6A.

95. "No More Aid for Nicaragua," *Today,* April 24, 1981, 13.

96. In its November 8, 1982, issue, *Newsweek* devoted its cover story to the covert war against Nicaragua. See "A Secret War for Nicaragua," pp. 42–55.

97. The justification for the Grenada invasion is taken from President Reagan's remarks on October 25, 1983. They are reprinted in "Grenada: Collective Action by the Caribbean Peace Force," *Department of State Bulletin* 83 (December 1983): 67.

98. The Reagan administration sought congressional repeal of the Clark Amendment,

an amendment passed in 1976 that prohibited aid to forces in Angola. The apparent aim of such an action was to allow the United States to support Jonas Savimbi and his UNITA forces, who were still fighting the Marxist government in Angola.

99. A chronology of these various actions is presented in William P. Bundy, ed., *America and the World 1981,* pp. 734–735. This chronology, and the subsequent ones in the other volumes of this series, were useful beginning points for unraveling the sequence of events in the Reagan administration.

100. The United States quickly suspended this agreement after the Israelis annexed the Golan Heights in December 1981. See Aron, "Ideology in Search of a Policy," in William P. Bundy, ed., *America and the World 1981,* p. 517.

101. Juan de Onis, "U.S. and Pakistanis Reach an Agreement on $3 Billion in Aid," *New York Times,* June 16, 1981, A1, A15. On the importance of both the AWACS and Pakistani sales, see Carol Housa, "Arms Sale Test, U.S.-Pakistan Ties," *Christian Science Monitor,* November 12, 1981, 3.

102. On the Reagan Initiative, see "Transcript of President's Address to Nation on West Bank and Palestinians," *New York Times,* September 2, 1982, A11.

103. The explanations for sending these forces into Lebanon are contained in the reports to Congress on August 24, 1982, and September 29, 1982, and in the Multinational Force Agreement between the United States and Lebanon of September 25, 1982. All of these are reprinted in *The War Powers Resolution: Relevant Documents, Correspondence, Reports,* Subcommittee on International Security and Scientific Affairs, House Committee on Foreign Affairs, December 1983, pp. 60–63 and 74–76.

104. See "Communique by the Common Market," *New York Times,* January 5, 1982, A7; and "Text of Declaration on Poland by the Foreign Ministers of NATO," *New York Times,* January 12, 1982, A8. Also see John Vincour, "Bonn Says Sanctions Are Not the Solution," *New York Times,* December 30, 1981, A1 and A7.

105. In West Germany, the proposed location for most of the theater nuclear forces, the opposition to the deployment of such weapons during 1983 assisted the Greens (a new antinuclear and environmental party) in gaining some seats in the legislatures of the Laender (or state) governments and eventually in the Bundestag (the national parliament). See "Focus on the National Elections in West Germany on March 6, 1983," p. 6, and "Focus on the Results of the National Elections in the Federal Republic of Germany on March 6, 1983," p. 2. Both are published by the German Information Center.

106. Paul E. Sigmund, "Latin America: Change or Continuity?" in William P. Bundy, ed., *America and the World 1981,* p. 636.

107. George Gallup, "Military Budget Boost Loses Support, Poll Hints," *Des Moines Sunday Register,* February 27, 1983, 5A.

108. A *Newsweek* poll as reported in the April 26, 1982, issue, p. 24, found that 68 percent of those who had heard of the nuclear freeze movement favored or strongly favored it. A *Newsweek* poll in the January 31, 1983, issue, p. 17, found that 64 percent of the public supported the nuclear freeze proposal.

109. The crowd estimates ranged from 500,000 to 700,000 or more as reported in Paul L. Montgomery, "Throngs Fill Manhattan to Protest Nuclear Weapons," *New York Times,* June 13, 1982, 1 and 43. For a survey of how the freeze movement reflects a diverse American public, see "A Matter of Life and Death," *Newsweek,* April 26, 1982, 20–33.

110. In a March 1981 interview with Walter Cronkite, President Reagan rejected the use of U.S. armed forces. See Francis X. Clines, "President Doubtful on U.S. Intervention," *New York Times,* March 4, 1981, A1 and A22. In a December 1981 interview, Secretary Haig ruled out American troops. On the interview, see Sigmund, "Latin America: Change or Continuity?" p. 641.

111. The quoted passage is from "Transcript of President's News Conference on Foreign and Domestic Issues," *New York Times,* November 8, 1984, 13.

112. George Shultz, "Managing the U.S.-Soviet Relationship Over the Long Term," address before the Rand/UCLA Center for the Study of Soviet International Behavior, October 18, 1984, reprinted in *Department of State Bulletin* 84 (December 1984): 2.

113. "Text of Inaugural Address," *Des Moines Register,* January 22, 1985, 4A.

114. On the changes in Soviet foreign policy, see David Holloway, "Gorbachev's New Thinking," and Robert Levgold, "The Revolution in Soviet Foreign Policy," in William P. Bundy, ed., *Foreign Affairs: America and the World 1988/89* 68 (1989): 66–98.

115. John E. Rielly, ed., *American Public Opinion and U.S. Foreign Policy 1987* (Chicago: The Chicago Council on Foreign Relations, 1987), p. 6.

116. For summits by other presidents, see Harold W. Stanley and Richard G. Niemi, *Vital Statistics on American Politics* (Washington, DC: CQ Press, 1988), pp. 293–294.

117. See the "Concluding Remarks: President Reagan, November 21, 1985," reprinted in *Department of State Bulletin* 86 (January 1986): 11.

118. "The Reykjavik Meeting," *GIST* (Washington, DC: Department of State, December 1986).

119. Steven B. Roberts, "Reagan Says He Was Moved by Contacts with Russians," *New York Times,* June 2, 1988, A16. On the third summit, see R. W. Apple, Jr., "Reagan and Gorbachev Report Progress on Long-Range Arms and Mute 'Star Wars' Quarrel," *New York Times,* December 11, 1987, 1 and 10.

120. President Reagan purposely described the occasion as not "a working summit" because there was no set agenda. See President Reagan's statement of December 3, 1988, in the *Department of State Bulletin* 89 (February 1989): 3.

121. "Joint Statement, Geneva, January 8, 1985," *Department of State Bulletin* 85 (March 1985): 30.

122. The complete text of the INF Treaty and its protocols are available in *Arms Control and Disarmament Agreements: Texts and Histories of the Negotiations* (Washington, DC: United States Arms Control and Disarmament Agency, 1990), p. 345–444.

123. Michael Mandelbaum, "The Luck of the President," in William G. Hyland, ed., *America and the World 1985* (New York: Pergamon Press, 1986), p. 408.

124. *Congressional Quarterly Almanac 1985* (Washington, DC: Congressional Quarterly, Inc., 1986), pp. 40, 56, 58.

125. Several sources were used to construct the description of events associated with the Iran–Contra affair. Among them were *Report of the Congressional Committees Investigating the Iran–Contra Affair* (Washington, DC: U.S. Government Printing Office, November 1987); *Report of the President's Special Review Board* (Washington, DC: U.S. Government Printing Office, February 26, 1987); Peter Hayes, ed., "Chronology 1987," *Foreign Affairs: America and the World 1987/88,* 66 (1988): 638–676; Peter Hayes, ed., "Chronology 1988," *Foreign Affairs: America and the World 1988/89* 68 (1989): 220–256; Clyde R. Mark, "Iran-Contra Affair: A Chronology," Report No. 86–190F (Washington, DC: The Congressional Research Service, April 2, 1987); and James M. McCormick and Steven S. Smith, "The Iran Arms Sale and the Intelligence Oversight Act of 1980," *PS* 20 (Winter 1987): 29–37. The Reagan quote on keeping the Contras "body and soul together" can be found in *Report of the Congressional Committees Investigating the Iran–Contra Affair,* p. 4. Finally, the data in this chapter on American hostages seized and released was drawn from BBC News, "Timeline: US–Iran Ties," at http://news.bbc.co.uk/go/pr/fr/-/1/hi/world/middle_east/3362443.stm. Published: 2004/01/02, accessed on March 14, 2004.

126. The change in support is from Sandra Burton, "Aquino's Philippines: The Center Holds," *Foreign Affairs: America and the World 1986* 65 (1987): 524–526.

127. Nadav Safran, *Israel: The Embattled Ally* (Cambridge, MA: The Belknap Press, 1978), p. 594.

128. Alan Cowell, "Arafat Urges U.S. to Press Israelis to Negotiate Now," *New York Times,* November 16, 1988, A1, A10.

129. "U.S. Makes Stunning Move Toward PLO," *Des Moines Register,* December 15, 1988, 3A. On the Palestine National Council deliberations, see "The P.L.O.: Less than Meets the Eye," *New York Times,* November 16, 1988, A30; and Youssef M. Ibrahim, "Palestinian View: A Big Stride Forward," *New York Times,* November 16, 1988, A10.

130. This discussion is based upon *Congressional Quarterly Almanac 1985* (Washington, DC: Congressional Quarterly, Inc., 1986), pp. 39, 40, and 85; and *Congressional Quarterly Almanac 1986* (Washington, DC: Congressional Quarterly, Inc., 1987), pp. 359–362.

5

Foreign Policy after the Cold War: The Bush and Clinton Administrations

The world leaves one epoch of cold war and enters another epoch. . . .
The characteristics of the cold war should be abandoned.

FORMER SOVIET PRESIDENT MIKHAIL GORBACHEV
AT THE MALTA SUMMIT WITH PRESIDENT GEORGE BUSH
DECEMBER 1989

The successor to a doctrine of containment must be a strategy of enlargement,
the enlargement of the world's free community of market democracies.

ANTHONY LAKE
NATIONAL SECURITY ADVISOR TO PRESIDENT CLINTON
SEPTEMBER 1993

George Bush, Ronald Reagan's vice president, was elected president in November 1988, less on a commitment to change the course of U.S. foreign policy and more as a result of the American people's desire for continuity in the approach to the world. Unlike Reagan, Bush came to office less as a foreign policy ideologue and more as a pragmatist without a strongly held worldview. In this sense, President Bush's initial foreign policy impulse leaned toward maintaining continuity with the recent past, rather than seeking change. However, his commitment to continuity was challenged by the dramatic events that began at the end of his first year in office: the demise of the Soviet empire, the emergence of new political, economic, and social openness in Eastern Europe, and the movement toward the reunification of Germany.[1] The end of the Cold War was at hand.

By 1990, therefore, President Bush had begun to modify the course of American foreign policy, away from one driven by the anti-Communist principles of the past and toward one driven by the changes in the Soviet Union and Eastern Europe. Iraq's invasion of Kuwait, and the American and allied response to it, gave further impetus for seeking a new direction for American foreign policy. Indeed, shortly after the beginning of the Persian Gulf War, President Bush acknowledged as much, when he announced that "we stand at a defining hour" in our foreign policy.[2] In that pursuit, the Bush administration sought to advance a new rationale for America's global involvement using the old rubric of a "new world order."

William Jefferson Clinton also ran for president on the theme of change—change in domestic policy and change in foreign policy.[3] With the end of the Cold War, candidate Clinton argued, American foreign policy must change to meet the challenges of the end of the twentieth century and to prepare for the twenty-first. What was needed for this new era, Clinton claimed, was "a new vision and the strength to meet a new set of opportunities and threats." "We face," Clinton continued, "the same challenge today that we faced in 1946—to build a world of security, freedom, democracy, free markets and growth at a time of great change."[4] Indeed, he contended that the Bush administration's leadership had been "rudderless, reactive, and erratic," while the country needed leadership that was "strategic, vigorous, and grounded in America's democratic values."[5] As such, Clinton promised a new direction in American policy, based on its traditional domestic values.

In this chapter, then, we review the foreign policy values, beliefs, and approaches of these two administrations as the Cold War was ending and a new era emerged. For the Bush administration, we outline the dramatic events that ultimately led to the demise of the Cold War and the Soviet Union, the initial efforts to build a "new world order," and the impact of the Persian Gulf War of 1991 and related events on American foreign policy in the early 1990s. For the Clinton administration, we identify its initial commitment to expanding free peoples and free markets around the world and assess the extent to which it succeeded in achieving those goals during its first term. With the altered political landscape at home, including Republican majorities in both houses of Congress, and with the successful reelection to a second term, we discuss how the administration's approach then evolved from its initial idealism to a more realist approach by the end of its time in office. Throughout these analyses, we survey numerous foreign policy actions to illustrate the administrations' approaches and assess values and beliefs that were now at the core of American foreign policy at the end of the twentieth century.

VALUES AND BELIEFS
OF THE BUSH ADMINISTRATION

In contrast to the Reagan administration's initial ideological approach, the Bush administration assumed office mainly seeking continuity but also willing to pursue modest change in foreign policy direction. Although the commitment to continuity was quickly challenged by the dramatic events in Central Europe and the Middle East, the foreign policy values and beliefs of the Bush administration remained markedly unchanged throughout its four years in office.

Pragmatic and *prudent* were favorite terms used to describe the Bush administration's basic values in directing American foreign policy.[6] President Bush did not come to office with a grand design or with a "vision thing" (as he himself might have said) for reshaping international politics. Instead, his administration's approach really reflected the values, beliefs, and temperament of Bush himself, a moderate, middle-of-the-road professional politician who was well trained in foreign affairs. After all, President Bush had a wealth of foreign policy experience—as director of the CIA, American representative to the People's Republic of China, ambassador to the United Nations, and vice president of the United States. Although at various times he claimed to be from Texas, Connecticut, or Maine, Bush had spent most of the twenty years prior to taking office deep within the establishment of Washington and was fully steeped in the foreign policy emanating from the nation's capital. Thus, he was prepared for the give and take of Washington and global politics.

The Commitment to Continuity:
A Problem Solver, Not a Visionary

Although President Bush might have described himself as a policy conservative, he was more than that. He was a problem solver who worked well with those with whom he disagreed.[7] His underlying political philosophy might best be summarized in this way: Getting results is more important than claiming ideological victory; getting results is the best way to achieve political success.

The tenets of realism (Chapter 4) come the closest to describing the general principles of Bush's foreign policy making. Bush essentially wanted to deal with the world as it existed and sought only those changes that would not be too unsettling for the international system as a whole. Further, the Bush administration was much more interested in relations with the strong (e.g., the Soviet Union and China) than with the weak (e.g., the Third World nations). In this sense, his policy orientation came closer to the balance of power approach that Nixon, Kissinger, and Ford brought to U.S. policy than to the staunchly anti-Communist, ideological approach of the Reagan years or the idealism of most of the Carter years. While these earlier principles continued to hold sway, the rapid unraveling of the Cold War from 1989 to 1991 compelled the Bush administration to adopt broader values and beliefs—largely from America's past—to guide U.S. policy for the future.

The personal style of decision making by President Bush gave further reason for asserting that personal values entered into the foreign policy process. Unlike the disengaged style of Reagan, Bush was actively involved in policy making—usually with a relatively small group of advisors. According to observers, he continuously "worked the phone" to accomplish his foreign policy objectives. Since he had served around the world and was vice president for eight years, he did indeed have a close working relationship with leaders from many nations. This personal dimension was most evident during the last half of 1990 and the early part of 1991, as Bush put together, and kept together, the anti-Iraq coalition prior to and during the Persian Gulf War.

Critics of the Bush administration viewed the president's initial pragmatic and cautious approach as indecisive, deliberate, and ad hoc. Most agreed that the designs of policy were nonexistent or, more charitably, still emerging. As Theodore Sorensen, a former Kennedy administration official, put it, the early part of the Bush administration was "all tactics, no strategy."[8] Another analyst, William Hyland, a former official in the Ford administration, was more supportive of the Bush administration's deliberate foreign policy approach. "It is the nature of the problems, however, not the style, that has dictated this approach," he contended at the time.[9] Other questions could be raised about Bush's "hand-on" approach to policy making and the dangers that may result from it. During his administration's decision to support the failed coup attempt in Panama in October 1989, for example, the president was apparently deeply involved in tactical decision making, perhaps much to his regret. By contrast, and perhaps indicative of his later style, he took a more detached approach to conducting the Persian Gulf War and left most tactical decisions to his military advisors. Even in this case, however, he did not stay too far away from the details, and was given frequent briefings and updates.[10]

Bush's Foreign Policy Team: "Sensibly Conservative"[11]

The foreign policy team that occupied Washington in the Bush years, conducted the initial policy review, and made policy decisions generally lent credence to this pragmatic, cautious-yet-realist description of the Bush administration's approach to foreign policy. Like Bush, the people chosen for the key cabinet and national security positions in the administration were individuals without strong ideological posture but given to practical solutions to problems. His choices for secretary of state, James Baker, and national security advisor, Brent Scowcroft, for instance, shared his commitment to incremental change in global affairs. According to one longtime foreign policy analyst, "The Baker-Scowcroft combination is the most competent-looking pair of people any new president has put in those jobs."[12]

The other key foreign policy participants in the Bush cabinet largely shared similar characteristics. At the Department of Defense, for instance, the appointment of Richard Cheney as Secretary of Defense reflected a choice of a policy maker of the same caliber as the others. While Cheney, a former member of Congress, had a conservative voting record, he was also viewed as pragmatic and reasonable in his approach to policy questions. His experience as chief of staff during the Ford administration demonstrated his pragmatic approach particularly well, and his handling of policy making during the Persian Gulf troop buildup and during the war itself won him high marks from several quarters. At the CIA, William Webster, Bush's first director and a holdover from the Reagan administration, was generally recognized as a top-flight professional without the ideological fervor of his predecessor, William Casey. At Treasury, Nicholas Brady, a personal friend of the president and a former U.S. senator, came from this moderate policy tradition, as did Carla Hills, the U.S. Trade Representative.

Despite the admiring characterizations of the administration's foreign policy advisors as "closely integrated and coherent" and "a parallel-minded team," few dissenters resided within the inner circle of advisors.[13] While the absence of such advisors may have appeared a problem, the personal Bush strategy of consulting widely diminished the potency of this criticism.

POLICY APPROACH
OF THE BUSH ADMINISTRATION

At the outset of the administration, President Bush called for a "policy review." The review process, centered in the National Security Council system, inevitably involved the entire foreign policy machinery. Moreover, it took almost four full months to complete and its results were mainly announced not through a single document, but through a series of speeches that Bush gave in April and May 1989.[14] While the speeches failed to reveal much in the way of foreign policy departures from the Reagan administration, they conveyed a positive approach toward working with the Soviet Union and Europe.

The Policy Review: Initial Ideas and Proposals

During the 1989 commencement address at Texas A&M University, President Bush spelled out his administration's approach for dealing with the Soviet Union and for the ending the Cold War. "We are approaching the conclusion of an historic postwar struggle between two visions: one of tyranny and conflict, and one of democracy and freedom. . . . And now, it is time to move beyond containment to a new policy for the 1990s—one that recognizes the full scope of changes taking place around the world and in the Soviet Union itself." His administration would therefore "seek the integration of the Soviet Union into the community of nations." To achieve that aim, President Bush outlined a number of changes in Soviet foreign policy that the United States would seek. First, the Soviet Union must change some of its global commitments (e.g., its support for the Sandinista regime in Nicaragua and its ties with Libya). Second, the Soviet Union must undertake several changes in Eastern Europe, including reducing Soviet troops there and tearing down the iron curtain. Third, the Soviet Union must work closely with the West in addressing conflicts in Central America, southern Africa, and the Middle East. Finally, it must also demonstrate a substantial commitment to political pluralism and human rights and must join with the United States in "addressing pressing global problems, including the international drug menace and dangers to the environment."

In response to these Soviet changes, the United States would seek completion of the START negotiations, move toward approving verification procedures to permit the implementation of two signed—but unratified—treaties between the United States and the Soviet Union limiting the size of nuclear tests, and support a renewal of the "open skies" policy between the two nations. Further, as soon as the Soviet Union reformed its emigration laws, the United States would seek a waiver of the requirements of the Jackson-Vanik Amendment for the Soviet Union, freeing up trade between the two countries.[15]

During another early address, President Bush was equally forthcoming with an expression of hope for a new era in Europe. Toward Eastern Europe, for instance, he applauded the emergence of democracy in Poland, offered various forms of assistance by the United States and the international community, and expressed a hope for more changes in Eastern Europe. Toward Western Europe, he expressed American support for the uniting of Europe into a single market in 1992, for the development of new mechanisms of consultation and cooperation with Europe, and for the maintenance of U.S. military forces in Europe "as long as they are wanted and needed to preserve the peace in Europe." Most important, on the occasion of the 40th anniversary of the NATO alliance, President Bush summarized his view of a new Europe in this way: "Let Europe be whole and free. . . . The Cold War began with the division of Europe. It can only end when Europe is whole."

Juxtaposed against this proposed strategy of Soviet-American cooperation and European integration, President Bush reaffirmed the commitment to a strong national security strategy for the 1990s largely consistent with the tradition of the Reagan administration. The United States would continue "to defend American interests in light of the enduring reality of Soviet military power." It would also seek to "curb the proliferation of advanced weaponry; . . . check the aggressive ambitions of renegade regimes; and . . . enhance the ability of our friends to defend themselves." Toward other areas, and particularly Third World trouble spots, the Bush administration was equally traditional in its approach, as revealed during the Persian Gulf War:

> In cases where the U.S. confronts much weaker enemies, our challenge will be not simply to defeat them, but to defeat them decisively and rapidly. . . . For small countries hostile to us, bleeding our forces in protracted or indecisive conflict or embarrassing us by inflicting damage on some conspicuous element of our forces may be victory enough, and could undercut political support for U.S. efforts against them.[16]

Early Actions: A Mix
of Moderation, Caution, and Realism

Unlike the bold speeches on the future of Eastern Europe and on ties with the Soviet Union or even the apparent advice on Third World trouble spots, the early policy actions of the Bush administration mainly reflected its impulses of pragmatism and moderation, albeit occasionally mixed with political realism. U.S. policy behavior in four major trouble spots reflected this policy mix and set the tone for the reaction of the Bush administration to the major political changes that occurred in Central Europe in late 1989 and throughout 1990.

In two early instances, the Bush administration reflected pragmatism and moderation in policy. The first involved policy accommodation with Congress over future support for the Nicaraguan Contras. Realizing that Congress was in no mood to provide further military support, the Bush administration quickly fashioned a bipartisan proposal that provided some support for the Contras, as the president wanted, and that committed the United States to the ongoing Central American peace, as Congress wanted.[17] The package called for $50 million of nonmilitary aid to the Contras, pledged the Bush administration to employ diplomatic and economic measures to pressure the Sandinistas to open up their political system, and allowed congressional involvement in suspending aid it deemed appropriate.[18] The second instance occurred in dealing with the ongoing civil war among the four parties competing to control the government of Cambodia. During the summer of 1990, in a sharp break with previous policy, the Bush administration withdrew its support from the three parties opposed to the Vietnamese-supported government in Cambodia and agreed to have direct talks with the Vietnamese government over the future of Cambodia.[19] This strategy, formulated in cooperation with the Soviet Union, was intended to motivate all parties to accept a UN peace plan for resolving the dispute, first through an internationally supervised cease-fire and then through an internationally supervised election. Indeed, within two months of this change in American policy, the four competing parties in Cambodia committed themselves to using the UN framework for settling the conflict.[20]

Policy accommodation, however, was not practiced everywhere by the Bush administration. Its actions toward Panama and the People's Republic of China reflected this pattern. For a number of years, the Panamanian government of General Manuel Antonio Noriega had been a source of annoyance and trouble for the Reagan administration, and then became so for the Bush administration. In February 1988, Noriega, a longtime CIA operative, was indicted on drug trafficking charges by a federal grand jury in Florida and was widely reported to be involved in numerous other unsavory international activities. Although the Reagan administration decided to impose economic sanctions on Panama and to use those and other economic measures as a way to force Noriega's resignation as the head of government,[21] none of its efforts proved successful. Once in office, the Bush administration continued these efforts. First, when Noriega nullified Panama's national election results in May 1989, the Bush administration asked the Organization of American States (OAS) to investigate. The OAS condemned the actions of the Noriega government and asked that he step down, but Noriega refused. Second, President Bush declared that Noriega's handpicked regime was illegitimate, called for the installation of the democratically elected government, and stated that the American ambassador to Panama, who had been called to Washington for consultations, would not return. In addition, Bush had earlier ordered more American forces into Panama, and, for political effect, the military had conducted exercises in Panama. All of these measures failed to budge Noriega's hold on power. Next, the Bush administration threw lukewarm support behind a coup attempt in October 1989, but it, too, failed within hours, much to the embarrassment of President Bush.[22] Finally, and as a last resort, President Bush ordered 13,000 American troops into Panama (in addition to the 11,000 already stationed at U.S. bases there) in December 1989. The invasion succeeded in a matter of days, and Noriega was captured and returned to the United States to stand trial on the drug trafficking charges. In essence, the Bush administration opted for and sustained a realistic approach in choosing the intervention course.

President Bush displayed the same reliance on political realism in his policy toward the People's Republic of China. During May and early June 1989, massive prodemocracy demonstrations, calling for political reforms within the country, occurred in Beijing and other Chinese cities. The Chinese government tolerated these demonstrations for a time, but it finally decided to put them down militarily. In a violent and bloody assault on the demonstrators in Beijing's Tiananmen Square, the Chinese military killed hundreds, and perhaps thousands, of demonstrators.[23] The Bush administration reacted initially by condemning the Chinese actions as violations of human rights and throwing its support behind the democracy movement within China. It immediately imposed a series of economic sanctions through an executive order; stopped arms sales; suspended visits between U.S. and Chinese military officials; offered humanitarian and medical assistance to those injured in the military crackdown; and instructed the U.S. immigration service to be sympathetic to Chinese students in the United States wishing to extend their stay. Yet, President Bush still wanted to maintain some ties with China, even in the context of continuing repression: "I understand the importance of the relationship with the Chinese people and the Government, it is in the interest of the United States to have good relations."[24] Indeed, the Bush administration vetoed legislation that would have allowed Chinese students to stay in the United States after their visas had expired, and it authorized high U.S. government officials to meet with Chinese officials, even though a ban on such visits was in effect.

POLITICAL CHANGE
AND EASTERN EUROPE

While Nicaragua, Cambodia, Panama, and China demonstrate the mixture of moderation and realism practiced by the Bush administration toward regional trouble spots, the imminent changes in Eastern Europe and within the Soviet Union were to pose the greatest challenge to its policy approach. Yet, in large measure, the Bush administration pursued the same policy mix, even as the Soviet Empire and the Soviet Union itself unraveled. Moderate and pragmatic responses, occasionally infused with doses of political realism, were still the governing principles.

The events of 1989 and 1990 can only be described as monumental in that they shook the foundations of U.S. foreign policy. In the space of less than two years, the Soviet Empire collapsed, with most of the states of Eastern Europe moving from socialist states to capitalist ones and from nondemocratic (Communist) states to democratic ones; the future of a divided Germany was resolved through reunification by the end of 1990; and, by the end of 1991, the Soviet Union itself was dissolved. In effect, the central issues of the Cold War—a divided Europe and Soviet-American antagonism—were seemingly resolved by these series of events.

The Collapse of the Soviet Empire

The initial changes within Eastern Europe began in Poland in early 1989.[25] Although *Solidarity,* the banned Polish trade union movement, had operated for many years in Poland, its success in gaining legal status by April 1989 rapidly set in motion the democratic reform process. By June 1989, Solidarity or Solidarity-backed candidates won all of the available seats in the lower house and 99 out of 100 seats in the upper house in free elections. By August 1989, a Solidarity member was chosen as the first non-Communist prime minister in an Eastern European state since the end of World War II, and a little more than a year later (November 1990), the founder of the Solidarity movement, Lech Walesa, was elected president.

Hungary and Czechoslovakia followed a similar pattern. In Hungary, the parliament took the first steps to guarantee individual liberties to its citizens in January 1989, and, by October 1989, it adopted a number of sweeping democratic reforms. Parliamentary elections were held in March and April 1990, with the democratic parties and their coalition partners capturing most of the seats. In Czechoslovakia, the change to democracy was even more rapid and equally nonviolent. While the first popular demonstrations for democracy occurred there later (November 1989) than elsewhere, once started, democratic change occurred quickly. By early December, Vaclav Havel, the playwright and leader of the reform movement, was named as president. By June 1990, free and democratic parliamentary elections were held in Czechoslovakia with democratic reform candidates faring very well.

In East Germany, pressures for democratic reform began as early as August 1989, when East Germans fled to West Germany, using Hungary, Czechoslovakia, and Austria as access routes, or sought asylum in the West German embassy in Czechoslovakia. By October 1989, the number of East Germans seeking asylum numbered almost 11,000. Popular demonstrations followed, and by March 1990, free and democratic elections were held in East Germany, with the conservative Alliance for Germany obtaining the greatest percentage of votes.

Nascent democratic movements characterized other Eastern European states, but their turn to democracy was slower and generally much less complete. Bulgaria, Romania, Yugoslavia, and Albania experienced calls for reform, but democratic reform was less assured in each case. Elections in Bulgaria, Romania, and Albania produced regimes that grew out of the former Communist parties or that were closely allied with them. Within the former Yugoslavia, a series of successor states emerged, but the degree of democratic reform was less certain immediately. Instead, intercommunal violence developed among the religious and ethnic groups within some of these new states (e.g., Bosnia) and between others (e.g., Serbia and Croatia).

The Unification of Germany

The unification of Germany was the second major Eastern European event of 1989–1990 and the one most directly related to the ending of the Cold War. Germany, which had been consciously divided by the victorious allies at the Yalta Conference in February 1945, and which had existed as two separate states from 1949 to 1990, was formally reunited on October 3, 1990.[26] Despite the pace of events elsewhere in Eastern Europe during the previous two years, both the ease and speed of this reunification—from mid-1989 through the end of 1990—were spectacular by any assessment. While the pressures for reunification began with the massive East German emigration to the West in August 1989, the opening of the Berlin Wall—the most tangible symbol of a divided city in a divided nation—on November 9, 1989, ignited even more calls for political reunification.

Despite Soviet President Mikhail Gorbachev's contention on November 15, 1989, that German unification "is not a matter of topical politics,"[27] West German Chancellor Helmut Kohl first proposed a "confederation" of the two Germanies in late November 1989. While the major wartime Allies—the United States, France, Britain, and the USSR—still retained rights over the future of Germany and, in particular, Berlin, this obstacle was quickly overcome. At a February 1990 meeting of the foreign ministers from these Allied countries and from East and West Germany, a formula was agreed upon for the eventual reunification of Germany. These so-called four plus two talks called for the two Germanys to discuss their plans for reunification and then to meet with the four Allied powers to resolve remaining security matters.

By May 1990, East and West Germany had worked out the terms for completing reunification. Existing borders were agreed upon; an economic union was initiated on July 1, 1990; a treaty setting out the legal and social bases of the new union was signed on August 31, 1990; a formal treaty among the Allied powers renouncing their rights and powers over German affairs was completed on September 12, 1990;[28] and formal reunification, under the name of the Federal Republic of Germany, took place on October 3, 1990.[29] Finally, democratic parliamentary elections across the unified German state were held in December 1990.

The Collapse of the Soviet Union

The Soviet Union itself was not immune to the changes that were sweeping Eastern Europe. While the changes in the Soviet state were not as rapid in 1989 and 1990 as they were elsewhere in Eastern Europe, change quickened by 1991, eventually producing the demise of the state itself. Initially, reform efforts were undertaken largely within the limits of maintaining a modified socialist system. In August 1991, however, the Soviet Union received a dramatic jolt: A coup attempt by Soviet hard-liners against the earlier reforms failed after three days, and internal change accelerated. Calls were now made for greater regional autonomy and greater democratization, and the future of the Soviet Union as a unified state appeared in doubt. By late 1991, moreover, the Baltic republics within the Soviet Union had achieved independence, and a looser confederation emerged among the Soviet republics. By December 1991, the Soviet Union itself collapsed. New nations replaced the former union and challenged long-held American thinking on foreign policy. These changes require more detail to appreciate their significance.

Prior to the August 1991 coup, two kinds of changes occurred within the Soviet Union: (1) efforts at institutionalizing democratic political reforms and Western-style market reforms; and (2) pressures for greater autonomy and even independence by some of the constituent republics. Indeed, democratic political reforms within the Soviet Union were essential parts of Mikhail Gorbachev's implementation of *glasnost* and *perestroika,* the mechanism for making the country more efficient and competitive globally (see Chapter 4). In March 1989, for example, in the freest election since the 1917 Revolution, voting was held for seats in the new legislative body, the Congress of People's Deputies.[30] Later in the year, an effort was even undertaken to eliminate the "leading role" of the Communist party in the Soviet Union.[31] Market reform progressed more slowly, but it, too, began. By the second half of 1990, a plan for a 500-day transition to a market economy was developed, but that one as well as less dramatic versions of it were shelved by the end of the year. During the last months of 1990 and early 1991, moreover, Gorbachev moved toward slowing down and even halting the political and economic liberalizations that he had initiated. Many of the internal reforms within the Soviet Union appeared stalled by the middle of 1991, and economic conditions worsened.

The other dramatic internal changes within the Soviet Union were the pressures for independence by several of the constituent republics. The three Baltic states of Latvia, Lithuania, and Estonia took the boldest steps in this regard by passing various measures declaring their independence or eventual independence from the central government in Moscow. In addition, other republics, such as Georgia and Armenia and even the largest Soviet republic, Russia, sought to achieve greater independence.

On the day prior to the signing of the proposed union treaty among the Soviet republics, a treaty in which greater power would have been dispersed to the constituent republics, a group of hard-line Communist party members and government officials (the "State Committee for the State of Emergency") deposed Mikhail Gorbachev and seized power briefly. The "three-day coup" (August 18–21, 1991) collapsed due to (1) massive protests in Moscow led by the popularly elected president of the Russian Republic, Boris Yeltsin, (2) the apparent failure of the KGB to attack the protestors surrounding the Russian parliament, and (3) the virtually unified international condemnation. Upon his return to power, Gorbachev called the failed coup "a majority victory for perestroika" and pledged "to move ahead democratically in all areas."[32] Ironically, though, the coup attempt had the effect of pressuring for more fundamental reform within the Soviet Union and further weakened the central government. With Gorbachev's power effectively curtailed in this new environment, he felt compelled to abandon his role as general secretary of the Communist party. Indeed, he called for a disbanding of the party itself because of its role in the coup. Furthermore, he consulted with the president of the Russian Republic, Boris Yeltsin, over the appointment of a number of key political offices and named several key officials from that republic to leadership posts within the central government.

Increased demands for independence by the constituent republics raised doubts about the future of the Soviet Union as a unified state. Within weeks of the coup, in fact, Lithuania, Latvia, and Estonia finally obtained their independence, and a new transitional confederative arrangement was devised between the central government and most of the republics. Eventually, a new constitution would be formulated for a new Soviet state structure, with more policy control to the constituent republics.[33] As with political change in Eastern Europe, the process of reform within the Soviet Union took on a life of its own, aided ironically by a coup that sought to topple the effort. By December 1991, the pressures for formal dissolution of the Soviet Union were rapidly building and, on December 25, 1991, the Soviet Union was formally dissolved, some 74 years after the Bolshevik Revolution of 1917.

AFTER THE COLD WAR: POLICY TOWARD CENTRAL EUROPE

Throughout the period of these changes in Central Europe and the Soviet Union, the Bush administration was largely an interested spectator, not an active participant. Its policy approach was to encourage change in Central Europe and in the Soviet Union without trying to shape it directly. The administration also was careful to avoid any actions that would embarrass the Soviet Union or the Eastern European governments as they sought to undertake change. Similarly, the United States sought to refrain from any actions that might appear as gloating over the extraordinary movement to democracy and capitalism in these countries. In short, its pragmatic and cautionary approach toward U.S. foreign policy remained intact, even in a context of dynamic and dramatic global change.

Perhaps indicative of the policy caution on the part of the United States was President Bush's restrained reaction on the day that the Berlin Wall was opened between East and West—undoubtedly one of the most dramatic moments in recent political history. Although President Bush claimed that he was "elated" by the development, he went on to justify his reserve by indicating that "I'm just not an emotional kind of guy," and that "We're handling this properly with the allies. . . ." Another administration official acknowledged the largely rhetorical nature of U.S. policy and argued for the measured American reaction to changing events: "I admit that when all is said and done it is a policy largely of stated desires and rhetoric. But what would you have us do? What we are dealing with in Eastern Europe, and to a lesser extent in the Soviet Union, is a revolutionary situation."[34]

Once these revolutionary changes were well under way, however, the Bush administration did outline tangible policy positions toward Central Europe, the reunification of Germany, and future relations with the Soviet Union. Toward Central Europe, the principal policy response was to provide some economic assistance to these new democracies and to encourage other European states (and particularly the European Community) to do so as well. The funds would aid efforts to stabilize the economy; foster private enterprise; provide food aid, trade credits, and environmental funds; and support agricultural programs, technical training, and scholarship and exchanges with the United States.[35]

Toward the future of Germany, the Bush administration added elements of realism to its accommodative stance, especially after the collapse of the Berlin Wall in November 1989. Beginning as early as December 1989, the Bush administration adopted the view that German reunification should proceed, that Germany's full sovereignty should be restored, and that other states (including the United States) would necessarily lose some of their rights over German territory. Somewhat later, it also made clear that it would accept only a reunified Germany that allowed the state to remain a full member of NATO.[36] This clear policy position proved significant in bringing about a unified Germany. In this respect, the Bush administration had clearly decided on its view of Germany's future and the kind of Central Europe that it sought.

AFTER THE COLD WAR: POLICY TOWARD THE SOVIET UNION

Toward the Soviet Union, and prior to its implosion, the Bush administration's policy was cautiously optimistic, albeit not fully developed. The administration sought first to end the Cold War formally and then to establish the foundation for a long-term cooperative relationship with the Soviet Union. In 1989 and 1990, two major summits were held, and important agreements were signed to reach the first goal; and several agreements and understandings on political, military, and economic cooperation were initiated to move toward the second goal. The Malta Summit was held in November 1989, and proved to be a watershed conference in ending the Cold War between the United States and the Soviet Union. As President Gorbachev indicated at that summit: "The world leaves one epoch of cold war and enters another epoch" and "the characteristics of the cold war should be abandoned."[37] At Malta, too, the Bush administration and the Soviet leadership committed themselves to make rapid progress on nuclear and conventional arms control. The Bush administration also threw its support behind the internal reforms initiated within the Soviet Union and pledged to assist the Soviet Union in joining the world economy.[38] In a matter of months, the Soviet Union gained observer status in the General Agreement on Tariffs and Trade (GATT) with U.S. assistance.[39] If the Malta Summit set the tone for the end of the Cold

War and for future relations, the leaders took several concrete steps to solidify the new relationship at the June 1990 Washington Summit. Agreements were signed (1) calling for the destruction of a substantial portion of each nation's chemical arsenal by the year 2002, (2) pledging both parties to accelerate negotiation on the Strategic Arms Reduction Treaty (START) and the Conventional (i.e., nonnuclear) Arms Forces in Europe (CFE) Treaty, and (3) initiating several cultural exchange pacts between the countries.[40]

Toward the end of 1990, the Bush administration made three other important commitments that served as the capstone for the ending of the Cold War in Central Europe and setting the stage for European politics for the 1990s and beyond.[41] First, at the Conference on Security and Cooperation in Europe (CSCE) in November 1990, the United States and its NATO allies and the Soviet Union and its Warsaw Pact allies signed the Conventional Armed Forces in Europe (CFE) Treaty, which provided for a substantial reduction in conventional forces on both sides. Second, these states also signed a declaration of nonaggression between the two sides to end, officially, the Cold War. Third, the parties to the CSCE (which includes the United States, Canada, and virtually all European states) signed an agreement to give the CSCE a greater role in future European affairs.

Yet another sign of the importance that the Bush administration attached to the new relationship with the Soviet Union was signaled with its attitude and policy toward the Soviet Union's effort to dissuade the Baltic Republics (Lithuania, Latvia, and Estonia) from pursuing independence in the spring of 1990 and the winter of 1991. In two instances, the Gorbachev government used economic sanctions and Soviet troops to stop these efforts. Although the Bush administration decried these actions, it did not do much more. In effect, the Bush administration's commitment to political realism and maintaining good relations with the Soviet Union was more important than supporting the independence of republics within that union.

In July 1991, the Bush administration took two additional policy steps—one military, another economic—as part of its effort to maintain good relations with the Soviet Union. In the military area, President Bush and President Gorbachev met after the London economic summit among leaders of the industrial democracies (United States, France, Britain, Canada, Germany, Italy, Japan, and the European Community) and completed work in principle on a Strategic Arms Reduction Treaty (START).[42] (The agreement was formally signed about two weeks later at a hastily arranged summit in Moscow.) Under this agreement, the first in which the long-range nuclear arsenals of the two superpowers would actually be reduced, each side would trim the number of nuclear warheads and the number of nuclear delivery vehicles (land-based missiles, sea-based missiles, and intercontinental bombers) in their arsenals. Document Summary 5.1 provides details on this treaty. In the economic area, another agreement, also completed after the London economic summit, called for economic assistance for the Soviet Union by the industrial democracies. While these countries would not provide immediate financial aid to the Soviet Union, they did agree upon several different measures to aid the economic reform under way there. These included "special association" status for the Soviet Union with the International Monetary Fund

Document Summary 5.1   Key Components
of the Strategic Arms Reduction Treaty, July 1991

Limitations on Numbers of Nuclear Warheads and Delivery Vehicles

	United States	USSR
Total nuclear delivery vehicles (land-based and sea-based ballistic missiles and intercontinental bombers) allowed	1,600	1,600
Total accountable warheads on all nuclear delivery vehicles allowed	6,000	6,000
Total warheads on land-based or sea-based ballistic missiles allowed	4,900	4,900
Total warheads allowed on mobile land-based missiles	1,100	1,100
Nuclear warheads not covered by the treaty	c. 4,400	c. 2,000

Inspection and Verification Provisions
- Exchange of information between the United States and the USSR on all strategic offensive weapons would take place prior to treaty signing.
- Twelve types of on-site inspections would be allowed under the agreement.
- Several types of cooperative procedures will be implemented to ensure verification.

Duration and Implementation of the Treaty
The treaty will be implemented over a seven–year period and will last for fifteen years. It may be continued in intervals of five years thereafter.

SOURCES: Eric Schmitt, "Senate Approval and Sharp Debate Seen," *New York Times,* July 19, 1991, A5 (including the accompanying table entitled "New Limits on Strategic Weapons"); and Office of Public Affairs, U.S. Arms Control and Disarmament Agency, "Strategic Arms Reduction Talks," *Issues Brief,* April 25, 1991.

and the World Bank, cooperation between the Soviet Union and all international economic institutions, the restoration of trade between the Soviet Union and its Central European neighbors, and closer contacts among the leaders of the industrial democracies and the Soviet Union.[43] While these actions may not have gone as far as the Soviet Union had initially hoped, they represented an extraordinary change in the economic relationship among the United States, the West, and the Soviet Union.

In the aftermath of the August coup within the Soviet Union and with the movement to a more confederative state in late 1991, the Bush administration faced calls to initiate new and wider economic and political ties with the constituent republics and the newly independent Baltic states. The Bush administration proceeded with diplomatic recognition for Lithuania, Latvia, and Estonia, albeit after several European states and the European Community had done so,[44] and promised to supply humanitarian aid to the Soviet Union as needed, albeit to the constituent republics, not the central government.[45] Yet, there were limits as to how far it would go in providing massive economic assistance. In general, the Bush administration did not deviate from its policy announced after the London summit which, in effect, withheld economic aid until significant and sustained policy reforms were carried out.

THE SEARCH FOR A
NEW WORLD ORDER?

With the international politics of the post–World War II period forever altered by the collapse of the Soviet Empire and the Soviet Union, the Bush administration sought to devise a new rationale and direction for U.S. foreign policy. The change was first hinted at in an address that President Bush gave to the UN General Assembly in September 1989, but it was more fully outlined in speeches to a joint session of Congress in September 1990, and the State of the Union address in January 1991, after Iraq's invasion of Kuwait.[46] The future direction, President Bush said, was to build "a new world order."[47]

President Bush described the new world order in this way: "a new era—freer from the threat of terror, stronger in the pursuit of justice, and more secure in the quest for peace, an era in which the nations of the world, East and West, North and South, can prosper and live in harmony." Such a world would be different from the one that had existed over the past 45 years. It would be "a world where the rule of law supplants the rule of the jungle, a world in which nations recognize the shared responsibility for freedom and justice, a world where the strong respect the rights of the weak."[48] In his State of the Union address, President Bush summarized this new world order as a condition "where diverse nations are drawn together in common cause to achieve the universal aspirations of mankind: peace and security, freedom, and the rule of law."[49]

Yet, President Bush was quick to add that the United States had a special role to play in creating this new world:

> For two centuries, America has served the world as an inspiring example of freedom and democracy. For generations, America has led the struggle to preserve and extend the blessings of liberty. . . . American leadership is indispensable. . . . we have a unique responsibility to the hard work of freedom.[50]

The new world order that the Bush administration envisioned, in effect, represented a reaffirmation of the traditional values that had shaped the birth of the nation and its foreign policy actions in its earliest years (see Chapter 1). Unlike the foreign policy at the beginning of the republic, however, the emphasis on traditional values was coupled with a commitment to sustained American involvement. In both tone and emphasis, moreover, the new world order of the Bush administration had the ring of Wilsonian idealism, which emphasized the League of Nations and collective security at the end of World War I. With the demise of the old order, the Cold War system, the new world order of the Bush administration envisioned an order grounded in the cooperation of all states and based upon greater involvement of the collective security actions of the United Nations. To be sure, Bush did not convey the same fervor in calling for this new system as had Wilson, and he continued to embrace the principles of political realism from time to time. Nonetheless, Bush did see his approach as an important departure from America's recent past (Cold War) behavior. His search to create a new world order quickly faced at least three major tests: the Iraqi invasion of Kuwait, the formation of policy toward a post Communist Russia, and the new challenges from global disorder in Bosnia, Somalia, and Haiti.

The Persian Gulf War

The event that sparked the effort to think about a new world order was Iraqi president Saddam Hussein's invasion of Kuwait on August 2, 1990. Iraq's action raised the question of whether the initial cooperation between the United States and the (then) Soviet Union could be sustained in another arena and whether the global community could rally around a common task. As events were to unfold, the first test of the new world order appeared to succeed: Soviet-American cooperation was sustained; the global community was largely supportive of this effort as well; and aggression was reversed.

In some respects, the vigorous response of the Bush administration to Iraq's action may have been unexpected. On the one hand, the United States had sought to better relations with Iraq during the 1980s: Diplomatic relations had been restored in 1984, after being ruptured since 1967, and the United States had "tilted" toward Iraq during the Iran–Iraq War from 1980–1988. On the other hand, the Reagan administration had its quarrels with Iraq: It had been displeased over Iraq's apparent mistaken attack upon the USS *Stark* in the Persian Gulf in May 1987, resulting in the death of 37 American sailors, and it had protested to Iraq in 1988 over its use of chemical weapons against its Kurdish ethnic minority.[51]

In keeping with its realist principles, however, the Bush administration decided early on to try to foster better relations with Iraq for both strategic and economic reasons. Iraq's location in the Persian Gulf area was important in efforts at achieving stability in the region, and its considerable oil reserves made Iraq crucial for global energy concerns. When Congress sought in early 1990 to enact economic sanctions against the Iraqi government over its abysmal human rights policy and the apparent effort to develop weapons of mass destruction, the administration argued against such an option.[52] Later, in the summer of 1990, when Iraq complained that Kuwait was responsible for keeping oil prices low (and hence hurting the Iraqi economy) by overproducing its oil quota, called for an OPEC meeting to raise oil prices, and threatened an invasion of Kuwait, the Bush administration's policy position did not really change. Furthermore, in testimony on Capitol Hill only days before the intervention, the administration did not issue any warning when asked about a possible Iraqi invasion into Kuwait.[53]

Despite the Bush administration's equivocal attitude in the summer of 1990, its response to the Iraqi invasion was immediate: It condemned the Iraqi action and called for its withdrawal from Kuwait, froze all Iraqi and Kuwaiti assets in the United States, and imposed a trade embargo on Iraq as well. The European Community and the Arab League condemned the invasion, too. Most important, the Soviet Union joined the United States in opposing the action in a joint statement issued by Secretary of State James Baker and Soviet Foreign Minister Eduard Shevardnadze.[54] A few weeks later, President Bush and President Gorbachev arranged a meeting in Helsinki, Finland, to deal with this crisis and concluded by jointly

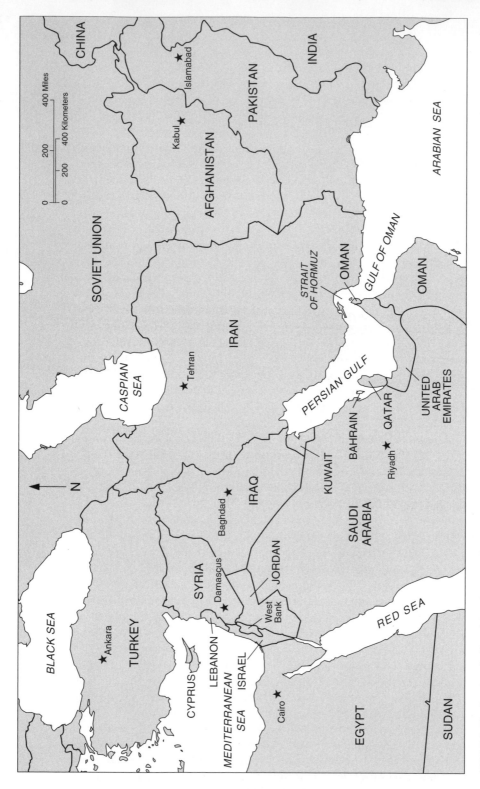

MAP 5.1 The Persian Gulf and Southwest Asia

stating that "Iraq's aggression must not be tolerated."[55] Within a matter of a few weeks, about 100 nations had condemned Iraq's invasion of Kuwait.

On August 8, 1990, the Bush administration announced that it was sending about 150,000 American forces into Saudi Arabia and the surrounding region for the purpose of helping that country defend its homeland against possible Iraqi aggression. President Bush outlined four policy goals that the United States sought to achieve in taking this action against Iraq: (1) "the immediate, unconditional, and complete withdrawal of all Iraqi forces from Kuwait"; (2) "the restoration of Kuwait's legitimate government"; (3) the protection of American citizens in Iraq and Kuwait; and (4) the achievement of "security and stability" in the Persian Gulf.[56] Two days later, the Arab League also voted to send forces to Saudi Arabia to stop further Iraqi aggression.[57] Within a matter of weeks, at least 28 nations from virtually every continent had sent forces to Saudi Arabia on behalf of this effort to deter further Iraqi aggression and to get Iraq out of Kuwait as well. Other nations (e.g., Germany and Japan) pledged financial assistance.[58]

The UN Security Council also quickly took concerted actions against the Iraqi government over its invasion of Kuwait. Within hours of the invasion, the Security Council condemned the invasion and further demanded the immediate withdrawal of Iraq. In all, the UN Security Council passed 10 resolutions against Iraq's invasion of Kuwait over the next several months. The resolutions sought to tighten the economic and political noose around Iraq to force it to leave Kuwait. They imposed mandatory economic sanctions against Iraq, invalidated Iraq's annexation of Kuwait, and condemned Iraq's holding of foreign nationals and diplomats. They also expanded the embargo to include sea and air embargoes as well. What was remarkable about these actions was not only their rapidity but also the unanimity among the permanent members on the Security Council (the United States, the Soviet Union, Britain, China, and France), a phenomenon rarely evident during the Cold War years.

On November 29, 1990, the Security Council passed its most significant resolution. It authorized member states "to use all necessary means to uphold and implement" the previous UN resolutions unless Iraq left Kuwait by January 15, 1991.[59] In effect, this resolution authorized the nations of the world to use force to expel Iraq from Kuwait. This call for collective security was only the second time in which the UN Security Council has authorized such action (the other was over the North Korean invasion of South Korea in 1950). When Iraq failed to leave Kuwait by the January 15 deadline and after the U.S. Congress had given the president the authority to use American forces to implement this UN resolution, the anti-Iraq coalition, now totaling over a half million troops, initiated a massive bombing attack against Iraq.

While it initially failed to budge the Iraqis, by mid-February, Iraq agreed to withdraw from Kuwait, albeit with conditions attached. The anti-Iraq coalition, led by the Bush administration, rejected that plan and imposed a 24-hour ultimatum on February 22, 1991, for the Iraqis to begin to leave Kuwait. When the deadline passed unanswered, the allied coalition mounted a massive ground, air, and sea assault to drive Iraq out. On February 27, 1991, President Bush declared that "Kuwait is liberated" and announced the suspension of hostilities beginning at midnight on February 28, officially ending the Hundred Hours War.

On March 3, 1991, the United Nations Security Council passed a resolution ending the hostilities and placing responsibilities upon the Iraqis for their invasion of Kuwait; on the same day, military commanders met in southern Iraq to formalize the terms of the military cease-fire and to work out arrangements for the exchange of prisoners of war.[60] Finally, on April 3, 1991, the United Nations Security Council passed a resolution formally ending the war and requiring Iraq to (1) destroy all of its chemical and biological weapons and ballistic missile systems with a range of more than 150 kilometers, (2) pay reparations to Kuwait, (3) reject support for international terrorism, (4) "not . . . acquire or develop nuclear weapons, and (5) respect the sovereignty of Kuwait.[61]

Ensuring a lasting peace within Iraq, and the region generally, ultimately proved more difficult than winning the short war. Almost immediately after the coalition victory, rebellions broke out in the north and south of Iraq.[62] In the north, the Kurdish people, an ethnic minority, rebelled against the Iraqi government but failed. In the south, the Shiite population, a religious Muslim minority, attempted to rebel against the authorities in Baghdad, but they too failed. Yet, the victors, and particularly the United States and NATO forces, imposed "no-fly zones" in the north and the south of Iraq to ensure the safety of these minority populations. They also sought to have UN inspectors investigate whether Iraqi facilities were producing nuclear materials, albeit with limited success (as succeeding American administrations would soon discover). Still, the first test of the new world order appeared to have been met with a unified international coalition freeing Kuwait from Iraqi intervention.

Relations with a Post-Communist Russia

A second test of the new order arose over devising an appropriate set of policies toward Russia and the other successor states of the old Soviet Union. In keeping with the instincts of the Bush administration, the policies were cautionary and pragmatic in both the economic and political-military areas, but significant commitments were made. By April 1992, the Bush administration decided to make a greater commitment to providing economic assistance to Russia and Ukraine, prodded on by its Group of Seven (G-7) partners; and, by the end of the Bush administration, another dramatic nuclear arms reduction agreement, the START II treaty, was completed with Russia.

On the diplomatic front, the Bush administration moved quickly to establish diplomatic ties with the new republics and to foster closer ties with President Boris Yeltsin of Russia. In February 1992, Presidents Bush and Yeltsin held discussions at Camp David, Maryland, on nuclear arms and on aid to Russia, and U.S. Secretary of State James Baker visited Moldova, Armenia, Azerbaijan, Tajikistan, and Uzbekistan to begin the normalization of relations with these new republics.[63] The highlight of these diplomatic efforts between Moscow and Washington was the June 16–17, 1992, summit conference between President Bush and President Yeltsin in Washington. The summit produced the outlines for a further reduction in nuclear weapons held by the two countries (what was to become the START II treaty), enabled President Yeltsin to speak to the U.S. Congress and request American assistance for Russia, and allowed for the development of vari-

---

Document Summary 5.2   Key Components of the START II Treaty

	START II Phase One	START II Phase Two
Total Strategic Warheads	3,800–4,250	3,000–3,500
MIRVed land-based missile warheads	1,200	0
Submarine-launched ballistic missile warheads	2,160	1,700–1,750
Heavy land-based missile warheads	650	0
Total strategic nuclear delivery vehicles	1,600	1,600

SOURCE: Abstracted from *U.S. Department of State Dispatch*, Vol. 4, no. 1, January 4, 1993, p. 6.

---

ous bilateral agreements dealing with cooperation in outer space, curbs on weapons of mass destruction, and American business activities in Russia.[64]

In the military area, two important actions were completed in 1992 and early 1993. In May 1992, a protocol to the START treaty was signed in Lisbon, Portugal, to recognize that the Soviet Union, as the original signatory of the treaty, had broken up, and the new states had to be incorporated into the pact.[65] After the June summit, too, final negotiations on the START II treaty were also completed (although they took longer than perhaps anticipated), and the final document was officially signed on January 3, 1993, about two weeks before President Bush left office. Under the pact, the United States and Russia would be required to reduce the number of strategic nuclear warheads to at least 3,500, in two phases, by 2003.[66] In addition, it called for the elimination of all multiple (or MIRVed) warheads on land-based missiles, prohibited warheads on either country's "heavy" (or the largest) land-based missiles, and maintained the total number of "strategic nuclear delivery vehicles" (or launchers) at 1,600. In an important stipulation, however, START had to be fully implemented before START II would come into effect. See Document Summary 5.2.

There was also progress in the economic area. In 1991 and early 1992, President Bush had been criticized for his failure to be more responsive to Soviet (and then Russian) requests for assistance.[67] Undoubtedly prodded in part by that criticism, President Bush announced on April 1, 1992, that the United States would participate in a $24 billion assistance program developed by the Group of Seven (G-7) to aid Russia. The plan was characterized "as a way for the United States and its allies to prevent economic collapse in Russia and stop a new authoritarianism from rising from the rubble of the Soviet empire."[68] This American aid plan was eventually written into law with the passage of the Freedom Support Act in October 1992. Under this legislation, the United States committed itself to provide $410 million in aid, authorized a $12.3 billion increase in its support of the International Monetary Fund as a mechanism to aid Russia and the other former Soviet republics, supported a $3 billion multilateral effort to stabilize the Russian currency, and offered various ways of increasing American cooperation and support for the former Soviet republics. In a unique feature, the Freedom Support Act authorized $800 million from the U.S. defense budget to help the former

Soviet republics dismantle nuclear weapons and other weapons of mass destruction.[69] These various components of the Freedom Support Act of 1992 reflected how far economic and political cooperation between the former Soviet Union and the United States had progressed in less than a year.

New Global Disorders: Bosnia, Haiti, and Somalia

The third major test in creating a new global order was over the direction of American policy toward new global disorders. Three particular problems captured the attention of the Bush administration and epitomized the difficulty confronting American foreign policy after the Cold War: the outbreak of ethnic fighting in Bosnia, the overthrow of democracy in Haiti, and the scourge of starvation in Somalia. The American response was different in each case. As a result, no clear direction appeared in U.S. foreign policy, which raised questions about the role of the United States in this new world order.

Bosnia Ethnic fighting in the former Yugoslavia erupted quickly after the end of the Cold War. With the declaration of independence by several constituent republics of that former country (e.g., Slovenia, Croatia, and Bosnia-Herzogovina in 1991 and 1992) and the determination of Serbia to maintain control of the former Yugoslav government and much of its territory, fighting among the differing ethnic and religious factions within Croatia and Bosnia quickly broke out. By early 1992, an uneasy truce was in place in Croatia, but by April 1992, an ethnic war erupted in Bosnia. The Bosnia conflict, moreover, would become the focal point of attention for the American administrations for the next several years. The fighting was among three major groups: Bosnian Serbs, Bosnian Muslims, and Bosnian Croats. In addition, there was a war between the Serbian government and the newly created Bosnian government, with the former seeking to extend greater Serbia and the latter seeking to maintain its independence.

The initial impulse of the Bush administration was to try to hold Yugoslavia together. It was reluctant to grant diplomatic recognition to the newly independent states carved out of the former Yugoslavia and instead sought a negotiated outcome. As acting Secretary of State Lawrence Eagleburger said, "the [Yugoslav] republics' unilateral and uncoordinated declarations of independence, which we unsuccessfully opposed, led inexorably to civil war."[70] The preferred policy was to have the parties negotiate a settlement and to have the Europeans (through the European Union, for example) and the United Nations take the lead in assisting the conflicting parties. While the United States eventually supported UN sanctions on Yugoslavia and the imposition of a NATO-run "no-fly zone" over Bosnia as mechanisms to stop the fighting and achieve a peaceful outcome, the Bush administration was unwilling to do much more. Indeed, Secretary of State James Baker declared that "we don't have a dog in that fight." By that assessment, the United States would limit its actions in aiding the restoration of peace and stability in the new era.[71]

Haiti In Haiti, however, the Bush administration faced another kind of post–Cold War problem, the promotion and maintenance of democracy. Here, it adopted a different response. In September 1991, the democratically elected government of President Jean-Bertrand Aristide was overthrown in a military-led coup.[72] While the United States was committed to Aristide's restoration, the Bush administration primarily limited its action to diplomatic and economic measures. The administration, for example, cut off economic assistance to Haiti and froze Haitian government assets in the United States. In turn, after the Organization of American States (OAS) enacted a trade embargo against Haiti, the Bush administration followed suit by participating in the embargo. Despite these and other efforts, no progress was made in restoring democracy, and the Bush administration was disinclined to do more.

By early 1992, another, and more complicating, problem arose over Haiti. Haitian refugees, seeking to flee the failing economy and the brutal regime there, took to a variety of boats and vessels in an attempt to reach American shores for asylum. Despite other efforts to help the Haitians, the Bush administration ultimately ordered the U.S. Coast Guard to stop the vessels and return them with their occupants to Haiti. By the end of the Bush administration, democracy had not been restored to Haiti, and the Haitian refugees had become a presidential campaign issue. The United States and the Bush administration were clearly limiting their actions in promoting and maintaining democracy after the Cold War.

Somalia The unrest in Somalia raised yet a third type of post–Cold War issue for the United States and a third type of response.[73] With the breakdown of the government within Somalia—and despite the efforts of international aid providers—starvation was rampant in that country by 1992. Estimates of death by starvation ranged up to 350,000. Relief convoys were systematically hijacked by rival "clans" within Somalia, and several cities and outlying villages simply were not receiving food aid. In July 1992, the United Nations acted and authorized the sending of UN peacekeepers to Somalia to aid the humanitarian efforts. At the time, too, the Bush administration authorized American military transport aircraft to help with the relief process. Despite these efforts, the situation continued to deteriorate in Somalia.

By early December 1992, the UN Security Council passed a resolution authorizing the United States to lead an effort to provide humanitarian assistance to Somalia. In an action dubbed "Operation Restore Hope," the Bush administration decided to intervene militarily. The administration directed that 28,000 American troops be sent to Somalia to make certain that humanitarian assistance reached the neediest people. While this action was carefully limited to providing food assistance and was successful initially, the Clinton administration would later expand the mission, and problems would develop.

CHALLENGES AND RESPONSES
TO THE NEW WORLD ORDER

Somalia evoked a markedly different response by the Bush administration to global disorders than had occurred in the earlier two cases. Was Somalia, then, the emerging model for establishing a new global order, or was the Bush administration's basic pragmatism operating in all of these instances after the Cold War? To many of the Bush administration's critics, of course, the answer was the latter. A coherent post–Cold War foreign policy had not been developed, and an ad hoc foreign policy approach remained. Despite these criticisms, former acting Secretary of State Lawrence Eagleburger, as he was leaving office, defended the efforts of the Bush administration to create a new world order.[74] Indeed, he argued that the administration did much more than it was credited with in pointing the way to a future foreign policy course for the United States. Moreover, he argued that the administration's alleged "ad hocism" in foreign policy was "a virtue, not a vice."

In particular, Eagleburger contended that the Bush administration successfully met three challenges. First, the Bush administration ended the Cold War peacefully by dealing with several major crises successfully—ranging from the democratic revolution in Eastern Europe to the reunification of Germany to the collapse of the Soviet Union. Second, the administration dealt with the "instabilities generated by the Cold War's demise" (e.g., the Persian Gulf War and Yugoslavia). Third, and what some may overlook, the Bush administration started the process of reform of the global institutions in terms of paving the way for the future. In particular, Eagleburger had in mind the development of NAFTA (the North American Free Trade Agreement), the trade organization among the United States, Canada, and Mexico; the creation of the Group of 24 [G-24] developed countries aiding Central and Eastern Europe; and the emergence of APEC (Asia-Pacific Economic Cooperation), an organization of 18 nations initially stretching across the Pacific from China and Japan in Northeast Asia to Australia and New Zealand, and to the United States and Canada. These largely economic organizations would be pivotal for the future. In short, Eagleburger argued, "there was a strategy behind the President's conduct of foreign policy" and "a certain degree of 'ad hocery' is a virtue, not a vice, when you are dealing with a world in crisis and chaos. . . ."

VALUES AND BELIEFS
OF THE CLINTON ADMINISTRATION

Unlike the ad hoc foreign policy pursued by the Bush administration, the Clinton administration was determined to have a foreign policy rooted in a clear set of principles, derived from America's past, guided by a coherent and workable strategy, and appropriate to the end of the Cold War. Domestic policy and foreign policy would be tied together in its approach, since only by shoring up America's economic and social strength at home would the United States be in a position to have an effective economic and security policy abroad. Indeed, candidate Clinton summarized his unified policy approach in this way: "We must tear down the wall in our thinking between domestic and foreign policy."[75]

Although American administrations often come into office with a commitment to a particular foreign policy approach, most have had to alter that approach during their years in power. For some administrations, this shift has occurred from the first to the second term; for others, it has occurred in response to dramatic domestic and international events; and for still others, it has occurred in response to the electoral cycle or the rhythms of domestic politics. In this respect, the Clinton administration was no different and the changes in value emphasis over the two terms of the Clinton administration are especially important to understand the direction of America's foreign policy after the Cold War and at the end of the twentieth century. Part of the explanation for these changes in the Clinton approach derive from the changing level of presidential interest in foreign policy and the changes in some of his advisors, but part of the explanation comes from the changing domestic and international environment that the administration faced. In the following sections, we discuss these factors as they relate to the change in foreign policy approach during the Clinton years.

Clinton, Foreign Policy, and His Foreign Policy Advisors

Unlike President Bush, who came to foreign policy with a broad background and interest, President Clinton, by virtually all accounts, was largely uninterested in foreign policy making. Indeed, his foreign policy background prior to assuming office was primarily confined to his two years at Oxford University, some travels in Western and Eastern Europe, and his personal anguish over American involvement in the Vietnam War. By contrast, his interest and involvement in a variety of domestic issues (e.g., educational reform, economic development) as governor of Arkansas were considerable. Thus, while Clinton may have justifiably been described as a policy wonk on domestic issues, that label was surely less accurate on foreign policy issues. Indeed, his initial attitude toward foreign policy was perhaps best summarized by what the political writer Elizabeth Drew identified as the task given to Anthony Lake, Clinton's campaign foreign policy advisor and later his first national security advisor: "Keep foreign policy from becoming a problem—keep it off the screen and spare Clinton from getting embroiled as he went about his domestic business." One senior administration official acknowledged the accuracy of this assessment in 1993: "We had hoped to keep foreign policy submerged."[76]

With President Clinton's limited interest in foreign policy and his apparent desire to keep foreign policy "submerged," the composition of his first foreign policy team thus became crucial for the development and implementation of his foreign policy agenda. Although Clinton had committed himself to appoint a cabinet that would "look like America" and did give some consideration to this idea, the top foreign policy posts of his first cabinet seemed more narrowly drawn: a very large number of previous foreign policy participants who had served in the Carter administration (e.g., Warren Christopher as secretary of state, Anthony Lake as national security advisor, and William Perry, his second secretary of defense), a few with Capitol Hill experience (most notably, the initial appointment of Les Aspin as secretary of defense and Madeleine Albright as U.S. ambassador to the United Nations), and some personal and campaign friends (e.g., Mickey Kantor as United States Trade Representative, Ron Brown as secretary of commerce, Samuel [Sandy] Berger as deputy national security advisor to Lake, and Strobe Talbott, first as ambassador at large for Russia, and later as deputy secretary of state).

By virtually all assessments, however, this foreign policy team, at least through the first two years of Clinton's initial term, had considerable difficulty developing policy, explaining it to the American people, and dealing with pressing global issues. After the appointment of William Perry to replace Les Aspin, a biting commentary in the British weekly *The Economist* noted that this appointment had now produced a "stealth" foreign policy team for the Clinton administration. It was comprised of "the little-known Mr. Perry, the camera-shy Anthony Lake, and the low-profile Warren Christopher as secretary of state." Each one seemingly competed, the analysts claimed, "for invisibility." Yet, "all too visible . . . are the global troubles they will have to cope with."[77]

While this description is surely overdrawn, it conveys the nagging personnel problem that the Clinton administration confronted in the foreign policy arena, especially early in its first term. "The whole national security apparatus of the President was in terrible disarray," in 1993 and 1994, as one later assessment put it. "There was poor central direction from the White House and a weak N.S.C. [National Security Council] staff—the worst since the first Reagan administration. They didn't know what they didn't know."[78] American foreign policy was being developed by a cacophony of voices without a strong leader or a strong spokesperson, resulting in a seemingly incoherent foreign policy to address the post–Cold War world. This difficulty was compounded somewhat by a president who appeared too detached to make foreign policy work effectively and by global events like Bosnia, Haiti, Somalia, and Russia that would not let the Clinton administration isolate foreign from domestic policy.[79]

While the performance of Christopher, Lake, and Perry improved from 1995 onward, and they enjoyed some foreign policy successes over Bosnia, Haiti, and the Middle East, the direction of American foreign policy remained unsteady, and a target of criticism. A frequent critic, Senator John McCain (R-Arizona), continued to fault the Clinton administration for its lack of "strategic coherence" in dealing with foreign policy, its "self-doubt" over the direction of American policy direction abroad, and its failure to identify key American interests in carrying out policy.[80]

For the second term, some changes were made. First of all, by then, Clinton had become more fully engaged in the foreign policy process and increasingly looked to it as a way to leave his mark on American policy. Indeed, some critics charged that the administration used foreign policy actions to deflect criticism from the domestic turmoil over the Lewinsky sex scandal and impeachment actions that surrounded President Clinton in 1997 and 1998. Second, President Clinton's foreign policy team changed, although it continued to draw from veterans of the Carter administration and close friends. Still, it now contained several individuals with foreign policy experience from Clinton's first term and with broader foreign policy views and experiences than those involved initially. To replace the relatively taciturn Warren Christopher as secretary of state, President Clinton chose Madeleine Albright, who served as American ambassador to the

United Nations during the first term. His new CIA director was George J. Tenet, the deputy director of the CIA at the time, and a former National Security Council staffer and Senate Intelligence Committee staff director. Anthony Lake's deputy and Clinton's longtime personal friend, Sandy Berger, assumed the national security advisor post. To replace Secretary of Defense William Perry, President Clinton chose retiring Republican senator William Cohen, a longtime student of defense and intelligence policy in the Senate. That appointment also reflected an attempt to reach across party lines to shape a bipartisan foreign and defense policy with Congress, especially since Cohen had been a frequent defender of congressional prerogatives in foreign affairs.[81]

This new foreign policy team was characterized as solid (rather than distinguished) in their foreign policy credentials. Yet still this team had its bumps along the road in creating a consistent and coherent foreign policy and increasingly turned away from the idealism of the early Clinton years to greater reliance on political realism as a foreign policy guide. To be sure, Madeleine Albright, the first woman secretary of state in American history, was a more articulate and outspoken secretary than Christopher had been. In this way, she was better able to explain the direction of foreign policy to the American public and the American Congress. Furthermore, Albright seemingly was able to rally more support internationally for the direction to be pursued by the United States. The new national security advisor, Sandy Berger, for the most part worked in an accommodative way with Albright, but, as with all recent national security advisors, came to dominate the foreign policy decision apparatus.[82] In some ways, the success of this team in forging a coherent and consistent policy hinged on the relationship between Berger and Albright, which often proved to be an admixture of competition and cooperation.

THE EVOLVING CLINTON ADMINISTRATION APPROACH TO FOREIGN POLICY

The Clinton administration displayed a shifting set of foreign policy priorities and approaches during its years in office, shaped by these advisors and by changing domestic and international environments. In essence, the Clinton administration's foreign policy approach evolved in three phases over the course of its eight years in office. Its initial approach was largely void of a comprehensive foreign policy approach and often relied more upon rhetorical flourishes than a well-developed foreign policy approach. To the extent that the administration fostered a foreign policy approach early on, it largely was oriented toward achieving success in foreign economic policy. This initial approach, which might be labeled "economic engagement," was quite idealist in content in that it sought to open new markets to American products and liberalize the international trading order as a means to foster American (and global) economic prosperity and cooperation. This approach fit nicely within the idealist or "liberal internationalist" approach to foreign policy, as discussed in Chapter 4.

As early as September and October 1993, however, this emphasis upon foreign economic policy as the administration's principal foreign policy orientation began to change. Through a series of speeches by key foreign policy advisors and by the president himself, the administration sought to give more coherence and structure to its foreign policy approach. This new phase might be described as the "democratic engagement and enlargement" phase or the "strategy of enlargement" phase, after the policy direction announced by National Security Advisor Anthony Lake. It lasted roughly from late 1993 through the end of 1994 (although elements remained through Clinton's entire time in office). During this period, the focus was on expanding the number of market democracies and market economies. This broader policy approach had even a fuller idealist underpinning in that it emphasized creating free markets and free societies as the fundamental goals of American foreign policy.

At least as early as 1995 (and perhaps sooner), and lasting through the entire second term, the administration's approach to foreign policy began to move in the direction of realism, driven largely by international events and the demands of domestic politics. By the beginning of the second term, the approach became decidedly more realist in focus and content, especially with its emphasis on bolstering alliance ties and working with traditional foreign policy partners. In short, a foreign policy of "selective engagement," driven more often by national interest considerations (although tempered by some idealist elements), best describes the Clinton administration's foreign policy approach during its last four years in office. A fuller discussion of each of these phases will convey the evolving values and beliefs that shaped foreign policy from 1993 through early 2001.

Phase One: Economic Engagement

The initial Clinton administration foreign policy approach focused on economic ties as the driving force in dealing with the global community. At his Senate confirmation hearings as secretary of state in January 1993, Warren Christopher outlined three principles to guide American foreign policy for the new administration: achieving economic security, reshaping defense, and promoting democracy—but the first priority that he discussed was the need to use the international system to foster greater economic prosperity for the American people.[83] Indeed, Christopher declared that the Clinton administration would "advance America's economic security with the same energy and resourcefulness . . . devoted to waging the Cold War." This emphasis upon foreign economic policy also nicely wedded foreign and domestic politics—a theme that candidate Clinton had struck during this campaign when he declared that "our first foreign priority and our first domestic priority are one and the same: reviving our economy."[84]

To achieve this economic security, the Clinton administration initially committed itself to several key initiatives at home and abroad. On the domestic level, the administration sought to develop an economic program to revive the Ameri-

---

Document Summary 5.3   Key Components of the North American Free Trade Agreement among Canada, Mexico, and the United States, Effective January 1, 1994

Tariffs—All tariffs on goods produced by the three countries and sold among them would be eliminated. These tariff reductions would occur over a five- to fifteen-year period. Strict "rules of origin" of goods would be observed.

Investments—All investments by the other agreement partners would be provided with "national treatment." Some restrictions were included, however, on national security grounds and, for example, in the areas of oil and the petrochemical industries for Mexico.

Services—Several areas, including banking, telecommunications, transportation, and government procurement, were to be opened to the agreement partners. Some restrictions still remained, however, in shipping, films, publishing, and oil and gas for the signatories.

Intellectual Property—Copyrights, industrial designs, trademarks, and other areas were provided protection under the pact.

Safeguards and Side Agreements—Under defined circumstances, temporary tariffs could be reimposed to protect some local industries. Side agreements were also completed to address environmental concerns and working condition issues among the participants.

SOURCE: Abstracted from "NAFTA Provisions," *Congressional Quarterly Almanac 1993* (Washington, DC: Congressional Quarterly, Inc., 1994), pp. 180–181.

---

can economy and to make American workers and companies more productive and competitive in the global marketplace. It sought to undertake actions to reduce the United States budget deficits and ensure that America was a more reliable trading partner. It also sought to infuse more economic components into the foreign policy making apparatus of the government. In this regard, the administration announced the creation of the National Economic Council (NEC) as the functional economic equivalent to the National Security Council (NSC) and as a mechanism to ensure that economic matters, foreign and domestic, received a full hearing in the executive branch. Economic advisors, too, became formal members of the national security committee structure. In addition, several economic officials and agencies gained greater authority: The United States Trade Representative (USTR) assumed a central role on trade policy; the Department of State created a new Office of the Coordinator for Business Affairs; and the Departments of Treasury and Commerce assumed more foreign policy responsibilities.[85]

On the international level, the Clinton administration moved quickly to complete two free trade agreements and to initiate several other multilateral and bilateral efforts to liberalize trade. Regarding the North American Free Trade Agreement (NAFTA), the administration began negotiations on important "side agreements" to protect worker rights and preserve environmental standards. When these agreements were secured, the Clinton administration set up an elaborate lobbying effort to secure passage in Congress. By November 1993, the House and the Senate passed NAFTA, although President Clinton ended up relying more upon votes from Republicans than Democrats to gain its final passage. Still, the congressional victory was hailed as an important foreign policy success of the Clinton administration—and remains so to this day. See Document Summary 5.3 for some details of this fact.

Document Summary 5.4   Key Components of the General Agreement on Tariffs and Trade (GATT) Changes, Fully in Force by July 1, 1995

Tariffs—Tariffs worldwide will be cut on approximately 85 percent of all world trade. These tariffs will be reduced from an average of 5 percent on industrial products currently to 3 percent at the end of this process. Cuts will be made over a five- to ten-year period.

Agriculture—For the first time, agriculture will be covered under this pact. On average, agricultural subsidies will be cut by 36 percent worldwide, and agricultural products exported with the help of governmental subsidies will drop by 21 percent. Quotas in agriculture will be converted to tariffs.

Textiles—Quotas placed on textiles imported from developing countries to the developed countries will be eliminated over a ten-year period.

Services—These kinds of transactions will now be covered by the GATT accord.

Subsidies, Intellectual Property—Government subsidies for particular industries will now be lowered and international protection will be accorded intellectual property such as semiconductor chip designs, books, films, and music.

World Trade Organization—As this round of GATT enters into effect, a new and expanded trading organization will be established to regulate global trade for the future.

SOURCES: Abstracted from "Highlights of GATT Accord," *Congressional Quarterly Almanac 1993* (Washington, DC: Congressional Quarterly, Inc., 1994), p. 183; and "The Shape of the Accord," *New York Times*, December 15, 1993, C18.

By November 1994, the Clinton administration had achieved another important victory with the completion and approval of the Uruguay Round of the General Agreement on Tariffs and Trade (GATT) and the creation of its successor organization, the World Trade Organization (WTO). Moreover, this agreement, too, required substantial lobbying by the administration on Capitol Hill, but it ultimately was approved by about two-thirds of the House and exactly three-quarters of the Senate. Along with NAFTA, the WTO signaled the centrality of economics for Clinton's foreign policy. See Document Summary 5.4 for the major components of this agreement.

With these agreements in place, President Clinton next moved to initiate two other multilateral trading pacts. In November 1994, the Clinton administration lent its support to the notion that the Asia-Pacific Economic Cooperation (APEC) forum establish a free trade area among its developed nation members by 2010 and its total membership by 2020. A month later, President Clinton proposed a free trade area by 2005 to the 34 Western Hemisphere countries that were meeting at the Summit of the Americas in Miami.

Beyond multilateral efforts, the Clinton administration undertook bilateral initiatives to foster American economic security. In January 1994, for instance, the administration identified 10 countries (Argentina, Brazil, China, India, Indonesia, Mexico, Poland, South Africa, South Korea, and Turkey) as the "big emerging markets" (BEMs) and set about seeking to gain access to them since they offer "the US its greatest opportunity for continued prosperity, enhanced competitiveness, and arenas of economic growth over the next several decades."[86] These states not only possessed sufficient land and population, but they were also undertaking the necessary market reforms to be engines of development in the future. Most instructive was the selection and inclusion of China among the BEMs. That nation, with over 1 billion people and with some market reforms under way, became a prime target for fostering economic security for the United States through enhanced trade and investment—even though it was hardly a model society in terms of democracy or human rights. In effect, economic considerations now trumped human rights or other foreign policy considerations when dealing with this crucial BEM nation.

Phase Two: Democratic Engagement and Enlargement

Although this economic focus dominated the foreign policy agenda during the early months (and years) of the Clinton administration, changing international conditions quickly drew the administration's attention elsewhere and led to an effort to define its foreign policy more broadly. The international events driving this change were the deteriorating situation in Bosnia, the unsettled conditions in Somalia and Haiti, and the changing political landscape in Russia and the Middle East. In Bosnia, ethnic cleansing continued, and the administration was unable to settle on a policy that was supported by its Western European allies. In Somalia, the effort to transform the humanitarian mission of late 1992 into a peace-building and nation-building mission in early 1993 met with strong resistance. In Haiti, the Governor Island accord was completed in the summer of 1993, but by fall, it failed to be implemented. In Russia, the Boris Yeltsin regime was meeting resistance, and the administration needed to decide whether to support him or not. The one bright spot in foreign affairs, the Israeli-PLO Accord of September 1993, required attention to put it into effect. In short, the international landscape called for more than economic engagement.

At home, too, the debate took another tack. An important question was whether foreign policy activities, beyond economics, were something that the United States should embrace. While isolationism overstates the sentiments of the public and some of its leaders at the time, many Americans did support some reassessment of the breadth of U.S. commitments worldwide. Indeed, in spring, 1993, the third-ranking official in the Department of State floated the idea of reducing American commitment around the world. Both questions of "will and wallet" in the foreign policy realm appeared in political discussions.

In effect, American foreign policy needed a clearer and broader road map than the Clinton administration had provided. By late September 1993, major foreign policy speeches by President Clinton, Secretary of State Warren Christopher, UN Ambassador Madeleine Albright, and especially by National Security Advisor Anthony Lake tried to do just that.[87] In their statements, these administration officials set out the fundamental premises of its foreign policy and the basic raison d'être of its foreign policy. Taken as a whole, the administration's foreign policy approach now embraced an even greater commitment to liberal internationalism than its initial approach.

First, the administration committed the United States to global involvement and leadership after the Cold War. Global engagement—not isolationism or neo-isolationism—would be the administration's policy. Warren Christopher put it one way ("I want to assure you that the United States chooses engagement"), and Madeleine Albright another ("Our nation will not retreat into a post–Cold War foxhole"). Second, the administration indicated that the United States would act in the world either unilaterally or multilaterally, and it would do so on a case-by-case basis. The United States acting either unilaterally or multilaterally, Christopher said, is a "false polarity. It is not an 'either-or' proposition." Additionally, Lake specified the basic criterion of that choice: "[O]nly one overriding factor can determine whether the U.S. should act multilaterally or unilaterally, and this is America's interests." Third, the administration committed the United States to use force when necessary. Although "diplomacy will always be America's first choice," Albright declared, "when diplomacy fails, we have both the capacity to use force effectively and the will to do so when necessary."

Finally, Lake provided the basic rationale and context for American engagement and leadership: It would be to strengthen and expand market democracies worldwide. This "strategy of enlargement," as he called it, would be the post–Cold War successor to the policy of containment. Its primary focus, Lake stated, would be on "strengthening our democratic core in North America, Europe, and Japan; consolidating and enlarging democracy and markets in key places; and addressing backlash states such as Iran and Iraq" that challenge market democracies. In a real sense, then, the new approach was to add creating liberal democracies to creating liberal markets around the world.

Put differently, two key concepts now formed the core of the Clinton foreign policy—free markets and free societies—and both concepts are key tenets of idealism or liberal internationalism. Importantly, the implicit assumption underpinning these concepts is that cooperation, not conflict, primarily motivates the behavior of states. The former concept assumes the pacifying effects of free markets: As states cooperate in more and more so-called low politics areas (e.g., in trading blocs or free market agreements), they become more interested in the absolute gains that their societies can achieve and less interested in their relative gains vis-à-vis neighbors or their trading partners. The latter concept assumes the pacifying effects of free societies: Democracies do not fight one another; they have peaceful mechanisms for resolving their disputes, and they respect the rights of their citizens.[88] Moreover, there would be a synergistic relationship between the two concepts: Sustained economic gains by democratic states would propel continued pacific relations among them, and democratic states would be equipped to pursue (and construct) more open markets in a peaceful way.

An important implication of relying on these two concepts was to emphasize the centrality of domestic values in shaping American foreign policy. The economic emphasis of the administration's approach could, of course, have a direct domestic effect on people's lives. The promotion of democracy could as well, especially since it was coupled with the promotion of human rights. In this way, the administration would seemingly be appealing to the deeply held values of most Americans and would restore some idealism to American foreign policy.

Despite the intuitive appeal of the enlargement of market democracies in the world, however, the approach never gained much support at home and never provided much policy guidance abroad—except in the most abstract sense. What it did become, however, was a ready target for criticism. Unsurprisingly, Henry Kissinger noted that the strategy was lacking in "operational terms."[89] Another critic noted that Clinton's foreign policy was too general and the administration approached "foreign policy as if it were on a supermarket shopping spree, grabbing whatever it takes a fancy to. . . ."[90] Still others viewed it less as a strategy (How would the administration bring about democratic development?) and more as a set of attractive principles (Who could challenge the promotion of democracy?). Disquieting, too, was that the administration's foreign policy appeared to be less focused on American national interests and more on universal global values.[91]

The Clinton administration's strategy of enlargement, and its foreign policy in general, also came in for criticism from within the administration itself, from Republicans on Capitol Hill, and from the American public. Secretary of State Warren Christopher reportedly saw it as "a trade policy masquerading as a foreign policy" and refused to use the *E* (or *enlargement*) word in his policy formulations.[92] Republicans, of course, seized upon the perceived failings of Clinton foreign policy by including several key foreign policy restrictions in its "Contract with America" during the 1994 congressional elections. Finally, in a national survey of public opinion on foreign policy conducted in late 1994, the Clinton administration's handling of foreign policy came under fire. Only 31 percent of the public judged it as "good" or "excellent."[93]

Equally important, the strategy of enlargement proved to be an incomplete guide to responding to the foreign policy challenges facing the administration in 1993–1994 and beyond. While the promotion of free markets was already a priority for the administration, the strategy did not provide a clear guide for how to promote democracy. While it surely served as a general rationale for promoting political liberalization in Haiti or Bosnia and comported with efforts to challenge backlash states, such as Iraq or North Korea, it did not provide much specificity about what actions should be taken prior to democratic development in these states. Furthermore, it was hardly a very precise guide to American policy toward the Middle East, Russia, or China, or for addressing ethnic killings in Rwanda.

Phase Three: Selective Engagement

As early as January 1995, and after some stinging criticisms over its lack of an effective foreign policy, the Clinton administration approach to foreign policy began to move away from the idealist design that the strategy of enlargement conveyed and toward a more substantive policy rooted in realist tenets. Secretary of State Warren Christopher outlined this movement in a speech at Harvard's Kennedy School of Government.[94] While reaffirming a commitment to American engagement and leadership, Christopher set out a series of concrete policy priorities for the Clinton administration. Although they were generally compatible with the liberal internationalism set out earlier, virtually all of them also had the ring of traditional American foreign policy goals. The United States, he declared, would seek cooperative ties with other states, build economic and security institutions, and support democracy and human rights. It would do so by liberalizing the trading order, building a new security structure in Europe, working to find a comprehensive peace in the Middle East, halting the proliferation of weapons of mass destruction, and combating international crime.

MAP 5.2   The Former Yugoslavia

A year later, in another address to the Kennedy School, Christopher outlined a similar set of foreign policy goals, but the hierarchical ordering of the goals seemed to signal a change in the administration's emphasis.[95] While reaffirming the overarching principles of the previous year ("pursuing peace in regions of vital interest," "confronting the new transnational security threats," and "promoting open markets and prospects"), the increasing emphasis on the security components of foreign policy could not be missed. The specific regional threats to peace that Christopher identified were familiar trouble spots—Bosnia, Central and Eastern Europe, Russia—and such problem states as Northern Ireland, Haiti, Cyprus, Angola, Burundi, Peru, and Ecuador. The new transnational security threats ranged from the proliferation of weapons of mass destruction and terrorism to international criminal activities and environmental damage. Finally, and significantly, promotion of open markets was listed third and mainly repeated trade liberalization efforts through NAFTA and APEC, and in the Americas. In addition, too, Christopher called for a continued commitment to seeking fast-track trading authority from the Congress. Except in the most generous interpretation, then, the strategy of enlargement was no longer central to the administration's foreign policy actions.

The Clinton administration's commitment to altering its foreign policy course seemed evident by the end of the first term, but the change was more fully signaled at the beginning of the second. In his 1997 State of the Union address, for instance, President Clinton stated that the first tasks for the United States is to "build . . . an undivided, democratic Europe" and "shape an Asia-Pacific community of cooperation, not conflict."[96] To be sure, he added that we needed to "expand our exports," but he also noted that the United States must "continue to be an unrelenting force for peace from the Middle East to Haiti, from Northern Ireland to Africa" and "must move strongly against new threats to our security." Further, he argued, the United States must strengthen and support its military and its diplomacy. Two months later, the new national security advisor, Samuel (Sandy) Berger repeated these very same objectives to a Washington audience.[97]

By May 1997, the administration's "National Security Strategy for a New Century" statement reinforced the change already under way.[98] That statement inverted two of the three key principles that Secretary of State Christopher had identified in 1993. (By 1994, this inversion had occurred, but arguably, the 1997 change was much stronger in tone.) The United States' principal objectives, in order, were now "to enhance our security with effective diplomacy and with military forces that are ready to fight and win, to bolster America's economic prosperity [and] to promote democracy abroad." Traditional political/military emphases gained primacy, while the economic goal and the democracy goal lost ground. Realism, or perhaps realism *lite,* now came to dominate the foreign policy agenda.

Defining Selective Engagement On a substantive level, selective engagement implied different policy assumptions from those outlined when the strategy of enlargement was announced in 1993. First, while the United States would remain engaged and lead in world affairs, it would now act (and justify its actions) on more narrowly drawn national, rather than global, interest criteria. Its agenda, too, as the statements by Christopher, Clinton, and Berger implied, would be more specific and more narrowly chosen. Second, although the United States would not wholly eschew multilateral actions in global affairs, the administration would be more amenable to utilizing unilateral actions—and would undertake them only if necessary. Third, while the United States would be willing to use military force, it would do so more carefully, probably more sparingly, and only after applying clear criteria. Finally, the context and goals for American engagement and leadership would change perceptibly: The United States would be less focused on remaking the international system through the expansion of market democracies and would be more focused on stabilizing relations among key states. In other words, conflict, rather than cooperation, was still a motivating force for states. Thus, the United States would now seek to dampen and manage conflicts, rather than to eliminate them quickly (i.e., the use of peacekeeping versus peace building). Put differently, and more in line with realist premises, the emphasis would be more on stabilizing the international order than seeking to restructure it. Importantly, though, elements of democracy and human rights promotion would continue to be commingled into the process by the Clinton administration at various points. Thus, realism lite is perhaps a more accurate theoretical descriptor of its evolving approach.

Several different types of behavior by the administration now reflected this security-based approach to foreign policy: its actions regarding interventions, its efforts in building or rebuilding alliances, its strictures on peacekeeping, its emphasis on nonproliferation, and its focus on a few key powerful states in the international system. Moreover, the actions and nonactions in Kosovo and the administration's approach to East Timor illustrate the continuance of selective engagement up to the very end of the administration. Furthermore, those episodes reveal how the administration grappled with "humanitarian interventions" in trying to devise a workable "Clinton Doctrine."

Implementing Selective Engagement   Shortly after the events in Somalia, the Clinton administration made perhaps its first decision in the direction of selective engagement by deciding not to take action over Rwanda but deciding to step up its actions in the Balkans. In April 1994, the administration refused to become deeply involved in the genocidal situation occurring in Rwanda. Instead, it issued Presidential Decision Directive-25 (PDD-25) a month later, which specified several decision criteria for American involvement in UN operations under Chapter VI and VII operations under the Charter. At about the same time, a different decision was made regarding the Balkans. That is, the Clinton administration began to move in the direction of taking more vigorous actions (including some selective bombing), in an effort to stabilize that region. Those efforts reached their height in the summer and fall of 1995, both with renewed support for the Bosnian government and with a vigorous diplomatic offensive. Eventually, too, those activities resulted in the Dayton Accords, the use of the NATO alliance to implement them, and the introduction of American troops to stabilize the fragile peace, albeit within strict rules of engagement. In short, a more vigorous but selective effort to stabilize global politics was being put into place by the Clinton administration by acting in Europe, but not in Africa.

Second, the administration's actions toward its allies also reflected this renewed interest in security. By late 1994, the president and his administration had endorsed the decision to go forward with NATO expansion, despite the objection of Russian leaders and despite its possible impact on Russian domestic politics. The aim of building a stable and secure Europe trumped assuaging Russian fears over Western encirclement and the possibility of dividing Europe. (In an anomalous way, of course, the decision to support NATO expansion had the side benefit of fostering democratic development within Europe.) Similarly, the Clinton administration initiated efforts to refurbish the Japanese-American alliance and strengthen alliance ties with South Korea. Further, the Clinton administration initiated and pursued the policy of "dual containment" toward Iran and Iraq and sought, rather unsuccessfully, to obtain the continued support of other nations in that endeavor. Still, the Clinton administration was now willing to go it alone, especially toward Iraq. As such, American military forces were rapidly dispatched to Kuwait in late 1994, and the United States periodically used American air power for selective sorties against Iraq over its violations of the no-fly zones.

Third, the Clinton administration started (or enhanced) several peace initiatives as a means of addressing traditional security concerns. The administration, for example, stepped up its efforts to seek peace in the Middle East after the 1993 Israeli-PLO Accords, inaugurated a mediating role in Northern Ireland that eventually resulted in the Good Friday Accords, and initiated a four-power effort to obtain peace on the Korean peninsula. For a time, too, the administration used a special advisor to seek movement on the Cyprus question between Greece and Turkey.

Fourth, the administration undertook at least three important actions to address the new dangers posed by the proliferation of various kinds of weapons of mass destruction. The administration completed work on the Chemical Weapons Convention and succeeded in getting the Senate to provide its advice and consent. Similarly, President Clinton signed the Comprehensive Test Ban Treaty, but, in a stinging defeat in the Senate, he was not able to get the approval of that body for that pact. Furthermore, in a switch in policy position for the administration, the president signed the National Missile Defense Act in 1999. Although the decision on the extent of deployment was ultimately left to Clinton's successor, the administration, with considerable congressional prodding, moved the nation in the direction of missile defense. In a related action in 1995, the administration, working with many other nations, succeeded in making the strictures in the nuclear nonproliferation treaty (NPT) permanent.

Fifth, a few key states now became the focal point of policy attention—even if their domestic situations did not comport with democratic practices or respect for human rights. For instance, the Clinton administration supported the Yeltsin (and later, Putin) regime in Russia, despite the human rights violations by the Russian military in Chechnya and despite the increasing concern over authoritarian processes within that society. The Clinton administration never wavered in its policy toward China, despite the widespread human rights abuse within that nation. Fostering American trade with China and maintaining stability in East Asia were greater priorities.

Finally, the actions by the Clinton administration over Kosovo and East Timor reflect the selective nature of its policy approach—both in areas where human rights were abused and where democracy was restricted. In the former area, the air campaign against Serbia over Kosovo in 1999 was strongly justified both on national interest grounds (peace in Europe; the stability of NATO) and on humanitarian values (protecting innocent lives) by President Clinton.[99] Yet the president placed strictures on this campaign by explicitly excluding the use of American ground forces in the region. Policy toward the atrocities in East Timor also more fully reflects this selective involvement principle by the administration. While the United States would provide logistical supplies for a multilateral operation, the Australians would largely be responsible for action on the ground in that island territory.

Both President Clinton and his national security advisor, Sandy Berger, reaffirmed the administration's selective engagement approach late in the second term. In a major foreign policy address in February 1999, the president identified five major challenges confronting the United States.[100] Significantly, the list—and its structure—emphasized the traditional political/military concern over economic/social ones. The first two challenges called for renewing alliances—whether through the expansion of NATO or through refurbishing ties with Japan and Korea—and for bringing Russia and China, America's principal adversaries during the Cold War, into the international system as "open, prosperous, stable nations." The third major challenge also emphasized the security dimension by focusing on the new threats and new dangers in the international system: drug trafficking, terrorism, proliferation, etc. Finally, only in the last two challenges—creating workable trading and financial order and promoting global freedom—was there any hint of the "economic engagement" or "democratic enlargement" emphases from 1993 and 1994. Rather, the message by now was clear: The United States should be engaged, it could do some good in the world, and its actions were ultimately more in the realm of traditional political/military areas than elsewhere.

Berger did likewise in his summation of the Clinton foreign policy record only a month or two before the administration left office.[101] In discussing the five principles that guided the administration, Berger lists four (reliance on allies in Europe and Asia, constructive relations with former adversaries, global consequences of local disputes, new security dangers produced by technology and permeable borders) that fully fit within this "selective engagement" approach and have the ring of realism in their prescriptions. Only one (the use of economic integration to reduce economic differences) harkened back to the early years of the Clinton administration and its liberal internationalist beginnings.

LINGERING POLICY EFFECTS
OF THE CLINTON
FOREIGN POLICY APPROACH

What are principal policy effects of the Clinton administration's foreign policies across these three phases? How did its foreign policy activities impact the United States and the rest of the world? In another analysis, I have provided a more detailed assessment of the major policy-making and policy legacies of the Clinton administration.[102] Here I draw upon that discussion to suggest several general and specific foreign policy effects from the Clinton years and outline the degree of continuity and change from earlier administrations.

General Policy Effects

The first and most important general effect of the Clinton administration on the conduct of American foreign policy was its commitment to maintaining American involvement and leadership in global affairs after the Cold War. As the extent of international engagement expanded and contracted from economic engagement to democratic engagement and enlargement to selective engagement, the president and his administration never wavered in their basic commitment to maintaining a central role for the United States in the international system. Virtually every pronouncement by the administration spoke of this global role for the United States. Early on when there was a hint of a reduced global role by Peter Tarnoff, the Undersecretary of State for Political Affairs, that trial balloon was promptly shot down by Secretary Christopher.[103] In this sense, continuity, rather than change, describes the action by the Clinton administration.

At the same time, some might well argue that the Clinton administration was so active across such a broad array of foreign policy issues—from economic to political/military to social/cultural issues—that the administration had the effect of expanding the American global role to new heights and making it difficult, if not impossible, for any subsequent administration to reduce significantly America's global engagement. Consider, for example, the initial impulse of the George W. Bush administration to promote a "distinctly American internationalism." That concept in effect meant a reduction of U.S. involvement on some issues. For instance, candidate Bush suggested that the presence of American forces in the Balkans and America's central role in the Middle East peace process would need to be reduced. Yet, the Bush administration had to alter its course on both fronts, even before the devastating events of September 11, 2001. In another context, one longtime Washington observer offered a possible explanation for why any policy change by the Bush administration might well be so difficult: The Clinton administration "occupied so much of the middle ground" across a broad set of foreign policy issues that it has really provided little maneuvering room for another administration.[104]

A second general effect of the Clinton years was the increased, not reduced, role for the president in foreign policy matters. Despite the initial impulse of the Clinton administration to reduce the role of foreign policy on its agenda, and despite President Clinton's apparent aversion to such issues, the administration actually left office with an imperative for greater, not lesser, executive involvement in foreign policy. Increasingly, the United States could not achieve success in the foreign policy realm without presidential involvement or leadership, both domestically and internationally. Whether seeking to pass NAFTA or to obtain fast-track trading authority, President Clinton's involvement (or noninvolvement) was crucial to the outcome. Whether negotiating NATO expansion or the refurbishment of the Japanese alliance, presidential involvement was paramount, to gain support both at home and abroad. Part of the reason presidential leadership became necessary was the divided nature of politics in the last six years of the administration (with Republicans controlling both houses of Congress). Another part of the reason was that there was less support for foreign policy without an overarching strategy such as the Cold War provided.

A third general effect of the Clinton foreign policy has been the extraordinary impact of domestic politics on virtually all foreign policy issues addressed by the administration. On one level, of course, it is hardly exceptional to assert that domestic politics affects foreign policy, but what is remarkable about the Clinton years is the extent to which domestic politics shaped the direction of foreign policy. In the first foreign policy phase, of course, the domestic effect was both by design and definition. Indeed, some of these actions were crassly calculated in terms of domestic politics. Consider this recent assessment of the two side agreements to the NAFTA pact negotiated in 1993. The side agreements "had to be sufficiently strong to sway domestic environmentalists, and to a lesser extent labor, in order to enable Democrats to vote for the agreement . . . while at the same time not being too strong as to alienate core Republican supporters of NAFTA and their business elites."[105] The continuance of the economic engagement phase was also driven by domestic political considerations, since the failure to gain fast-track trading authority for the president (see Chapter 8) impeded the rapid completion of further economic pacts, especially some multilateral ones. Certainly the lack of movement on a trade agreement for the Americas, the expansion of NAFTA, or more progress on an APEC accord derive in part from the failure to secure fast-track authority.

In the second phase, too, the strategy of enlargement was equally driven by consideration of domestic politics. The assumption was that free markets and free peoples would have considerable domestic appeal. The problem was that the design was perhaps too grandiose and was viewed too skeptically by the public at large, and the strategy never really caught on. In reality, of course, domestic politics compelled the Clinton administration to move in the direction of selective engagement, after the Republicans gained control of both houses of Congress and as security questions once again (and perhaps inevitably) came to dominate the international agenda.

Finally, the limitations on American actions during the selective engagement phase flows in large part from domestic politics as well. Most noteworthy, of course, was the public's aversion to the use of American ground forces abroad, and the Clinton administration's policy caution as a result. Similarly, NATO expansion, the decision to sign legislation including the Helms-Burton amendment, the administration's changed position on missile defense, and a change in defense policy generally all reflect the increased effects of domestic politics.

Specific Policy Effects

Undoubtedly the first and most important specific policy effect of the Clinton administration for American foreign policy—and an important change from earlier administrations—was the placement of global economic policy at the center of American foreign policy. The completion of NAFTA, WTO, about 300 other trade accords (including the approval of permanent normal trading relations with China by Congress in late 2000), and the initiation of several multilateral pacts in different areas of the world represent a lasting foreign policy impact by the Clinton administration. Significantly, too, Clinton's actions in the foreign economic arena have made it incumbent upon future American presidents to assist in managing the global economy in much the same way as American presidents have become responsible for managing the American domestic economy. To be sure, the globalization of the economic policy has been a two-edged sword. While these efforts transformed and improved the lives of the citizens in many countries throughout the world, they have also created innumerable dislocations for others. The prolonged and violent protests at the WTO Ministerial meetings in December 1999 (and more recently, the violent protests at the Western Hemisphere meeting in Quebec City, the European Union meeting in Goteborg, and the G-8 meeting in Genoa) illustrate the growing concerns that the global economic transformations have produced.

A second specific policy effect by the Clinton administration was to stabilize the relationship between the United States and its principal alliance partners. The expansion of NATO and the prodding of NATO to take actions in "out-of-area" missions are important effects of the Clinton years. These actions also had the effect of moving the allies in the direction of greater security responsibilities, including the incipient development of the European Defense and Security Initiative (EDSI). The refurbishment of alliances in Asia appears not to have progressed as far as Europe, but, still, the Clinton administration began that process. In this sense, alliance stability represented continuity, but the nature of some alliance actions (e.g., within NATO) represented change.

A third specific effect was the effort to stabilize the relationship with China and Russia after the Cold War, actions portending more continuity than change. By the end of its second term, neither of these nations was the strategic partner originally envisioned by the Clinton administration, but once again, the process has begun. The granting of permanent normal trading relations (PNTR) to China and the expenditure of significant foreign aid to Russia are important factors in stabilizing the relationships with these former adversaries. Moreover, these significant policy actions make it difficult for any future administration to turn abruptly in a different policy direction.

A fourth specific effect has been for the United States to take the lead in conflict resolution efforts. Although this area of American actions does not represent great change by the United States or the Clinton administration, it was an area where the administration devoted a great deal of foreign policy time and energy. The record from these activities, however, is largely mixed. Still, the general conclusion is that these efforts were more positive than negative; thus, the administration left important opportunities for its successors in these areas. The Dayton Accords and the Middle East peace discussions top the list of these activities, but the efforts to address the conflicts in Northern Ireland and over the Korean peninsula were important as well. Yet, by the end of the Clinton presidency, significant and sustained progress was still unrealized. None of these efforts produced the level of conflict resolution perhaps originally hoped or envisioned by the administration. In fact, the Middle East negotiations were sharply frayed and in danger of collapse by the end of 2000 (despite the Wye Plantation Accords of 1998 and a last ditch effort in 2000 by the Clinton administration), and the situation in Bosnia from the Dayton Accords was fragile, with the likelihood of American military presence there for some time to come. The Good Friday Accords for Northern Ireland also yielded some initial promise, but, once again, by the end of the Clinton years, they were on the verge of collapse. The four-power talks over Korea were also stalled as a new president assumed office.

At least three other specific policy efforts had similar incomplete outcomes and represent more continuity than change from past American actions. First, the efforts to reduce the dangers to global peace and stability from weapons of mass destruction have not progressed very far. To be sure, the counterproliferation initiative announced by the Clinton administration early in its first term sent a signal that the United States would use both prevention and protection measures against these dangers, and the successful ratification of the Convention on Chemical Weapons was also an important step. However, the failure to gain the Senate's approval of the Comprehensive Test Ban Treaty, the failure to resolve the issue of missile defense (and the ABM Treaty debate), the ambiguous outcome from the 1994 agreement with North Korea over halting its nuclear weapons program, the remaining dangers from possible weapons development by Iraq, and the nuclear weapons testing by India and Pakistan in 1998 all suggest that this policy legacy was perhaps more negative than positive and represents a real challenge for future administrations.[106]

Second, the policy impact of the Clinton administration on the promotion of democracy and human rights in American foreign policy remains ambiguous as well. Although the administration came to office with a substantial commitment to human rights and the promotion of democracy, its policy efforts in these areas often were overshadowed by the requirements of other policy priorities. The administration's hesitancy to become involved in the Balkans, its reluctance to challenge China over human rights, and its decision to not become involved in Rwanda lend credence to this position. The military interdiction in Haiti, the response under the Dayton Accords, and the actions in Kosovo suggest a different effect, but, by most measures, the promotion of democracy and human rights during the Clinton administration cannot be characterized as unqualified successes.

By its second term, the Clinton administration actually suggested a different path to improve global human rights. That is, the administration seemingly decided to place greater emphasis on *multilateral* and *indirect* means of improving human rights, although they indicated that unilateral and direct means would not be wholly abandoned.[107] Increasingly, then, American actions would be directed to resolving conflicts and disputes and encouraging the building of political institutions and holding elections as an indirect way of improving human rights conditions. Moreover, the United States would work with other state and nonstate actors in pursuing these goals. Finally, and importantly, the negative effects of globalization still need to be incorporated into any policy addressing democracy and human rights by a new administration.

Third, the issue of when and under what conditions the United States would intervene with American forces also remained unresolved at the end of the Clinton years. The administration took several steps to clarify American policy, but questions continued. In May 1994, and in response to the Somalia fiasco, the Clinton administration issued Presidential Decision Directive 25 (PDD-25), which outlined the specific conditions required for the United States to participate in multilateral peace support operation; in May 1997, the administration issued another directive, PDD-56, which outlined the intragovernmental procedures for preparing for, and executing, a humanitarian intervention,[108] and in June

1999, after the Kosovo bombing, President Clinton made a sweeping pledge to assist those endangered around the world: "[W]hether you live in Africa, or Central Europe, or any other place, if somebody comes after innocent civilians and tries to kill them en masse because of their race, their ethnic background or their religion, and it's within our power to stop it, we will stop it."[109]

The pledge has been labeled the Clinton Doctrine on humanitarian intervention and seemed to represent a new departure on intervention policy.[110] Such a statement, however, is controversial. Were American policy makers wholly committed to such universal action, especially in light of the limited actions over Rwanda and East Timor? Would the American people support such interventions in light of previous limited support for the use of force involving internal conflicts, although more so for humanitarian ones?[111] Future administrations will need to decide whether this doctrine will indeed become a feature of post–Cold War and post–September 11 American foreign policy.

CONCLUDING COMMENTS

Although the George H. W. Bush administration came to office focused primarily on some continuity in policy approach, the end of the Cold War and the collapse of the Soviet Union compelled it to attempt a different course in foreign affairs. Instead of Soviet-American relations serving as the centerpiece for American foreign policy as they had for the past forty years, a new international order would be sought. That order would be based upon a shared set of global values, involve cooperation among nations, and be grounded in the leadership of the United States. While the Bush administration surely achieved some success in uniting a coalition in the Persian Gulf War around this vision, its efforts in other areas of the world—whether toward Russia, Somalia, Haiti, or Bosnia—met with a more mixed reception from the American people. Any new world order led by the United States remained elusive.

The Clinton administration, too, was determined to pursue a foreign policy grounded in a set of principles and guided by a clear strategy, it, too, found that enunciating principles was easier than implementing a strategy. As such, its ultimate legacy was more continuity in policy than change. Still, it left some important effects on the direction of American foreign policy at the end of the twentieth century.

First, despite initial attempts to downplay foreign policy, the Clinton administration maintained an important place for it and promoted a central role for American "engagement and leadership" in the post–Cold War era, much as during the Cold War years. Second, despite some initial attempts to set a new direction for American foreign policy, the Clinton administration ultimately failed to do so and largely reverted to a policy agenda closely akin to its predecessors. That is, it initially sought to give economic policy a more central role in the foreign policy process, and it did so. Yet these efforts ultimately were overshadowed by pressing international events and problems (whether in the Balkans, the Middle East, or with China and Russia) and by the constraints of domestic politics, especially after the Republican congressional victories in the 1994 elections. Third, the Clinton administration sought initially to infuse a greater sense of idealism into American foreign policy with its efforts to restructure the international system through its promotion of free markets and the expansion of democracy. Although strands of those assumptions shaped its policy actions throughout its eight years in office, the administration ultimately moved in the direction of more traditional political/ military concerns dominating its decision making. In large measure, the administration's policy actions were more in step with stabilizing the existing international order than in significantly changing it. In this way, then, these efforts reflected a movement back toward realism with a primary focus on refurbishing and restructuring some traditional alliances and stabilizing relations among the great powers.

NOTES

1. Throughout this chapter, before the breakup of the Soviet empire in 1989–1990, the use of the term *Eastern Europe* shall refer to those countries that were Communist allies of the Soviet Union (East Germany, Poland, Czechoslovakia, Hungary, Romania, Bulgaria) and formed part of the "Soviet bloc." After its breakup, the term *Central Europe* shall refer to these countries, since it is more descriptive of their proper geographical location.

2. "Text of President Bush's State of the Union Message to Nation," *New York Times,* January 30, 1991, A8.

3. Part of this chapter and its arguments appeared in James M. McCormick, "Assessing Clinton's Foreign Policy at Midterm," *Current History* 94 (November 1995): 370–374.

4. Governor Bill Clinton, "A New Covenant for American Security," address at Georgetown University, December 12, 1991.

5. "Remarks of Governor Bill Clinton," Los Angeles World Affairs Council, August 13, 1992.

6. These concepts are discussed in and drawn from Charles W. Kegley, Jr., "The Bush Administration and the Future of American Foreign Policy: Pragmatism, or Procrastination?" *Presidential Studies Quarterly* 19 (Fall 1989): 717–731, especially p. 717.

On the Bush presidency, also see Barbara Kellerman and Ryan J. Barilleaux, *The President as World Leader* (New York: St. Martin's Press, 1991), pp. 210–216.

7. See Elaine Sciolino, "Bush Selections Signal Focus on Foreign Policy," *New York Times,* January 17, 1989, 1, for this depiction of Bush as a problem solver and not as a visionary.

8. Theodore C. Sorensen, "Bush's Timid 100 Days," *New York Times,* April 27, 1989, 27.

9. William G. Hyland, "Bush's Foreign Policy: Pragmatism or Indecision?" *New York Times,* April 26, 1989, 25.

10. Evan Thomas with Thomas M. DeFrank and Ann McDaniel, "Bush and the Generals," *Newsweek,* February 4, 1991, 27.

11. The description was written by Charles William Maynes and is quoted in Sciolino, "Bush Selections Signal Focus on Foreign Policy," p. 1.

12. Noted analyst I. M. Destler is quoted in John Felton, "Will Bush-Hill Honeymoon Bring Bipartisanship?" *Congressional Quarterly Weekly Report,* February 18, 1989, 334.

13. Sciolino, "Bush Selections Signal Focus on Foreign Policy," p. 1; and Thomas, "Bush and the Generals," p. 27.

14. The National Security Council staff confirmed that there was not a publicly

available summary of the "policy review" and that these speeches summarized the essence of the policy positions of the Bush administration at that time. The speeches, which are quoted below, were supplied by the NSC staff and consisted of the following: "Remarks by the President to the Citizens of Hamtramck," April 17, 1989; "Remarks by the President at Texas A&M University," May 12, 1989; "Remarks by the President at Boston University Commencement Ceremony," May 21, 1989; "Remarks by the President at the Coast Guard Academy Graduation Ceremony, " May 24, 1989; and "Remarks by the President at Rheingoldhalle," Mainz, Germany, May 31, 1989.

15. See Chapter 8 for a complete discussion of the Jackson-Vanik Amendment.

16. Quoted in Maureen Dowd, "Bush Moves to Control War's Endgame," *New York Times,* February 23, 1991, 5.

17. John Felton, "Bush, Hill Agree to Provide Contras with New Aid," *Congressional Quarterly Weekly Report,* March 25, 1989, 655–657.

18. See *Congressional Quarterly Weekly Report,* April 15, 1989, 853–854.

19. Steven Erlanger, "Hanoi's Partial Victory," *New York Times,* July 20, 1990, A1, A2.

20. Steven Erlanger, "Ending Talks, All Cambodia Parties Commit Themselves to U.N. Peace Plan," *New York Times,* September 11, 1990, A3.

21. The following discussion draws upon "U.S. Invasion Ousts Panama's Noriega," and "From U.S. Canal to Invasion . . . A Chronology of Events," *Congressional Quarterly Almanac 1989* (Washington, DC: Congressional Quarterly, Inc., 1990), pp. 595–609 and 606–607, respectively; and Stephen Engelberg, "Bush Aides Admit a U.S. Role in Coup and Bad Handling," *New York Times,* October 6, 1989, 1 and 8.

22. Ibid.

23. Nicholas D. Kristof, "Beijing Death Toll at Least 200; Army Tightens Control of City But Angry Resistance Goes On," *New York Times,* June 5, 1989, 1. A summary of the Bush administration's actions over this episode can be found in "Repression in China Leads to Sanctions," *Congressional Quarterly Almanac 1989* (Washington, DC: Congressional Quarterly, Inc., 1990), pp. 518–526, and it was used here.

24. "President's News Conference on Foreign and Domestic Issues," *New York Times,* June 9, 1989, 12.

25. The chronology of events in the next three sections is based upon several sources: Peter Hayes, ed., "Chronology 1989" *Foreign Affairs: America and the World 1989/90* 69 (1990); 213–257; Peter Hayes, ed., "Chronology 1990" *Foreign Affairs: America and the World 1990/91* 70 (1991): 206–248; "East Bloc Political Turmoil . . . Chronology of Big Changes" *Congressional Quarterly Weekly Report,* December 9, 1989, 3376–3377; and the chronologies in The 1990 World Book, *Yearbook* (Chicago: World Book, Inc., 1990), and the 1990 Britannica, *1990 Book of the Year* (Chicago: Encyclopedia Britannica, Inc., 1990). For changes in Yugoslavia and Albania in 1991, see "2 Republics Split From Yugoslavia," *Des Moines Register,* June 26, 1991, 1A and 12A; and Thomas L. Friedman, "300,000 Albanians Pour into Streets to Welcome Baker," *New York Times,* June 23, 1991, 1 and 4.

26. Serge Schmemann, "Two Germanys Unite After 45 Years with Jubilation and a Vow of Peace," *New York Times,* October 3, 1990, A1, A9.

27. Quoted in "German-NATO Drama: 9 Fateful Months," *New York Times,* July 17, 1990, A6. It provides a useful chronology of the reunification process, which we also used here.

28. "'Two Plus Four' Treaty Signed; Germany Regains Full Sovereignty," *The Week in Germany,* September 14, 1990, 1–2. The formal name of the treaty is Treaty on the Final Provisions Regarding Germany.

29. The details of the unification treaty can be found in "Bonn, GDR Sign Unification Treaty," *The Week in Germany,* September 7, 1990, 1–2.

30. On these elections, see Bill Keller, "Soviet Savor Vote in Freest Election Since '17 Revolution," *New York Times,* March 27, 1989, A1 and A6.

31. "Reforms in the Soviet Union," *Des Moines Sunday Register,* February 11, 1990, 1C.

32. The quotations are taken, respectively, from "Gorbachev's First Remarks: 'They Failed,'" *New York Times,* August 23, 1991, A9; and his first post-coup press conference: "The Gorbachev Account: A Coup 'Against the People, Against Democracy,'" *New York Times,* August 23, 1991, A10.

33. See Serge Schmemann, "Gorbachev, Yeltsin and Republic Leaders Move to Take Power From Soviet Congress," *New York Times,* September 3, 1991, A1 and A6; "Excerpts From Soviet Congress: Time for Drastic Changes," *New York Times,* September 3, 1991, A7; and Serge Schmemann, "Soviet Congress Yields Rule to Republics to Avoid Political and Economic Collapse," *New York Times,* September 6, 1991, A1 and A6.

34. The president and the "senior Bush Administration policy maker" are quoted in Thomas L. Friedman, "U.S. Worry Rises Over Europe's Stability," *New York Times,* November 10, 1989, 10.

35. "Poland, Hungary Aid Launched in 1989," *Congressional Quarterly Almanac 1989* (Washington, DC: Congressional Quarterly, Inc., 1990), pp. 503–504.

36. Karl Kaiser, "Germany's Unification," in William P. Bundy, ed., *Foreign Affairs: America and the World 1990/91* 70 (1991): 179–205.

37. The quotations are from "Transcript of the Bush-Gorbachev New Conference in Malta," *New York Times,* December 4, 1989, A12. Also see Andrew Rosenthal, "Bush and Gorbachev Proclaim a New Era for U.S.-Soviet Ties; Agree on Arms and Trade Aims," *New York Times,* December 4, 1989, A1 and A10; and Frances X. Cline, "Economic Pledges Cheer Soviet Aides," *New York Times,* December 4, 1989, A11.

38. "As Iron Curtain Falls, Superpowers Thaw," *Congressional Quarterly Almanac 1989* (Washington, DC: Congressional Quarterly, Inc., 1990), pp. 477–484.

39. Peter Hayes, ed., "Chronology 1990," p. 208.

40. "Text of the Statement on Long-Range Arms," "Summary of U.S.-Soviet Agreement on Chemical Arms," "The Other Agreements in Brief," *New York Times,* June 2, 1990, 8.

41. James Baker, "The Gulf Crisis and CSCE Summit," *Dispatch,* 1 (November 19, 1990): 273–274; Pat Towell, "Historic CFE Treaty Arms, Marks the End of Cold War," *Congressional Quarterly Weekly Report,* November 24, 1990, 3930–3932; and "CSCE Summit in Paris Shapes 'New Europe,'" *The Week in Germany,* November 23, 1990, 1. The Warsaw Pact was officially disbanded as of March 31, 1991. See Christine Bohlen, "Warsaw Pact Agrees to Dissolve Its Military Alliance by March 31," *New York Times,* February 26, 1991, A1 and A10.

42. R.W. Apple, Jr., "Superpower Weapons Treaty First to Cut Strategic Bombs," *New York Times,* July 18, 1991, A1, A6; Thomas L. Friedman, "Bush and Gorbachev Close Era in U.S.-Soviet Relations," *New York Times,* July 18, 1991, A8; Eric Schmitt, "Senate Approval and Sharp Debate Seen," *New York Times,* July 19, 1991, A5 (including accompanying table entitled "New Limits on Strategic Weapons"); and Office of Public Affairs, U.S. Arms Control and Disarmament Agency, "Strategic Arms Reduction Talks," *Issues Brief,* April 25, 1991.

43. Steven Greenhouse, "7 Offer Moscow Technical Help," *New York Times,* July 18, 1991, A1, A8; and "Excerpts From Talks by Gorbachev and Major: Investing and Accepting," *New York Times,* July 18, 1991, A6.

44. Andrew Rosenthal, "Baltics Recognized," *New York Times,* September 3, 1991, A1, A8.

45. Clifford Krauss, "U.S. and Britain Will Send Some Food Aid to Republics," *New York Times,* August 30, 1991, A10.

46. See George Bush, "Outlines of a New World of Freedom," an address before the 44th session of the UN General Assembly, New York City, September 25, 1989, and "Toward a New World Order," an address before a joint session of Congress, September 11, 1990. Both are published by the Department of State, Bureau of Public Affairs, Washington, DC. Also see "Text of

President Bush's State of the Union Message to Nation," A8.

47. President Bush's national security advisor, Brent Scowcroft, is given credit for developing this phrase and the strategy behind it. See Andrew Rosenthal, "Scowcroft and Gates: A Team Rivals Baker," *New York Times,* February 21, 1991, A6.

48. "Toward a New World Order," p. 2.

49. "Text of President Bush's State of the Union Message to Nation," A8.

50. Ibid.

51. Daniel C. Diller, ed., *The Middle East,* 7th ed. (Washington, DC: Congressional Quarterly, Inc., 1990), pp. 164–165.

52. Ibid., p. 3.

53. On the evolution of the crisis, see Tom Matthews, "The Road to War," *Newsweek,* January 28, 1991, pp. 54–65. On the failure of the United States to issue a warning to Iraq, see Elaine Sciolino with Michael R. Gordon, "U.S. Gave Iraq Little Reason Not to Mount Assault," *New York Times,* September 23, 1990, 1. The former source provided useful background information that was relied upon for this section. On the controversy over what the American ambassador to Iraq said or did not say to Saddam Hussein prior to the crisis, see Thomas L. Friedman, "Envoy to Iraq, Faulted in Crisis, Says She Warned Hussein Sternly," *New York Times,* March 21, 1991, A1 and A7.

54. Peter Hayes, ed., "Chronology 1990," p. 228.

55. The joint statement is reprinted in "US-USSR Statement," *Dispatch* 1 (September 17, 1990): 92.

56. George Bush, "The Arabian Peninsula: U.S. Principles," an address to the nation from the Oval Office of the White House, August 8, 1990, provided by the Department of State, Bureau of Public Affairs, Washington, DC.

57. See "How the Arab League Voted in Cairo," *New York Times,* August 11, 1990, 4.

58. The most commonly cited number of countries in the anti-Iraq coalition in public descriptions was 28 nations, but see Steven R. Bowman, "Iraq-Kuwait Crisis: Summary of U.S. and Non-U.S. Forces" (Washington, DC: Congressional Research Service, The Library of Congress, December 27, 1990), in which slightly more nations are identified as having contributed some contingent of forces.

59. UN Security Council Resolution 678 (1990), reprinted in Marjorie Ann Browne, "Iraq-Kuwait: U.N. Security Council Resolutions—Texts and Votes" (Washington, DC: Congressional Research Service, The Library of Congress, December 4, 1990). This source provides complete texts and a summary of the previous 11 UN resolutions, while "U.N. Resolutions on Iraq," *New York Times,* February 16, 1991, 6, provides a summary of them. The latter source was used for the discussion here.

60. Andrew Rosenthal, "Bush Calls Halt to Allied Offensive; Declares Kuwait Free, Iraq Beaten; Sets Stiff Terms for Full Cease-fire," *New York Times,* February 28, 1991, A1; R.W. Apple, Jr., "U.S. Says Iraqi Generals Agree to Demands 'On All Matters'; Early P.O.W. Release Expected," *New York Times,* March 4, 1991, A1, A6; and "New U.S. Hint About Hussein," *New York Times,* March 4, 1991, A6. On Iraqi and American battlefield deaths, see Patrick E. Tyler, "Iraq's War Toll Estimated by U.S.," *New York Times,* June 5, 1991, A5; and "The Reluctant Warrior," *Newsweek,* May 13, 1991, 22.

61. Paul Lewis, "UN Votes Stern Conditions for Formally Ending War; Iraqi Response Is Uncertain," *New York Times,* April 4, 1991, A1, A7; "UN Conditions," *Des Moines Register,* April 4, 1991, 14A; and Resolution 687 (1991) at http://www.fas.org/news/un/iraq/sres/sres0687.htm.

62. On the outbreak of these rebellions, see, among others, "Apocalypse Near," *Newsweek,* April 1, 1991, 14–16.

63. This discussion draws upon Patricia Lee Dorff, ed., "Chronology 1992," *Foreign Affairs: America and the World 1992/93*: 215–218, 230–233.

64. Ibid. Also see Michael Wines, "Bush and Yeltsin Agree to Cut Long-Range Atomic Warheads: Scrap Key Land-Based Missiles," *New York Times,* June 17, 1992, A1 and A6.

65. U.S. Senate, *The START Treaty,* Report of the Committee on Foreign Relations,

United States Senate (Washington, DC: U.S. Government Printing Office, 1992), p. 3.

66. The treaty details are summarized more fully in "START II Treaty," U.S. Department of State *Dispatch* 4, January 4, 1993 (Washington, DC: Bureau of Public Affairs, 1993), pp. 5–7, from which our discussion draws.

67. See "Bush Signs Freedom Support Act," *Congressional Quarterly Almanac 1992* (Washington, DC: Congressional Quarterly, Inc., 1993), pp. 523–524.

68. Andrew Rosenthal, "Bush and Kohl Unveil Plan for 7 Nations to Contribute $24 Billion in Aid to Russia," *New York Times,* April 2, 1992, A1.

69. "Freedom Support Act Highlights," *Congressional Quarterly Almanac 1992* (Washington, DC: Congressional Quarterly, Inc., 1993), p. 526. Also see U.S. Department of Defense, "Semi-Annual Report on Program Activities to Facilitate Weapons Destruction and Nonproliferation in the Former Soviet Union," April 30, 1994.

70. Lawrence Eagleburger, "Charting the Course: U.S. Foreign Policy in a Time of Transition," *Dispatch* 4 (Washington, DC: Bureau of Public Affairs, 1993), p. 3.

71. Former secretary of state James Baker is quoted in Elizabeth Drew, *On the Edge: The Clinton Presidency* (New York: Simon & Schuster, 1994), p. 139. The chronology of events here was drawn from that source and from Dorff, "Chronology 1992," pp. 221–230.

72. The sequence of events here draws upon Patricia Lee Dorff, ed., "Chronology 1991," *Foreign Affairs: America and the World 1991/92* 71 (1991/92): 217–220; and Dorff, "Chronology 1992," pp. 243–245.

73. The sequence of events draws upon ibid., pp. 248–251. Also see John R. Bolton, "Wrong Turn in Somalia," *Foreign Affairs* 73 (January/February 1994): 56–66.

74. Eagleburger, "Charting the Course: U.S. Foreign Policy in a Time of Transition."

75. "Remarks of Governor Bill Clinton."

76. Both quotes are from Drew, *On the Edge: The Clinton Presidency,* p. 138. The first is Drew's assessment (for a similar characteri-

zation, see p. 28), the other is her quoting of a senior official.

77. "Enter Mr. Stealth," *The Economist,* January 29, 1994, A28.

78. A former national security council staffer during the Bush administration is quoted in Tim Weiner, "Clinton as a Military Leader: Tough On-The-Job Training," *New York Times,* October 28, 1996, A1.

79. For a discussion of these two reasons that help explain the Clinton administration's difficulty in foreign policy, see Anthony Lewis, "Foreign Policy Morass," *New York Times,* October 11, 1993, A11.

80. John McCain, "Imagery or Purpose? The Choice in November," *Foreign Policy* 103 (Summer 1996): 20–34.

81. See, for example, Gordon Silverstein, *Imbalance of Powers* (New York: Oxford University Press, 1997), pp. 5–6; and Adam Clymer, "A Career Bipartisan: William Sebastian Cohen," *New York Times,* December 6, 1996, A1 and A16.

82. Steven Erlanger, "Albright May Be Facing Unfamiliar Tests," *New York Times,* December 7, 1996, 5.

83. Warren Christopher, "Statement of Warren Christopher before the Committee on Foreign Relations of the United States Senate," January 13, 1993.

84. "Remarks of Governor Bill Clinton."

85. See James M. McCormick, "Clinton and Foreign Policy," in Steven E. Schier, ed., *The Postmodern Presidency: Bill Clinton's Legacy in U.S. Politics* (Pittsburgh: University of Pittsburgh, 2000), pp. 78–79.

86. James M. Scott, "Trade and Trade-Offs: The Clinton Administration and The 'Big Emerging Markets' Strategy," *Futures Research Quarterly* 13 (Summer 1997): 38–39.

87. The four speeches were: President Clinton, "Confronting the Challenges of a Broader World," address to the UN General Assembly, September 27, 1993; Secretary Christopher, "Building Peace in the Middle East," address at Columbia University, September 20, 1993; Anthony Lake, Assistant to the President for National Security Affairs, "From Containment to Enlargement," address at John Hopkins University School

of Advanced International Studies, September 21, 1993; and Madeleine K. Albright, "Use of Force in a Post–Cold War World," remarks at the National War College, September 23, 1993. All quoted passages by the various individuals in the next several paragraphs are from these addresses.

88. See McCormick, "Assessing Clinton's Foreign Policy at Midterm," pp. 370–374.

89. See Henry A. Kissinger, *Diplomacy* (New York: Simon & Schuster, 1994). A portion was excerpted in *Time,* March 14, 1994 and the relevant passage is in *Time* at p. 74.

90. George Szamuely, "Clinton's Clumsy Encounter with the World," *Orbis* 38 (Summer 1994): 393.

91. Michael Mandelbaum, "Foreign Policy as Social Work," *Foreign Affairs* 75 (February 1996): 16–32

92. Douglas Brinkley, "Democratic Enlargement: The Clinton Doctrine," *Foreign Policy* 106 (Spring 1997): 121.

93. John Rielly, ed., *American Public Opinion and U.S. Foreign Policy 1995* (Chicago: The Chicago Council on Foreign Relations, 1995), p. 16.

94. Warren Christopher, "Principles and Opportunities for American Foreign Policy," *Dispatch* 6, no. 4 (January 23, 1995): 41–46.

95. Warren Christopher, "Leadership for the Next American Century," *Dispatch* 7, no. 4 (January 22, 1996): 9–12.

96. Bill Clinton, "Address Before a Joint Session of the Congress on the State of the Union," February 4, 1997. *Public Papers of the Presidents of the United States: William J. Clinton 1997.* Book I—January 1 to June 30, 1997 (Washington, DC: United States Government Printing Office, 1998).

97. Samuel R. Berger, "Remarks by Samuel R. Berger, Assistant to the President for National Security Affairs," Center for Strategic and International Studies, Washington, DC, March 27, 1997, at http://www.pub. whitehouse.gov/uri-res/12R?urn:pdi:// oma.eop.gov.us/1997/3/28/1.text1, July 12, 1999.

98. United States, Executive Office of the President, *A National Security Strategy for a New Century,* National Security Council, Washington, DC, May 1997, at http:// www.whitehouse.gov/WH/EOP/NSC/ Strategy/, August 4, 1999. In fact, in its 1994 National Security Strategy Report to Congress, the Clinton administration had already placed security concerns above the pursuance of economic prosperity, and democratic promotion abroad, but it was not until the 1997 National Security Strategy Report that "there was a new focus on enumerating priorities for America abroad." See Don M. Snider and John A. Nagl, "The National Security Strategy: Documenting Strategic Vision," in Joseph R. Cerami and James F. Holcomb, Jr., eds., *U.S. Army War College Guide to Strategy,* pp. 135–136 online. Available: carlisle-www.armymil/ssi/pubs/ 2001/gidstrat/gidstrat.pdf.

99. Bill Clinton, "Statement by the President to the Nation," The Oval Office, Washington, DC, March 24, 1999, at http://www.pub.whitehouse.gov/uri-res/ 12R?urn:pdi://oma.eop.gov.us/1999/3/25/ 1.text1, June 27, 1999.

100. Bill Clinton, "Remarks by the President on Foreign Policy," Grand Hyatt Hotel, San Francisco, California, February 26, 1999 at http://library.whitehouse.gov/ ThisWeek.cgi?type=pdate=2&briefing=2, February 28, 1999.

101. Samuel R. Berger, "A Foreign Policy for a Global Age," *Foreign Affairs* 79 (November/December 2000): 22–39.

102. McCormick, "Clinton and Foreign Policy," pp. 74–83.

103. J. F. O. McAllister, "Secretary of Shhhhh!" *Time International,* June 7, 1993, 26.

104. Confidential interview with longtime Washington observer, May 2001.

105. Maxwell A. Cameron and Brian W. Tomlin, *The Making of NAFTA: How the Deal Was Done* (Ithaca, NY, and London: Cornell University Press, 2000), p. 201.

106. See Stephen M. Walt, "Two Cheers for Clinton's Foreign Policy," *Foreign Affairs* 79 (March/April 2000): 72–74, for a somewhat more positive assessment in this area.

107. James M. McCormick, "Human Rights and the Clinton Administration: American Policy at the Dawn of a New

Century," in Robert G. Patman, ed., *Universal Human Rights?* (New York: St. Martin's Press, 2000), pp. 128–131.

108. Alton Frye, *Humanitarian Intervention: Crafting a Workable Doctrine* (New York: Council on Foreign Relations, Inc., 2000), pp. 77–85.

109. Ibid., p. 76.

110. Ibid., p. 74.

111. See Bruce W. Jentleson and Rebecca L. Britton, "Still Pretty Prudent," *The Journal of Conflict Resolution* 42, no. 4 (August 1998): 395–418, on public support for various interventions.

6

Before and After September 11: The Foreign Policy of the George W. Bush Administration*

America must be involved in the world. But that does not mean our military is the answer to every difficult foreign policy situation . . . American internationalism should not mean action without vision, activity without priority, and missions without end. . . . A distinctly American internationalism.

GEORGE W. BUSH
NOVEMBER 19, 1999

Every nation, in every region, now has a decision to make. Either you are with us, or you are with the terrorists. From this day forward any nation that continues to harbor or support terrorism will be regarded by the United States as a hostile regime.

GEORGE W. BUSH
SEPTEMBER 20, 2001

---

*"Before and After 9/11: The Foreign Policy of the George W. Bush Administration" by James M. McCormick is from: *High Risk and Big Ambition: The Presidency of George W. Bush,* Steven E. Schier, ed., © 2004 by University of Pittsburgh Press. Used by permission of the University of Pittsburgh Press.

During the 2000 election campaign, George W. Bush announced that he would pursue a "distinctly American internationalism" in foreign policy.[1] Unlike the Clinton administration, he wanted the United States to be more "humble" in global affairs and to recognize its limits in changing the international system.[2] Put differently, he sought to have a foreign policy that placed greater emphasis on American national interests than on the global interests of the Clinton years. While the George W. Bush administration initially sought to move American foreign policy in this direction, the events of September 11, 2001, changed both the content of its foreign policy and the process by which American foreign policy was made. As a result, the administration came to pursue a foreign policy that was universal in scope and that viewed virtually all actions in the international arena as affecting American interests. The universal nature of its policy came to be summarized by its effort to build a "coalition of the willing" to find and defeat "terrorists and tyrants" on a worldwide scale.[3]

In this chapter, we discuss the evolution in both foreign policy content and policy making during the George W. Bush administration. We begin by identifying and analyzing the Bush administration's assumptions and its policy positions adopted prior to the events of September 11, 2001. The initial approach reflected a commitment to classical realism in foreign policy. Next, we assess the impact of those events on the policy approach of the Bush administration and how the policy-making process and the policy content of the administration were altered in response to September 11. In particular, the Bush administration adopted an approach that combined defensive realism and idealism in foreign policy. The efforts to remove the Taliban from power in Afghanistan, pursue Osama bin Laden and al-Qaeda globally, and disarm and pursue regime change in Iraq demonstrate the fundamental direction of the Bush administration's foreign policy approach. In addition, we discuss how this change in direction after September 11 was also manifested in its policy toward other great powers (e.g., Russia and China) and allies (e.g., Britain, France, and Germany). We conclude by evaluating the foreign policy approach that the administration adopted, the criticisms leveled against it, and the implications of the approach for future American foreign policy.

FOREIGN POLICY LEGACIES
AFTER THE COLD WAR

An important point of departure for understanding the foreign policy of George W. Bush is to recall the foreign policy legacies that he inherited from the Clinton administration and from his father's (George H. W. Bush) administration. Both of those previous administrations experienced the seismic foreign policy shock that the end of the Cold War wrought, and both administrations sought to put different stamps on the directions of American foreign policy to replace the anti-Soviet and anti-Communist principles that had for so long guided policy. Neither administration was wholly successful in setting the United States on a new foreign policy course, and both left different kinds of legacies for the George W. Bush administration. In addition to dealing with those legacies, George W. Bush also had to respond to a more fundamental shock, the tragic events of September 11, 2001. In all, these foreign policy legacies and the events of September 11 left the George W. Bush administration with a daunting task in seeking to shape and anchor a consistent foreign policy for the United States at the beginning of the twenty-first century.

George W. Bush's father, George H. W. Bush, largely came to office with a commitment to continue the course that President Ronald Reagan had pursued during his second term: a more moderate, less ideological commitment to political realism. As such Bush's initial impulse was toward a practical political realism (or what might be called *realism lite*) in which he sought to manage the relationship with the Soviet Union and to stabilize relations with other great powers, even as he dealt with other foreign policy issues. As noted in Chapter 5, this commitment to continuity in foreign policy was quickly undermined by the dramatic events that occurred near the end of the first year in office: the opening of the Berlin Wall on November 9, 1989 and the floodgate of other changes that followed in Central Europe. By 1990, the Bush administration began to change American foreign policy from one driven by anti-Communist principles and toward one addressing the new issues facing the international arena. In all, the new policy response took several different forms: The quick American (and coalition) response to the Iraqi invasion of Kuwait in August 1990 was one kind of reaction. The administration's more cautious (and largely noninvolved) response to the ethnic and communal conflicts in the former Yugoslavia was another. And the administration's limited humanitarian intervention to the tragedy in Somalia was yet a third. While these responses were done under the rubric of creating a "new world order," the foreign policy approach of the George H. W. Bush had hardly identified a clear and consistent course for American foreign policy.

Candidate Bill Clinton seized upon this uncertainty to argue for a new direction in policy. During its two terms in office, the Clinton administration sought to forge this new direction. Its initial impulse was to rely upon a commitment to expanding the number of market democracies, since, the administration contended, these kinds of societies offer the best prospect of creating a more pacific international system. This "liberal international" approach, which focused upon promoting free markets and free peoples around the world as a way of creating international peace and stability, stood in sharp contrast to the realism of the first Bush administration. Yet, the Clinton administration had to confront the new realities of the post–Cold War world, with its frequent ethnic and communal conflicts in various parts of the world and with the emergence of competing centers of power from Russia and China. As a result, the administration took a decided turn toward political realism and away from liberal internationalism by its second term in office, as witnessed by its action in Kosovo and by its efforts to strengthen ties with traditional allies.[4] Nonetheless, as the first full-fledged post–Cold War administration, it left an array of foreign policy legacies for the new Bush administration: a commitment to global involvement, a commitment to liberal internationalism in economic and social affairs, and a commitment to humanitarian intervention (or what came to be labeled the Clinton Doctrine) in the political-military arena. As also noted in Chapter 5, these legacies had controversies associated with them from several different quarters.

VALUES AND BELIEFS
OF THE BUSH ADMINISTRATION:
PRIOR TO SEPTEMBER 11

Because the George W. Bush administration was more philosophically inclined toward a foreign policy approach closer to that of his father's administration, the Clinton foreign policy legacies were particularly not welcomed by the Bush administration. Indeed, those legacies were a target of attack by candidate Bush and his foreign policy advisors in the 2000 election and beyond since they represented a more universal and multilateral approach (liberal internationalism) than the new Bush administration envisioned. Yet George W. Bush did not come to office with much foreign policy experience or with his own vision of America's role in the world. In this sense, he was highly dependent upon his foreign policy advisors. As such, the foreign policy team that he chose provided considerable insight into the direction that his administration's foreign policy would pursue. For the most part, Bush selected political realists, foreign policy conservatives, and veterans of recent Republican administrations in Washington as his advisors.

BUSH'S FOREIGN POLICY TEAM:
POLITICAL REALISTS AND VETERANS
OF REPUBLICAN ADMINISTRATIONS

His vice president, Dick Cheney, would quickly become a key foreign policy advisor. Cheney, of course, had been a member of two previous administrations, as chief of staff in the Gerald R. Ford administration and secretary of defense in the George H. W. Bush administration. In addition, he had represented Wyoming in the U.S. Congress for several terms. In this sense, he was readily familiar with Washington and the policy-making process. His views, too, were well established. He was generally regarded as conservative, as reflected in his voting record in Congress, and a strong advocate for promoting American primacy in the world. He quickly came to advance those views in the Bush White House and sometimes got ahead of the administration policy, especially in promoting a more vigorous approach toward Iraq in the months preceding the war with that country.[5]

A second crucial Bush advisor was Condoleezza Rice, who was quickly named as assistant to the president for national security affairs or national security advisor. A veteran of the George H. W. Bush administration, where she had worked on the National Security Council (NSC) staff dealing with Soviet/Russian affairs, she was now named to head the NSC staff and the NSC "system" (see

Chapter 10). Moreover, on foreign policy matters, Rice quickly became Bush's "alter ego," much as she had served in that role during the 2000 election campaign. While she is not viewed as the "master global strategist like Henry Kissinger" and largely sees her role as sharpening the differences among other key advisors,[6] she has ready access to the president and can surely shape the direction of policy by her (largely) private advice. Moreover, one recent indicator of President Bush's confidence in her foreign policy acumen was his fall 2003 directive to have her lead the Iraq Stabilization Group, a group responsible for advancing reconstruction efforts in postwar Iraq.

For the Department of State, President Bush appointed Colin Powell, a veteran of several previous administrations and possessor of a wealth of foreign policy experience, as his secretary of state. During the Reagan administration, for example, Powell had served as national security advisor, and during the George H. W. Bush administration and the early days of the Clinton administration, he had served as Chairman of the Joint Chiefs of Staff.[7] While he was instinctively a political realist, he was probably the most moderate among the key foreign policy advisors to the Bush administration. His deputy secretary of state, Richard Armitage, who also had served in several different foreign policy making posts in the Reagan and previous Bush administration, largely in the Department of Defense, had views compatible with Powell, though perhaps a bit more conservative than those of his boss.

At the Department of Defense, the two top officials appointed were largely conservative voices on American foreign policy, and both came to their positions with substantial policy-making experience. Donald Rumsfeld was appointed for a second time as secretary of defense, since he previously served in the post during the Ford administration. Beyond that appointment, his Washington experience included several terms in Congress during the 1960s, a stint in the Nixon administration, and service as U.S. Ambassador to NATO in the early 1970s. In 1998 and 2000, he served on commissions evaluating missile defense and national security strategy for space.[8] His foreign policy views tended toward promoting American primacy, and his policy impact became especially pronounced in the post–September 11 period. Rumsfeld's deputy secretary of defense, Paul Wolfowitz, shared many of Rumsfeld's views about a more vigorous and singular role for the United States in shaping global order after the Cold War and after September 11. Indeed, in many ways, Wolfowitz was often viewed as the leader of the neoconservatives in the Bush administration, who wanted to reshape American foreign policy utilizing the Reaganite model of the 1980s.[9]

George Tenet remained as Director of Central Intelligence from the Clinton Administration. He, too, brought a considerable amount of Washington experience. He previously served as deputy director at the CIA before assuming the directorship, worked on the National Security Council staff, and spent time on the Senate Intelligence Committee. This kind of experience was viewed as an asset by the new administration.

In all, then, the key Bush advisors were experienced Washington and foreign policy veterans, but they surely tended to be more ideological and more unilateralist than their predecessors in the Clinton administration. As a group, too, they tended to endorse a more realist view of the world and were comfortable with utilizing American power to shape the world after the Cold War. In this sense, George W. Bush and his advisors were more inclined toward a foreign policy that embraced the components of classical realism.

CLASSICAL REALISM AND BUSH'S INITIAL FOREIGN POLICY PRINCIPLES

As noted in Chapter 4, classical realism starts with several important assumptions about states and state behavior that had direct implications for American foreign policy actions. First, classical realists assume that states are the principal actors in foreign policy and that actions *between* states would trump any efforts to change behaviors *within* states. In this sense, the quality of relations between states is the major way in which to evaluate a country's foreign policy, and American policy would focus principally on state-to-state relations. Second, for the classical realist, a state's "interests are determined by its power (meaning its material resources) relative to other nations."[10] As a state's relative power increases, it would seek to expand its political influence, but this expansion of influence would not be done in a mad frenzy. Instead, it would be pursued only after a careful cost/benefit analysis. In this regard, American power can and should be used to restrain states that could clearly harm the United States and its interests, but American power should be used carefully and selectively. Third, classical realists focus upon managing relations among the major powers, since these states are the ones that are likely to be the major threats in the international system. A guiding principle for realists is that no great power, or coalition of great powers, should dominate or endanger a nation or a group of nations. In this sense, some of the broader issue agenda items from the Clinton years—for example, failed states or transnational issues like drug trafficking or terrorism—would not be high priorities for a classical realist. Instead, the United States should focus on strengthening its alliances and on challenging some states. In all, then, the classical realism approach implies that the United States can and should aid global stability from its position of strength, but—and importantly—it should do so in a highly prudent and selective manner.

What the Bush Administration Initially Supported

Other foreign policy values and policy positions flowed from the initial commitment to classical political realism by George W. Bush and his advisors. By considering what the Bush administration initially supported and what it initially opposed in the foreign policy realm, we can gain a better appreciation of how fully classical political realism permeated much of the administration's initial months in office.

First and foremost, George W. Bush and his principal advisors came to office as foreign policy internationalists, although a particular kind of internationalist. Bush characterized his approach as one that sought to develop a "distinctly American internationalism," as we noted earlier. What that phrase connoted, however, was an approach that was more unilateralist than his predecessor and even his father. The phrase, too, implied a much narrower definition of the American national interests than his immediate predecessors, including his father's presidency a decade earlier.[11]

Second, candidate Bush made clear that a top priority of his administration would be to refurbish America's alliance structure around the world as a tangible manifestation of managing great power relationships. Europe and Asia—and not other areas of the world—would be the highest foreign policy priorities, since those regions contain longtime allies—and potential rivals. In refurbishing these alliances, too, all allied countries must be real partners, not satellites, and they must share burdens and risks with the United States. Europe and Japan, for example, should do more to support their own defense.

Third, Russia and China would be viewed in a more skeptical way than the Clinton administration had done, and American military capacity would be important for exercising American influence with these nations. China, for example, should be viewed as an emerging power and as "a competitor, not a strategic partner."[12] Candidate Bush went on to say that "we must deal with China without ill will, but without any illusion." Before the 2000 election, future national security advisor Condoleezza Rice suggested the policy approach: "It is important to promote China's internal transition through economic interaction while containing Chinese power and security ambitions. Cooperation should be pursued, but we should never be afraid to confront Beijing when our interests collide."[13]

According to the Bush administration, the United States should deal with Russia in a somewhat different way, albeit with more skepticism than in the past. We need to be concerned "less by Russia's strength," Rice noted, and more by its "weakness and incoherence."[14] Hence, the focus must be on the security of its nuclear arsenal and the dangers that loose nuclear weapons pose. Furthermore, she argued, we must always be aware that Russia, like China, will continue to have interests at variance with those of the United States.

Fourth, candidate (and President) Bush valued the role of "hard power" over "soft power" for the United States.[15] Hard power refers to the utility of military capacity, sanctioning behavior, and threat behavior, among other coercive measures, as ways to influence the behavior of nations. Soft power relies upon the appeal of American culture and American values to enable the United States to influence the behavior of other states. In Bush's view, hard power is to be preferred, since there are still adversaries in the world who do not like what the United States represents and will take actions to harm America. Moreover, the forces hostile to the United States today only understand traditional hard power; they are unlikely to be dissuaded by soft power.

Fifth, and in line with refurbishing alliances and with the use of hard power, candidate Bush made clear that remaking and strengthening the American military would be a top priority. Hence, increased military pay and increased military spending would be key priorities for his administration. Perhaps the poster child for the Bush administration's commitment to military preparedness was its commitment to develop and deploy a national missile defense as a protection against rogue states or against groups with access to weapons of mass destruction.

What the Bush Administration Initially Opposed

Both candidate and President Bush also knew what foreign policy actions he opposed. Most fundamentally, the administration sought to narrow the number of American actions around the world and focus only on strategically important ones. This position, too, is highly compatible with classical realism.

First, the United States would not be as involved in trying to change other states internally or create political democracy within other countries. As candidate Bush stated:

> America cherishes [its] freedom, but we do not own it. We value the elegant structures of our own democracy—but realize that, in other societies, the architecture will vary. We propose our principles, but we must not impose our culture.[16]

In other words, the United States would invite other states to imitate its values and political structure, but it would not seek to impose them on other states.

Second, Bush opposed American humanitarian interventions without a clear strategic rationale for being involved in such missions. Thus, American involvement in communal and regional conflicts would be rare. Condoleezza Rice made the point forcefully. The American military is neither "a civilian police force" nor "a political referee," in internecine and communal conflicts. "And it is most certainly not designed to build a civilian society."[17]

The administration demonstrated its reluctance to become involved in regional and communal conflict early on. In the election campaign, candidate Bush proposed to bring American military forces home from its peacekeeping duties in the Balkans if elected. Later, President Bush indicated that the administration would pull back from American involvement in Middle East discussions. The administration also sought to move away from negotiations with the North Koreans during its first months in office. In all, there was a reluctance to engage the United States in important ethnic, communal, and regional conflicts that existed in the world.

Third, the Bush administration eschewed involvement with international institutions and opposed several key international agreements. For example, the administration rejected the Kyoto Protocol to control global warming, opposed the Comprehensive Test Ban Treaty as a means of stopping the spread of nuclear weapons to new nations, and indicated its willingness to withdraw from the 1972 ABM Treaty in order to deploy national missile defense. While the Bush administration endorsed efforts at freeing up global trade, it was undoubtedly more cautious about embracing environmental and labor standards within the World Trade Organization. More generally, the administration looked skeptically on the United Nations as a key instrument of American foreign policy.

Fourth, and like past American administrations, the Bush administration was not inclined to afford much influence to the Congress in the conduct of American foreign policy or to America's allies. Despite winning the presidency by the narrowest of margins, the administration tended to pursue its foreign policy (and its domestic agenda) in a manner that suggested a wider mandate than it possessed. Similarly, and given Bush's general approach to foreign policy, he was more inclined to pursue an international agenda singularly—without being encumbered too greatly by the views of allies.

THE IMPACT OF SEPTEMBER 11

Much as December 7, 1941 was a "day of infamy" for earlier generations of Americans, September 11, 2001, will be such a day for the current American generation. Indeed, it is one of those days in which every American will always remember where they were, and what they were doing, when they first heard that American Airlines flight 11 crashed into the north tower of the World Trade Center, or a few minutes later when United Airlines flight 175 crashed into the south tower. Few, too, will forget where they were a little while later when American Airlines flight 77 crashed into the Pentagon and United Airlines Flight 93 crashed in a field in Pennsylvania after an attempt by the passengers to overpower their hijackers.

From an analytic point of view, the events of that day represent one of those rare and spectacular political events that can change the mindset or the image of the public and its leaders regarding foreign policy. Such watershed events are rare indeed, as one political scientist noted many years ago, but when they do occur, they can reverse or change the views toward the international system of a generation or more.[18] The Vietnam War—or the "searing effects of Vietnam" to use the words of a political scientist at the time—was another of those spectacular events that had a jarring effect on attitudes toward war and peace and toward the use of American force abroad in an earlier period.[19] More recently, the collapse of the Berlin Wall and the implosion of the Soviet Union—the ending of the Cold War—might be cited as similar spectacular events in affecting foreign policy. Yet September 11 appears to rank at the top end of these spectacular events because of its pervasive effect not only for the generation being socialized to politics at the time, but also for the leveling effect it had on foreign policy beliefs across generations.

In this sense, September 11 has had a more profound effect than these other spectacular events—whether Pearl Harbor, the Vietnam War, or the Berlin Wall— for at least three reasons. First, it was the first substantial attack upon the American continental homeland since the burning of Washington in the War of 1812. The American public had always assumed the security of the U.S. homeland, and these events shattered that assumption. September 11 demonstrated that no state or person was secure from those determined to do them harm. Second, September 11 was fundamentally an attack upon American civilians, not military personnel (although, to be sure, military personnel were killed at the Pentagon). Even Pearl Harbor and its devastation had fundamentally been directed at military personnel.

Third, and important, the terrorist attack was the deadliest in American history—costing almost 3,000 lives and surpassing the total at Pearl Harbor by almost 1,000 deaths. In all, then, September 11 produced a profound and pronounced effect, whether measured by the changed attitudes among the American public toward foreign policy, the changed agenda within Congress with new levels of support for the president on foreign policy issues, or the changed nature of the presidency itself.

Impact on the Public and Congress

The impact of September 11 on the American people was evident almost immediately after the attacks. Hosts of Americans were suddenly flying flags from their car windows, wearing them on their lapels, and pasting them to the front windows of their homes. People of all walks of life and from all parts of the country exhibited a huge outpouring of support for the victims of September 11, 2001, and their families. Support, too, for President Bush and his foreign policy actions increased across party lines. Bush's approval went from 51 percent just prior to September 11, 2001 to 86 percent approval immediately after the event. The "rally 'round the flag" effect by the American public (35 points) was the largest ever recorded by the Gallup polling organization. Indeed, within a short time, Bush's approval rating had reached 90 percent.[20]

Although the immediate outpouring of patriotism and support for the president by the public is not surprising given the gravity of the events of September 11, what was unusual was the lasting effect of this so-called rally effect. The average level of public support for Bush during the first four months after September 11, 2001 was 84 percent.[21] A year after September 11, 2001, his public approval was still at 70 percent. After a total of eighteen months in office, Bush's average approval over that time frame was 72 percent, the highest cumulative average of any post-Vietnam president, and the third highest for that time period (after Kennedy and Johnson) of any post–World War II president.[22] To be sure, his support began to decline prior to the war with Iraq in early 2003, rose with the outbreak of war,[23] and began to decline as post-Iraqi reconstruction proved difficult.[24] Still, the lingering support for President Bush (even in the midst of recession and a weak economy) seemed tied to the residual impact of September 11.

After September 11, 2001, the American public's foreign policy attitudes took a sharp turn away from those that it had held as recently as the 1998 Chicago Council on Foreign Relations survey.[25] Now, those attitudes supported a more robust American approach abroad. In particular, while the public continued to provide strong support for nonmilitary measures to address terrorism, the public was now willing to endorse a variety of military measures as well. The public supported the use of American air strikes and ground troops against terrorists and would even support the assassination of terrorist leaders when such efforts were done with multilateral support. A large majority of the public, too, favored the use of American troops against Iraq, although they favored a multilateral approach toward the invasion of that country. The public gave strong support for more spending on defense and more spending on gathering intelligence. Sixty-five percent of the public wanted to increase spending on homeland security. A majority of the public also supported the maintenance of American military bases overseas. In all, then, the public was hardly a constraint on the foreign policy actions of the president after September 11; instead, it appeared to be endorsing the actions that the administration was already pursuing or contemplating.

September 11 had a similar effect on Congress and its role in policy making, especially when compared to that institution's role over the previous three decades. The end of the Cold War accelerated the pluralistic decision-making process that had emerged after the Vietnam War and enhanced the role of Congress. With the collapse of the Soviet Empire and the breakup of the Soviet Union, for instance, the America's foreign policy issue agenda changed dramatically, and a broad array of new economic, environmental, social-cultural, and security issues now took center stage. Many of these issues allowed or required congressional action, and many of them did not immediately produce common positions among the American people or among members of Congress. As a result, foreign policy issues became increasingly partisan and contentious. Indeed, the Clinton administration fought numerous difficult battles with the Republican-controlled Congress on foreign policy during its time in office, and it had a decidedly mixed record in this new political environment.[26]

In large measure, the events of September 11 changed all that, and, much like the impact on public attitudes, these events served as a watershed in congressional-executive relations on foreign policy. In particular, September 11, 2001, seems to have resurrected an aphorism popular during the height of the Cold War: "Politics stops at the water's edge." Much as the public rallied behind the president after September 11, members of Congress appeared to put aside partisan divisions to confront international terrorism. Symbolically, President Bush's embrace of Senator Tom Daschle, leader of the Senate majority at the time, after a speech in the House of Representatives, aptly portrayed this new sense of unity. Substantively, the impact of September 11 on congressional behavior manifested itself in the high degree of bipartisan support for legislation to combat international terrorism.

Within a week of the September 11, 2001, attack, Congress had enacted Senate Joint Resolution 23 authorizing the president to use force "against those nations, organizations, or persons, he determines planned, authorized, committed, or aided the terrorist attacks." Just over a month later, Congress passed the USA PATRIOT Act that afforded the executive branch greater discretion in pursuing terrorist suspects and narrowed some previous civil liberty protections. Over the next several months, Congress passed several pieces of legislation that afforded the executive greater power in dealing with international terrorism, ranging from waiving previous restrictions on aid to Pakistan and enhancing border security and visa entry requirements to aiding the victims of terrorism, increasing intelligence authorization, and amending the immigration statute. As Table 6.1 shows, some 21 pieces of legislation were passed as part of the congressional response to September 11.[27]

Table 6.1 also shows that these pieces of legislation were largely passed without much dissent on the part of the members of Congress. In all, only five pieces

Table 6.1 Legislation Related to the Attack on September 11

	Date	Public Law #	Vote: House	Vote: Senate
Congressional Sentiment	9/18/01	107-39	Without Objection	100–0
Authorization for Use of Military Force	9/18/01	107-40	Without Objection	98–0
Public Safety Officer Benefits bill	9/18/01	107-37	413–0	Unanimous Consent
Emergency Supplemental Appropriations Act	9/18/01	107-38	422–0	Unanimous Consent
Air Transportation Safety and System Stabilization Act	9/22/01	107-42	356–54	Unanimous Consent
A bill to amend the Immigration and Nationality Act	10/1/01	107-45	Without Objection	Unanimous Consent
USA PATRIOT Act	10/26/01	107-56	357–66	98–1
Foreign Assistance Waivers	10/27/01	107-57	Voice Vote	Unanimous Consent
Aviation and Transportation Security Act	11/19/01	107-71	410–9	Voice Vote
Designating September 11 as Patriot Day	12/18/01	107-89	407–0	Unanimous Consent
Afghan Women and Children Relief Act	12/21/01	107-81	Voice Vote	Unanimous Consent
National Defense Authorization Act for Fiscal Year 2002	12/28/01	107-107	382–40	96–2
Intelligence Authorization Act for Fiscal Year 2002	12/28/01	107-108	Voice Vote	100–0
Higher Education Relief Opportunities for Students Act	1/15/02	107-122	Voice Vote	Unanimous Consent
Victims of Terrorism Relief Act of 2001	1/23/02	107-134	418–0	Unanimous Consent
Extended Unemployment Compensation bill	3/25/02	107-154	Voice Vote	Unanimous Consent
Enhanced Border Security and Visa Entry Reform Act	5/14/02	107-173	411-0	97–0
Bioterrorism Response Act of 2001	6/12/02	107-188	425–1	98–0
Export-Import Bank Reauthorization Act	6/14/02	107-189	344–78	Unanimous Consent
Police and Fire Chaplains Public Safety Officers' Benefit Act	6/24/02	107-196	Without Objection	Unanimous Consent
Terrorist Bombings Convention Implementation Act	6/25/02	107-197	381–36	83-1

SOURCE: http://thomas.loc.gov/house/terrorleg/htm.

of legislation produced any opposition, and this opposition was confined to the House of Representatives. Even the five pieces of legislation that garnered opposition—the Air Transportation Safety and System Stabilization Act, the USA PATRIOT Act, the Terrorist Bombings Convention Implementation Act, the

Export-Import Bank Reauthorization Act, and the National Defense Authorization Act—had only a modest number of votes against them. The percentage of opposition among these five, for instance, included two votes with 9 percent opposed, and the other three votes with 13, 16, and 18 percent opposed. In all, then, there was overwhelming congressional support for the president in the first year after September 11.

This level of congressional support continued in the second year as well, though not quite at the same level. In October 2002, Congress passed a joint resolution authorizing the president to use force "as he determines to be necessary and appropriate in order to defend the national security of the United States against the continuing threat posed by Iraq and enforce all relevant United Nations Security Council Resolutions regarding Iraq," and it did so by a large margin in each chamber (House by a vote 296–133, Senate by a vote of 77–23). The Department of Homeland Security Act of 2002 was passed by a wide margin in the House (295–133), but the bill was stalled in the Senate for a time. After the Republicans' and President Bush's success in the 2002 congressional elections, the Senate acted quickly, passing that measure by a 90–9 vote in November 2002 and establishing one of the largest governmental bureaucracies in the history of the American Republic. In all, then, despite occasional questioning of the administration's policy on terrorism by some members of Congress, there was bipartisan support and interbranch cooperation on this issue.

Impact on the President

Finally, and importantly, the events of September 11, 2001, appeared to have had a profound impact on George W. Bush himself. This effect was evidenced at both a personal and policy level. On the night of those tragic events, President George W. Bush dictated for his diary that "the Pearl Harbor of the 21st century took place today."[28] With that assessment, President Bush appeared to realize that he had new responsibilities. "He was now a wartime president,"[29] as Bob Woodward noted, with all the implications of that judgment for his leadership.

Analyst Fred Greenstein, a longtime student of presidents, provided an important window on how the president was affected by comparing Bush's leadership style before and after the events of that day.[30] In particular, by assessing Bush's leadership on six qualities—emotional intelligence, cognitive style, political skill, policy vision, organization capacity, and effectiveness as a public communicator—Greenstein finds that Bush's cognitive style and his effectiveness with the public were the areas most affected and the other four leadership qualities were sometimes strengthened.

In the area of emotional intelligence, for example, the events of September 11 strengthened Bush's ability to face this national tragedy, and his political skills were sharpened as well by the need to try to put together a coalition against terrorism. While Bush had always had a fairly clear policy vision and possessed the ability to maintain a strong organizational team, September 11 strengthened his resolve in these areas. In the two other areas, September 11 had a greater effect. While Bush was routinely criticized during the 2000 campaign as lacking "intellectual curiosity" and not "drawn to the play of ideas," he appeared transformed by September

11, 2001. Now Bush had become more "thoughtful" and more "focused" in his thinking. Furthermore, and perhaps the most important leadership transformation, Bush became a more effective communicator to the American public and beyond. As Greenstein noted, "Bush has made himself a public presence." Through his visits to the World Trade Center and the Pentagon and with his eulogy at the National Cathedral, Bush conveyed his transformation in this area.

Two other scholars who focus upon the role of personality in policy making largely reach the same conclusion about the impact of September 11 on President George W. Bush's increased attention on foreign policy. As Preston and Hermann note: "[Bush's] normal lack of interest in foreign affairs and desire to delegate the formulation and implementation of foreign policy to others, which had been the dominant pattern within his advisory system before the terrorist attacks, was forced to give way to his current, more active and involved pattern."[31] In this sense, foreign policy became a real focal point for him. Nonetheless, Preston and Hermann also contend that Bush continued to see global issues in black-and-white terms (an approach that he used to convey a sense of moral clarity in the public arena), and he still relied upon a "like-minded inner circle of advisers for policy guidance."[32] In this sense, his leadership style on foreign policy showed elements of continuity, even as it changed after September 11.

VALUES AND BELIEFS OF THE BUSH ADMINISTRATION: AFTER SEPTEMBER 11

If several aspects of President Bush's leadership style were affected by the tragic events at the World Trade Center and the Pentagon, the administration's approach to foreign policy and its content was as well. Almost overnight, the administration changed its course in important ways. While these events ironically confirmed some of the administration's assumptions about the world and its approach (e.g. the importance of hard power over soft power and the need for enhanced military preparedness), they also suggested the limitation of the Bush's commitment to classical realism. While the administration did not do a *volte-face* in policy, it appeared to change its approach from classical realism to defensive realism and incorporated a distinct form of idealism to its foreign policy actions.

Defensive Realism/Limited Idealism

While defensive realism makes many of the same assumptions as classical realism, it differs in one meaningful aspect: the importance of "insecurity" as the motivating force for state actions. Fareed Zakaria summarizes the fundamental difference when he compares defensive realism and classical realism:

> While the latter implies that states expand out of confidence, or at least out of an awareness of increased resources, the former maintains that states expand

out of fear and nervousness. For the classical realist, states expand because they can; for the defensive realist, states expand because they must.[33]

The new threatening environment after September 11, 2001, thus propelled the Bush administration to change some of its foreign policy assumptions and actions—and eventually to create a new security strategy statement that incorporated elements of defensive realism rather than classic realism.

Combined with this new defensive realism, the Bush administration also embraced a form of idealism in foreign affairs, especially as it related to combating international terrorism in the post–September 11 era. A nation pursuing an idealist foreign policy approach is motivated by a moral imperative in its actions and seeks to promote common values within and across states. In this sense, foreign policy becomes more than state-to-state relations among the strong and instead seeks to advance universal norms worldwide. In the post–September 11 period, the Bush administration sought to do just that as it promoted a worldwide imperative against terrorism. As such, it became increasingly concerned about the actions of all states (and groups) and the internal composition of many states, especially concerning their attitude toward terrorism. Put somewhat differently, the administration appeared to embrace the Wilsonian tradition in American foreign policy, albeit an idealism driven rather singularly on combating international terrorism.[34]

Changes in Assumptions

At least three initial foreign policy assumptions that the Bush administration had embraced were changed in the immediate post–September 11, 2001, world.[35] First, and perhaps most significant, the Bush administration moved from a narrow or particularistic foreign policy approach to a more universal one. That is, it moved from a concern with narrowing American national interests as compared to the Clinton years to broadening those interests to pursue universal security for all states threatened by international terrorism. Indeed, the administration, in various ways, equated American security from terrorism to universal security for all states. Second, the Bush administration moved away from its rather narrowly defined unilateralist approach to American foreign policy to a greater multilateral effort, albeit a multilateralism with a unilateralist option for the United States.

Its involvement against terrorism with a broad array of states, with regional and international institutions, and with its multiple activities at home reflected this evident, but reluctant, multilateralism. In all of these arenas, the United States sought to pursue multilateral efforts, although President Bush threatened to act unilaterally, if multilateral support did not develop—much as the war against Iraq ultimately demonstrated. In this sense, the depth of the administration's commitment to multilateralism has been rightly questioned by numerous critics.

Third, the administration moved from its reliance on a stark realist approach to foreign policy—without much concern with the internal dynamics of states—to a version of idealism—with a clear concern about the internal dynamics of some states. For other states, the United States became more concerned with the attitudes and policies of some states regarding terrorism and less concerned with other internal conditions within those states. In this regard, humanitarian interventions, peacekeeping efforts, and peacemaking actions within states had now become part and parcel of the Bush foreign policy approach, not unlike his immediate predecessor.

Some Change in Policy Direction

The universal nature of the post–September 11, 2001, foreign policy approach is captured best in President Bush's address to a joint session of Congress shortly after September 11. Instead of embracing a policy of a "distinctly American internationalism," as he had done in the 2000 election campaign, President Bush now adopted what we might call a "comprehensive American globalism," albeit narrowly defined and animated by the moral outrage against the attacks on the World Trade Center and the Pentagon. That is, President Bush committed the United States to fighting terrorism, and states that support terrorism everywhere—and with all means. As he noted:

> Our enemy is a radical network of terrorists, and every government that support them. . . .

> Our war on terror begins with al Qaeda, but it does not end there. It will not end until every terrorist group of global reach has been found, stopped and defeated.[36]

In words reminiscent of the Truman Doctrine at the start of the Cold War, President Bush outlined the dichotomous and stark nature of the global struggle—a struggle between the way of terror and the way of freedom, a struggle between those states who support terror and those who do not, and a struggle between the uncivilized and civilized world. Recall what he said:

> These terrorists kill not merely to end lives, but to disrupt and end a way of life. With every atrocity, they hope that America grows fearful, retreating from the world and forsaking our friends. They stand against us, because we stand in their way.

> [W]e will pursue nations that provide aid or safe haven to terrorism. Every nation, in every region, now has a decision to make. Either you are with us, or you are with the terrorists. From this day forward any nation that continues to harbor or support terrorism will be regarded by the United States as a hostile regime.

> This is not . . . just America's fight. And what is at stake is not just America's freedom. This is the world's fight. This is civilization's fight.[37]

The President also conveyed the multilateral nature of this new foreign policy approach in his initial speech on the war on terrorism, and it was demonstrated by the actions that the administration immediately undertook.

President Bush declared:

> Our response involves far more than instant retaliation and isolated strikes. Americans should not expect one battle, but a lengthy campaign, unlike any

other we have ever seen. . . . We will starve terrorist of funding, turn them one against another, drive them from place to place, until; there is no refuge or no rest. . . .

We ask every nation to join us. We will ask, and we will need, the help of police forces, intelligence services and banking systems around the world. The United States is grateful that many nations and many international organizations have already responded—with sympathy and with support. Nations from Latin America, to Asia, to Africa, to Europe, to the Islamic world.[38]

What was most dramatic about the approach was the decision to embrace a coalitional effort, the speed with which it was put together, and the variety of participants that it included—especially in light of the foreign policy assumptions of the Bush administration when it took office. Table 6.2 lists some of the bilateral and multilateral actions within the first 20 days of September 11 as summarized by the Department of State. It nicely conveys the sense of collective effort undertaken to address the events of September 11, 2001. In addition, of course, cooperative efforts were sought to freeze financial assets of known or suspected terrorist organizations within the United States and around the world. The Office (and later Department) of Homeland Security was created at home, new security standards were imposed at airports, and stricter standards were initiated for immigration into the United States. In short, law enforcement efforts at home and abroad were dramatically enhanced.

By the time that a military operation was commenced in Afghanistan on October 7, 2001, several allied countries (Britain, Canada, Australia, Germany, and France, among others) pledged to assist with the operation. And more than forty nations, by that time, had approved American overflight and landing rights.[39] These expressions of assistance came from several continents and regions (Middle East, Africa, Europe, and Asia). Furthermore, Operation Anaconda in Afghanistan eventually included contributions from some 20 countries from around the world.

A third dimension to this post–September 11 change was the administration's interests and actions regarding communal and regional conflicts. The decision to focus upon the internal situation in Afghanistan is hardly surprising in light of the September events, but what is surprising is the extent to which the administration committed itself to changing or assisting in changing the domestic situations in a series of other countries. These range from the effort to pursue the "axis of evil" countries—Iran, Iraq, and North Korea—to the commitments for military training and advisory units to several countries throughout the world—the Philippines, Yemen, Georgia—and to efforts to use American naval power around Sudan to block possible escaping al-Qaeda fighters.

The administration's efforts at seeking conflict resolution in the Middle East, between India and Pakistan, and opening up discussions with the North Koreans illustrated a newfound concern about internal dynamics of various countries and regions. Almost immediately after September 11, the administration appointed a special envoy, General Anthony Zinni, to the Middle East, and Secretary of State Colin Powell traveled to India and Pakistan in an attempt to defuse the situation over Kashmir. President Bush reiterated his willingness to open discussions with the North Koreans over peace and stability on the Korean peninsula (although this

Table 6.2 Some Examples of Bilateral and Multilateral Efforts to Assist the United States Immediately after September 11

- Russia was the first nation to call the United States and offer to share information and the use of its airspace for humanitarian efforts
- China, India, and Pakistan immediately offered to share information and/or offered support
- Twenty-seven nations offered American overflight and landing rights regarding actions against Afghanistan
- Forty-six declarations of support from multilateral organizations
- One hundred nations offered to provide intelligence support to the United States
- The UN Security Council adopted a resolution instructing all nations to pursue terrorists and their supporters
- Australia invoked Article IV of the ANZUS Treaty and declared that September 11, 2001, was an attack on Australia
- NATO invoked Article V, thus viewing September 11, 2001, as an attack on them

SOURCE: Drawn from Department of State, "Operation Enduring Freedom Overview," accessed at http://www.state.gov/s/ct/rls/fs/2001/5194.htm, March 27, 2003.

was a position adopted as early as Summer 2001 by the administration). At the same time, the administration was willing to look past internal concerns about some nations (e.g. China, Russia, Pakistan), and especially their human rights conditions, since their cooperation on the war on terrorism was more important than anything else for the United States.

In sum, the new approach, quickly labeled the Bush Doctrine, sought to hunt down terrorists, and those that supported terrorists, on a worldwide scale. While cooperation and support from other countries would be sought, the United States would go it alone if necessary. The globalism of this effort and the motivation for its actions represent the major transformations of the policy approach of the Bush administration after September 11, 2001.

FORMALIZING THE BUSH DOCTRINE

In September 2002, almost exactly one year after the attacks upon New York and Washington, the Bush administration issued a fuller statement and rationale for its foreign policy approach. This statement, *The National Security Strategy of the United States of America*, postulated that the fundamental aim of American foreign policy was "to create a balance of power that favors freedom."[40] To create such a balance, the administration asserted that the United States "will defend the peace by fighting terrorists and tyrants . . . will preserve peace by building good relations among the great powers . . . [and] will extend the peace by encouraging free and open societies on every continent." The statement demonstrates how much American actions would now be motivated by the new threatening environment—and how singularly important that environment would be in dictating

United States actions—much as defensive realism would postulate. Yet also note the idealist and universal nature of this proposed foreign policy agenda with its concerns for the internal makeup and operations of states and groups. A summary and assessment of this statement provide a fuller understanding of the Bush administration's policy content.[41]

The administration recognized and accepted the fact that the United States "possesses unprecedented—and unequaled—strength and influence in the world" and acknowledged that "this position comes with unparalleled responsibilities, obligations, and opportunity." It also recognized that the task of building this new balance of power for freedom would be much more difficult than in earlier eras, since the United States "is now threatened less by conquering states than we are by failing ones . . . less by fleets and armies than by catastrophic technologies in the hands of the embittered few."

The Bush administration outlined seven courses of action to promote this fundamental goal of promoting freedom and advancing the "nonnegotiable demands of human dignity":

1. Strengthen alliances to defeat global terrorism and work to prevent attacks against us and our friends

2. Work with others to defuse regional conflicts

3. Prevent our enemies from threatening us, our allies, and our friends, with weapons of mass destruction

4. Ignite a new era of global economic growth through free markets and free trade

5. Expand the circle of development by opening societies and building the infrastructure of democracy

6. Develop agendas for cooperative action with other main centers of global power

7. Transform America's national security institutions to meet the challenges and opportunities of the twenty-first century.[42]

Although these courses of action together constitute the effort to construct this new balance of power for freedom, some of them contribute directly to one of the three peace themes identified earlier. In order to provide a better sense of the direction of American foreign policy and to identify the policy emphasis within the administration, we group these courses of actions under what appears to be the proper theme of either defending, preserving, or extending the peace.

Defending the Peace

The first three courses of actions explicitly focus on defending the peace against terrorists and rogue states. Under the first course of action, the administration seeks to rally nations and alliances around the world to defeat terrorism. The new adversary is now "not a single political regime or person or religion or ideology." Instead, it is an "elusive enemy" who "will be fought on many fronts" and "over an extended period of time. Progress will come through the persistent accumulation of successes—some seen, some unseen." Moreover, a broad array of actions will be used to defeat terrorism—disrupting the funding of terrorists through various means, taking direct actions against terrorists and terrorist organizations, denying territorial sanctuaries to terrorist groups in failed countries, addressing domestic conditions that breed terrorism, and strengthening homeland security. While the national strategy statement makes clear that regional and international organizations would be used in pursuing this objective, it also states that the United States would act alone or through a "coalition of the willing" if necessary.

A second course of action to defend the peace is to address the regional conflicts in the world today. These conflicts "can strain our alliances, rekindle rivalries among the great powers, and create horrifying affronts to human dignity." The Bush administration therefore committed itself to taking a variety of actions to reduce the impact of these regional conflicts on global stability and, where possible, to aid in their resolution. The administration made clear, though, that there are limits to how much the United States can and will do: "The United States should be realistic about its ability to help those who are unwilling or unready to help themselves."

A third dimension of defending the peace focuses on those rogue states and terrorists that might gain access to weapons of mass destruction (WMD). That is, the Bush administration uses the threat of WMD as a way to link terrorists and rogue states and to identify both as the combined enemies of American foreign policy. These rogue states, while small in number, are states "that brutalize their own people"; "display no regard for international law"; "are determined to acquire weapons of mass destruction"; "sponsor terrorism around the globe; and reject human values and hate the United States and everything for which it stands." A major policy imperative for the United States is thus to defend itself, its allies, and friends from these states and groups that would seek to acquire weapons of mass destruction.

In particular, the United States must be prepared to "deter and defend" against terrorists and rogue states, strengthen nonproliferation efforts against them, and have "effective consequence management" against the effects of WMD, if deterrence fails. In one of the most controversial sections of the national strategy statement, the United States must have available "the option of preemptive actions to counter a sufficient threat to our national security." The administration's argument is based upon the view that the terrorists and rogue states that possess these weapons will not be deterred and will use acts of terrorism and weapons of mass destruction in any effort to achieve their ends. Under appropriate safeguards, then, the United States must be prepared to act preemptively against such adversaries.

Preserving the Peace

While the first three courses of action would also contribute to preserving the peace, the sixth course of action—developing cooperation with other centers of power—is the one course of action explicitly focused on that goal. Under this course of action, the United States would seek to lead a broad coalition, "as broad as practicable," as the document puts it, to promote a balance of power in favor of freedom. This broad coalition, moreover, would thus join together as a means to achieve the first three courses of action—namely defending the peace against terrorists and rogue states.

The coalition-building effort would involve America's traditional allies, such as NATO (and an expanded NATO), Japan, Australia, Korea, Thailand, and the Philippines, but it would also include Russia, India, and China. In this sense, the Bush administration advocated submerging differences that might exist between the United States and key countries (e.g., Russia, China, India, and Pakistan) in an effort to build a larger and nearly universal coalition against international terrorism. What is particularly noteworthy about this section of the document is its relative silence on the role of international organizations, save for some discussion of NATO and the European Union.

Extending the Peace

The fourth and fifth courses of action—igniting global economic growth and expanding the number of open societies and democracies—reflect the economic and political components of the administration's foreign policy approach (as contrasted with the security dimension so evident in the other courses of action). They also reflect the administration's effort to bring more states into this balance of power for freedom and some of its idealistic underpinnings as well. In substance, these two courses of action share a considerable continuity of policy with the Clinton administration's effort to enlarge the number of market democracies, but they convey the priorities of the Bush administration in these areas as well.

The Bush administration's view is that economic growth "creates new jobs and higher incomes. It allows people to lift their lives out of poverty, spurs economic and legal reform, and the fight against corruption, and it reinforces the habits of liberty." Thus, the United States is committed to "a return to economic growth in Europe and Japan" and "to policies that will help emerging markets achieve access to larger capital flows at lower costs." In particular, the Bush administration reaffirmed its commitment to global, regional, and bilateral free trade initiatives as the way to foster global economic growth and development. The protection of the environment should accompany this commitment to economic growth. As such, the administration pledged to reduce U.S. greenhouse gas intensity by 18 percent during the next 10 years as its contribution to a better environment. (This commitment, however, would be accomplished outside the Kyoto Protocol.)

The Bush administration's development aims are closely tied to its economic growth goals. The national strategy statement recognizes that "a world where some live in comfort and plenty, while half . . . lives on less than $2 a day, is neither just nor stable." As such, development is "a moral imperative" for the United States. The administration thus pledged to increase its development assistance by 50 percent, work to reform the World Bank and its activities to help the poor, develop measures to document progress within countries, and increase the amount of funding in the form of grants, as opposed to loans. At the same time, the administration continued to view trade and investment as "the real engines of economic growth." Finally, the administration continued to emphasize basic needs within poor countries, such as improving public health, education, and agricultural development, as its top priorities.

The last course of action in the statement calls for transforming national security institutions at home. While such a transformation would have an impact on all three themes of defending, preserving, and expanding peace, the priorities listed focus primarily on improving the military and the intelligence communities and strengthening homeland security to meet the demands of defending the peace at home and abroad. There is a brief mention of improving diplomacy and the Department of State, but the emphasis is surely more on the "hard power" agencies than the "soft power" ones.

Overall, then, Bush's national strategy statement outlines an approach to enlist a worldwide campaign to address the threats posed by terrorists and rogue states and to create a new balance of power favoring human freedom. The security threats posed by these groups and states seem paramount in the Bush administration's actions toward others. The responses of other states toward these threats will increasingly trump concerns about political differences on other issues and will likely dominate efforts to foster economic and political development as well. Increasingly, the United States will judge states on their commitment to addressing the dangers of terrorism and rogue states and will work to engage other states in a grand coalition against such threats. At the same time, the national strategy statement concludes by emphasizing the commitment of the Bush administration to act unilaterally if collective efforts fail: "In exercising our leadership, we will respect the values, judgment, and interests of our friends and partners. Still, we will be prepared to act apart when our interests and unique responsibilities require."

POLICY IMPLICATIONS
OF THE BUSH DOCTRINE:
IRAQ AND OTHER ROGUE STATES

After Afghanistan, the first real test of the Bush Doctrine of pursuing terrorists and tyrants was, of course, the pursuit of Saddam Hussein's Iraq. Indeed, discussion of Iraq by the Bush administration occurred almost immediately after September 11, 2001. In the first set of meetings by policy makers after those events, Secretary of Defense Donald Rumsfeld "raised the question of Iraq," although the Pentagon "had been working for months on developing a military option for Iraq."[43] At that time, however, President Bush wanted more attention directed toward Afghanistan—particularly al-Qaeda and the Taliban. As such, Iraq was placed on the back burner for a time.

Policy toward Iraq

By early 2002, however, Iraq once again gained the attention of President Bush and key policy makers because Saddam Hussein's regime represented a state that had used chemical and biological weapons against its own people and had started the development of a nuclear weapons program as well. While its link to terrorists

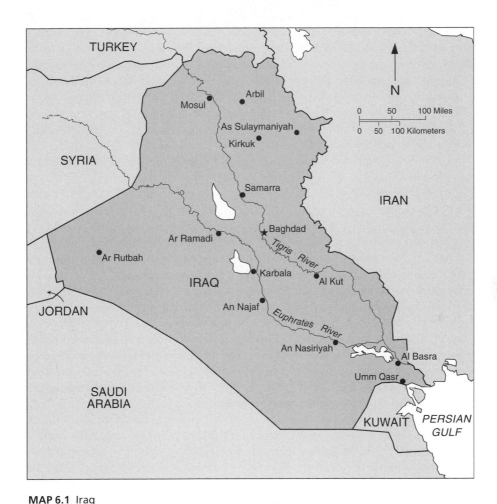

MAP 6.1 Iraq

Source: http://www.cia.gov/cia/publications/factbook/geos/iz.html

was still unclear to many, the possibility of the joining together of a "rogue state" (in the administration's definition) with nonstate terrorist groups was a lethal combination for the United States and the international community.

By summer 2002, the issue had set off a pitched debate within the administration. Some key advisors supported quick and unilateral action to remove Saddam Hussein, while others, most prominently Secretary Colin Powell and his deputy, Richard Armitage, argued that this approach had "risks and complexities" that needed more analysis.[44] In addition, the discussion of pursuing a war strategy against Hussein had alienated Republican allies in Congress and former officials from previous administrations, notably former secretary of state Henry Kissinger and former national security advisor Brent Scowcroft. While these officials supported the need to remove Saddam Hussein, they were concerned that the administration's approach had risked "alienating allies, creating greater instability in the Middle East, and harming long-term American interests."

By fall 2002, the Bush administration decided to challenge the international community, and the United Nations, to address the issue of weapons of mass destruction in Iraq by seeking a multilateral solution. In a speech to the United Nations, President Bush challenged the United Nations to address this issue of Iraq and weapons of mass destruction. As President Bush noted:

> [O]ur principles and our security are challenged today by outlaw groups and regimes that accept no law of morality and have no limit to their violent ambitions. . . . [O]ur greatest fear is that terrorists will find a shortcut to their mad ambitions when an outlaw regime supplies them with the technologies to kill on a massive scale.

> In one place—in one regime—we find all these dangers, in their most lethal and aggressive forms. . . .[45]

After five weeks of negotiation, the UN Security Council passed Resolution 1441 unanimously on November 8, 2002.[46] The resolution found Iraq in "material breach" of a previous UN Resolution (687). (UN Resolution 687, passed at the end of the Gulf War in 1991, called for Iraq's disarmament of its weapons of mass destruction.) In addition, 1441 required Iraq to report within 30 days on all aspects of its programs related to weapons of mass destruction and ordered that Iraq shall immediately allow UN and IAEA (International Atomic Energy Agency) inspectors back into the country. Significantly, the resolution stated "that the Council has repeatedly warned Iraq that it will face serious consequences as a result of its continued violations of its obligations."

In accordance with this resolution, Iraq provided a report to the UN in December 2002 on its weapons program and allowed the UN and IAEA inspectors back into the country. Over the next several months, the chief inspectors provided reports to the UN Security Council on the status of the inspections and the disarmament. In all, these reports indicated that Iraq was not fully complying with the resolution and with the inspectors, but the inspectors requested more time from the Security Council to continue their work.

By March 2003, the Bush administration's patience had run out on the failure of the UN Security Council to act against Iraq. At the urging of Prime Minister Tony Blair of Great Britain, the United States, Britain, and Spain circulated another draft UN resolution to once again find Iraq in "material breach" and implicitly to get approval for military action to enforce UN Resolution 1441. This resolution never reached a vote, since several nations on the UN Security Council, led principally by French opposition and the potential use of its veto, indicated that they would not support it. Indeed, France indicated that it would not support any resolution that would lead to war.

As a result, President Bush issued an ultimatum to Iraq and its leadership on March 17, 2003: "Saddam Hussein and his sons must leave Iraq within 48 hours. Their refusal to do so will result in military conflict, commenced at a time of our choosing."[47] When the Iraqi leadership refused to do so, the United States attacked a command bunker in Baghdad, and the war, called Operation Iraqi Freedom, had begun. The president took this action without another UN resolution and instead relied upon the congressional resolution passed in October 2002. The administration put together a "coalition of the willing" (some 42 nations initially), much as the national security strategy statement of a few months earlier had implied. Yet, the United States and the United Kingdom carried out the principal military action, with some assistance from Australia and a few other countries. In all, the Bush administration was willing to act alone (or with an informal coalition) in addressing the issues of tyrants and terrorists and in implementing its national security strategy.

The war campaign went well and quickly for the United States and Great Britain, with the loss of relatively few lives. The United States gained control of Baghdad by April 9, only three weeks after the war's initiation, and President Bush declared "major combat operations" over on May 1. Still, winning the peace and establishing a stable democratic government proved more difficult. Indeed, Americans continued to be killed over the following months as Iraqi resistance remained. Equally challenging was the effort to uncover clear evidence of the existence of weapons of mass destruction—the fundamental rationale for the war—and to capture Saddam Hussein. While Hussein was ultimately captured in December 2003, the Bush administration's foreign policy came increasingly under greater scrutiny and greater criticism, both at home and abroad, as violence in Iraq continued.

Policy toward North Korea, Iran, and Libya

In his January 2002 State of the Union address, President Bush also identified North Korea and Iran as part of the "axis of evil," and the Bush Doctrine thus had important implications for American policy toward those two states as well. Indeed, both became important targets for sustained effort to deter their attempts to develop weapons of mass destruction, but the approach toward each was markedly different from the one directed toward Iraq. In both instances, deterrence and diplomatic efforts continued to be the preferred strategy.

In particular, North Korea became a source of increased attention and international tension when, in October 2002, that country informed a "visiting American delegation to Pyongyang that it had maintained a clandestine nuclear weapons program."[48] Furthermore, North Korea announced in December 2002 that it would reopen a previously closed nuclear facility at Yongbyon in violation of the 1994 Agreed Framework between the United States and North Korea. A month later, North Korea renounced its adherence to the Nuclear Non-Proliferation Treaty (NPT). In all, North Korea claimed that it needed to have a nuclear capability to deter the United States from taking action against it, especially after the perceived aggressive statements by the Bush administration.

Unlike its policy toward Iraq, however, the United States did not pursue a preemptive approach; instead, the Bush administration sought to employ a multilateral diplomatic effort to deter and roll back the North Korean actions. While North Korea called for direct, bilateral talks with the United States and initially demanded a nonaggression pact between the two countries to move away from its nuclear program, the Bush administration held out for a joint effort by interested states and the international community. By August 2003, initial six-power talks—

among the United States, North Korea, South Korea, Japan, China, and Russia—were held in Beijing.[49] While progress through such talks was slow and at best episodic, the Bush Doctrine clearly yielded a different policy toward North Korea than toward Iraq.

Toward Iran, the Bush policy looked more like that adopted toward North Korea than toward Iraq, even as the administration continued to insist that Iran possessed chemical, biological, and nuclear programs. In the heady days immediately after the fall of Baghdad, the administration appeared to make a veiled threat about moving against Iran, but those comments were quickly downplayed. Instead, the diplomatic and economic tracks continued to be pursued. By December 2003, John Bolton, Undersecretary of State for Arms Control and International Security, continued to maintain that the Bush administration's basic strategy over Iran's nuclear policy was "to use bilateral and multilateral pressure to end" this threat.[50] Moreover, the approach to Iran's biological and chemical weapons appeared to follow the same pattern.

To some extent, the administration's approach on Iran's nuclear policy yielded progress by the end of 2003. In November of that year, the Board of Governors of the International Atomic Energy Agency (IAEA) passed a resolution that "strongly deplores" the failure of Iran to adhere to its obligations under its Safeguard Agreement pursuant to the Nuclear Non-Proliferation Treaty. Fearing that the IAEA might go to the United Nations Security Council, Iran agreed in mid-December to an accord that would allow United Nations experts "full access" to various nuclear research facilities in that country. The Bush administration saw the accord as "a useful step in the right direction," but continued to be skeptical that Iran was being fully forthcoming.[51] As such, the administration continued to challenge the Iranian argument that it was developing nuclear capability only for peaceful purposes, and it also continued to pursue multilateral diplomatic efforts to enforce greater compliance to international standards by Iran.

Libya, although not explicitly mentioned by President Bush in his "axis of evil" statement in 2002, also became a target of administration action over that country's efforts to acquire weapons of mass destruction. While the United States had imposed economic sanctions on Libya for some time over its past involvement with terrorism, it had also been concerned about Libya's efforts to acquire (and even use) weapons of mass destruction over the years. Indeed, its mercurial leader, Colonel Muammar el-Qaddafi, had been accused of developing and using chemical weapons by Washington going back to the 1980s. In a key diplomatic initiative in March 2003, the Bush administration, in conjunction with Great Britain, began secret discussions with Libya at the very time that it was initiating war against Iraq. Nine months later, in late December 2003, those efforts proved successful when British Prime Minister Tony Blair and President Bush announced that Qaddafi "had agreed to give up all of his nuclear, chemical, and biological weapons" and to submit to international inspections.[52] Although Libya claimed that it made this decision of its own "free will," the Bush administration cited it as support for its policy of confronting countries with weapons of mass destruction.[53] Once again, however, the administration's policy instruments to produce this dramatic decision on the part of Libya were largely economic and diplomatic, although it was done against the backdrop of the Iraq War. In this sense, coercive diplomacy might well be a more apt description of the policy approach toward Libya.

POLICY IMPLICATIONS OF THE BUSH DOCTRINE: RUSSIA AND CHINA

Although the Bush Doctrine was fundamentally directed against terrorists and those states that might obtain weapons of mass destruction, it also had an effect on U.S. relations with other major powers, its allies, and friends around the world. Indeed, the events of September 11 and the application of the doctrine toward Iraq had the effect of altering the initial approach of the Bush administration toward two key states, Russia and China. While the administration initially sought to treat each of those powers more as competitors than as partners (in contrast to the Clinton administration's approach), the events of September 11 changed that policy. After September 11, both Russia and China immediately provided support for the United States, and the Bush administration reciprocated with closer ties with each one.

The change in ties began when President Vladimir Putin was the first to call the United States after September 11, declaring that "we are with you."[54] In short order, too, Putin offered his diplomatic support, Russian aid in fighting terrorism, and expressed a willingness to work more closely with NATO. Putin also accepted the American decision to withdraw from the Anti-Ballistic Missile (ABM) Treaty and pledged to continue good relations with the United States despite this decision. In turn, the United States made several concessions to Russia. The United States agreed to a new strategic arms pact—the Treaty of Moscow—that further reduced the number of nuclear warheads available to the two states, down to a range of 1,700 to 2,200 by 2010; designated Russia as possessing "market economy" status in the world; and offered full membership to Russia in the Group of Eight (G-8) countries. Additionally, the United States toned down its criticism of Russia over its policy actions in Chechnya and began to encourage closer ties to NATO for Russia as well.[55] In short, a strategic partnership increasingly seems to characterize the relationship.

The formal enunciation of the Bush Doctrine and the movement toward war with Iraq dampened the increasingly closer ties, but only modestly. Russia, as a former patron of Iraq, was not supportive of such a war and announced that it would oppose such action by the UN Security Council. While the war itself did not erase the progress that had been made in Russian-U.S. ties, it did have the effect of cooling the ties between the two states for a time. After the major fighting in Iraq was over, Russia was willing to work with the United States in the United Nations to pass resolutions calling for aid from other states and working toward democracy in that country, too. Importantly, in December 2003, Russia agreed to cancel a large portion of the debt owed by the former Iraqi government to assist with the reconstruction process. By the end of 2003, some further deterioration in relations took place, especially over American concerns over Russian interference into the internal affairs of Ukraine and Georgia and over the "managed democracy" in Russia itself, where some freedoms were coming under increased pressures from the Putin government. In early 2004, the United States expressed concerns over the level of democratic participation in the Russian presidential election, raising the ire of Moscow, too. In sum, while the close ties immediately after September 11 had waned, U.S.-Russian relations remained stable, despite some clear differences in interests and outlook.

The events of September 11 and then the Iraq War had a parallel effect on U.S.-Chinese relations. After September 11, China provided immediate diplomatic support in the United Nations and acquiesced in America's military action in Afghanistan. At the ensuing Asia-Pacific Economic Cooperation (APEC) forum in Shanghai shortly after September 11, the United States toned down its criticism of China over such vexing issues as Taiwan, its sales of missiles abroad, and its treatment of Tibetans. Additionally, a "cooperative tone continued" during President Bush's visit to Beijing in February 2002.[56]

Once again, the proclamation of the Bush Doctrine and the time prior to the war with Iraq began to sour those immediate post–September 11 ties, but they did not fissure them. China, like Russia, was opposed to American action against Iraq, and it made its position known. It largely favored allowing more time for UN inspections to do their work, rather than using military force against Saddam Hussein's regime. China did not contribute to reconstruction efforts in Iraq, but it did not veto efforts by the United States to get resolutions passed to promote reconstruction efforts in Iraq.

While the application of the Bush Doctrine through preemptive action toward Iraq thus created some stress on Chinese-American relations, the stability in ties between the two powers remained. Indeed, one Asian analyst described the relationship that has evolved as a "selective partnership" in which the two countries cooperate when they can. That is, the relationship is neither the strategic competition that the Bush administration portended nor the strategic partnership that the Clinton administration had hoped.[57] In this sense, the change in the U.S.-Chinese relationship since the first days of the Bush administration "has been one of the biggest foreign policy shifts of this administration," in the view of another Asian expert.[58] Part of the explanation for such change may be tied to the events of September 11, but it is also undoubtedly related to the recognition by both nations of the converging and conflicting interests that continue to shape their relationship.

POLICY IMPLICATIONS OF THE BUSH DOCTRINE: AMERICA'S ALLIES

If September 11 and the application of the Bush Doctrine toward Iraq had the dual effect of improving ties with Russia and China and then chilling those relations for a time, the same can be said of the impact of these events on some of America's traditional allies in Europe and Canada, albeit with an important difference. The difference appears to be a more sustained chill over the implications of the Bush Doctrine. Only in late 2003 and early 2004 was there any evidence of improving ties with some key allies.

U.S. ties with all European states grew closer in the immediate aftermath of September 11. As one analyst noted, "even the traditionally skeptical French press declared, 'We are all Americans.'"[59] As we noted earlier, too, NATO invoked Article 5 of the treaty after the attack. In addition, support from many countries was quickly provided, even for an American administration that had already evidenced a unilateralism (e.g., over the Kyoto Protocol and national missile defense) that had irritated many European states.

While this support and cooperation with allies lasted throughout the 2001–2002 campaign in Afghanistan, relations with some European states—notably France and Germany—quickly soured as the Bush administration turned its sights toward Iraq and its presumed weapons of mass destruction. In addition, the national security strategy statement with its unilateral option for the United States appeared to signal once again that the Bush administration was reverting to a more unilateral approach in global affairs.

While Britain under the leadership of Tony Blair joined with the Bush administration in his effort to confront Iraq, France and Germany, in particular, counseled for a slower and more multilateral approach. (In fact, the Bush administration ultimately went to the United Nations to obtain UN Security Council Resolution 1441, calling for more international inspections in Iraq.) The opposition of these two nations became particularly intense when the United States sought a second resolution in the United Nations to support the initiation of war against Iraq in early 2003. When that effort failed, the United States worked to put together a "coalition of the willing" to initiate the war. France and Germany, along with a number of other traditional allies, including Canada, refused to join that coalition. Some Western and Eastern European nations, including Spain, the Netherlands, Poland, and Italy, ultimately lent their support, but the fissure in American and Western European ties was clearly wrought by the Iraq War.

Indeed, the divisions between France and Germany and the United States continued in the post-Iraq war period as well. The two European powers continued to pressure the United States to turn more reconstruction activities in Iraq over to the United Nations and to turn political control over to that international organization as well. When the United States was unwilling to make these changes immediately, political differences continued. Moreover, the electoral defeat in March 2004 of the Spanish political party whose leader had supported the United States in the Iraq War and the massive demonstrations in allied and friendly countries on the first anniversary of the war convey the sense of opposition to elements of the Bush Doctrine.

These differences were more broadly manifested in changing European opinion of the United States and its foreign policy. Increasingly, the European public took a less favorable view of the United States and its policies after the Iraq War, especially when compared to the post–September 11 period. In Germany, for example, the percentage of the public viewing the United States favorably fell from 61 percent in the summer of 2002 to 45 percent about a year later. In France, the decline was even steeper, from 63 percent favorable in summer 2002 to only 43 percent in 2003. Even in Canada, the public's favorable view of the United States declined nine percentage points from 72 percent to 63 percent.[60] In another survey at about the same time, 64 percent of Europeans surveyed across seven countries—France, Germany, Italy, Britain, Netherlands, Poland, and Portugal—disapproved of the Bush administration's foreign policy. One analyst noted, however, that European anger with the United States goes deeper than opposition to President Bush himself and his policies. As he said in discussing the survey results:

> But would it [European anger] go away if a Democrat took over the White House? Frankly, I don't think so. The poll suggests that Bush's policies are pretty well in sync with American public opinion. If you had a Democrat, they would still have to work basically within those kinds of public constraints. The policies that annoy most Europeans would still be there.[61]

In this sense, the divisions between Europe and America are more long-term, and they are not amenable to a quick fix over one policy position.

The Bush administration did begin to undertake some actions to improve ties with its alliance partners, and they responded in kind. In mid-2003, bilateral discussions at the G–8 summit meetings and other diplomatic initiatives (see the discussion below) began to produce a thaw in the strained ties. By fall 2003, the Europeans and the Americans were cooperating on new United Nations resolutions to address the reconstruction in Iraq, and those actions represented compromises on both sides. By the end of 2003, in a dramatic shift in policy, Germany and France indicated that they would be willing to provide debt forgiveness to Iraq and thus contribute to the reconstruction effort in that country.[62] In December 2003, Canada, under the leadership of a new Prime Minister, Paul Martin, indicated that improving the relationship with the United States was a key priority and that steps would be taken to do so. In all, then, some progress appears possible, but the Bush Doctrine and its implications for American unilateralism remain troublesome to U.S. allies and are likely to be source of tension for some time.

CRITIQUING THE BUSH DOCTRINE

Reactions to the national security strategy statement in 2002 provided the first careful evaluations of the Bush Doctrine, but the policy debates prior to and after the war with Iraq brought into sharp relief the key questions about the Bush approach to foreign policy and its implications for America's role in the world. None of these criticisms succeeded in altering the fundamental approach of the Bush administration, but they highlight the issues surrounding the Bush Doctrine.

Daalder, Lindsay, and Steinberg provided one of the earliest critiques of the national security strategy statement and framed their assessment around five major concerns with it.[63] First, they noted that the goals of promoting freedom and liberty and opposing terrorism and rogue states are laudable, but they also pointed out that the national security strategy statement does not spell out how to achieve these goals in any systematic way. In this sense, a strategy is largely missing. Second, the goals may lead to contradictory actions since some states that oppose terrorism fail to respect freedom within their own countries. Put somewhat differently, the document seems to imply that antiterrorism support from some states is more important than supporting freedom within those states for the administration—especially since the administration is willing to cooperate with states with questionable records on advancing freedom. Third, the national strategy statement had too much emphasis on preemption without much specification regarding what circumstances would justify that course of action. As they noted, deterrence remained the fundamental strategy, but it is somewhat lost in the discussion within the document. Fourth, they disagreed with the emphasis on a "coalition of the willing" versus the use of formal international institutions because the latter can assist American interests more than the former and the creation of the former appears more difficult than the Bush administration acknowledges. Finally, the efforts to promote global prosperity and development were commendable, but they do not go far enough in addressing the institutional needs of failed states. These kinds of states are unlikely to satisfy the conditions (e.g., "fight corruption, respect basic human rights, embrace the rule of law, invest in health care and education") that the administration set out to qualify for this new American assistance. As a result, Daalder, Lindsay, and Steinberg argued: "There is a risk that the countries that need help the most will not be eligible for it, and the countries eligible for it will be the ones that need it least."

An assessment of the national security strategy by John Lewis Gaddis is more favorable than Daalder, Lindsay, and Steinberg's, but Gaddis raised some similar concerns. Gaddis saw the approach as "a grand strategy" that "could represent the most sweeping shift in U.S. grand strategy since the beginning of the Cold War."[64] In that sense, he believed that the strategy has real possibilities for American foreign policy, especially in comparison to the last one developed by the Clinton administration. Yet the strategy also had "potential stresses," as he puts it. The first is what he calls "multitasking"—addressing terrorists at the same time as tyrants may create a problem by stretching attention, resources, and support from others. Other presidents in American history have focused on several foreign policy tasks at once, but such an effort would be difficult and pose a serious challenge for the Bush administration. Second, will the United States be "welcomed" by people in countries in which we act to combat terrorism and tyrants? Put differently, Gaddis wondered whether there is domestic support in other countries for this grand strategy. Such support is necessary to success (and the postwar difficulties in Iraq obviously lend credence to Gaddis's concern). Third, will the United States have the "moral high ground" for this strategy? Implicitly, there is a need for multilateralism for the Bush administration's grand strategy to make it work. As Gaddis readily acknowledges, the Bush administration has not always done a very good job of seeking the support of others. Too often, the administration has "depleted the reservoir of support from allies it ought to have in place before embarking on such a high-risk strategy." In short, unilateralism is simply unlikely to succeed.

Prior to and after the 2003 Iraq War, the Bush Doctrine was subject to additional criticism from several different quarters—both for its policy content and the policy-making process that produced it. All tended to focus on some common themes: The Bush approach was too unilateralist and too ideological in its policy content, and it was too secretive and too ideological in its policy making. Several critics, for example, pointed to a strategic plan developed in the early 1990s by officials in the first Bush administration (and who are now in the second Bush administration) as evidence of the ideological underpinning of current Bush Doctrine. That plan called for a "policy of U.S. global domination."[65] In 1997 some of those same individuals (e.g., Richard Cheney, Donald Rumsfeld, and Paul Wolfowitz) helped initiate the Project for a New American Century, an organization that "called for an aggressive American policy of global domination." With these individuals now in prominent positions in the George W. Bush administration, these officials were simply carrying out the plans developed earlier. Further, the kind of "unipolarism" now pursued by the Bush administration, a critic wrote, is essentially "a nationalistic and militaristic version of the liberal international vision of world democracy," and "the U.S. makes a mockery of its democratic ideals when it bullies other nations to serve U.S. interests and pretends that its bullying deserves to be called justice or idealism." In short, to these critics, neither the unipolarism employed nor the values promoted in the Bush Doctrine serve the long-term interests of the United States.

As the number of American deaths in postwar Iraq continued to mount and as weapons of mass destruction were not found by summer 2003, criticism of Bush policy also arose from the bureaucracy and Capitol Hill. Some charged that the administration had skewed intelligence data to support its desire to pursue the war against Iraq or pressured intelligence analysts to provide supportive estimates. And the Pentagon was accused of developing its own "hard-line view of intelligence related to Iraq" to justify American military actions there.[66] While the Bush administration denied such charges, skeptics remained, and Congress initiated inquiries into these matters. By July 2003, foreign policy criticisms appeared to reach a crescendo when the administration was forced to admit that a passage in the president's 2003 State of the Union regarding Iraq's efforts to obtain uranium from an African nation was not supported by American intelligence. George Tenet, director of Central Intelligence, took formal responsibility for this error,[67] but the episode reinforced the view that the administration was determined to find evidence to justify military action against Iraq. Furthermore, the integrity of the Bush administration's policy making was called into question, and the Senate Intelligence Committee called hearings to investigate.

By this time, too, foreign policy arose in the incipient 2004 presidential election campaign. As Democratic presidential candidates began to test the waters in early caucus and primary states, the Bush administration's foreign policy was now a legitimate subject of debate. Former Vermont governor Howard Dean and Representative Dennis Kucinich, who opposed the war in Iraq, had voiced criticism for some time, but other presidential contenders (Representative Richard Gephardt and Senator John Kerry) who had supported the war followed suit by the summer and fall of 2003. Representative Gephardt, for example, charged the president with "stunning incompetence" in the area of foreign policy.[68] Senator

Kerry accused the administration of failing to have a plan to win the peace in Iraq, pointing to the "arrogant absence of any major international effort to build what's needed" in Iraq.[69] And another contender for a time, Senator Bob Graham, called for further investigations into Bush's policy making. In this sense, foreign policy, and the Bush Doctrine in particular, were again sources of domestic debate after a long hiatus since September 11.

The Bush administration sought to deflect some of these criticisms both by engaging in some diplomatic initiatives on other pressing problems and by initiating some postwar policy in Iraq. It did not, however, alter its fundamental course on terrorism. Indeed, its initial action as the war in Iraq was ending was to hint at possible actions toward Syria and Iran over their policies toward terrorism and weapons of mass destruction. Still, the administration moved away from that approach somewhat by undertaking several significant actions to broaden its foreign policy agenda. First, and perhaps most important, the administration issued its "Roadmap for Peace" on April 30, 2003, regarding the Israelis and the Palestinians, and promptly began to work on implementing it. A Palestinian prime minister had been appointed; Israeli prime minister Ariel Sharon agreed to pull back some settlements in the West Bank; and a cease-fire was negotiated among Israel, the Palestinians, and the groups responsible for the suicide bombing in the region (Hamas and Islamic Jihad), albeit briefly. And Bush visited the Middle East as a further stimulus to supporting this road map. Second, the Bush administration was successful in getting approval for UN Security Council Resolution 1483 lifting sanctions against Iraq and encouraging other nations and international institutions to assist with the reconstruction of that nation. In addition, the resolution established a Special UN Representative for Iraq to oversee the reconstruction process there. In fall 2003, too, the administration also succeeded in getting UN Security Council Resolution 1511 passed. This resolution called for states to contribute to a multinational force in Iraq and directed the Iraqi Governing Council to develop a timetable and a program for a new constitution and democratic elections. Third, President Putin of Russia and President Bush exchanged instruments of ratification of another strategic arms reduction treaty, signaling continued cooperation with a nation that had opposed the war in Iraq. Fourth, as noted earlier, Bush met with European leaders at the G-8 (and most notably with French president Jacques Chirac) to begin to repair the rift with alliance partners that the war against Iraq had created. Fifth, Bush went on a five-day trip to Africa, becoming only the third U.S. president to visit that continent, to promote his AIDS/HIV initiative and to demonstrate a broader foreign policy agenda than the war on terrorism had connoted. Furthermore, the administration sent some U.S. peacekeeping forces to aid strife-torn Liberia, although that action was driven both by security (that is, failed states are likely havens for terrorists) and by humanitarian concerns. Sixth, during a state visit to Great Britain in November 2003 (and earlier to an American audience), President Bush sought to expand the rationale for American foreign policy by emphasizing anew that the promotion of democracy was a key pillar of U.S. action abroad, much as its efforts in postwar Iraq demonstrated. Finally, though, as Iraqi insurgent attacks against the American military continued in late fall 2003, the administration accelerated its efforts to turn over more responsibilities to Iraqis and aimed for the return of sovereignty to the Iraqi people by the summer of 2004.

None of these actions, as noted, reflected a fundamental shift in policy approach by the Bush administration from the one adopted after September 11. Indeed, terrorist incidents in Saudi Arabia in both the spring and fall 2003 and Morocco in the spring of 2003 (and attributed to al Qaeda) only reinforced the administration's stance. Still, the mounting criticism at home and abroad of the administration's unilateral and ideological approach appeared to introduce a more cautionary note in considering further military responses, whether against North Korea, Iran, or elsewhere. For the near term, then, the administration appeared determined to pursue its combination of defensive realism and limited idealism in shaping U.S. foreign policy—albeit at a more muted level than actions against Afghanistan and Iraq implied. The approach, moreover, will likely remain as long as the American public continues to be supportive, the Congress remains relatively acquiescent (as evidenced by its support of $87 billion in military and reconstruction spending for Iraq and Afghanistan in fall 2003), and the international community fails to challenge American primacy successfully. An important unknown is the direction of reconstruction and reconciliation within Iraq. As attacks on Americans continue and the death toll exceeds the total during major combat in March and April 2003, opposition increases at home and public and congressional criticism continue to mount. That situation will likely remain an important factor influencing the direction of Bush foreign policy as well.

CONCLUDING COMMENTS

The events of September 11, 2001, had a significant impact on both the Bush administration's theoretical and policy approaches to American foreign policy. On a theoretical level, September 11 significantly changed the administration's foreign policy approach, from largely embracing classical realism before those events to pursuing defensive realism after them. On a policy level, September 11, 2001, has had a similar effect, from altering the foreign policy-making process at home to changing the content of Bush administration's actions abroad.

The Bush administration came to office committed to creating a "distinctly American internationalism" in which it sought to limit American involvement abroad and to pursue a narrower interpretation of the national interest than the Clinton administration had followed. In effect, this approach was a commitment to classical realism where relative capabilities largely shaped actions abroad and relations with major powers principally dominated the agenda. With the events of September 11, however, the Bush administration jettisoned its classical realist approach and embraced defensive realism, where foreign policy actions were driven more by the threat environment. That is, the broadening threat environment that terrorism posed compelled the administration to pursue a more globalist strategy than it initially envisioned. This new environment, too, saw the administration embrace elements of idealism by pursuing regime (and internal) change abroad, most notably reflected in the war with Iraq, and in providing military support to states threatened by internal (and terrorist) insurgencies (e.g., Georgia and the Philippines).

The effects of these changes were evidenced both on the processes of policy making and its content. On the policy-making side, for example, September 11 enhanced the authority of the president, increased the degree of congressional deference to the executive, rallied public opinion behind the actions of the president, and narrowed America's foreign policy agenda. On the content side, September 11 altered some initial foreign policy assumptions that the Bush administration brought to office (e.g., opposition to humanitarian interventions and a global strategy), but it confirmed others (e.g., the need for hard power over soft power; the importance of security issues over political and economic issues). At the same time, September 11 also afforded the Bush administration the opportunity to attempt to forge a "grand strategy" of foreign policy for the years ahead. That strategy is grounded in the belief that terrorism and rogue states are the major adversaries and that a "coalition of the willing" should be developed worldwide to isolate and defeat those adversaries. Importantly, the United States reserved the right to act alone if necessary and engage in preemptive actions, especially when weapons of mass destruction are in the hands of adversaries.

In all, the combination of defensive realism and idealism of the George W. Bush administration represents a determined effort to restore a more consistent, coherent, and universal foreign policy approach, something that had largely eluded his immediate predecessors, William Clinton and George H. W. Bush. Indeed, in practice, Bush's approach probably resembles more closely the early years of his father's immediate predecessor, Ronald Reagan. Although the context was markedly different in the early 1980s and the early years of the new century, the ideological and universal nature of American actions during each of these administrations—one staunchly anti-Communist, the other staunchly antiterrorist—bear striking similarity to one another. Both were strongly committed to setting a clear course to direct American actions abroad, and both were willing to act alone and use America's military capacity, if necessary. Moreover, the administration of George W. Bush remains committed to that course even in light of recent challenges at home and abroad.

The larger implication of the Bush administration's strategy for American foreign policy, however, remains unclear. Will it usher in a new foreign policy consensus that the American public and policy makers will embrace for the foreseeable future? Or will it isolate the United States from the rest of the global community? On the one hand, the approach has an underlying moral content—so important to the American public in addressing foreign policy—and it is also aimed at a focused threat that the American public can understand and grasp—unlike the diffuse set of threats identified by administrations at the end of the Cold War. On the other hand, the foreign policy approach has the potential of alienating the United States from the rest of the global community, especially at this important time in global politics. As political analyst Fareed Zakaria noted just prior to the initiation of the war against Iraq: "Never will [America] have waged a war in such isolation. Never will have so many of its allies been so firmly opposed to its policies. Never has it provoked so much public opposition, resentment, and mistrust."[70] Not only have America's traditional allies, France and Germany, opposed the unilateralism implicit in applying the Bush Doctrine, but America's many friends and supporters after September 11, 2001, notably Russia and China, have as well. In addition, the larger international community, including the United Nations, has raised serious doubts about this approach, largely through its inaction. Importantly, too, anti–Americanism among states, fueled by opposition to the Iraqi War, has increased.[71] And as the Iraqi occupation wore on with more Americans dying there and questions arose over intelligence analyses prior to that war, public support began to erode. In this sense, the Bush Doctrine may well produce the opposite effect from what the administration had intended, and it may undermine international efforts to confront the many transnational threats, including international terrorism, which it had initially sought.

NOTES

Substantial portions of this chapter appeared previously in "The Foreign Policy of the George W. Bush Administration," by James M. McCormick from *High Risk and Big Ambition: The Presidency of George W. Bush,* Steven E. Schier, ed., © 2004 by University of Pittsburgh Press. Used by permission of the University of Pittsburgh Press.

1. George W. Bush, "A Distinctly American Internationalism," delivered at the Ronald Reagan Presidential Library, November 19, 1999, online. Available: http://www. georgewbush.com/speeches/foreignpolicy/ foreignpolicy.asp.

2. "Election 2000 Presidential Debate II with Republican Candidate Governor George W. Bush and Democratic Candidate Vice President Al Gore," Wait Chapel, Wake Forest University, Winston, North Carolina, October 11, 2000, online. Available: http://www.c-span.org at "Presidential Debates 2000."

3. *The National Security Strategy of the United States of America,* September 17, 2002, online. Available: http://www.whitehouse. gov/nsc/nss.html.

4. Clinton argued that American actions in Kosovo were motivated by a "moral imperative" to aid the persecuted people in this province (and hence were consistent with principles of liberal internationalism), but he also contended that American actions involved "protecting our interests" and demonstrating the continued effectiveness of NATO. See my "Clinton and Foreign Policy: Some Legacies for a New Century," in Steven E. Schier, ed., *The Postmodern Presidency* (Pittsburgh: University of Pittsburgh Press, 2000), pp. 60–83.

5. See Evan Thomas, "Condoleezza Rice, Bush's Secret White House Weapon," *Newsweek,* December 16, 2002, 26, in which Rice apparently had to moderate some of Vice President Cheney's remarks on Iraq.

6. Ibid, p. 27

7. The biographical information on Colin Powell is taken from http://www.state.gov/ r/pa/ei/biog/1349.htm.

8. The biographical information on Donald Rumsfeld and Paul Wolfowitz is from http://www.defenselink.mil/bios/ secdef_bio.html and http://www. defenselink.mil/bios/depsecdef_bio.html.

9. The commitment to this Reaganite foreign policy model is derived in part from Rumsfeld and Wolfowitz's involvement with the Project for a New American Century, in which both (as well as Dick Cheney) signed on to a statement of principles in June 1997. See the statement at the following Web site: http://www.newamericancentury.org/ statementofprinciples.htm.

10. Fareed Zakaria, *From Wealth to Power: The Unusual Origins of America's World Role* (Princeton, NJ: Princeton University Press, 1998), pp. 8–9.

11. Bush, "A Distinctly American Internationalism."

12. Ibid.

13. Condoleezza Rice, "Promoting the National Interest," *Foreign Affairs* 79 (January/February 2000): 57.

14. Ibid., p. 58.

15. George W. Bush, "A Period of Consequences," delivered at The Citadel, September 23, 1999, online. Available: http://www.georgewbush.com/speeches/defense/citadel.asp.

16. Bush, "A Distinctly American Internationalism."

17. Rice, "Promoting the National Interest," p. 53.

18. Karl W. Deutsch, "External Influences on the Internal Behavior of States," in R. Barry Farrell, ed., *Approaches to Comparative and International Politics* (Evanston, IL: Northwestern University Press, 1966), pp. 5–26.

19. Bruce Russett, "The Americans' Retreat from World Power," *Political Science Quarterly* 90 (Spring 1975): 1–22.

20. "Rallying behind the Country's Leaders and Institutions," September 25, 2001, online. Available: TuesdayBriefing@Gallup.com; and Shoon Kathleen Murray and Christopher Spinosa, "The Post-9/11 Shift in Public Opinion: How Long Will It Last?" in Eugene R. Wittkopf and James M. McCormick, eds., *The Domestic Sources of American Foreign Policy: Insights and Evidence,* 4th ed. (Lanham, MD: Rowman & Littlefield, 2004), pp. 97–115.

21. Frank Newport, "Terrorism Fades as Nation's Most Important Problem," January 14, 2002, online. Available: http://www.gallup.com/poll/releases/pr020114.asp.

22. Murray and Spinosa, "The Post-9/11 Shift in Public Opinion: How Long Will It Last?"

23. Lydia Saad, "Iraq War Triggers Major Rally Effect," March 25, 2003, online. Available: http://www.gallup.com/poll/releases/pr0300325.asp.

24. Lydia Saad, "Bush's Job Rating Still Above 60%," July 2, 2003, online: Available: http://www.gallup.com/poll/releases/pr030702.asp; and David Moore, "Fewer Say Iraq Worth Going to War Over," July 1, 2003, online. Available: http://www.gallup.com/poll/releases/pr030701.asp.

25. The Chicago Council on Foreign Relations, "A World Transformed: Foreign Policy Attitudes of the U.S. Public after September 11th," September 4, 2002, online. Available: http://www.worldviews.org/key_findings/us_911_report.htm.

26. McCormick, "Clinton and Foreign Policy: Some Legacies for a New Century," pp. 60–83.

27. This table was constructed from the legislation identified by the House of Representatives at http://thomas.loc.gov/ and the accompanying votes available through that Web site.

28. Bob Woodward, *Bush at War* (New York: Simon & Schuster, 2002), p. 37.

29. Ibid., p. 37.

30. Fred Greenstein, "The Changing Leadership of George W. Bush: A Pre- and Post-9/11 Comparison," in Eugene R. Wittkopf and James M. McCormick, eds., *The Domestic Sources of American Foreign Policy: Insights and Evidence,* pp. 353–362.

31. Thomas Preston and Margaret G. Hermann, "Presidential Leadership Style and the Foreign Policy Advisory Process," in Eugene R. Wittkopf and James M. McCormick, eds., *The Domestic Sources of American Foreign Policy: Insights and Evidence,* p. 370.

32. Ibid., p. 377.

33. Zakaria, *From Wealth to Power,* pp. 8–9. For a critique of defensive realism and a discussion of offensive realism, see Jeffrey W. Taliaferro, "Security Seeking Under Anarchy," *International Security* 25 (Winter 2000/01): 128–161. Considerable debate—and confusion—surround these two concepts, and their use, often sparking a lively discussion of a country's foreign policy.

34. For a critique of this approach, see Gary Dorrien, "Axis of One," *Christian Century* 120 (March 8): 30–35.

35. For another recent analysis, see Ivo Daalder and James M. Lindsay, "The Bush

Revolution: The Remaking of America's Foreign Policy," revised version of a paper prepared for presentation at The George W. Bush Presidency: An Early Assessment Conference, April 25–26, online. Available: http://www.wws.princeton.edu/bush-conf/DaalderLindsayPaper.pdf. Daalder and Lindsay argue that the events of September 11 afforded the Bush administration the opportunity to put into place a foreign policy design that they had already embraced. In this sense, the administration's foreign policy was less changed than actualized by September 11.

36. George W. Bush, "Address to a Joint Session of Congress and the American People," September 20, 2001, online. Available: http://www.whitehouse.gov/news/releases/2001/09/20010920–8.html.

37. Ibid.

38. Ibid.

39. U.S. Department of State, "Operation Enduring Freedom Overview," October 1, 2001, online. Available: http://www.state.gov/s/ct/rls/fs/2001/5194.htm; U.S. Department of State, Office of the Historian, "The United States and the Global Coalition Against Terrorism, September–December 2001: A Chronology," December 31, 2001, online. Available: http://www.state.gov/r/pa/ho/pubs/fs/5889.htm; and U.S. Embassy Islamabad, "Fact Sheet: Coalition Contributions to the War on Terrorism," May 25, 2002, online. Available: http://usembassy.state.gov/posts/pk1/wwwh02052502.html.

40. *The National Security Strategy of the United States of America,* 2002.

41. Also see Ivo H. Daalder, James M. Lindsay, and James B. Steinberg, "The Bush National Security Strategy: An Evaluation," October, 2002, online. Available: http://www.brookings.edu/comm/policybriefs/pb109.htm, upon which we draw.

42. *The National Security Strategy of the United States of America,* 2002. The rest of the quoted material in this section is from the document as well.

43. Woodward, *Bush at War,* p. 49.

44. Todd S. Purdom and Patrick E. Tyler, "Top Republicans Break with Bush on Iraq Strategy," *New York Times,* August 16, 2002, online. Available: http://www.nytimes.com.

45. George W. Bush, "President's Remarks at the United Nations General Assembly," September 12, 2002, online. Available: http://www.whitehouse.gov/news/releases/2002/09/2002/09.

46. "Text of U.N. Resolution on Iraq," November 8, 2002, online. Available: http://www.cnn.com/2002/US/11/08/resolution.text/.

47. George W. Bush, "President Says Saddam Hussein Must Leave Iraq Within 48 Hours," March 17, 2003, online. Available: http://www.whitehouse.gov/news/releases/2003/03/20030317-7.html.

48. Young Whan Kihl, "Nuclear Issues in U.S.-Korea Relations: An Uncertain Security Future," *International Journal of Korean Studies* 7 (Spring/Summer 2003): 79–97. The quoted passage is at p. 84.

49. Ibid., pp. 94–95.

50. See the texts of remarks to be delivered by John R. Bolton, Undersecretary of State for Arms Control and International Security, to the Conference of the Institute for Foreign Policy Analysis and the Fletcher School's International Security Studies Program, December 2, 2003, online. Available: http://web.lexis-nexis.com/universe/document?_m=db581af8ba84e819eda4030efc04a4c2&_docnum=35&wchp=dGLbVtb-zSkVb&_md5=6de8dd06a0293b590c3fed55080cedea.

51. Vanessa Gera, "Iran to Open Nuclear Facilities to UN," Associated Press Online, December 18, 2003, online. Available: http://web.lexis-nexis.com/universe/document?_m=221a4f9a4668a390861be5a6ecf8076f&_docnum=44&wchp=dGLbVlb-zSkVA&_md5=76216dc29c2cc73e8b809758550716d7.

52. David E. Sanger and Judith Miller, "Libya to Give Up Arms Programs, Bush Announces," *New York Times,* December 20, 2003, A1, A8.

53. Ibid., A8.

54. The listing of the items of cooperation and accommodation between Russia and the United States in this paragraph are drawn from Jessica T. Matthews, "September 11,

One Year Later: A World of Change," *Policy Brief,* Special Edition 18, (Washington, DC: Carnegie Endowment for International Peace, 2002), p. 3.

55. Ibid.; and James Steinberg, "Counterterrorism," *Brookings Review* 20 (Summer 2002): 5.

56. Ibid., p. 6.

57. Peter Grier and Amelia Nemcomb, "US, China Find a New Middle Way," *Christian Science Monitor,* December 11, 2003, 1, online. The expert quoted here is Minxin Pei from the Carnegie Endowment for International Peace. Available: http://web. lexis-nexis.com/universe/document?_ m=02fa823a2fc5ab2c8c706501cf453339&_ docnum=16&wchp=dGLbVzb-zSkVA&_ md5=b081383f4b4dfa53ec8ccbe05e7a9afb.

58. Ibid. The expert quoted here is Elizabeth Economy at the Council on Foreign Relations.

59. Steinberg, "Counterterrorism," p. 6.

60. The data are from Pew Global Project Attitudes. *Views of a Changing World June 2003* (Washington, DC: The Pew Research Center for the People & the Press, 2003), 19.

61. These survey results are reported in Glenn Frankel, "Poll: Opposition to U.S. Policy Grows in Europe," *The Washington Post,* September 4, 2003, A15, online. The quotation is from Craig Kennedy, president of the German Marshall Fund, one of the organizations involved in conducting the poll. Available: http://web.lexis-nexis. com/universe/document?_m=34c2cfeb 8e1198a4ae1d474516397b48&_docnum= 56&wchp=dGLbVlz-zSkVb&_md5= ac6f8a32239f9ae57606112211cf6d96.

62. Dana Milbank, "The 'Bush Doctrine' Experiences Shining Moments," *The Wash-ington Post,* December 21, 2003, A26, online. Available: http://web.lexis-nexis. com/universe/document?_m=5f4ea6a41c2d b8c6aef626b89b0e4dac&_docnum=7&wch p=dGLbVlb-zSkVA&_md5=7fb3cfa95ba 18af75f73dc8c027db0d2.

63. Daalder, Lindsay, and Steinberg, "The Bush National Security Strategy: An Evaluation"; and Ivo H. Daalder, James M. Lindsay, and James B. Steinberg, "Hard Choices: National Security and the War on Terrorism," *Current History* 101 (December 2002): 409–413.

64. John Lewis Gaddis, "A Grand Strategy," *Foreign Policy* (November/December 2002): 50–57. The quoted passages are from pp. 50, 55, and 56.

65. Dorrien, "Axis of One," pp. 30–31, and 33 for the quoted passages. Also see the Web site for the New American Century at http://www.newamericancentury.org.

66. Eric Schmitt, "Aide Denies Shaping Data to Justify War," *New York Times,* June 5, 2003, online. Available: http://www. nytimes.com.

67. David E. Sanger and James Risen, "C.I.A. Chief Takes Blame in Assertion on Iraqi Uranium," *New York Times,* July 12, 2003, A1, A5.

68. Thomas Beaumont, "Gephardt Takes Aim at Bush," *The Des Moines Register,* July 14, 2003, 1B.

69. Dan Balz, "Kerry Raps Bush Policy on Postwar Iraq," *The Washington Post,* July 11, 2003, A1, A6.

70. Fareed Zakaria, "Why America Scares the World and What to Do About It," *Newsweek* (March 24, 2003): 20.

71. See Pew Global Project Attitudes, *Views of a Changing World June 2003.*

PART II

The Process
of Policy Making

Now that the reader is generally familiar with the basic values and beliefs that have shaped American policy over time, we shift our focus to policy making itself. In Part II, we examine in some detail the policy-making process and how various institutions and groups—the executive, the Congress, several bureaucracies, political parties, interest groups, and the public at large—compete to promote their own values in American policy abroad. In this section, our goal is to provide essential information on the principal foreign policy makers, assess their relative influence within the decision-making process, and evaluate how their power has changed over time. In this way, the student may be better able to understand how and why particular values, beliefs, and policies are adopted by the United States toward the rest of the world.

Chapters 7 and 8 examine the institutional competition between the two most important participants in the foreign policy process, the president and the Congress. While each branch of government has constitutionally prescribed power over particular aspects of the formulation and conduct of foreign policy, each shares responsibility in shaping America's foreign policy. Because these institutions share responsibilities, conflict inevitably occurs regarding who should hold sway over the process. Chapter 7 explains why the values and beliefs of the executive branch often dominate the foreign affairs machinery of the American government. Chapter 8 discusses the post-Vietnam through the post–September 11 efforts of the Congress to reassert some of its constitutional prerogatives and to engage more fully in a foreign policy partnership with the executive branch.

Chapters 9 and 10 focus upon the bureaucratic structures within the executive branch that compete for policy influence. At least three reasons justify this emphasis upon bureaucracies in analyzing American foreign policy: first, the growth of executive institutions associated with foreign affairs (e.g., the National Security Council, the Department of State, and the Department of Defense) and the expansion of policy activities by other bureaucracies not normally viewed as participants in foreign policy making (e.g., the Office of the United States Trade Representative, Department of the Treasury, the Department of Agriculture, and the Department of Commerce); second, the emergence of competition among bureaucracies over policy options (e.g., the National Security Council vs. the Department of State) and the importance of this competition in understanding policy; and third, the ability of some bureaucracies to dominate policy, not always with adequate control by the executive branch, the Congress, or the public at large (e.g., the Central Intelligence Agency). Chapter 9 examines the role of the Department of State, the National Security Council, and key economic departments in the policy process, while Chapter 10 examines the impact of the Department of Defense, the intelligence community, and the newly created Department of Homeland Security. In the latter chapter, too, we explain how policy making has been coordinated among these various bureaucracies by the president through a system of interagency groups.

The final participants in the foreign policy process are political parties, interest groups, the media, and public opinion. Political parties seek to influence foreign policy making by gaining control of the machinery of government—the presidency, the Congress, and the bureaucracy. Interest groups and public opinion attempt to shape foreign policy making, indirectly rather than directly, by influencing these institutions. The media are important transmission vehicles through which the public and the policy makers learn about important issues. The media also may provide a discreet influence on what issues are on the agenda, how they are analyzed, and how they are decided. Chapter 11 discusses the role of political parties and interest groups and their impact on foreign policy. In the first part of that chapter, we outline the bipartisan tradition that the Democrats and Republicans have often claimed to follow in policy making and demonstrate how this tradition has eroded significantly in the last two decades. Further, we show how the two parties are moving farther apart on foreign policy as ideological differences become stronger, but how the events of September 11 have also affected the political process. In the second half of Chapter 11, we identify the myriad types of interest groups that attempt to influence foreign policy. To illustrate how influence has been exercised by interest groups, we focus in particular on two types that, arguably, have enjoyed the greatest success in the postwar period: economic interest groups and ethnic interest groups. Finally, Chapter 12 is devoted to a discussion of the role of the media and public opinion in the foreign policy making process. In the first part of this chapter, we analyze the growth in media coverage of foreign affairs and the differing roles, as analysts argue, that the media play in the foreign policy. In the second half of this chapter, we highlight several factors that limit the influence of public opinion on foreign policy making, but we also demonstrate that the public can and does affect the actions of foreign policy makers.

7

The President and the Making of Foreign Policy

I think that, clearly, the Constitution leaves to the President,
for good and sufficient reasons, the ultimate decision-making
authority [in foreign policy].

PRESIDENT BILL CLINTON

OCTOBER 1993

On October 7, 2001, on my orders, U.S. armed forces began combat actions
in Afghanistan against al-Qaeda terrorists and their Taliban supporters. . . .
I have taken these actions pursuant to my constitutional authority to conduct
U.S. foreign relations as Commander in Chief and Chief Executive.

PRESIDENT GEORGE W. BUSH

OCTOBER 2001

As a response to the September 11, 2001, attacks against the Pentagon in Washington and the World Trade Center in New York, President George W. Bush deployed American forces to a number of locations around the world on September 24 and began military operations against al-Qaeda and the Taliban in Afghanistan on October 7. In explaining his decision to take these actions, President Bush cited his constitutional authority as a Commander in Chief and as Chief Executive of the United States. He also indicated that he would unilaterally take other actions as necessary: "I will direct such additional measures as necessary in exercise of our right to self-defense and to protect U.S. citizens and interests."[1] Clearly, President Bush views his role as preeminent in the direction of American foreign policy.

Other recent American presidents have as well. In October 1993, when President Clinton was faced with possible congressional restrictions on his ability to use force in Haiti, he too asserted his presidential prerogative in foreign policy. While President Clinton acknowledged that he had a "big responsibility" to "appropriately consult with members of Congress," he, like virtually every president—at least since Franklin Roosevelt—sought to retain his control over foreign policy: "I think that, clearly, the Constitution leaves to the president, for good and sufficient reasons, the ultimate decision-making authority."[2] More than a decade earlier, two former presidents, Jimmy Carter and Gerald Ford, enunciated this long-standing view in a joint appearance. In foreign policy, there is "only one clear voice," Carter said, and that is the president's; Ford endorsed this view by adding that Congress is too large and too diverse to handle foreign policy crises.[3] Presidential dominance, in short, is the usual way to characterize U.S. foreign policy making.

Over the past four decades, however, the U.S. Congress has increasingly challenged the presidency by seeking a larger role in the making of American foreign policy. This congressional resurgence began in the early 1970s, fueled by the Vietnam and Watergate experiences, and resulted in several initiatives that sought to curb executive prerogatives in foreign affairs. That assertiveness continued in the 1980s with major roles for Congress in shaping Central American, Middle Eastern, and Soviet-American policy. As the Cold War ended and as Republican majorities were elected to Congress in the mid-1990s, congressional initiatives did not diminish, and the Clinton administration faced continuous foreign policy challenges from Capitol Hill. At the outset of the George W. Bush administration, it, too, faced criticism from Congress over the direction that it was taking American foreign policy. While the campaign against terrorism in the second half of 2001 muted the congressional voices on foreign policy for a time, congressional challenges of presidential power started to emerge in the early months of 2002. In this sense, the debate between these two branches over the control and direction of U.S. foreign policy persists to this day.

In this chapter and the following one, we examine the struggle between the president and Congress to make American foreign policy. In these two chapters the analysis explores the following themes: (1) why and how the executive has dominated the foreign policy process; (2) why and how Congress has tried to curb presidential power recently; and (3) what is likely to be the relationship between the president and Congress in the twenty-first century.

CONSTITUTIONAL POWERS
IN FOREIGN POLICY

Under the Constitution, both the legislative and executive branches of government have been delegated specific foreign affairs powers. Both branches, too, were directed to share some foreign policy responsibility with the other. This arrangement ensured that Congress and the president could each check the actions of the other in foreign policy, much as the two branches do in domestic policy. Throughout the history of the republic, however, the division of these foreign policy powers between the legislature and the executive has not always been clear. Indeed, political disputes have often arisen over it. In order to appreciate American foreign policy making more fully, we begin our analysis by identifying the foreign policy powers of each branch and the areas of dispute between them.

Presidential Powers

Under Article II of the Constitution, the president is granted several foreign policy powers. First, the president is granted the plenary power to be chief executive, which extends to the foreign policy arena ("The Executive Power shall be vested in a President" and "he shall take Care that the Laws be faithfully executed").[4] He is also granted the power to command the armed forces ("The President shall be Commander in Chief of the Army and Navy of the United States"). And the president is granted the power to be the chief negotiator and the chief diplomat ("He shall have power, by and with the advice and consent of the Senate, to make Treaties . . . shall appoint Ambassadors . . . and he shall receive Ambassadors and other public Ministers. . . ."). The president, in short, is to wear at least three different hats in foreign policy: chief executive, chief diplomat, and commander in chief of the armed forces. With such power at his disposal, the president seemingly possesses the constitutional mandate to dominate foreign affairs.

This delegation in our Constitution of foreign policy powers to the executive branch represented a marked change from the arrangements under the earlier Articles of Confederation, which had no executive branch. During that period prior to 1787, it was Congress that controlled foreign policy through its Committee on Foreign Affairs. Such a process, however, did not work very well. Congress's inability to manage trade policy, maintain and protect America's national boundaries, and deal effectively with Britain and Spain contributed to the need for a new constitutional structure for the young Republic. Indeed, according to one assessment, "*the mismanagement of foreign affairs by Congress*" contributed to the holding of the Constitutional Convention.[5]

While the founders at the Constitutional Convention agreed on the need to strengthen the national government over the states, they were divided over how strong the foreign policy powers of the executive should be. Although they were familiar with Locke's *The Second Treatise on Government,* in which various foreign policy prerogatives rested with the executive, and with Sir William Blackstone's *Commentaries on the Laws of England,* in which the king enjoyed significant prerogatives in foreign affairs as well, the founders largely rejected these models. Instead, they were concerned about too much executive power and were careful to share presidential powers in making treaties, appointments, and war and peace with the legislative branch.[6] Even as strong a proponent of executive power as Alexander Hamilton was led to conclude that the president under the Constitution would have fewer substantive foreign affairs powers than the King of England.[7]

Congressional Powers

Under Article I of the Constitution, Congress does in fact enjoy several significant foreign policy powers. Congress has the right to make and modify any laws and to appropriate funds for the implementations of any laws ("No money shall be drawn from the Treasury, but in Consequence of Appropriations made by Law"). Congress has the right to provide for the national defense and to declare war (Congress is authorized to "provide for the common Defence . . . ; To declare War . . . ; To raise and support Armies . . . ; To provide and maintain a Navy"). Congress is also delegated the responsibility to regulate international commerce ("To regulate commerce with foreign nations") and to use the implied powers (the right to "make all Laws which shall be necessary and proper" for carrying out its other responsibilities).

Constitutional scholar Louis Henkin has argued that Congress has even more powers, what he calls the "Foreign Affairs Powers." These are powers that are not explicitly derived from the Constitution, but derive from the fact that the United States has sovereignty and nationhood. Thus, Congress enjoys additional authority to support legislation to regulate and protect "the conduct of foreign relations and foreign diplomatic activities in the United States." These undefined powers, too, allow congressional legislation in such areas as immigration, the regulation of aliens, the authorization of international commitments, and the extradition of citizens to other states. Moreover, Henkin rather boldly concludes that today there is no matter in foreign affairs "that is not subject to legislation by Congress."[8] In this sense, Congress has a constitutional mandate to be involved in foreign policy, just as the executive branch does.

"The Twilight Zone" and Foreign Policy

While the nation's founders delegated separate foreign policy responsibilities to each branch, they went further by stipulating the sharing of some foreign policy power between them as well. While the president is the chief executive of the United States, Congress decides what laws are to be enforced; while the president may command the armed forces, Congress decides whether wars should be initiated; and while the president may negotiate treaties, Congress (or more accurately, the Senate) must give its advice and consent. (Table 7.1 shows three areas of shared foreign policy powers as outlined in Articles I and II of the Constitution.)

The constitutional ideal of shared foreign policy powers is more easily described than it is put into effective operation. Often, the actions of one branch seemingly cross over into the responsibilities of another branch. The president will rely upon his commander-in-chief power to initiate conflict with another nation, even though only Congress has the power to declare war. Congress will seek to

**Table 7.1 Some Foreign Policy Powers Shared
between the President and the Congress**

President	Congress
War making	
"Commander in Chief of the Army and Navy of the United States"	the power "to declare war"; "to raise and support armies"; to "provide for the Common Defence"
Commitment making	
"He shall have Power . . . to make Treaties"	"provided two thirds of the Senators present concur"
Appointments	
"He shall nominate . . . and shall appoint Ambassadors"	"by and with the advice and Consent of the Senate"

restrict the deployment of troops into a particular region, even though the president has the power to direct the deployment of armed forces. What has emerged, in the words of Supreme Court Justice Robert Jackson, has been "a zone of twilight in which [the president] and Congress may have concurrent authority, or in which its distribution is uncertain."[9]

The result of this shared responsibility has been an historical tension over who ultimately controls foreign policy, owing to this constitutional ambiguity. Perhaps one of the earliest debates reflecting the ambiguity of these divided powers was provided by two founders, Alexander Hamilton and James Madison, writing under pseudonyms in the early 1790s. Hamilton (or "Pacificus," as he wrote), in defense of President Washington's declaration of neutrality in 1793 (over France's war against Great Britain, Spain, and the Netherlands), made the classic case for a strong executive who would dominate foreign policy: The powers and responsibilities over foreign policy rested with the executive, Pacificus argued, except for those powers specifically delegated to Congress. Madison (or "Helvidius," as he wrote) viewed presidential powers in foreign affairs in a more limited way: Only those powers expressly delegated to the executive were allowed under the Constitution, and there was not such an unrestrained delegation of power to that branch.[10] Moreover, other foreign policy powers were necessarily left to Congress to serve as a counterweight to the presidency. In short, no exact division was spelled out between the two branches.

In the modern era, several scholars attest to the problem of delineating the foreign policy powers between the two branches. Historian Arthur Schlesinger, in his book *The Imperial Presidency,* describes the division of power between the two governmental branches in the Constitution as "cryptic, ambiguous, and incomplete," thus contributing to policy-making disputes between the two institutions.[11] Constitutional scholar Henkin notes that "the constitutional blueprint for the governance of our foreign affairs has proved to be starkly incomplete, indeed skimpy."[12] Edward S. Corwin, the noted scholar on constitutional and presidential power, has probably provided the most often cited summary of this dilemma: The

Constitution has really provided "an invitation to struggle for the privilege of directing American foreign policy."[13]

A CYCLICAL INTERPRETATION OF FOREIGN POLICY DOMINANCE

To some analysts, a cyclical pattern of control has resulted from this "invitation to struggle": one branch dominating during a particular epoch, the other dominating during another. The exact period of executive or legislative dominance may not be the same for all analysts.[14] Others would see the presidency as having emerged as more successful than Congress over the history of the republic, and especially in the post–World War II years. In this view, only in recent decades (i.e., since the Vietnam War) has the legislative branch attempted to wrest some foreign policy making from the executive branch. Both views merit our attention, although the latter view, especially as we focus upon the post–World War II era, will receive more detailed analysis here.

The Early Years of the Republic

According to the cyclical interpretation, during the early decades of the country, presidential dominance was on the rise, and congressional involvement in foreign policy was often limited. When President Washington took several unilateral actions—appointing diplomats abroad, refusing to share information on the Jay Treaty, and issuing a neutrality declaration over fighting between Britain and France—with only limited congressional involvement, presidential ascendancy was assured. Other early presidents—Adams, Jefferson, and Madison—largely followed this pattern, epitomized by the executive initiatives in securing the Louisiana Purchase and in issuing the Monroe Doctrine. (These particular actions are described in more detail in the next section.) Congressional involvement was not entirely abandoned in these early years, as illustrated by the role of Congress in precipitating the War of 1812. In particular, Congress sought to enact various embargo bills—especially against the British. As a result, political scientist Holbert Carroll has subsequently judged that a "congressional war" was actually initiated.[15]

With the presidency of Andrew Jackson and generally continuing until the presidency of Abraham Lincoln (with the exception of James Polk), the congressional role became more assertive in the foreign policy realm. Jackson, for example, deferred to Congress when action seemed called for over attacks upon American ships off South America and when France was reluctant to pay claims owed to the United States. When Texas revolted against Mexico and then sought American recognition as an independent state, President Jackson turned to the U.S. Congress for its guidance on American policy.

During the presidency of James Polk, presidential dominance arose once again. Without asking Congress for authorization, President Polk ordered the U.S. military into the territory that was in dispute between Texas and Mexico. What resulted was an attack upon American forces by Mexico, and a rather quick declaration of war by Congress.[16] With the presidency of Lincoln, however, this executive dominance in foreign policy extended even further as the Civil War president sought to hold the Union together. A wide range of executive actions were initiated without congressional involvement, as we catalog below, and the height of the powerful presidency was upon us.

Congressional Dominance after the Civil War

After the Civil War, however, the "golden age of congressional ascendancy" emerged.[17] Congress once again asserted its role, passing a resolution to stop the acquisition of future territories after Seward's purchase of Alaska in 1867. In 1869, the Senate refused to take action on a treaty "permitting de facto annexation of Santo Domingo." Indeed, over the next 30 years or so, congressional-executive relations were so strained that the "Senate refused to ratify any important treaty outside of the immigration context."[18]

By roughly the turn of the century, however, the pendulum began to swing back toward the executive. From Presidents McKinley and Roosevelt to Wilson (and with Taft as the exception), the presidency reigned over foreign policy. Consider Teddy Roosevelt's robust action in the Western Hemisphere and McKinley's in Asia. President Wilson, too, sought to enlarge the role of the presidency in foreign affairs with his proposal of a global collective security system and his endorsement of the League of Nations. As the U.S. Senate rejected the Versailles Treaty and membership in the nascent League of Nations, presidential dominance waned once again. By the time of the "return to normalcy" of the interwar years, Congress largely shaped foreign policy through the passage of neutrality acts to keep America out of foreign involvement and through restrictive trade and immigration laws (e.g., the Smoot-Hawley Tariff and the National Origins Act).

Despite the congressional role in the nineteenth century and into the early twentieth century, political scientist Holbert Carroll aptly describes Congress's overall involvement in foreign policy as "episodic and fitful."[19] Moreover, the congressional involvement was to change dramatically with the emergence of World War II, when executive dominance emerged once again. President Roosevelt, for example, acted to aid the British with the "destroyers for bases" deal, an arrangement in which the United States sold 50 destroyers to Britain in exchange for access rights to British bases "in the Atlantic and Caribbean,"[20] and he got congressional approval for the Lend-Lease Act, an American aid effort to support the allies already in World War II. With the emergence of the Cold War, presidential power was to change even more dramatically. Indeed, by the late 1940s and early 1950s, executive dominance in foreign affairs was fully in place.

EXECUTIVE DOMINANCE
AFTER WORLD WAR II:
THE IMPERIAL PRESIDENCY

Some of the reasons for the growth of presidential power after World War II are the result of long-term historical trends, but other reasons are particularly associated with the rise of American globalism in the post–World War II years. In the main, though, the president has been the one to dominate foreign affairs matters owing to several key factors:

1. Important historical executive precedents
2. Supreme Court decisions
3. Congressional deference and delegation
4. Growth of executive institutions
5. International situational factors

Important Historical Executive Precedents

An important first factor that contributed to executive dominance of foreign affairs consists of those actions taken by the various presidents throughout history. By assuming that they possessed control of foreign policy over particular issues and by taking action, the early presidents set a pattern—a precedent—for how future executives would act. These precedents ranged across several key foreign policy areas: the right of the president to negotiate with other nations, the right to recognize other governments, the right to withhold information from the Congress on certain foreign policy matters, the right to initiate the conduct of foreign policy, the right to begin conflict and even war with other nations, and the right to make commitments with other governments. In this regard, the actions of the first president, George Washington, were particularly pivotal in establishing these precedents, since he put into effect the meaning of the Constitution "in response to events."[21] Other early presidents followed Washington's lead and were to give the presidency preeminence in these foreign policy areas.

Negotiating with Other Nations In the area of representing the United States abroad, President Washington made it clear that the executive would be that representative. He sent personal emissaries to represent him in negotiations abroad and simply informed Congress of his actions. In 1791, for instance, President Washington informed the Senate that Gouverneur Morris, who was in Great Britain at that time, would confer with the British over their adherence to the treaty of peace. A short time later, Washington sent his friend Colonel David Humphrey to Spain and Portugal as his personal representative.[22] By such actions, Washington established the principle that the president would conduct relations with other states.

Recognizing Other Nations President Washington established another important precedent: The chief executive would be the one to recognize other states. When Washington received Edmond Genet ("Citizen Genet"), the first minister to the United States from the French Republic, he went a long way toward legitimizing that nation's revolutionary government. Similarly, when Genet seemingly violated his power by seeking to enlist Americans against the British, it was up to Washington to demand that he be recalled.[23]

Withholding Foreign Policy Information   In a similar vein, President Washington provided another precedent by declining to share important diplomatic information with the House of Representatives when negotiating the Jay Treaty. Although his rationale was that the House had no standing in the treaty process, the implications of his actions went further. In Corwin's view, the allowance of this precedent broadened presidential power so that "a President feels free by the same formula to decline information even to his constitutional partner in treaty-making. . . ."[24]

Initiating Policy   President Washington also established the precedent of executive initiation of foreign policy. In unilaterally declaring neutrality between France and Britain in 1793, he began the process of presidential direction for foreign policy matters. After this declaration, Congress largely followed the president and passed a neutrality act in conformity with Washington's wishes.[25] President Monroe followed a similar approach with his unilateral declaration of the Monroe Doctrine in 1823, although the Congress still held the right to deny funding for any Western Hemisphere activity.

By these actions of sending emissaries abroad and receiving representatives from other states, President Washington gave meaning to the constitutional power of appointing and receiving ambassadors. In effect, the executive power in this area came to eclipse any congressional prerogative. When President Washington followed the Hamiltonian notion of inherent executive power by initiating foreign policy actions, he seemed to imply that the powers of the executive derived from the fact that the United States was a sovereign state and that the president was the representative of that sovereignty. In short, President Washington gave meaning to the characterization of the presidency by a future chief justice of the United Sates, John Marshall: "The President is the sole organ of the nation in its external relations, and its sole representative with foreign nations."[26]

Other early presidents followed Washington's lead of a strong executive carrying on relations with other states. For instance, President Adams used his executive power to extradite an individual under the Jay Treaty without congressional authorization. Likewise, Adams vigorously defended his right to recognize other states. President Jefferson, too, although a proponent of legislative dominance in the affairs of state, still exercised considerable individual control over the Louisiana Purchase. Still later, President James Monroe refused to relinquish the president's right to recognize other governments, especially with regard to several Latin American states. The result, as Corwin concludes, was to "reaffirm the President's monopoly of international intercourse and his constitutional independence in the performance of that function."[27] This presidential preeminence in the recognition of, and negotiation of relations with, other states continued through the rest of the nineteenth century and into the twentieth century. As a result, the president's right to recognize and to negotiate with states is little challenged to this day.

Initiating Conflicts and War   Another area in which actions by early executives set a precedent was in war making. Although Congress was granted the right to declare war under the Constitution, to what extent could the executive use military force without the explicit authorization of the legislative branch? Put differently, how far could the president go under the commander-in-chief clause of the Constitution before it intruded on the congressional prerogative to declare war?

Early presidents generally were quite careful about extending the meaning of the commander-in-chief clause, but not always. Only in the case of attacks upon Americans or American forces did the president occasionally provide immediate military responses. As Arthur Schlesinger points out, however, even in those instances, the early presidents were quite meticulous in involving Congress in any actions.[28] When President Thomas Jefferson was faced with the question of using force against Tripoli because of its attack upon American shipping, he did send U.S. frigates to the Mediterranean, but he supposedly limited them to defensive action. Some evidence presented by Schlesinger, however, suggests otherwise. Jefferson apparently "sent a naval squadron to the Mediterranean under secret orders to fight the Barbary pirates, applied for congressional sanctions six months later and then misled Congress as to the nature of the orders."[29] Moreover, at about the same time, Jefferson sent a message to Congress declaring that "his actions . . . [were] in compliance with constitutional limitations on his authority in the absence of a declaration of war."[30] In this sense, executive assertiveness in war making may have begun quite early in the republic.

By the 1840s, however, some transformation in the commander-in-chief clause was already evident. As noted earlier President James K. Polk was instrumental in using his power as head of the armed forces to precipitate a declaration of war against Mexico. By moving American troops into land disputed with Mexico—resulting in a Mexican attack upon these forces—President Polk was able to obtain a war resolution from Congress.[31] By using his constitutional power as commander in chief, President Polk was able to force Congress's hand on the war powers.

The boldest precedents with the commander-in-chief clause came during the presidency of Abraham Lincoln. Combining the powers granted under this clause with the executive power to take care that the laws were carried out, President Lincoln effectively made the "war power" his own, as analyst Edward Corwin said. Because of the Civil War, President Lincoln, without consulting Congress, "proclaimed a blockade of the Southern ports, suspended the writ of habeas corpus in various places, and caused the arrest and military detention of persons 'who were represented to him' as being engaged or contemplating 'treasonable practices.' . . ."[32] In addition, Lincoln enlarged the Army and Navy, pressed into service the state militias, and called into service 40,000 volunteers. Despite outcries that the president was going beyond his limits, neither Congress nor the courts challenged him. In fact, Congress gave approval to his actions after the fact, and the Supreme Court upheld his actions in the *Prize Cases* by a narrow margin of 5–4.[33] While these presidential actions were taken in the context of a civil war (and their relevance to foreign wars is debatable), the expansion of the presidential power in war making was not lost on future presidents.

While congressional acquiescence to Lincoln's actions did not produce any expansion of war making by his immediate successors, it did establish important precedents for later commanders in chief.[34] The dispatch of troops to China by President McKinley in 1900, the interventions by Presidents Theodore Roosevelt and William Howard Taft in the Caribbean in the early 1900s, and even the sending of American forces to Korea (albeit with a UN resolution) were done without congressional authorization.

Furthermore, several interventions by the United States during the height of the Cold War (Lebanon, Bay of Pigs, Dominican Republic, and Vietnam) occurred without the benefit of congressional actions before the fact. Moreover, even Lyndon Johnson was able to boast that there was a large body of precedent for his Vietnam policy by citing the actions of previous commanders in chief. On one occasion, for instance, President Johnson was able to cite some 125 cases in which previous presidents took military action to protect American citizens. On another occasion, he was to cite some 137 cases in which earlier chief executives had unilaterally employed force to protect U.S. citizens.[35] Later on, during the Vietnam War, President Nixon justified the Cambodian invasion in 1970 by stating: "I shall meet my responsibility as Commander in Chief of our Armed Forces to take the action necessary to defend the security of our American men."[36]

The pattern has continued throughout the 1980s, 1990s, and to the present. In 1982, President Reagan initially sent American troops into Lebanon as a "peace-keeping force" without congressional approval and justified that action through the commander-in-chief clause of the Constitution. In April 1986, too, President Reagan unilaterally initiated a retaliatory attack against Libya over that country's involvement with a terrorist attack upon Americans in West Berlin. In December 1989, President George H. W. Bush justified the U.S. intervention into Panama on the basis of his "constitutional authority with respect to the conduct of foreign relations," his responsibility "to protect American lives in imminent danger," and "as Commander in Chief" of American military forces.[37] In August 1990, President Bush once again used a similar kind of constitutional rationale for sending some American military personnel into Saudi Arabia to protect that country from Iraq's Saddam Hussein, who had seized Kuwait. When the president actually decided to use force against Iraq over its seizure of Kuwait, he did seek congressional authorization, as we discuss below.

President Clinton expressed the same presidential prerogative with regard to the use of force in Haiti, Bosnia, and Kosovo during his time in office. When Congress raised the possibility of restricting Clinton's use of force to intervene in Haiti in September 1993, the president said he was determined to "strongly oppose" congressional restrictions on the right to use force there and elsewhere. In a sharply worded letter to the leaders in the Senate, President Clinton stated that he opposed several amendments at the time because they would "unduly restrict the ability of the President to make foreign policy" and because they would weaken the commander-in-chief power as well.[38] In 1995, President Clinton sent American peacekeeping forces to Bosnia without congressional approval as part of the NATO-led Dayton Accords. In sending these forces, he noted that these commitments were made "in conjunction with our NATO allies" and consistent with his constitutional authority as president.[39] In 1999, in initiating bombing in Kosovo against Serbian atrocities, Clinton actually asked Congress for its support, although he indicated that he was doing so "without regard to our differing views on the Constitution about the use of force." Still, when he reported to Congress shortly after the bombing was started, Clinton, like other presidents, stated that he was taking such actions "pursuant to my constitutional authority to conduct U.S. foreign relations and as Commander in Chief and Chief Executive."[40]

More recently, President George W. Bush has followed these past precedents after September 11. As we noted earlier, President Bush cited his constitutional powers in this area to initiate a military response to the terrorism that the United States had experienced by those events. As a result, American forces were dispatched to Afghanistan to pursue al-Qaeda and the Taliban, and other forces were sent to several countries (e.g., Philippines, Yemen) to aid in combating terrorists. While these actions were taken on presidential authority, Congress, in an unusual move, passed a sweeping resolution granting the president broad authority to take military actions abroad (see the discussion of Public Law 107–40 later in this chapter). In fall 2002, Congress also passed a sweeping resolution (Public Law 107–243) authorizing the president to take use force "as he determines" against the threat posed by Iraq. In turn, of course, President Bush used that authority as well as his commander-in-chief powers to initiate war with Iraq in March 2003.

According to critics, then, the commander-in-chief clause had been expanded to include the power not only to conduct a war already begun, but to initiate a conflict if necessary. The growth of this executive precedent has caused Congress to react strongly to this apparent incursion into its area of responsibility. As we shall discuss in the next chapter, the War Powers Resolution was passed in an attempt to curb executive war making, but it has been far from successful.

Making Foreign Commitments   Yet another area of executive precedent was in the making of foreign policy commitments. Instead of relying on the treaty as the basic instrument of making commitments to other states, presidents have come to rely on the so-called executive agreement as a principal means of establishing bonds with other nations. By such precedent, the treaty power of Congress has been eroded, and congressional involvement in this aspect of foreign policy making has been weakened. In this way, once again, the president has enhanced his ability to make and carry out foreign policy by executive action only.

The executive agreement is an agreement made by the president or the president's representative, usually without congressional involvement, with another country. Its most important distinction from a treaty is that it does not require the advice and consent of the Senate, yet it has the same force of law as a treaty. An executive agreement actually may take two forms. One type is based solely on the constitutional power of the president; the other type is based on congressional legislation authorizing or approving the president's making a commitment with another nation. The former relies upon powers granted in Article II, and especially the commander-in-chief clause. An example would be an agreement made by the United States for use of naval facilities in Bahrain in 1971. A State Department official testified before Congress that the "President, as Commander in Chief, has constitutional authority to make arrangements for facilities for our military personnel." The latter type, the so-called statutory executive agreement, relies on some precise piece of earlier congressional authorization or a treaty. An example would be an agreement with Portugal for military rights on the Azores in 1971, which was based upon a 1951 Defense Agreement between the two countries in accordance with the NATO Treaty.[41]

Overall, the statutory executive agreement is the more prevalent form of the executive agreement and the more controversial.[42] While the statutory agreement allows Congress to be involved procedurally in the agreement process, the extent of substantive congressional involvement remains an important question. It is not always clear that Congress is fully aware of the considerable discretion that it is affording the president in making commitments abroad or how far statutory authority is expanded to cover a contemplated executive agreement. In some instances, Congress may be providing legislation that might later be viewed as a "blank check" for presidential action.

Table 7.2 provides some data on the use of executive agreements (including both the statutory agreement and the "pure" constitutionally based agreements in one category) and treaties over the history of the republic. As these data show, the executive agreement—instead of the treaty—was used moderately at first, but its use has grown dramatically in the last century or so.[43] By the 1889–1929 period, the number of executive agreements was almost twice that of the treaty form. By comparison, the executive agreement in the post–World War II period has virtually exploded in usage, dwarfing the treaty mechanism as the principal instrument of commitment abroad. Over the history of the nation, about 90 percent of all agreements have been executive in nature. Since 1950, though, 94 percent of all commitments have been made through executive agreements.

Despite the limited use of the executive agreement in the first century of the republic, important commitments were still made via this route. For instance, the agreement between the British and the Americans to limit naval vessels on the Great Lakes (the Rush-Bagot Agreement of 1817) was made through an exchange of notes by executive representatives of both governments. Later, President McKinley agreed to the terms for ending the Spanish-American War by executive agreement. President Theodore Roosevelt entered into a secret agreement with Japan over Korea and into a "Gentlemen's Agreement" in 1907 to restrict Japanese immigration into the United States.[44]

In the modern era, the executive agreement was used frequently and for important commitments. The actions of President Franklin Roosevelt set the pattern for recent presidents. Roosevelt, for instance, completed the destroyers-for-bases deal of 1940 with an executive agreement. Similarly, the Yalta Agreement of 1945 was completed through this mechanism. President Truman followed this pattern with the Potsdam Agreement, also by executive agreement. Later,

Table 7.2 Treaties and Executive Agreements, 1789–1999

Years	Treaties	Executive agreements	% of Total as executive agreements
1789–1839	60	27	31%
1839–1889	215	238	53
1889–1929	382	763	67
1930–1939	132	154	54
1940–1949	116	919	89
1950–1959	138	2,229	94
1960–1969	114	2,324	95
1970–1979	173	3,039	95
1980–1989	166	3,524	96
1990–1999	249	2,857	92
Totals/Average %	1,745	16,074	90%

SOURCES: The agreement data for 1789–1929 are from Michael Nelson, ed., *Congressional Quarterly's Guide to the Presidency* (Washington, DC: Congressional Quarterly, Inc., 1989), p. 1104; while the agreement data for 1930–1999 are from *Treaties and Other International Agreements: The Role of the United States Senate,* A Study Prepared for the Committee on Foreign Relations, United States Senate (Washington, DC: U.S. Government Printing Office, 2001), p. 39. Column 3 was calculated by the author.

President Truman made an oral commitment to defend the newly independent state of Israel in 1948 and started a pattern of support for this nation through executive declaration.[45]

Following these initiatives, the other postwar chief executives proceeded to make numerous important political and military commitments through the executive agreement. As a Senate Foreign Relations subcommittee investigation reported in the late 1960s and early 1970s, numerous political, military, and intelligence commitments (some verbal and some secret) were extended to a diverse group of nations, ranging from Thailand and Laos, to Spain, Ethiopia, and the Philippines, among others, through executive action only. Congress was kept almost entirely in the dark about these commitments.[46]

A later analysis has also documented the extent to which important foreign military commitments have taken the form of executive agreements in the postwar years.[47] The commitment of military missions in Honduras and El Salvador in the 1950s, pledges to Turkey, Iran, and Pakistan over security in 1959, the permission to use the island of Diego Garcia for military purposes from the British in the 1960s, and the establishment of a military mission in Iran in 1974 were all done by executive agreement. Further, the analysis revealed that some "understandings" and arrangements with nations are handled by executive agreements. For instance, a message by President Nixon to aid the reconstruction of North Vietnam as part of a peace effort was handled in this way, and an "understanding" regarding the role of American military personnel in the Israeli-Egyptian disengagement agreement of 1975 was as well. Similarly, the Offensive Arms Pact of the Strategic Arms Limitation Talks (SALT I) took the form of an executive agreement.

More recently, presidents have carried out important commitments via executive agreements as well. Presidents Carter and Reagan completed the release of American hostages in Iran through an executive agreement. Moreover, the controversy over this unilateral executive action led to a court challenge (*Dames & Moore v. Regan*) during the Reagan administration, but the Supreme Court held that President Carter had the authority to carry out this pact by executive agreement even though the agreement nullified various judicial directives, returned Iranian assets, and altered private economic claims against Iran.[48] In October 1994, too, President Clinton completed a significant commitment with this instrument: An executive agreement between the United States and North Korea was signed over that country's future nuclear program. If this pact were fully implemented, North Korea would forgo any nuclear weapons development program, open up its nuclear power sites to international inspection, and receive two light-water nuclear power reactors from an international consortium (probably Japan and South Korea) in return.[49] Needless to say, with the rising fear of nuclear proliferation, this pact was highly significant for foreign policy.

Finally, various pledges at the superpower summits or presidential meetings have also taken this form. President George H. W. Bush made unilateral commitments to former Soviet President Mikhail Gorbachev at summits in 1990 and 1991 regarding future relations, and President Clinton took similar actions with Russian President Boris Yeltsin, such as seeking to establish a "strategic relationship" between the two countries and greater economic cooperation. More recently, President George W. Bush and President Vladimir Putin met and developed several understandings on the war on terrorism through executive consultations. Indeed, President Bush developed several such understandings with other nations over dealing with terrorism through this mechanism. Similarly, the various agreements by the Group of Eight (G-8), the industrial democracies of the United States, Britain, France, Germany, Japan, Italy, Canada, and Russia, at their annual meeting epitomize these kinds of executive agreements in action. Congress may still become involved in some of these commitments, especially if commitments are made to change the status of a nation under a treaty or convention (e.g., granting most favored nation trading status to China, for example) or when additional funding of some program is required (increasing foreign aid for Ukraine or Russia, or restoring aid to Pakistan), but the executive agreement remains a potent foreign policy tool for the president.

Issuing Executive Orders A final area of presidential power in foreign policy is the use of executive orders. These orders are directives that the president unilaterally makes for particular areas of policy, both domestic and foreign. Some orders are like statutory executive agreements in that they implement a statute passed by Congress. For example, President Bush issued a directive continuing the national emergency with respect to Burma and its human rights policy under a national emergency act passed by Congress in May 2001. A few months earlier (February 2001) he reported to Congress over the continuance of a similar executive order against Iraq, originally issued by his father in August 1990.[50] Other orders initiate a new direction for American foreign policy. For example, President Ford issued a 1976 executive order outlawing the use of political assassination by the United States as an instrument of foreign policy. Executive orders thus deal with significant matters—and significant foreign policy matters, as it turns out. Political scientists Kenneth Mayer and Kevin Price analyzed a sample of executive orders from 1936 through 1999.[51] Based upon stringent criteria, they found that 149 of the 1,028 executive orders that they sampled were "significant" in that they affect policy and society in important ways. Of those 149, moreover, we estimated that 58 (or 39 percent) dealt with foreign policy. In this way, executive orders afford presidents yet another avenue of impacting foreign affairs.

In sum, executive precedents in several different areas—negotiating with and recognizing other states, withholding information from Congress, initiating foreign policy actions, starting conflicts or interventions with other nations, and making unilateral commitments abroad—have given operational meaning to the delegation of executive foreign policy powers as outlined in Article II of the Constitution. In some instances, too, these precedents have expanded presidential authority in foreign policy well beyond what the founders envisioned. As a result, precedents alone have contributed significantly to making the president the chief executive, the chief diplomat, and if necessary, the chief war maker in the conduct of foreign policy.

Supreme Court Decisions

The Supreme Court has also aided the president in gaining ascendancy in the foreign policy arena. With few exceptions, the Court's decisions have supported presidential claims to dominance over foreign policy matters. It has done so in two different, but important ways. First the Court, particularly in the twentieth century, has largely ruled on the merits in favor of the executive over the Congress on foreign policy matters. Second, and increasingly in recent decades, the Supreme Court and lower courts have refused to rule on cases challenging executive authority in foreign policy. The courts have done so either because the case under consideration raises political, not legal, questions (the "political question doctrine") or because the case is not ready for adjudication since all avenues have not been exhausted by the Congress or the plaintiff (the "ripeness" issue). Let us discuss these two different ways in greater detail.

Some Rulings Supporting the Executive   During the past century, when the Court has decided foreign policy cases, it has largely ruled in favor of the position supported by the executive branch. In turn, these decisions for the executive have become important precedents for the Court as other cases are brought before it. We highlight five important court decisions from the early twentieth century that illustrate the extent to which the Supreme Court has deferred to the president in matters dealing with international politics—even prior to America's extensive global involvement after World War II. We also discuss a ruling on the "legislative veto" from the 1980s that had significant implications for presidential foreign policy powers. By finding in support of the president in this instance, the Court once again provided the president considerable latitude in policy making and weakened the role of Congress.

Curtiss-Wright The most important and most sweeping grant of presidential dominance over foreign policy was set forth in the Supreme Court's decision in *U.S. v. Curtiss-Wright Export Corporation et al.* (1936).[52] In effect, this case gave special standing to the executive in foreign policy matters. A brief summary of the issues in dispute will make this clear.

The case dealt with a joint congressional resolution that authorized the president to prohibit "the sale of arms and munitions of war . . . to those countries engaged . . . in armed conflict" in the Chaco region of South America, if he determined that such an embargo would contribute to peace in the area. On May 28, 1934, President Franklin Roosevelt issued such a proclamation and put the resolution into effect. Later, in November 1935, he revoked this resolution with a similar proclamation. As a result of the original proclamation, however, the Curtiss-Wright Corporation was indicted on the charge that it conspired to sell fifteen machine guns to Bolivia, beginning in May 1934.

Several issues were raised before the Supreme Court by the corporation to deny any wrongdoing in this matter. Curtiss-Wright contended that the joint resolution was an invalid delegation of legislative power, that the joint resolution never became effective because of the failure of the president to find essential jurisdictional facts, and that the second proclamation (lifting the ban) ended the liability of the company under the joint resolution.[53] While the Court rejected all of the arguments, its reasoning on the first was the most important for enlarging presidential power in foreign affairs.

The Court held that the delegation of power to the executive—to apply the ban or not—was not unconstitutional because the issue dealt with a question of external, not internal, affairs. In these two areas, the Court said, the powers of delegation are different. In internal affairs, the federal government can exercise only those powers specifically enumerated in the Constitution (and such implied powers as are necessary and proper), but in the external area, such limitation do not apply. Because of America's separation from Great Britain, and as a result of being a member of the family of nations, the United States possesses external sovereignty and the powers associated with it. "The powers to declare and wage war, to conclude peace, to make treaties, to maintain diplomatic relations with other sovereignties, if they had never been mentioned in the Constitution, would have vested in the federal government as necessary concomitants of nationality."[54]

Most important, the Court held that the president was the representative of that sovereignty ("the President alone has the power to speak or listen as a representative of the nation"). Therefore, the executive's powers in foreign affairs go beyond the actual constitutional delegation of power. Furthermore, the president is to be granted considerable discretion in his exercise of these powers as compared to the domestic arena. As the Court said, "it is quite apparent that if, in the maintenance of our international relations, embarrassment—perhaps serious embarrassment—is to be avoided and success for our aims achieved, congressional legislation which is to be made effective through negotiation and inquiry within the international field must often accord to the President a degree of discretion and freedom from statutory restriction which would not be admissible were domestic affairs alone involved."[55]

In light of such a view and numerous precedents that the decision cites, the Court held that the joint resolution was not an unlawful delegation of legislative power. Most important, the decision established that foreign policy and domestic policy were different arenas, with a special position for the president in the former. In sum, the Curtiss-Wright case made clear that the president's power in foreign policy could not be gleaned only from constitutional directives; there were "extra-constitutional" powers tied to the sovereignty of the United States and the executive's role as the representative of that sovereignty. Subsequent cases and legal analyses have challenged this interpretation, but they have not fully undermined the notion of the executive's primacy in foreign affairs.[56]

Missouri v. Holland A second important Supreme Court decision, *Missouri v. Holland* (1920), clarified, and actually enlarged, the treaty powers given to the executive. In this case, the Court held that the treaty powers could not be limited by any "invisible radiation" of the Tenth Amendment to the Constitution.[57] Put differently, the power of the president in making treaties with other nations was ensured against any intrusion by states' rights advocates.

The particulars of the case will once again point to the significance of the Court's decision. The dispute involved the constitutionality of the Migratory Bird Act, which was passed by Congress pursuant to a treaty between the United States and Great Britain. Missouri contended, however, that this act was void because Article I of the Constitution did not delegate the regulation of such birds to Congress; therefore, the states were reserved this power by the Tenth Amendment. In two earlier cases, moreover—before the treaty was signed—two U.S. district courts had voided such a congressional act. But now the Court decided differently, mainly because of the intervening treaty. Justice Holmes, in his opinion for the majority, wrote:

> Acts of Congress are the supreme law of the land only when made in pursuance of the Constitution, while treaties are declared to be so when made under the authority of the United States. We do not mean to imply that there are no qualifications to the treaty-making power; they must be ascertained in a different way. It is obvious that there may be matters of the sharpest exigency for the national well being that an act of Congress could not deal with but that a treaty followed by such an act could, and it is not lightly to be assumed that, in matters requiring national action, "a power which must belong to and somewhere reside in every civilized government" is not to be found.[58]

Justice Holmes argued further that the regulation of migratory birds was best left to the federal government. Although he acknowledged that the Constitution was silent on this issue, such silence was not sufficient to support the claim made by the State of Missouri. In addition, Justice Holmes held that "a treaty may override" the powers of the state.[59]

In sum, *Missouri v. Holland* was highly significant for the powers of national government versus the states, but it also aided the president. It legitimized his role of using the treaty process to add to the constitutional framework of the nation, in conjunction with the Senate; it arguably reduced the implied powers of the states and Congress, since those powers could be overridden through the treaty power; and it began a series of twentieth-century Court decisions giving special deference to the president in foreign affairs.

Belmont and Pink   The third and fourth important Supreme Court decisions, one prior to World War II and the other during the war (*U.S. v. Belmont* [1937] and *U.S. v. Pink* [1942]), dealt with the legal status of executive agreements.[60] The decisions in these cases gave the president another means of enhancing his foreign policy powers.

The *Belmont* case involved whether the federal government could recover the bank account of an American national, August Belmont, who owned obligations belonging to a Russian company before the establishment of the Soviet Union. The bank accounts were held in the State of New York. The federal government tried to reclaim such accounts because, under the Litvinov Agreement—which established diplomatic relations between the United States and the Soviet Union—these accounts had been assigned to the U.S. government. While the state courts held that the federal government could not claim such accounts, the Supreme Court held otherwise. Justice Sutherland argued that the external powers of the United States must be exercised without regard to the constraint of state law or policies.

The *Pink* case also dealt with the legitimacy of the Litvinov Agreement and involved some of the same issues as the Belmont case. It was an action brought by the U.S. government against the New York State Superintendent of Insurance to acquire the remaining assets of the First Russian Insurance Company. When the Soviet Union was established, all properties—wherever located—were nationalized. Under the Litvinov Agreement, as we noted, all such assets were assigned to the American government. Superintendent Pink claimed, however, that the nationalization action had "no territorial effect" and that the U.S. government action was improper.[61] The Supreme Court held otherwise, and Justice Douglas stated the Court's view in this forceful passage:

> We hold that the right to the funds or property in question became vested in the Soviet Government as the successor to the First Russian Insurance Co.; that this right has passed to the United States under the Litvinov Assignment; and that the United States is entitled to the property as against the corporation and the foreign creditors.[62]

The *Belmont* and *Pink* cases are important because the Litvinov Agreement between the United States and the Soviet Union was an executive agreement. Thus, these decisions have been interpreted as giving legitimacy to executive agreements as the law of the land—without any congressional action—and the supremacy of those agreements over rights of an individual state (the State of New York in both cases) within the American union. Once again, these cases strengthened the president's hand in the conduct of foreign affairs. Moreover, Louis Henkin argues that the language and reasoning in the *Belmont* and *Pink* cases were sufficiently general to apply to any executive agreement and to ensure its supremacy over any state law.[63]

INS v. Chadha   Perhaps the most recent sweeping court decision in the foreign policy area was *Immigration and Naturalization Service v. Chadha* (1983). In this case, the Supreme Court found the "one-house legislative veto" unconstitutional. At the time of the Chadha decision, at least 56 statutes, including several important foreign policy statutes, contained one or more legislative vetoes.[64] The decision thus had far-ranging implications for congressional-executive relations generally and foreign policy in particular. It also illustrated the Court's continuing deference to the executive branch, often at the expense of the legislative branch. Some background on the legislative veto and the case itself will convey the significance of this ruling.

Originally devised in the 1930s, the legislative veto was a procedural device that allowed Congress "to relegate policy making authority to the executive branch in areas constitutionally delegated to the legislature," but which also "allowed Congress to retain ultimate oversight in the form of a veto power."[65] While this policy mechanism grew gradually until about 1960, its incorporation into new legislation expanded rapidly after that date. Foreign policy and defense legislation was hardly immune from this instrument. While the veto mechanism did not appear in foreign policy legislation until the 1950s and 1960s, immigration and defense legislation had such vetoes included as early as the 1940s.[66]

Specifically, the legislative veto works in the following way: Congress would explicitly incorporate a provision in a piece of legislation that allowed Congress to stop or modify the executive's subsequent implementation of the statute by simply declaring its objection. The legislative branch could register its "veto" of executive action in several different ways, depending upon how the statute was written: (1) by a single chamber passing by a simple majority a veto resolution (either the Senate or House); (2) by both chambers passing by a simple majority a veto resolution (called a concurrent resolution); or, in some instances, (3) by a committee in Congress passing by a majority a veto resolution.[67] The most important point is that none of these forms of veto resolutions allowed the executive to approve or disapprove the action. In other words, when the legislative veto was incorporated within an act of Congress, the legislative branch could pass legislation and then could, unilaterally, monitor and modify the implementation of that legislation by the executive branch. In this sense, congressional power was gained at the expense of executive power.

The particulars of the *Chadha* case will make clear how the legislative veto operated in this instance. The case involved an East Indian student who was born in Kenya and held a British passport. He overstayed his student nonimmigrant visa and was ordered deported by the INS. He appealed the deportation, and his deportation was suspended by immigration authorities. By a provision that was incorporated into previous immigration legislation, however, Congress (either the House or the Senate) could pass a simple majority resolution objecting to this suspension of the deportation order. In this case, the House of Representatives did so; in effect, the House called for Chadha's deportation promptly.

Once the case reached the Supreme Court, a majority of the justices held that this "legislative veto" in the earlier legislation was invalid for two important constitutional reasons. It violated the presentment clause of the Constitution.[68] That is, "every Bill which shall have passed the House of Representatives and the Senate, shall, before it becomes a Law, be presented to the President of the United States" for his consideration. Such a presentment did not occur in this case, since the House acted unilaterally to rescind the action of the executive branch. Second, the legislative veto also violated the principle of bicameralism (i.e., all legislation must be passed by majorities in both the House of Representatives and the United States Senate).[69] As such, the legislative veto could not stand.

Although the *Chadha* decision dealt only with the "one-House" legislative veto, the Supreme Court expanded its decision about two weeks later by declaring the "two-house" legislative veto as unconstitutional as well.[70] Since the legislative veto was a prominent device used by Congress in the 1970s and early 1980s to reign in executive power in foreign affairs (as we shall discuss in Chapter 8), the *Chadha* decision has had considerable impact on the extent of congressional resurgence.

Some Rulings Challenging the Executive Although the president has usually gotten his way with the Court on foreign policy questions, we also need to highlight important instances in which he did not. One important case in the 1950s and two in the 1970s fit into this category. Still, even these successful challenges to executive power in foreign policy have been overshadowed by the precedents from the earlier cases and the nonrulings in favor of the president in numerous others (as we discuss shortly). Furthermore, the basis for deciding against the president in the 1970s cases was less an effort to reduce his foreign policy powers and more an effort to maintain some fundamental American freedoms.

Youngstown Sheet & Tube Co. et al. v. Sawyer Unlike the earlier cases, the Supreme Court's decision in the Youngstown case restricted the foreign policy powers of the president, especially as those powers seem to delve into domestic policy. In so deciding, the Court thus preserved a role for Congress over some areas of foreign policy. In particular, the *Youngstown* case, decided in 1952, addressed the question of whether the chief executive and commander-in-chief clauses of the Constitution enabled the president to seize control of the nation's steel mills to avert a national strike and to protect national security. President Truman had made just such a claim and had issued an executive order to his secretary of commerce (Sawyer) to take over the operation of the steel mills. The Court held that such action was unconstitutional. Justice Black wrote in the majority opinion for the Court that there was no statutory authorization for such action:

> The President's power, if any, to issue the order must stem either from an act of Congress or from the Constitution. There is no statute that expressly authorizes the president to take possession of property as he did here. Nor is there any act of Congress to which our attention has been directed from which such a power can fairly be implied.[71]

Likewise, Justice Black contended that there was no constitutional basis for such an action either:

> The order cannot properly be sustained as an exercise of the President's military power as Commander in Chief of the Armed Forces. . . . Even though "theater of war" be an expanding concept, we cannot with faithfulness to our constitutional system hold that the Commander in Chief of the Armed Forces has the ultimate power as such to take possession of private property in order to keep labor disputes from stopping production. . . . Nor can the seizure order be sustained because of the several constitutional provisions that grant executive power to the President.[72]

In sum, the *Youngstown* case made clear that there are indeed limits on the foreign policy powers of the president. This decision stands in contrast to the earlier cases that largely deferred to president's authority in foreign affairs and, indeed, afforded the president wide discretion as well.

In another intriguing aspect to this decision, Justice Jackson wrote a concurring opinion in which he, while agreeing with the decision, sought to set forth more fully the division of foreign policy powers between the president and Congress. In particular, Justice Jackson said that there were clear strictures on the foreign policy powers of the president:

1. When the President acts pursuant to an express or implied authorization of Congress, his authority is at its maximum, for it includes all that he possesses in his own right plus all that Congress can delegate. . . .

2. When the President acts in absence of either a congressional grant or denial of authority, he can only rely upon his own independent powers, but there is a zone of twilight in which he and Congress may have concurrent authority, or in which its distribution is uncertain. . . .

3. When the President takes measures incompatible with the expressed or implied will of Congress, his power is at its lowest ebb, for then he can rely only upon his own constitutional powers minus any constitutional powers of Congress over the matter.[73]

Justice Jackson concluded that this particular case fell into the third category and was least sustainable for the executive branch. By one recent analysis, moreover, Justice Jackson's arguments sought to challenge the court's earlier decision in the *Curtiss-Wright* case.[74]

New York Times v. United States **and** *U.S. v. Nixon*   The two presidential defeats from the 1970s are arguably less sweeping in their implications for foreign policy than *Youngstown,* but they, too, convey important limitations on executive power. In *New York Times v. United States* (1971), popularly known as the *Pentagon Papers* case, the Court held that the executive's claims of national security could not stop the publication of these volumes chronicling American involvement in Southeast Asia. First-amendment freedoms proved to be more persuasive than any immediate national security needs. In *U.S. v. Nixon* (1974), the Court decided that President Nixon had to turn over tape recordings and records dealing with the Watergate investigation. The Supreme Court held that "neither the separation of powers nor the confidentiality of executive communications barred the federal courts from access to presidential tapes needed as evidence in a criminal case." At the same time, the Court was less than precise over whether specific claims of "national security" would have led to another result. As Chief Justice Burger put it, the president did not "claim . . . [a] need to protect military, diplomatic, or sensitive national secrets," as such.[75]

Nonrulings Supporting the President   A second important way in which the Court has supported the executive on foreign policy has been through *nonrulings*—deciding not to consider cases brought before it. In doing so, the Court has allowed the executive actions that have already been taken to stand.

One justification for adopting this nondecision posture by the Court is the "political question" doctrine. In effect, the Court has held that the issue before it is a political, not a legal or constitutional, dispute between the branches of government—normally Congress and the presidency—and hence is not subject to judicial remedy. While the basis for the doctrine is not well developed or wholly understood in constitutional law, the doctrine seemingly has been invoked under several differing circumstances by the Court: when the Court believed it lacked the authority to decide the case because the constitutionally prescribed activities of another branch of government were involved, when the effective solution involved a political remedy that would favor one branch of government over another, and when the Court wanted to avoid a question brought before it.[76]

Another justification for the Court's nondecisions on foreign policy cases is the "ripeness" criterion, mentioned at the beginning of this section. By this criterion, the Court has claimed that when members of Congress, for example, file suit against the president over the use of force abroad or the abrogation of a treaty, they must first use all available avenues within the political system (e.g., completing the legislative process and legislative routes) before pursuing a legal challenge. Only, then, the Court has held, may the issue be appropriate for judicial judgment.

Several recent cases have relied upon these two justifications as reasons for not ruling in particular cases, and a brief discussion of several of them will reveal the Court's rationale in each instance. In particular, the discussion will reveal how these nondecisions have strengthened the president's hand in policy making over the use of force as commander in chief and as well in the use of the treaty powers.

The first case deals with the breaking of the 1954 Mutual Defense Treaty with Taiwan (Chapter 2) as part of the process of establishing diplomatic relations with the People's Republic of China. In *Goldwater et al. v. Carter* (1979), several U.S. senators charged that President Carter could not terminate the 1954 Mutual Defense Treaty with Taiwan in establishing diplomatic relations with the People's Republic of China without either a two-thirds majority of the Senate or a majority of both houses of Congress. The Supreme Court, however, divided along several lines in rendering its judgment. Four justices held that the case was "nonjusticiable" because it involved a political issue, another said that is was not ripe for court action since Congress, as a body, had taken no formal action to challenge the president, and only one decided the case on the merits and argued that the president acted within his constitutional power to recognize states.[77] The upshot of this ruling was to dismiss the challenge to the president and his treaty powers.

A year earlier, in *Edwards v. Carter* (1978), 60 members of Congress challenged the Panama Canal Treaty and charged that both houses of Congress must approve any transference of property by Article IV of the Constitution. The District of Columbia Court of Appeals ruled that the Constitution was ambiguous on the disposal of American property and "that the power was not *exclusively* congressional." Moreover, the transference of the Canal was tied to a larger foreign policy action under the Panama Canal Treaty and "it was valid in this case."[78] The Supreme Court ultimately let this decision stand by simply refusing to hear the case.

Several attempts were made to challenge the constitutionality of the Vietnam War in the 1970s, but, in virtually all instances, the Court refused to hear these cases since it judged them to deal with a political question between the two branches.[79] Much the same reasoning, albeit with an exception or two, prevailed in the cases dealing with presidential actions in El Salvador, Grenada, and the Persian Gulf during the 1980s. In *Crockett v. Reagan* (1983) 29 members of Congress contended that the sending of U.S. military advisors and military aid to El Salvador was a violation of the War Powers Resolution and the Foreign Assistance Act. The lower court held that the issue was nonjusticiable because the issue was a "political question" between the branches and because it could not determine all the facts in the case. The Supreme Court refused to hear the case when it was appealed to it. In *Conyers v. Reagan* (1985), 11 members of Congress, led by John Conyers of Michigan, charged that the executive branch had gone beyond its powers and had usurped Congress's war-making powers in sending U.S. forces to invade Grenada. The district court dismissed the case by asserting that it lacked jurisdiction, and the appeals court held the issue as moot, since the invasion had ended. In *Lowry v. Reagan* (1987), 110 members of Congress wanted the president to report to Congress under the War Powers Resolution because American forces were being used to keep the Persian Gulf open during the Iran–Iraq War. Once again, the district court dismissed the case as a political matter between the two branches, and no further action was taken.[80]

In two cases in the 1990s involving the president's war-making powers, the decisions by the courts largely followed these precedents. In *Dellums v. Bush* (1990), 54 members of Congress sought a federal injunction to negate President Bush's right to go to war against Iraq without a congressional declaration of war or some congressional authorization. The federal district court in Washington, DC, heard that case, but ruled against the members. The judge held that the issue was not "ripe" for decision because Congress as a body had not taken a formal stand on whether it wanted President Bush to seek a congressional authorization. While both leaving the door open for such a decision if Congress acted and rejecting the executive claim that the courts could not intrude into "political question" disputes, the judge's ruling did not formally restrict executive power in this area.[81]

In decisions in two recent cases, similar kinds of arguments were made by the court. In *Campbell v. Clinton* (2000), 31 members of Congress challenged President Clinton's decision to use American forces in the 1999 campaign against Yugoslavia in Kosovo. The suit claimed that the president violated the War Powers Resolution (see Chapter 8) and the constitutional war powers granted to Congress. The district court dismissed the suit because it argued that the members of Congress lacked standing to sue. The appeals court concurred by contending the members of Congress could seek other remedies, such as passing a law to stop the operation in Kosovo, cutting off funding, or even impeaching the president. Yet, Congress as a body did not pursue options, so its members lacked standing.[82] Finally, in the summer of 2002, 32 members of Congress, led by Dennis Kucinich (D-OH), filed a suit against President George W. Bush's decision to withdraw the United States from the 1972 Anti-Ballistic Missile Treaty. The suit charged that President Bush did not have the right to withdraw from the treaty without approval from Congress. In December 2002, the case was dismissed by a district court judge who wrote that the "issues concerning treaties are largely political questions best left to the political branches of the government, not the courts, for resolution."[83] The judge also held that this group of members of Congress lacked standing to sue since they were not authorized to initiate this action for the entire House of Representatives.

While the *Youngstown Steel* case (and particularly Justice Jackson's argument) seemed to argue strongly for a more balanced interpretation of constitutional powers over foreign policy, many of the cases over the past three decades reflect the extent to which the Supreme Court and other federal jurisdictions continue to defer to the executive in the conduct of foreign policy, often at the expense of Congress. Indeed, constitutional analyst Gordon Silverstein sums up the Court's actions during the current period as a difficult one for the Congress when seeking to challenge the president on foreign policy. When "Congress is formally or clearly opposed" to the president, he argues, "the Court will support Congress."[84] Increasingly, however, the Court is demanding clearer and clearer direction when the Congress seeks to do so. If the Congress does not exhaust all avenues to assert its power (satisfying the ripeness criterion) or is at all unclear in its legislative intent or ambiguous in the language that delegates authority to the president, the Court is likely to support the executive.

Congressional Deference and Delegation

A third factor that has added to the presidential preeminence in foreign policy has been the degree of congressional support for presidential initiatives, particularly since World War II. In addition, Congress has sometimes gone further than giving its support to the executive; it has, on occasion, delegated some of its foreign policy prerogatives to the president. A brief survey of this factor will illustrate how the president's foreign policy control has been strengthened by congressional support and how it has met some challenge recently.

Congressional Leadership Legislative support for the president in foreign policy can be seen in the statements and policy actions of members of both houses of Congress. This support was often couched in a commitment to bipartisanship in the conduct of foreign policy; "politics must stop at the water's edge" was a frequent postwar refrain. This tradition of bipartisanship probably dates from the pledge of Senator Arthur Vandenberg, Chairman of the Senate Foreign Relations Committee, to support President Harry Truman in his foreign policy efforts in the immediate post–World War II years. The Vandenberg Resolution, for example, worked out in close consultation with the Department of State and passed in June 1948, called upon the executive branch to proceed with the development of the North Atlantic Treaty and with reforms of the United Nations. What it also did, however, was to usher in an era of congressional-executive cooperation in the making of foreign policy. Throughout this era, and running to this day, the president has generally taken the initiative, and Congress has often legitimized an executive program.[85]

Leaders of Congress, and particularly leaders of the foreign affairs committees in both the House and the Senate, have often—until relatively recently—viewed their role primarily as carrying out the president's wishes in the foreign policy area. Thomas (Doc) Morgan, chair of the House Foreign Affairs Committee from 1959 to 1976, stated this view directly: "Under the Constitution, the President is made responsible for the conduct of our foreign relations. . . ." He saw himself as "only the quarterback not the coach of the team." Moreover, congressional scholar Richard Fenno reports that Chairman Morgan saw his committee, "in *all* matters, as the subordinate partners in a permanent alliance with the executive branch. And as far as he is concerned, the group's blanket, all purpose decision rule should be: support all executive branch proposals."[86] Morgan's successor from 1977 to 1983, Clement J. Zablocki, despite his activism for congressional reform, still adopted this bipartisan approach. According to the committee staff and State Department officials, Congressman Zablocki worked with the executive, generally trying to get the president's program through the committee.[87] At the same time, Zablocki allowed liberal critics ample opportunity to express their views. Further, despite his own moderate-to-conservative beliefs, Zablocki continued to express support—albeit not always enthusiastically—for such 1980s congressional initiatives as the nuclear freeze and the ending of covert aid to the Nicaraguan rebels.[88]

Senator J. William Fulbright, chair of the Senate Foreign Relations Committee from 1959 to 1974, also enunciated this commitment to bipartisanship in foreign affairs at least until 1965. As Chairman Morgan had done, Senator Fulbright relied upon a football analogy to express his support of, and deference to, the president: "No football team can expect to win with every man his own quarterback. . . . The Foreign Relations Committee is available to advise the President, but his is the primary responsibility."[89] While this bipartisanship by Fulbright and the Senate Foreign Relations Committee waned with the deepening

American involvement in Vietnam during the 1960s, the tradition of support for the president by the Committee was not entirely abandoned by subsequent leaders. Nonetheless, by the early 1980s, Senator Charles Percy, a former chair of the Senate Foreign Relations Committee, lamented the "partisan gap" that had developed over foreign policy and renewed the call for bipartisanship "if the United States is to maintain a leadership role in the world."[90]

By the early 1980s, and continuing to the present, policy cooperation between Congress and the executive began to erode, and the congressional leadership was not as willing to follow the lead of the president. Speakers of the House of Representatives Thomas P. ("Tip") O'Neill and Jim Wright in the 1980s clashed bitterly with the Reagan administration over Central American policy. The sending of American forces into Lebanon and the exchange of arms for hostages with Iran and the transfer of profits to the Nicaraguan contras (the so-called Iran–Contra affair) further weakened the notion of congressional support for executive action. The establishment of two committees in 1987 to hold hearings on executive decision making during the Iran–Contra affair reflects the suspicion with which Congress held the president's explanation of this whole episode. Throughout these years of confrontation, calls for bipartisanship and for greater executive prerogatives in foreign affairs were never quite quelled by congressional debate over alleged executive abuses.

Sensing the need to renew the foreign policy process between Congress and the executive, President George H. W. Bush called for the establishment of the "old bipartisanship" in his 1989 inaugural address. Some congressional leaders were responsive to this initiative. Proposals were made for increasing consultation between the White House and Congress by holding monthly meetings to review foreign policy issues, for congressional changes in the foreign aid bill to allow greater presidential flexibility in implementing it, and even for changing the restrictiveness of the War Powers Resolution.[91] While none of these could reshape the suspicions of the immediate past, they do suggest the inclination by congressional leaders to defer to presidential leadership on foreign policy.

The chair of the House Foreign Affairs Committee at the time, Dante Fascell, generally applauded this call for bipartisan renewal, but he also wanted the democratic process to work. In his view, "a bipartisan foreign policy does not mean a unilateral decision by the president, rubber-stamped by the Congress." Yet, "if it gets to the point where consensus is asked for and consensus is reached on a specific policy decision, which the president will undertake, then obviously there is a responsibility for the congressional leadership to do what it can to drive that policy." If such a consensus were not reached, though, Fascell favored letting the "democratic process take over."[92] Fascell's successor, Lee Hamilton of Indiana, largely adopted this view on relations between Congress and the White House. While he committed to making the constitutional system work, he conveyed traditional congressional deference to the foreign policy powers of the executive: "I do not fool myself about the role of Congress on foreign policy. It is an important actor, but presidential leadership is by far the most important ingredient in a successful foreign policy. Only the president can lead. . . . We in the Congress . . . can help and support him."[93]

After the 1994 elections, the new Republican congressional foreign policy leadership, however, were much less to willing to defer to a Democratic president. As such, they were more assertive of a congressional role, and more confrontational than recent Democratic foreign affairs leaders toward President Clinton's initiatives in the foreign affairs realm. For example, both Senator Jesse Helms, chair of the Senate Foreign Relations Committee, and Congressman Benjamin A. Gilman, chair of the International Relations Committee, offered legislation to restructure the foreign affairs bureaucracy within the executive branch and proposed significant cuts in American foreign assistance. In this sense, any automatic deference toward presidential leadership seems to be waning.

With the 2000 election of Republican president George W. Bush, the Republican leadership in the House and the Senate was ready to defer to executive leadership on foreign policy matters. After the events of September 11, the Democratic leadership in both Houses, Representative Richard Gephardt, the House minority leader, and Senator Tom Daschle, Senate majority leader, were also quick to endorse President Bush's actions against international terrorism. The leaders of the key foreign policy committees (House International Relations Committee chair, Representative Henry Hyde, and Senate Foreign Relations Committee chair, Senator Joseph Biden, and, after the 2002 election, Senator Richard Lugar) were also supportive of executive leadership on foreign policy after these events. To be sure, that leadership support began to fray as the reconstruction in Iraq unraveled in 2003–2004 and as human rights abuses there were revealed.

Supportive Legislative Behavior   Although the bipartisanship call by congressional leaders over the years is one indicator of legislative deference to presidential wishes on foreign policy matters, congressional action on executive branch proposals is an even better one. Aaron Wildavsky, in a 1966 article on the presidency, documented the level of congressional support for presidential initiatives, and then contended that:

> In the realm of foreign policy there has not been a single major issue on which Presidents, when they were serious and determined, have failed. The list of their victories is impressive: entry into the United Nations, the Marshall Plan, NATO, the Truman Doctrine, the decisions to stay out of Indochina in 1954 and to intervene in Vietnam in the 1960s, aid to Poland and Yugoslavia, the test-ban treaty, and many more.[94]

Moreover, Wildavsky went on to demonstrate that on presidential proposals to Congress during the 1948 to 1964 period of his study, the president prevailed about 70 percent of the time in defense and foreign policy matters, but only 40 percent of the time on domestic matters.[95] Thus, the president is not only successful on foreign policy matters with Congress, but he is 75 percent more effective on foreign policy matters than on domestic policy matters. In this sense, Congress has been highly supportive of the president's wishes on issues beyond the water's edge.

Other studies have shown that this extraordinary support for the president's priorities in foreign policy has remained even into the 1970s and beyond, a period

Table 7.3 Presidential Victories on Foreign Policy Votes in the Congress: From Harry S Truman to George W. Bush

Administration	House		Senate	
Truman	68%	(N=78)	77%	(N=110)
Eisenhower	85	(N=94)	88	(N=217)
Kennedy	89	(N=47)	88	(N=109)
Johnson	86	(N=111)	81	(N=231)
Nixon	75	(N=85)	80	(N=181)
Ford	59	(N=46)	76	(N=106)
Carter	75	(N=180)	85	(N=215)
Reagan	64	(N=275)	84	(N=325)
Bush	48	(N=132)	77	(N=127)
Clinton	47	(N=217)	72	(N=136)
Bush (through 2002)	77	(N=30)	85	(N=26)

Note: Entries are the percentage of presidential victories on congressional foreign policy votes upon which the president took a position.

SOURCES: Calculated by the author and Eugene R. Wittkopf from congressional roll calls made available by the Inter-University Consortium for Political and Social Research and from reported votes in *Congressional Quarterly Weekly Reports* and *CQ Weekly* (various issues). The president's position was based upon *Congressional Quarterly Almanac* (various years), *Congressional Quarterly Weekly Reports* (various issues), and *CQ Weekly* (various issues) assessments for Eisenhower through Bush and was determined for Truman by a survey of *Congressional Quarterly Almanac* and presidential papers in collaboration with Eugene R. Wittkopf of Louisiana State University.

sometimes described as producing a congressional "revolution" in foreign affairs. LeLoup and Shull, for instance, demonstrate the congressional approval of presidential foreign policy initiatives remained high for the period of 1965 to 1975, although the average level of support has decreased to about 55 percent, compared to 70 percent for the 1948 to 1964 period.[96]

Similarly, a considerable difference remained between congressional approval of foreign policy versus domestic policy issues advanced by the president (55 percent compared to 46 percent on average). Further, when LeLoup and Shull categorized the domestic policy questions into social welfare, agriculture, government management, natural resources, and civil liberties, presidential proposals in the foreign and defense area still received greater congressional support than any of the other individual issues.[97] Fleisher and Bond, in a study through the first term of the Reagan administration, found that presidential foreign policy success remained substantial in both the House and the Senate through the Reagan years, although Nixon and Ford did not obtain as much support as did some of the other administrations. Similarly, Carter and Reagan did not do as well in the House as they did in the Senate, compared to earlier presidents.[98]

In our calculation of the degree of presidential success from Harry S Truman to George W. Bush on foreign policy voting in Congress, we also found that the recent presidents have been enormously successful in getting votes for issues on which they took a position. Table 7.3 shows the results of these calculations.

Overall, presidential success has been greater, on average, in the Senate than in the House, but both chambers have been supportive of presidential votes. In the Senate, presidents (from Truman through Clinton) averaged an 82 percent success rate, while in the House, presidents won about 66 percent of the time.[99]

In another study, analyzing the impact of the president on the voting behavior of individual members of Congress, political scientist Aage Clausen found a high degree of congressional deference to the executive's positions on foreign policy issues. In his *How Congressmen Decide,* Clausen reported that legislative voting on "international involvement" issues showed a considerably different pattern than did legislative voting on issues involving agricultural assistance, social welfare, government management, and civil liberties during the years 1953–1964 and 1969–1970. Only on foreign policy questions did "presidential influence" significantly help to explain congressional action in both the House and the Senate. Moreover, this factor did better than region, constituency influence, and party.[100] Here again, then, we find that the role of the president is pivotal in the actions of Congress, especially as they relate to foreign policy matters, and likely remain so to this day.

Changing Legislative Behavior? Foreshadowing our discussion of congressional resurgence in the next chapter, some evidence exists that congressional support for the president on foreign policy matters has waned over the years. Political scientist Lee Sigelman has shown that, when one examines "key votes," the degree of support for the president has declined in recent years, especially since 1973 and especially among the opposition party to the president in power.[101] Moreover, he suggests that despite what Wildavsky and others had contended earlier, the difference in congressional support for presidential initiatives on foreign policy versus domestic policy on key votes was never very great from 1957 to 1972 (74 percent vs. 73 percent) and has only slightly widened from 1973 to 1978 (60 percent vs. 57 percent).[102] In this sense, the argument about greater congressional support on foreign policy matters than on domestic matters is not demonstrable when key votes are examined. Nonetheless, the support by Congress for the president's foreign policy agenda even on key votes was still very high, at least until 1973.

LeLoup and Shull and our own analyses provide additional evidence that executive success with Congress has weakened somewhat in recent years. LeLoup and Shull demonstrate that the congressional approval of foreign policy initiatives for Nixon and Ford was considerably lower than for the other three presidents in their analysis (Eisenhower, Kennedy, and Johnson).[103] In this sense, the degree of congressional deference to executive proposals began to wane in the decade of the 1970s. The data in Table 7.3 show a similar pattern for recent administrations. This weakening of presidential success, however, is confined more to the House than to the Senate. Note that President Gerald Ford's success rate was only 59 percent in the House, Jimmy Carter's was higher at 75 percent, but Ronald Reagan's at only 64 percent, George H. W. Bush's lower at 48 percent, and Bill Clinton's lower still at 47 percent. In the Senate, by contrast, Carter and Reagan are actually at about the same rate as the earlier administrations, although Ford's and Bush's success rates were a bit lower. During the eight years of the Clinton administration, its support was only 72 percent, the lowest of any administration since the end of World War II.

Through the first two years of President George W. Bush's tenure, presidential foreign policy success bucked these trends, with congressional support returning to some earlier levels. Bush received 77 percent support in the House and 85 percent support in the Senate. Such levels of support were no doubt aided by the war on terrorism and are based upon only a few important votes (30 in the House and 26 in the Senate). Hence, it remains to be seen whether this level of support will be sustained, especially in face of the challenging situation in reconstructing Iraq after the 2003 war, or whether the George W. Bush administration will face the same changing congressional behavior as recent presidents have.

Another changing congressional behavior on foreign policy questions has also been identified in recent years. Several recent assessments of specific foreign policy issues show that partisanship and ideology are now good predictors of congressional behavior. Analyses of congressional voting patterns on the antiballistic missile issue in the late 1960s and early 1970s, the Panama Canal Treaties in the late 1970s, the call for a nuclear freeze, the B-1 bomber debate, and the fight over aid to the Nicaraguan Contras in the 1980s demonstrate that ideology in particular was a potent factor in explaining individual member's votes, seemingly more important than presidential influence.[104]

Finally, originator of the "two-presidencies" thesis also has recognized the substantial change in relations between Congress and the White House over the years. In a 1989 study, coauthored with Duane Oldfield, Aaron Wildavsky contended that his earlier (1960s) argument was "time and culture bound." As the public and the political parties have become more ideological, the building of bipartisan support for the president has become much more difficult in the current era. Yet, Oldfield and Wildavsky argue that the president still has other means of exercising his power, much as our survey here suggests.[105] Overall, though, the foreign policy debate has become more politicized than in the past.

In the aggregate, then, while we can surely conclude that there has been some change in congressional deference to the executive, presidential success remains pronounced. Nonetheless, as we shall demonstrate in Chapter 8, specific areas of foreign policy did elicit changes in congressional procedures in dealing with the executive.

Legislative Delegation Not only has Congress shown this deference by its approval of presidential actions, but it has occasionally gone even further in granting some of its powers to the executive. Most notably, this delegation of its foreign policy powers has occurred in authorizing the president to use armed forces as he sees fit, in affording the president discretion in the distribution of foreign aid, and in implementing trade policy abroad. In effect, these delegations transferred some congressional responsibility to the executive.

This transference of power in the post–World War II period has been most dramatic in the use of armed forces at the president's discretion. In the Formosa Resolution in January 1955, Congress granted to President Eisenhower the power to use armed forces to defend Quemoy and Matsu from attack by the Chinese Communists as well as to protect Formosa and the Pescadores Islands. The language was quite sweeping in its tone: "the President of the United States is authorized to employ the Armed Forces of the United States *as he deems necessary.* . . ."[106]

As we noted in Chapter 2, Congress also granted to President Eisenhower a broad mandate to deal with the threat of international communism in the Middle East. Popularly called the Eisenhower Doctrine, this congressional resolution appeared to grant to the president the right "to use armed forces to assist any such nation or group of nations requesting assistance against armed aggression from any country controlled by international communism" in the Middle East.[107] Once again, what was so remarkable about this resolution was the apparently broad grant of power given to the executive in the war-making area, although the Congress weakened the grant slightly by requiring the affected country to request assistance and by declaring that the United States (not the president per se) "is prepared to use armed forces to assist" such a country. Furthermore, President Eisenhower pledged to keep Congress informed about these activities.[108]

Perhaps the most famous grant of war-making power by Congress to the executive was the Gulf of Tonkin Resolution, approved by the House on a vote of 416–0 and in the Senate by 89–2 in August 1964 at the beginning of substantial American involvement in Vietnam. This resolution granted to the president the right "to take all necessary steps, including the use of armed forces, to assist any member or protocol state of the Southeast Asia Collective Defense Treaty requesting assistance. . . ."[109] Moreover, the determination as to when to use these forces was left to the president, but he did have this prior congressional approval as a basis for action. This resolution was eventually viewed as the "functional equivalent" of war by the Johnson administration and was used to expand American involvement in Vietnam and Southeast Asia in the 1960s.[110]

In the wake of the terrorist attacks of September 11, 2001, both houses of Congress quickly passed a sweeping resolution granting the president broad military power to respond to these events and to pursue international terrorists. By Public Law 107–40,

> the president is authorized to use all necessary and appropriate force against those nations, organizations, or persons he determines planned, authorized, committed, or aided the terrorist attacks that occurred on September 11, 2001, or harbored such organizations or persons, in order to prevent any future acts of international terrorism against the United States by such nations, organizations, or persons.

Much like the Gulf of Tonkin resolution, P.L. 107–40 was overwhelming approved by the House (420–1) and by the Senate (98–0), indicating the broad consensus allowing presidential discretion in this area.

In fall 2002, Congress passed Public Law 107–243 again granting the president broad authority to take military action against Iraq. The operative section afforded the president wide latitude:

> The President is authorized to use the Armed Forces of the United States *as he determines to be necessary and appropriate* [emphasis added] in order to (1) defend the national security . . . against the continuing threat posed by Iraq; and (2) enforce all relevant United Nations Security Council resolutions regarding Iraq.

In both chambers, the resolution was passed by wide margins, although not as unanimously as some others. In the House, the vote was 296–133, while in the Senate, it was 77–23.

Beyond these rather dramatic examples in the war-making area, Congress has had a tendency to grant to the executive considerable discretion in implementing trade and foreign assistance statutes. In recent foreign assistance legislation, for example, the president is still afforded latitude in authorizing development assistance "on such terms and conditions as he may determine," in providing economic support funds "on such terms and conditions as he may determine . . . to promote economic or political stability," and to provide military assistance in a similar fashion that "will strengthen the security of the United States." While this legislation also imposed considerable restrictions on the executive, considerable residual presidential authority still remains.[111]

The congressional delegation of trade responsibility to the president predates the Cold War years, going back at least to the Reciprocal Trade Agreements Act of 1934, but it continues to this day. Under the 1934 act, the president was authorized to negotiate tariff reductions and implement such agreements. Moreover, these reductions could involve as much as 50 percent reduction without any congressional involvement. This delegation also occurred in subsequent reciprocal trade acts into the 1950s.[112] More recent trade acts, such as the Trade Act of 1974 and the Trade Act of 1979, continued this process by authorizing the president to negotiate the elimination of nontariff barriers as well. In the Omnibus Trade and Competitiveness Act of 1988, too, the president's prerogatives were reaffirmed in negotiating and implementing trade legislation. The president was authorized to enter into tariff agreements, both bilaterally and multilaterally. He could also change the U.S. tariff schedules "if the President determines such action to be in the interest of the United States." While the legislation gave more power to the U.S. Trade Representative in implementing many of the provisions, this representative would still be responsible to the president.[113] Finally, congressional approval of the North American Free Trade Agreement (NAFTA) and American entry into the World Trade Organizations (WTO) yielded even more control over trade policy to the executive. The only exception in the WTO approval was a review mechanism mandating withdrawal from the organization under specified conditions.[114]

In an even broader piece of congressional legislation enacted at the end of 1977, the International Emergency Economic Powers Act, the president was authorized to declare a national emergency to deal with any "extraordinary threat, which has its source in whole or substantial part outside the United States, to the national security, foreign policy, or economy of the United States." Under this authority, the president may "investigate, regulate, or prohibit" a wide array of actions, albeit largely economic ones.[115] In addition, however, this grant of authority was conditioned upon several requirements dealing with consulting and reporting to Congress. In this sense, the seemingly broad sweep of the legislation was actually to be more restrictive than what earlier legislation dating back to the Roosevelt era had allowed. Yet subsequent Supreme Court decisions in the early 1980s weakened the congressional role and, in the estimation of one analyst, "freed the president . . . to conduct widespread economic warfare merely by declaring a national emergency with respect to a particular country. . . ."[116]

Part of this discretion is understandable in that individual cases might arise that Congress would not be able to foresee, or, alternatively, that Congress might not have the time or inclination to handle expeditiously. In this sense, presidential discretion was reasonable, since the presidential responsibility was to execute the law. At the same time, such discretion inevitably has led to a greater concentration of foreign policy powers in the hands of the president—usually at the expense of the legislative branch. In the words of one well-known trade analyst, I. M. Destler, the "Congress legislated itself out of the business of making product-specific trade law," despite the constitutional mandate that it shall "regulate commerce with foreign nations."[117]

Growth of Executive Institutions

A fourth reason for presidential dominance in foreign policy has been the expansion of executive institutions. Since the end of World War II, the foreign policy machinery of the president has grown quite substantially, while the capacity of Congress has grown only modestly. As a result, presidential control of the foreign policy apparatus and foreign policy information has increased sharply, leaving Congress at a distinct disadvantage in both areas.

With congressional passage of the National Security Act of 1947, the foreign policy machinery of the executive branch was both consolidated and enlarged.[118] This act provided for the establishment of the National Security Council, the Central Intelligence Agency, and the organization of the separate military forces under the National Military Establishment (later the Department of Defense). In addition, the civilian position of the secretary of defense was mandated to head this National Military Establishment, and the Joint Chiefs of Staff was organized to advise the secretary of defense.

All of these new agencies and individuals ultimately were to assist the president with the conduct of foreign policy. The National Security Council, for instance, composed of the president, vice president, the secretary of state, secretary of defense, and others that the president may designate, was "to advise the president with respect to the integration of domestic, foreign, and military policies relating to the national security. . . ."[119] This council to the executive enabled him to make foreign policy with little involvement on the part of the other branches of government, and even without much involvement on the part of the rest of the executive branch. Moreover, as the National Security Council system has evolved—especially with the enhanced role of the national security advisor in more recent administrations—the executive control of the foreign policy machinery became firmly entrenched in the office of the president. One indicator of the growth of the National Security Council system is the size of the staffs under each succeeding president in the postwar years.

Under President Truman, for instance, National Security Council personnel numbered 20 in 1951. This total increased to 28 in 1955 under President Eisenhower; grew to 50 in 1962 under President Kennedy; remained at 50 in 1966 under President Johnson; rose to 75 under President Nixon; decreased to 64 under President Carter in 1979; and again declined to 62 in 1982 under President Reagan and to 61 in 1990 under President Bush. For the Clinton administration, the estimated number of National Security Council personnel by 2000 was 100. In contrast, the George W. Bush administration committed itself to reduce the size of the staff by one-third and to have a more "strategically focused operation." Overall, then, while the size of the National Security Council staff has fluctuated over time, it has surely grown from its initial years.[120] More importantly, it has grown in power and influence in the actual formulation of foreign policy within the executive branch (see Chapter 9).

The Central Intelligence Agency was established by the National Security Act for the purpose of developing intelligence estimates and for advising and making recommendations to the National Security Council. The agency also was to assist in coordinating the activities of other intelligence agencies within the U.S. government. Further, the CIA was "to perform such other functions and duties related to intelligence affecting the national security as the National Security Council may from time to time direct."[121] This last function was used as the rationale for "covert actions" by the American government as the CIA developed.

The National Security Act also begat the National Military Establishment in 1947. Under this provision of the act, the Departments of the Army, Navy, and Air Force came into existence, with the secretary of defense heading this overall organizational arrangement. By 1949, amendments to the act created the present Department of Defense to replace the National Military Establishment. Moreover, the secretary of defense, who was the head of this new cabinet department, was required to be a civilian and to be "the principal assistant to the President in all matters relating to the national security."[122]

Finally, the 1947 act provided for the creation of the Joint Chiefs of Staff. This group would consist of the Army and Air Force chiefs of staff, the chief of naval operations, and the chairman of the Joint Chiefs. Their duties would consist of preparing strategic plans and forces, formulating military policies, and advising the president and the secretary of defense on military matters.

By one congressional act, then, the president was provided an intelligence advisor (the director of the CIA), a military advisor (chairman of the Joint Chiefs of Staff), and a national security advisor (the secretary of defense). In addition, the president was provided with a bureaucratic mechanism for gathering intelligence (the Central Intelligence Agency), for making policy (the National Security Council), and for carrying out the military options (the National Military Establishment). All of these forums were in addition to the Department of State and the secretary of state, traditionally the principal foreign affairs bureaucracy and its spokesperson.

Later in the postwar period, some agencies were established to assist the president, and other agencies assumed a larger role in foreign policy matters. Three new agencies illustrate how the executive branch continued to gain greater control over various aspects of foreign policy. In 1961, the Agency for International Development (AID) was established by Congress to coordinate the distribution of foreign assistance abroad.[123] In the same year, the Arms Control and Disarmament Agency (ACDA) was mandated by Congress to coordinate arms control activities.[124] The director of ACDA was to be the principal advisor to the president on these foreign policy questions. In 1963, the Office of the Special Trade Representative was created by an executive order, and the duties of the individual who would be U.S. Trade Representative has been institutionalized and expanded in subsequent trade acts passed by Congress.[125] The U.S. Trade Representative, for instance, now has the responsibility for directing all trade negotiations and for formulating trade policy as well. Other bureaucracies within the executive branch (e.g., the departments of Commerce, Treasury, Agriculture, and Justice) have also become increasingly involved in international affairs.[126] Finally, in the post–September 11 era, Congress created the Department of Homeland Security in 2002 to provide the executive branch with additional assistance to address foreign (and domestic) threats. In short, with all of these agencies in place, the president, and the executive branch more generally, are in a better institutional position to shape foreign policy than the executive's traditional rival, Congress.

Such structural and hierarchical arrangements have markedly aided the president and his advisors in gathering information and in making rapid foreign policy decisions. Some years ago it was estimated that, at any one time, more than 35,000 people within the executive branch are working on matters related to foreign policy.[127] With all of these people ultimately answerable to the president and with all of these sources of information, centralized and quick decision making can usually result. Thus, the executive can *usually* respond quickly to an international situation, ranging from the use of military force to negotiating arms control to the distribution of foreign assistance. As we note in Chapters 9 and 10, however, bureaucratic politics can and does impede the assumed efficiency of the executive branch. The discerning student needs to keep this important exception in mind as we discuss the bureaucracies of the executive.

By contrast, Congress *usually* does not enjoy such advantages, and a number of its bureaucratic, procedural, and informational arrangements have been criticized. Congress is a large and often unwieldy body, with 535 members who are sometimes described as parochial, not national or international, in their outlook. As constituency service has become an increasingly important mechanism for political survival, national and foreign policy interests may well suffer. Congress has a cumbersome bureaucratic system, with numerous committees and subcommittees claiming foreign policy responsibilities, and thus hindering quick foreign policy decision making. Congress does not enjoy many large independent information sources on foreign policy matters, and it has been often highly dependent upon the executive branch. Further, many complain that the size of congressional staffs has been inadequate to do the necessary background work on foreign policy questions.

Several of these criticisms about Capitol Hill are accurate, and some issues are being addressed by reforms within Congress, beginning in the 1970s and continuing to the present. Members are becoming more expert on foreign policy, and foreign policy issues can actually work to a member's advantage within a constituency, especially as the boundaries between domestic and foreign policy questions erode (e.g., agricultural trade policy for a midwestern member of Congress). Information sources have expanded, too. The General Accounting Office (GAO), an arm of the U.S. Congress, has the responsibility to investigate and to provide evaluations to members of the House and the Senate. GAO has 13 "teams" to address policy questions, including at least three with foreign policy responsibilities—Defense Capabilities and Management, Homeland Security and Justice, and International Affairs and Trade. The Congressional Research Service, a department within the Library of Congress, was expanded under the Legislative Reform Act of 1970 and now has a separate division, the Foreign Affairs, Defense and Trade Division, to work on foreign policy analyses for members of Congress. The Office of Technology Assessment, also a creation of the 1970s, was another source of information on highly specialized topics for Congress (until it was eliminated during budget-cutting efforts in 1995).[128]

Beginning with the establishment of the Joint Committee on the Organization of Congress in 1992, members of the House and Senate held discussions into 1994 on how to streamline the congressional system and to make it more effective. Because of partisan bickering, these reforms were not enacted into laws.[129] In 1995, as the new Republican majority took control of the House and Senate, some changes did occur—with a reduction in the number of committees and subcommittees, new internal congressional rules on handling and expediting legislation, and the enactment of a bill applying national workplace rules to the House and the Senate. While, arguably, these reforms will have limited impact in the overall operation of Congress, they are meant to increase efficiency and accountability in carrying out the legislative process.

International Situational Factors

The final factor affects all of the previous ones. Throughout the greater portion of the years since World War II, the United States has made foreign policy within a Cold War environment. Such a perceived dangerous environment had the effect of muting foreign policy debate over long-term goals and instead focused on short-term tactics (see Chapter 2). Another consequence, given the dangerous global situation, was a tendency by both Congress and the American public to defer to the executive on foreign policy matters. If an emergency arose, the president, not Congress, could react immediately. If decisions had to be made about the use of force or diplomacy, the president, not Congress, had to be prepared to act quickly. Furthermore, with the advent of nuclear weapons and instantaneous global communication, centralized control of the foreign policy machinery seemed more necessary than ever. More generally, too, the president was often the most admired person among the American people, and this admiration was transferred to trust in his conduct of foreign affairs.[130] As a result, there was a tendency to defer to the executive, with the assumption that the "president knows best."[131]

In recent decades, such deference to the president has eroded somewhat, for a variety of domestic and international reasons, although this factor cannot be wholly dismissed as a source of presidential power. Now Congress and the public are more willing to question presidents on foreign policy matters. This new posture probably had its beginnings with the Watergate events of the early 1970s, when the credibility of President Nixon suffered greatly. President Ford's reputation, in turn, was hurt by his pardoning of the former president over the Watergate matter. Later on, President Carter's foreign policy credibility was diminished by his inability to deal effectively with the Iran hostage crisis.

In the 1980s, President Reagan had a similar difficulty, at least with regard to his Central American policy. Despite Reagan's overall popularity among the public and several addresses to the American people appealing for their support and that of their representatives in Congress, he was never able to obtain their approval for his Contra aid policy in Central America. Public opinion polls consistently opposed this aspect of his foreign policy throughout his administration. Similarly, although President George H. W. Bush enjoyed substantial popular support, he had to fight vigorously with Congress over his policy toward China after the Tiananmen Square massacre of June 1989, had to employ his veto power to stop restrictive trade policy toward Japan, and had to spar with that body over his right to conduct American policy unilaterally with Iraq over its seizure of Kuwait. Further, with the rapidly changing events in Central Europe and the Middle East, and with no evident consensus on what American policy should be in the world, President Bush had perhaps less than automatic support for his foreign policy agenda from the American people or its representatives.

With the end of the Cold War, President Bill Clinton failed to obtain this seemingly "automatic" deference that earlier presidents received on foreign policy matters. Several reasons appeared to account for this situation. With a direct nuclear threat to the United States having diminished as a result of the demise of the Soviet Union, the public (and Congress) seemed unwilling to defer to the president. With the public unsure of the future role of the United States in global affairs, and with the Clinton administration seemingly unable to define such a role satisfactorily, the public were initially reluctant to embrace the policies of the president. As a result, the public's support of President Clinton's handling of foreign policy was usually below the 50 percent level (averaging in the mid-40s generally) during much of the first term, actually falling to 34 percent support in August 1994 and 36 percent in April 1995.[132] By Clinton's second term, the public's approval of his handling of the presidency increased, as did its foreign policy support. By late 1998, 55 percent of the public now rated his foreign policy performance as "excellent" or "good."[133] With the opposition still in control of Congress, that body continued to challenge the president on a range of foreign policy issues, from the use of force in Bosnia and Kosovo and the level of spending for defense to the rejection of the Comprehensive Test Ban Treaty and fast-track trading authority for the president.

The events of September 11, 2001, restored the level of support and deference to the presidency by the Congress and the public. Prior to September 11, the average level of support for George W. Bush as president was 57 percent. After September 11, and through mid-January 2002, Bush's support averaged 87 percent, an increase of 30 percentage points.[134] Moreover, his approval rating remained high through much of 2002 and into 2003. In this same international environment and during this same time, Congress was equally supportive of the presidential initiatives on terrorism and other priorities were put aside.[135] While this level of support eroded in the aftermath of the Iraq War, this international situational factor, like some of the other factors discussed in this chapter, are still a source of presidential preeminence in the conduct of foreign policy.

CONCLUDING COMMENTS

Historical precedents as well as Supreme Court decisions and nondecisions continue to serve as important reservoirs of presidential domination of foreign policy making. Similarly, the capacity of the executive branch to control the foreign policy bureaucracy and the demands for rapid decision making in global events are usually supportive of the preeminence of the president in making American foreign policy (as the response to September 11 emphasized). Legislative deference and delegation of power to the executive also aid the president, even as these sources of executive strength have begun to change. In this sense, these are now sources of challenge to presidential power in foreign policy, but executive preeminence largely remains.

In Chapter 8, we examine the role of Congress more fully in foreign policy making. In particular, we shall focus upon the major areas in which Congress has tried to reassert its prerogatives and, at the same time, has sought to reduce the degree of executive dominance. After that analysis, we then turn to discuss how to address the inevitable policy-making conflict between these two branches.

NOTES

1. "President's Letter to Congress on American Response to Terrorism," October 9, 2001, at http://www.whitehouse.gov/news/releases/2001/10/20011009–6.html, accessed on July 16, 2002.

2. Thomas L. Friedman, "Clinton Vows to Fight Congress on His Power to Use the Military," *New York Times,* October 19, 1993, A18.

3. "The McNeil-Lehrer Report," Public Broadcasting Service, February 10, 1983.

4. Michael J. Glennon in his *Constitutional Diplomacy* (Princeton, NJ: Princeton University Press, 1990), p. 20, says that a "'plenary presidential power' is one that is not susceptible of congressional limitation." Thanks to James M. Lindsay for this point about plenary powers.

5. See Cecil V. Crabb, Jr., and Pat M. Holt, *Invitation to Struggle: Congress, the President,* *and Foreign Policy* (Washington, DC: Congressional Quarterly Press, 1980), p. 34. Emphasis in original.

6. See Louis Fisher, *Presidential War Power* (Lawrence, KS: University Press of Kansas, 1995), pp. 1–6, for this argument.

7. Federalist No. 69 can be found in Clinton Rossiter, ed., *The Federalist Papers* (New York: A Mentor Book, 1961), pp. 415–423.

8. Louis Henkin, *Foreign Affairs and the Constitution* (Mineola, NY: The Foundation Press, Inc., 1972). The quotations are at pp. 74 and 76. An early court case, *Little v. Barreme* 6 U.S. 170 (1804), reveals the degree to which the Congress held sway over foreign policy and how the president must yield to its authority. See Glennon, *Constitutional Diplomacy,* pp. 3–8, for a discussion of this case.

9. Quoted in Louis Henkin, "Foreign Affairs and the Constitution," *Foreign Affairs*

66 (Winter 1987/1988): 285, from *Youngstown Sheet & Tube Co. v. Sawyer* (1952).

10. Cited in ibid., p. 292.

11. Arthur M. Schlesinger, Jr., *The Imperial Presidency* (Boston: Houghton Mifflin Company, 1973), p. 2.

12. Henkin, "Foreign Affairs and the Constitution," p. 287.

13. Edward S. Corwin, *The President: Office and Powers 1787–1957* (New York: New York University Press, 1957), p. 171.

14. See Arthur Schlesinger, Jr., "Congress and the Making of American Foreign Policy," *Foreign Affairs* 51 (October 1972): 78–113; James L. Sundquist, *The Decline and Resurgence of Congress* (Washington, DC: The Brookings Institution, 1981), pp. 21–29; and Harold Hongju Koh, *The National Security Constitution* (New Haven, CT: Yale University Press, 1992). For a brief description of the "pendulum theory" of foreign policy powers between the president and Congress, see Thomas M. Franck and Edward Weisband, *Foreign Policy by Congress* (New York: Oxford University Press, 1979), pp. 5–6. Also, these are the sources for the discussion of the different phases in executive and legislative dominance.

15. Holbert N. Carroll, *The House of Representatives and Foreign Affairs* (Pittsburgh: University of Pittsburgh Press, 1958), p. 10. Sundquist, *The Decline and Resurgence of Congress,* pp. 22–23, views this early period slightly differently, with seemingly more power for Congress.

16. In reality, Congress passed a resolution that acknowledged that "a state of war exists." This passage is quoted in Fisher, *Presidential War Power,* p. 33.

17. The quoted phrase is from Sundquist, *The Decline and Resurgence of Congress,* p. 25.

18. The last two quoted passages are from Koh, *The National Security Constitution,* p. 86.

19. Carroll, *The House of Representatives and Foreign Affairs,* p. 14. Much of this section on the cyclical interpretation of foreign policy control also draws upon James M. McCormick, "Congress and Foreign Policy," in *The Encyclopedia of U.S. Foreign Relations* (New York: Oxford University Press, 1997), pp. 312–328.

20. Fisher, *Presidential War Power,* p. 65.

21. Henkin, "Foreign Affairs and the Constitution," p. 290.

22. Corwin, *The President,* p. 206.

23. Henkin, "Foreign Affairs and the Constitution," p. 291, and Robert H. Ferrell, *American Diplomacy: A History,* 3rd ed. (New York: W. W. Norton and Company, 1975), pp. 78–79.

24. Corwin, *The President,* p. 182.

25. Schlesinger, "Congress and the Making of American Foreign Policy," p. 82. Also see Fisher, *Presidential War Power,* pp. 21–22.

26. Quoted in Corwin, *The President,* p. 177.

27. Ibid., p. 188.

28. Schlesinger, "Congress and the Making of American Foreign Policy," pp. 83–87. Also, however, see the 1989 edition (and its epilogue) of *The Imperial Presidency* (Boston: Houghton Mifflin Company, 1989), p. 442 in particular.

29. Ibid.

30. Johnny H. Killian, ed., *The Constitution of the United States: Analysis and Interpretation* (Washington, DC: Congressional Research Service, 1987), p. 338.

31. Schlesinger, "Congress and the Making of American Foreign Policy," p. 86.

32. Corwin, *The President,* p. 229.

33. For a discussion of the *Prize Cases,* see *Guide to the U.S. Supreme Court* (Washington, DC: Congressional Quarterly, Inc., 1979), pp. 187–189.

34. Schlesinger, "Congress and the Making of American Foreign Policy," pp. 89–91. Also see pp. 91–95 for the interventions mentioned and others done by presidents without congressional authorization.

35. Francis D. Wormuth, "Presidential Wars: The Convenience of 'Precedent,'" in Martin B. Hickman, ed., *Problems of American Foreign Policy,* 2nd ed. (Beverly Hills: Glencoe Press, 1975), p. 96.

36. Richard M. Nixon, "Cambodia: A Difficult Decision," *Vital Speeches of the Day* 36 (May 15, 1970): 451. This speech was originally delivered to the American public on April 30, 1970.

37. Taken from the "Letter to the Speaker of the House and the President Pro Tempore of the Senate on United States Military Action in Panama," *Weekly Compilation of Presidential Documents* 25 (December 25, 1989): 1985.

38. The quoted passages by the president are reported in Friedman, "Clinton Vows to Fight Congress on His Power to Use the Military," p. A1.

39. Ryan Hendrickson, *The Clinton Wars: The Constitution, Congress, and War Powers* (Nashville: Vanderbilt University Press, 2002), p. 87.

40. Ibid., pp. 127, 129.

41. These two examples are drawn from the testimony of U. Alexis Johnson, undersecretary of state for political affairs, and reported in "Department Discusses Agreements on Azores and Bahrain Facilities," *Department of State Bulletin* (February 28, 1972): 279–284. The quoted passage is at p. 282. Johnson did add that Congress would have to approve the rental payment for the use of the Bahrain facilities.

42. For some evidence illustrating that the bulk of the executive agreements in the postwar period have been pursuant to statute, see Loch Johnson and James M. McCormick, "The Making of International Agreements: A Reappraisal of Congressional Involvement," *The Journal of Politics* 40 (May 1978): 468–478.

43. The agreement data are in part from Michael Nelson, ed., *Congressional Quarterly's Guide to the Presidency* (Washington, DC: Congressional Quarterly, Inc., 1989), p. 1104. Louis Fisher in his *The President and Congress: Power and Policy* (New York: Free Press, 1972), p. 45, reports similar data through 1970. See Table 7.2 for another source from the U.S. Senate.

44. Schlesinger, *The Imperial Presidency,* pp. 86–88.

45. On this point, see "National Commitments," Senate Report 91-129, 91st Cong., 1st sess., April 16, 1969, 26.

46. The hearings on American commitments with other countries were held in 1969 and 1970 by a subcommittee of the Committee on Foreign Relations (Subcom-mittee on United States Security Agreements and Commitments Abroad), chaired by Senator Stuart Symington of Missouri. A summary of these hearings, popularly known as the Symington Subcommittee, is reported in "Security Agreements and Commitments Abroad," *Report to the Committee on Foreign Relations of the United States Senate by the Subcommittee on Security Agreements and Commitments Abroad,* December 21, 1970.

47. Loch Johnson and James M. McCormick, "Foreign Policy by Executive Fiat," *Foreign Policy* 28 (Fall 1977): 117–138.

48. Koh, *The National Security Constitution,* p. 138.

49. The pact was entitled "The Agreed Framework Between the United States and the Democratic People's Republic of Korea," and was signed in Geneva, Switzerland, on October 21, 1994.

50. See "Notice: Continuation of Emergency with Respect to Burma," signed by President George W. Bush on May 15, 2001, and "To the Congress of the United States," signed February 8, 2001. Both are available at http://www.whitehouse.gov and were accessed on July 9, 2002.

51. Kenneth R. Mayer and Kevin Price, "Unilateral Presidential Powers: Significant Executive Orders, 1949–99," *Presidential Studies Quarterly* 32 (June 2002): 367–386. The author classified the significant executive order as foreign policy–related from the listing at pp. 380–384 and calculated the resulting numbers.

52. 299 U.S. 304 (1936).

53. Ibid., p. 314.

54. Ibid., p. 318.

55. Ibid., pp. 319, 320. The "extra-constitutional" description below is from Henkins, *Foreign Affairs and the Constitution,* p. 22. For another discussion (upon which we draw) on the courts (and other factors) and foreign policy, see Howard Bliss and M. Glen Johnson, *Beyond the Water's Edge: America's Foreign Policies* (Philadelphia: J. P. Lippincott Company, 1975), pp. 133–137.

56. See Adler, "The Constitution and Presidential Warmaking: The Enduring Debate," *Political Science Quarterly* 103 (Spring 1988):

30–36. See especially his discussion of the *Steel Seizure Case* and *Reid v. Covert* at p. 32 as particular challenges to this broad "extra-constitutional" interpretation of presidential power. For a detailed analysis of *Curtiss-Wright,* see Glennon, *Constitutional Diplomacy,* pp. 18–34.

57. 252 U.S. 433.

58. Ibid.

59. Ibid.

60. 301 U.S. 324 (1937), 315 U.S. 203 (1942).

61. Jean Edward Smith, *The Constitution and American Foreign Policy* (St. Paul: West Publishing Company, 1989), p. 127.

62. 315 U.S. 234 (1942).

63. Henkin, *Foreign Affairs and the Constitution,* p. 185.

64. These statutes are listed in Appendix I of *INS v. Chadha* 462 U.S. 919 (1983).

65. Martha Liebler Gibson, "Managing Conflict: The Role of the Legislative Veto in American Foreign Policy," *Polity* 26 (Spring 1994): 442–443.

66. Joseph Cooper and Patricia A. Hurley, "The Legislative Veto: A Policy Analysis," *Congress & Presidency* 10 (Spring 1983): 1–24, especially at pp. 1 and 4.

67. For a fuller discussion of the origin and development of the legislative veto, see Gibson, "Managing Conflict: The Role of the Legislative Veto in American Foreign Policy," 441–472; Martha Liebler Gibson, *Weapons of Influence: The Legislative Veto, American Foreign Policy, and the Irony of Reform* (Boulder, CO: Westview Press, 1992); and Cooper and Hurley, "The Legislative Veto: A Policy Analysis," pp. 1–24.

68. These details are taken from the Chadha decision and from David M. O'Brien, *Constitutional Law and Politics,* vol. 1 (W. W. Norton and Company, 1991), p. 355.

69. 462 U.S. 947–959 (1983).

70. Frederick M. Kaiser, "Congressional Control of Executive Actions in the Aftermath of the Chadha Decision," *Administrative Law Review* 36 (Summer 1984): 242.

71. 343 U.S. 585 (1952).

72. 343 U.S. 587 (1952).

73. 343 U.S. 635, 647 (1952).

74. Koh, *The National Security Constitution,* p. 108.

75. Quoted in Smith, *The Constitution and American Foreign Policy,* from the decision itself at p. 169. The earlier quotation is from Smith's analysis at the same page.

76. This discussion is gleaned and simplified somewhat from Henkin, *Foreign Affairs and the Constitution,* pp. 210–215. The "political doctrine" question is more complicated than this brief summary conveys and remains a complex issue of constitutional law.

77. Warren Christopher, "Ceasefire Between the Branches: A Compact in Foreign Affairs," in James M. McCormick, *A Reader in American Foreign Policy* (Itasca, IL: F. E. Peacock Publishers, Inc., 1986), pp. 253–254.

78. The case summary and quoted passages are from Gordon Silverstein, "Judicial Enhancement of Executive Power," in Paul E. Peterson, ed., *The President, The Congress, and The Making of Foreign Policy* (Norman and London: University of Oklahoma Press, 1994), p. 38. Emphasis in original.

79. See, for example, *Altee v. Richardson* 411 U.S. 911 (1973).

80. The discussion is drawn from *Crockett v. Reagan* 720 F. 2d 1355 (1983); *Conyers v. Reagan* 765 F. 2d 1124 (1985); and *Lowry v. Reagan* 676 F. Supp. 333 (D.D.C. 1987).

81. Neil A. Lewis, "Lawmakers Lose War Powers Suit," *New York Times,* December 14, 1990, A9. Also see 752 F. Supp 1141 (D.D.C. 1990).

82. The details are taken from http//www.ll.georgetown.edu/FedCt/Circuit/dc/opinions/99-5214a.html, where the opinion of the District of Columbia Circuit Court is printed for *Campbell v. Clinton.* This site was accessed on October 31, 2000. Also see *Campbell v. Clinton,* 203 F.ed 19 (D.C. Cir. 2000).

83. The discussion of the filing of this suit is in "Congressmen Sue Bush," *Detroit Free Press,* June 12, 2002, 5A, while the decision and the quoted passage by the court is from "ABM Treaty Dismissed," December 31, 2002, from http://www.cnn.com/2002/LAW/12/31/abm.treaty.suit.

84. Silverstein, "Judicial Enhancement of Executive Power," pp. 23–45, especially pp. 34–45. The quoted passage is at p. 26.

85. On the Vandenberg Resolution, see James A. Robinson, *Congress and Foreign Policy-Making,* rev. ed. (Homewood, IL: The Dorsey Press, 1967), pp. 44–46. Also see Table 2-1 at p. 65, which shows the small degree of congressional initiation in foreign policy and the considerable degree of executive influence within Congress.

86. Richard F. Fenno, Jr., *Congressmen in Committees* (Boston: Little, Brown and Company, 1973), p. 71. Emphasis in original.

87. Interview, House Foreign Affairs Committee, Washington, DC, June 1982; and Department of State, Washington, DC, October 1981.

88. John Felton, "Foreign Affairs Committee Changes Seen Under Fascell," *Congressional Quarterly Weekly Report* 41 (December 10, 1983): 2622–2623. In fact, Zablocki was the principal sponsor of nuclear freeze resolutions in the House in 1982 and 1983.

89. Fenno, *Congressmen in Committees,* p. 163.

90. Charles H. Percy, "The Partisan Gap," *Foreign Policy* 45 (Winter 1981–1982): 15.

91. On the "perpetual crisis in executive-legislative relations" during the Reagan years and on these proposals to improve this situation in the Bush years, see John Felton, "Will Bush-Hill Honeymoon Bring Bipartisanship?" *Congressional Quarterly Weekly Report* (February 18, 1989): 332–337. The quotations are from p. 335.

92. The description of Fascell is taken from Felton, "Foreign Affairs Committee Changes Seen Under Fascell," pp. 2622–2623.

93. Lee H. Hamilton, "American Foreign Policy: A Congressional Perspective," speech at the Department of State, Washington, DC, December 14, 1993.

94. Aaron Wildavsky, "Two Presidencies," *Trans-action* 3 (December 1966): 8.

95. Ibid., p. 8. For several cogent arguments questioning the utility of roll-call analysis in evaluating presidential success, see James M. Lindsay and Wayne P. Steger, "The 'Two Presidencies' in Future Research: Moving Beyond Roll-Call Analysis," *Congress & The Presidency* 20 (Autumn 1993): 103–117. For some arguments supporting the use of roll-call analysis, see Jon R. Bond and Richard Fleisher, *The President in the Legislative Arena* (Chicago and London: The University of Chicago Press, 1990), pp. 66–71.

96. Lance T. LeLoup and Steven A. Shull, "Congress Versus the Executive: The 'Two Presidencies' Reconsidered," *Social Science Quarterly* 59 (March 1979): 707.

97. Ibid., pp. 712–713.

98. Richard Fleisher and Jon R. Bond, "Are There Two Presidencies? Yes, But Only for Republicans," *The Journal of Politics* 50 (August 1988): 747–767. Table 1 at p. 754 is the source of these conclusions. Also see their book, which in part addresses this issue: Bond and Fleisher, *The President in the Legislative Arena.*

99. These results were calculated from roll-call data made available through the Inter-University Consortium of Political and Social Research (the Consortium bears no responsibility for the analyses and interpretations reported here) and from recorded votes reported in *Congressional Quarterly Almanac* (various years) and *Congressional Quarterly Weekly Report* (various issues). Foreign policy votes were identified for the Eisenhower through the first two years of the George W. Bush administration on which the president took a position, based upon *Congressional Quarterly Almanac, Congressional Quarterly Weekly Report,* and *CQ Weekly* assessments, and then the president's success or failure was calculated across each administration. The foreign policy votes for the Truman years were identified from the roll-call data, and Truman's position was determined by an assessment of available *CQ Almanacs* and presidential papers. The assistance of Eugene R. Wittkopf of Louisiana State University in identifying the 1947–1996 foreign policy votes, in collecting some of the Clinton votes, and in determining Truman's position on those particular votes is appreciated. A more detailed discussion of the data collection process is reported in James M. McCormick and Eugene R. Wittkopf,

"Bipartisanship, Partisanship, and Ideology in Congressional-Executive Foreign Policy Relations, 1947–1988," *The Journal of Politics* (November 1990): 1077–1100.

100. Aage R. Clausen, *How Congressmen Decide: A Policy Focus* (New York: St. Martin's Press, 1973), pp. 192–212, 222–230. Clausen qualifies this conclusion by stating that presidential influence "appears to be effective only on congressmen of the same party as the president" (p. 209).

101. See Lee Sigelman, "A Reassessment of the Two Presidencies Thesis," *The Journal of Politics* (November 1979): 1195–1205, especially 1200–1201. Drawing upon *Congressional Quarterly,* Sigelman defined a key vote as one involving "'a matter of major controversy,' 'a test of presidential or political power,' or 'a decision of potentially great impact on the nation and lives of Americans.'" The number of such votes ranged between 10 and 36 for the years of his study (p. 1199).

102. Ibid., pp. 1200–1201.

103. LeLoup and Shull, "Congress Versus the Executive: The 'Two Presidencies' Reconsidered," p. 710.

104. See Robert A. Bernstein and William Anthony, "The ABM Issue in the Senate, 1968–1970: The Importance of Ideology," *American Political Science Review* 68 (September 1974): 1198–1206; James M. McCormick and Michael Black, "Ideology and Voting on the Panama Canal Treaties," *Legislative Studies Quarterly* 8 (February 1983): 45–63; James M. McCormick, "Congressional Voting on the Nuclear Freeze Resolutions," *American Politics Quarterly* 13 (January 1985): 122–136; Richard Fleisher, "Economic Benefit, Ideology, and Senate Voting on the B-1 Bomber," *American Politics Quarterly* 13 (April 1985): 200–211; James M. Lindsay, "Parochialism, Policy, and Constituency Constraints: Congressional Voting on Strategic Weapons Systems," *American Journal of Political Science* 34 (November 1990): 936–960; and Eugene R. Wittkopf and James M. McCormick, "The Domestic Politics of Contra Aid: Public Opinion, Congress, and the President," in Richard Sobel, ed., *Public Opinion in U.S. Foreign Policy: The Controversy over Contra Aid* (Lanham,

MD: Rowman & Littlefield Publishers, Inc., 1993), pp. 73–103.

105. Duane M. Oldfield and Aaron Wildavsky, "Reconsidering the Two Presidencies," *Society* 26 (July/August 1989): 54–59. The quotation is at p. 55. For a good summary of the recent debates over the "two presidencies" argument, see Steven A. Shull, ed., *The Two Presidencies: A Quarter Century Assessment* (Chicago: Nelson/Hall Publishers, 1991).

106. See P.L. 85-7, in *United States Statutes at Large,* Vol. 69 (Washington, DC: Government Printing Office, 1955), p. 7. Emphasis added.

107. P.L. 85-7, in *United States Statutes at Large,* Vol. 71 (Washington, DC: Government Printing Office, 1958), p. 5.

108. See Fisher, *Presidential War Powers,* pp. 107–110 for the controversies surrounding this resolution. Also see "'Eisenhower Doctrine' for the Middle East," *Congressional Quarterly Almanac 1957* (Washington, DC: Congressional Quarterly, Inc., 1957), pp. 573–579. The quote indicating that America "is prepared to use armed forces" is at p. 573. Also see Gordon Silverstein, *Imbalance of Powers* (New York: Oxford University Press, 1997), pp. 78–79.

109. P.L. 88-408.

110. See the testimony by Undersecretary of State Nicholas Katzenbach in "U.S. Commitments to Foreign Powers," Hearings before the Committee on Foreign Relations, 90th Cong., 1st sess., August 16, 17, 21, 23, and September 19, 1967, p. 82. Two other resolutions were passed by Congress in 1962 "expressing the determination of the United States" to use armed forces if necessary to stop Cuban aggression and to defend Berlin. Neither resolution, however, expressly granted the presidential discretion that the Formosa and Gulf of Tonkin resolutions did. See P.L. 87-733 (October 3, 1962) and H. Con. Res. (October 10, 1962).

111. These passages are taken from the Foreign Assistance Act of 1961, as amended, and reported in *Legislation on Foreign Relations Through 1985* (Washington, DC: U.S. Government Printing Office, April 1986). The quoted passages are at pp. 32, 141, and 129, respectively.

112. See I. M. Destler, *American Trade Politics* (Washington, DC: Institute for International Economics and New York: The Twentieth Century Fund, June 1992), p. 12. Also see Sharyn O'Halloran, "Congress and Foreign Trade Policy," in Randall B. Ripley and James M. Lindsay, eds., *Congress Resurgent: Foreign and Defense Policy on Capitol Hill* (Ann Arbor: The University of Michigan Press, 1993), pp. 283–303.

113. The quoted passage is from P.L. 100-418 at 102 Stat. 1143. A summary of the bill is in *Congressional Quarterly Almanac 1988* (Washington, DC: Congressional Quarterly, Inc., 1989), pp. 209–215.

114. Stephen D. Cohen, Joel R. Paul, and Robert A. Blecker, *Fundamentals of U.S. Foreign Trade Policy* (Boulder, CO: Westview Press, 1996), p. 272.

115. 91 Stat. 1626.

116. Koh, *The National Security Constitution,* pp. 46–47. The quoted passage is at p. 47.

117. Destler, *American Trade Politics,* p. 13.

118. P.L. 253, in *United States Statutes At Large,* Vol. 61, part 1, 80th Cong., 1st sess., pp. 495–510.

119. Ibid., p. 496. The membership of the National Security Council has changed slightly over time. This membership represents the current required composition, although the president may invite other members to participate.

120. These data are taken from the Budget of the United States Government for the appropriate years. The data for the Clinton administration in 2000 was taken from Ivo H. Daalder and I. M. Destler, "A New NSC for a New Administration," Brookings Policy Brief #68, p. 6, at http://www. brook.edu. dybdocroot/comm/policybriefs/pb068/ pb68.htm, accessed on July 22, 2002. The information for the George W. Bush administration is from Karen DeYoung and Steven Mufson, "A Leaner and Less Visible NSC Reorganization Will Emphasize Defense, Global Economics," *The Washington Post,* February 10, 2001, p. 1 at http:// washingtonpost.com/wp-dyn/world/ europe/A50937-2001Feb9.html, accessed on February 12, 2001.

121. P.L. 253, p. 498.

122. Ibid., p. 500.

123. See P.L. 87-194.

124. See P.L. 87-297. By a reorganization plan, part of AID (effective April 1, 1999) and all of ACDA (October 1, 1999) were incorporated into the Department of State. See P.L. 105-277 at 112 Stat. 2681-797.

125. *U.S. Government Manual 1989/1990,* July 1, 1989, p. 95.

126. For a discussion of the role of some of these bureaucracies in the foreign policy process, see Chapter 9.

127. Charles W. Kegley, Jr., and Eugene R. Wittkopf, *American Foreign Policy: Pattern and Process,* 3rd ed. (New York: St. Martin's Press, 1987), p. 340.

128. For a discussion of these services for Congress, see *Executive Legislative Consultation on Foreign Policy: Strengthening Foreign Policy Information Sources for Congress* (Washington, DC: Government Printing Office, February 1982), pp. 27–37; Evelyn Howard, *The Congressional Research Service* (Washington, DC: Congressional Research Service, August 14, 1989); *General Accounting Office, National Security and International Affairs Division: Organization and Responsibility* (Washington, DC: Government Printing Office, 1989); and http://www.gao.gov/orgchart.html for current organizational structure information on the GAO.

129. See "No Action Taken on Congressional Reform," *Congressional Quarterly Almanac 1993* (Washington, DC: Congressional Quarterly, Inc., 1994), pp. 21–29.

130. For some evidence on how admired presidents have been in the postwar period, see John E. Mueller, *War, Presidents and Public Opinion* (New York: John Wiley and Sons, 1973), pp. 179–195.

131. The phrase is taken from Daniel Yankelovich, "Farewell to 'President Knows Best,'" in William P. Bundy, ed., *America and the World 1978* (New York: Pergamon Press, 1979), pp. 670–693, who discusses this deferential tradition in the American public and its decline in the middle 1970s.

132. For some summary poll numbers on foreign policy support for the Clinton administration among the American public, see "Opinion Outlook" in various issues of

National Journal. See, for examples, the following issues: January 14, 1995, p. 130; February 11, 1995, p. 385; March 11, 1995, p. 642; April 8, 1995, p. 889; and May 6, 1995, p. 1129.

133. John E. Rielly, *American Public Opinion and U.S. Foreign Policy 1999* (Chicago: The Chicago Council on Foreign Relations, 1999), p. 35.

134. Gallup Poll Analyses, "Despite Sharp Increase in Bush Approval Since 9/11, Race Gap Persists," http://www.gallup.com/poll/releases/pr020108.asp, accessed on January 17, 2002.

135. For an example of the Congress's changed priorities after September 11, see Miles A. *CQ Weekly,* October 27, 2001, 2551–2558.

8

Congressional Prerogatives and the Making of Foreign Policy

The Framers . . . gave to Congress the responsibility for deciding matters
of war and peace. The President, as Commander in Chief, was left
with the power to "repel sudden attacks." . . . Whenever the President
acts unilaterally in using military force against another nation,
the constitutional rights of Congress and the people are undermined.

CONSTITUTIONAL SCHOLAR LOUIS FISHER
DECEMBER 1995

It's very important for the President to seek approval of the Congress
[before sending troops to Bosnia]. The title of Commander in Chief
is one thing. But the power of the purse is the greatest power
in our Constitutional system.

SENATOR ROBERT BYRD (D-WEST VIRGINIA)
OCTOBER 1995

The unrest at home over America's involvement in Vietnam, the perceived growth in the foreign policy powers of the president, and the weakening of executive authority as a result of the Watergate incident all contributed to efforts by the legislative branch to reassert its foreign policy prerogatives beginning in the early 1970s. Congress achieved some success in placing limitations on the foreign policy powers of the president in four principal ways:

1. Requiring the executive to report all commitments abroad
2. Limiting the war powers of the president
3. Placing restrictions on foreign policy funding
4. Increasing congressional oversight of the executive branch in foreign policy making

Several of these limitations have become institutionalized practices between Congress and the president, others had been altered or largely abandoned, and, in some instances, new ones added. In this sense, the struggle over foreign policy continues between the two branches.

In this chapter, we review some of the foreign policy restrictions enacted by Congress over the past three decades, assess how well they have worked, and discuss how they have affected congressional-executive relations in American foreign policy making.

COMMITMENT MAKING

The first area of congressional resurgence in the 1970s involved commitment making by the executive. This effort to rein in executive power was not particularly new, since a similar attempt was undertaken in the 1950s, but it did prove to be more successful than the earlier one. The two efforts differed in several ways: The earlier effort took the form of a proposed constitutional amendment restricting the kind of treaties and executive agreements the president might initiate; the later focused upon requiring the president to report to Congress on commitments already made. The earlier effort was led by congressional conservatives, the latter by congressional liberals.

The Bricker Amendment

The 1950s effort at curbing the president was motivated by America's increasing global involvement and was led by Senator John Bricker of Ohio. In a series of constitutional amendments, Bricker proposed that any treaty or executive agreement that infringed upon the constitutional rights of American citizens shall be unconstitutional and that Congress shall have the right to enact appropriate legislation that will be required to put into effect any treaty or executive agreement made by the president. Bricker was concerned that the United Nations Treaty, and human rights treaties and agreements under consideration by the UN at the time, might commit the United States to particular domestic actions and reduce congressional or state prerogatives under the Constitution.[1] Bricker did not want these domestic actions to obtain constitutional legitimacy simply because a treaty or agreement had been agreed to by the president.[2] In effect, his amendments were designed (1) to alter the constitutional principle established for treaties in *Missouri v. Holland* and executive agreements in *U.S. v. Belmont* and *U.S. v. Pink* (see Chapter 7), (2) to stop self-executing treaties (i.e., treaties not requiring implementing legislation on the part of Congress) from occurring, and (3) to ensure a larger congressional role in implementing all treaties and executive agreements domestically.

Several votes were taken in the Senate on these various amendment proposals. Only one ballot came close to passage. That vote in 1954 failed by only one vote to obtain the necessary two-thirds majority needed to pass a constitutional amendment. Similar proposals were made throughout the mid-1950s, but support waned, and President Eisenhower's opposition to such legislation remained.

The Case–Zablocki Act

With the escalating involvement in Vietnam, primarily through presidential initiative, and with the revelations of secret commitments to a variety of other nations during the 1950s and 1960s, the congressional liberals of the 1970s sought to enact some limitations on executive commitments abroad.[3] In June 1969, the Senate passed a "sense of the Senate" resolution stating that the making of national commitments should involve the legislative as well as the executive branch (The National Commitments Resolution).[4] When the executive branch went ahead with executive agreements with Portugal and Bahrain, another "sense of the Senate" resolution was passed stating that agreements with these states for military bases or for foreign assistance should take the form of treaties.[5] Although these resolutions provided an avenue for venting congressional frustration over executive actions abroad, they were largely symbolic, since they did not legally bind the executive branch to alter its previous policies.

By the middle of 1972, however, Congress passed the first significant piece of legislation in the commitment-making area, the Case–Zablocki Act, named after Senator Clifford Case (R-New Jersey) and Congressman Clement Zablocki (D-Wisconsin). This law required the executive branch to report all international agreements to Congress within 60 days of their entering into force. (Classified agreements would be transmitted to the House Foreign Affairs [now, the International Relations] Committee and the Senate Foreign Relations Committee under an injunction of secrecy.[6]) In 1977, this act was amended and strengthened to require that all agreements made by all agencies within the executive branch must be reported to the Department of State within 20 days for ultimate transmittal to Congress under the provisions of the original act.[7]

Even with this reporting arrangement (further strengthened under the Foreign Relations Authorization Act of 1979), Congress has enjoyed only mixed success in obtaining all agreements in a timely fashion. While a large number of agreements (both public and classified) have been reported to Congress, the number of late transmittals to Congress remains quite substantial. In 1976, for example,

Table 8.1 Late Reporting of International Agreements by the Executive Branch to the Congress, Selected Years

	NUMBER OF AGREEMENTS						
	1978	*1981*	*1988*	*1992*	*1996*	*1999*	*1978– 1999*
Agreements transmitted to Congress	520	368	412	296	225	166	7091
Agreements reported after 60 days	132	99	79	56	41	31	1245
Reported late from the Department of State	45	69	39	38	28	18	675
Reported late from other agencies to the Department of State	87	30	40	18	13	13	570

	PERCENTAGE OF AGREEMENTS						
	1978	*1981*	*1988*	*1992*	*1996*	*1999*	*1978– 1999*
Agreements transmitted to Congress	100%	100%	100%	100%	100%	100%	100%
Agreements reported after 60 days	25.4	27	19.2	18.9	18.2	18.6	17.5
Reported late from the Department of State	8.7	18.8	9.5	12.8	12.4	10.8	54.2
Reported late from other agencies to the Department of State	16.7	8.2	9.7	6.1	5.7	7.8	45.8

SOURCE: Constructed from information available in Committee on Foreign Relations, United States Senateb *Treaties and Other International Agreements: The Role of the United States Senate,* A Study Prepared for the Committee on Foreign Relations, United States Senate, by the Congressional Research Service (Washington, DC: U.S. Government Printing Office, January 2001), pp. 226–227.

39 percent of all agreements were reported late; by the first half of 1978, the percentage had dropped to 32 percent.[8] By 1981, 27 percent of all agreements were still transmitted to Congress beyond the 60-day period. By 1988, reporting had improved, but almost one-fifth of all agreements were still reported late.[9] By 1999, the situation had changed very little with 19 percent still being reported late. While other agencies besides the Department of State had contributed to the tardiness of agreements in 1977, the bulk of the late agreements in 1981 had emanated from the Department itself. By 1988, both the Department of State and other agencies had about equally contributed to the tardiness in reporting. In the 1990s, however, the Department of State was again the most frequent agency that was late in reporting. Table 8.1 provides a summary of the agreements that were reported late in selected years from 1978 to 1999.

Late reporting or nonreporting prompts concern by Congress for at least two reasons: Late reports are inconsistent with the procedural requirements of the Case–Zablocki and Case legislation, and late reporting could also affect the substance of policy. Although one can readily acknowledge that the late reporting of some executive agreements dealing with administrative details (e.g., water and electricity agreements for American bases in a particular country) may not be terribly problematic, other executive agreements (e.g., intelligence agreements with other countries) may be. The failure of Congress to know about the latter type of agreements in a timely fashion may well preclude that body from taking any action or even staying informed on current policy. In this sense, prompt reporting of commitments abroad facilitates the role of Congress in foreign policy making.

Beyond Case–Zablocki

While the Case–Zablocki Act required only the reporting of commitments, it did signal congressional determination to participate in the agreement-making process. In fact, some members of Congress were sufficiently dissatisfied with the limitation of just the reporting requirement that they sought to go further in strengthening the legislative role in this entire process. Various attempts were made by members of the House and the Senate to allow Congress to have the right to reject a commitment made by the executive branch within a prescribed period of time (usually 60 days). In the Senate, for example, Senator Sam Ervin (D–North Carolina) introduced several measures that would have allowed both houses to veto any executive agreement within 60 days, while Senator John Glenn (D–Ohio) introduced a similar bill that would have allowed only the Senate the right of disapproval of these executive agreements.[10] In the House, similar measures were introduced. The most intriguing was one by Congressman Thomas (Doc) Morgan (D–Pennsylvania), then chairman of the House Foreign Affairs Committee. In the Executive Agreements Review Act of 1975, he proposed that both houses of Congress have the right of disapproval of executive agreements, but only for those involving "national commitments"—mainly those agreements regarding the introduction of American military personnel or providing military training or equipment to another country.[11] None of these proposals became law.

The reform initiative that came closest to going beyond the simple reporting of executive agreements was that undertaken by Senator Dick Clark (D–Iowa) on behalf of his Treaty Powers Resolution in 1976 and after. Under this resolution:

> the Senate may . . . refuse to authorize and appropriate funds to implement those international agreements which, in its opinion, constitute treaties and to which the Senate has not given its advice and consent to ratification.[12]

In other words, the Senate would be able to reject any measure that it thought should have been a treaty and, instead, had been done by executive action. The emergence of this resolution (and others) set the stage for the passage of some reform procedures between Congress and the executive that were incorporated into the Foreign Relations Authorization Act for Fiscal Year 1979.[13] Under the provisions of this act, the president must now report yearly to Congress on each agreement that was late in being transmitted to Congress; the Secretary of State must now determine what arrangements constitute an international agreement; and oral agreements must now be "reduced to writing."[14] In effect, this act further strengthened the original idea behind Case–Zablocki, without going much beyond it.

At the time, too, the Department of State worked out an informal arrangement with the Senate Foreign Relations Committee for periodic consultation regarding which international agreements should take the form of treaties.[15] In practice, these procedures involve the periodic transmittal of a list of agreements under negotiations by the Department of State (or other agencies) to the House and Senate foreign policy committees. These lists include "a citation of the legal authority for the agreement, and the expected form the agreement would take (treaty or executive agreement)." In turn, they "are circulated and filed in a manner similar to the procedures used for classified agreements under the Case [–Zablocki] Act."[16]

In sum, although Congress nurtured the beginning of a resurgence in the commitment-making area, it was unwilling to go very far. Except for the formal list procedure and more informal congressional staff–Department of State consultations, Congress has not ventured much beyond the reporting mechanism for trying to control agreement making by the executive.

WAR POWERS

Frustrated over the use of the commander-in-chief and executive clauses of the Constitution to intervene abroad, Congress adopted several measures to limit the war-making ability of the president in the 1970s. The first important action was the 1970 congressional repeal of the Gulf of Tonkin resolution, which had allowed the president a virtual free hand in conducting the Vietnam War.[17] Although the repeal was more symbolic than substantive, Congress, by this action, was beginning to assert its role in war making. The executive branch, however, still claimed it had the power to continue the war even without the resolution in place.

Spurred on by the Nixon administration's indifference to its repeal of the Gulf of Tonkin resolution, Congress proceeded to work on a proposal that would limit the war-making powers of the president more generally. The resulting War Powers Resolution, passed over President Nixon's veto in November 1973, remains the most significant congressional attempt to reassert its control over committing American forces abroad.[18]

Key Provisions of the War Powers Resolution

This resolution has several important provisions that require presidential consultation and reporting to Congress on the use of United States forces abroad, limit the time of deployment of such forces, and provide Congress a mechanism for withdrawing these forces prior to this time limit as well. These provisions are worth summarizing in detail.[19]

First, the president may introduce United States Armed Forces "into hostilities or into situations where imminent involvement in hostilities is clearly indicated by the circumstances" under only three conditions: "(1) a declaration of war, (2) specific statutory authorization, or (3) a national emergency created by attack upon the United States, its territories, or its armed forces." The significance of this provision is that, for the first time, Congress specified the conditions under which the president could use armed forces. Previously, and excepting a declaration of war, presidential power to use force abroad was more discretionary and ambiguous.

Second, the president "in every possible instance shall consult with Congress" before sending American forces into hostilities or anticipated hostilities and "shall consult regularly with Congress" until those forces have been removed. Put differently, the resolution expected Congress to be involved in the process from beginning to end.

Third, for those circumstances in which forces were introduced without a declaration of war, the president must submit a written report to the Speaker of the House and the President pro Tempore of the Senate within 48 hours of deploying American forces, explaining the reasons for the introduction of troops, the constitutional and legislative authority for taking such actions, and the "estimated scope and duration of the hostilities or involvement." Further, the president was directed to "report to the Congress periodically on the status of such hostilities or situation as well as on the scope and duration of such hostilities or situation" at least every six months, if troops remained that long.

Fourth, and perhaps its core feature, the resolution placed a time limit on how long forces may be deployed. The resolution specifically authorized the president to use American forces for no longer than 60 days, unless there had been a declaration of war or a specific congressional authorization to continue the use of such forces beyond this period. An extension of 30 days was possible, according to the resolution, if the president certified that military requirements precluded troop withdrawal within the 60-day period. In an important ambiguity in the resolution, however, unless the president reports under the appropriate section (Section 4 [a] [1]), the 60-day time limit does not automatically begin. Alternately, however, Congress may begin the 60-day clock by invoking the resolution itself.[20] In any event, the beginning of the 60-day time limitation is a bit more ambiguous than an initial review of the resolution might suggest.

Finally, the congressional resolution included a provision that allowed Congress to withdraw the troops prior to the expiration of the 60-day limitation. By passing a concurrent resolution (a resolution in both houses but without presidential approval) by a simple majority, Congress could specify that the troops be withdrawn from the hostilities immediately. Moreover, the resolution provided time limits on the hearings in committee on such a resolution and required that a vote must be taken expeditiously. In other words, safeguards were provided so that the concurrent resolution would not become tied up within Congress without ever reaching a vote.

The clear intent of the war powers legislation was to stop the president from introducing American troops abroad and getting them mired in a conflict without a clear objective. Put more simply, it was to reduce the possibility of future Vietnams. At the same time, the intent of the resolution was also to reassert the expressed war powers of Congress under Article I of the Constitution. Despite these combined aims, the resolution would not prevent the president from taking military action if and when necessary; instead, the War Powers Resolution would promote the sharing of responsibility between the executive and legislative branches for dispatching American military personnel abroad.

Despite its obvious legal requirements, the War Powers Resolution also had another important purpose: It served as a political and psychological restraint on presidential war making. By this legislation, the president would now have to calculate whether Congress and the American public would support the sending of American forces to foreign lands. In addition, he would need to provide a formal justification for his taking military action and might well have to submit to formal congressional scrutiny.

Presidential Compliance

The record of presidential compliance with the requirements of this resolution is, at best, mixed. Some of the reporting requirements and the time limitation on troop deployments, as specified in the War Powers Resolution, have been nominally adhered to since 1973, but controversy continues to surround the precise situations requiring its applicability, the extent and manner of presidential compliance with all aspects of the resolution, and its overall effectiveness in curbing the expansion of executive power in this area. In addition, the Chadha decision on the congressional veto, as noted in Chapter 7, has seemingly made the concurrent resolution provision of the law unconstitutional.

Over the past several administrations (through August 2003), 109 reports had been forwarded to Congress in accordance with the provisions of the War Powers Resolution.[21] Table 8.2 lists the number of reports for each administration. The Clinton administration filed the most reports with 60, while the Nixon administration did not submit any reports in the brief time in office after the enactment of the resolution. The other administrations ranged from one by Carter, four by Ford, seven by George H. W. Bush, fourteen by Reagan, and twenty-three (through August 2003) by George W. Bush.

The reports cover a variety of military activities by the United States under the various administrations. A sampling will provide a sense of the type of activities reported. President Ford, for example, filed reports over the evacuations of refugees and American personnel from Vietnam and Cambodia and over the use of force to free the crew of the *Mayaguez* in May 1975. President Carter's lone report concerned the abortive 1980 attempt to rescue the American hostages in Iran. President Reagan's reports ranged from one on the dispatch of the American military personnel to participate in the Multinational Force and Observers (MFO) in the Sinai Peninsula in accordance with the Egyptian-Israeli Peace Treaty and three on the deployment of American forces to Lebanon in 1982 and 1983 to the use of American forces to invade Grenada in 1983 and to retaliate against Libya for a Libyan-sponsored terrorist attack against Americans in 1986. President George H. W. Bush's reports focused upon such actions as sending American air support to the Philippines to assist the government in restoring order and protecting American lives, dispatching 25,000 American forces to invade Panama and capture General Manuel Noriega, ordering forces to Saudi Arabia after the seizure of Kuwait by Iraq in August 1990, and directing actions against Iraq in the Persian Gulf War.

President Clinton forwarded the most reports to Congress. Most of the Clinton administration's reports covered American military deployments to Bosnia,

**Table 8.2 The War Powers Resolution
and Presidential Reports to Congress**

Administration	Number of reports
Richard Nixon	0
Gerald Ford	4
Jimmy Carter	1
Ronald Reagan	14
George H. W. Bush	7
William Clinton	60
George W. Bush (August 2003)	23

SOURCE: Richard F. Grimmett, *The War Powers Resolution: After Twenty-Eight Years,* Congressional Research Service, November 30, 2001; and Richard F. Grimmett, *IB81050: War Powers Resolution: Presidential Compliance,* Congressional Research Service, June 12, 2002 and updated September 16, 2003.

East Timor, Haiti, Kosovo, Macedonia, and Somalia in various peacekeeping and peacemaking operations. These deployments often required multireports, thus accounting for the high frequency of reports by this administration. In addition, the Clinton administration reported on the deployment of forces to provide evacuation support to Americans in such trouble spots as Cambodia, Central African Republic, Kenya, Liberia, and Rwanda. Finally, the Clinton administration also reported on the American retaliation against Afghanistan and Sudan in 1998 after the terrorist bombing of U.S. embassies in Kenya and Tanzania and deployment of military personnel to Yemen in 2000 after the terrorist attack on the U.S.S. *Cole*.

President George W. Bush's reports so far have focused upon several different areas. Six of them have focused upon the deployment of forces in Bosnia as part of the stabilization effort there, five have focused on the continuation of American presence in Kosovo to stabilize that province in the former Yugoslavia, three addressed the limited presence in East Timor as part of the continuing American support for the UN peacekeeping mission there, and four on American forces sent to the Philippines to aid antiterrorist effort and to Liberia and Ivory Coast over evaluation or stabilization effort in those countries. The remaining reports focus upon American actions in Afghanistan in response to the bombing of the World Trade Center and the Pentagon in September 2001 and American military intervention in Iraq in March 2003.

Continuing Controversies

Despite these reports, Congress has been dissatisfied with the level and depth of executive notification. Since the passage of the resolution, none of the seven presidents has fully complied with it, and each president has viewed the resolution as an unconstitutional intrusion on the president's commander-in-chief powers. Furthermore, several controversies continue to plague its operation.

Failing to Comply Fully Executive reservations about the resolution are evident by the fact that presidents carefully phrase their congressional reports and do not fully comply with the resolution's requirements. In virtually every report that the presidents have sent forward, they have used the same language. They are providing the report "in accordance with my desire that Congress be fully informed on this matter, and consistent with the War Powers Resolution."[22] In none of the reports do the presidents acknowledge that they were complying with the War Powers Resolution. Indeed, only in President Ford's report on the Mayaquez incident in 1975 did he cite the operative section (section 4 [a][1]) of the resolution (and, hence, acknowledge the 60-day deployment limitation of the resolution), although he did so only after the military conflict had ceased. In a few other cases, presidents cited section 4 of the Resolution in reporting. President Ford, for example, cited section 4 (a) (2) in the reports on American evacuation efforts from Vietnam and Cambodia, and President Reagan cited "section 4 (a) (2) of the War Powers Resolution," in reporting on the deployment of American military personnel sent into the Sinai Desert for peacekeeping purposes between Israel and Egypt. Yet that section of the resolution does not set into operation the part of the act limiting the deployment to only 60 days.[23] Further, in a few presidential reports to Congress (e.g., President George H. W. Bush's report on sending a reinforced rifle company to Liberia, and President Clinton's report on the use of American air power against Bosnian Serb forces in August 1994), no specific reference was made to the War Powers Resolution.

Failing to Report Beyond the kind of reporting by presidents, the failure to report some instances at all has also weakened the impact of the resolution. Critics charged, for instance, that President Richard Nixon failed to report to Congress when U.S. forces were used to evacuate Americans from Cyprus during the ethnic conflict on that island nation in 1974. President Jimmy Carter raised the ire of Representative Paul Findley for his failure to report to Congress after placing some American forces on alert and for sending U.S. transport aircraft to Zaire (now Congo) during secessionist activities in that country in May 1978.[24]

President Reagan became embroiled in controversy with Congress over the applicability of the War Powers Resolution to Central America and the Middle East. After President Reagan indicated in early 1981 that he was going to increase the number of American military advisors in El Salvador, questions were raised over whether the War Powers procedures needed to be invoked. The executive's position was that these U.S. military personnel were not being introduced into hostilities, nor were they in a situation where "imminent hostilities might occur," as the War Powers Resolution required.[25] Over a deployment to Lebanon, President Reagan's position was that American forces, first dispatched there in 1982, were on a "peacekeeping mission" at the request of the Lebanese government and that they were neither involved in hostilities nor in any immediate danger. By the fall of 1983, however, Congress was unwilling to accept that position, especially after two Marines were killed on August 29, 1983. Instead, Congress sought to start the 60-day clock under the War Powers Resolution. To head off this time limit on American forces in Lebanon, President Reagan proceeded to work out a compromise agreement, the Multinational Force in Lebanon Resolution (October 1983), authorizing the president to use American forces in Lebanon for 18 months.

In addition, some other episodes that appeared to be covered by the War Powers Resolution were not reported to Congress. The Reagan administration, for instance, did not report to Congress on the United States Navy's interception of an Egyptian airliner carrying the hijackers of the *Achille Lauro* in 1985 or on the sending of American Army assistance to the Bolivian government in antidrug efforts in 1986. President George H. W. Bush failed to report to Congress on sending American military advisors in the Andean countries of Colombia, Bolivia, and Peru as part of a new antidrug strategy and did not report the American efforts to convey Belgian troops into Zaire during September 1991. In 1998, President Clinton did not report to Congress on American bombing of Iraq as part of an effort to destroy facilities capable of nuclear, biological, or chemical weapons and to attack Iraqi military targets.[26]

Failing to Consult The "prior consultation" requirement has caused even greater difficulty between Congress and the executive branch. Members of Congress have generally held that the president has not really "consulted" with them before using American military forces, but that he has often merely "informed" them of his intended action.[27] The executive branch, on the other hand, has insisted that it has generally consulted with Congress and has kept Congress informed of its action.

The evidence is, at best, mixed based upon the limited instances available. President Ford, for example, "advised" members of the congressional leadership on his plans for the evacuation from Southeast Asia in 1975; President Reagan held a meeting with congressional leaders before the actual invasion of Grenada in 1983, but after he had signed the order; and President Reagan also met with congressional leaders after ordering the air strike against Libya in 1986, although, again, after he had directed it to be carried out; and President Bush met with congressional leaders seven hours before the invasion of Panama was to begin and informed them of his decision.[28]

In other instances, when presidents have chosen not to consult with Congress, they have defended their actions by pointing to the need for secrecy in carrying out the operation, the limited time available for consultation, and the inherent presidential power to act. When President Jimmy Carter, for instance, was confronted by Congress over his failure to consult prior to the Iran rescue mission in 1980, his legal counsel offered this staunch defense of presidential authority:

> His inherent constitutional power to conduct this kind of rescue operation, which depends on total surprise, includes the power to act before consulting Congress, if the President concludes, as he did in this case, that to do so would unreasonably endanger the success of the operation and the safety of those to be rescued.[29]

In 1989, when President Bush failed to consult Congress over his use of American aircraft to assist Corazon Aquino's government in the Philippines in avoiding an insurrection, his national security advisor, Brent Scowcroft, defended his action by stating that "the nature of the rapidly evolving situation required an extremely rapid decision very late at night and consultation was simply not an option."[30]

Inadequate prior consultation also characterized the Clinton administration. Although President Clinton has acknowledged that he has "a big responsibility to try to appropriately consult with members of Congress . . . whenever we are in the process of making a decision which might lead to the use of force," he also asserted that the president retained "the ultimate decision-making authority."[31] Still, the Clinton administration did little to consult with Congress prior to its intervention in Haiti in September 1994 and subsequently acknowledged that it adopted a strategy that was not likely to allow congressional action. Instead, according to one executive branch official, the strategy was "to get as much positive impact as we could without opening a debate that would be harmful, not helpful."[32] With the use of air action over Bosnia by American forces, too, the Clinton administration generally acted and then informed Congress. In early April 1993, for example, the first American action in Bosnia was promptly reported to Congress, but consultation with "about two dozen congressional leaders on potential future action" took another two weeks for the administration.[33]

A recent analysis, however, suggests that the Clinton administration, while acting "very much like past administrations in dealing with Congress" over war powers, did reach "out to Congress in a manner that was uncharacteristic of recent presidents." In particular, this analysis suggests that Clinton consulted with Congress prior to the bombing of the headquarters of Osama Bin Laden in August 1998, prior to the bombing of Kosovo in March 1999, and used the "*rhetoric* of 'consultation'" prior to implementing the Dayton Accords over Bosnia in 1995.[34] Finally, after September 11, President George W. Bush also offered some indication of his willingness to consult with Congress, even as he defended the prerogatives of the presidency. On the occasion of signing Public Law 107-40 on September 18, 2001 (see Chapter 7), President Bush stated that he had enjoyed the "benefit of meaningful consultations with members of Congress" since the terrorist attack. At the same time, however, he reasserted the "President's constitutional authority to use force."[35]

While the problem of eliciting presidential cooperation in the consultative process on a regular basis continues, several questions also remain about the process of consultation. Three, in particular, seem crucial.[36] First, when should consultation take place? That is, what kind of situations require discussions with Congress? Since the War Powers Resolution does not spell out all such circumstances, ambiguity remains. Second, what actions by the executive constitute consultation? Is informing or meeting with members of Congress on a presidential decision sufficient? Or does the course of action still need to be in doubt to justify full consultation? Third, with whom should the executive branch consult? Is consultation (in whatever meaning) with the congressional leadership sufficient? Or should only certain foreign policy committees be involved in the process? Congress and the executive have differing views on these items, and they have yet to be resolved.

Recent Events and the War Powers Resolution

While the War Powers Resolution has hardly been without controversy since its passage, several recent foreign policy episodes have sharply rekindled the debate over its utility and practicality for managing congressional-executive relations in this area. The first, the Persian Gulf War during the Bush administration, seemingly enhanced the standing of Congress when President Bush sought congressional approval to use American forces against Iraq over its invasion of Kuwait. The second, the use of American forces in Somalia, Haiti, Bosnia, and Kosovo during the Clinton years, did not advance the congressional role; instead, they actually contributed to an unsuccessful effort to repeal the resolution and produced a court case that failed to challenge successfully presidential prerogatives in this area. The third, the passage of resolutions delegating broad authority to the president after September 11th and authorizing the use of force against Iraq, appeared to erode congressional war powers even more.

The Gulf War Although President Bush reported to Congress regarding his August 1990 decision to send American forces to Saudi Arabia to protect that country from possible Iraqi aggression after the seizure of Kuwait, he failed to acknowledge compliance with the War Powers Resolution or even its applicability to the situation. Initially, members of Congress did not object and did not take any action to start the 60-day clock under the War Powers Resolution. In November 1990, however, when President Bush announced that he was enlarging the American presence in the Persian Gulf to include an "offensive capability" against Iraq, congressional clamor began. Several members of Congress complained that the president needed to seek congressional authorization if he contemplated going to war. Calls were heard from both Republicans and Democrats that Congress should come back into a special session after the election to take up this issue. The president denied that any authorization was necessary and insisted that he had the necessary presidential powers. Indeed, some congressional leaders were willing to wait for a presidential request and until the new Congress was seated.[37]

The clamor did not stop, however. Opinion pieces appeared in elite newspapers challenging the president's interpretation of his powers. Public opinion polls indicated that the president ought to seek congressional support. Eventually, 54 members of Congress filed a suit in district court claiming that the president needed congressional authorization to use force, and hearings were held in the House and Senate Armed Services Committee, the Senate Foreign Relations Committee, and the House Foreign Affairs Committee debating the wisdom of continuing sanctions against Iraq or going to war.

Adding further fuel to the issue between Congress and the president was the fact that the Bush administration had requested—and received—authorization from the United Nations Security Council to use force against Iraq, if necessary. UN Security Council Resolution 678, passed on November 29, 1990, authorized member states "to use all necessary means to uphold and implement" the previously passed resolutions calling for Iraq to leave Kuwait after January 15, 1991.[38] By contrast, no such request was made of Congress.

Finally, in early January 1991, President Bush changed his mind and sought legislative authorization after he sensed that his request would be successful in Congress.[39] After a soul-searching debate in both chambers, the House voted by a margin of 250–183 and the Senate by a margin of 52–47 to grant such authorization. More specifically, the "Authorization for Use of Military Force Against Iraq Resolution" endorsed the president's decision to use U.S. military forces to implement the UN Security Council resolutions regarding occupied Kuwait, if all diplomatic and peaceful means had been exhausted by the U.S. government. The measure made specific mention of the War Powers Resolution by noting that this Iraqi resolution constituted a specific statutory authorization as prescribed in the act and that it "supersedes any requirement of the War Powers Resolution."[40] The resolution required the president to report to Congress every 60 days on whether Iraq was complying with the applicable UN Security Council resolutions. While the resolution did not declare war explicitly, it was the functional equivalent because the president could use force if all the stipulations had been met.

To proponents of congressional prerogatives in foreign policy, then, the very act of the president's requesting congressional authorization was significant. It acknowledged the role of Congress in the use of force abroad, and it might establish a precedent for future American involvements. Further, the president's signing of this authorization, with the explicit references to the War Powers Resolution incorporated into it, was also significant. Since all presidents had denied its constitutionality,[41] President Bush's signing of the Iraqi resolution without challenging this section was a glimmer of hope that the War Powers Resolution may have come to assume some legitimacy.

Somalia, Haiti, Bosnia, and Kosovo   Any hopes that the War Powers Resolution had gained any new standing with the executive branch, however, were quickly dashed with American military involvement in Somalia, Haiti, and Bosnia. In each instance, Presidents Bush and Clinton reverted to a more familiar pattern since the resolution's passage in 1973. In the case of Somalia, when the United States (and United Nations) humanitarian and peace-building situation deteriorated in the summer and fall of 1993, Congress had to reassert its own prerogatives toward that country, since the Resolution had not served as a deterrent to sustained involvement. In this sense, the relative power of the resolution was diminished. As noted earlier, Congress did succeed, however, by adding an amendment to a defense appropriations bill, requiring the ending of American involvement in Somalia by March 31, 1994. While that amendment has been portrayed by one analyst as supporting the president's wishes on Somalia,[42] it also reflected Congress's resolve to more fully manage the sending of American forces abroad, even outside the War Powers Resolution.

In the case of Haiti in the fall of 1993 and 1994, Congress again attempted to restrict the Clinton administration's military options when the perception was that American forces were going to be sent there to restore democracy without prior congressional involvement. As one might expect, the White House strongly opposed such action. Yet the Senate passed a nonbinding resolution by a vote of 100–0 opposing the sending of United States forces to Haiti and entertained stronger measures as well. Such an action seemingly had little effect, since the Clinton administration initially deployed some 2,000 American troops to Haiti in mid-September 1994 and the force was expected to grow to 15,000 from 25 nations shortly thereafter.[43] While reporting occurred under the War Powers Resolution, the report sent forward was informational ("informing the Congress" once again), and the consultation was minimal, as we noted earlier.

In the case of Bosnia, congressional frustration over the Resolution was heightened even further. During the summer of 1995, the Senate and the House passed a measure to lift the arms embargo and the Senate also sought to restrict the conditions for the use of American forces in that troubled country to only assisting in extracting UN peacekeepers, and then only under particular circumstances.[44] President Clinton vetoed the measure, but then he later reversed his administration's policy somewhat by deciding to use American air power as part of a NATO response to an apparent Bosnian Serb rocket attack on Sarajevo, the capital of Bosnia. Moreover, the NATO effort continued for several days and began to bring about some movement toward negotiations among the parties. By late 1995, as peace prospects brightened a bit, a new debate emerged between Congress and the president over sending American soldiers to enforce any peace settlement.

Once the Dayton peace accords over Bosnia were initialed in November and then formally signed in December 1995, the Clinton administration had fully committed American troops as part of that arrangement, despite congressional opposition. By then, Congress was unwilling to withdraw support from the military. As a result, the House and Senate could do little but pass a resolution supporting the troops, even as they opposed the overall Clinton administration policy. The episode illustrated once again the difficulty of making the War Powers Resolution operate effectively. Indeed, throughout the congressional debate on Bosnia, there was virtually little discussion of the resolution itself.

President Clinton's executive decision to use American air power force against Serbian-held Kosovo in the former Yugoslavia beginning in March 1999 produced a flurry of congressional actions to try to recoup lost ground and to put a congressional stamp on this warmaking.[45] Ultimately, it failed to take clear and decisive action, and, in this sense, it appeared to diminish the overall effectiveness of the War Powers Resolution. President Clinton cited the actions of NATO to justify American force toward Kosovo, but he failed to seek the advice of Congress on this action. As a result, both Houses considered several resolutions on this matter. In the House, for example, a bill was passed to stop the use of American ground forces in Kosovo, but resolutions directing the president to abide by the 60-day time limit in the War Powers Resolution and declaring war on Yugoslavia failed. Further, though, the House failed to pass (on a tie vote) a previously passed Senate resolution supporting the military strikes that the president had initiated. In the Senate, that body passed a resolution supporting the air strikes, but it failed to adopt a measure that would authorize the use of force toward Yugoslavia. In addition, the Senate tabled two other measures that would have limited military actions in Kosovo.

The other significant action that came out of these congressional actions was a lawsuit filed by Congressman Tom Campbell (R-CA) and other members of

Congress challenging the president's authority to initiate these actions against Kosovo without congressional authorization. As discussed in Chapter 7, the lawsuit (*Campbell v. Clinton*) ultimately failed, further diminishing the War Powers Resolution and the powers of the Congress in the war-making area.

Public Laws 107-40 and 107-243   In the aftermath of the September 11 attack on the World Trade Center and the Pentagon, as noted earlier, the Congress passed P.L. 107-40 (or S.J. Res 23) in which the president was authorized to use force "against those nations, organizations, or persons, he determines planned, authorized, committed, or aided the terrorist attacks. . . ." This resolution was thus a broad grant of authority and went beyond previous measures in that it granted the president authority to pursue "organizations" or "persons," not just nations. As also discussed earlier, in October 2002, Congress passed P.L. 107-243 (or H.J. Res. 114) in which the president was authorized to use U.S. armed forces "as he determines to be necessary and appropriate in order to (1) defend the national security of the United States against the continuing threats posed by Iraq, and (2) enforce all relevant United Nations Security Council resolutions regarding Iraq."

From the perspective of the War Powers Resolution and congressional authority, these resolutions had their pros and cons. On the one hand, Congress passed both resolutions pursuant to the appropriate section of the War Powers Resolution and as constituting "specific statutory authorization" by Congress to the president. On the other hand, in signing P.S. 107-40, President Bush maintained "the longstanding position of the executive branch regarding the President's constitutional authority to use force . . . and regarding the constitutionality of the War Powers Resolution."[46] In the view of one analyst, this statement, and subsequent actions by the president on the war on terrorism, demonstrated how "the President and the Congress . . . maintained their respective positions on the constitutionality of the War Powers Resolution and the responsibilities under it." Additionally, the second resolution, while requiring the president to report periodically to the Congress, explicitly declared that "the president has authority under the Constitution to take action in order to deter and prevent acts of international terrorism against the United States." Further, the grant of authority in this resolution is quite broad since it authorizes action to "enforce all relevant United Nations Security Council resolutions," apparently past or future.[47] With such grants of authority incorporated into these statutes, the president continues to maintain his prerogatives, despite the existence of the War Powers Resolution.

Reforming or Repealing the War Powers Resolution?

While such controversies continue to fuel the war powers debate, a larger, lingering question concerns the constitutionality of the resolution, in whole or part. In his veto message back in 1973, President Nixon questioned the constitutionality of that portion of the War Powers Resolution dealing with the withdrawal of troops prior to the 60-day limitation through the use of a concurrent resolution and the imposition of a 60-day limit on the use of such troops. In the *Chadha* decision (see Chapter 7), the Supreme Court seemingly resolved part of this question by invalidating the use of the concurrent resolution, or the "legislative veto," by Congress. Indeed, Congress acknowledged as much by passing legislation in late 1983 requiring a joint resolution for any withdrawal of troops prior to the 60-day period.[48] (A joint resolution differs from a concurrent resolution in that it requires the approval of a majority of both houses of Congress and the president, while the concurrent resolution requires only majorities within Congress.) The constitutionality of the time limit, identified by the executive branch as a challenge to presidential powers in foreign affairs, has yet to be resolved by the Court or even to be directly challenged there. Yet, it remains a major reason why every president since Nixon has challenged the constitutionality of the entire resolution.[49]

Although some recommendations have been made to change the resolution to resolve these and other concerns, no effort has been successful. Numerous proposals were offered in 1988, for example, and extensive hearings were held in the House and the Senate, sparked by the use of American force in the Persian Gulf in 1987–1988. Some proposed the repeal of the resolution, others suggested strengthening the consultation procedures, and still others would have dropped the 60-day limitation on the use of force and required an affirmative congressional vote on the use of force by the president.[50]

In June 1995, this frustration reached a peak when the House of Representatives voted on a repeal of the resolution. By a narrow margin (217–201), the House voted not to repeal the measure. Despite frustration over the resolution and the increasing belief of many members that the president should have a freer hand in the conduct of foreign policy, a sufficient number of representatives did not want to go quite that far. With the troubling situation in Bosnia at the time, a conservative Republican member was reluctant to give the president a freer hand toward that problem ("The deepening crisis in the Balkans may lead us at some point to invoke the War Powers," he declared). Yet this member was also concerned about preserving congressional prerogatives, as weak as this measure had proved to be ("Every President finds Congress inconvenient. But we're a democracy, not a monarchy"). A moderate Democratic member relied upon the constitutional argument more directly in defending the resolution: "The core principle behind War Powers is that sending troops abroad requires the sound collective judgment of the president and the Congress. I do not think that principle should be abandoned."[51] In sum, barring a real constitutional crisis in which the executive fails to comply in any fashion with the resolution over a sustained period of time, the prospects for significant reform or full repeal seem slim.

Yet, in a broader sense, and despite the unhappiness over presidential compliance, the War Powers Resolution seems to have served at least some of its original purposes: It has generally limited the executive branch's use of military force without involving Congress in *some fashion;* it has prevented long-term military involvements by the executive (such as the Vietnam War had been); and, perhaps more important, it probably has made the president more circumspect and cautious in his foreign military actions than before the resolution's enactment.[52]

Finally, although a counterfactual by definition cannot be demonstrated empirically, it has probably prevented the use of American ground forces by the president in some instances (e.g., in Central America during the 1980s).

CONTROLLING THE PURSE STRINGS

A third area of congressional response to executive power has been to use its funding power (the "purse strings") to reduce executive discretion and to increase congressional direction of American foreign policy. Legislative funding provisions were increasingly used in the 1970s and 1980s to achieve a variety of broad foreign policy objectives: (1) to reduce American military involvement abroad, (2) to cut off covert actions in the Third World, (3) to allow congressional review of the sale of weapons and the transference of nuclear fuels to other countries, (4) to specify the trading relations with other nations, and (5) to limit the transfer of American economic and military assistance to countries with gross violations of human rights, among other things. In several instances, specific countries were identified by Congress and restrictions imposed upon them as a means of shaping foreign policy. Specific human rights restrictions were applied to the transfer of military assistance to El Salvador, for example, and, for a time, Congress cut off all funding for the Nicaraguan Contras as a means of changing the Reagan administration's policy toward that country. "Earmarking" of foreign assistance funds, too, became a particularly popular mechanism as Congress has sought to affect foreign affairs.

Most of these measures, moreover, continue in use in the present era. And the power of the purse remains a potent one as longtime Democratic chairman of the Senate Appropriations Committee Senator Robert Byrd (D–West Virginia) reminded the Clinton administration over the prospect of sending American forces into Bosnia: "It's very important for the President to seek approval of Congress. The title of Commander in Chief is one thing. But the power of the purse is the greatest power in our Constitutional system."[53] More recently, the members of the House and Senate Appropriations Committee echoed this sentiment when President George W. Bush asked to have the authority to transfer budget authority within the new Department of Homeland Security.[54]

Cutting Off and Conditioning Funding

First of all, Congress has sometimes used (or tried to use) a blunt instrument to shape policy: the elimination of funds for foreign policy actions that it opposed. From 1966 to 1973, Congress cast 94 roll calls on questions relating to American involvement in Southeast Asia, but only a few of these votes succeeded in affecting American policy.[55] By 1973, however, the situation had changed, and Congress succeeded in passing a sweeping measure that stopped funding as of August 15, 1973, for military activities "in or over or from off the shores of North Vietnam, South Vietnam, Laos, or Cambodia."[56] Later, in 1975, when President Ford asked Congress to approve new assistance to Vietnam shortly before its fall, Congress refused.[57]

Spurred by these efforts of using funding measures to shape policy in Vietnam, Congress enacted other funding restrictions over the years. In 1975, Congress cut off military and economic aid to Turkey because of its invasion of Cyprus earlier in that year.[58] (In that invasion, Turkey had used American-supplied weapons in violation of statutory requirements that they not be used for offensive purposes.) In 1976, Congress attached the Clark Amendment, a measure prohibiting American assistance to any group in the Angolan civil war, to the Arms Export Control Act.[59]

In the 1980s, Congress continued to use the funding mechanism, but now with a more nuanced approach to policy: Congress placed restrictions or conditions on the use or continuance of funding. In 1981, for example, Congress attached a human rights reporting requirement to the International Security and Development Cooperation Act of 1981 as a condition for continued military assistance to El Salvador.[60] In 1983, Congress succeeded in placing one further restriction on military aid to El Salvador by specifying that 30 percent of all military aid for fiscal 1984 would be withheld until those accused of murdering four U.S. churchwomen were brought to trial and a verdict rendered.[61] In another prominent attempt to guide American foreign policy in Central America during this period, Congress relied upon a combination of conditioning aid and cutting it off. From 1982 to 1986, Congress passed a series of Boland Amendments to first restrict and then prevent the Reagan administration from aiding the Nicaraguan Contras, who were fighting the Sandinista government at the time. As the Iran–Contra investigation was to reveal, however, violations of the Boland restrictions had already taken place during a two-year period (1984–1986) when no military assistance to the Contras was allowed.

Throughout the 1990s and to the present, Congress has continued to use the funding mechanism to shape policy and the policy process. In recent authorization bills for foreign assistance and for the State Department, the House of Representatives has sought to reshape the foreign policy bureaucracies (e.g., by consolidating all or part of three former independent agencies, the Arms Control and Disarmament Agency, the United States Information Agency, and the Agency for International Development within the Department of State) and by making cuts in foreign assistance and by eliminating some programs.[62] A long-running dispute between Congress and the executive throughout much of the 1990s was over funding for the United Nations and whether American funds would be used to support abortions in particular. While this dispute was ultimately resolved near the end of the Clinton administration, it is a poignant illustration of how funding cutoffs can affect the operation of foreign policy.

More generally, the level of funding for the foreign policy budget serves as an important measure of policy influence by the Congress. Near the end of his time as secretary of state in October 1996, Warren Christopher bemoaned the fact that congressional support for international affairs spending had declined by 51 percent since 1984, after taking account of inflation, and that now such spending constituted only 1.2 percent of the federal budget.[63] This concern continued with Christopher's successor, Madeleine Albright, and was also an important agenda item for George W. Bush's secretary of state, Colin Powell. In one of his first appearances before Congress in 2001, Secretary of State Powell asked that body to increase funding for foreign operations and promised in exchange that he would undertake reforms to improve efficiencies.[64] Overall, then, by its funding decisions (or nondecisions), Congress has indeed affected American foreign policy and also indicated its policy disputes with the executive branch in this way.

Earmarking of Funds

Congress may also shape foreign policy more specifically through *earmarking* funds for particular purposes. Legislation designating funds for specific regional or functional programs (e.g., African Development Foundation, refugee assistance programs) would qualify as earmarks, as would prohibition on the use of funds for particular countries (e.g., Cuba, Iraq, Libya, North Korea, Iran, Sudan, and Syria were excluded from direct or indirect assistance for fiscal year 2003).[65] Yet, the more common use of the term refers to "specific amounts of foreign aid for individual countries."[66]

The data in Table 8.3 illustrate countries that received earmarked amounts of foreign assistance during fiscal year 2003. Israel and Egypt continue to be the principal beneficiaries of both economic and military earmarks, as they have for over two decades now. Three former republics of the Soviet Union (Ukraine, Georgia, and Armenia) have now been earmarked for United States economic assistance, while strategically important countries in the Middle East (Jordan, Lebanon, and Cyprus) have received that designation as well, largely as part of incentives for maintaining or securing peace in the region or specific countries. In addition, two Asian countries with recent political unrest and economic difficulty (Indonesia and East Timor) are earmarked in this legislation as well.[67] While earmarks have their critics in that they restrict executive discretion and place a certain rigidity into the foreign assistance program, their defenders point to this mechanism as an important, and perhaps a principal, way for Congress to shape foreign policy.

Specifying Trade and Aid Requirements

By the 1970s and continuing into the 1980s, Congress also sought other vehicles to ensure greater legislative participation in United States foreign policy. Trade and foreign aid legislation proved to be readily available mechanisms. Increasingly, Congress sought to add amendments to both kinds of legislation in order to work its will in foreign policy making. Several of these amendments, although passed several decades ago, continue to play an important role in the policy process today.

In the early 1970s, for instance, Congress added two important amendments to the Trade Act of 1974: the Jackson–Vanik and Stevenson amendments.[68] The Jackson–Vanik Amendment directed that the United States could grant most-favored-nation (MFN) status only to those countries that fostered a free emigration policy and did not impose "more than a nominal tax" on citizens wishing to emigrate. Without mentioning any country by name, the clear intent of the amendment was to prohibit the Soviet Union from gaining that status. The action

Table 8.3 Some Earmarked Foreign Assistance Funds by Country in Fiscal Year 2003

	Economic aid	Military aid
Israel	$720 million	$2.04 billion
Egypt	$655 million	$1.3 billion
Ukraine	$154 million	
Jordan	$150 million	$75 million
Georgia	$90 million	
Armenia	$90 million	$4 million
Indonesia	$50 million	
Lebanon	$35 million	
East Timor	$25 million	
Cyprus	$15 million	

SOURCE: Taken from P.L. 107-115, January 20, 2002.

proved successful, inasmuch as the Soviet Union rejected this provision as an intrusion on its national sovereignty. Still, the restrictions in the legislation came to affect other states (e.g., China) and affect American policy toward them. The Stevenson Amendment was a more direct affront to the Soviet Union. By limiting the amount of credit available to the Soviet Union from the United States to no more than $300 million this amendment effectively reduced the potential for expanded trade between the two countries.

Similarly, Congress passed the Nelson–Bingham Amendment to the 1974 Foreign Assistance Act.[69] Under this amendment, Congress now had the right to review for 20 days any intended arms sale of $25 million or more. Moreover, Congress reserved the right to reject such a sale by passing a concurrent resolution of disapproval. In the International Security Assistance and Arms Export Control Act of 1976, this provision was modified to allow congressional review of any offer to sell defense articles or services totaling $25 million or more, or any major defense equipment of $7 million or more.[70] The time limit for congressional review was extended from 20 to 30 days, but the right of Congress to reject such a sale by concurrent resolution was maintained. Through an informal agreement with the Ford administration, the Congress was afforded an additional 20-day period of "informal notification"—a policy that has been continued by the succeeding administrations.[71]

In the same security assistance legislation (and in earlier legislation on economic assistance), Congress added human rights considerations in dealing with other countries.[72] Neither security assistance nor economic assistance would be granted to those nations whose government "engages in a consistent pattern of gross violations of internationally recognized human rights." Similar provisions were added to United States funding for the multilateral banks, such as the World Bank, the Inter-American Development Bank, the African Development Fund, and the Asian Development Bank.[73]

During the 1990s and beyond, congressional measures specifying foreign aid and trade requirements continued. In 1992, for example, Congress was instrumental in shaping the content of the Freedom Support Act, the principal initial effort by the United States to provide economic assistance to the former states of the Soviet Union. While the administration had requested broad spending discretion toward those states, Congress enacted limitations on aid levels and imposed conditionality on that aid. In addition, Congress passed legislation to assist the states of the former Soviet Union in dismantling their nuclear weapons in accordance with the START and START II treaties.[74] This legislation, popularly known as the Nunn–Lugar amendments, was an important initiative to deal with the newly emerging threat of "loose nukes" in the global arena.

Congress also initiated and passed the Horn of Africa Recovery and Food Security Act of 1992. This measure demonstrated Congress's ability to impose conditions placed upon foreign aid to countries in that region of the world: Under this law, prior to the granting of aid, "[t]he President must certify that the [recipient] government had begun to implement peace or national reconciliation agreements, demonstrated a commitment to human rights and democracy, and held or scheduled free or fair elections."[75] In *Plan Colombia,* a $1.3 billion antidrug foreign assistance program for Colombia passed in 2000, the Congress imposed a series of conditions—aimed primarily at possible human rights violations by the military—for that government to receive any aid. In particular, the Colombian government was required to issue an order specifying that military personnel charged with human rights violations would be tried in civilian, not military, courts, and that military personnel facing human right violations be suspended from duty. In addition, the Colombian government would need to devise a strategy to eliminate coca and poppy production by 2005, and develop and utilize a judge advocate general corps to investigate military misconduct.[76]

In the trade area, Congress's record is perhaps uneven, but some efforts were made to direct policy in recent years. Perhaps the most celebrated effort centered on denying MFN trade status to China, owing to its abysmal human rights records. (Presidents over the years had invoked an exemption clause from the Jackson–Vanik amendment to grant this status to China on a yearly basis.) Resolutions were introduced and, on occasion, passed by both houses of Congress, only to be vetoed by the president. This pattern continued until the Clinton administration "de-linked" trade policy with China and human rights. Near the end of the Clinton administration, the Congress actually passed new legislation granting China permanent normal trading relations (PNTR) with the United States.[77]

In two recent pieces of trade legislation, Congress facilitated expanded trade with Africa and the Caribbean, while restricting it with Libya and Iraq. In 2000, for instance, the Congress lowered American tariffs and removed quotas mainly on textiles from sub-Saharan, the Caribbean, and Central America as a way to assist the economies in those countries. In 2001, Congress tightened sanctions on businesses that invested more than $20 million in the energy industry in either Libya or Iran and extended them for five years. This action was partly in response to the Libyan involvement in the 1988 bombing of Pan Am flight 103 and both countries' involvement with international terrorism and the development of weapons of mass destruction.[78] (When Libya agreed to dismantle its weapons program, some of these sanctions were lifted in 2004.)

Congress also put its imprint on policy in another region. It initiated, and passed, tougher economic sanctions against Cuba. The Cuban Democracy Act of 1992 directed that prohibitions be placed on United States subsidiaries in other countries from trading with Cuba.[79] While the measure was opposed by the administration, and some presidential flexibility was eventually incorporated into the legislation, it did reflect this continued congressional effort on trade policy. In 1996, after an anti-Castro plane was shot down in international waters off Cuba, Congress passed, and the president agreed to sign, a measure to tighten sanctions further. Under the Helms–Burton legislation, foreign individuals who traded with Cuba would be denied access to the United States, and foreign companies in Cuba who used property formerly belonging to Americans could be sued in American courts.[80]

In sum, then, Congress increasingly uses the funding power and its commerce powers to affect American foreign policy. Moreover, these vehicles will likely remain important ones, and their use will continue to take a variety of forms from cutting off funds, earmarking appropriations, or imposing some form of restrictions on spending.

CONGRESSIONAL OVERSIGHT

The fourth area of congressional resurgence is in the area of *oversight*. Oversight refers to Congress's reviewing and monitoring of executive branch action—in this case, of foreign policy actions. In general, oversight has expanded because Congress now has placed more and more reporting requirements on the executive branch, and congressional committees have increased their review activities as well. In particular, the resurgence in activity by key congressional committees—the International Relations (formerly, Foreign Affairs) and Armed Services (briefly National Security) Committees in the House, the Foreign Relations and Armed Services Committees in the Senate—has been much more pronounced recently and has contributed to greater foreign policy oversight.[81]

Expansion of Reporting Requirements to Congress

The major mechanism of renewed congressional oversight of foreign policy has been the expansion of reporting requirements placed upon the executive branch. That is, the executive branch must file a written report on how a given aspect of American foreign policy was carried out. As we have noted, important pieces of foreign policy legislation already incorporate this kind of requirement (e.g., the Case–Zablocki Act or the War Powers Resolution), but the extent of such reporting requirements goes beyond these specific instances. By one estimate, in the late 1980s, Congress had imposed approximately 600 foreign policy reporting requirements on the executive, a threefold increase from the early 1970s. Moreover, these reporting requirements are a valuable "tool to oversee executive branch implementation of foreign policy" and "are [the] workhorses of congressional oversight."[82] And these requirements largely continue today.

Three main types of reports are required of the executive branch: periodic or recurrent reports, notifications, and one-time reports. The periodic reporting requirement directs the executive branch to submit particular information to Congress every year, every six months, or even quarterly.[83] In the mid-1970s, for example, an amendment was added to the Foreign Assistance Act that required an annual assessment of human rights conditions around the world. This report must be forwarded to Congress early in each new calendar year and becomes an important source of information on human rights globally. Another example of these annually required reports directs the executive branch to outline the foreign policies pursued by member countries of the United Nations. The aim of the report is to assess how the policies of those countries comport with the policies and interests of the United States.[84] Yet another piece of legislation instructs the executive branch to prepare "a single, comprehensive and comparative analysis of the economic policies and trade practices of each country with which the United States has an economic or trade relationship."[85]

A second kind of report is a notification. These are by far the most frequent form of reporting and require the executive branch to inform the Congress that a particular foreign policy action is contemplated or has been undertaken. The notifications on executive agreements or on the use of military force fall into this category, but a series of notifications on arms sales, arms control measures, and foreign assistance constitute the bulk of these kinds of reports. Perhaps the most frequent notification occurs with changes in funding levels of foreign assistance toward particular countries. Under current law, the executive branch must notify Congress whenever it "reprograms" economic or military assistance funds from one program or project to another in a country and sometimes places special notification requirements for some countries.[86]

The third type of report is the one-time report, calling upon the executive branch to examine a particular issue or question. While these reports are probably the most infrequent, they can be very helpful in assisting Congress to understand an issue or in shaping future policy on the question. In the mid-1980s, with the passage of the Anti-Apartheid Act, for example, Congress called for 10 one-time reports from the executive branch. Reports were sought on the degree to which the United States depended upon South Africa for minerals, the kind of programs available to help black South Africans, and the efforts that the United States undertook to obtain international cooperation to end apartheid.[87] In another piece of legislation, Congress required the Secretary of Defense to complete "a study of the functions and organization of the Office of the Secretary of Defense" and to submit a copy of that report to Congress within one year of enactment of the legislation.[88]

In one recent appropriations measure for foreign assistance, for example, Congress required a one-time report on the extent to which developing countries were contributing to the "greenhouse effect" and what efforts would be most beneficial in reducing harmful emissions. In the renewal of sanctions against Iran and Libya in 2001, that we referenced earlier, Congress directed the president to submit a report to it on the effectiveness of the sanctions in the 18 months from passage.[89]

These differing kinds of reports are, of course, more than informational and more than record keeping on the part of Congress; they also can affect policy. The reports alert Congress to changes or potential changes in administration policy and may well set off "fire alarms" in some quarters of the House and the Senate. For instance, reports provided on proposed new arms sales to Arab states or to Israel may elicit reactions from different segments of Congress. Reports on new covert operations in various corners of the world may have a similar effect. As a result, such policy proposals may turn out to be stillborn or changed dramatically before enactment by Congress. On the other hand, even a one-time or yearly report can prove to be significant. Because the Department of State must report annually on global human rights conditions, members of Congress may be able to use that information to monitor the changing situation within a country and use the report in an attempt to impose new restrictions or to lift past ones. In numerous ways, then, these reports may prove beneficial to Congress and to the policy process.

Senate Foreign Relations Committee

In the first three decades after World War II, the Senate Foreign Relations Committee was viewed as the focal point for congressional monitoring of the foreign policy actions of the president, but in more recent decades its influence has declined. The committee can and does affect the foreign policy process from time to time, though perhaps not as regularly as in earlier decades. Several reasons account for the committee's real and potential influence.

First, the committee has constitutional and oversight responsibilities. Not only does the Senate Foreign Relations Committee have responsibility for monitoring foreign affairs activities, but it also is required to advise on and consent to treaties and presidential nominations for various diplomatic posts.[90] The committee also has been viewed as the most prestigious in the Senate (and perhaps in Congress) and provides a ready forum for those members seeking to shape foreign policy and national politics. Furthermore, the committee provides valuable foreign policy experience for those members who entertain presidential ambitions. Indeed, a number of committee members over the years have actively sought the presidential nomination of their party.

Second, the quality of the committee's leadership in the immediate post–World War II years contributed initially to its activism and influence. Particularly prominent among recent committee chairs was the Senator J. William Fulbright (D-Arkansas), who served for 15 years in this role. His penetrating hearings on American involvement in Vietnam contributed significantly to the national debate on this issue and to America's eventual withdrawal from Southeast Asia.[91] Further, his active involvement in the numerous reform efforts by Congress in the late 1960s and early 1970s assured the committee's prominence in the shaping of the nation's foreign policy.

Committee chairs in the 1970s and 1980s did not gain the same stature as Fulbright, and the prestige and activism of the Senate Foreign Relations Committee began to wane.[92] An exception to this generalization would be Senator Richard Lugar, a conservative Republican from Indiana who chaired the Committee in the 1980s for a short time. While Lugar initially supported the Reagan administration ("I think it is fair to say that I share the basic assumptions of the President and the Secretary of State in regard to foreign policy"[93]), he also led the committee "by charting a course and sticking with it, working behind the scenes to build consensus through compromise and patient prodding."[94] As a consequence, the committee was able to exert influence on several issues, including passage of South African sanctions and the ouster of Ferdinand Marcos in the Philippines, during his tenure.

By the mid–1990s, and with the Republicans again in control of the Senate, Senator Jesse Helms (R–North Carolina) was selected as chair of the committee. He came to the committee with a reputation for a strong ideological view of both foreign and domestic policy questions, and, as expected, his views came to dominate committee operations. Although Helms initially seemed to veer away from his strongly held views (as evidenced by his dropping his opposition to the START II treaty and tempering his initial hostility to the North Korean–United States nuclear agreement negotiated in October 1994), he still served as a staunch watchdog over the direction of policy, holding up several foreign policy nominees by the Clinton administration.[95] By mid-1995, Helms was locked in a battle with the Clinton administration over the restructuring of the United States foreign affairs bureaucracy and a variety of other foreign policy matters. In particular, Helms wanted to restructure the Department of State in a way that would effectively eliminate three semiautonomous bureaucracies, the Agency for International Development (AID), the Arms Control and Disarmament Agency (ACDA), and the United States Information Agency (USIA). The result would be a considerable downsizing of the foreign affairs bureaucracy, and, to critics, a severe downsizing of the American assistance program, too. In its place, Helms wanted to install a nongovernmental foundation to manage U.S. assistance abroad.[96] While this debate over reorganization went on for several years, it finally resulted in an incorporation of both USIA and ACDA into the Department of State in 1999. While AID retained some of its autonomy, parts of its bureaucracy also went to the Department of State.[97]

To get this reorganization accomplished, Senator Helms employed his power as chair of the Senate Foreign Relations Committee to hold up committee and Senate action on State Department promotions, some 30 ambassadorial appointments, and several important treaties, including the START II treaty and the Chemical Weapons Convention.[98] The impasse was finally broken when the Clinton administration yielded and agreed to have Senate Democrats work with Senate Republicans to come up with legislation acceptable to both sides for reshaping the foreign affairs bureaucracy.[99] Still, the episode demonstrates the ability of one committee—and, indeed, one pivotal member of a committee—to affect the operation of foreign policy, at least for a time. Furthermore, the episode also illustrates that the Senate Foreign Relations Committee can play a pivotal role in the oversight of foreign policy making if it chooses to do so.

Helms's successors as chair of the Senate Foreign Relations Committee were Senator Joseph Biden (D-Delaware) and Senator Richard Lugar (R-Indiana). Over the years as the ranking Democrat, Biden worked well with Helms to forge some movement within the Committee. As chair, he continued to do so, though he was the principal foreign policy critic of the Bush administration. In the war on terrorism, he has been a supporter of the administration on the general direction of America's response, even as he expressed some reservations about the specifics of Bush's approach. Still, Biden differed with the Bush administration on a number of issues, including the development of national missile defense, the efforts to reduce American forces in Bosnia, and the level of support for Taiwan.[100] His successor after the 2002 election was Senator Lugar, who, as noted, had previously been chair of the committee. While Lugar largely supported the Bush administration's policy, he also consistently called for greater multilateralism than the administration pursued. He became increasingly critical of the Bush administration's implementation of postwar reconstruction in Iraq, including its failure to provide a fuller assessment of the costs and time for the transformation of that society after the American intervention.

International Relations Committee

Unlike the Senate Foreign Relations Committee, the House Committee on International Relations (called the Committee on Foreign Affairs throughout most of the post–World War II period) was seen as less prestigious than the Senate Foreign Relations Committee and some other committees in the House.[101] Unlike the other House committees, too, International Relations was less likely to assist the constituency or biennial reelection goals of a member of the House directly. It was also less useful than the Senate Foreign Relations Committee as a springboard to national prominence on foreign policy matters. Furthermore, the House Committee had a more limited agenda, confined mainly to the preparation of the foreign assistance bill, and lacked the wide sweep of responsibilities that the Senate Foreign Relations Committee had.[102]

By the 1970s, however, the House Foreign Affairs Committee underwent a series of changes that produced a considerable resurgence of activity in this committee. The oversight function, for instance, increased rather sharply as a result.[103] The newfound zeal for oversight derived from the changing composition of the committee, the structural changes in the committee system within the House of Representatives, and a resurgent interest in foreign policy matters.[104] During that time, too, the committee increasingly was composed of younger, more liberal members of the House, who viewed foreign policy matters as an important part of their legislative activities. Often elected in opposition to the Vietnam War, these new members were more determined than ever to make American foreign policy accountable to the House. Moreover, this trend of the committee being more liberal than the House as a whole continued into the 1990s.[105]

Structural reforms within the House also assisted the invigorated oversight process. In an effort to open up the congressional process, limitations were placed on the authority of the committee chairs in the appointment of subcommittee chairs (they were now elected by the committee caucus) and in the number of subcommittees that any member could chair (the number was limited to one).[106] As a result, more liberal members of the committee emerged as subcommittee chairs. In addition, because of some jurisdictional changes, the House Foreign Affairs Committee (and consequently its subcommittees) gained more review power over international economic issues.[107] One result of this enlarged agenda was a change in subcommittee organization, from primarily regional subcommittees to new functional ones. Although the committee eventually settled on a combination of functional and regional subcommittees, the pattern of increased responsibility was set in motion.[108]

Yet another congressional reform of the 1970s also aided the House International Relations Committee. The committee and subcommittee staffs were enlarged and placed formally under the chairs of the particular committees or subcommittees. While these changes regarding the subcommittee chair's control of his or her staff were already in place on this committee, the rule changes in the House formalized them and staff grew.[109] One important consequence of these changes has been the significant increase in committee and subcommittee hearings by Foreign Affairs. In the 1970s and early 1980s hearings by the committee and its subcommittees numbered more than 700 in a given Congress. Since then they have fallen off a bit, but still number about 500 per Congress.[110]

In short, the International Relations Committee has played a larger role in both the formulation and review of American foreign policy since the 1970s through the early 1990s under Democratic control. With the Republicans in control of the committee after the 1994 elections, its assertiveness and legislative oversight appeared to have changed very little. The committee quickly proceeded to change its name from Foreign Affairs to International Relations, reduced the number of subcommittees, and took decisive action on its principal legislative measure, the foreign aid bill. With rather remarkable speed, and under the somewhat reluctant leadership of Benjamin Gilman (R–New York), who had long supported foreign assistance legislation, the committee passed a pared down foreign aid bill by mid-1995. Like the Senate measure discussed above, this bill abolished three foreign affairs agencies—AID, ACDA, and USIA—and it called for sharp cuts in total foreign assistance.[111]

When Gilman's leadership ended after three terms as chair by internal rules, Henry Hyde (R–Illinois) succeeded him in 2001. By one assessment, Hyde's presence "could restore some luster and influence" to the Committee. While he generally adopts positions consistent with the center of Republican thinking, he also has prompted tougher positions toward China and the Palestinian Authority. In all, though, he is likely to work with the Bush administration on most issues.[112]

Across party control of the committee, then, the International Relations Committee and its subcommittees continue to be active participants in the oversight and legislative process, matching and perhaps even surpassing their Senate counterparts at various times. In this sense, the House International Relations

Committee continues to exercise a somewhat more independent role in the monitoring and shaping of foreign policy than in its past.

Armed Services Committees in the House and Senate

The House and Senate Armed Services Committees have also enjoyed a bit of a renaissance in their foreign policy oversight activities in recent years. Throughout the 1950s and 1960s, both committees were often regarded as committees largely supportive of the Pentagon's point of view on policy matters. One study, focusing on data to 1970, found that these committees relied upon the Department of Defense for information about military matters and "usually ratified administration proposals." Another analysis described its role up to the early 1970s as both an "advocate" and as an "overseer," with the House Armed Services Committee less of an overseer and more of an advocate than the Senate Armed Services Committee.[113] Yet, a recent analysis claims that the "stylized image" of the two committees as protector of a strong national defense and of local military bases and defense contractors remains, but that two changes—a move toward yearly military authorization procedures and an innovative approach to handling military base closings—have begun to alter this image.[114]

More generally, the changes in rules in Congress and in congressional procedures during the 1970s—coupled with changes in leadership—have enabled the armed services committees to match or approach what we described as happening with the House International Relations Committee. While the extent of legislative oversight of defense policy changed modestly at first, by the 1980s, the activities increased even more with the emergence of what one political scientist has called the "outside game" in defense policy making.[115] Because Congress as a whole was increasingly more interested in scrutinizing defense policy, the committees, too, had to examine legislative policy more carefully if they were to retain any legitimacy. While this did happen, one concern was that the committee's responsibilities will be eroded with continued Congress-wide involvement.

Both armed services committees have also benefited from more assertive leadership since the 1980s. In the House, Les Aspin (D-Wisconsin) gained the chairmanship of the Armed Services Committee by leaping over other members with greater seniority and by offering a policy posture that tended to be more critical of Pentagon requests than previous leaders. Aspin's successor, Ron Dellums (D-California), headed the committee for only a two-year period, and, although traditionally an outspoken critic of the military establishment, he appeared to manage it in a more moderate, middle-of-the-road, manner than might have been initially expected.

Dellum's Republican successor after the 1994 election was Floyd Spence (R-South Carolina). The Armed Services Committee (renamed the House National Security Committee for a time), under Spence's leadership, sought to implement the Republican "Contract with America" pledge for strengthening American military capabilities through the emphasis on greater readiness of United States military personnel and through greater defense spending levels as well. Indeed, he (and others) proposed "their own multiyear, hundred billion dollar plans to increase military spending and shift defense priorities" shortly after the beginning of the 104th Congress.[116] By the end of this Congress, the Committee—and the House and Senate as a whole—had passed a defense spending bill surpassing what the Clinton administration had proposed.

Representative Bob Stump (R–Arizona), the chair of the House Armed Services Committee by 2001, did not match the flair and global strategy of Aspin or Nunn (in the Senate) in this role, but he was a strong defender of military interest. His particular area of interest is dealing with military personnel issues and veterans' issues.[117] Stump's successor, Representative Duncan Hunter (R–California), was equally a voice for a strong defense and a bit more assertive than his immediate predecessor.

In the Senate, recent chairs have stimulated new life into the Armed Services Committee. Sam Nunn of Georgia, chair of Armed Services from 1987 to 1995, did not automatically prove to be a supporter of the military. Instead, he, too, demonstrated a willingness to challenge the Department of Defense and the administration in office with his own defense plans.[118] At the same time, Nunn sought to improve America's armed forces by increasing efficiency within the Pentagon and enhancing the conditions of military personnel. He also evidenced a streak of independence over military affairs by continuing to support economic sanctions rather than military actions prior to the Persian Gulf War and by vigorously opposing the Clinton administration's effort to overturn existing policy on gays in the military. Finally, Nunn's Republican successors, Strom Thurmond (R–South Carolina) and John Warner (R–Virginia), brought altered priorities to the Senate Armed Services Committee, ones more in line with its earlier tradition of being receptive to the Pentagon's wishes. In particular, Thurmond sought to increase military spending as a means of enhancing U.S. force readiness.

In 2001, Warner's successor, Senator Carl Levin (D–Michigan), represented a bit more skepticism on defense policy. While Levin supported the promilitary tilt of the committee, he also remained a persistent critic or questioner of some administration defense policy. A student of defense issues, he was well versed in the intricacies of defense policy and could successfully spar with those holding opposing views. As such, he was critical of the Bush administration's call for national missile defense and its abandonment of the ABM Treaty, and he questioned aspects of the war on terrorism. In doing so, he continued to make the Senate Armed Services Committee an important player in responding to September 11 and devising American defense strategy for the future.[119] After the 2002 election, Senator John Warner returned as chair of the committee, and he largely espoused a position fully in line with the Bush administration's wishes, while still seeking to have the committee exercise some policy influence.

MECHANISMS
OF CONGRESSIONAL INFLUENCE

A useful way to summarize the congressional role in the foreign policy process that we have been describing so far is to use some categories of influence that prominent political scientists have developed.[120] In the broadest sense, we may categorize congressional actions on foreign policy as either legislative or nonlegislative. Within the legislative category, Congress can pass substantive legislation on foreign policy or impose procedural legislation on the executive branch. Within the nonlegislative category, we can subdivide those mechanisms into institutional actions (i.e., action by Congress to express its view) and individual actions (i.e., action by members to convey their policy prescriptions) to affect foreign policy.

Legislation: Substantive and Procedural

While Congress has the ability to legislate foreign policy with a particular bill or act (e.g., imposing sanctions on South Africa or Cuba, lifting the arms embargo against Bosnia, or granting trade preferences to African states), those substantive pieces of legislation are relatively rare in terms of all of the activities that Congress undertakes. Political scientist Barbara Hinckley reports that, on average, only about seven to eight substantive pieces of foreign policy legislation have been approved by the House of Representatives per administration from the Kennedy years to the first three years of the George H. W. Bush administration. In the Senate, the average of substantive foreign policy legislation is even lower, averaging five per administration. While Hinckley notes that foreign policy related resolutions, primarily of a symbolic nature, have increased, the substantive amount of foreign policy legislation has remained markedly stable and small over the years.[121]

Procedural legislation, however, has grown dramatically, as our earlier discussion sought to convey. In such diverse areas as war powers, commitments abroad, covert operations, foreign aid, and trade, Congress has developed a wide array of procedures for discerning executive action and, in some instances, seeking to play a more direct role in changing or altering executive policy. In addition, as political scientist James Lindsay has pointed out, these procedural measures include the reporting and monitoring of policy and the creations of new bureaucracies and new offices within bureaucracies to allow greater congressional insight and involvement in the process.[122] The U.S. Trade Representative, for example, was a creation of Congress and has now been given increased powers over trade policy. Accompanying these enhanced powers in fact has been a requirement that five House members be designated as advisors to the USTR on trade policy issues.

Nonlegislative Actions:
Institutional and Individual Actions

Nonlegislative actions by Congress have also assumed an increasingly larger role in congressional efforts to influence foreign policy.[123] Nonlegislative institutional actions by Congress range from holding hearings by standing committees, such as the Senate Foreign Relations or the International Relations Committee over

American policy toward international terrorism, to the use of select committees, such as the Iran–Contra committees in the 1980s or the House Select Committee on Homeland Security in 2002, to address particular issues. While such hearings may not, and in most instances will not, lead directly to legislation, they do serve to convey to the executive branch and to the public at large the congressional view on these matters. A second nonlegislative institutional action is the formal executive-congressional consultation that is called for in the War Power Resolution or the formal and informal notification procedures in the selling of arms abroad. Yet a third, and popular, nonlegislative institutional mechanism is the passing of various kinds of nonbinding resolutions (e.g., a concurrent or two-house resolution or a single ["sense of the House" or "sense of the Senate"] resolution) on a current foreign policy issue. In 1999, for instance, the Senate passed a nonbinding resolution supporting President Clinton's actions toward Kosovo, while the House rejected such a resolution but passed a similar nonbinding resolution directing the president to follow the War Powers Resolution over Kosovo.[124] As these resolutions suggest, such nonbinding actions are not always followed, but they do put the executive on notice about the interest and intention of Congress on particular issues.

A final nonlegislative way for Congress to express its views on foreign policy activities is through individual actions. These ways are myriad, but a few illustrations will demonstrate how legislators over the years have attempted to affect the foreign policy process. Some members have used newsletters and policy analyses to convey their views on foreign policy issues. Others have written individual letters directly to the president or an executive branch office, or they have joined with their colleagues in sending such letters. Still others have used the floor of the House and Senate, either during regular debate or at the beginning or end of the legislative day when time has been set aside for individual members to speak. Finally, too, members of Congress have increasingly used network media programs (morning, evening, or weekend interview shows) to make their cases about foreign policy issues.

Two other intriguing and more potent nonlegislative mechanisms have also been used by individual members: (a) dealing directly with foreign governments, and (b) filing court challenges to the executive's foreign policy actions. In the case of the former, two examples will illustrate this phenomenon. In the late 1980s, former House Speaker Jim Wright (D-Texas) prepared a peace plan for ending the conflict in Central America between the Contras and the Sandinista government in Nicaragua and then provided his plan to regional governmental representatives and to the State Department. While his plan was not ultimately adopted, his actions got the attention of the White House and stimulated some progress toward peace within the region. In the mid-1990s, Senator Sam Nunn (D-Georgia), at the behest of President Clinton, joined with former president Jimmy Carter and former chairman of the Joint Chiefs of Staff (and now secretary of state) Colin Powell to seek to remove the Haitian junta that had overthrown the democratically elected government of Jean-Bertrand Aristide.

In the case of court challenges, numerous lawsuits have been filed by individual members or groups of members of Congress to thwart actions taken by the president in foreign policy. These range from Senator Barry Goldwater's effort to stop President Carter from breaking the defense treaty with Taiwan without Senate approval (*Goldwater et al. v. Carter,* 1979) to Representative Ron Dellums (D-California) filing a suit to stop the Bush administration from going to war in the Persian Gulf in 1990 (*Dellums v. Bush,* 1990) to the 2002 suit filed by Representative Dennis Kucinich (D-OH) over President George W. Bush's decision to withdraw from the 1972 Anti-Ballistic Missile Treaty. Other lawsuits (described in Chapter 7) have been filed by members of Congress, primarily to stop the use of force without congressional authorization. While these measures have gained considerable attention and notoriety for the members of Congress, they have largely failed to affect policy outcomes.

On balance, these various legislative mechanisms appear to have a mixed record of success, but one recent analysis suggests that they have an effect. As Rebecca Hersman argues, "individualized power and strong issue leaders have enhanced Congress's obstructive powers" in foreign policy. "The very strength of these obstructive powers makes them effective leverage against the executive branch. . . ."[125]

CONGRESSIONAL CHANGE AND FUTURE FOREIGN POLICY MAKING

Have all of these congressional changes over the past three decades permanently altered the foreign policy relationships between Congress and the executive that have evolved since World War II? Alternate views abound from within and outside the executive and legislative branches and from analysts as well.

The Degree of Change

Writing two decades ago, congressional-executive scholars Thomas Franck, Edward Weisband, and I. M. Destler believe so.[126] They point to the structural and procedural arrangements that Congress put in place for dealing with foreign policy; the various pieces of legislation giving Congress more political clout; the larger foreign policy staffs on Capitol Hill and constituencies among the American public; and the adjustments that the president has made in his relationship with Congress (perhaps grudgingly).

More recently, and writing in a similar vein, analyst Jeremy Rosner points to "the new tug-of-war," between the branches, largely as a result of the end of the Cold War. In this new environment, Rosner argues that the relationship between the two branches will vary by issue and will be dependent upon the degree of presidential involvement with the Congress. On those issues involving security, the president will likely prevail if he takes an early and determined stance. On those issues not directly involving security (e.g., international peacekeeping or human rights), Congress will likely dominate, especially if the president does not push these issues. Since more issues are likely to reflect the latter than the former in the years ahead (although Rosner wrote before September 11, 2001), Congress will be "more assertive relative to the executive branch than during the late years of the Cold War."[127]

Constitutional lawyer Harold Hongju Koh and political scientist Barbara Hinckley, however, raise doubts about whether the changes over the years have been very significant or important to the policy process. Koh argues that the Congress ultimately has assented to presidential wishes because the reforms undertaken have been inadequate and the political will has been insufficient to stop the executive.[128] Hinckley is as skeptical as Koh—if not more so—about the impact of this presumed congressional activism. She argues that conflict between the two branches is "in large part an illusion." There has been "no shift from a conventional to a reform pattern of policy making, as some popular wisdom leads us to expect."[129] Indeed, the level of activity and the degree of foreign policy legislation have changed very little since the 1960s, in her judgment, and Congress has largely continued to defer to the executive in the foreign policy realm.

Yet, considerable other evidence from recent administrations seems to provide at least some support for the earlier view. The Reagan administration, for example, was locked in heated policy battles with Congress on several foreign policy fronts during its time in office. Most prominent, of course, was the six-year struggle with Congress over the funding of the Nicaraguan Contras. It also fought with Congress over the reflagging of Kuwaiti vessels in the Persian Gulf and congressional war powers, the imposition of economic sanctions on South Africa over its apartheid policy, and the congressional initiatives on international trade policy, among others.[130] Reagan's successor, George H. W. Bush also sparred with Congress over both substance and procedure in foreign policy making. President Bush used his veto power four times in his first year to alter foreign policy legislation with which he did not agree—an extraordinarily high usage of the veto on foreign policy legislation in such a short time.[131] Furthermore, he was sharply critical of the attempted congressional restrictions on his foreign policy prerogatives. In all instances, President Bush was successful, but this rancor indicated the intensity of the congressional-executive rivalry in foreign affairs.

The Clinton administration experienced the same tumult with Congress over foreign policy making as did previous administrations. The debacle in Somalia in mid to late 1993, and the congressional response to end American involvement there formally by the end of March 1994, were early examples. Later ones focused on the American military role in Bosnia and Kosovo and over funding the Mexican peso bailout and refunding the International Monetary Fund at the time of the Asian financial crisis. Perhaps the most critical debates, and direct losses for the president, were over Congress's failure to renew fast-track trading authority for the Clinton administration and the Senate's stinging defeat of the Comprehensive Test Ban Treaty (CTBT). Even on foreign policy battles that the Clinton administration won, such as the passage of NAFTA and GATT, they required the use of considerable political capital and deal making by the president.

The George W. Bush administration has also had its disputes with Congress, although their acrimony has been tempered by the events of September 11. Early in the administration, members of Congress looked with skepticism on the approach that the Bush administration took toward such issues as North Korea, Russia, and missile defense. Initially, the administration was not interested in continuing a dialogue with North Korea and also appeared to be reluctant to move on improving ties with Russia. In general, members on both sides of the political aisle in Congress criticized these positions. Similarly, the Bush administration's decision to push forward with national missile defense and to abrogate the ABM Treaty with Russia also elicited congressional opposition. Although the terrorist attacks of September 11, 2001, dramatically dampened any criticism of the administration's foreign policy by members of Congress for a time, foreign policy criticisms began to emerge by mid–2002.

Such conflicts between the branches have been lamented by a number of high officials, as they point to the difficulties of conducting foreign policy with a Congress constantly intruding on, or at least limiting, the president's freedom of action. A principal complaint, for instance, is that coherent foreign policy cannot result with this continuous struggle between Congress and the president. This view was most forcefully expressed not by a member of the executive branch, but by a former member of the Senate, John Tower of Texas, some two decades ago: "Five hundred and thirty-five Congressmen with different philosophies, regional interests and objectives in mind cannot forge a unified foreign policy that reflects the interests of the United States as a whole."[132] Moreover, virtually every president since these various reforms were enacted have complained about congressional intrusions in the foreign policy areas, and each one has sought to pursue and to protect presidential foreign policy prerogatives. In this sense, the struggle between the two branches continues.

Congressional Reform and Policy Impact

A key question, of course, is how much effect these reforms have had on American foreign policy. For several different reasons, the substantive impact of the various reforms on American foreign policy have been much less widespread than might be anticipated by only examining the original legislation and thus lend support to those analysts who are skeptical about the degree of congressional activism.

First, the measures have been used relatively infrequently. Despite the arms sales review procedures, for instance, no arms deal has actually been denied to the executive branch since 1974, although the composition and timing of some arms sales may have been altered. The human rights requirements did not markedly change the economic or security assistance policies of the subsequent administrations, although they did result in the cutting off of aid to a few nations (e.g., Argentina, Chile) and the rejection of aid by some others (e.g., Brazil). When necessary, legislative loopholes or exceptions were often found for strategically important states. After September 11, for instance, Congress rapidly waived sanctions against Pakistan (imposed after that country's nuclear tests in 1998) as a way to obtain Pakistan's cooperation in the war on terrorism.[133]

The apparent weak public record should not be pushed too far, however. Some significant actions have been taken by Congress to stop executive action, and some administrations have been dissuaded from pursuing some policy options because of evident congressional opposition. In the first category, the use of the Jackson–Vanik Amendment to restrict most-favored-nation status with the former Soviet Union and, more recently, with China illustrates how congressional legislation can be significant. Indeed, it took affirmative action by Congress before China was actually granted permanent normal trading relations (PNTR) with the United States in 2000. In the second category, the rapid completion of the Chemical Weapons Convention by the Senate was slowed down by congressional opposition and prerogatives and the CTBT was actually defeated in the Senate.[134] In this sense, the presence of procedural requirements and congressional prerogatives had a tangible effect on policy.

A second factor that weakens congressional authority in foreign affairs is that much of this legislation has "escape clauses" for the president. If, for example, the president certifies that an arms sale must go forward for national security reasons despite a congressional rejection, he may proceed. The most-favored-nation requirement in the Trade Act of 1974 also has an escape clause allowing the president the right to grant such a status if he so wishes. Indeed, this clause has been used since 1980 (until the 2000 legislation) to grant such status to the People's Republic of China. The human rights requirements in the economic assistance legislation also can be waived, if the executive branch certifies that the aid will reach "needy people" in the recipient nation "and if either house of Congress didn't disapprove the waiver within thirty days."[135] Two more recent action reflect this same pattern. In 1995, the congressional effort to lift the arms embargo toward Bosnia contained a presidential waiver provision. Under the legislation, the United States would end the embargo only after a United Nations withdrawal of forces "or 12 weeks from the date of a request by the Bosnian Government for a pullout of forces." Yet, the legislation also granted the president "the right to ask for unlimited thirty-day waivers if he certified that they were necessary for a safe withdrawal."[136] In effect, the lifting of the Bosnian arms ban would still be at the president's discretion. Similarly, the Helms–Burton Act tightening economic sanctions against Cuba also included a presidential waiver for a portion of the act. Under Title III of the legislation, American citizens could sue in court over properties seized in Cuba after the Castro Revolution. Yet the act also allowed the president to waive this portion if "necessary to the national interest of the United States" and if the president decided the waiver "will expedite a transition to democracy in Cuba."[137] President Clinton immediately waived its application for six months and continued to do so throughout his second term. President George W. Bush has continued this practice as well.

A third reason for the limited impact of these congressional reforms focuses on the legislative veto, declared unconstitutional by the Supreme Court in *Immigration and Naturalization Service v. Chadha*.[138] Several of the important congressional reforms in foreign policy making (e.g., the War Powers Resolution and the arms sales amendment) incorporate this veto provision. While the removal of this veto power does not wholly paralyze congressional participation in any of these areas, it does make it more difficult to halt presidential action quickly. The president would still be restricted to 60 days for sending troops abroad, for example, but now Congress could not remove them before this time period without a joint resolution (instead of through the concurrent resolution provision previously). In effect, then, this kind of legislation would require a two-thirds majority to override an expected presidential veto, not just a simple majority under the concurrent resolution procedure.

While the elimination of the legislative veto has meant a weakening of the foreign policy capability of Congress, its impact also should not be pushed too far, since the reporting and review mechanisms continue. In addition, Congress has developed and used other instruments of action. Congress has sought to employ "conditions bills," tougher measures specifying the actions of the president on trade policy beyond what the legislative veto will allow, and to use its informal consultations to threaten congressional action on trade agreements not submitted to it.[139] In addition, informal arrangements have evolved between the legislative and executive branches. A recent analysis of selling frigates to Turkey, amending sanctioning legislation toward Pakistan, and passing the Chemical Weapons Convention illustrate the informal approach adopted by Congress and the executive.[140] Finally, members of Congress, and particularly members of the Senate, can place "holds" on measures, temporarily stopping action on foreign policy items that they do not want to take up until they obtain some concession from the executive branch.

Yet a fourth factor reduces the substantive effect of the congressional reforms of the 1970s and 1980s. Despite the desire of members of Congress to assert their role in foreign affairs, they still perceive limits as to how far they should go in restricting the executive. Many members of Congress still rely upon the president for the initiation and execution of foreign policy. In a series of lectures on congressional-executive relations in 1999 and 2000, former congressman and former chair of the House Foreign Affairs Committee Lee H. Hamilton (D-Indiana) perhaps best summarized the prevailing congressional perspective: "There is simply no substitute for presidential leadership. Only the president is accountable to, and speaks for, all Americans, and possesses the authority to implement policy. On rare occasions, Congress seizes the initiative on foreign policy, but most decisions follow a proposal by the president."[141]

In short, what Congress seeks is to be involved in the formulation of policy, in conjunction with the president, but the implementation of policy is left to the executive branch. While members of Congress are unlikely to turn back to an earlier era of congressional acquiescence, they appear equally unlikely to pass many new restrictions on presidential power.[142] Instead, members of Congress will remain alert to exercise their prerogatives in foreign affairs without seeking to direct American policy unilaterally.

CONCLUDING COMMENTS

As Chapters 7 and 8 have emphasized, Congress and the president share foreign policy making powers under the Constitution, and hence foreign policy is likely to remain a "contest" between them for the foreseeable future. Neither side is likely to yield its foreign policy prerogatives, nor is any structural change ultimately going to alter the inherent constitutional dilemma between these two branches. Instead, as Arthur Schlesinger, Jr., correctly noted at the beginning of these congressional reform efforts, the problem is "primarily political,"[143] and will undoubtedly require efforts at cooperative solutions in procedural, rather than legislative, remedies. As such, greater consultation and institutional respect for the role of the other remains the best prescription for dealing with the continuing foreign policy debate between the president and Congress.[144]

While these two institutions are the preeminent actors in foreign policy making, they are not the only ones involved in the process. Within the executive branch in particular, diverse and important foreign policy bureaucracies—the Department of State, the Department of Defense, the National Security Council, the intelligence community, and several economic bureaucracies—can and do affect the formulation of American foreign policy. The next two chapters analyze these key bureaucracies and begin to offer a more complete picture of the foreign policy process.

NOTES

1. See Natalie Hevener Kaufman, *Human Rights Treaties and the Senate* (Chapel Hill and London: The University of North Carolina Press, 1990). For other discussions of the Bricker Amendment, see Stephen A. Garrett, "Foreign Policy and the American Constitution: The Bricker Amendment in Contemporary Perspective," *International Studies Quarterly* 16 (June 1972): 187–220; and Duane Tananbaum, *The Bricker Amendment Controversy: A Test of Eisenhower's Political Leadership* (Ithaca, NY, and London: Cornell University Press, 1988).

2. See Michael Nelson, ed., *Congressional Quarterly's Guide to the Presidency* (Washington, DC: Congressional Quarterly, Inc., 1989), pp. 512–513; and *Congressional Quarterly's Guide to Congress,* 3rd ed. (Washington, DC: Congressional Quarterly, Inc., 1982), pp. 303–304.

3. See "Security Agreements and Commitments Abroad," Report to the Committee on Foreign Relations of the United States Senate by the Subcommittee on Security Agreements and Commitments Abroad, December 21, 1970.

4. The text of the resolution can be found in the *Congressional Record,* 91st Cong., 1st sess., June 25, 1969, 17245.

5. The text of the amended resolution can be found in "Agreements with Portugal and Bahrain," Senate Report No. 92-632, 92nd Cong., 2d sess., February 17, 1972, 1.

6. See P.L. 92-403.

7. See section 5 of P.L. 95-45 for the text of the Case amendment.

8. The data are from Report of the Comptroller General of the United States, "Reporting of U.S. International Agreements by Executive Agencies Has Improved," Report ID-78-57, October 31, 1978, p. 22.

9. The late reporting by agencies in 1977 is given in ibid., p. 23, while the rest of the data cited in this paragraph are from Committee on Foreign Relations, United States Senate. *Treaties and Other International Agreements: The Role of the United States Senate,* A Study Prepared for the Committee on Foreign Relations, United States Senate, by the Congressional Research Service (Washington, DC: U.S. Government Printing Office, January 2001), pp. 226–227.

10. For a brief review of the Ervin bill, see Marjorie Ann Browne, Executive Agreements and the Congress, *Issue Brief Number 1B75035* (Washington, DC: Congressional Research Service, The Library of Congress, 1981), p. 7. The Glenn bill was S. 1251, 94th Cong., 1st sess., introduced on March 20, 1975.

11. See H.R. 4439, 94th Cong., 1st sess., introduced on March 6, 1975.

12. The section of the Treaty Powers Resolution (S. Res. 434) quoted is from the *Congressional Record,* 94th Cong., 2nd sess., April 14, 1976, 10967.

13. See Section 708 of P.L. 95-426, October 7, 1978.

14. Ibid. These reforms are also summarized in "Reporting of U.S. International Agreements by Executive Agencies Has Improved," p. 8.

15. The exchange of letters establishing this process are reproduced in "International Agreements Consultation Resolution," Senate Report 95-1171, August 25, 1978, 2–3.

16. *Treaties and Other International Agreements: The Role of the United States Senate,* pp. 233–234.

17. P.L. 91-672. For the executive claim of not needing the Gulf of Tonkin Resolution to continue the war, see *Congress and the Nation Volume III 1969–1972* (Washington, DC: Congressional Quarterly, Inc., 1973), p. 947.

18. The entire text of the resolution can be found in *The War Powers Resolution: Relevant Documents, Correspondence, Reports,* Subcommittee on International Security and Scientific Affairs, House Committee on Foreign Affairs, December 1983, pp. 1–6.

19. The following analysis is based upon the text of the War Powers Resolution (P.L. 93-148). A section-by-section analysis of the Resolution is provided in Robert A. Katzmann, "War Powers: Toward A New Accommodation," in Thomas E. Mann, ed., *A Question of Balance* (Washington, DC: The Brookings Institution, 1990), pp. 46–49.

20. Ibid., pp. 50 and 58, on this point.

21. The cases of presidential reports to the Congress discussed in this section are drawn from Richard F. Grimmett, *War Powers Resolution: After Twenty-Eight Years* (Washington, DC: Congressional Research Service, November 30, 2001) and Richard F. Grimmett, *IB81050: War Powers Resolution: Presidential Compliance* (Washington, DC: Congressional Research Service, June 12, 2002 and September 16, 2003).

22. This language is taken from President Bush's report on the Panama invasion, which is printed in *Weekly Compilation of Presidential Documents* 25 (December 25, 1989): 1985.

23. Grimmett, *War Powers Resolution: After Twenty-Eight Years,* pp. 53–54.

24. Jeffrey Frank, "Vietnam, Watergate Bred War Powers Act . . . Controversy Still Surrounds Law's Effects," *Congressional Quarterly Weekly Report,* October 1, 1983, 2019.

25. See the reply to Congressman Zablocki's letter of inquiry by Richard Fairbanks, former assistant secretary of state for congressional relations, in *The War Powers Resolution: Relevant Documents, Correspondence, Reports,* pp. 52–54.

26. Grimmett, *War Powers Resolution: After Twenty-Eight Years,* p. 69.

27. Katzmann, "War Powers: Toward A New Accommodation," p. 61.

28. Ellen C. Collier, "The War Powers Resolution: Fifteen Years of Experience," Congressional Research Service, August 3, 1988, pp. 29–31; and Collier, "War Powers Resolution: Presidential Compliance," Congressional Research Service, Issue Brief 81050, February 16, 1990, p. 3.

29. "Legal Opinion of May 9, 1980, by Lloyd Cutler, counsel to Former President Carter, on War Powers Consultation Relative to the Iran Rescue Mission," reprinted in *The War Powers Resolution: Relevant Documents, Correspondence, Reports,* p. 50.

30. Collier, "War Powers Resolution: Presidential Compliance," p. 5.

31. President Clinton is quoted in Thomas L. Friedman, "Clinton Vows to Fight Congress On His Power to Use the Military," *New York Times,* October 19, 1993, A18.

32. The official is quoted in Elaine Sciolino, "On the Brink of War, a Tense Battle of Wills," *New York Times,* September 20, 1994, A13, and the White House strategy for moving toward intervention is also set forth there.

33. Collier, "War Powers Resolution: Presidential Compliance," p. 49.

34. Ryan Hendrickson, *The Clinton Wars* (Nashville: Vanderbilt University Press, 2002), pp. 161–162. Emphasis in original.

35. Grimmett, *War Powers Resolution: After Twenty-Eight Years,* p. 46.

36. Collier, "The War Powers Resolution: Fifteen Years of Experience," pp. 27–29.

37. Adam Clymer, "Congress in Step," *New York Times,* January 14, 1991, A11.

38. UN Security Council Resolution 678 (1990), reprinted in Marjorie Ann Browne, *Iraq-Kuwait: U.N. Security Council Resolutions—Texts and Votes* (Washington, DC: Congressional Research Service, The Library of Congress, December 4, 1990).

39. Clymer, "Congress in Step," p. A11.

40. "Text of Congressional Resolution on the Gulf," *New York Times,* January 14, 1991, A11.

41. For a dissenting view on this conclusion, see Michael J. Glennon, *Constitutional Diplomacy* (Princeton, NJ: Princeton University Press, 1990), p. 93. He argues that only Nixon and Reagan viewed the withdrawal of troops requirements in the War Powers Resolution as unconstitutional.

42. Barbara Hinckley, *Less Than Meets the Eye* (Chicago and London: The University of Chicago Press, 1994), pp. 195–196.

43. For a discussion of the Senate vote on nonbinding resolutions, see Louis Fisher, *Presidential War Power* (Lawrence: University Press of Kansas, 1995), p. 156; also see Larry Rohter, "2,000 U.S. Troops Land without Opposition and Take Over Haiti's Ports and Airfields," *New York Times,* September 20, 1994, A1.

44. See Donna Cassata, "Congress Bucks White House, Devises Its Own Bosnia Plan," *Congressional Quarterly Weekly Report,* June 10, 1995, 1653.

45. The events in Congress over Kosovo in the following paragraphs are outlined in Grimmett, *War Powers Resolution: After Twenty-Eight Years,* pp. 39–40.

46. Quoted in ibid., p. 46.

47. The first quote by an analyst is from ibid., p. 47, while the point about the broad authority in the second is from Richard F. Grimmett, *War Powers Resolution: Presidential Compliance,* Congressional Research Service, updated September 16, 2003, p. 16.

48. Collier, "The War Powers Resolution: Fifteen Years of Experience," pp. 9–11; and Grimmett, *War Powers Resolution: After Twenty-Eight Years,* p. 9.

49. See Glennon, *Constitutional Diplomacy,* p. 93, for a dissenting view as discussed in footnote 41.

50. Katzmann, "War Powers: Toward A New Accommodation," pp. 66–69; *Committee on Foreign Affairs, Congress and Foreign Policy 1988* (Washington, DC: U.S. Government Printing Office, 1989), p. 9; and Collier, "The War Powers Resolution: Fifteen Years of Experience," pp. 45–50.

51. See Carroll J. Doherty, "House Approves Overhaul of Agencies, Polices," *Congressional Quarterly Weekly Report,* June 10, 1995, 1655–1656; and Katharine Q. Seelye, "House Defeats Bid to Repeal 'War Powers,'" *New York Times,* June 8, 1995, A5. The first two quoted passages are by Toby Roth (R-Wisconsin). The first can be found in the former source at p. 1656, while the second can be found in the latter source, p. A5. The last quoted passage is by Lee Hamilton (D-Indiana) and can be found in the first source at pp. 1655–1656.

52. David P. Auerswald and Peter F. Cowhey, "Ballotbox Diplomacy: The War Powers Resolution and the Use of Force," *International Studies Quarterly* 41 (September 1997): 505–528.

53. Quoted in Eric Schmitt, "Senators Query U.S. Role in Bosnia," *New York Times,* October 18, 1995, A12.

54. Curt Anderson, "Bush Seeks More Powers, Money for National Safety," *Des Moines Register,* July 17, 2002, 1A.

55. The analysis of voting during the 1966–1972 period is drawn from "Congress Took 94 Roll-Call Votes On War 1966–72," *Congress and the Nation,* Volume III, 1966–1972 (Washington, DC: Congressional Quarterly Service, 1973), pp. 944–945. Senator Frank Church (D-Idaho) was able to get a defense appropriation bill amended to bar the "introduction of U.S. ground combat troops into Laos or Thailand" in 1969, and he, along with Senator John Sherman Cooper (R-Kentucky), was also able to get an amendment passed to bar "U.S. military operations in Cambodia after July 1, 1970." The quoted passages are from this source, too.

56. See P.L. 93-126 of October 18, 1973.

57. *Congressional Quarterly Almanac 1975* (Washington, DC: Congressional Quarterly, Inc., 1976), pp. 306–315.

58. See Keith R. Legg, "Congress as Trojan Horses? The Turkish Embargo Problem, 1974–1978," in John Spanier and Joseph Nogee, eds., *Congress, The Presidency, and American Foreign Policy* (New York: Pergamon Press, 1981), pp. 107–131, and especially the chronology of events at pp. 108–109 for the passage of the arms embargo.

59. See Section 404 of P.L. 94-329. 90 Stat. 757.

60. See Section 728 of P.L. 97-113.

61. See P.L. 98-151. A description of the law is provided by John Felton, "Omnibus Bill Includes Foreign Aid Programs," *Congressional Quarterly Weekly Report,* November 19, 1983, 2435–2436.

62. See Doherty, "House Approves Overhaul of Agencies, Policies," p. 1655; and Carroll J. Doherty, "Bill Slashing Overseas Aid Gets Bipartisan Support," *Congressional Quarterly Weekly Report,* June 10, 1995, 1658.

63. "Force, Diplomacy and the Resources We Need for American Leadership," address by U.S. Secretary of State Warren Christopher, U.S. Military Academy, West Point, New York, October 25, 1996, available through the Internet. In inflation-adjusted spending, the international affairs budget (spending by the Department of State, the U.S. Information Agency, the Arms Control and Disarmament Agency, and the Agency for International Development) had declined from $37.5 billion in 1984 to $18.6 billion for 1996. See Thomas W. Lippman, "The Decline of U.S. Diplomacy," *The Washington Post National Weekly Edition,* July 22–29, 1996, for a State Department table showing the yearly changes in this budget from 1984 to 1996.

64. Miles A. Pomper, "Powell Calls on Hill to Remedy State Department Underfunding," *CQ Weekly,* March 10, 2001, pp. 547–548.

65. See P.L. 107-115 at sec. 507 and sec. 523 on these prohibitions.

66. "Most Aid Earmarked," *Congressional Quarterly Weekly Report,* January 20, 1990, 198.

67. P.L 107-115. at 115 Stat. 2124-2128.

68. See sections 402 and 613 of the Trade Act of 1974 (P.L. 93-618).

69. See Section 36 of P.L. 93-559.

70. See Section 36h of P.L. 94-329. The dollar totals were subsequently raised to $50 million and $14 million, respectively. See John Felton, "Hill Weighs Foreign Policy Impact of Ruling," *Congressional Quarterly Weekly Report,* July 2, 1983, 1330.

71. See *Congressional Quarterly Almanac 1981* (Washington, DC: Congress Quarterly, Inc., 1982), p. 132.

72. The economic aid legislation was the International Development and Food Assistance Act of 1975 (P.L. 94-161). The human rights provision can be found at Section 116. In the International Security and Arms Report Control Act, the human rights provision is Section 502b.

73. See P.L. 95-118, Section 701, and P.L. 94-302, Section 28. Also see the discussion of this human rights legislation in Lars Schoultz, "Politics, Economics, and U.S. Participation in Multilateral Development Banks," *International Organization* 36 (Summer 1982): 537–574.

74. These examples are taken from Ellen C. Collier, "Congress and Foreign Policy 1992: Introduction" in Committee on Foreign Affairs, *Congress and Foreign Policy 1992* (Washington, DC: U.S. Government Printing Office, 1993), pp. 1–21; and U.S. Congress, Office of Technology Assessment, *Dismantling the Bomb and Managing the Nuclear Materials.* OTA-O-572 (Washington, DC: U.S. Government Printing Office, September 1993), p. 130.

75. Collier, "Congress and Foreign Policy 1992: Introduction," p. 6.

76. Jennifer S. Holmes, "The Colombian Drug Trade: National Security and Congressional Politics," in Ralph G. Carter, ed., *Contemporary Cases in U.S. Foreign Policy: From Terrorism to Trade* (Washington, D.C.: CQ Press, 2002), p. 103.

77. "Lawmakers Hand Clinton Big Victory in Granting China Permanent Trade Status," *Congressional Quarterly Almanac 2000* (Washington, DC: Congressional Quarterly, Inc., 2001), p. 20–23.

78. "African-Caribbean Initiative Lower Tariffs, Quotas on Some Foreign-Made

Apparel," *Congressional Quarterly Almanac 2000* (Washington, DC: Congressional Quarterly, Inc., 2001), p. 20–24; and "Iran, Libya Sanctions," *CQ Weekly,* December 22, 2001, 3039.

79. Collier, "Congress and Foreign Policy 1992: Introduction," p. 11.

80. Patrick J. Haney and Walt Vanderbush, "The Helms-Burton Act: Congress and Cuba Policy," in Ralph G. Carter, ed., *Contemporary Cases in U.S. Foreign Policy: From Terrorism to Trade,* pp. 270–290.

81. We do not mean to imply that other committees are not involved with foreign policy issues, but rather that these are the principal foreign policy authorizing committees. Appropriations, Governmental Affairs (Senate), Government Reform and Oversight (House), Judiciary, and Select Intelligence, among others, are regularly involved as well. Further, the Foreign Operations Subcommittee of the House and Senate Appropriations Committees are extraordinarily important in appropriating foreign policy funding.

82. Ellen C. Collier, "Foreign Policy by Reporting Requirement," *The Washington Quarterly* 11 (Winter 1988): 81, 77. This article is the source for the subsequent discussion as well.

83. The types of reports and the description of each are taken from ibid.

84. Committee on Foreign Affairs and Committee on Foreign Relations, *Legislation on Foreign Relations Through 1985* (Washington, DC: U.S. Government Printing Office, April 1986), p. 956.

85. *Country Reports on Economic Policy and Trade Practices,* Report to the Committee on Foreign Relations and Committee on Finance of the U.S. Senate and Committee on Foreign Affairs and Committee on Ways and Means of the U.S. House of Representatives (Washington, DC: U.S. Government Printing Office, February 1994).

86. A more complete description of reprogramming reporting is available in James M. McCormick, "A Review of the Foreign Assistance Program," memo prepared for the Office of the Honorable Lee Hamilton.

87. Collier, "Foreign Policy by Reporting Requirement," p. 80.

88. See P.L. 99-433, enacted on October 1, 1986.

89. The examples of required reporting are taken from the Committee on Foreign Relations and Committee on International Relations, *Legislation on Foreign Relations Through 1994,* Volume I-A (Washington, DC: U.S. Government Printing Office, June, 1995), pp. 658, and "Iran, Libya Sanctions," p. 3039.

90. For a more complete discussion of the changing role of the Senate Foreign Relations Committee and its oversight responsibilities, see James M. McCormick, "Decision Making in the Foreign Affairs and Foreign Relations Committees," in Randall B. Ripley and James M. Lindsay, eds., *Congress Resurgent: Foreign and Defense Policy on Capitol Hill* (Ann Arbor: University of Michigan Press, 1993), pp. 115–153.

91. *Congressional Quarterly's Guide to Congress,* p. 289.

92. Ibid.

93. Bernard Gwertzman, "Senator Planning Sweeping Hearing on Foreign Policy," *New York Times,* December 9, 1984, 20.

94. Helen Dewar, "Senate Foreign Relations Panel Founders," *Washington Post,* October 10, 1989, A12.

95. Dick Kirschten, "Where's the Bite?" *National Journal,* March 25, 1995, 739–742.

96. Ibid.

97. See P.L. 105-277.

98. Elaine Sciolino, "Awaiting Call, Helms Puts Foreign Policy on Hold," *New York Times,* September 24, 1995, 1.

99. Elaine Sciolino, "Helms to Allow Action in Senate on Clinton Diplomatic Nominees," *New York Times,* September 30, 1995, 1.

100. "Foreign Relations: The Power Broker," *CQ Weekly,* May 26, 2001, 1228.

101. Foreign Affairs is not ranked as the most popular committee in the House; it still ranks behind Ways and Means and Appropriations as a desirable committee assignment. See Fenno, *Congressman in Committees* (Boston: Little, Brown and Company, 1973), pp. 16–20. For a different ranking, see Randall B. Ripley, *Congress: Process and Policy,*

2nd ed. (New York: W. W. Norton and Company, 1978), p. 166.

102. See Fenno, *Congressman in Committees,* pp. 15–151, on the importance of the Senate Foreign Relations Committee. On the limited responsibilities of the House Foreign Affairs agenda, see ibid., pp. 213–215.

103. See Fred Kaiser, "Oversight of Foreign Policy: The U.S. House Committee on International Relations," *Legislative Studies Quarterly* 2 (August 1977): 259; and Fred M. Kaiser, "The Changing Nature and Extent of Oversight: The House Committee on Foreign Affairs in the 1970s," paper presented at the 1975 Annual Meeting of the Midwest Political Science Association, Chicago, Illinois.

104. Fred M. Kaiser, "Structural Change and Policy Development: The House Committee on International Relations," paper presented at the 1976 Annual Meeting of the Midwest Political Science Association; and Fred M. Kaiser, "Structural and Policy Change: The House Committee on International Relations," *Policy Studies Journal* 5 (Summer 1977): 443–451.

105. Interviews with majority and minority staff in June 1982, reveal that they view the committee as more liberal than the House as a whole. Also see James M. McCormick, "The Changing Role of the House Foreign Affairs Committee in the 1970s and 1980s," *Congress & The Presidency* 12 (Spring 1985): 1–20; and James M. McCormick "Decision Making in the Foreign Affairs and Foreign Relations Committees," pp. 132–137.

106. *Origins and Development of Congress* (Washington, DC: Congressional Quarterly, Inc., 1976), p. 159.

107. Kaiser, "Structural and Policy Change: The House Committee on International Relations," p. 446.

108. For a listing of the subcommittees and for a brief history of the House Foreign Affairs Committee, see *Survey of Activities, 99th Congress* (Washington, DC: Government Printing Office, 1987).

109. Kaiser, in "Structural Change and Policy Development," pp. 21–22.

110. See the data on committee and sub-committee hearings in Committee on *International Relations, Legislative Review Activities of the Committee on International Relations.* One Hundred Fourth Congress (Washington, DC: U.S. Government Printing Office, 1997), p. 123.

111. Carroll J. Doherty, "Republicans Poised to Slash International Programs," *Congressional Quarterly Weekly Report,* May 13, 1995, 1334–1336; and Carroll J. Doherty, "Gilman Under Pressure," *Congressional Quarterly Weekly Report,* May 13, 1995, 1335.

112. Miles A. Pomper, "International Relations: Rep. Henry J. Hyde of Illinois," *CQ Weekly,* January 6, 2001, 17.

113. The first study is one by Carol Goss cited in Edward J. Laurance, "The Congressional Role in Defense Policy: The Evolution of the Literature," *Armed Forces & Society* 6 (Spring 1980): 437; the second is "Armed Services Committees: Advocates or Overseers?" *Congressional Quarterly Weekly Report,* March 25, 1972, 673–677.

114. Christopher J. Deering, "Decision Making in the Armed Services Committees," in Randall B. Ripley and James M. Lindsay, eds., *Congress Resurgent: Foreign and Defense Policy on Capitol Hill* (Ann Arbor: University of Michigan Press, 1993), pp. 155–182.

115. James M. Lindsay, "Congress and Defense Policy: 1961 to 1986," *Armed Forces & Society* 13 (Spring 1987): 371–401, for a discussion of these committees in the 1970s and 1980s. As he correctly notes, the Defense subcommittees on the House and Senate Appropriations Committee are equally important—or even more important—players on defense policy issues.

116. Cited in Paul Stockton, "Beyond Micromanagement: Congressional Budgeting for a Post–Cold War Military," *Political Science Quarterly* 110 (Summer 1995): 239.

117. Pat Towell, "Armed Services: Rep. Bob Stump of Arizona," *CQ Weekly,* January 6, 2001, 14.

118. See Stockton, "Beyond Micromanagement: Congressional Budgeting for a Post-Cold War Military," pp. 237–240 for mention of Nunn's and Aspin's effort. For a fuller discussion, see Paul N. Stockton, "Congress and U.S. Military Policy Beyond the Cold War," in Ripley and Lindsay, eds.,

Congress Resurgent: Foreign and Defense Policy on Capitol Hill, pp. 235–259.

119. Pat Towell, "Armed Services: Missile Defense Skeptic," *CQ Weekly,* May 26, 2001, 1221.

120. The subsequent discussion here draws upon the insightful analyses by Eileen Burgin, "Congress and Foreign Policy: The Misperceptions," in Lawrence C. Dodd and Bruce I. Oppenheimer, eds., *Congress Reconsidered* (Washington, DC: CQ Press, 1993), pp. 333–363; and James M. Lindsay, "Congress and Foreign Policy: Avenues of Influence," in Eugene R. Wittkopf, *The Domestic Sources of American Foreign Policy: Insights and Evidence,* 2nd ed. (New York: St. Martin's Press, 1994), pp. 191–207.

121. See Barbara Hinckley, *Less Than Meets the Eye,* pp. 26–29, esp. Tables 2.1 and 2.2. Given Hinckley's definition of what to include and exclude as legislation (see p. 25), the congressional role might be somewhat understated. Also, it is not clear which legislation is initiated by Congress and which is initiated by the president.

122. See Lindsay, "Congress and Foreign Policy: Avenues of Influence," pp. 198–201. Also see his "Congress, Foreign Policy, and the New Institutionalism," *International Studies Quarterly* 38 (June 1994): 281–304.

123. See Burgin, "Congress and Foreign Policy: The Misperceptions," for the types of nonlegislative actions upon which we draw throughout this section and for more examples of these activities.

124. Grimmett, *The War Powers Resolution: After Twenty-Eight Years,* pp. 39–40.

125. Rebecca K. C. Hersman, *Friends and Foes* (Washington, DC: The Brookings Institution, 2000), p. 106.

126. Thomas M. Franck and Edward Weisband, *Foreign Policy by Congress,* (New York: Oxford University Press, 1979), pp. 6–9; and I. M. Destler, "Dateline Washington: Congress as Boss?" *Foreign Policy* 42 (Spring 1981): 167–180.

127. Jeremy D. Rosner, *The New Tug-of-War: Congress, the Executive Branch and National Security* (Washington, DC: Carnegie Endowment for International Peace, 1995).

128. Harold Hongju Koh, *The National Security Constitution* (New Haven, CT, and London: Yale University Press, 1990), p. 117.

129. Hinckley, *Less Than Meets the Eye,* pp. 5 and 47, respectively.

130. Committee on Foreign Affairs, *Congress and Foreign Policy, 1988;* and Committee on Foreign Affairs, *Congress and Foreign Policy 1987* (Washington, DC: U.S. Government Printing Office, 1989).

131. "Bush's Dozen Vetoes," *New York Times,* June 16, 1990, 8; and "State Department Bill Clears, But Faces Bush's Veto," *Congressional Quarterly Weekly Report,* November 18, 1989, 3189.

132. John G. Tower, "Congress Versus the President: The Formulation and Implementation of American Foreign Policy," *Foreign Affairs* 60 (Winter 1981–1982): 233.

133. "Pakistan Waivers," *CQ Weekly,* December 22, 2001, 3040. Also see P.L. 107-57.

134. On the difficulties of approving the Chemical Weapons Conventions, see Hersman, *Friends and Foes,* pp. 85–104.

135. Norman J. Ornstein and David W. Rohde, "Shifting Forces, Changing Rules, and Political Outcomes: The Impact of Congressional Change on Four House Committees," in Robert L. Peabody and Nelson W. Polsby, eds., *New Perspectives on the House of Representatives,* 3rd ed. (Chicago: Rand McNally, 1977), p. 259. This description, however, was before the *Chadha* decision.

136. Sciolino, "Defiant Senators Vote to Override Bosnian Arms Ban," *New York Times,* July 27, 1995, A8.

137. Haney and Vanderbush, "The Helms-Burton Act: Congress and Cuba Policy," pp. 278, 283. On the continued suspension of Title III in the Clinton and Bush administrations, see Mark P. Sullivan and Maureen Tuff-Morales, "Cuba: Issues for Congress," Congressional Research Service, January 6, 2003. Received through the CRS Web at http://www.fpc.state.gov/documents/organization.6563.pdf.

138. See Felton, "Hill Weighs Foreign Policy Impact of Ruling," pp. 1329–1330, for an assessment of the Supreme Court ruling

on the legislative veto for foreign policy, and 462 U.S. 919 (1983).

139.   Jessica Korn, *The Power of Separation* (Princeton, NJ: Princeton University Press, 1996), pp. 99–110, 116–119.

140. See Hersman, *Friends and Foes* for these cases. She also discusses the use of "holds."

141. Lee Hamilton, "The Role of the U.S. Congress in American Foreign Policy," Elliott School Special Lecture Series, The George Washington University, 1999–2000, p. 16.

142. These views are based on interviews with staff of the House Foreign Affairs Committee (June 1982), officials of the Department of State who deal with congressional relations (October 1981), some participant observation in the House of Representatives in 1986 and 1987, and continued observation of the political process.

143.   Schlesinger, "Congress and the Making of American Foreign Policy," *Foreign Affairs* 51 (October 1972): 106.

144. For a listing of suggestions for addressing this consultation problem, see Hamilton, "The Role of the U.S. Congress in American Foreign Policy," pp. 1–10.

9

The Diplomatic
and Economic
Bureaucracies:
Duplication
or Specialization?

The Armed Forces are just . . . one part of our national security team. . . .
If you confirm me, I will become the leader of one of the most vital elements.
It is the State Department and its talented and dedicated professionals
who are in the forefront of our engagement in the world.

SECRETARY OF STATE DESIGNATE COLIN POWELL
SENATE CONFIRMATION HEARING
JANUARY 17, 2001

Trade policy is the bridge between the President's international
and domestic agendas. . . . [T]he free exchange of goods
and services sparks economic growth, opportunity, dynamism,
fresh ideas, and democratic values, both at home and abroad.

ROBERT B. ZOELLICK
U.S. TRADE REPRESENTATIVE BEFORE THE HOUSE
WAYS AND MEANS COMMITTEE
MARCH 7, 2001

Although the president may dominate the Congress's role in the foreign policy process, he cannot act alone. The president needs information and advice from his assistants and the various foreign affairs bureaucracies within the executive branch to formulate policy. The president also needs the aid of the executive branch to implement any foreign policy decision. Thus, while the president may ultimately choose a foreign policy option, such as economic sanctions against Saddam Hussein in Iraq in the 1990s or the use of force against the Taliban and al-Qaeda in Afghanistan in 2001, the bureaucratic environment in which he operates greatly influences the decision process and the implementation of his choices.

The variety of agencies with an interest in foreign policy may be surprising. While the Department of Agriculture may seem primarily concerned with domestic farm issues, it also encourages the granting of foreign trade credits to countries such as Russia or Poland to promote American farm exports. While the Department of Treasury may monitor the money supply at home, it also advises the president on the need for a shift in the value of the U.S. dollar against the Euro or the Japanese yen to aid American trade abroad. While the Justice Department may be interested in controlling the use of illegal drugs at home, it also has an interest in drug production in several South American countries as well. One of the Justice Department's long-standing divisions (before it was folded into the new Department of Homeland Security), the Immigration and Naturalization Service (INS), was responsible for monitoring America's borders, but especially after September 11, 2001, it was also interested in developing cooperative arrangements with other countries to control international terrorism. More than any other department, the newly created Department of Homeland Security illustrates how domestic and foreign concerns are intermingled within an agency. In short, the principal foreign policy bureaucracies that we often think of (and even ones we may not immediately think of) compete to get the "president's ear" on international issues and to shape an outcome favorable for its bureaucracy. With the globalization of so many issues, and the growth and expansion of the agendas of many bureaucracies, understanding domestic bureaucratic politics has become critically important to understanding American foreign policy.

BUREAUCRATIC POLITICS
AND FOREIGN POLICY MAKING

The "bureaucratic politics" approach to foreign policy making stands in contrast to the earlier discussions in which we emphasized the values and beliefs of American society as a whole, the values of particular presidents and administrations, or even the effects of institutions like Congress and the presidency on United States foreign policy. This approach views the emergence of policy from the interactions among the various bureaucracies as they compete to shape the nation's actions abroad. Policy thus becomes less the result of the values and beliefs of an individual political actor in the process (although each can surely have an effect) and more the result of the interaction process between and among several bureaucracies.

Put differently, policy making is the result of the "pulling" and "hauling" among competing institutions.[1] Compromise within bureaucracies and coalition building across them become important ways in which policy ultimately emerges. In this sense, the *process* of policy making becomes an important mechanism to arrive at the substance of policy.

While the bureaucratic politics model has long been used to study domestic policy, its sustained application in foreign policy dates from the early 1970s and the imaginative work by political scientist Graham Allison on the Cuban Missile Crisis, as well as to a more general work by political analyst Morton Halperin.[2] These two pioneering analyses sparked a more general interest in this approach, and it has now become a standard mode of foreign policy analysis.

A recent study analyzed "the sale of dual-use technology to Iraq" by the United States during the 1980s and early 1990s (prior to the Persian Gulf War) through the bureaucratic politics lens and provides an illustrative example of how this approach may be applied to understanding American foreign policy.[3] According-ing to proponents of the bureaucratic politics model, "where you stand depends on where you sit." That is, the policy priority of a particular bureaucracy would likely predict its position in any decision situation.[4] In the case of arms sales to Iraq the aphorism seemed to work especially well.

On the one hand, the Department of Defense continuously argued against the sales of technology to Iraq because it potentially could be used for military pur-pose. On the other hand, the Department of Commerce argued that the promo-tion of such sales were a part of its mission and they aided America's trade balance. Interestingly, the Department of State joined the Department of Commerce in promoting export sales for its own reason: These sales served as a means of im-proving political-military ties with Iraq, an important nation in the Persian Gulf and the Middle East. The decision and implementation processes took on an even greater bureaucratic cast because policy making over controlling export policy was so dispersed within the United States government. As a result of these various factors, "the Pentagon never had a chance," according to this analyst. In short, by this account, bureaucratic politics, as contrasted to other explanations, largely ac-counted for Saddam Hussein's ability to secure American technology from 1984 through August 1990, right up to his invasion of Kuwait.

A similar bureaucratic policy debate arose in mid-2002, also over the appropri-ate policy actions toward Iraq. While some officials in the George W. Bush admin-istration favored taking immediate military actions to remove Saddam Hussein from power over his development of weapons of mass destruction, other administra-tion officials in the Department of State, including Secretary of State Colin Powell and Deputy Secretary of State Richard Armitage, raised concerns about the "risks and complexities" of such an approach.[5] Members of Congress, too, coun-seled against quick military action, as did foreign policy officials from George H. W. Bush's administration. Further, a Senate Foreign Relations Committee hear-ing in July 2002 illustrated the array of views over taking immediate action against Iraq. Finally, there were reportedly divided opinions even within the Department of Defense itself: Civilian officials there favored immediate military actions, while military officials in the Pentagon were more cautious about such actions.

The bureaucratic politics approach thus allows us to apply another perspective in order to interpret and understand American foreign policy. To apply this approach, however, we must examine the key foreign policy bureaucracies within the executive branch, describe each one's role in the policy process, and assess their relative policy influence. In this way, we begin to evaluate the relative success of some bureaucracies in the shaping of foreign policy on particular issues as compared to others.

In particular, we analyze four central foreign policy bureaucracies in detail: the Department of State, the National Security Council, the Department of Defense, and the intelligence community. We will also survey the increasing important economic bureaucracies and their role in shaping foreign economic policy. In particular, we focus on the Office of the U.S. Trade Representative, the Department of Treasury, the Department of Commerce, and the Department of Agriculture. In the last part of Chapter 10, we bring the discussion of the various bureaucracies together by showing how the individual foreign policy bureaucracies coordinate with one another through the process of forming interagency groups (IGs) or policy coordinating committees (PCC). Throughout both chapters, we discuss a crucial question of the bureaucratic politics approach: How are foreign policy choices the result of both efforts at interdepartmental coordination and interdepartmental rivalries?

THE DEPARTMENT OF STATE

The oldest cabinet post and the original foreign policy bureaucracy in the American government is the Department of State. The department was established originally in 1781 under the Articles of Confederation as the Department of Foreign Affairs and became the Department of State in 1789 with the election of George Washington.[6] Over its 215-year history, the department has evolved into a large and complex bureaucracy with a variety of functions. Among those key functions are assisting the president in policy formulation on all international issues and implementing America's foreign relations abroad. In this way, the Department of State coordinates the U.S. overseas programs that emanate from Washington, DC.[7] At the same time, the Department has had its influence weakened by internal and external problems over the years.

The Structure of State at Home

While the Department of State has always been arranged in a complex and hierarchical fashion, recent organizational changes aimed to rationalize its organizational structure and obtain greater operational efficiency.[8] In particular, the department has sought to streamline its internal structure through reorganization and restructuring of decision-making responsibilities and by downsizing its foreign operations (about 40 embassies and consulates were closed during the 1990s).

Secretary of State, Office of the Secretary, and the Executive Secretariat
Figure 9.1 displays the internal organizational structure of the Department of

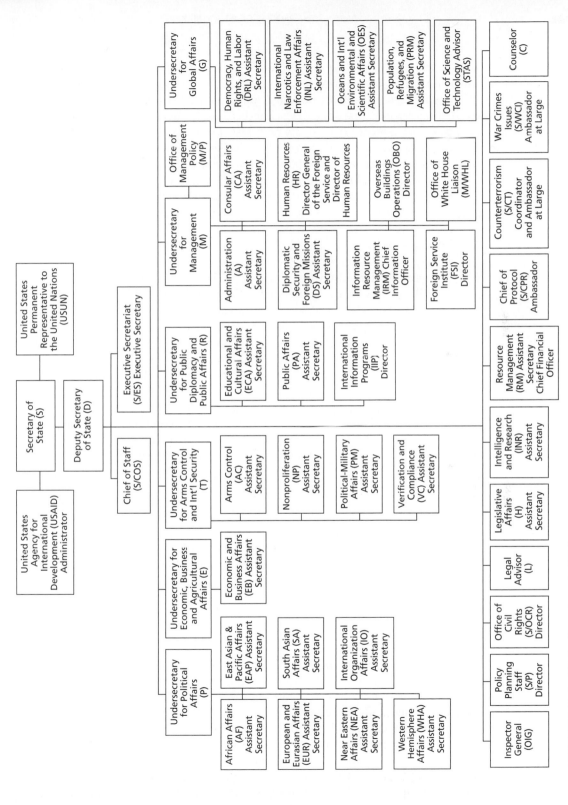

FIGURE 9.1 United States Department of State

SOURCE : http://www.state.gov/documents/organization/8792.pdf

State. At the top of the structure is the Secretary of State. The secretary is the principal foreign policy advisor to the president and, in theory, "is responsible for the overall direction, coordination, and supervision of U.S. foreign relations and for the interdepartmental activities of the U.S. government abroad."[9] The secretary's principal assistant is the deputy secretary of state, who reports directly to the secretary. Also included at the top of the organizational structure is the Office of the Secretary, consisting of the chief of staff and deputy, the executive secretary, and several staff assistants to aid the secretary. The Executive Secretariat consists of the executive secretary and four deputies. Its function is to coordinate activities among the secretary, deputy secretary, undersecretaries, and the various bureaus. It also has responsibility to work with "the White House, the National Security Council, and other Cabinet agencies."[10] Several different departmental individuals, bureaus, and activities report directly to the secretary. These range from the Policy Planning Staff, the Bureaus of Legislative Affairs, and the Bureau of Intelligence and Research to the activities of the Office of Counter Terrorism and the War Crimes Office. The overall goal of this design is to have a more sharply focused decision process among the principal policy formulators within the department than in the past.

The Role of Undersecretaries An important second level of authority is the undersecretaries, who have varying responsibilities and report directly to the secretary as well. The change to a larger number of undersecretaries was completed during the Clinton administration. It was done to strengthen their role in the policy process and to have them serve as "the principal foreign policy advisors to the Secretary."[11] These officials (and their divisions) are now responsible for managing and coordinating the principal activities under their aegis and serving as a "corporate board" to the secretary of state.

The undersecretary for political affairs now oversees the six regional bureaus (Bureau of African Affairs, Bureau of East Asian and Pacific Affairs, European and Canadian Affairs, Inter-American Affairs, Near Eastern Affairs, and South Asian Affairs) and the Bureau of International Organization Affairs. The undersecretary for economic, business, and agricultural affairs is responsible for the Bureau of Economic and Business Affairs. More important, within this Bureau is the Office of Commercial and Business Affairs. This Office "coordinates State Department advocacy on behalf of U.S. businesses," assisting American companies in gaining business access abroad, incorporating business interests in foreign policy decision making, and working with the "Commerce Department's U.S. and Foreign Commercial Service for posts where that State Department is directly responsible for trade promotion and commercial services."[12] The undersecretary for arms control and international security affairs has primary oversight of a wide range of security and defense questions through the Bureau of Political-Military Affairs, which now answers directly to this undersecretariat. The undersecretary for public diplomacy and public affairs is a recently created undersecretariat with responsibilities for such activities as educational and cultural affairs, international information programs, and public affairs. In effect, this bureau assumed responsibilities from the former United States Information Agency, when that former semiautonomous agency was folded into the Department of State in 1999. The undersecretary for global affairs manages a number of functional bureaus dealing with several different policy questions: human rights and democracy, international narcotics, environmental affairs, and population, refugees, and migration. Finally, the undersecretary for management oversees many of the common internal administrative activities of the department, ranging from operating the Foreign Service Institute, which provides language, political, cultural, and now business-promotion training for American governmental personnel assigned abroad, and managing the department's Human Resources Office. This secretariat also manages the Bureaus of Administration, Consular Affairs, Diplomatic Security and Foreign Missions, and the Office of Information Resource Management.

An assistant secretary of state (20 in all currently) heads each of the bureaus within the department's structure and answers to either the secretary's office or to the appropriate undersecretary.[13] Because the recent reorganization has emphasized the need for the undersecretaries to concentrate on broad overviews of policy, the assistant secretaries possess considerably greater latitude in policy formulation and decision making. As a result, these officials are likely to represent their bureaus within interagency groups consisting of other foreign affairs bureaucracies, in testimony before congressional committees or subcommittees, and perhaps with the secretary of state directly (although the chain of command goes through the appropriate undersecretary). Further, several functional activities were combined into new or consolidated bureaus in recent reorganizations: Several offices dealing with nuclear issues were consolidated into the Bureau of Political-Military Affairs, while several international business activities were consolidated in the Bureau of Economic and Business Affairs.

Semiautonomous Agencies Until the congressional-mandated changes in 1999, there were four semiautonomous agencies associated with the Department of State. Two of them, the United States Information Agency (USIA) and the United States Arms Control and Disarmament Agency (ACDA), were incorporated into the Department of State in 1999. USIA, created in 1953, had the tasks of explaining American policy abroad, seeking to build good relations with peoples and nations overseas, and advising the government on foreign attitudes about the United States. ACDA, created in 1961, had responsibility for fostering global arms restraint, seeking arms control agreements with other states, and monitoring compliance with agreements already in effect. The incorporation of these agencies into the Department of State was done both to streamline and improve efficiency, but it was also undertaken to provide the Department of State with greater control over these two aspects of American foreign policy. The two remaining semiautonomous agencies connected with the Department of State complete the diplomatic apparatus of the United States Government: the Office of the U.S. Permanent Representative to the United Nations and the U.S. Agency for International Development. They are also shown at the top of Figure 9.1.

The establishment of an Office for the U.S. Permanent Representative to the United Nations in the Department of State, an innovation originally undertaken by the Clinton administration, aims to allow America's UN ambassador to coordinate activities more directly with the Department of State and the Bureau of International Organization Affairs within the department. This has continued with the George W. Bush administration. During the Clinton administration, the permanent representative to the UN was on the Principals Committee of the National Security Council, but the Bush administration has not continued this practice. The U.S. Agency for International Development (USAID) was created by Congress in 1961, and is the principal foreign aid bureaucracy of the U.S. government. While USAID operates as an independent agency, it receives its "overall foreign policy guidance from the Secretary of State." Further, under the 1999 reorganization in which USIA and ACDA were folded into the Department of State, USAID also lost some of its autonomy of earlier decades. USAID's overall objectives are "to support long-term and equitable economic growth" and to advance "U.S. foreign policy objectives" in four regions of the world: sub-Saharan Africa, Asia and the Near East, Latin America and the Caribbean, and Europe and Eurasia. Its specific objectives in these regions are to promote economic growth by promoting trade and agricultural development, but it also promotes global health, the development of democracy, conflict prevention, and humanitarian assistance. More generally, USAID provides aid "to countries recovering from disaster, trying to escape poverty, and engaging in democratic reforms."[14]

Organizationally, USAID seeks to achieve these goals through a series of regional and functional bureaus and through its various AID missions or posts located in countries throughout the developing world. Its budget is quite small, at approximately one-half of one percent of the U.S. federal budget (e.g., in fiscal year 2003, the administration requested $8.5 billion),[15] but, by combining its efforts with and through private and voluntary organizations (PVOs) and nongovernmental organizations (NGOs) working around the world, USAID points to numerous successes such as saving more than three million lives yearly through its immunization program, raising literacy rates by 33 percent worldwide in the past three decades, reducing the number of undernourished people by 50 percent, eradicating smallpox worldwide, and providing assistance to millions of entrepreneurs all around the world.

The Structure of State Abroad

The State Department also has the responsibility to represent America abroad through U.S. missions, usually located in the capital city and with consulates in other major cities of host countries. As of 2003, the United States operated about 260 embassies, missions, consular agencies, consulates general, and other offices abroad.[16] It also had 10 missions at the headquarters of various intergovernmental organizations (e.g., the United Nations, the European Union, Organization of American States, and the International Civil Aviation Organization). In all, the United States conducts diplomatic relations with more than 180 nations; there are only a few nations with whom the United States does not presently have diplomatic relations: Bhutan, Cuba, Iran, and North Korea.

The U.S. embassy is headed by a chief of mission, usually an ambassador, who is the personal representative of the president and who is authorized to conduct U.S. foreign relations toward that country.[17] The ambassador is assisted by the deputy chief of mission (DCM), who is largely responsible for conducting the day-to-day operation of the embassy staff. While political, economic, consular, and administrative foreign service officers from the Department of State serve the embassy, it also has representatives from several other executive departments housed within it. The composition of the "country team" of a U.S. mission might consist of an agricultural counselor from the Department of Agriculture, a commercial counselor from the Department of Commerce, a labor official from the Department of Labor, an environmental officer from the Environmental Protection Agency, a defense attaché from the Department of Defense, and a military advisory group from the Department of Defense as well. Other agency representatives may also be present, ranging from the Drug Enforcement Agency to the Internal Revenue Service. In addition, officials from the Central Intelligence Agency—using a cover of some other positions—are often represented in the country team. In all, numerous departments and agencies serve within a single U.S. mission abroad. On average, more personnel from agencies and departments other than the Department of State often populates an embassy or mission. By one assessment, "63 percent of those now under the authority of our ambassadors and other chiefs of mission are not State Department employees."[18]

The actual size of the mission will be a function primarily of the size of the nation where the U.S. mission is located and the perceived political and strategic importance of that nation. The sizes of American missions abroad have ranged widely, from a mission with 1,100 U.S. direct hires in Germany (and an additional 800 foreign nationals) to a one-person mission in the Former Yugoslav Republic of Macedonia. By one analysis, the median size of a U.S. mission abroad in the 1990s was roughly 100—equally divided between Americans and foreign nationals.[19]

As this overview indicates, the structure of the Department of State (and its affiliated agencies) appears to be quite large and complex. Yet, in reality, the department itself is one of the smallest bureaucracies within the executive branch. Currently, the State Department has about 24,000 employees with about 4,400 foreign service officers, 3,600 foreign service specialists, 6,500 civil service personnel, and 9,730 foreign service nationals. (By contrast, the Department of Defense has about 669,000 civilian employees.[20]) It is smaller in size than all but four other cabinet departments (Department of Energy, Department of Labor, Department of Housing and Urban Development, and Department of Education).[21] Furthermore, the budget of the Department of State is one of the smallest within the government, at about $7 billion, and especially small when compared with other foreign affairs sectors of the government, such as the Department of Defense or the Central Intelligence Agency.[22]

The Weakened Influence of State

Despite its role as the principal foreign policy bureaucracy, and as the one that will usually offer the nonmilitary option for conducting foreign policy, the Department of State has been criticized for its effectiveness in both policy formulation and policy implementation.[23] As a consequence, the Department of State has not played the dominant role in recent administrations that its central diplomatic position might imply. Indeed, a departmental report has now formally acknowledged that the Department of State should not be the focus point for coordinating foreign policy. Instead, the *State 2000* report asserted "that the National Security Council (NSC) [should] be the catalyst and the point of coordination for this new, single foreign policy process."[24]

In this sense, the *policy influence* of the Department of State is comparatively less than that of other foreign policy bureaucracies in the U.S. government. The factors that have reduced the policy influence of the State Department range from a series of *internal* problems, such as its increasing budget problems, its size, the kind of personnel within this bureaucracy, the "subculture" within the organization, and the relationship between the secretary of state and the department to a series of *external* problems, such as the relationship between the president and the secretary, the relationship between the president and the department, and the perception of the public at large, as well as the growth of other foreign policy bureaucracies (e.g., the National Security Council and the Office of the U.S. Trade Representative). Let us examine several of these factors in more detail to give some sense of the weakened influence of the Department of State.

The Problem of Resources   The first problem that the Department of State faces in the competition to influence foreign affairs and to carry out its responsibilities is resources. The small operating budget of the department has been a perennial problem over the last two decades, with the Congress reluctant to fund all of its needs. By contrast, the funding for the Department of Defense and the intelligence community grew in the 1980s, suffered from budgetary pressures after the end of the Cold War, and received enlarged funding at the beginning of the new century as part of America's effort to combat global terrorism. The Department of State, however, has not enjoyed such substantial budget increases.

The Department of State's budget has increased from about $700 million in 1979 to about $7 billion in 2003, but the effects of inflation, congressional mandates for establishing new departmental bureaus, and the expansion of foreign affairs responsibilities worldwide have caused a real problem. Moreover, the Congress has not always been responsive to the department's needs and, indeed, has sought to stop some activities with which it disagrees (e.g., several controversial foreign assistance programs). In February 1987, Secretary of State George Shultz became so frustrated that he commented that state's budget problems were "a tragedy." As a result, "America is hauling down the flag. . . . We're withdrawing from the world." By November 1987, the department began hinting that 1,200 jobs would have to be eliminated, and several embassies and consulates around the world would need to be closed because of these mounting budget problems.[25]

During the Clinton administration, the closing of numerous foreign posts (consulates and embassies) had become a reality. From 1993 to 1997, the State Department closed 32 embassies and consulates. Many of these closings were consulates in peripheral locations around the world (e.g., consulates in Brisbane, Australia; Cebu, the Philippines; Udorn, Thailand; Bilbao, Spain; and Matamoros, Mexico) and represented efforts to consolidate operations within a country. A few, however, were embassies (e.g., Equatorial Guinea, Western Samoa, and the Sey-chelles).[26] Nonetheless, all of these closings reduce American presence globally and increase the workload for other posts.

In addition, reductions in State Department staff occurred as well. In May 1995, Secretary of State Warren Christopher indicated that 500 State Department positions would be eliminated to save money, streamline the policy process, and forestall even greater reductions by the Republican-controlled Congress. Six months later, the Department of State reported that more than 1,100 jobs had been trimmed.[27] By late 2001, however, this trend had started to reverse itself with the Department of State hiring "about 475 foreign service generalists (offi-cers) and about 350 foreign service specialists each year. These numbers decline marginally in FY05 but should remain at similar levels."[28]

Still, one of Colin Powell's first stops after being named Secretary of State was the U.S. Congress, to implore it to provide more funding to the department. Although Powell promised reform as part of the request for more congressional funding, he was met by some skepticism. As one member put it: "The most relevant question . . . is not have we provided enough money, but rather . . . is the State Department up to the task of responsibly managing the money it's been given and the mission given to it by the Congress?"[29]

In the views of those at the Department of State, serious policy implications accompany these continuing funding problems. First, State Department person-nel are not adequately compensated or supported under such circumstances. Start-ing salaries are relatively low in the low $30,000 to low $40,000 range (compared to similar positions in the private sector), and salary increases are often small. As a result, top-quality staff becomes more difficult to keep and less easy to recruit. While concerns have been expressed that new recruits do not match the quality of those of earlier years, regular recruiting has been forestalled, at least until recently. The foreign service exam, the principal mechanism to screen new foreign service officers, was not even offered in two years in the 1990s. Second, budget restraints also mean that individuals are asked to carry greater and greater workloads, and, inevitably, the quality of their work suffers. Third, morale also suffers as officials are asked to do more with less and, sometimes, even to work without pay. Finally, America's foreign policy representation around the world potentially pays a price in this kind of environment. Both the collection of information and implementa-tion of policy by the departmental personnel are unlikely to be as complete under such circumstances. All in all, then, from the Department of State's view, the con-tinuing budget problem reduces both the incentives and the capacities of the department for competing with other bureaucracies in shaping U.S. foreign policy.

The Problem of Size   A second problem of the Department of State, as it attempts to compete with other bureaucracies, focuses on its size. It is, at once, too large and too small. It is too large in the sense that there are "layers and layers" of bureaucracy through which policy reviews and recommendations must pro-gress. At the present time, for example, there are six geographical and eighteen functional bureaus involved in policy making. In most instances, policy recom-mendations must go through the appropriate regional and functional bureaus before they can reach the "seventh floor," where the executive offices of the department are located.

As one former secretary of state reported in his memoir, getting things done at state can be a challenge: "Different floors of 'the building' [the State Department] had their own unique views on events: 'The seventh floor [where the secretary and undersecretaries are located] won't want it that way.' 'The sixth floor [where the assistant secretaries are] wants to reclama on that.' . . . 'EUR [the Bureau of European and Canadian Affairs] is out of control.' "[30] In this sense, the structure of state's bureaucracy hinders its overall effectiveness and reduces efficiency in developing policy.

At the same time, the department has been criticized as too small, because it is dwarfed by the other bureaucracies in terms of political representation in the National Security Council interagency process (see Chapter 10). Furthermore, staff does not often carry the same domestic political clout as other large bureaucracies. Consider the lobbying power of the Department of Defense, the Department of Commerce, Department of Treasury, or even the Department of Agriculture; all these agencies have large and vocal constituencies to argue their policy position with the American people, the Congress, and, ultimately, the president. By contrast, the Department of State lacks a ready constituency within the American public to offer support and political lobbying within the Congress.[31] The State Department must therefore lobby by itself through the testimony of its officials during congressional hearings, through its informal contacts with congressional staff through the implementation of legislative action programs (LAPs), and through the interagency process. Suffice it to say, these avenues do not always yield political success for the Department of State.

The Personnel Problem A third problem of the Department of State focuses on its personnel and the environment in which they operate. Foreign service officers, foreign policy specialists, and civil service personnel from the U.S. Foreign Service comprise the principal officials of the department. Primary policy responsibility, however, rests with the approximately 4,400 foreign service officers (FSOs) in the department.[32] These officers have sometimes been depicted in the past as an "eastern elite," out of touch with the country and determined to shape policy in line with their own foreign policy views. According to this line of criticism, many of these foreign service officers share the same educational background (e.g., Princeton, Harvard, Yale, Johns Hopkins, Fletcher School of Law and Diplomacy), overrepresent the eastern establishment, and adopt a rather inflexible attitude toward global politics. However, several careful analyses of the foreign service officer corps challenge some of these stereotypes, and midcareer ("lateral entry") and minority recruitment efforts have been used for some time to address this issue.[33] Nonetheless, this elitist image persists, as more recent assessments confirm, and it reduces the effectiveness of the Department of State.[34]

At least two additional personnel problems are perceived among members of Congress, the foreign affairs bureaucracy, and the public at large. One is the charge of "clientelism," or "clientitis."[35] That is, in an FSO's zeal to foster good relations with the country in which he or she is serving, the officer becomes too closely identified with the interests of that state, sometimes at the expense of American interests and the requirements of American domestic politics. While the criticism is largely overdrawn, it becomes an important excuse of members of Congress or the executive branch who want to avoid relying too closely on the recommendations of the State Department.

Another is the level of expertise the State Department personnel and FSOs possess on increasingly specialized issues. While these individuals are undoubtedly capable generalists, the level of specific knowledge on technical subjects—and some reluctance to recruit outside experts—foster the charge that the quality of work is inadequate:

> Critics complain the State Department studies are too long and too descriptive and often unsatisfactory. Based heavily on intuition, and almost never conceptual, many of the analyses are unaccompanied by reliable sources and information, or reflect the FSO's lack of adequate training and expertise; papers are so cautious and vague as to be of little use to policymakers who long ago concluded that such "waffling" constitutes the quintessential character of the "Fudge Factory at Foggy Bottom."[36]

The other side of this personnel complaint is exactly the reverse: "The tendency to assume that others do not understand foreign affairs as well as the Foreign Service."[37] With the emergence of sound academic programs, research institutes, and Washington think tanks on many specialized issues, and with political appointees in and out of government on a regular basis, State Department FSOs should be more willing to look to these individuals for policy advice.

The Subculture Problem   Accompanying this kind of personnel problem is a related one. Even if the individuals themselves are not the source of the problem for the Department of State, the environment of the department creates a personnel problem. A bureaucratic "subculture" has developed in the State Department that emphasizes the importance of "trying to be something rather than . . . trying to do something."[38] "Don't rock the boat" is the dominant bureaucratic refrain. Because of these institutional norms, obtaining regular promotions and ensuring career advancements become more important than creating sound, innovative policy: "Subcultural norms discourage vigorous policy debate within the Department. . . . The Department is not inclined toward vigorous exploration of policy options and it is not inclined to let anyone else do the job for it."[39] Another analyst describes the subculture in this way: "The prudent course is the cautious course. 'Fitting in' has a higher value than 'standing out.'"[40]

Once again, a recent secretary of state confirms the persistence of this State Department subculture. In his experience, "the State Department has the most unique bureaucratic culture I've ever encountered."[41] While acknowledging the skills of most foreign service officers, he also found that "some of them tend to avoid risk-taking or creative thinking" because of the bureaucratic environment.[42] As a result, he found that sole reliance on State Department officials in policy making was not possible.

The President and the Secretary of State A fifth problem of the Department of State focuses on its relationship with the president and the secretary of state.[43] Postwar presidents and secretaries of state have often not made extensive use of the department for policy formulation. Instead, presidents have tried to be their own "secretary of state" or have relied on key advisors instead of the appointed secretary of state for foreign policy advice. For these reasons, the power of the secretary of state in policy making may be more apparent than real. Even when the secretary of state enjoys the confidence of the president for formulating policy, he sometimes chooses not to involve the department widely and instead relies on a few key aides. Because of these patterns, the State Department's role has once again been diminished.

The relationship between recent presidents and their secretaries of state illustrate the problem. President Richard Nixon did not view Secretary of State William Rogers as his key foreign policy advisor; instead, National Security Advisor Henry Kissinger was the primary architect of foreign policy during those years. President Carter initially tried to create a balance in policy making between Secretary of State Cyrus Vance and National Security Advisor Zbigniew Brzezinski, but he depended more on Brzezinski for shaping his response to global politics. President Reagan came to office committed to granting more control of foreign policy to the secretary of state but his national security advisors over the years proved to be quite influential in policy making.[44]

Even the two early post–World War II presidents who relied on the secretary of state for policy formulation did not often go beyond him to enlist the full involvement of the department itself. Dean Acheson and George Marshall, secretaries of state under President Harry Truman, were primarily responsible for making their own foreign policy without much input on the part of the department.[45] Similarly, John Foster Dulles, secretary of state under President Dwight Eisenhower, was given wide latitude in the formulation of foreign policy.

The recent administrations of George H. W. Bush and William Clinton tried to combine these various policy patterns. President George H. W. Bush viewed foreign policy as an area of his own expertise since he had served as U.S. ambassador to the United Nations, director of the CIA, and the American representative to the People's Republic of China. As such, he assumed a large role in policy formulation, but relied on his close friend and secretary of state, James Baker, and his national security advisor, Brent Scowcroft. By contrast, during his first term, President Clinton eschewed the importance of foreign policy and largely left its oversight to Anthony Lake, his national security advisor, and Warren Christopher, his secretary of state. In his second term, he was more directly involved, but his national security advisor, Samuel Berger, and his secretary of state, Madeleine Albright, remained key formulators of policy. Still, both Bush and Clinton placed the national security advisor and his staff at the center of foreign policy making, with ultimately a lesser role for the secretary of state.[46]

President George W. Bush's secretary of state, Colin Powell, was initially thought to have a central role to play in the shaping of American foreign policy. In the first several months of the administration, though, Secretary Powell's views appeared not to dominate Bush administration policy, as the new president veered from the secretary's view on dealing with North Korea and on policy toward Iraq.[47] After September 11, however, Secretary Powell quickly came to assume a larger role in shaping the direction of America's response to terrorism. Still, President Bush continued to rely closely on the advice of his national security advisor, Condeleezza Rice, much as recent presidents have done. Complicating the situation further for Secretary Powell was the fact that the president also sought foreign policy advice from his vice president, Dick Cheney.[48] As a result, the secretary of state in the Bush administration could not be seen as the central or only foreign policy spokesperson for the administration.

In sum, under any of the arrangements for the past six decades—where the secretary of state was primarily responsible for foreign policy, where the president relied upon other advisors for policy making, or where the president tried to be his own secretary of state—the Department of State's role in the formulation of foreign affairs has been reduced in comparison with other executive institutions or key individuals.

The President and the Department Yet another aspect of the problem between the Department of State and the president was summarized by a former foreign service officer, Jack Perry, in this way: "the Foreign Service does not enjoy the confidence of our presidents." Too often, foreign service officers are perceived as potentially "disloyal" to the president. Instead, they are seen as being loyal "either to the opposition party or else to the diplomat's own view of what foreign policy should be."[49]

The percentage of ambassadorships that go to political friends—mainly large campaign contributors with limited foreign policy experience—reflects this degree of suspicion between the president and state. These appointments reduce the opportunities available for career foreign service officers, whose aspirations may be to gain ambassadorships to cap their long service to the Department of State. While some analyses focusing on only the first year or so of an administration found somewhat higher percentage of appointments going to political friends as opposed to career diplomats,[50] the entire record of ambassadorial appointment by presidents from Kennedy through the early years of the George W. Bush administration reveals that slightly less than one-third went to political friends and campaign contributors. The percentage of such appointments ranged from 24 percent for Carter to 33 percent for Kennedy and Reagan (see Figure 9.2).

While these percentages have remained relatively stable over the past nine administrations, what these numbers fail to reveal are that some key and prestigious ambassadorships in several administrations have not gone to presumably the most skilled foreign policy officials; instead, they have gone to large campaign contributors and political allies. President Clinton, for example, appointed the late Pamela Harriman, who had contributed $132,000 to Democrats in recent years, to be ambassador to France, and a successful hotel operator in California, M. Larry Lawrence, who donated $196,000 to the Democratic party, as ambassador to Switzerland. Other large contributors received ambassadorial appointments to the Netherlands, Austria, and Barbados. For the George W. Bush administration, this trend has continued. Ambassadorships to Britain, Ireland, Canada, France, Den-

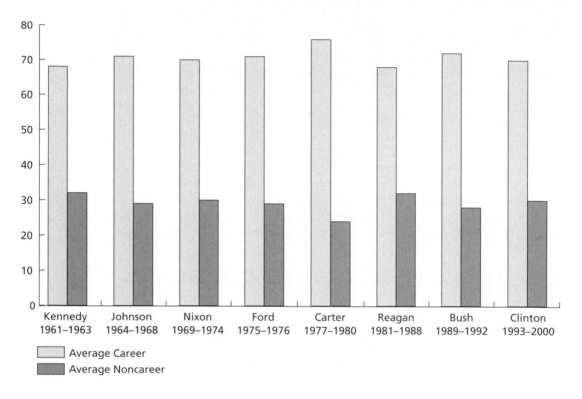

FIGURE 9.2 Percentage of Career and Noncareer Appointments as Ambassadors, Kennedy through the Clinton Administration

SOURCE: American Foreign Service Association at http://www.afsa.org/ ambassadorsgraph2.html, accessed on August 19, 2002.

mark, the Vatican, and Switzerland, among others, went to prominent political donors and key political friends. Will Farish, a family friend of Bush's, and Richard Egan, a major political contributor, were appointed to London and Dublin, respectively. Stuart Bernstein, who previously headed a Republican National Committee for donors contributing $100,000 or more, was appointed to Copenhagen, and Howard Leach, who contributed $282,000 to Bush and others, to Paris. Former Massachusetts governor Paul Cellucci was assigned to Ottawa, former senator and presidential chief of state Howard Baker to Tokyo, and former chair of the Republican National Committee Jim Nicholson to Vatican City.[51]

Aside from the influence of money in politics, critics see serious problems with such appointments from a policy point of view. They reduce the role of the Department of State in the foreign policy process, and the political appointees' inexperience may be damaging to the conduct of U.S. foreign policy. Furthermore, these ambassadors may feel much freer to circumvent the State Department in shaping policy and use "back channels" to the White House. In doing so, they alienate the career personnel within an embassy and further weaken an orderly foreign policy process. One senator described such appointments starkly: They are "ticking time bombs moving all over the world."[52]

The U.S. ambassador to a small Asia–Pacific nation, and a political appointee of the Clinton administration, however, defends these kinds of appointments. The political appointee as ambassador, he argues, has better access to the president than nonpolitical appointees. Furthermore, the president may be more willing to listen to his or her personal appointee than to a career diplomat. The Australian ambassador to the United States, commenting on the American political appointments sent to his country as ambassador, made the same point in a different way: "What you want is a quality person who is taken seriously in his own capital."[53] In this way, these kinds of appointments may actually enhance American diplomacy by better serving both the United States and the host country.

The use of political appointees within the Department of State and the weighing of political loyalties in appointing foreign service officers as ambassadors also exemplify the often-found suspicion between state and the president. One tactic, for instance, has been to engage in a "purge" of bureaus and personnel that were perceived as not fully committed to the administration's policy. The Bureau of Inter-American Affairs suffered this fate early in the Reagan administration because it was not fully in tune with the priorities of the White House. The assistant secretary of state of this bureau was replaced with a career diplomat perceived as more loyal to the administration's goal, albeit lacking in Latin American experience. When the diplomat began to waver on policy, he was ultimately replaced by a political appointee who was a staunch conservative and wholly committed to the policy of aiding the Nicaraguan Contras.[54]

The George H. W. Bush administration employed a number of political appointees, particularly at the top of the State Department bureaucracy. The four key political operatives for Secretary of State James Baker came from outside the department, and one of them was responsible for screening all papers that reached the secretary. By one account, the department's attitude "evolved from deep hostility to ambivalence" toward Baker and these appointees. The career foreign service people "felt altogether shut out for a time. . . ."[55] They were, however, pleased that Secretary Baker was personally close to the president because, if they could break through to the leadership, they could play a greater role in policy making.

For the Clinton administration, the most notable political appointment within the Department of State was President Clinton's longtime friend and one-time Oxford University roommate and a former journalist, Strobe Talbott.[56] Talbott was initially appointed as an ambassador at large with special responsibilities to the Secretary of State regarding policy toward the former Soviet Union. By the end of President Clinton's first year in office, however, Talbott was appointed as deputy secretary of state, with numerous career officers being passed over. With his new title, Talbott largely continued his work on policy toward Russia, and his policy importance was manifest in that "only Talbott was in the room for Clinton's one-on-one with Yeltsin," during a Moscow summit in 1994.[57]

Sometimes, the policy direction of an administration can cause grumbling within the State Department ranks and the political appointments to state by an administration can cause problems elsewhere, notably in Congress. In early 1994, five State Department officials resigned from the Clinton administration and others protested to the secretary over Bosnia policy.[58] While some were surely unhappy over the failure to heed the views of the foreign policy analysts within the Department and over policy changes by the administration, morale still remained "level," according to one close observer.[59] For the George W. Bush administration, the appointment of staunch conservatives to two important State Department posts, John Bolton as undersecretary for arms control and international security, and Otto Reich as assistant secretary for Inter-American affairs, caused delays and drew criticism from the Senate.

Overall, then, the role of the career officials at the Department of State continues to erode, with increasing numbers of political appointees, both as ambassadors and as key departmental leaders. In a slightly different context, one former foreign service officer perhaps said it best almost two decades ago: "Creeping politicization has corrupted foreign service professionalism." In turn, this former FSO added, politicization "has hindered American diplomacy."[60]

The Public's View A final reason for the Department of State's weakened influence derives from the domestic setting: The department has never really enjoyed a sound reputation among the American public. Beyond the view that the State Department is out of step with the nation as a whole, members of Congress and the executive branch have also called for making the department more efficient and effective. While the negative public image has perhaps waned over the decades, it, along with the other restraints evident within the department, has produced a certain caution in policy choices advanced by State Department personnel.

THE NATIONAL SECURITY COUNCIL

The National Security Council (NSC) and its staff remains the bureaucracy that has enlarged its role in the foreign policy process over the last four decades. The NSC has grown from a relatively small agency with solely a policy-coordinating function to one with a separate bureaucratic structure and major policy-making function. Its head, now designated as the assistant to the president for national security affairs (or the national security advisor), is viewed as a major formulator of U.S. foreign policy, often surpassing the influence of the secretary of state and the secretary of defense.

Because of this evolution, an important distinction ought to be kept in mind as we discuss two different, but related, bureaucratic arrangements operating under the "National Security Council" label. One bureaucratic arrangement refers to the "NSC system" and focuses on the departmental memberships on the National Security Council itself and the subsequent interagency working groups established by presidents to coordinate policy making across the existing bureaucracies. That coordination process remains intact and is the focus of the last portion of Chapter 10. The other bureaucratic arrangement, and one that has become more commonly discussed lately, refers to the "NSC staff" (or simply "the NSC"), the separate bureaucracy that has developed over the years and which has increasingly played an independent role in U.S. foreign policy making.[61] The following discussion focuses on the growth of that bureaucracy and its policy-making role and leaves the discussion of the NSC system to the next chapter.

The Development of the NSC Bureaucracy

As originally constituted under the National Security Act of 1947, the National Security Council was to be a mechanism for coordinating policy options among the various foreign affairs bureaucracies. By statute, members were to be limited to the president, the vice president, secretary of state, and secretary of defense, with the director of central intelligence and the chairman of the Joint Chiefs of Staff as advisors; these members, along with others that the president might choose to invite, met to consider policy options at the discretion of the president.[62] Over time, the NSC system has evolved with a set of interdepartmental committees to support the National Security Council itself.

Table 9.1 portrays the composition of the National Security Council under the George W. Bush administration. The composition includes those required by statute, but it also included the assistant to the president for national security (national security advisor), the chief of staff to the president, and the assistant to the president for economic policy. Other possible attendees for specific topics include the counsel to the president, the attorney general, and the director of the office of management and budget. In addition, the heads of other departments or senior officials may be invited to attend NSC meetings. What is important to note about these attendees is that economic advisors to the president attend, a pattern begun by the Clinton administration, and that other officials (e.g., attorney general, president's chief of state) who might normally not deal with foreign policy are also present.[63]

Under the original legislative mandate for the National Security Council, the assumption was that the staff of the NSC was to be small and its responsibilities focused largely on facilitating the coordination of activities among the various foreign affairs departments. Indeed, the NSC staff originally had only three major components: "(a) the Office of the Executive Secretary; (b) a Secretariat . . . and (c) a unit simply called 'the staff.'" The executive secretary and the secretariat were the permanent employees and generally undertook the actual coordinating activities of the council. The staff "initially consisted wholly of officials detailed on a full-time basis by the departments and agencies represented on the Council" and was assisted by a full-time support group as well.[64] Their responsibilities focused on preparing studies on various regional and functional questions. Nonetheless, the staff members continued to maintain and coordinate their work with the respective departments from which they were drawn. Coordination across departments appeared to be more important than an independent assessment that they might undertake.

Table 9.1 Composition of the National Security Council

Regular Attendees (Statutory and Nonstatutory)
President
Vice President
Secretary of State
Secretary of Treasury
Secretary of Defense
Assistant to the President for National Security Affairs
Director of Central Intelligence (attends as advisor)
Chairman of the Joint Chiefs of Staff (attends as advisor)
Other Attendees
Chief of Staff to the President
Assistant to the President for Economic Policy
Counsel to the President
Attorney General
Director of the Office of Management and Budget

SOURCE: National Security Presidential Directive 1, The White House, Washington
DC, February 13, 2001, at http://www.fas.org/irp/offdocs/nspd/nspd-1.html.

Presidents Truman and Eisenhower used the NSC as a coordinating body, too. Because President Truman had relatively strong secretaries of state, and because he tended to employ them for policy advice, he used the National Security Council meetings primarily as an arena for the exchange of ideas (often not attending the meetings himself until the outbreak of the Korean War). President Eisenhower, by contrast, met with the National Security Council on almost a weekly basis and relied upon it for decision-making discussions. (By one account, Eisenhower attended 306 out of 338 NSC meetings during his presidency.) Actual policy decisions, however, seemed to have been made outside this forum, especially as Secretary of State John Foster Dulles gained decision-making influence.[65] For neither of these presidents, though, was the NSC staff the independent policy influencer that it was to become.

Under Eisenhower, however, the structure and staff of the National Security Council bureaucracy began to change and gain some greater definition. Eisenhower, for instance, created the post of special assistant to the president for national security affairs for Robert Cutler and named him the "principal executive officer" of the NSC.[66] The staff structure was also revamped and enlarged, and the mandate and duties of the NSC itself expanded. Most notably, President Eisenhower stated that members of the NSC were "a corporate body composed of individuals advising the President in their own right, rather than as representatives of their respective departments and agencies." In a later revision, however, he did indicate that "the views of their respective departments and agencies" ought to be stated as well.[67] While Cutler and the NSC staff continued to perform their coordinating role, President Eisenhower's statements were the first hints of a more independent policy role for the NSC bureaucracy and its staff. Moreover, such a view of the NSC bureaucracy would eventually become a reality during the succeeding administrations.

The Rise of the National Security Advisor

By the time of the Kennedy administration, the role of the National Security Council began to change, and a more prominent role for the national security advisor ("special assistant for national security affairs") emerged. Now more reliance was placed on key ad hoc advisors, including the national security advisor, but not on the NSC as such by the president. In fact, few meetings of the council were held during the Kennedy years. Instead, the national security advisor began to emerge as a source of policy making, rather than as only a policy coordinator. As a result of Kennedy's reorganization of the NSC staff, the national security advisor had a number of previous staff responsibilities consolidated into his office. As a consequence, McGeorge Bundy became the first national security advisor to serve in a policy-formulating and policy-coordinating capacity.[68]

The role of national security advisor was enhanced even more during the administration of President Lyndon Johnson. Walt W. Rostow, successor to Bundy during much of President Johnson's term, and a small group of advisors (the "Tuesday Lunch" group) played an increasingly large role in the formulation of American foreign policy, and especially Vietnam policy.[69] As during the Kennedy years, the national security advisor gained influence, but the National Security Council, as a decision or discussion forum, actually declined in importance.

The full implication of this changed decision-making style became most apparent during the administration of President Richard Nixon.[70] In particular, the appointment of Henry A. Kissinger as national security advisor further transformed the use of the national security advisor in foreign policy making. Henry Kissinger, an academic and consultant to previous administrations, was familiar with, and critical of, the bureaucratic machinery of government. In large measure, he saw the bureaucracy as being an impediment to effective policy making and as hindering the job of the "statesman."[71] Through his considerable personal skill, Kissinger was able to reorganize the decision-making apparatus of the foreign policy bureaucracies so that he was able to dominate all the principal decision machinery, and the National Security Council and staff were to become the focal point of all policy analyses.

Kissinger accomplished this transformation through the development of a series of interdepartmental committees flowing from the National Security Council system. These committees included representatives from the other principal foreign policy bureaucracies, but, at the same time, they excluded those institutions from ultimate authority for making policy recommendations. In fact, Kissinger set up a senior review group, which he himself chaired, for examining all policy recommendations before they were sent to the National Security Council and the president.[72] Even when Kissinger became secretary of state (as well as national security advisor) in September 1973, and when Gerald Ford became president in August 1974, this pattern of National Security Council staff dominance continued.

The National Security Advisor:
The Carter and Reagan Administrations

Under President Jimmy Carter, the initial impulse was to reduce the role of the national security advisor and his staff (partly in reaction to the role that Henry Kissinger had played in the previous eight years) and to place more responsibility for foreign policy in the hands of the secretary of state. More accurately, President Carter's goal was to balance the advice coming to the president from the secretary of state and from the national security advisor. The elaborate NSC committee system developed during the Kissinger years was initially pared back to only two.[73] Ultimately, however, National Security Advisor Zbigniew Brzezinski was able to play a more dominant role in the shaping of foreign policy and to work his will in the policy process due to the force of his personality, his strong foreign policy views, and the challenge of global events (e.g., the seizure of American diplomats in Iran in November 1979 and the Soviet invasion of Afghanistan in December 1979).[74] This development only continued the pattern of moving away from the Department of State and toward the national security advisor in the formulation of American foreign policy.

Under the Reagan administration, a return to the earlier pattern of collegial policy making was once again attempted. President Reagan's first secretary of state, Alexander Haig, came to office determined to restore the dominance of the Department of State (and especially the office of secretary) and to make himself the "vicar" of foreign affairs. In part to facilitate this reversion to the earlier model of policy making, a relatively inexperienced foreign policy analyst, Richard Allen, was appointed by President Reagan to be the national security advisor. In this environment, it seemed possible that the secretary of state could reassert his authority as the dominant force in the shaping of policy.

Although Secretary of State Haig achieved some initial success in shaping the foreign policy of the Reagan administration, he failed to dominate the process. Ultimately, he was forced to resign when policy frictions developed among the White House staff and the secretaries of state and defense and when a new national security advisor, William Clark, who was closer to President Reagan, was appointed. Power seemed to be shifting more perceptibly back to the White House and the national security advisor.

George Shultz, Haig's successor as secretary of state, appeared to be given some latitude in policy making, but National Security Advisor William Clark soon eclipsed this role. A series of events reflected this shift in decision making. Whether over arms control policy (e.g., the Strategic Defense Initiative), Central American policy (the removal of the ambassador to El Salvador and the firing of the assistant secretary of state for Inter-American affairs), or Middle Eastern policy (e.g., a change in the President's personal representative), the decisions once again illustrated the shift in policy dominance toward the NSC and away from the Department of State.[75] Indeed, by one assessment, Clark "became the most influential foreign policy figure in Reagan's entourage" in a very short time.[76] The shift was so perceptible that Shultz reportedly complained directly to the president that he could not do his job effectively if foreign policy decisions were made without his participation.[77]

Only under Clark's successor as NSC advisor, Robert McFarlane, and after the disclosure of the Iran–Contra affair did Shultz gain policy dominance. Because McFarlane was not personally close to President Reagan and because he felt constrained by the president's insistence on "cabinet-style" government, the pattern began to change somewhat. Still, crucial national security decision directives were issued by McFarlane's office, often without prior departmental clearance.[78] After November 1986 and the domestic political fall-out from the Iran–Contra affair, things changed more perceptibly.

While the Iran–Contra affair in one sense demonstrated the extent to which the NSC had dominated policy making (after all, the episode seemed to be directed entirely by individuals within the NSC), it also showed the dangers of such a procedure. Both investigations of this affair—the presidential inquiry, known as the Tower Commission, and the report of the two congressional committees—cited the dangers of allowing the National Security Council staff to run covert operations without presidential accountability, faulted the poor operation of the NSC system under the Reagan administration, and recommended reforms in the decision-making system itself.[79] After the firing of John Poindexter as national security advisor, Poindexter's two successors—first, Frank Carlucci and then Colin Powell—were much more inclined to serve as policy coordinators than as policy formulators. As a result, Secretary of State George Shultz increasingly dominated the policy process.

The National Security Advisor:
The George H. W. Bush and Bill Clinton Administrations

At least by formal design, the Bush administration returned to a more familiar pattern of NSC dominance of foreign policy making. In National Security Directive 1 (NSD-1), President Bush placed his national security advisor, Brent Scowcroft, and his deputy at the head of the foreign policy-making machinery by appointing them as chairs of the two key coordinating committees of the NSC system: the NSC/Principals Committee and the NSC/Deputies Committee (see Chapter 10 for details on these committees).[80] As heads of these two committees, the NSC and its staff were in a strong position to dominate the Departments of State and Defense in the shaping of policy. Further, the national security advisor, albeit in consultation with the secretaries of state and defense, was given responsibilities for establishing appropriate interagency groups to develop policy options, as the need arose.

With James Baker as secretary of state and with Baker's close personal ties to President Bush, some raised doubts about Scowcroft's ability to dominate the process. However, with his previous experience as national security advisor under President Ford and with his background in bureaucratic politics, Scowcroft fared quite well. He did not seek the limelight, he put together a staff that was generally applauded, and he quickly undertook a broad review of American policy. Content to allow Baker to do more of the public relations side of foreign policy (e.g., congressional relations and trips abroad), Scowcroft ultimately was identified as the principal molder and the real "mover and shaker" of American foreign policy within the foreign policy hierarchy.[81]

Clinton's first national security advisor, Anthony Lake, was cut from the same cloth as Scowcroft and was less like, say, a Kissinger or Brzezinski in carrying out this foreign policy assignment. Lake did not seek the limelight and rarely got it. By one assessment, he was "surely the only national security advisor ever to stand beside the President in a *New York Times* photograph and be described as an 'unidentified' man."[82] While that comment surely understated his importance, it conveyed his style of influence: a quiet, behind-the-scenes approach.

Lake's influence derived from his geographical closeness to the president and Clinton's limited foreign policy experience and foreign policy interest. He saw the president every day to brief him on global development and served as the arbiter among the conflicting bureaucracies whether State, Defense, or the intelligence community. While Lake said that he was careful "that the President is getting all points of view," he also offered his own views. As he gained more confidence in his role, Lake assumed a more assertive posture in the policy debate. He was more likely to assert his own position sooner in the process "because it helps move issues to a resolution."[83] Despite a self-effacing personal style, Lake, after the president and vice president, was perhaps "the most powerful influence on foreign affairs."[84]

Lake's successor was his former deputy, Samuel (Sandy) Berger, appointed in December 1996. As with Lake, he appeared to enjoy considerable policy influence, based upon his knowledge of foreign affairs and his close ties with the president. He had previously worked for Lake in the Department of State during the Carter administration and, in turn, worked for four years as Lake's top aide on the National Security Council during Clinton's first term. In addition, he had a long personal relationship with President Clinton, beginning with their involvement in the McGovern campaign for president in 1972. In time, moreover, he came to dominate the foreign policy process and to eclipse the influence of the secretary of state, Madeleine Albright.[85]

The National Security Advisor: George W. Bush Administration

With the arrival of the George W. Bush administration, the same question emerged over whether the national security advisor would again come to dominate the foreign policy-making process. For several reasons, the national security advisor might not. First, the foreign policy credentials of the new secretary of state, Colin Powell, seemed to indicate that he would be able to eclipse the national security advisor. After all, Powell has served in several previous administrations, starting with the Nixon administration, was national security advisor for a time during the Reagan administration, and also was Chairman of the Joint Chiefs of Staff during parts of the George H. W. Bush and Clinton administrations. Second, the national security advisor appointed by President Bush, Condoleezza Rice, although personally close to Bush and with experience on President George H. W. Bush's NSC staff, indicated that she would not be a "policy initiator or implementer."[86] Instead, she saw her role, according to administration officials, as ensuring that the president was properly briefed and as "serving as an honest broker of differences among the major policy players." Rice also indicated that she intended to be seen and heard less than the previous national security advisor, Sandy Berger. Third, Rice reorganized and trimmed the national security staff as a means of producing a more efficient staff operation: Three regional offices of the NSC staff were consolidated into directorate on Europe and Eurasia, a new Asia/Southeast Asia directorate and an Africa/Near East directorate were created, other functional offices were combined into a single directorate for democracy, human rights, and international operations. In addition, the professional staff was trimmed from 100 to 70 in a further effort to streamline operations.[87]

Despite this initial intention to move back toward a policy coordinating role for the national security advisor and staff, Condoleezza Rice has, in fact, come to play a major role in policy formulation and implementation. At the outset of the Bush administration, some policy differences—over dealing with North Korea, the role of the United States in the Middle East, and policy toward China—developed. In these initial bureaucratic struggles, the national security advisor's position appeared to prevail more than the secretary of state. Part of the reason was that President Bush's "comfort level is highest with her," compared to other foreign policy advisor, according to one administration source.[88] As a result, he tended to rely upon her more than others. Indeed, by August 2001, questions were being raised about the role of the secretary of state in foreign policy making. In addition, rather than being invisible in discussing foreign policy matters as initially suggested, Rice appeared to be very much in the limelight with numerous media interviews.

The events of September 11 brought Secretary of State Powell and Secretary of Defense Rumsfeld back onto the center stage of foreign policy making, and the national security advisor was a bit less evident. Moreover, Powell and Rumsfeld largely directed the immediate American response toward the Taliban and al-Qaeda in Afghanistan. Still, on other major foreign policy issues facing the administration—notably national missile defense and policy toward Iraq—National Security Advisor Rice often took the lead for the administration. Moreover, at least one assessment saw the decision making after September 11 as aiding the national security advisor since more NSC meetings were being held (three a week rather than twice a month) and the president's involvement on foreign policy discussion and decisions were now much more regular and more intense.[89] Furthermore, when postwar reconstruction efforts appeared to falter in Iraq, President Bush appointed Condoleezza Rice to head a new NSC group to coordinate policy more directly from the White House on this crucial foreign policy issue. In this sense, it is "'madness' to think that the genie of NSC dominance [on foreign policy making] can or should be put back in the lamp."[90]

WHY TWO DEPARTMENTS OF STATE?

With the National Security Council and the Department of State competing for influence, the foreign policy apparatus of the United States has actually evolved into what political scientist Bert Rockman calls two Departments of State.[91] There are now "regular" channels (through the Department of State) and "irregular" channels (through the National Security Council) for foreign policy making. Yet, even this simple division is too narrowly drawn in reality; instead, the division ought to be stated more boldly. The division is really between the irregular channels, epitomized by the National Security Council, and the regular channels, including the Department of State and all the other foreign policy bureaucracies with foreign policy responsibilities. After all, the NSC controls the interagency process within the government (as we shall discuss in Chapter 10). Still, it is important to consider why these irregular processes have been in ascendancy and have actually come to dominate the foreign policy process, and why the regular channels have lost ground as a result.

System overload is one reason.[92] Overload refers to the tremendous amount of information and policy analyses available to the president from the various regular bureaucracies. With the end of the Cold War and the expansion of the foreign policy issue agenda, the national security staff provides a ready arena for coordinating and distilling such a volume of material for the president—something that a single formal bureaucracy would not likely be able to do.[93] As Rockman acknowledges, however, while overload might account for the coordination of policy within the NSC, it does not actually explain the decision-making growth of the NSC system. For this explanation, he looks to institutional and organizational arrangements within the foreign policy bureaucracies and the political culture within Washington.

Because the bureaucracies have their own parochial interests to protect, political advantage is often sought by one institution over another. A favorite tactic is the use of the press leak to undermine some unfavorable policy or position, especially in politically conscious Washington. This approach, moreover, is particularly endemic to the personnel in the regular channels, who believe that they are being left out of the decision process or who have, inevitably, divided loyalties—to the president on the one hand, and to their institutions on the other. Individuals in the irregular channels, however, would be less prone than disgruntled departmental officials to "go public" over a policy dispute, bound as they are to the president by appointment and ideology. Therefore, to protect his policy options, the president would prefer the confidentiality of his White House staff and the NSC system.

Along with the political rivalries, the regular channels (i.e., the Department of State) have institutional norms and bureaucratic subcultures that would be more prone to deflect (or "bury") innovative policy ideas that diverge too greatly from the status quo. By contrast once again, the irregular channels, presumably more committed to innovation and more committed to translating the president's views into policy, would be receptive to new ideas and might well be the catalyst of policy change themselves. In this way, too, the president's preferred position can be put into effect more quickly.

Finally, the political culture of Washington only exacerbates these bureaucratic tendencies. Because the nation's capital operates on "bureaucratic politics" (the competition between departments), the president is constantly in danger of becoming only an arbitrator between agencies, rather than a policy maker, if he cannot control this infighting. Since the ties between the White House and the departments are never as strong as between the White House and its immediate staff, there is a tendency for a "we versus them" relationship to develop between these two groupings, with an attempt to isolate the departments. If the national security advisor and her/his staff are performing their role properly, they can be the "honest broker" for the president on policy options.[94] In this way, incentives exist for the executive to feel more confident making foreign policy through his staff rather than through regular departments, including the Department of State.

BUREAUCRACIES AND FOREIGN ECONOMIC POLICY MAKING

Our discussion in this chapter so far has focused on two key foreign affairs bureaucracies that deal primarily with the political aspects of policy making. In the next chapter, we focus on bureaucracies that deal with military or quasi-military (covert operations) aspects of policy making. Yet a third aspect of the foreign policy-making bureaucracy addresses economic questions. While those bureaucracies are often avoided or given cursory treatment in books on foreign policy, they are increasingly crucial to the actions of the United States abroad.[95] After all, roughly 25 percent of the American economy comes from international trade, and jobs tied to international exports accounted for about 25 percent of the private sector jobs created in the early years of the 1990s.[96] As more foreign policy questions address issues of international economics and finance such as trade, debt policy, and investment, American foreign policy making becomes, more than ever, foreign economic policy making. Indeed, the Clinton administration recognized the importance of economic security as a foreign policy during its tenure, and the George W. Bush administration continues to emphasize its importance, especially after the economic shock that the events of September 11 produced.

Several bureaucracies that were often viewed as dealing only with domestic policy have actually emerged over the last four decades to assume important roles in shaping America's foreign economic policy. To illustrate both the breadth and growth of these bureaucracies, we identify several of them, describe the principal ways in which they contribute to foreign policy making, and discuss some issues with which they have been associated recently. We shall first discuss the newest economic bureaucracy, the Office of the U.S. Trade Representative, then turn to discuss the role of the Departments of State and Defense in economic issues, and finally describe the responsibilities of the Department of Treasury, Department of Commerce, and Department of Agriculture in the area of foreign economic policy. Some of these bureaucracies are more pivotal than others, and we shall try to specify the importance of each one.

Before we proceed, however, we ought to note several important characteristics of policy formulation in the foreign economic area, especially as it relates to trade policy.[97] First, only in the twentieth century (and usually dating from the passage of the Reciprocal Trade Agreements Act of 1934) has the executive branch assumed a lead role in the trade policy area, even though Congress still retains the constitutional prerogative to regulate foreign commerce. Second, the executive branch has increasingly been the focus point for trade policy making, especially since recent presidents have been granted "fast-track authority" (now labeled "trade promotion authority" during the George W. Bush administration) by Congress to expedite negotiations with other nations. This authority gives the executive branch the authority to negotiate trade pacts and limits congressional action to an up-or-down vote, without amendments, of any trade agreement negotiated by the president. Third, the formulation of trade policy is often quite diffuse within the executive branch. Some decisions are made wholly within a particular bureaucracy (e.g., at the deputy assistant secretary level in one of the relevant departments), others are made at the interagency group level (through coordination among the bureaucracies), and still others are ultimately resolved by the president. Fourth, various bureaucracies are more likely to deal with different aspects of international economic policy (e.g., import policy/export policy or international debt financing). Such dispersion reinforces the decentralized nature of foreign economic policy. The principal consequence of these various characteristics is that, perhaps more than other foreign policy-making questions, the process is highly subject to the vagaries of bureaucratic politics.

Office of the U.S. Trade Representative

The most important foreign economic bureaucracy is the newest and the smallest: the Office of the U.S. Trade Representative. It has been described the "*primus inter pares*" (first among equals) within the executive branch and is responsible "for developing and coordinating U.S. trade, commodity, and direct investment policy" and for "leading negotiations with other countries on these matters."[98] The U.S. Trade Representative has cabinet-level status and acts as "the President's principal trade advisor, negotiator, and spokesperson on trade and related investment matters."[99] Further, the USTR, both the agency and the individual heading the office, has wide-ranging responsibilities for coordinating the interagency process within the United States government, leading trade delegations abroad, and preparing policy questions for presidential decision making. As a result, the USTR has been at the center of such negotiations as the North American Free Trade Agreement (NAFTA), the creation of the World Trade Organization (WTO) from the General Agreements on Tariffs and Trade (GATT), the negotiations with China for establishing permanent normal trading relations (PNTR), and, more recently, for developing and promoting the Free Trade of the Americas (FTAA) initiative.

The creation of the Office of the USTR is relatively new, and its role in directing trade policy is even more recent. The USTR, congressionally mandated by the Trade Expansion Act of 1962, was formally established by an executive order in 1963.[100] Only in the 1970s and 1980s, however, were its powers and responsibilities enhanced. In the Trade Act of 1974, USTR gained cabinet-level status and assumed responsibility for coordinating policy on trade matters. By an executive reorganization plan in 1980, its responsibilities expanded even further when its head was designated as the "chief trade negotiator" and as America's official representative to the major trade organizations. In addition, the staff of the office doubled in size to about 80. With the passage of the Omnibus Trade and Competitiveness Act of 1988, the powers of the Office of the USTR were reaffirmed, and the head of the office (the USTR) was designated as having primary responsibility for undertaking trade retaliation actions against unfair trading partners of the United States (section 301 of the act). Furthermore, the staff of USTR continues to grow, almost doubling once again to about 150 by the late 1990s.[101]

As Figure 9.3 shows, the organizational structure of the USTR has become increasingly complex, too. The office has special negotiators on textile and agricultural issues, and it also has two deputy USTRs, headquartered in Washington, with responsibilities for America's trade with different regions and in different functional areas. A third deputy USTR has primary responsibility for monitoring WTO activities at that organization's headquarters in Geneva. Finally, the office has designated staff to deal with Congress and intergovernmental affairs and to coordinate its activities with important parts of the private sector (e.g. labor and industry).

In the policy-making area, the USTR has primary responsibility for coordinating and chairing two important interagency committees on trade policy.[102] The first is the Trade Policy Staff Committee (TPSC), the principal operating committee with a wide array of representation throughout the government, encompassing more than 60 subcommittees to deal with a myriad set of trade questions. The second is the Trade Policy Review Group (TPRG), composed of the deputy USTR and undersecretary level appointees from other federal agencies and offices. The TPRG resolves questions that the Trade Policy Staff Committee cannot resolve and addresses particularly important policy questions. Importantly, the TPRG fits into the "NSC system" (see Chapter 10) as one of the separate policy-coordinating committees within that larger structure. The final component of this interagency system for trade policy making is the National Economic Council (NEC).[103] This council, established by the Clinton administration and continued by the George W. Bush administration, was created to give more prominence to economic issues (both domestic and foreign) in the policy process. The NEC is ultimately headed by the president and has ultimate decision-making authority on trade policy questions theoretically beyond the USTR.

The Office of the USTR also represents the convergence of trade policy making in two other important ways: It serves as a focal point for congressional involvement in affecting trade policy making, and it serves as the formal contact point for a series of private-sector advisory groups on trade-related policy questions. Beginning with the Trade Act of 1974, and through expansion in subsequent legislation (e.g., the Trade Acts of 1979 and 1988), five members of the House and the Senate serve as official advisors to the USTR. Similarly, the private

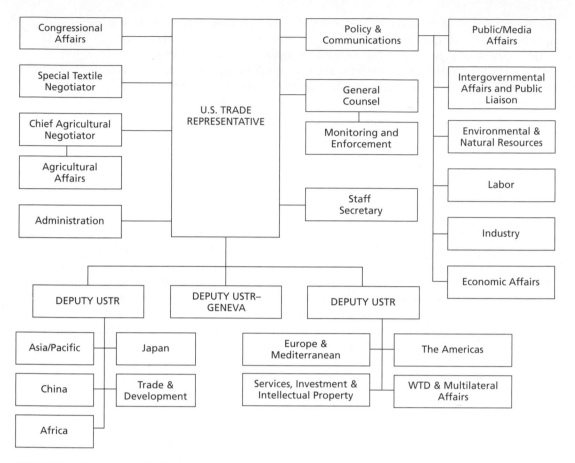

FIGURE 9.3 Office of the U.S. Trade Representative

SOURCE: Office of the U.S. Trade Representative Human Resources, 600 17th Street—Winder Building—Room 115, Washington, DC.

sector has an elaborate system of advisory groups to the USTR to aid in shaping America's negotiating posture and general trade policy abroad. The Advisory Committee on Trade Policy and Negotiations, the Agricultural Policy Advisory Committee, the Industry Sector Advisory Committee, the Trade and Environment Policy Advisory Committee, and the Labor Advisory Committees, among others, give a sense of the variety of technical and functional area committees that interact on a regular basis with the USTR. In short, the Office of the USTR, with these myriad ties and responsibilities, has become "at least nominally, the lead agency" for "U.S. trade and investment policies," and it "plays a major role in managing the interagency coordination process."[104]

Besides the USTR, however, political analysts Stephen Cohen, Joel Paul, and Robert Blecker make clear that other "players" at the White House level considerably affect foreign economic policy making. While the cabinet-level economic coordinating bodies, such as the National Economic Council, play a crucial role in ultimately finalizing and ratifying policy formulation as noted above, other White House offices, such as the economic officials on the National Security Council (NSC), the Council of Economic Advisors (CEA), and the Office of Management and Budget (OMB), play a more secondary and advisory role in policy formulation.[105]

Departments of State and Defense

The two bureaucracies that are normally thought of as political-military ones do play important roles in foreign economic policy making. As our earlier discussion implies, the Department of State retains a crucial role, since its goal is to coordinate security and economic policy toward the rest of the world and toward particular countries. Indeed, by one assessment, State's role was dominant on economic policy-making questions up until World War II. During the Cold War, however, as political and security concerns came to dominate assessments at state, the department lost some of its clout in the economic arena. Beginning in the 1960s, the Department of State's economic role has "evolved into the role of an important participant in the making of international economic policy rather than one . . . of leadership." While State has largely continued in that role to the present, it regained some clout as "economics consciousness-raising" occurred within the department in the late 1980s and 1990s. The Department of State may still be pivotal on policy if the circumstances are right. As one analyst put it, State "is sufficiently influential and ubiquitous in the decision-making process to be in a position to prevent interagency consensus on almost any international economic issue if a clear national security threat can be credibly demonstrated."[106] After September 11, moreover, the Department of State may just be in those kinds of circumstances.

The other political-military bureaucracy, the Department of Defense, plays a less pivotal role in foreign economic policy than the Department of State, but it still can affect America's economic actions abroad, especially in advising on sensitive exports and the transfer of American technology.[107] Defense's role can be especially crucial when considering a sale of "dual-use" technology—technology with potential military and nonmilitary applications—to an unfriendly, or potentially unfriendly, country. During the Cold War years, the monitoring of such exports by the Department of Defense (and Commerce) was often pivotal. The United States developed an extensive list of restricted or prohibited trade items, and it cooperated with the efforts of other Western nations through the Coordinating Committee on Multilateral Export Controls (COCOM) to stop the transfer of sensitive technologies to Communist states. In both arenas, Defense played a key role in assessing the interests of the United States and the impact of any transfers on national security.[108]

As the Cold War waned and finally ended in the early 1990s, both the unilateral and multilateral export control lists were sharply revised; consequently, the department's role in the export process has lessened. Even in the mid to late 1980s, for example, the Department of Defense was not very successful in stopping exports to Iraq, despite objections that the dual-use technology being considered for export had "the high likelihood of military end use."[109] In 1992, moreover, the department was invited to assess the implications of selling new technology (e.g., a new supercomputer) to China and to weigh into the policy debate over whether the licensing of this sale should go forward. While it opposed such a sale to China, the Departments of State and Commerce were on the other side for business and political reasons, and Defense's view was not persuasive.[110]

Several factors appear to explain the lack of defense's clout on such policy questions. First, defense's role is more consultative than statutory. Second, unlike the Department of Commerce, defense lacks a public constituency that might aid it in the inevitable bureaucratic clashes over the promotion of such sales abroad, especially in an era of trade liberalization. Third, and with particular reference to export policy, the Department of Commerce retains the final authority on issuing export licenses.[111] Finally, since the COCOM standards have been replaced by the Wassenaar Agreement (a multilateral mechanism for monitoring the transfer of dual use goods and conventional armaments), an interagency group develops the United States position and the Department of Defense participates but does not dominate the process.[112] Much as with the Department of State, one important caveat needs to be noted about this assessment. Since the terrorist attack of September 11, 2001, the political-security bureaucracies are more likely to be heeded than before. In this sense, Defense's assessment in interagency debate on technology and arms transfer is likely to carry more weight.

Department of the Treasury

The Department of Treasury today enjoys increased policy-making clout, especially in international financial matters. Unlike the Department of State, which has had an historical role in foreign economic matters, Treasury's rise in influence has been more recent, primarily dating from the end of World War II. Indeed, the department has been described as the "enfant terrible" in the making of international economic policy, and as the one that now often dominates the rest of the bureaucracy on international financial matters.

The growth of the Department of the Treasury in policy influence has been attributed to a variety of factors: (1) the relative decline of American economic power globally; (2) the increased recognition that external economic policies affect the domestic economy; (3) the acknowledgment that international financial shocks needs American attention; (4) congressional legislation that grants the Treasury Department a greater global economic policy responsibility; and (5) the enhanced role of the secretary of the treasury in economic policy making. Furthermore, "the Treasury Department has undisputed jurisdiction over U.S. international monetary policy . . . and international financial policy." In addition, Treasury has responsibility for policy making on aiding former communist countries transitioning toward market economies and in aiding emerging counties with currency problems. In all, only the Department of State is equally as interested in the range of foreign economic policy as the Department of Treasury.[113]

While Treasury has an elaborate bureaucratic structure in which various divisions could potentially have an impact on foreign economic policy making, the center of its activity are the offices and bureaus directed by the undersecretary for international affairs. In particular, the undersecretary has policy responsibility for running the Office of International Affairs, which monitors the whole array of foreign economic issues, including international monetary policy, trade and investment, global debt, and America's role in international financial institutions (e.g., International Monetary Fund and the World Bank). Aided by the assistant security and the several deputy assistant secretaries, this office and the undersecretary play a pivotal role in coordinating policy with the other major market democracies (G-8 countries) and in preparing the U.S. position for the annual meetings among these countries. Finally, Treasury also handles all international tax treaty issues with other countries and has two important bureaus, especially after September 11, under its jurisdiction: the U.S. Customs Service (for monitoring tariff compliance by other nations) and the Office of Foreign Assets Control (for enforcing economic sanctions policy toward other countries). With the creation of the Department of Homeland Security in 2003, the U.S. Customs Office was transferred to that department.[114]

Several recent actions illustrate Treasury's policy-making importance in the foreign economic area: In the 1980s, Treasury was instrumental in producing the so-called Plaza Pact, the Baker Plan, and the Brady Plan. The Plaza Pact sought to reduce the value of the dollar against other leading currencies as a means of helping the United States and world economies. The pact took its name from the Plaza Hotel in New York, where representatives of the United States, Japan, West Germany, France, and Great Britain met. These representatives agreed that "further orderly appreciation of the main non-dollar currencies against the dollar is desirable" and that their governments would encourage this kind of an outcome.[115] The Baker Plan, a proposal offered by U.S. Secretary of the Treasury James Baker to the 1985 annual meeting of the World Bank and the International Monetary Fund, aimed to address the burgeoning international debt crisis. It called for commercial banks to assist 15 particularly indebted nations (e.g., Mexico, Argentina, and Brazil in Latin America; Nigeria and Morocco in Africa; and the Philippines in Asia) by pledging to provide $20 billion in new loans through 1988, and for international lending institutions (e.g., the World Bank and the Inter-American Development Bank) to provide $9 billion more. In exchange, the debtor nations would be asked to follow "anti-inflationary fiscal and monetary policies."[116] They would also be asked "to strengthen their private sectors, mobilize more domestic savings, facilitate investment, liberalize trade and pursue market-oriented approaches to currencies, interest rates, and prices."[117] The Brady Plan, named after President George H. W. Bush's secretary of the treasury, was a debt-reduction proposal.[118] Under this design, the commercial banks in rich countries would be encouraged to write off a portion of debt owed by Third World countries. A variety of schemes would be used, ranging from getting international financial institution to fund poor countries' effort to buy back a portion of the debt in exchange for some debt reduction to the use of "debt–equity swaps" in which banks got some property or asset within a country or accepted repayment of debt in local currency (probably at reduced value).

In the 1990s, Treasury was deeply involved in addressing two major international financial crises: the Mexican bailout of 1995 and the Asian flu or contagion of 1997–1998. In December 1994, the value of the Mexican peso had declined dramatically, from about 3.5 pesos to the U.S. dollar to more than 5.5 pesos by the end of that month, and eventually to almost 6.5 pesos to the dollar by early February 1995. The reason for this sharp drop in the value of the peso was the weakening Mexican economy. Over the previous several years, the Mexican government, banks, and businesses had borrowed heavily to fuel the rapid expansion of the economy. When investor confidence began to erode in 1993 and 1994, however, the Mexican government was forced to use its revenue to protect the value of the peso in the face of increasing pressure to devalue the currency. By the end of 1994, that effort had largely failed, and the value of the peso plummeted.[119]

This sharp decline in the peso's value foreshadowed a dramatic decline in Mexico's living standard, but it also had important implications for the United States. First, a weak Mexican economy would have direct and immediate consequences for the health of the American economy.[120] Since a significant portion of Mexican debt was held by American banks, mutual funds, and insurance companies, U.S. pension plans with Mexican investments and American workers producing goods for export would be hurt. Second, a weak Mexican economy would have profound consequences for the success of the recently implemented North American Free Trade Agreement (NAFTA). Third, a weak Mexican economy would have political and economic consequences within Mexico itself. Market and political reforms to make Mexico's economy more open and its political system more democratic would now be in jeopardy. Fourth, a weak Mexican economy would likely spark increased illegal immigration to the north, creating social and political dislocations in the United States. Finally, the collapse of the Mexican economy would likely lead to reverberations throughout the international global economy.[121]

The Clinton administration moved quickly to devise an assistance plan for Mexico, with the Department of Treasury taking the lead in developing and promoting such a plan.[122] The first plan developed by the Clinton administration provided for $40 billion in new loan guarantees by the United States to Mexico and about $13 billion in loans from the International Monetary Fund.[123] The plan, however, required congressional action, and opposition quickly developed in both the House and the Senate. As a result, President Clinton abandoned this approach and adopted an alternative strategy. Under this new plan, emanating from the Department of Treasury as well, the United States decided to provide $20 billion to forestall a default by Mexico, to ask the International Monetary Fund to provide $17.5 billion in assistance and the Bank for International Settlements to add $10 billion, and to invite Canada and Latin American countries to contribute $2 billion more.[124] The new American-devised $50 billion rescue plan was implemented and provided an immediate shot in the arm to the Mexican economy, and Mexico ended up repaying the entire debt two years early in January 1997.[125]

As the 1990s ended and the new century arrived, the Department of Treasury again took a leading role in developing foreign economic policy. In response to the Asian financial crisis of 1997–1998, the Department of Treasury and Secretary of the Treasury Robert Rubin developed a plan to respond to this global economic challenge and work diligently to get congressional approval. The Asian crisis refers to the collapse of the value of the currencies and the economies in a number of Southeast Asian countries beginning in the summer of 1997.[126] The collapse of the value of the Thai baht is usually marked as the beginning point of this process, but the loss of confidence in the currencies in the region quickly spread from Thailand to Indonesia, South Korea, and the Philippines, among others. As the investments in these countries failed as a result of, for example, the collapse of large construction projects, and banks began to fail because businesses could not pay their loans, international investors withdraw their capital (or reduced further investment). The loss of these markets and these investment opportunities for a number of developed economies had a ripple effect on the entire global economy. As a result, it was imperative for the United States to act to stabilize this situation, not only for the states in the region, but for the entire global economy.

While the Clinton administration did not respond very sympathetically to the Thai situation initially,[127] it eventually proposed a bailout plan through the International Monetary Fund (IMF). Moreover, the administration requested $17.9 billion in new congressional funding for the IMF as an important part of this effort in December 1997. Some in Congress balked at this request because it was seen as more of a bailout for bankers and investment speculators than really aiding these countries. Treasury Secretary Rubin, however, became a strong advocate for this bailout package and the leading spokesperson on Capitol Hill in lobbying for these funds. After much partisan bickering and political maneuvering, Congress passed the IMF replenishment in the fall of 1998, although it required the Department of Treasury to be involved in providing various certifications to Congress over the IMF and the use of the funds.

After September 11, 2001, the mandate of the Department of Treasury has been both reaffirmed and broadened. Its immediate response was to become more deeply involved in identifying and freezing assets of front organizations within the United States that may be funneling monies to terrorist organizations abroad and to work with finance officers in other countries to elicit their cooperation in taking similar action. Those efforts have indeed been successful in closing down a number of front organizations at home and abroad that had links to terrorism. Treasury, too, has continued to take a lead role in seeking actions that would bolster and revive the American economy after the shock of September 11 both domestically and internationally. With a new secretary, John Snow, succeeding Paul O'Neill in 2003, the Department of the Treasury has worked vigorously to make the American economy more competitive and to pull it out of recession with the help of the international system through such actions as pursuing more free trade agreements (e.g., with Chile and Singapore) and through some weakening of the U.S. dollar to make American goods more attractive abroad. At the same time, Treasury has been reluctant to intervene directly in some countries facing currency and export problems. Most notably, the Bush administration largely adopted a hands-off policy when Argentina experienced severe currency devaluation problems.

Department of Commerce

The fifth key department in the foreign economic policy area is the Department of Commerce. Like the Office of the USTR, Commerce benefited from the 1980 executive reorganization act by gaining a wider mandate in formulating and implementing U.S. trade policy. It now has the principal responsibility for administering all import-export programs of the United States.[128] Two major divisions within the department are directly involved in these tasks. They are the Bureau of International Trade Administration and the Bureau of Industry and Security, each headed by an undersecretary of commerce. (The latter bureau, as its name implies, also has responsibilities to regulate "the export of sensitive goods and technologies . . . ; [and] enforcing export control, anti-boycott, and public safety law . . ." as well.[129])

The International Trade Administration has the responsibility for all U.S. trade policy (except agricultural products) and for assisting the U.S. Trade Representative in all trade negotiations. These activities range from formulating and implementing foreign economic policy, shaping all import policies, and promoting and developing American markets around the world. Although the USTR would likely take the lead role, ITA can provide valuable assistance.

Importantly, the ITA also has the responsibility for operating the U.S. and Foreign Commercial Service (US & FCS), the primary agency that aids American businesses seeking to export nonagricultural products. Through some 100 export centers within the United States and through 140 posts in 78 countries, this agency conducts a variety of activities to showcase American products and works with other government agencies and foreign organizations to aid American business.[130] In particular, US & FCS provides information on new markets to businesses, counsels and arranges contact between American companies and local businesses abroad, and holds trade shows and "trade events" to demonstrate the range of American products, especially those from small and medium-sized companies.[131]

Another important new function for the Department of Commerce is on the import side of the trade equation: the enforcement of antidumping and countervailing trade statutes to protect American businesses from unfair trade practices from abroad (prior to 1980, these responsibilities rested with the Department of the Treasury). Antidumping statutes deal with monitoring imports from other countries to make certain that goods being sold in the United States are not below "fair market value," while countervailing statutes focus on whether production costs have been subsidized in a foreign country, hence making imported goods less costly within the American market.[132] In either instance, if such a determination were made, the department could recommend retaliation, and import duties, for example, could be added to the products in question.[133] With the ever increasing American trade deficits over the past three decades and with the rising tide of protectionism in various markets, the monitoring of imports and the recommending of appropriate action have become crucial aspects of foreign economic policy for the United States.[134] Furthermore, with the completion of several new trade agreements to lower tariffs and eliminate nontariff barriers—such as the North American Free Trade Agreement (NAFTA) and the World Trade Organization—these monitoring activities now take on even more significance.

Indeed, the Department of Commerce has gained some bureaucratic influence through this very power, but it has also obtained some influence through its efforts to open foreign markets to American products. The actions of the Commerce Department, particularly during the Clinton administration, arguably had a greater impact on American foreign policy than at any time since the department shaped trade policy with the Soviet Union during the Nixon administration.[135] Commerce was able to obtain this influence by organizing numerous promotional trips for American corporate executives to potentially new U.S. markets, ranging from South Africa and Northern Ireland to China and the Middle East. (Indeed, at the time of his fatal plane crash in April 1996, Secretary Ron Brown was leading a delegation of a dozen or more corporate executives to assist with reconstruction in Bosnia.[136]) Furthermore, the department was able to tie these economic development efforts to domestic policy as a means of promoting greater prosperity for the American economy at home, and to foreign policy as a means of promoting peace and democracy abroad through economic development. In this way, too, the department was able to stave off efforts to eliminate it as a cabinet-level department, as originally proposed by the Republican-controlled Congress in 1995.

Still, Commerce's overall role in the trade area remains more on the operational side than on the shaping of overall policy.[137] American trade policy toward Japan over the past two decades, for instance, demonstrates the limitations of Commerce's influence. Commerce has long been working to pry open the Japanese market for American products. Yet this vigorous approach has met resistance—not only from the Japanese, but from other foreign affairs bureaucracies. The Department of the Treasury, a seeming natural ally on economic policy, took a more cautious approach for its own reasons. As one Treasury official said several years ago: "We take a very broad macroeconomics view of U.S.-Japan relations. We don't worry much about specific products and industries." Another added: "We rely importantly on Japanese investment capital to help finance our trade and current account deficits."[138] Resistance also came from other foreign affairs bureaucracies that examine the Japanese relationship from a political-military perspective. The State and Defense Departments were reluctant to endorse the stronger position of the Department of Commerce because they had to worry about the political-military implications of such an approach as the Cold War ended and the post–Cold War began.[139] In this sense, Commerce is more likely to have success in influencing the way policy is implemented (i.e., what countervailing duties are imposed, which companies get sales licenses) than in shaping trade and economic policy at the outset.

Department of Agriculture

A sixth important economic bureaucracy with direct foreign policy responsibilities is the United States Department of Agriculture (USDA). This department enters into the foreign policy arena through its involvement with agricultural trade and agricultural aid. Under several pieces of legislation, the USDA has the responsibility to monitor agricultural imports (and to suggest quotas if necessary) and to promote the export of American agricultural products. Under Public Law 480 (P.L.-480), the Agricultural Trade Development and Assistance Act, the USDA has primary responsibility for providing food aid to needy countries throughout the world.[140]

The Foreign Agricultural Service (FAS), the principal agency for formulating and implementing both agricultural trade and aid policy, is located in the Farm and Foreign Agricultural Services division of the Department of Agriculture. As the primary promoter of U.S. agricultural sales abroad, FAS does so in several different ways. First and foremost, it relies upon FAS attachés, who are posted at 80 American embassies abroad (covering 130 countries) and supported through an extensive support staff of agricultural experts in Washington. These individuals have a wide array of duties, which include observing the agricultural policies of host countries, monitoring agricultural imports at home and making recommendations for quotas when necessary, analyzing agricultural trading patterns and trading prospects worldwide, and promoting American agricultural exports at home and abroad.

Second, about two decades ago, the FAS opened Agricultural Trade Offices (ATOs) abroad as yet another mechanism to promote American agricultural exports. In mid-2002, for example, 16 offices were operating. There are three offices in China, two in Japan, and offices in Hong Kong; Taiwan; São Paulo, Brazil; Seoul, South Korea; Mexico City, Monterrey, Mexico; and Jakarta, Indonesia, with another to open in Manila, the Philippines. Through these ATOs, the Foreign Agricultural Service is involved in sponsoring trade exhibitions to showcase the variety and quality of American agricultural products.[141]

Third, FAS operates in conjunction with the funding from the Commodity Credit Corporation (CCC) in USDA, the Export Credit Guarantee program, the Export Enhancement Program (EEP), the Dairy Export Incentive Program (DEIP), and the sale of surplus commodities. These various programs are further efforts to build markets abroad.[142] The DEIP, for instance, provides support to dairy exporters in an effort to broaden American markets abroad, sometimes leading to market clashes with other dairy exporters (e.g., Australia and New Zealand).

On the aid side, the FAS plays a central role in managing the Public Law 480 (P.L.-480) program, which provides both loans and grants in the form of food assistance and offers various incentives to help developing countries expand their agricultural sectors. The U.S. food aid effort totaled $1.2 billion in FY03, a figure representing about 10 percent of the total U.S. foreign assistance budget. In particular, FAS has responsibility for managing the food loans (Title I) of P.L.-480, while the Agency for International Development (AID) has responsibility for food grants for emergency humanitarian and relief efforts (Title II) and for food aid that fosters food security and market reforms (Title III). Title III, however, has not been funded for several years.[143] In addition, the Department of Agriculture provides food assistance through the Food for Progress (FFP) program, which aids countries that are expanding market principles in their agricultural sectors. The USDA also operates another program (the 416 [b] program) in which the United States donates surplus American commodities to needy countries, although this program is now being phased out. Finally, FAS's International Cooperation and

Development program, in collaboration with the Agency for International Development and other funding agencies, works to share U.S. agricultural and scientific knowledge with other countries (mainly middle-income and developing countries) and to foster global cooperation in these crucial areas.[144]

According to one analysis, the policy impact of the USDA on international agricultural trade is mixed. On the one hand, the Foreign Agricultural Service has a "major input when agricultural trade matters are concerned" in the policy-making process and its clout has increased "as U.S. agricultural trade has expanded."[145] When Clayton Yeutter served as secretary of agriculture during the George H. W. Bush administration, his presence added further clout to the USDA in shaping agricultural trade policy, since he had a sustained interest in trade policy (as a former U.S. Trade Representative) and was a strong believer in free trade in agriculture.[146] President Clinton's appointments of Mike Espy and Dan Glickman as his secretaries of agriculture did not emphasize the international trade side within USDA as fully as had Yeutter's appointment. Yet, both secretaries quickly became advocates of free-trade policies as a way to strengthen American agriculture, with Espy strongly endorsing NAFTA for example, and Glickman eventually endorsing the opening of international markets.[147] Ann Veneman, secretary of agriculture during the George W. Bush administration, is closer to the Yeutter role in affecting agricultural trade policy. She comes to the position with a strong interest and background in this area. She previously served as deputy undersecretary of agriculture for International Affairs and Commodity Programs and early on in her career had worked for the Foreign Agriculture Service (FAS) for the department. In addition, she reportedly worked very well with the USTR, Robert Zoellick, on matters related to developing and promoting foreign agricultural policy: They are often in "lockstep" with one another, according to one close observer.[148]

The principal mechanism for USDA to affect overall trade policy, however, is less through the secretary and more through the committee structures established under the Trade Act of 1974. Under the formula emerging from that legislation, USDA and the private sector participate in the agricultural advisory committees for trade and through the five agricultural technical advisory committees for trade. These committees make policy recommendations to the secretary of USDA and to the U.S. Trade Representative. Moreover, these mechanisms have worked quite well in past negotiations and serve as a ready means of incorporating the public and private agricultural sectors into international trade negotiations. For example, the Trade Policy Staff Committee, headed by the Office of the USTR, is an important forum for USDA to affect policy formation on international agricultural policy. Indeed, according to one official at USDA, "many, most, [international agricultural initiatives] originate" at the Department of Agriculture, and the Foreign Agricultural Service has a whole division dealing with Multilateral Trade Negotiations to monitor and develop policy options.[149]

Nevertheless, the Department of Agriculture does not always work its will in agricultural trade or sales abroad, as the case of agricultural credits for Iraq illustrates. In the late 1980s and early 1990s, the USDA's Commodity Credit Corporation (CCC) was providing substantial credits to Iraq for purchasing American agricultural products.[150] Despite some growing concerns over Saddam Hussein's

Iraq and its creditworthiness in the late 1980s, the CCC still allocated $30 million in additional loan guarantees in September 1988, just prior to a new fiscal 1989 credit of $1 billion. A year later, USDA's CCC again recommended $1 billion in credits for Iraq. By then, however, there were serious concerns in the Federal Reserve and the Department of Treasury regarding Iraq's financial standing. In a compromise, USDA agreed to lower its recommendation to $400 million. Shortly thereafter, USDA investigators found diversion of funds and evidence of corruption by Iraq. As a result, it suspended its recommendation for any further credit. At that juncture, the State Department and the White House engaged in a flurry of activities to get the original policy back on course and eventually carried the day.[151] Through considerable bureaucratic maneuvering and substantial political pressure, the original $1 billion proposal was reborn and put into effect as policy.[152] This decision was consistent with the national security policy of the time, which sought to employ "economic and political incentives for Iraq to moderate its behavior and to increase our [United States] influence with Iraq."

As this case illustrates, security interests ultimately continue to govern policy decisions, even as USDA and its constituents were benefiting as a result of this reinstatement of policy orchestrated by the Department of State and the White House. More generally, albeit in another context, some analysts have argued that the Department of State, the Department of Commerce, the Office of Budget and Management, and the National Security Council have increased their interest and expertise in agricultural trade policy and, in this way, are in a position to challenge the role of the Department of Agriculture.[153] Still, the USDA can and does play an important role, especially in affecting the agricultural component of America's foreign economic policy.

CONCLUDING COMMENTS

As this review of the Department of State, the National Security Council, and several economic bureaucracies demonstrates, the process of foreign policy making is much more complex than is often realized, and more actors are involved in the process than we immediately think. Although the Department of State may often be identified as the center of U.S. foreign diplomacy, the National Security Council has increasingly assumed a larger role in the shaping of American foreign policy. Similarly, while political and military issues are also often assumed to be pivotal in the foreign policy arena, economic issues are increasingly claiming more attention. Hence, the role of economic bureaucracies has been enlarged, with the Office of the U.S. Trade Representative and the Department of Treasury particularly prominent in shaping America's foreign economic policy.

Although the foreign policy bureaucracies discussed so far are important to policy making, other bureaucracies cannot be left out of this discussion. In the next chapter, therefore, we complete this survey of the foreign affairs bureaucracies by looking at the Department of Defense and the several bureaucracies associated with the intelligence community, and the newly created Department of Homeland

Security. In that chapter, too, we shall take a closer look at the structural and procedural arrangements used by recent presidents to coordinate the policy-making process among these various bureaucracies within the executive branch.

NOTES

1. Graham Allison, *Essence of Decision: Explaining the Cuban Missile Crisis* (Boston: Little, Brown, 1971), p. 144. This idea is also at p. 158, where Allison quotes from Roger Hilsman's *To Move a Nation* (Garden City, NY: Doubleday Publishing, 1964), p. 6.

2. Allison, *Essence of Decision: Explaining the Cuban Missile Crisis;* and Morton H. Halperin with the assistance of Priscilla Clapp and Arnold Kanter, *Bureaucratic Politics and Foreign Policy* (Washington, DC: The Brookings Institution, 1974).

3. Christopher M. Jones, "American Prewar Technology Sales to Iraq: A Bureaucratic Politics Explanation," in Eugene R. Wittkopf, ed., *The Domestic Sources of American Foreign Policy: Insights and Evidence,* 2nd ed. (New York: St. Martin's Press, 1994), pp. 279–296. The quoted passages for the Iraqi case are at pp. 280 and 293, respectively, in this paragraph and the next one.

4. Note, however, that Allison, *Essence of Decision,* pp. 164–165, identifies not only bureaucracies as determinants of policy position. Instead, he refers to the variety of "players" in the process. Kim Richard Nossal, "Bureaucratic Politics and the Westminster Model," in Robert O. Matthews, Arthur G. Rubinoff, and Janice Gross Stein, eds., *International Conflict and Conflict Management: Readings in World Politics* (Scarborough, Ontario: Prentice-Hall of Canada, Inc., 1984), p. 125, makes this point from which we draw.

5. Todd S. Purdom and Patrick E. Tyler, "Top Republicans Break with Bush on Iraq Strategy," *New York Times,* August 16, 2002, A1.

6. *Department of State Completes 200 Years* (Washington, DC: United States Department of State, Bureau of Public Affairs, 1982), p. 1.

7. Report of the U.S. Department of State Management Task Force, *State 2000: A New Model for Managing Foreign Affairs* (Washington, DC: U.S. Department of State Publication 10029, January 1993).

8. Much of the discussion of the organizational and structural details of the Department of State is drawn from "The United States Department of State: Structure and Organization," *Dispatch Supplement* 6 (May 1995), Supplement No. 3, 1–8. Also see Warren Christopher, "Department of State Reorganization," *Dispatch* 4 (February 8, 1993): 69–73. We also rely upon the Department of State Web site during the George W. Bush administration for recent changes.

9. *The United States Government Manual 2001/2002,* June 1, 2001, p. 295.

10. "Department Organization," p. 2, from State Department Web site at http://www.state.gov, accessed on July 21, 2002.

11. Christopher, "Department of State Reorganization," p. 69. Former Secretary of State James Baker notes in his memoirs that the organization whereby the undersecretaries report to the secretary and the assistant secretaries to the undersecretaries was actually started during his time at the department during the George H. W. Bush administration. See James A. Baker III with Thomas M. DeFrank, *The Politics of Diplomacy: Revolution, War and Peace, 1989–1992* (New York: G. P. Putnam's Sons, 1995), pp. 35–36.

12. "Department Organization," p. 5.

13. "Assistant Secretaries and Those of Equivalent Rank," from the State Department Web site at http://www.state.gov/r/pa/ei/biog/c129.htm, accessed on August 16, 2002.

14. The information and quoted materials in these two paragraphs on USAID are drawn from the USAID Web site at http://www.usaid.gov/about, accessed on August 16, 2002.

15. Ibid. The USAID budget data are from "Summary of USAID Fiscal Year 2003 Budget" at http://www.usaid.gov/press/releases/2002/fs2003budget.html, accessed on August 27, 2002. See a list of USAID accomplishments at "A Record of Accomplishment," http://www.usaid.gov/about/accompli.html, accessed on August 16, 2002.

16. "Diplomacy: The State Department at Work," at http://www.state.gov/r/pa/ei/rls/dos/4078.htm, accessed on October 22, 2003.

17. See "Diplomacy at Work: A U.S. Embassy" and "A U.S. Embassy at Work" at http://www.state.gov/r/pa/c61777.htm, and http://www.state.gov/r/pa/8710.htm, respectively. Both were accessed on July 21, 2002.

18. Strobe Talbott, "Globalization and Diplomacy: The View from Foggy Bottom," in Eugene R. Wittkopf and James M. McCormick, eds., *The Domestic Sources of American Foreign Policy: Insights and Evidence,* 3rd ed. (Lanham, MD: Rowman & Littlefield Publishers, Inc., 1999), p. 191. For a brief and interesting description of the working of an embassy and the responsibilities of political officers, see Robert Hopkins Miller, *Inside an Embassy: The Political Role of Diplomats Abroad* (Washington, DC: Congressional Quarterly, Inc., 1992).

19. *Overseas Presence: Staffing at U.S. Diplomatic Posts,* General Accounting Office Report (GAO/NSIAD-95–50FS, December 28, 1994): 33.

20. The data on the size and composition of the Department of State's personnel come from "Speaker's Briefing Notes for DOS Requirement," April 30, 2001, p. 4. The data on the size of the Department of Defense come from "DoD at a Glance," Department of Defense web site at http://www.dod.gov/pubs/lamanac/almanac/at_a_glance.html, accessed July 26, 2002.

21. Bureau of Public Affairs, Department of State, "The International Affairs Budget—A Sound Investment in Global Leadership: Questions and Answers," October 1, 1995, via the Internet.

22. See Miles A. Pomper, "Powell Calls on Hill to Remedy State Department Underfunding," *CQ Weekly,* March 10, 2001, 547,

for comparative budget of state and defense. In the wake of September 11, the CIA has reportedly received a large increase in funding to over $30 billion and perhaps as much as $35 billion per year (or more).

23. Among some readings that criticize the effectiveness of the Department of State are the following: I. M. Destler, *Presidents, Bureaucrats, and Foreign Policy* (Princeton, NJ: Princeton University Press, 1974), pp. 154–190; John Franklin Campbell, "The Disorganization of State," in Martin B. Hickman, ed., *Problems of American Foreign Policy,* 2nd ed. (Beverly Hills: Glencoe Press, 1975), pp. 151–170; Robert Pringle, "Creeping Irrelevance at Foggy Bottom," *Foreign Policy* 29 (Winter 1977–1978): 128–139; Andrew M. Scott, "The Department of State: Formal Organization and Informal Culture," *International Studies Quarterly* 13 (March 1969): 1–18; and Andrew M. Scott, "The Problem of the State Department," in Martin B. Hickman, ed., *Problems of American Foreign Policy,* pp. 143–151.

24. *State 2000: A New Model for Managing Foreign Affairs,* p. 4.

25. Elaine Sciolino, "Austerity at State Dept. and Fear of Diplomacy," *New York Times,* November 15, 1987, 1, 8; and John M. Goshko, "State Dept. Budget Faces New Cuts," *The Washington Post,* April 27, 1987, A6. The quoted passages are from the latter.

26. For a listing of 16 of 17 posts closed in 1993 and 1994, see *State Department: Overseas Staffing Process Not Linked to Policy Priorities,* General Accounting Office Report (GAO/NSIAD 94-228, September 20, 1994): 18–19; and for those scheduled for closing by the end of 1996, see U.S. State Department Daily Press Briefing, July 18, 1995. The total of 32 closures comes from Talbott, "Globalization and Diplomacy: The View from Foggy Bottom," p. 188, who was deputy secretary of state at the time.

27. See Steven Greenhouse, "Christopher to Cut Jobs at State Dept.," *New York Times,* May 7, 1995, 4; and "The International Affairs Budget—A Sound Investment in Global Leadership: Questions and Answers."

28. Personal communication with a State Department official, March 25, 2004.

29. Pomper, "Powell Calls on Hill to Remedy State Department Underfunding," p. 548.

30. Baker with DeFrank, *The Politics of Diplomacy: Revolution, War and Peace, 1989–1992,* p. 28.

31. On this point, see Henry T. Nash, *American Foreign Policy: Changing Perspectives on National Security* (Homewood, IL: The Dorsey Press, 1978), p. 139. Also, see Nash's excellent discussion on the problems of state, from which our overall discussion draws.

32. "Speaker's Briefing Notes for DOS Requirement," April 30, 2001, p. 4.

33. David Garnham, in particular, has looked at some of these stereotypes about the Department of State. While he finds that the background characteristics of FSOs differ from the general population, he reports that the FSOs do not differ from other groups in American society on psychological flexibility. Overall, he judges that this elitism has not negatively affected the conduct of U.S. foreign policy. See his "State Department Rigidity: Testing a Psychological Hypothesis," *International Studies Quarterly* 18 (March 1974): 31–39; and "Foreign Service Elitism and U.S. Foreign Affairs," *Public Administration Review* 35 (January/February 1975): 44–51.

34. Duncan L. Clarke, "Why State Can't Lead," *Foreign Policy* 66 (Spring 1987): 135; and Baker with DeFrank, *The Politics of Diplomacy: Revolution, War, and Peace, 1989–1992,* p. 28.

35. Clarke, "Why State Can't Lead," p. 134. Also, see Baker with DeFrank, *The Politics of Diplomacy: Revolution, War and Peace, 1989–1992,* p. 29.

36. Clarke, "Why State Can't Lead," p. 133–134. "Foggy Bottom" refers to the area of Washington, DC, where the Department of State and several executive agencies are located. Indeed, it is so familiar to Washington residents that it has its own metro stop named "Foggy Bottom."

37. Baker with DeFrank, *The Politics of Diplomacy: Revolution, War and Peace, 1989–1992,* p. 29.

38. Scott, "The Problem of the State Department," p. 146. Emphasis in original.

39. Scott, "The Department of State: Formal Organization and Informal Culture," p. 6.

40. Clarke, "Why State Can't Lead," p. 136.

41. Baker with DeFrank, *The Politics of Diplomacy: Revolution, War and Peace, 1989–1992,* p. 28.

42. Ibid., p. 31.

43. Nash, *American Foreign Policy: Changing Perspectives,* p. 139.

44. Hedrick Smith, *The Power Game: How Washington Works* (New York: Ballantine Books, 1988), pp. 558–562; and Theodore C. Sorensen, "The President and the Secretary of State," *Foreign Affairs* 66 (Winter 1987–1988): 231–248. But also see Leslie H. Gelb, "McFarlane Carving His Niche," *New York Times,* March 28, 1984, B10.

45. Nash, *American Foreign Policy: Changing Perspectives,* p. 100.

46. For a detailed assessment of the relationship between President Bush and Secretary of State James Baker, see Maureen Dowd and Thomas L. Friedman, "The Fabulous Bush and Baker Boys," *The New York Times Magazine,* May 6, 1990, 36. Other analyses available to assess the close ties between Bush and Baker and the enhanced role of the national security advisor under Bush can be found in John Newhouse, "Profiles (James Baker)," *The New Yorker,* May 7, 1990, 50–82; and Bernard Weinraub, "Bush Backs Plan to Enhance Role of Security Staff," *New York Times,* February 2, 1989, 1 and 6. On Berger's emergence as preeminent over the secretary of state, see Jane Perlez, "With Berger in Catbird Seat, Albright's Star Dims," *New York Times,* December 14, 1999, A14.

47. Jane Perlez, "Washington Memo: Divergent Voices Heard in Bush Foreign Policy," *New York Times on the Web,* March 12, 2001, at http://www.nytimes.com/201/03/12/world/12DIPL.html, accessed March 18, 2001.

48. On the importance of Vice President Cheney in foreign policy making, see Karen DeYoung and Steven Mufson, "A Leaner and Less Visible NSC," *The Washington Post,* February 9, 2001, at http://washingtonpost.com/wp-dyn/world/europe/A50937-2001Feb9.html, accessed on February 12, 2001.

49. Jack Perry, "The Foreign Service in Real Trouble, But It Can Be Saved," *Washington Post National Weekly Edition,* January 16, 1984, 21.

50. See, for John M. Goshko, "Appointing Loyalists as Envoys," *Washington Post,* April 28, 1987, A16, who reports that during the Reagan administration just under 40 percent of all ambassadors went to political appointments; and Elaine Sciolino, "Friends as Ambassadors: How Many Is Too Many?" *New York Times,* November 7, 1989, A1, A8, who reports higher figures for Kennedy through Bush when focusing only on the first few months.

51. On the Clinton appointments, see Steven Greenhouse, "Clinton Is Faulted on Political Choices for Envoy Posts," *New York Times,* April 13, 1994, A16. On the Bush appointments, see Marc Lacey and Raymond Bonner, " A Mad Scramble by Donors for Plum Ambassadorships," *New York Times,* March 17, 2001, at http://www.nytimes.com/2001/03/17/world/18AMBA.html, accessed March 18, 2001, and the Department of State Web site for chiefs of mission/country at http://www.state.gov/r/pa/ei/biog/c130.htm, accessed on July 21, 2002.

52. Sciolino, "Friends as Ambassadors: How Many Is Too Many?" p. A8.

53. The first point is based on the author's conversation with the U.S. ambassador of a small Asia-Pacific nation, July 1995, while the Australian ambassador is quoted in Lacey and Bonner, "A Mad Scramble by Donors for Plum Ambassadorships."

54. See John M. Goshko, "Clout and Morale Decline," *Washington Post,* April 26, 1987, A12.

55. Newhouse, "Profiles (James Baker)," p. 76.

56. "The State Roster," *Congressional Quarterly Weekly Report,* January 23, 1995, 185.

57. Barry Schweid, "Warren's World," *Foreign Policy* 94 (Spring 1994): 144.

58. See the commentary by two former Balkan specialists in the State Department who resigned in 1993 to protest Clinton administration policy: Marshall Freeman Harris and Stephen W. Walker, "America's Sellout of the Bosnians," *New York Times,* August 23, 1995, A15.

59. Schweid, "Warren's World," p. 143.

60. Perry, "The Foreign Service in Real Trouble, But It Can Be Saved," p. 21.

61. I am grateful to Smith, *The Power Game: How Washington Works,* p. 589, for drawing this distinction between the two. "The NSC" is his term.

62. Membership on the National Security Council has varied slightly by statute over time, but these are the ones that have remained continuously on the Council.

63. See National Security Presidential Directive 1, February 13, 2001, for the list of NSC members for the George W. Bush administration at http://www.fas.org/irp/offdocs/nspd/nspd-1.htm, accessed on July 15, 2002.

64. James S. Lay, Jr., and Robert H. Johnson, "Organizational History of the National Security Council during the Truman and Eisenhower Administrations," Report prepared for the Subcommittee on National Policy Machinery, August 11, 1960, p. 8.

65. Destler, "National Security Advice to U.S. Presidents: Some Lessons from Thirty Years," *World Politics* 24 (January 1977): 148–151, 153–159. Also see Nash, *American Foreign Policy: Changing Perspectives,* pp. 140, 172–174. On Truman's and Eisenhower's attendance of NSC meetings, see Lay and Johnson, "Organizational History of the National Security Council during the Truman and Eisenhower Administrations," pp. 5 and 24.

66. Ibid., p. 26. The characterization of Cutler as "the principal executive officer" is Lay and Johnson's.

67. Ibid., p. 30, and footnote 61.

68. For a discussion of how President Kennedy transformed the role of the national security advisor with Bundy, see I. M. Destler, "National Security Management: What Presidents Have Wrought," *Political Science Quarterly* 95 (Winter 1980–1981): 578–580; and Bromley K. Smith, "Organizational History of the National Security Council During the Kennedy and Johnson Administrations,"

monograph written for the National Security Council, February 1987.

69. Townsend Hoopes, *The Limits of Intervention* (New York: David McKay, 1968) for a discussion of the important influence of Rostow on LBJ, especially at pp. 20–22 and 59–62. For the identity, and critique, of the "Tuesday Lunch" group, see Irving Janis, *Victims of Groupthink* (Boston: Houghton Mifflin Company, 1972), pp. 101–135.

70. Destler, "National Security Management: What Presidents Have Wrought," p. 580.

71. Henry A. Kissinger, "Domestic Structure and Foreign Policy," in James N. Rosenau, ed., *International Politics and Foreign Policy,* rev. ed. (New York: Free Press, 1969), pp. 261–275, especially pp. 263–267.

72. See the diagram of the "Kissinger National Security Council System," in Nash, *American Foreign Policy: Changing Perspectives,* p. 197.

73. Elizabeth Drew, "A Reporter at Large: Brzezinski," *The New Yorker,* May 1, 1978, 94, reports that the initial National Security Council under Brzezinski consisted of only two committees: the Policy Review Committee and the Special Coordination Committee.

74. See the discussion of Brzezinski's role in Chapter 4. Also see Zbigniew Brzezinski, *Power and Principle: Memoirs of the National Security Advisor, 1977–1981* (New York: Farrar, Straus & Giroux, 1983).

75. On the disputes that precipitated Haig's firing, see Steven R. Weisman, "Aides List Clashes," *New York Times,* June 26, 1982, 1, 5; Leslie H. Gelb, "A Year in Office, Shultz Still Mapping His Way Through Diplomacy's Thicket," *Milwaukee Journal,* August 7, 1983, Accent on the News section, p. 2.

76. Smith, *The Power Game: How Washington Works,* p. 593. The characterization of Clark's role in pushing the Strategic Defense Initiative is from pp. 594–599.

77. See "Shultz: No More Mr. Nice Guy?" *Newsweek,* August 22, 1983, 17; and "Shultz Peeved, Magazine Says," *Des Moines Register,* August 15, 1983, 8A. For Secretary of State Shultz's denial of the report, see "Aide Denies Shultz Losing His Influence," *Des Moines Register,* August 16, 1983, 1A, 2A.

78. Leslie H. Gelb, "McFarlane Carving His Niche," *New York Times,* March 28, 1984, B10.

79. *Report of the President's Special Review Board* (Tower Commission Report) (Washington, DC: U.S. Government Printing Office, February 26, 1987); and *Report of the Congressional Committees Investigating the Iran–Contra Affair* (Washington, DC: U.S. Government Printing Office, November 1987).

80. Weinraub, "Bush Backs Plan to Enhance Role of Security Staff," pp. 1, 6; and National Security Council statement, "National Security Council Organization," mimeo, April 17, 1989, 3 pp.

81. John Barry with Margaret Garrard Warner, "Mr. Inside, Mr. Outside," *Newsweek,* February 27, 1989, 28; and R.W. Apple, Jr., "A Mover and Shaker Behind Bush Foreign Policy," *New York Times,* February 6, 1989, 3.

82. Jason DeParle, "The Man Inside Bill Clinton's Foreign Policy," *New York Times Magazine,* August 20, 1995, 34.

83. Lake is quoted in ibid. at p. 37.

84. Ibid., p. 34.

85. "Clinton Chooses a Foreign Policy Team," *New York Times,* December 23, 1992, A13; and James Bennet, "A Trusted Adviser, and a Friend," *New York Times,* December 6, 1996, A16.

86. DeYoung and Mufson, "A Leaner and Less Visible NSC" p. 2.

87. See ibid., pp. 7–9, and Ivo H. Daalder, "How Operational and Visible an NSC?" February 23, 2001, The Brookings Institution on the Web at http://www.brook.edu/dybdoocroot/webcache/www.brook.edu-80/p.15/a0004415.312.htm, p. 1, accessed on July 22, 2002.

88. "Condoleezza Rice, National Security Adviser," *BusinessWeek online,* February 11, 2002, p. 1

89. Ibid., p. 2.

90. DeYoung and Mufson, " A Leaner and Less Visible NSC," p. 6.

91. Bert A. Rockman, "America's Departments of State: Irregular and Regular Syndromes of Policy Making," *The American Political Science Review* 75 (December 1981): 911–927.

92. Ibid., pp. 914–918. While this section draws upon Rockman's explanations, some of my own interpretations are added to his insights.

93. See Ivo H. Daalder and I. M. Destler, "How National Security Advisers See Their Role," in Eugene R. Wittkopf and James M. McCormick, *The Domestic Sources of American Foreign Policy: Insights and Evidence,* 4th ed. (Lanham, MD: Rowman and Littlefield Publishers, Inc., 2004), pp. 171–181 for this and other reasons for the expansion of the role of this official.

94. Ibid.

95. Two books that both address these economic bureaucracies and influenced the following discussion are Kegley and Wittkopf, *American Foreign Policy: Pattern and Process,* 5th ed. (New York: St. Martin's Press, 1996); and Howard J. Wiarda, *Foreign Policy Without Illusion* (Glenview, IL: Scott, Foresman, Little Brown Higher Education, 1990).

96. Bruce Stokes and Pat Choate, *Democratizing U.S. Trade Policy* (New York: Council on Foreign Relations, Inc, 2001), p. 6.

97. The following principles are largely drawn from the discussion in Stephen D. Cohen, Joel R. Paul, and Robert A. Blecker, *Fundamentals of U.S. Foreign Trade Policy* (Boulder, CO: Westview Press, 1996), pp. 105–108.

98. The first quote is from ibid., p. 109, while Stephen D. Cohen, *The Making of United States International Economic Policy,* 5th ed. (Westport, CT: Praeger, 2000), p. 58.

99. "USTR's Role," at http://www.ustr.gov/about-ustr/ustrrole.shtml, accessed on July 26, 2002.

100. The discussion is drawn from Cohen, *The Making of United States International Economic Policy,* 5th ed., pp. 58–60; and from Cohen, Paul, and Blecker, *Fundamentals of U.S. Foreign Trade Policy,* pp. 109, 153–154.

101. See Cohen, *The Making of United States International Economic Policy,* 5th ed., p. 60.

102. "USTR's Role."

103. Ibid.

104. Cohen, *The Making of United States International Economic Policy,* 5th ed., p. 60, and Cohen, Paul, and Blecker, *Fundamentals of U.S. Foreign Trade Policy,* pp. 109- 110.

105. Ibid., and Cohen, *The Making of United States International Economic Policy,* 5th ed., pp. 61–62.

106. Ibid., pp. 46–55. The quotes are at p. 52, 55, and 53, respectively.

107. Ibid., p. 64.

108. Cohen, Paul, and Blecker, *Fundamentals of U.S. Foreign Trade Policy,* p. 47.

109. Quoted in Jones, "American Prewar Technology Sales to Iraq: A Bureaucratic Politics Explanation," p. 286.

110. Stephen D. Cohen, *The Making of United States International Economic Policy,* 4th ed. (Westport, CT: Praeger, 1994), p. 182.

111. Jones, "American Prewar Technology Sales to Iraq: A Bureaucratic Politics Explanation," p. 286.

112. Cohen, *The Making of United States International Economic Policy,* 5th ed., p. 92.

113. The quoted passages and the set of factors to explain Treasury's growth in influence are ibid., pp. 47, 47–49, and 49, respectively.

114. Ibid., pp. 49–52. On the transfer of the U.S. Customs Office on March 1, 2003, see http://www.treas.gov/bureaus/index.html. Accessed on March 25, 2004.

115. The quote is from Robert D. Hormats, "The World Economy Under Stress," in William G. Hyland, ed., *America and the World 1985* (New York: Pergamon Press, 1986), p. 469. Another source used here was Congressman Lee Hamilton, "The Decline of the Dollar," *Washington Report,* February 25, 1987.

116. S. Karene Witcher, "Baker's Plan to Relieve Debt Crisis May Spur Future Ills, Critics Say," *The Wall Street Journal,* November 15, 1985, 1.

117. Hormats, "The World Economy Under Stress," p. 474.

118. The plan was devised by Undersecretary David C. Mulford. See John R. Cranford, "Members Press for Details on Brady Proposal," *Congressional Quarterly Weekly Report,* March 18, 1989, 572, for this point and some examples of how the plan would work; and John R. Cranford, "Brady Signals Shift in Policy Toward Debt Reduction," *Congressional Quarterly Weekly Report,* March

11, 1989, 510–513, for an earlier discussion of the plan.

119. Peter Passell, "2 Views of the Peso: Wall St. vs. Main St.," *New York Times,* February 2, 1995, A6.

120. Patrick J. Lyons, "Mexico's Ripple Effects: Subtle Risks for Americans," *New York Times,* February 1, 1995, A11.

121. Bruce Stokes, "Tottering Markets," *National Journal,* February 18, 1995, 424.

122. The central role of the Department of Treasury in devising this plan can be gleaned from the active involvement of the secretary of the treasury in seeking congressional support (see, for example, David E. Sanger, "U.S. Seeks Mexican Steps in Bid to Aid Bailout Plan," *New York Times,* January 26, 1995, A14) and from the importance of the undersecretary of the treasury, Lawrence Summers, in securing the agreements on the final package (see, for example Douglas Jehl, "Slow-Building Despair Led to Decision on Aid," *New York Times,* February 1, 1995, A10).

123. David E. Sanger, "Clinton Offers $20 Billion to Mexico for Peso Rescue; Action Sidesteps Congress," *New York Times,* February 1, 1995, A1.

124. Ibid.

125. White House Press Release, "Remarks By the President at Signing of U.S.-Mexico Loan Agreement Protocol," January 15, 1997, via the Internet.

126. For details on the Asian crisis and upon which we draw here, see Ralph G. Carter and James M. Scott, "Funding the IMF: Congress versus the White House," in Ralph G. Carter, ed., *Contemporary Cases in U.S. Foreign Policy* (Washington, DC: CQ Press, 2002), pp. 339–363.

127. Joseph E. Stiglitz, *Globalization and Its Discontents* (New York: W.W. Norton and Company, 2002), p. 93. This book provides a stinging critique of the IMF/Treasury actions during the Asian crisis, see especially pp. 89–132.

128. Cohen, *The Making of United States International Economic Policy,* 5th ed, p. 55.

129. See the Web site of the Commerce Department at http://www.commerce.gov. Formerly, the two bureaus were the Bureau of International Trade Administration and the Bureau of Export Administration, but the latter was changed by the Bush administration. Also see the *U.S. Government Manual 2002/2003,* p. 135–142. The quoted passage is from ibid., p. 138.

130. Ibid., pp. 140–141; International Trade: Coordination of U.S. Export Promotion Activities in Pacific Rim Countries. General Accounting Office Report (GAO/GGD-94 192, August 29, 1994): 5; and Cohen, *The Making of United States International Economic Policy,* 5th ed, p. 57.

131. Ibid., pp. 56–57; and Kegley and Wittkopf, *American Foreign Policy: Pattern and Process,* 5th ed., 414.

132. Ibid.

133. The procedures for these countervailing duties and antidumping actions are spelled out in *Summary of Statutory Provisions Related to Import Relief* (Washington, DC: United States International Trade Commission, July 1993).

134. The total yearly U.S. trade deficit through July 2003 was about $475 billion. See *The World Almanac and Book of Facts, 2004,* p. 39.

135. Richard W. Stevenson, "A Role as Nation's Chief Salesman Abroad," *New York Times,* April 4, 1996, A7.

136. Leslie Eaton, "A Dozen Companies Await Word," *New York Times,* April 4, 1996, A7.

137. Cohen, *The Making of United States International Economic Policy,* 5th ed., p. 56.

138. These officials are quoted in Robert Pear, "Confusion Is Operative Word in U.S. Policy Toward Japan," *New York Times,* March 20, 1989, 6.

139. The prominence of political-military concerns over economic ones with Japan was the reaffirmation of the defense treaty even in the middle of trade disputes. See Steven Erlanger, "As Clinton Visits Changing Asia, Military Concerns Gain Urgency," *New York Times,* April 15, 1996, A1 and A6.

140. The discussion and what follows mainly draws upon *U.S. Government Manual 2001/2002,* pp. 119–122; and *U.S. Government Manual 2002/2003,* pp. 119–122; supplemented with Cohen, *The Making of United States International Economic Policy,* 5th ed., pp. 62–63. I also rely upon several phone

interviews with officials from the Department of Agriculture in Washington, DC, in August 2002. I am also indebted to my late colleague, Ross B. Talbot, for sharing his insight on agricultural policy making.

141. The number of current ATOs was based upon an interview with a knowledgeable official in the Department of Agriculture, August 26, 2002. For an earlier critical assessment of ATOs, see *International Trade: Agricultural Trade Offices' Role in Promoting U.S. Exports Is Unclear,* General Accounting Office Report (GAO/GGD-92-65, January 16, 1992).

142. *U.S. Government Manual 2001/2002,* p. 121, and a phone interview with a Department of Agriculture official in August 2002.

143. Jonathan E. Sanford, with the assistance of Pamela D. Richardson, *Foreign Assistance: An Overview of U.S. Aid Agencies and Programs,* CRS Report for Congress (Washington, DC: Congressional Research Service, April 18, 1995), pp. 4, 6; Larry Q. Nowels, "Foreign Aid Budget and Policy Issues for the 104th Congress," *CRS Issue Brief* (Washington, DC: Congressional Research Service, April 3, 1996), p. 7; and phone interviews with Department of Agriculture officials, August 2002.

144. "The Foreign Agricultural Service-Mission Statement," U.S. Department of Agriculture, Foreign Agricultural Service, June 1996, pp. 4–5; and a phone interview with a Department of Agriculture official in August 2002.

145. H. Wayne Moyer and Timothy E. Josling, *Agricultural Policy Reform: Politics and Process in the EC and the USA* (New York: Harvester Wheatsheaf, 1990), pp. 124 (note 6), 120.

146. George Athan, "Yeutter Likely to Push for Free Trade, Exports," *Des Moines Register,* December 15, 1988, 1A, 11A.

147. See Dan Looker, "The Politics of NAFTA Heat Up," *Successful Farming* 91 (September 1993): 8; and Dan Glickman, "U.S. Opportunities" [Landon Lecture, Kansas State University] *Vital Speeches* (October 15, 1995): 5–10.

148. The background on Secretary Veneman comes from http:www//usda.gov/ agencies/gallery/veneman.htm, accessed on August 27, 2002; and from an interview with a Department of Agriculture official on August 27, 2002. The last characterization of Veneman comes from the interview as well.

149. "Agricultural Advisory Committees for Trade," U.S. Department of Agriculture, Foreign Agricultural Service, July 1995, p. 1, and an interview with a Department of Agriculture official on August 27, 2002.

150. The details of the Iraqi case here are drawn from Bruce W. Jentleson, *With Friends Like These* (New York and London: W. W. Norton and Company, 1994), pp. 83, and 128–132.

151. Ibid., pp. 132–138.

152. The quoted passage is from National Security Directive 26 (NSD-26) and is taken from ibid., p. 94.

153. See Raymond F. Hopkins and Donald J. Puchala, *Global Food Interdependence: Challenge to American Foreign Policy* (New York: Columbia University Press, 1980), pp. 110–115, for a discussion of tensions between the Department of State and the USDA and the expansion of agricultural capacities in other bureaucracies in the 1970s.

10

The Military
and Intelligence
Bureaucracies:
Pervasive
or Accountable?

Our job is to work to prevent another attack like the one we experienced on
September 11th—before it happens. There is only one way to do so—by taking
the battle to the terrorists, and those who give them support and sanctuary.

SECRETARY OF DEFENSE DONALD RUMSFELD'S TESTIMONY
BEFORE A SENATE APPROPRIATIONS COMMITTEE
SEPTEMBER 24, 2003

A lot went wrong.

SENATOR RICHARD SHELBY, COMMENTING ON THE INVESTIGATION
OF THE INTELLIGENCE COMMUNITY'S ACTIVITIES
PRIOR TO THE EVENTS OF SEPTEMBER 11
JULY 24, 2003

This chapter continues the discussion of bureaucracies and foreign policy by examining the Department of Defense and the intelligence community. These bureaucracies increased their foreign and national security influence over the post–World War II years, but both now have come under closer scrutiny in the post–Cold War and post–September 11 years. Our discussion highlights the changes in influence over time and assesses each bureaucracy's relative policy role in the early years of the twenty-first century. In addition, the chapter includes an initial discussion of the newly created Department of Homeland Security and its implications for American foreign policy. Finally, we outline the mechanisms that the executive branch uses to coordinate policy making across the different bureaucracies discussed in the last two chapters. While individual bureaucracies may impact foreign policy making directly, the combined effect of several bureaucracies—or the success of one bureaucracy over another—occurs most often through the interagency or interdepartmental coordination process that all recent presidents have used.

THE DEPARTMENT OF DEFENSE

The Department of Defense may well be perceived as a bureaucracy that only implements policy, but, in fact, the Department of Defense contributes substantially to the formulation of foreign policy decisions. Its overall power has grown significantly over the past 60 years, but its role in foreign policy formulation remains a source of some debate. Some would contend that it is but one bureaucracy within the foreign policy apparatus, albeit a powerful one.[1] Others would argue that it has a pervasive effect on American foreign policy making—often surpassing the competing bureaucracies within the executive branch.[2] Still others would suggest that it is the beginning point for the "military-industrial complex," a structure woven into American society (see Chapter 11).[3] Yet another view, and one especially prevalent today, claims that the military and its role ought to be changed substantially to meet the new international threats after the Cold War and after the events of September 11, 2001. In this connection, too, a new concern has arisen over the military-civilian gap and the implications of that gap for policy making. Whatever view the reader adopts about the military and its role, there can be little doubt that the Department of Defense has increased its foreign policy-making influence and that such policy-making influence will likely remain substantial for the foreseeable future, especially in the post–September 11 environment.

The Structure of the Pentagon

The perceived influence of the Department of Defense begins with its considerable size and presence in the foreign policy decision-making apparatus of the government. As Figure 10.1 shows, the Pentagon (located across the Potomac River from the nation's capital in Arlington, Virginia, and named for the shape of the Department of Defense's headquarters) is a large and complex bureaucracy organized into key major divisions. These major divisions are further subdivided into a

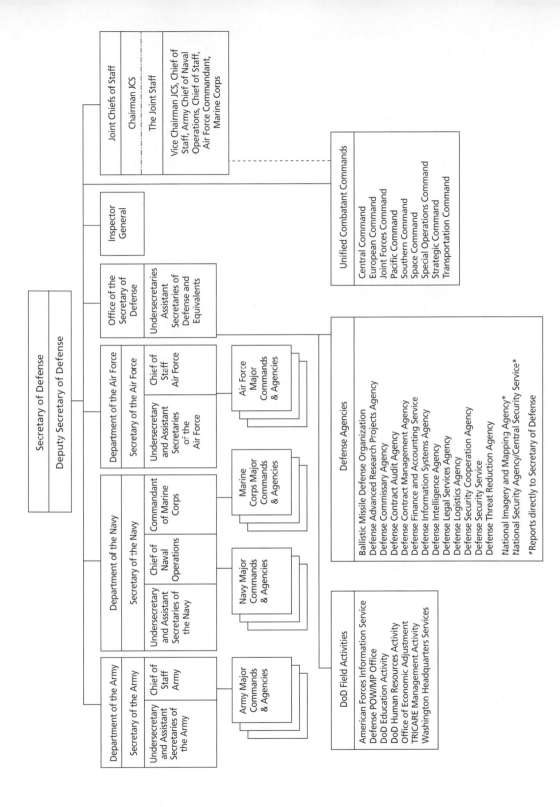

FIGURE 10.1 Department of Defense

SOURCE: Department of Defense Organizational Structure, U.S. Department of Defense Web site (http://www.defenselink.mil/odam/omp/pubs/GuideBook/DoD.htm#Department%2oof% 20Defense)

variety of departments, agencies, and offices that potentially affect many areas of American life.

The Department of Defense affects the American public through the awarding of defense contracts, through domestic and foreign jobs created for U.S. corporations, and through the number of men and women serving in the military services. In fiscal year 2002, for example, more than $170 million in prime defense contracts were awarded to American and international corporations, with virtually every state and the District of Columbia sharing in those awards and the thousands of jobs they create.[4] In fact, by one estimate, more than 5 million American jobs are related to national defense spending. In 2003, the Department of Defense directly employed about 669,000 civilians, 1.4 million active-duty military personnel, and 1.2 million National Guard and reserve forces. More generally, the level of national defense outlays represents one of the largest items in the U.S. national budget with estimated outlay for fiscal year 2003 at about $380 billion. In the aftermath of September 11, moreover, projections are that these outlays will reach about $443 billion by fiscal year 2007.[5] In this sense, the impact of the Department of Defense expenditures on American society remain pronounced, fueled by concerns over the spread of weapons of mass destruction (e.g., biological, chemical, and nuclear) and the persistence of terrorist threats around the world.

In terms of foreign policy formulation, three sectors of the Department of Defense are pivotal: (1) the secretary of defense; (2) the Joint Chiefs of Staff (JCS); and (3) the office of the secretary of defense (OSD). The last, the office of the secretary of defense, is the newest, and potentially the greatest, source of influence in affecting foreign policy formulation. OSD, the staff arm of the secretary of defense, consists of a variety of offices and agencies that deal with managing the department and developing foreign policy recommendations. The OSD's mandated duties include the responsibility to "develop and promulgate policies in support of United States national security objectives, provide oversight to ensure the effective allocation and efficient management of resources consistent with Secretary of Defense approved plans and programs, develop appropriate evaluation mechanisms to provide effective supervision of policy implementation and program execution . . . , [and] provide the focal point for departmental participation in the United States security community and other Government activities."[6] As the office of the secretary of defense has grown over the years, it has become the principal focus for policy development and administration within the Department of Defense.

Office of the Secretary of Defense

The policy division of OSD, headed by an undersecretary of defense for policy and a principal deputy, illustrates the crucial policy-formulating function within OSD. Within this division, several important policy offices operate, too: International Security Affairs, International Security Policy, Net Assessment, and Special Operations and Low-Intensity Conflict, among others. Each office, headed by an assistant secretary of defense, has an important stake in policy development.

Two of the middle-level offices within OSD illustrate the increased policy formulation role of the Department of Defense over the years: the Office of International Security Affairs (ISA) and the Office of International Security Policy (ISP). The former, in particular, gained prominence during the Vietnam War period when it was instrumental in offering policy advice.[7] Moreover, its responsibilities today include developing security and political-military policy for various regions of the world (Africa, Asia and the Pacific, Near East and South Asia, and the Western Hemisphere), overseeing security assistance abroad through the Defense Security Cooperation Agency, and monitoring prisoner of war/missing in action issues through the Defense POW/Missing Personnel Office.[8] Over the years, ISA had gained such prominence in policy making that it has been labeled the "little State Department," since it provides a political component to the military analysis at the Pentagon. The ISA, however, declined in influence from Nixon to Carter, through some structural and procedural realignments.[9]

During the Reagan administration, the Office of International Security Policy (ISP) assumed a larger role within the Department of Defense for policy influence. Its responsibilities encompassed policy development on NATO and European affairs, including nuclear and conventional forces, strategic and theater arms negotiations, nuclear proliferation questions, and oversight of existing agreements.[10] During those years, the assistant secretary of defense for international security policy was particularly prominent in speaking out on arms policy. Richard Perle often took the lead in shaping policy on the question of deploying intermediate-range nuclear missiles in Europe in the early 1980s and in developing the U.S. bargaining position on both intermediate-range and long-range nuclear forces at the arms control talks in Geneva. Indeed, his role in these negotiations, and in policy development generally, was so substantial that it has been chronicled in great detail by a political analyst, a rarity for a middle-level official in the foreign policy bureaucracy.[11]

Although these offices did not gain the same recognition in the George H. W. Bush administration, their status returned during the Clinton years. Two assistant secretaries heading these offices were prominent policy analysts on leave from Harvard University: Joseph Nye, a leading scholar of international relations and foreign policy, headed the Office of International Affairs for a time; and Ashton Carter, a leading thinker and analyst in the nuclear weapons area, headed the Office of International Security Policy. Both sought to put an imprint on policy, and Nye, in particular, was deeply involved in shaping U.S. policy toward Asia.[12]

During the George W. Bush administration, the undersecretary of defense for policy, and the offices within his responsibility, once again gained some notoriety. After September 11, Undersecretary Douglas Feith created an intelligence team to assess whether terrorist links existed between Iraq and other countries. About a year later, in October 2002, he also appointed a special planning team to prepare for a possible war with Iraq. Both teams became controversial in the aftermath of the Iraqi War because of their possible influence on the policy-making process. Indeed, the intelligence team's finding about the "suspected linkages between Iraq and Al Qaeda, a conclusion doubted by the C.I.A. and D.I.A." was particularly a source of interest to those assessing the quality of American intelligence prior to the Iraqi War.[13] Nonetheless, this kind of controversy suggests the potential foreign policy impact of the Department of Defense on the direction of American policy. Ultimately, though, the importance of OSD—and any office within it—will be a function of how the secretary of defense or even the president wants to use them to shape foreign policy.

The Joint Chiefs of Staff

The Joint Chiefs of Staff (JCS) is a second set of important policy advisors within the Department of Defense. The JCS, composed of the chief of staff of the Army, the Chief of Naval Operations, the chief of staff of the Air Force, the commandant of the Marine Corps, and the chairman of the Joint Chiefs, has been described as "the hinge between the most senior civilian leadership and the professional military."[14] The responsibility of the JCS is to provide the president and the secretary of defense with strategic planning and to coordinate the integration of the armed forces for use if necessary. In addition, the JCS recommends to the president and the secretary of defense the military requirements of the United States and how they are to be accomplished. Finally, the chairman of the Joint Chiefs, appointed by the president with the advice and consent of the Senate, is the primary military advisor to the secretary of defense, the National Security Council, and the president.[15]

Policy-making Constraints Despite its statutory foreign policy duties, the Joint Chiefs of Staff probably has generally been less effective in shaping American policy since World War II than the civilian side of the Pentagon for at least two reasons.

First, the Joint Chiefs has enjoyed only mixed favor with both presidents and secretaries of defense since 1947.[16] In fact, some presidents and secretaries have been at odds with the JCS and have tried to reduce its policy impact. President Eisenhower, for instance, was determined to "balance the budget and restrict military spending"—something the JCS did not favor.[17] With his own vast military experience in World War II, Eisenhower did not see the need to rely upon the JCS for advice and assistance, especially after it had publicly criticized his policy. Under President Kennedy, the situation for the JCS only worsened, as Secretary of Defense Robert McNamara attempted to streamline and modernize the management and operation of the Pentagon. Any initial confidence that President Kennedy might have placed in the JCS was quickly eroded as a result of what he perceived as bad policy advice on the Bay of Pigs invasion in April 1961.[18]

Relations between the JCS and the president improved from Johnson through Ford. During the Johnson administration, relations warmed a bit—especially after the disaffection and ultimately the resignation of Secretary of Defense McNamara in 1967—when the president increasingly became dependent upon the JCS for policy advice on the Vietnam War. Even before this occurrence, however, there is some evidence of President Johnson's more favorable tilt toward the Department of Defense, if not directly to the Joint Chiefs, in foreign policy making.[19] Under Presidents Nixon and Ford and when Melvin Laird was secretary of defense, the

Joint Chiefs was clearly in the ascendancy in terms of influence, even though it did not apparently shape the critical policy positions during those years.[20]

Under the Carter and Reagan administrations, the situation changed once again, and reliance on the JCS fluctuated. Carter's major policy decisions on troop withdrawals from Korea and the scrapping of the B-1 bomber were adopted with minimal JCS involvement.[21] By contrast, the Reagan administration appeared initially to be more receptive to the views of the JCS. At one point in his administration, President Reagan reportedly sent written praise to the Joint Chiefs for its policy advice.[22] Despite such praise, policy making for the Reagan administration was largely located elsewhere within the executive branch and the Department of Defense.

Second, each Joint Chief's commitment to his own service has reduced combined policy impact.[23] That is, each JCS member has the responsibility of managing his own military service as well as advising the president and the secretary of defense through the Joint Chiefs structure. In the estimate of one defense analyst, this individual service responsibility consumes an important portion of Joint Chiefs' time and diminishes their combined foreign policy formulation role. The divided loyalties among JCS members also produces policy differences within the Joint Chiefs themselves, and, in turn, policy recommendations reflect a compromise position among them which may not be vigorously supported by all members.[24]

Indeed, criticisms of the Joint Chiefs' recommendations have been particularly harsh. President Jimmy Carter's secretary of defense, Harold Brown, for instance, characterized the advice from the JCS as "worse than nothing." Another former high-ranking Pentagon official labeled it as "a laughingstock." Yet a third official—a former aide to Brown—said the advice was like a "bowl of oatmeal." Despite President Reagan's praise of the JCS, Secretary of Defense Caspar Weinberger rejected or ignored the advice of the Joint Chiefs on such major issues as the basing mode for the MX and on the requirements of the Rapid Deployment Force.[25] Perhaps even more telling regarding the weakened influence of the JCS was President Reagan's failure to even remember the name of the chairman of the Joint Chiefs during a major portion of his administration. When testifying during the Iran–Contra trial of John Poindexter, President Reagan was asked if he recognized the name of John Vessey, chairman of the Joint Chiefs during much of his term in office. While he said that the name sounded "very familiar," he could not be certain as to who Vessey was.[26]

Policy-making Reforms In the Defense Reorganization Act of 1986 (also known as the Goldwater–Nichols Reorganization Act, after its congressional sponsors), Congress changed the power and authority of the Joint Chiefs of Staff to address these problems. In effect, the changes reduced the clout of the individual services in policy recommendations and increased the impact of the JCS as a whole.

One key change was to give more power to the chairman in policy formulation and recommendation. The chairman (and not the Joint Chiefs as such) was designated as the president's primary military advisor, and he was responsible for providing the executive with the range of military advice on any matter requested. Thus the chairman would not have to "water down" his recommendation to accommodate his JCS colleagues. The chairman also assumed statutory responsibility for preparing strategic military plans, future military contingency plans, and budget coordination within the military itself. Finally, the Joint Staff reported directly to the chairman, as did a newly appointed vice chairman.[27]

A second key change was in the command structure. The unified commanders or the commanders in chief (CinCs, in military parlance), those responsible for coordinating the four different services operating in a particular region of the world, gained much greater authority. Under the previous arrangement, the individual services retained substantial authority in directing forces, but, under the reorganization, new authority now rested with those directing multiservice operations, greatly increasing the integration of forces across the branches.

In fact, the Goldwater–Nichols legislation has been characterized as "the most important piece of military legislation . . . in the last forty years . . . [and] the most dangerous."[28] In this view, the reorganization was important because it enhanced the power of the JCS chairman, but it was dangerous because it challenged civilian control of the military. This concern was seemingly given support with the appointment of General Colin Powell as chairman of the Joint Chiefs of Staff during the George H. W. Bush administration.

Described as a "military intellectual," who took a "pragmatic and collegial approach" to policy making, General Powell was well versed in all aspects of national security policy.[29] Aided by the legal basis for policy influence offered by the Goldwater–Nichols Act, Powell was thus in a position to "become the most influential JCS chairman in U.S. history."[30] Indeed, Powell was soon appointed to a new executive defense committee established by the secretary of defense and became a key influence on policy formulation. Significantly, he played a central role in designing the American response to Iraq's intervention into Kuwait, including the resulting American buildup in Saudi Arabia and the Persian Gulf. By one assessment, moreover, Powell was "responsible for shaping the U.S. military response in the gulf," and his strategy of deploying "maximum force" was fully endorsed by President Bush.[31]

When Powell continued in office during the Clinton administration, policy analyst Richard Kohn argued that Powell was in a strong position to defy "a young, incoming president with extraordinarily weak authority in military affairs" in policy making, as he initially did over Bosnia. Further, he would be in a position to invite "resistance all down the line."[32] In this way, traditional civil-military relations might be transformed with greater military influence. Yet as Powell pointed out after his retirement from the JCS chairmanship, any perceived crises in civil-military relations simply did not exist: "[T]hings were not out of control . . . Presidents Bush and Clinton, and Secretaries Cheney and Aspin, exercised solid, unmistakable control over the Armed Forces and especially me."[33] Nonetheless, the JCS chairman's power and influence increased with the passage of Goldwater–Nichols.

Powell's successor, General John Shalikashvili, also benefited from Goldwater–Nichols. Shalikashvili lacked the significant political background of Powell in

Washington (although he served as an aide to Powell in 1991 and 1992 and acted as a representative to the Department of State for Powell on occasions[34]), but he had directed two politically sensitive military operations successfully before he assumed the chairmanship: one in aiding the Kurds in northern Iraq after the Gulf War, the other in planning possible air strikes in Bosnia in 1992 and 1993 as NATO commander. As such, Shalikashvili soon proved to be an important policy participant in the Clinton administration's policy making over Haiti and Bosnia in 1994 and 1995 and an articulate spokesperson for the administration on Capitol Hill. In short, the chairman of the Joint Chiefs had begun to play a more central role in policy making, even for an administration whose first secretary of defense (Les Aspin) sought to rely more on civilian leadership within the Pentagon.[35]

The two most recent chairmen of the Joint Chiefs of Staff, General Henry Hugh Shelton and General Richard Myers, did not quite match the policy-making impact of their immediate predecessors. Shelton served in the last years of the Clinton administration and the first year of the George W. Bush administration. He was more reserved and less assertive than his predecessors and was skeptical of the United States fighting small wars and engaging in peacekeeping operations around the world.[36] Instead, he preferred to work with the troops than to work in the corridors of the Pentagon or the halls of Congress. As such, he was less a policy influencer than was General Powell only a few years earlier.

Because the attacks of September 11 occurred at the very end of General Shelton's watch (he was scheduled to retire on September 30, 2001), he was not a key player in the American response to those tragic events. Neither was his successor, Air Force General Richard Myers. Both were overshadowed by Bush's secretary of defense, Donald Rumsfeld, who quickly took charge of American military policy in the post–September 11 era. General Myers, a skilled and knowledgeable expert in the area of space and missile defense, however, could play an important role in the effort to reshape the American military in the twenty-first century. He soon proved to be an articulate and effective military spokesperson in American actions against Afghanistan in 2001 and 2002 and during the war against Iraq in 2003. Still, his impact on policy itself appears to be overshadowed by others within the Bush bureaucracy.

While Goldwater–Nichols thus benefited the JCS and several of its recent chairmen, it significantly benefited the regional commanders in chief (CinCs) who were given joint command over all branch of American military forces in their area. In doing so, the ability of the CinCs to shape American policy increased. In particular, the military officials heading the five regional commands around the world (Pacific, Southern, European, Central, and Northern) have increasingly assumed a larger and larger role in policy formulation and implementation. This increased power for the CinCs has also been aided by the decline in the capacity of the State Department through continuous budget cuts and the attrition of staff and through the diminished role of the service chiefs of the Army, Navy, and Air Force in affecting policy. As one analyst put it, "Washington came to rely ever more on the regional CinCs to fill a diplomatic void."[37]

In the Gulf War of 1991, for example, General Norman Schwartzkopf became a bit of a folk hero over his direction of the war and his political impact as well. In the Iraq War of 2003, General Tommy Franks, the head of the Central Command, did likewise. Other CinCs in the past decade have assumed important role whether in shaping policy in Asia (Admiral Dennis Blair), Europe (General Wesley Clark), or the Middle East (General Anthony Zinni).[38] Indeed, President Bush called upon General Zinni in late 2001 and early 2002 to serve as his special envoy to try to get the Middle East peace process back on track after the September 11 attack upon the United States.

In all, then, uniformed military officials—whether the chairman of the Joint Chiefs of Staff or the regional commanders in chief—have played a larger role in the shaping of policy as well as implementing it, and the Goldwater–Nichols reforms were important in aiding this process.

The Secretary of Defense

After the office of the secretary of defense and the Joint Chiefs of Staff, the third policy advisor within the Department of Defense is the secretary himself. Over the postwar years, the secretary's role in policy making has been enhanced considerably. As the secretary's control of the department increased through the reform acts of 1953 and 1958, and as the confidence of presidents in their secretaries of defense rose, the influence of the office in foreign policy making expanded.[39] Two analyses challenge this view and contend that the powers of the secretary of defense are less than the responsibilities of the office and that the relative influence of the secretary can be easily overstated.[40] While noting the cautionary signs that have been raised over the power of the secretary of defense, a good case can still be made that the secretaries of defense on particular issues, and in some administrations, have often commanded as much influence as the secretary of state. A brief survey of the most important occupants of this post supports this view, especially for recent decades.

Past Influential Secretaries   The most influential of the twenty-one secretaries of defense since 1947 has been Robert McNamara, who was secretary of defense throughout President Kennedy's years in office and for most of President Lyndon Johnson's term. With his close ties to both presidents, McNamara, more than any other cabinet officer, exercised policy influence.[41] Given a wide mandate to modernize the Pentagon, McNamara was also allowed substantial latitude in shaping America's strategic nuclear policy. Moreover, he was the spokesperson who announced the change in strategic doctrine in two important areas: (1) the nuclear strategy toward the Soviet Union and (2) the defense strategy for NATO. In the former area, McNamara moved the United States nuclear strategy from one of "massive retaliation," in which the United States reserved the right of engaging in an all-out nuclear attack for an act of aggression by the Soviet Union, to one of "mutual assured destruction" (MAD). In the latter area, McNamara was instrumental in developing the strategy of flexible response for the United States and its European allies. This strategy called for the use of both conventional and nuclear forces to respond to any Soviet or Warsaw Pact aggression in Central Europe. Once again, the notion behind this strategy was to move away from simply a reliance upon an all-out nuclear response and instead to use conventional (i.e., nonnuclear) forces and short-, intermediate-, and long-range nuclear weapons in maintaining stability in Central Europe. Like MAD, this strategy remained a core element of America's defense posture throughout the Cold War.

Harold Brown, who served during the Carter administration, continued a pattern of secretaries of defense who were increasingly influential on foreign and defense policy making. Originally one of the "whiz kids" in the Department of Defense under Robert McNamara, Brown was able to shape Pentagon policy toward his own views and toward those of the president. On such controversial issues as the B-1 bomber, the Panama Canal treaties, and SALT II, Secretary Brown was quite successful in getting the military to follow his lead.[42] In turn, he was able to work well with the White House on several contentious policy questions. Furthermore, Brown enjoyed good relations with Zbigniew Brzezinski, the national security advisor to the president, who came to dominate policy during much of the Carter administration.[43]

Caspar Weinberger, secretary of defense until the last year of the Reagan administration, was an equally influential participant in the foreign policy process, particularly in bolstering defense expenditures. Aided by strong support from President Reagan, Weinberger achieved virtually all his requests for a conventional and strategic military buildup. Only by 1983 were the requests of the secretary and the Department of Defense for defense spending compromised.[44] Still, by fiscal year 1985, the Department of Defense's budget authority reached the highest in real terms for any period in the 1980s, a total of $295 billion. In subsequent years, however, Weinberger was not as successful, with the budget declining about 3.5 percent a year from fiscal year 1986 through fiscal year 1988. Nonetheless, Weinberger had been able to move the defense budget from less than $200 billion per year to nearly $300 billion per year in a very brief period of time.[45] Moreover, Weinberger's political influence lay in his close ties with President Reagan and with the president's second national security advisor, William Clark.[46]

Recent Secretaries of Defense under Bush and Clinton   President George H. W. Bush's secretary of defense, Richard Cheney, was hailed by friends and adversaries as "bright, articulate, fair, unflappable, and eminently likable."[47] While Cheney's policy-making clout did not seem to match that of his immediate predecessors, he proved to be a competent manager of the department, where he quickly put together a plan to reduce the size of the U.S. military for the post–Cold War era, and an articulate spokesman for the military on Capitol Hill, where he previously served as Wyoming's representative in the U.S. House for six terms. He also enjoyed the support of the public. In fact, during the crisis immediately after Iraq's intervention into Kuwait and then during the conduct of the Gulf War itself, Cheney's stature rose appreciably.[48] Along with General Colin Powell, he had primary responsibility for negotiating the initial commitment of U.S. forces to Saudi Arabia in August 1990, consulting with Congress over more arms sales to Saudi Arabia, and developing the shape of U.S. foreign policy in the region.

Clinton's three secretaries of defense had more mixed records in terms of policy influence. His first, Les Aspin, a congressman from Wisconsin and chairman of the House Armed Services Committee at the time of his move to the Pentagon, proved to be a better strategic thinker than a manager of the Department of Defense. Indeed, he was forced to resign by the end of the first year of the Clinton administration over the Somalia fiasco, some policy differences with the White House, and his leadership style at the Pentagon.[49] Despite his short tenure at the Department of Defense, Aspin initiated three important evaluations of America's defense posture for the post–Cold War years during his brief tenure. His most important accomplishment was the completion of the "Bottom-Up Review," the study that outlined U.S. defense strategy after the Cold War and set forth the restructuring of the military to meet the threats of the new era. He also announced and set into motion the Counterproliferation Initiative—to use both prevention and protection to counteract the emerging threats from weapons of mass destruction around the world. His third major endeavor, a review of U.S. nuclear posture after the Cold War, was not completed until after he had left office.

Clinton's second secretary of defense was William Perry, a mathematician and former undersecretary of defense for research and engineering during the Carter administration.[50] In contrast to Aspin, Perry was more reserved and formal. He had earned his credentials as a Pentagon bureaucrat and enjoyed the respect of the defense brass and Congress alike. He also had the bureaucratic skills to manage what has been described as "the largest corporate entity in the world."[51] On the other hand, his political and policy-making skills were suspect, and he had little background as a public spokesperson on security issues.[52] Still, Perry proved to be more successful than initially predicted. In the management of the Pentagon, Perry did quite well. He tightened up the running of meetings at the Defense Department, "pushed for reforms in the Pentagon's byzantine procurement system," sought to enhance the industrial base undergirding U.S. defense policy, and reaffirmed an emphasis on new technology to bolster America's defense.[53] In shaping policy, Perry worked to implement the "Bottom-Up Review," proposed an easing in American "dual-use" technology exports to aid American businesses, and sought to develop a new concept-preventive defense to guide future security policy. In particular, preventive defense would be "the first line of defense of America, with deterrence the second line of defense, and with military conflict the third and last resort."[54]

Perry's successor in the second term of the Clinton administration, former Republican senator William Cohen, brought a bipartisan cast to national security policy, but he did not prove to be an important shaper of foreign or defense policy. Instead, he was largely overshadowed by Secretary of State Madeleine Albright and National Security Advisor Sandy Berger. However, Cohen, a veteran member of the Senate Armed Services Committee and an acknowledged expert on defense issues, engaged in a great deal of international travel, "courted foreign defense ministers and even presidents and prime ministers," and consulted on myriad agreements with foreign countries.[55] In this sense, he contributed to the Department of Defense's effort to play a larger role in America's diplomatic effort worldwide. Within the Pentagon bureaucracy, though, he was often overshadowed by the increasing influence of the regional commanders within the Pentagon (i.e., the CinCs as discussed earlier) and did not leave the kind of policy mark that Aspin or his other predecessors had in their tenure as Clinton's secretaries of defense.

Secretary of Defense in the George W. Bush Administration   By contrast, President George W. Bush's secretary of defense, Donald H. Rumsfeld, has arguably returned this office to be an important force in the shaping of foreign and defense policy, especially in the post–September 11 period. Rumsfeld was appointed as secretary of defense in December 2000 to a second tour in this role, having previously served in the Ford administration. During his previous tenure, Rumsfeld had worked closely with Vice President Cheney, and he originally hired Cheney for a position in the Nixon administration. In this sense, he was well connected to the Bush White House through Cheney and was thus perhaps poised to exercise more foreign policy influence than other secretaries of defense. He also came to office steeped in some current defense issues, important to candidate George W. Bush. In particular, Rumsfeld led a 1998 independent commission that reviewed and evaluated the threat posed by ballistic missiles from North Korea and Iran, and the commission's report brought the issue back on the national agenda.[56] Furthermore, Rumsfeld had a mandate to undertake a "defense transformation"— an effort to change the way the United States would wage war during the twenty-first century.

His initial efforts to exercise significant policy influence and to effect this transformation of the military were largely undermined by his own style and by bureaucratic politics. His brass and brusque style did not immediately win him favor with Pentagon officials or even with his policy-making counterparts in the Bush administration. His tendency to dress down senior military officials and his generally caustic style of policy making won him few friends, either in the Pentagon or on Capitol Hill. Indeed, some military officers found themselves treated less well than during the Clinton administration.[57] Even the White House "quickly countermanded" a commitment to seek a supplemental defense appropriation from Congress.[58] Furthermore, the proposed $18 billion defense increase ultimately approved by the administration did not go very far in addressing the transformation of the American military. In short, the first nine months of Rumsfeld's tenure were largely unsuccessful and frustrating.

The events of September 11, however, had a telling effect on Rumsfeld's role within the Pentagon, and his impact on policy making changed appreciably after those events. Indeed, Secretary Rumsfeld and the military assumed an importance and a centrality in policy making that they had not had in many years. Rumsfeld immediately became the point person in the policy discussions over how to respond to al-Qaeda and the Taliban in Afghanistan. During the first set of meetings after September 11, for example, Rumsfeld immediately "raised the question of Iraq" with President Bush.[59] As American military actions were under way in Afghanistan in 2001 and 2002 and then later in Iraq in 2003, Rumsfeld often held press conferences explaining American actions and defending policy decisions. Indeed, his skills in explaining policy and deflecting criticism enhanced his policy role in the administration. In short, along with Deputy Secretary of Defense Paul Wolfowitz, Secretary of Defense Rumsfeld was increasingly the principal shaper of American foreign policy in the immediate months after September 11.

Within the Pentagon, too, Rumsfeld's stock improved appreciably after September 11. The appointment of a new chairman of the Joint Chiefs of Staff, General Richard Myers, the increased funding for defense from Congress (quickly edging toward $400 billion yearly), and the ability to use the war on terrorism to reshape the military all contributed to his effort to undertake a defense transformation of the Pentagon. In time, though, Rumsfeld had to confront some new challenges. As the reconstruction effort in Iraq stalled, as human rights abuses occurred there, and as American forces were stretched thin around the world, the Defense Department and Secretary Rumsfeld increasingly became targets of criticisms at home over the direction of American policy. (Indeed, one long-serving member of Congress, David Obey of Wisconsin, called for his resignation over Iraq policy in the summer of 2003, and other members did in 2004 over the Iraq prisoner abuse scandal.) While the policy debate over Iraq and other political-military issues continue, one thing seems certain: The Department of Defense and the secretary of defense remain important influences on the direction of American foreign policy in the early years of the twenty-first century, perhaps as much as at any time in several decades.

THE INTELLIGENCE AGENCIES

Another key structure within the foreign affairs bureaucracy is the intelligence community. Although the growth of America's intelligence apparatus owes much to the Cold War, the role of intelligence has increased dramatically in the post–September 11 era. Indeed, in a world increasingly fraught with dangers from international terrorism and political and economic instabilities, the ability of policy makers to evaluate effectively the global political, economic, and social conditions is arguably more important than ever before. With continued incidents of global terrorism (e.g., in Saudi Arabia, Morocco, and Iraq in 2003 and Spain in 2004), the possession of nuclear weapons by North Korea and possibly other states, and the occurrence of potential ecological issues worldwide (e.g., global warming), sound intelligence remains as necessary—maybe even more so—than ever before. Importantly, the 2003 Joint Congressional Intelligence Report into the Terrorist Attack of September 11, 2001, emphasized the continuing need for intelligence, even as it outlined the changes necessary in the intelligence community after that event.[60]

While the intelligence community is often associated with the Central Intelligence Agency (CIA), it is really much more comprehensive than that single agency. There are intelligence units within the Department of Defense, the Department of Energy, the Department of the Treasury, the Federal Bureau of Investigation, Department of State and, since 2003, Department of Homeland Security (discussed separately below). Each intelligence unit concentrates on various aspects of information gathering and intelligence analysis.

Within the Defense Department, for example, the Defense Intelligence Agency (DIA) operates such a service as does each branch of the military within that bureaucracy.[61] The Department of Defense also has three additional intelligence agencies under its organizational structure. First, the National Security Agency (NSA) has responsibility for gathering signal intelligence (or SIGINT) from a variety of electronic and nonelectronic sources from foreign countries, breaking transmission codes of these sources, and developing secure transmission codes for several American government agencies.[62] Second, the National Reconnaissance Office (NFO) also operates under auspices of the Department of Defense and its "core responsibilities have included overseeing and funding the research and development of reconnaissance spacecraft and their sensors." It is also responsible for "procuring the space systems and their associated ground stations, determining launch vehicle requirements . . . , and disseminating the data collected."[63] The National Imagery and Mapping Agency develops and analyzes imagery intelligence. This office produces maps, topography, and imagery support for the Department of Defense, the CIA, and other governmental agencies, as needed, and works closely with the Department of Defense and CIA personnel employed in similar areas.[64] Figure 10.2 portrays the components of the intelligence community—those elements under the Department of Defense, those outside the DOD, and the independent agency.

The exact size and budget of the intelligence community is difficult to estimate, shrouded as it is in secrecy within Department of Defense funding, but some estimates have been available over the years. In the early 1970s, the intelligence community consisted of about 150,000 individuals, with a budget in excess of $6 billion annually, and by 1980, the total budget grew to over $10 billion. During the Reagan administration, spending on intelligence reportedly "sharply increased . . . for the CIA and other intelligence activities."[65] Indeed, the budget of the 1990s had increased threefold from the 1980s: The Bush administration reportedly asked Congress for $30 billion in funding for intelligence activities during fiscal year 1991, and that figure represented only a "moderate increase" from 1990.[66] In mid-1994, Congress inadvertently published the budget figure for the intelligence community (about $28 billion) in a declassified transcript of a Senate hearing, and, later, a House committee reported a budget breakdown for major intelligence components, with about $3.1 billion to the CIA, $13.2 billion to NSA, DIA, and the National Reconnaissance Office, and $10.4 billion to the intelligence units of the military branches.[67] In 1997, the director of central intelligence revealed that the aggregate budget for intelligence was $26.6 billion for fiscal year 1998, and acknowledged that the intelligence budget was roughly 10 percent of the size of the defense budget.[68] In the aftermath of the events of September 11, 2001, the spending on defense has increased sharply, and it is reasonable to expect that the intelligence budget continued to follow the previous pattern as well. If it does so, the spending on intelligence may reach about $40 billion per year.

As Figure 10.2 illustrates, the director of central intelligence (DCI) stands at the center of the intelligence community. The exact responsibility of the DCI and each agency within the intelligence community was spelled out in an executive

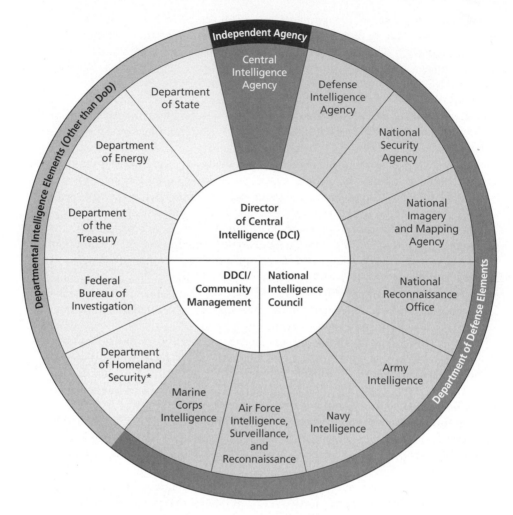

Figure 10.2 The Intelligence Community

*According to an executive order, only those posts of the Department of Homeland Security dealing with "analyses of foreign intelligence" are in the intelligence community.

SOURCE: The Intelligence Community, *Factbook on Intelligence,* Central Intelligence Agency Web site (www.cia.gov).

order issued by President Reagan in December 1981, and that order remains in effect.[69] The order established that the DCI was responsible for developing the intelligence program and its budget and for directing the collection of all intelligence throughout the various agencies. In general, the DCI was given much greater control over intelligence matters by that order than in the original National Security Act of 1947 or the Central Intelligence Act of 1949.

Under the order, too, the director of central intelligence was specifically designated the primary advisor to the president and the National Security Council for intelligence matters. The order also provided that the National Security Council could establish "such committees as may be necessary to carry out its functions and responsibilities under this Order."[70] Recent presidents have used different mechanisms for implementing the order.

The Reagan administration, for example, formed the Senior Interagency Group, Intelligence (SIG-I), to advise the NSC on intelligence matters. The membership on the committee varied from time to time, but it was mainly composed of the following: the director of central intelligence, the national security advisor, the deputy secretary of state, the deputy secretary of defense, the chairman of the Joint Chiefs, the deputy attorney general, the director of the FBI, and the director of the National Security Agency. This committee, under the leadership of the director of central intelligence, was to be the principal intelligence group within the U.S. government and was to oversee the collection of intelligence and the implementation of any intelligence decisions by the National Security Council. Later in the Reagan administration, the National Security Planning Group, a smaller and more select group of the National Security Council, assumed responsibility for monitoring covert intelligence activities.[71]

The George H. W. Bush administration established a different arrangement. It relied upon the NSC Deputies Committee and a NSC Policy Coordination Committee on intelligence for monitoring intelligence activities. The latter interagency committee had initial responsibility over intelligence activities and was chaired by an individual appointed by the director of the CIA, while the Deputies Committee, headed by the deputy national security advisor, had been given particular responsibility in the area of covert operations within the national security system. President Bush's directive on the organization of the National Security Council system explicitly called for "a representative of the Attorney General" to be in attendance when this committee discussed covert actions.[72]

The Clinton administration followed a similar arrangement as the George H. W. Bush administration. Presidential Decision Directive 2, an order establishing the membership on the National Security Council committees, was silent on the actual responsibility for reviewing and authorizing covert operations, but it did specify an additional member to the Deputies Committee of the NSC when considering intelligence operations. "When meeting on sensitive intelligence activities, including covert actions, the attendees shall include the appropriate senior representative of the Attorney General."[73]

President George W. Bush's *National Security Presidential Directive-1* is likewise silent on managing intelligence, but the structure and membership on the Deputies Committee of the National Security Council strongly suggests that the pattern established by the Clinton administration remains in effect.[74] In this connection, then, the Deputies Committee appears to have primary responsibility over reviewing operations anticipated by the intelligence community. With the perception of intelligence failures after the events of September 11, 2001, with the creation of the Department of Homeland Security, and with congressional calls for further changes in intelligence operations (see below), intelligence arrangements within the administration are likely to change.

Relative Influence in Policy Making

The policy-making impact of the CIA, and of the intelligence community more generally, stems from a central role in providing information about international issues and in evaluating different foreign policy options. Several different types of intelligence products developed by the intelligence community as a whole and by its components (i.e., CIA, DIA, etc.) enable the community to affect the policy formulation process. By one estimate, the community regularly produces at least a dozen different intelligence products for policy makers.[75] On a daily basis, for example, the intelligence community produces the *President's Daily Brief* and the *National Intelligence Daily.* These reports deal with immediate issues, using both open and classified sources. On an annual basis, the intelligence community produces its more familiar, and more comprehensive, intelligence products: the National Intelligence Estimates (NIEs) and the Special Estimates (previously they were called Special National Intelligence Estimates or SNIEs). NIEs are in-depth analyses of a particular country, region, or issue. The number of these reports completed each year varies by administration, but they can range from several dozen upward, although their total has dropped in recent years.[76] The Special Estimates, as their name implies, are special intelligence reports in response to current developments around the world. Their exact number varies from year to year, depending upon the changing global events and the tasking from the intelligence leadership. In addition to these estimates, each of the major intelligence agencies produces a variety of separate intelligence reports for use and reference by policy makers and analysts.[77]

The National Intelligence Council (NIC) oversees and authorizes the production of the intelligence estimates for the community as a whole (also see Figure 10.2). It is composed of CIA intelligence officers, representatives from other departments with intelligence responsibilities (e.g., state, defense), and civilians from universities and nonprofit organizations, and is the central decision-making body on intelligence production and analysis. In turn, the National Foreign Intelligence Board—the heads of the principal components of the intelligence community as outlined in Figure 10.2—"review[s] and approve[s] each estimate before it is published and sent to the president and other top officials."[78]

Despite these numerous reports and analyses, the intelligence community's effectiveness in the policy process remains difficult to gauge because of the secrecy surrounding its role and its activities. Since policy makers are heavily dependent upon the intelligence community for information about policy options, a reasonable inference is that its influence is quite substantial. Assessments of the intelligence community's analytic capabilities vary widely, but the quality of its work, and how policy makers use intelligence, has especially come under criticism since the events of September 11, 2001.

Acclaim for Its Policy Assessments Marchetti and Marks, two severe critics of the CIA generally, nonetheless hint at the quality of its intelligence estimates, especially during the Cold War. While CIA estimates on relative U.S.-USSR strength during those years were not always successful in shaping policy and were subject to abuse on occasion, they argue, these estimates often served as a counter-weight to the influence of the military planners in debates between the president and Congress. These analysts also point to the success of the agency in gathering intelligence leading to the showdown with the Soviet Union over missiles in Cuba in 1962.[79]

Others also point to the utility of the CIA's analytic assessments as well. One analyst points to the accuracy of its estimates during the early policy making on Southeast Asia—although the CIA's recommendations were not always followed by presidents and their advisors.[80] The CIA also reportedly assessed the situation in the Middle East correctly just prior to the outbreak of the Six-Day War in 1967. Policy makers, however, were unable to take effective action to prevent the war's occurrence.[81] Furthermore, the intelligence community painted a grim picture of the Soviet economy near the end of the country's existence, characterizing it as in a "near crisis," and pointed out that some modest decline in Soviet military spending had occurred.[82] Such estimates undoubtedly assisted policy makers in deciding on the degree of United States support to provide for *perestroika* in the USSR.

Other threads of evidence also have emerged that point more directly to the policy influence of the CIA in different regions of the world. Prior to the fall of the Shah of Iran in 1979, for example, the CIA reportedly exercised considerable influence over U.S. relations with Iran. Because the CIA assisted in establishing the Nicaraguan Contras, the forces opposed to the Sandinista regime, and because those forces were a key element in American policy toward Nicaragua throughout much of the 1980s, the intelligence community enjoyed a leading role in the formulation of policy in that area, too. Indeed, both the Department of State and the Department of Defense deferred to the intelligence community on this issue for a time, leaving policy largely to the CIA and to key White House allies.[83] Even after Congress cut all American military assistance to the Contras in October 1984, we now know, in light of the Iran–Contra investigation, that the CIA and National Security Council operatives, such as Admiral John Poindexter and Oliver North, remained active in supporting the Contras. Yet a third area where the intelligence community played a pivotal role in policy was aiding Afghanistan after the Soviet invasion in late 1979. The CIA ran an arms smuggling operation there for several years until the Soviets finally abandoned their effort in that country.[84]

Criticisms for Its Policy Assessments   At the same time, the intelligence community has been the object of severe criticism by presidents and others both for the quality of its intelligence and for its efforts to shape foreign policy. President Kennedy, in particular, lost confidence in the CIA over its policy recommendations that led to the ill-fated Bay of Pigs invasion.[85] As a result, Kennedy was later reluctant to accept fully the agency's intelligence advice and options on Southeast Asia or the Cuban Missile Crisis. Instead, he sought advice from other agencies and individuals to assist him in policy making. Later in the 1960s, the CIA was criticized over the loss of the intelligence ship USS *Liberty* during the Six-Day War in the Middle East, and the capture of the Navy spy ship the *Pueblo* by the North Koreans in 1968.[86] In the early 1970s, the intelligence community again came under attack for its failure to evaluate accurately the likelihood of the Yom Kippur War between Israel and its neighbors in October 1973.[87]

In the late 1970s, the quality of American intelligence came in for criticism yet again. At the time that the Shah of Iran was losing power in 1978, President Carter was moved to send off a sharply worded memo to his key advisors: "I am not satisfied with the quality of political intelligence. Assess our assets and as soon as possible give me a report concerning our abilities in the most important areas of the world. Make a joint recommendation on what we should do to improve your ability to give me political information and advice."[88] Indeed, an "Iran Post-mortem" report on intelligence lapses over the Iranian revolution of 1979 noted myriad problems in assessing the internal situation of that country and in arriving at sound intelligence estimates: lack of intelligence sources near the Shah or in all the opposition groups; little discussion of CIA intelligence estimates within the bureaucracy or the airing of disagreements on those estimates; the inadequate use of publicly available sources; and conflicting meanings drawn from the words and phrases used in the intelligence estimates.[89] Furthermore, doubts were also raised about the failure of the intelligence community to assess more accurately the Soviet military buildup of the 1970s and the strength of the Soviet economy in the 1980s.[90]

In the 1980s and as the Cold War ended, the criticisms continued. Questionable intelligence estimates recommended the use of a grain embargo against the Soviet Union over that country's invasion of Afghanistan but failed to predict the bombing of the marine barracks in Lebanon in October 1983, which killed 241 Americans. Intelligence lapses over the changing events in Eastern Europe—whether it was over the opening of the Berlin Wall in November 1989, the sudden, violent fall of Nicolae Ceausescu in Romania in December 1989, or the initial reforms within the Soviet Union throughout 1989 and 1990—raised anew doubts about the CIA's analytic abilities. Even the successes during the Persian Gulf War of 1991 did not come without some intelligence failures: U.S. intelligence estimates placed the number of Iraqi forces in the Kuwait theater at 540,000, when the number was really closer to 250,000; they placed the number of mobile Scud launchers at 35, when the number totaled nearly 200; and they reported that Iraq had many chemical weapons in the Kuwaiti theater although none were found.[91]

More dramatic was the failure of the intelligence community to predict the collapse of the Soviet Union in 1991. To be sure, the intelligence community did predict an economic slowdown in the Soviet Union, but it was not successful in predicting the economy's collapse. Nor was it successful in pointing to the political demise of the Soviet Union itself (although, in fairness, few others did so either). Still, this shortcoming, coupled with other failures, led one senator to call for the CIA's functions to be turned over to the Department of State.[92]

This criticism of the intelligence community perhaps reached its peak in the aftermath of the events of September 11, 2001. In a report issued in the summer of 2003, a joint investigation by the two congressional intelligence committees noted an array of failings by the intelligence community prior to the attacks. As the chairman of the Senate Intelligence Committee at the time noted, the attacks "could have been prevented if the right combination of skills, cooperation, creativity and some good luck had been brought to the task," but "no evidence surfaced . . . to show that the government could have prevented the attacks." Still "a lot went wrong," another senator observed.[93]

The congressional investigation found two important problems: (1) available information on the future terrorists and information on the suspicious activity by others had not been fully examined or utilized by the intelligence community; and (2) information was inadequately shared among the CIA, FBI, National Security Agency, and others prior to the attacks. Consider the following examples from the intelligence report that illustrate these problems. First, the intelligence community had developed information about Osama bin Laden and his terrorist activities "that was clearly relevant to the September 11 attacks, particularly when considered for its collective significance" (including information that terrorists were considering the use of aircrafts as weapons), but it was not fully recognized and utilized. Second, the intelligence community gathered information on two future hijackers in early 2000 but failed to act on it fully. It knew, for example, that these two future hijackers "had numerous contacts with a long time FBI counterterrorism informant in California," but apparently it did not share that information with the FBI office in San Diego handling the informant. Third, the FBI had information from its Phoenix field office about Osama bin Laden sending students for aviation training in the United States, but "FBI headquarters did not take the action requested by the Phoenix agent prior to September 11, 2001" to follow up on this information. Fourth, the FBI field office in Minneapolis had detained Zacarias Moussaoui, who was pursuing flight training in Minnesota (but whom the FBI suspected of being invoked in a hijacking plot), and the field office wanted "to obtain a court order to search Moussaoui's belongings." Because of disagreement and misunderstanding regarding what was needed to obtain such an order, valuable time was lost just prior to the events of September 11. In all, then, available intelligence information was not fully analyzed and fully shared among the appropriate agencies, and some intelligence opportunities were lost because they were not always adequately pursued.[94]

In the months leading up to the March 2003 war with Iraq (and even after it), controversy and criticism also surrounded the intelligence community and its assessments. In his 2003 State of the Union address, President Bush claimed that Iraq had sought to purchase uranium from the nation of Niger and used that information to bolster his case that Iraq was seeking to develop nuclear weapons. An October 2002 national intelligence estimate (NIE) had in fact stated that "a foreign government service reported" on a possible arrangement between Iraq and Niger (and possibly two other countries), but the estimate also noted that "we cannot confirm whether Iraq succeeded in acquiring uranium ore and/or yellowcake from these sources."[95] Despite this assessment (and a footnote in the NIE that the State Department was dubious of such a claim), the assessment still was utilized by President Bush in his January speech. In July 2003, though, when the British House of Commons noted that the initial report about Niger was wrong, the administration was forced to retract the "16 words" from the State of the Union address dealing with the matter. In turn, the director of central intelligence,

George J. Tenet, assumed responsibility for failing to delete this reference from the prepared text.[96] Once again, then, concerns were raised over both the quality of the intelligence analysis and the way in which intelligence assessments were being used by policy makers.

Some Reasons for Intelligence Problems   Several reasons seem to account for these intelligence and policy failures over the years, including the terrorist attacks of September 11, 2001. One focuses on the quality of intelligence produced by CIA analysts. As one of President George H. W. Bush's advisors put it with reference to the changes in Eastern Europe in the late 1980s and early 1990s, the CIA is "good at analyzing trends," and "poor at predicting the timing of events in the collapse of Eastern Europe." Testifying before Congress after the bombing of the American military complex in Saudi Arabia in the summer of 1996, Secretary of Defense William Perry pointed to another limitation in intelligence analyses: "The intelligence was not useful at a tactical level. It didn't specify the nature of the threat or the timing of the threat, and therefore it was not what we might call actionable intelligence in terms of doing our planning."[97] Another former CIA official raised questions about the adequacy of "fact-checking" by CIA analysts and the possible problem of exaggeration with the use of increasingly popular oral briefings of policy makers.[98] In part, of course, the incomplete evaluations of a 2002 intelligence report that Iraq sought to purchase nuclear materials from several African countries illustrate this problem. As a result, unverified information eventually made its way into President Bush's State of the Union address. In sum, the general issue surrounding the quality of intelligence analysis was bluntly stated by a former Defense Department official: "The CIA's analysts 'collect a lot of facts and organize them very nicely. But their predictions are wrong.'"[99]

A second reason focuses on excessive reliance upon technology for intelligence assessments at the expense of human intelligence and analysis. With the increasing use of satellites and electronic interceptions of messages, for example, less reliance has been placed on agents in the field. Even those analysts who are at work are criticized as either too timid in their assessments—more interested in protecting their reputation than in taking risks—or overzealous—too often driven by ideological bias. Further, some intelligence analysts lack the necessary skills. While political analysts are plentiful, sometimes analysts with sociological and anthropological backgrounds are needed to assess more fully the changes occurring in a foreign society.[100] Evaluating the determination of Iraq's Saddam Hussein and his Revolutionary Council to keep Kuwait as well as estimating the loss of morale on the part of the Iraqi military from the U.S. air war required more than electronic intelligence in the Gulf War of 1991. Similarly, assessing al-Qaeda or similar terrorist organizations and their capabilities and intentions today requires more than technical surveillance if either attacks like September 11 are to be stopped or if attacks on American solders in postwar Iraq are to be prevented.

A third reason for the failure of intelligence is competition among the various bureaucracies. As one official noted: "In intelligence, what you foresee is often affected by where you work."[101] The Defense Intelligence Agency (DIA), for example, often gives different intelligence estimates than the CIA. During the Cold War, the DIA tended to be more hawkish on Soviet intentions than the CIA, and the two agencies also sparred over estimates in particular regions (e.g., the likelihood of Soviet success in Afghanistan) or particular weapons systems (e.g., the capabilities of Soviet air defenses) in the past.[102] Such competing estimates will occur more frequently, when more diverse actors and issues complicate global politics than they did during the Cold War. In the months prior to the war with Iraq, the intelligence estimates from the State Department on the danger that Iraq poses differed from the estimate provided by the Department of Defense. Under such circumstances, intelligence estimates sent to policy makers may simply become "compromises" between or among several intelligence bureaucracies, or they allow policy makers simply to chose the estimate that fits most favorably with their ideological or prior sets of beliefs. The controversy over the "16 words" in President George W. Bush's 2003 State of the Union address discussed earlier illustrates how intelligence estimates can be used, abused, or even ignored in the disputes among various bureaucracies dealing with intelligence assessments.[103]

Yet a fourth reason often identified for intelligence shortcomings is the structure of leadership within the intelligence community. The director of CIA is also the head of the entire intelligence community, which cuts across many different foreign policy bureaucracies outlined above. Therefore, the degree to which the director can be an honest broker among these bureaus has been called into question, whether in distilling intelligence estimates or in assigning areas of responsibility. As a result, the intelligence community's "product" has not always been as useful as it might be with this kind of organizational structure. Indeed, the need for separating these two roles has been identified as a necessary reform for some time,[104] and it remains so. Undoubtedly in recognition of this persistent problem, the first recommendation in the 2003 report issued by congressional intelligence committees investigating the September 11 attack was a pointed call for creating a director of national intelligence to oversee the community's operation. The director, in the report's words, would possess "the full range of management, budgetary and personnel responsibilities needed to make the entire U.S. Intelligence Community operate as a coherent whole," and this official would hold no other position within the intelligence community.[105]

Recent Cases and Pressures for Reform:
From Aldrich Ames to September 11

Two recent events—one in 1994, the other in 2001—particularly shook the mooring of the intelligence community and sparked calls for fundamental reforms. The first was the revelation that a Soviet/Russian mole was operating in the Central Intelligence Agency, the other, of course, was the terrorist attacks on the World Trade Center and the Pentagon in September 2001. While many recommendations have been made after both events, the record of reform remains spotty overall.

The case of Aldrich "Rick" Ames, a Soviet counterintelligence agent in the CIA, was the first shock to the intelligence community. Ames was arrested in

February 1994, plea-bargained for life imprisonment for himself (and a lesser sentence for his wife), and was quickly convicted of spying for the Soviet Union during the previous nine years. In the course of his lengthy espionage, however, Ames had shared literally hundreds of highly classified documents with the Soviet Union and identified a number of individuals from the Soviet Union and its allies who were working for the CIA. Ten of those identified were subsequently executed by the Soviets, and dozens of others were imprisoned.[106]

The Ames case caused damage both to the intelligence community's internal operations but also to its policy-making role. First, Ames's lengthy espionage contributed to a flawed perception of the Soviet Union by the American intelligence community during the crucial years at the end of the Cold War. After the Soviet agents working for the United States were executed, for instance, the Soviet Union was able to use a series of double agents to feed false and misleading information to the United States about Soviet military strength.[107] Second, while the amount of intelligence damage to United States and its interests was considerable, the entire extent may never be known. While Ames was required by his plea-bargain agreement to cooperate fully with intelligence officials, he claimed that he could not remember everything that he revealed because he was always drunk when he met with his Soviet handlers (yet, almost every time he took a lie-detector test after his conviction, he failed to pass it).[108] Third, the Ames case also called into questions the internal workings of the intelligence community and raised the question over whether the intelligence community "culture" went too far to protect its members. As the subsequent investigations revealed, Ames had long had a serious drinking problem, received poor performance ratings, violated intelligence procedures, and appeared to be living beyond his government salary. Yet, such seeming indicators of a possible personnel problem were not recognized.[109]

Although the Ames case produced several investigations and calls for reform, only limited actions were ultimately taken. At least three different internal intelligence community investigations were initiated—one to improve security procedures, a second to evaluate the damage that Ames had done, and a third to assess the quality of the operational supervision of Ames. Virtually all the reports turned out to be unflattering to the operation of the CIA. As a result, some changes took place, and others were called for. CIA Director James Woolsey, for example, was forced to resign and new personnel, committed to reform, were appointed. Congress, too, initiated some actions. The congressional intelligence committees, for example, called for a substantial overhaul of the intelligence community and a bipartisan commission was set up by Congress to examine the future of the intelligence community.[110] Still, the numerous problems were not fixed.

After the events of September 11, there were immediate calls for investigations of what went wrong and for actions to prevent such attacks in the future. One immediate change was congressional passage of the USA PATRIOT Act in October 2001. This act granted the executive branch, and particularly the intelligence community, more investigatory tools to pursue terrorist suspects. In doing so, though, the legislation narrowed some domestic civil liberties and sparked some domestic protests, especially as the administration has sought to expand the act with new legislation. A second important response was the investigation by the congressional intelligence committees and the report that they issued in July 2003. Their report calls for a sweeping restructuring of the intelligence community to provide greater coordination and cooperation among the various components and set forth a number of specific actions for strengthening the counterterrorism activities of the United States. (Some of the specific recommendations of this report are discussed below). In addition, with his signing of the intelligence authorization legislation for fiscal year 2003, President Bush established the National Commission on Terrorist Attacks Upon the United States for another investigation of September 11 and the intelligence community. The formal mission of this panel, headed by former New Jersey governor Thomas Kean and former congressman Lee Hamilton, was to prepare "a full and complete accounting of the circumstances surrounding the September 11, 2001 terrorist attacks," and "provide recommendations to guard against future attacks."[111] While the commission held numerous hearings, perhaps the most explosive were those held in March 2004 in which Clinton and Bush administration officials testified. While these officials outlined diplomatic and military efforts to track down Osama bin Laden and al-Qaeda prior to September 11, they acknowledged that those efforts were unsuccessful. Further, one former Bush administration official with counterterrorism responsibilities testified that the administration did not act urgently on the perceived terrorist threat before September 11 and that the war against Iraq had diverted attention from the anti-terrorist efforts. Bush administration officials denied such accusations. Increasingly, though, intelligence analyses and recommendations were being politicized. Nonetheless, the report of the commission ought to provide impetus for needed changes within the intelligence community.

CIA "SPECIAL ACTIVITIES" AND POLICY INFLUENCE

While the analysis side is a crucial component of the intelligence community, it is not the only one. The other "side" of the intelligence community consists of covert operations. This side of the intelligence community, too, has often been criticized for its lack of accountability and control and for its considerable influence on the direction of American foreign policy. Indeed, some critics have called for the elimination of these operations, on both policy and ethical grounds. These activities are not effective, they contend, and they are inconsistent with the ethical standards of the American people.[112]

Yet, American covert intelligence operations, or "special activities" as they are euphemistically called, are far more numerous than we often think, and they form important aspects of foreign policy making. These activities have included propaganda campaigns, secret electoral campaign assistance, sabotage, assisting in the overthrow of unfriendly governments, and, apparently, even assassination attempts on foreign officials. Covertly supplying funds to Afghan tribal groups to fight against the Taliban in the fall of 2001 illustrates one recent type of covert action, while sending covert operatives into Iraq three months prior to the 2003 war "to forge alliances with Iraqi military leaders and persuade commanders not to fight" represents another.[113]

Many times, too, these covert activities involve counterintelligence activities, activities "concerned with protecting the government's secrets."[114] Part of this work involves such mundane efforts as classifying sensitive documents to keep them out of the public domain and providing adequate physical security for American secrets. Yet, part of counterintelligence also involves infiltrating the intelligence services of foreign governments, subverting and blackmailing agents through unethical means (e.g., creating compromising situations for foreign agents), and using measures to thwart the techniques that are being used against the United States.

Such covert (and not so covert) operations immediately raise questions about their compatibility with democratic values and ethical standards as well as how accountable the agents are for their actions. The public has often been divided on the wisdom of such activities and has expressed this uneasiness in public opinion polls. In 1995, for example, 48 percent of the public thought these activities were acceptable but 40 percent did not.[115] After September 11, however, the public seemingly had become more supportive of at least one such type of activity. In a 2002 survey, 66 percent of the American people "favor[ed] the assassination of individual terrorist leaders" (although the question did not specify whether this should be done overtly or covertly).[116] For most administrations over the years, though, any ambivalence or support among the American public over covert operations has apparently not mattered very much: Covert activities have been widely used by the government. As we shall see, though, these operations have occasionally stirred serious concerns about their accountability among policy makers and the American people.

Origins and Usage of Covert Operations

Under the National Security Act of 1947, the CIA was not only authorized to collect intelligence, but it was also authorized "to perform such other functions and duties related to intelligence . . . as the National Security Council may from time to time direct."[117] By successive directives from the NSC and succeeding presidents, it has continued to hold that imperative. In President Reagan's 1981 executive order (still the one operating today), these covert operations were defined as "those activities conducted in support of national foreign policy objectives which are planned and executed so that the role of the United States government is not apparent or acknowledged publicly, and functions in support of such activities, but which are not intended to influence United States political process, public opinion, policies, or media, and do not include diplomatic activities or the collection and production of intelligence or related support functions."[118] As this directive suggests, the mandate is broad and open-ended.

The appeal of these measures to various presidents has been unmistakable: "Clandestine operations can appear to the President as a panacea, as a way of pulling the chestnuts out of the fire without going through all the effort and aggravation of tortuous diplomatic negotiations. And if the CIA is somehow caught in the act, the deniability of these operations, in theory, saves a President from taking any responsibility—or blame."[119] These activities, then, are not designed to be traceable to the White House.

The use of these activities has indeed been substantial since World War II, even if the exact number is not readily available. In its final report in 1977, the Senate Select Committee on Intelligence Activities (the Church Committee, named after its chair, Senator Frank Church of Idaho), which investigated the covert activities of the CIA over the postwar period, hints at the broad usage of these activities over the years and provided some figures as well:

> [C]overt actions operations have not been an exceptional instrument used only in rare instances. . . . On the contrary, presidents and administrations have made excessive, and at times self-defeating, use of covert action. In addition, covert action has become a routine program with a bureaucratic momentum of its own.[120]

Between the years 1949 and 1952, the Church Committee reported that the director of central intelligence approved some 81 projects. In the Eisenhower administration, 104 covert operations were approved; in the Kennedy administration, 163; and in the Johnson administration, 142.[121]

Yet the exact totals go well beyond these numbers, as evidenced by a 1967 CIA memorandum that noted that only 16 percent of the covert operations received approval from a special committee to monitor them. By yet another estimate, several thousand covert actions were undertaken from 1961 on, with only a small percentage (14 percent) receiving review by the National Security Council or its committees.[122] Along with the number of activities, the justifications for undertaking covert operations have greatly expanded, "from containing International (and presumably monolithic) Communism in the early 1950s, to merely serving as an adjunct to American foreign policy in the 1970s."[123]

Covert operations, moreover, were an important instrument of foreign policy for the Reagan administration and remained for subsequent American administrations. As Reagan's former National Security Advisor Robert McFarlane has noted, the United States must have an option between going to war and taking no action when a friendly nation is threatened. In McFarlane's view, there must be something available between "total peace" and "total war" in conducting foreign policy.[124] Covert activity seemed to fit that middle category for a number of American administrations. Because President George H. W. Bush served for a time as the director of the CIA in the 1970s, he was particularly attuned to the role that covert operations can play in providing another foreign policy alternative for the United States. Brent Scowcroft publicly endorsed covert actions several years before serving as Bush's national security advisor: "In many cases, covert action is the most effective, easiest way to accomplish foreign policy objectives. It is only effective if it remains covert."[125]

There is little evidence to suggest that this view does not continue during the George W. Bush administration, especially with its all-out war on international terrorism. Indeed, the use of covert operations has undoubtedly increased, as have the calls for the continued use of such operations. One of the first actions after the September 11 attacks on the United States was for the director of the CIA, George Tenet, to outline for the president and his advisors a plan for "a full-scale covert attack on the financial underpinnings of the terrorist network, including clandestine computer surveillance and electronic eavesdropping to locate the assets of al-Qaeda and other terrorist groups." In addition, he brought along to this meeting a draft intelligence finding "that would give the CIA power to use the full range of covert instruments, including deadly force" against these adversaries. Finally, illustrating the pervasiveness of covert operations worldwide, CIA Director Tenet produced a document outlining "covert operations in 80 countries either underway or that he was now recommending" in the war against terrorism.[126]

Furthermore, the congressional intelligence committees' report investigating the September 11 attacks strongly endorsed the continued use of covert operations. Specifically, that report recommended that the intelligence community "maximize the effective use of covert actions in counterterrorist efforts" and that the intelligence community "facilitate the ability of CIA paramilitary units and military special operations forces to conduct joint operations against terrorist targets."[127]

In sum, special (and covert) operations became an important staple of American policy, especially in the late twentieth century, and, with the Bush administration's war on terrorism, they apparently remain so in the early years of the twenty-first century.

Accountability and Covert Actions

The Church Committee Report and several other investigations questioned the degree of political accountability for covert operations. Because the lines of accountability were not always operating, and because the CIA often carried on special activities without the full approval of the rest of the government, and particularly the White House, the agency's influence on policy was substantial. In effect, the agency could seemingly shape foreign policy.

Such discretionary powers were in operation from the beginning of the agency. In the initial 1947 NSC directive for covert operations (NSC-4), no formal guidelines were established to approve or coordinate these activities. The only requirement was that the director of central intelligence would be certain, "through liaison with State and Defense, that the resulting operations were consistent with American policy." Up to 1955, for instance, there were still no clear procedures for approval of CIA covert operations. At best, the National Security Council required that consultation take place with the Department of State and the Department of Defense, although formal consultation with the president or his representative was not required. In fact, during the period from 1949 to 1952, the director of central intelligence apparently granted approval for covert operations without assistance.[128]

Even when clear NSC directives were issued for committee approval of covert operations (beginning in 1955), the procedures were not without some loopholes. As a CIA memorandum in 1967 reports:

> The procedures to be followed in determining which CA [covert action] operations required approval by the Special Group or by the Department of State and the other arms of the U.S. government were, during the period 1955 to March, 1963, somewhat cloudy, and thus can probably best be described as having been based on value judgments by the DCI [Director of Central Intelligence].[129]

Although new directives were issued in 1963 and 1970, slippage in accountability remained. Not all covert actions were discussed and approved by the new NSC committee, the Forty Committee (a committee established to review and monitor covert operations). Nor were the covert action proposals always coordinated with the Departments of State and Defense.[130]

Coupled with this weakness in executive branch accountability for CIA activities was the lack of any greater accountability by Congress during the bulk of the post–World War II years. Although in principle the Armed Services and the Appropriation Committees in the House and the Senate had oversight responsibility (and the CIA argued that it reported fully to the appropriate subcommittees), in practice, the CIA was under only "nominal legislative surveillance" throughout much of the Cold War period.[131] Chairs of these committees did not want to know of, or did not make concerted efforts to monitor, CIA activities. Further, Congress as a whole seemed reluctant to inquire significantly into intelligence activities.

One analysis has dubbed this inaction on the part of Congress a result of the "buddy system," a cozy relationship between top CIA officials and the several "congressional barons," usually key committee chairs or ranking minority members in the House and Senate Armed Services and Appropriations Committees.[132] Such members as Senators Richard Russell (D–Georgia) and Leverett Saltonstall (R–Massachusetts) and Congressmen Carl Hayden (D–Arizona), Mendel Rivers (D–South Carolina), and Carl Vinson (D–Georgia) did not always want to know about all CIA activities or, at least if they did, they were able to squelch any attempts to let knowledge of these activities get beyond a small group. As a result, CIA covert activities were at best shared with a small congressional constituency whose inclination was not to challenge or disrupt any "necessary" CIA activity.

What such procedures allowed was that the CIA could by itself begin to shape, although perhaps not direct, American foreign policy. Without adequate accountability or control, the CIA could take actions that might be outside the basic lines of American policy or, at the very least, might create difficulties for the overt foreign policy of the United States. This latter problem in particular arose once covert actions were revealed. In this sense, the foreign policy influence of the intelligence community through the use of its covert side could be quite substantial. The exact significance of the CIA's influence cannot be fully determined, owing once again to the secrecy surrounding its operation.

The Hughes–Ryan Amendment

By the early 1970s, several key events weakened this congressional acquiescence to CIA covert operations and ultimately produced more congressional oversight. First, the Bay of Pigs attack against Castro's Cuba in 1961, almost solely a CIA-designed operation, proved to be a fiasco. As a result, President Kennedy became increasingly suspicious of reliance on that organization in policy formation. Second, the Vietnam War produced a large increase in CIA covert operations which, in turn, stimulated more congressional interest in these kinds of activities. Third, investigations over America's involvement in destabilizing the government of Salvador Allende raised questions about CIA activity abroad, too. And finally, the "Watergate atmosphere" of 1972–1974 emboldened Congress to challenge executive power across a wide spectrum, including intelligence activities.[133]

The first result of this new congressional interest was the Hughes–Ryan Amendment. Sponsored by Senator Harold Hughes (D-Iowa) and Representative Leo Ryan (D-California), this amendment to the 1974 Foreign Assistance Act began to impose some control on the initiation and use of covert activities. Its key passage is worth quoting in full:

> No funds appropriated under the authority of this or any other Act may be expended by or on behalf of the Central Intelligence Agency for operations in foreign countries, other than activities intended solely for obtaining necessary intelligence, unless and until the President finds that each such operation is important to the national security of the United States and reports, in a timely fashion, a description and scope of such operation to the appropriate committees of the Congress.[134]

Thus this amendment required that the president be informed about covert operations (hence eliminating the "plausible denial" argument for the executive) and that he must certify that each operation is "important to the national security of the United States." Further, the amendment directed the president to report, "in a timely fashion," any operation to the "appropriate" committees of the U.S. Congress. Under this provision, eight committees needed to be informed: the Committees on Armed Services and Appropriation in the House and the Senate, the Senate Foreign Relations Committee, the House Foreign Affairs (now, International Relations) Committee, and, later, the Senate and House intelligence committees established in 1976 and 1977, respectively.

In addition to these new reporting requirements under the Hughes–Ryan Amendment, two separate investigations by the executive and legislative branches recommended several other changes in the monitoring of intelligence operations. An executive-ordered inquiry into intelligence activities in 1975 (the Rockefeller Commission) and a legislative inquiry by the Senate in 1975 and 1976 (the Church Committee) recommended several substantive and procedural changes in the operation of the Central Intelligence Agency, especially regarding covert operations. New legislative acts were proposed for gaining greater oversight of the CIA through joint or separate intelligence committees in Congress, through the establishment of an intelligence community charter by Congress, and through more stringent control over covert actions. The investigations also recommended consideration of a more open budgeting process, a limitation on the term of the directorship of the CIA, and the consideration of appointing a director from outside the organization.[135]

Aside from the establishment of intelligence committees in each house of Congress, few of these recommendations actually became law; some reforms, however, were incorporated in executive orders issued by Presidents Ford and Carter. President Ford issued an executive order in February 1976, in which the lines of authority over covert operations were spelled out and which expressly prohibited political assassination as an instrument of American policy. Two years later in January 1978, President Carter issued another executive order on the reorganization of the intelligence community, which included some recommended reforms, too.[136] Even though few reforms were translated into statutes, the various reform proposals did have the effect of calling attention to the accountability problem of the intelligence community as a whole, and especially to its covert side. As a result, the reforms did serve to lessen the influence of the intelligence community in foreign policy making.

Furthermore, Stansfield Turner, CIA director during the Carter administration, proceeded to undertake an organizational reshuffling to increase the powers of the director and to focus more on analytic intelligence than on covert operations. Turner also initiated a reduction in personnel within the CIA's Directorate of Operations, the bureau that handles clandestine operations. Veteran intelligence officers were dismissed from the intelligence service; by one account, more than 800 members of the intelligence community were forced out by the end of 1977.[137] Not surprisingly, both of these actions were said to have hurt morale within the agency, and especially within the clandestine services.

Intelligence Oversight Act of 1980

Despite these efforts at greater control, the intelligence community and its allies were successful in stopping any further legislative restrictions. Most notably, proposed legislation to establish an intelligence community charter never became law. In fact, by 1980, the intelligence community was able to persuade Congress to repeal the Hughes–Ryan Amendment and its reporting requirements and to pass legislation that was deemed more workable.

This act, the Intelligence Oversight Act of 1980, retained the Hughes–Ryan provision that the president must issue a "finding" for each covert operation, but it modified the reporting requirements of that earlier act. (An intelligence finding is a statement, later required to be a written statement, in which a covert operation is defined and in which the president has certified that the operation is "important to the national security of the United States.") Now, the executive branch (either the director of central intelligence or the appropriate agency head) was required to report only to the Select Committee on Intelligence in the Senate and the Permanent Select Committee on Intelligence in the House.[138] Prior notification of all covert operations, however, was now specified in the law and not simply "in a timely fashion," as required under the Hughes–Ryan language. Further, the act also required that the executive branch report to the committees any intelligence failures, any illegal intelligence activities, and any measures undertaken to correct such illegal activities.

Some reporting discretion was also afforded to the president by two exemptions that were included in the statute. First, if the president deemed that a covert operation is vital to national security, he may limit prior notification to a smaller group (the "Gang of Eight," as they came to be called) listed in the statute: the chairs and the ranking minority members of the House and Senate intelligence committees, the Speaker and minority leader of the House, and the majority and minority leaders of the Senate. Even in these exceptional instances, though, the president must ultimately inform the entire intelligence committees "in a timely fashion."

Second, a more oblique, and potentially more troubling, exemption was also incorporated. The statute specified that reporting of covert operations was to be followed "to the extent consistent with all applicable authorities and duties, including those conferred by the Constitution upon the executive and legislative branches of the Government." While the meaning of this passage is purposefully vague, it invites the executive branch to claim constitutional prerogatives on what information it will share with the legislative branch. (And, indeed, the Reagan administration apparently invoked this exemption to defend its delay in disclosing covert operations surrounding the Iran–Contra affair.)

By this legislation, a balance seemed to have been struck between the requirements of secrecy, as demanded by the intelligence community and the executive branch, and public accountability, as sought by the United States Congress and the public. The intelligence community gained the repeal of the Hughes–Ryan legislation, which it disliked, and Congress was able to gain knowledge of covert actions prior to their occurring, except in rare instances.

The initial application of even these requirements was not without controversy, however. When it was publicly revealed, in April 1984, that the CIA was involved in the mining of Nicaraguan harbors, the Senate Intelligence Committee reacted strongly in the belief that it had not been properly informed. (In fact, Senator Daniel Patrick Moynihan, vice-chair of the Senate panel, resigned in protest for a time, although he later withdrew his resignation when CIA Director William Casey apologized for not keeping the committee fully informed.) Subsequent evidence indicated that, in fact, the CIA had informed the House and Senate committees, although the briefing on the Senate side was not as complete as it might have been. As a result of this episode, the CIA pledged to notify the Senate and the committee in advance of "any significant anticipated intelligence activity."[139] On balance, then, this incident demonstrates that the congressional intelligence committees seemed determined to preserve accountability on covert operations ordered by the executive branch.

The Iran–Contra Affair:
Failed Accountability of a Covert Operation

Only two years later, the revelations surrounding a series of events that came to be called the Iran–Contra affair again raised questions about how accountable covert operations were to such congressional directives. After Congress had cut off CIA funds to the Contras, a group of rebels fighting the Nicaragua's Sandinista government, through the passage of the Boland Amendment, and after the seizure of several American hostages in Lebanon in the early 1980s, members of the Reagan administration initiated covert operations to assist the Nicaraguan Contras and to sell arms to Iran to help free the American hostages in Lebanon. In turn, and without President Reagan's knowledge (according to his testimony), these two operations were linked when a portion of the Iran arms sales profits were funneled to the Contras. These covert actions unfolded from 1984 to 1986 without any congressional accountability or knowledge. Indeed, the House and Senate intelligence committees were kept in the dark about all of these activities until CIA Director William Casey testified before the committees on November 21, 1986.

A Failure to Comply with Existing Statutes Critics charged that the Iran–Contra episode was an example of the executive branch's failure to comply with the requirements of the Boland Amendment and the Intelligence Oversight Act. The joint report of the House and Senate select committees investigating this episode outlined numerous specific violations of the legislative statutes and agreed-upon congressional-legislative procedures.

Three general violations serve to illustrate the difficulty of congressional oversight of covert operations.[140] First, contrary to the prohibitions in the Boland Amendment, CIA and NSC staff of the Reagan administration sought a private organization (called "the Enterprise") "to engage in covert activities on behalf of the United States." This organization became involved in both the arms sales to Iran and in aiding the Nicaraguan Contras, used "private and non-appropriated money" to carry on these activities, and received support from CIA personnel around the world. Beyond the specific prohibition of the Boland Amendment, this covert operation violated the Intelligence Oversight Act, since the Congress was not kept informed. Second, the covert arms sales to Iran were also carried out in a manner inconsistent with the Intelligence Oversight Act. Intelligence findings were neither properly prepared and approved by the president in all instances, nor were they reported to Congress "in a timely fashion." The first arms sale to Iran in August–September 1985 was completed only through an oral finding. According to President Reagan's testimony, however, he could not remember exactly when he approved this sale. A retroactive finding was prepared to cover the CIA's involvement in the second arms sale to Iran in November 1985, but this finding was ultimately destroyed by National Security Advisor John Poindexter in February 1986. Finally, a finding for arms sales to Iran was signed and approved by the president on January 17, 1986, but this finding was never shared with the intelligence committees of Congress or even the smaller Gang of Eight, as allowed under the Intelligence Oversight Act, until the episode was publicly revealed in November 1986. Third, the transfer to the Nicaraguan Contras of a portion of the funds from the arms sales to Iran was inconsistent with government policy. It not only violated the Boland Amendment regarding military aid to the Contras, but it was done largely outside the established channels of government and represented a significant privatization of U.S. covert operations.

Recommendations of the Investigating Committees The investigating committees acknowledged that the episode "resulted from the failure of individuals to observe the law, not from deficiencies in existing law or in our system of governance." Therefore, their "principal recommendations . . . [were] not for new laws but for a renewal of the commitment to the constitutional government and sound processes of decisionmaking." Nonetheless, the committees suggested that "some changes in law, particularly relating to oversight of covert operations" may be helpful.

Their recommendations fell into three categories. The first set of recommendations focused on improving the preparation and dissemination of presidential "findings" on covert operations. Findings should be in writing and reported in that form to Congress "prior to the commencement of a covert action except in rare instances and in no event later than 48 hours after a Finding is approved." They should include the names of all U.S. agencies involved in such operations but should restrict National Security Council members from participating in covert operations. Findings also should be limited to one-year duration (before possible recertification). All National Security Council members should be informed of such findings. And finally, no finding should recommend actions that are presently illegal under existing law. The second set of recommendations called for a series of executive branch changes in monitoring the participation of private individuals used in covert operations, in preserving executive documents of such operations, and in strengthening treaties regarding foreign bank records of U.S. individuals so that the executive and congressional branches can gain access to them. In addition, Congress called for improved legal review of covert operations. The third set of recommendations focused on steps that Congress could take to improve its oversight capacity by reviewing the adequacy of contempt statutes currently on the books, the effectiveness of several laws dealing with arms sales and arms transfers, and congressional procedures for safeguarding classified information.

Executive/Legislative Changes in Accountability
after the Iran–Contra Affair

Prior to the final report of the two investigating committees, President Reagan issued a new directive outlining several changes that conformed with the committee recommendations, although at least one did not.[141] Under Reagan's executive order, all executive branch agencies (and private individuals) participating in these operations were ordered to report in the same manner as currently required of the Central Intelligence Agency. An intelligence finding for a covert operation must be in writing and completed before the operation begins, except when an "extreme emergency" arises. Oral and retroactive findings were no longer to be permitted. All findings must be available to members of the National Security Council, thus ensuring that the secretary of state and the secretary of defense will be informed of such operations. And finally, all findings must be limited in duration and periodically reviewed.

Concerning the notification of Congress, though, President Reagan's directive did not necessarily represent a tightening of reporting requirements; instead, it opened up the possibility of even more delay. That is, Reagan pledged that his administration would notify Congress within two working days after a covert operation had begun, "in all but the most exceptional circumstances." Thus, a real possibility existed that the reporting of more and more covert operations would be delayed until after they had begun and, in some instances, perhaps very long after they had begun.

In 1988 and 1989, Congress enacted several legislative remedies as a result of the Iran–Contra affair. The first legislation dealt with "third parties" transferring American supplies to another country. It specifically required the president to allow Congress 30 days to pass legislation to block such transfers from taking place. Under this legislation, Congress would now have the right to stop such action within 30 days of being notified of it, if Congress were inclined to do so. A second legislative measure strengthened prohibitions on the sales of arms to countries supporting global terrorism. The third required the president to appoint an independent inspector general for the Central Intelligence Agency as one mechanism for closer monitoring of covert actions. And finally, a provision was added to a foreign aid appropriations bill that prohibited the use of such aid to be used as a lever to gain support for some foreign policy activity (e.g., aiding the Contras).[142]

In 1991, Congress took further action by enacting new legal procedures to govern covert operations. The law, in effect, finally put into statute some of the changes that were originally part of President Reagan's 1987 executive order, albeit in a more flexible way. The law provided a legal definition for a covert operation for the first time, required that the president approve, in writing, all covert activity by any executive agency, and outlawed all retroactive finding of covert actions. Still, some discretion was afforded the executive discretion in the use of third parties to carry out covert operations, and the president was allowed "a few days" to notify Congress of the initiation of such operations.[143] In essence, the law continued to affirm the president's prerogative to assert "his constitutional authority to withhold information for more than a few days."[144]

These standards of accountability by and large remain in effect today, although some changes (and calls for others) have been made, especially to fight the war on terrorism. For instance, Congress has now changed the rules about conducting wiretaps on foreigners and American citizens "who are associated with suspected terrorist groups" and has "relaxed the conditions under which courts may authorize warrants for national security wiretaps and searches." Congress has also considered, but not yet changed, an internal CIA policy dating back to 1995 that requires "the Directorate of Operations headquarters to approve the recruitment of sources believe to have serious criminal or abusive human rights records." The

concern of some former officials now is that such a policy hinders efforts to infil-
trate terrorist organizations since potential recruits are hardly likely to have satisfactory records in this area, although good reasons remain for keeping it. As a
result, calls remain for changing this internal policy directive. Finally, some have
called for reconsidering the ban outlawing "intelligence agencies from assassinat-
ing foreign political leaders." To date, such a ban has not been rescinded, and there
are sound policy and ethical reasons for not doing so.[145]

THE INTELLIGENCE COMMUNITY: AFTER THE AMES CASE AND SEPTEMBER 11

With the alarming disclosures from the Aldrich Ames case and September 11, the
intelligence community remained under increasing pressures to make significant
reforms. After the Ames case, the Clinton administration and Congress sought to
reorganize and streamline the intelligence community. The amount of change in
the intelligence community proved to be more incremental than step-level. After
September 11, the calls for reform were even more dramatic, although they fundamentally focused on counterterrorism efforts by the American government.
While some changes were undertaken and a new security bureaucracy created
(i.e., the Department of Homeland Security, which we discuss below), the intelligence community likely remains a target for greater oversight and reforms by both
the executive and legislative branches.

Attempted Reforms during the Clinton Years

President Clinton made some important structural changes in the intelligence
community during his latter years in office. Presidential Decision Directive 24
abolished an existing counterintelligence facility and established a new National
Counterintelligence Policy Board that would report to the president through the
national security advisor. Senior representatives from the National Security Council, CIA, FBI, the Department of Defense, Department of State, Department of
Justice, and a military service with a counterintelligence unit would lead this
board. The same directive created a National Counterintelligence Center, consisting of members from the FBI, CIA, the Department of Defense, and the military
services, whose task is to coordinate counterintelligence activities within the government. These new structures also directed closer collaboration between the FBI
and the CIA in addressing counterintelligence problems.[146] All of these changes
had the effect of weakening the dominance of the Central Intelligence Agency in
conducting counterintelligence activities.

On the congressional level in the 1990s, numerous changes were proposed,
but the action taken were largely modest, either structurally or operationally. On a

structural level, a March 1996 commission report from a commission proposed several changes: (1) a new deputy for the director of the CIA to assist with overall coordination of the intelligence community; (2) the consolidation of the imagery and mapping operations within the community; (3) increased coordination between intelligence actions and law enforcement to deal with proliferation threats, terrorism, drug trafficking, and organized crime; and (4) an open budget for the intelligence community. Importantly, the commission rejected the establishment of a new intelligence czar to coordinate overall activities and opposed the use of the intelligence community to engage in industrial spying.[147] On an operational level, Congress did take a number of actions: It trimmed the intelligence community's budget, established a new conditional fund for covert operations, provided funds specifically for a covert operation against Iran, pushed for buying new and small spy satellites to improve analytic capabilities, and slowed efforts to consolidate agencies within the intelligence community. In addition, Congress allowed the CIA greater latitude in checking the credit records of individuals during counterintelligence operations.[148]

Proposed Reforms after September 11

While no major overhaul of the intelligence community has occurred in the post–September 11 period, the outlines of future changes are foreshadowed in some of the statements and proposals made so far. These changes also focus on both structural and operational reforms within the intelligence community. The fullest statement of the structural and operational reforms envisioned is contained in the July 2003 report issued by the joint investigation of September 11 by the two congressional intelligence committees.[149]

On a structural level, that report calls for Congress to create a statutory position of the director of national intelligence. This individual would have full authority over the entire intelligence community and would not occupy any other position within the intelligence community. Second, a National Intelligence Officer for Terrorism would be created and would sit on the National Intelligence Council to make certain that this issue gets sustained attention. Third, "an effective all-source terrorism information fusion center" should be developed within the Department of Homeland Security. Fourth, the director of national intelligence should move to upgrade the skill levels of intelligence personnel in counterterrorism training, information sharing among intelligence personnel, language capabilities, and require more "joint tours" between intelligence and law enforcement personnel "to broaden their experience and help bridge existing organizational and cultural divides through service in other agencies." Finally, the budgeting process for intelligence should be changed by considering a separate intelligence community budget and for more "long-term investment in counterterrorism."

On an operational level, the report calls upon the president to "take action to ensure that clear, consistent, and current priorities are established and enforced throughout the intelligence community." It also calls for the development of a comprehensive government strategy to combat terrorism. Importantly, too, from a cooperation and integration standpoint, the report calls for a wide-ranging set of actions to improve the domestic intelligence capacities and performance of the FBI, and it proposed that the director of the National Security Agency develop a detailed plan of the "technological challenges for signals intelligence" and how best to integrate intelligence by the NSA with the CIA and the FBI.

While these proposed changes are likely to undergo considerable scrutiny and reformulation, they appear to offer a good blueprint to address some of the shortcomings of the intelligence community in the early part of the twenty-first century.

A Democratic and Ethical Challenge

About a decade ago or so, a veteran government official, Roger Hilsman, called for a more fundamental overhaul of the intelligence community generally and the CIA in particular—away from the structural or operational changes that we have discussed. Hilsman argued that "the United States should get out of the business of both espionage and covert political action."[150] The contribution of espionage "to wise decisions in foreign policy and defense is minimal. But the cost in lives, treasure, and intangibles is high." Similarly, he contended that "covert action has been overused as an instrument of foreign policy," and it has tarnished the image of the United States. "While one action, taken in isolation, might seem worth the cost of slightly tarnishing the national image, the cumulative effect of several hundred blots has been to blacken it entirely, thus corroding one of America's major political assets—a belief abroad in American intentions and integrity." In short, the CIA's role should be only as "an independent research and analysis organization," and other intelligence operations in the rest of the government should be transferred to it.

Hilsman's argument compels us to conclude this discussion with some vexing and important questions about intelligence operations, especially covert activities, and their compatibility with democratic and ethical values. First, how consistent are intelligence activities with American democracy? And second, what about the ethical standards that such actions portend for the United States in conducting its foreign policy? A free and democratic society surely seems at odds with the kinds of intelligence activities that we have described. Moreover, they stand in sharp contrast to the openness and public discussion of issues that Americans demand and promote at home. Similarly, do not some of these activities (e.g., entrapping and enticing foreign agents to engage in unethical conduct) affront the ethical standards of the society? Do they not place the United States in the awkward position of endorsing "the ends justifying the means" proposition with virtually any (unethical) behavior acceptable in pursuing foreign policy ends? With the war on terrorism so much the focal point of attention in recent years, these kinds of questions may not be confronted very directly or very often, since the rationale for fighting terrorism can be so easily and quickly evoked by some. Still, these and related questions need to be raised and addressed anew in deciding on the structure and operation of the intelligence community.

DEPARTMENT OF HOMELAND SECURITY

Another consequence of the intelligence failures associated with the events of September 11 was the creation of a new bureaucracy charged with ensuring homeland security and now also included in the larger intelligence community. In October 2001, by executive order, the Office of Homeland Security was established within the Executive Office of the President, and former Pennsylvania governor Tom Ridge was named as head of this office, or, more formally, as the assistant to the president for homeland security. The mission of this office was "to develop and coordinate the implementation of a comprehensive national strategy to secure the United States from terrorist threats or attack."[151] In addition, a Homeland Security Council, consisting of the president, vice president, the assistant to the president for homeland security, and other key cabinet secretaries, was also created to assist in the development of homeland security policy and to ensure its effective implementation across the U.S. government.

Within a very short time, however, members of Congress called for the creation of a cabinet-level department on homeland security, since a department would be answerable both to the legislative and executive branches rather than to the president only. While President Bush initially balked a creating a cabinet-level department, he changed his mind by mid-2002 and sought to create just such a cabinet department. The House of Representatives quickly passed such a proposal by a wide margin (295–133), but the issue was stalled in the Senate during much of fall 2002 due to differences over work rules that would govern employees within the new department. After the 2002 congressional elections in which Republicans did better than expected with the help of President Bush's personal campaigning on national security issues, Senate opposition waned, and that body quickly passed the Department of Homeland Security Act of 2002 by a margin of 90–9. The bill, creating the new Department of Homeland Security, was signed into law at the end of November 2002.

Like the Office of Homeland Security, the Department of Homeland Security (DHS) has as its "first priority . . . to protect the nation against further terrorist attacks" after the September 11 tragedy.[152] At the same time, DHS combines its mission of protecting American citizens against foreign threats with its mission of "protecting the rights of American citizens and enhancing public services, such as natural disaster assistance and citizenship services." In this sense, it is the prototype "intermestic" agency within the American government—a bureaucracy with responsibilities both domestically and internationally. While our focus is primarily on its foreign policy responsibilities, the dual role of the Department of Homeland Security should be kept in mind.

DHS formally came into existence in early 2003 when twenty-two domestic agencies from several different existing departments were combined to create the third-largest government bureaucracy (170,000 employees and $36 billion budget). The creation of DHS was characterized as "the most significant transformation of the U.S. government since 1947, when President Truman merged the various branches of the armed forces into the Department of Defense better to coordinate the nation's defense against military threats."[153]

Figure 10.3 displays the organizational structure of the Department. DHS consists of five major directorates—Border and Transportation Security, Emergency Preparedness and Response, Science and Technology, Information Analysis and Infrastructure Protection, and Management—and four other divisions housed within it—Coast Guard and Secret Service, Citizenship & Immigration Services, State & Local Government Coordination, and Private Sector Liaison. While all of these divisions have some components that deal directly with foreign policy, the Border and Transportation Security and the Science and Technology directorates are probably the central focus for foreign affairs. The former directorate houses the U.S. Customs Service and the former Immigration and Naturalization Service, while the latter directorate houses programs and centers analyzing environmental dangers, animal diseases, and biological warfare threats, among other issues. Importantly, too, a separate division housing the Coast Guard is also integral to the foreign policy aspects of the DHS.

The department initiated a wide range of activities in the first 100 days of its existence to protect threats from abroad and at home. It put into place, for example, a technologically sophisticated entry-exit system that will make it more difficult for visitors to enter the country illegally. DHS has also "developed new technologies and tools at land, air and sea borders" to protect the homeland and has undertaken a "reorganization of the border agencies . . . to increase departmental services and capabilities." The Science and Technology division (S&T) within DHS developed the Biowatch program. This is a program "to detect terrorist agents like anthrax in time to distribute life-saving pharmaceuticals to affected citizens."[154] More generally, new emergency preparedness training was initiated throughout the country.

The most widely known homeland security mechanism that DHS has developed is the "Homeland Security Advisory System."[155] This system is a five-level, color-coded system to warn the American public about the level of threat detected by the intelligence community. Level 1, or the green level, indicates "a low risk of terrorist attacks," and general procedures of readiness among the public should be followed. Level 2, or the blue level, connotes an assessment of "a general risk of terrorist attacks," and, when this condition is invoked, federal agencies are advised to review and update their response procedures and provide the public with additional warning information if necessary. Level 3, or the yellow level, indicates "a significant threat of terrorist attacks." During this condition, government agencies are to increase surveillance of key locations, coordinate emergency planning, and implement "contingency and emergency response plans." Level 4, or the orange level, connotes "a high risk of terrorist attacks." When this condition is specified, officials and agencies will seek to coordinate activities across the various levels of government, undertake precautionary measures at public events, restrict access to some facilities, and prepare to carry out contingency procedures. Finally, Level 5, or the red level, indicates "a severe risk of terrorist attacks." In this condition, officials should increase personnel to key emergency needs, preposition and mobilize responders and resources, monitor or close some transportation facilities, and close some public facilities.

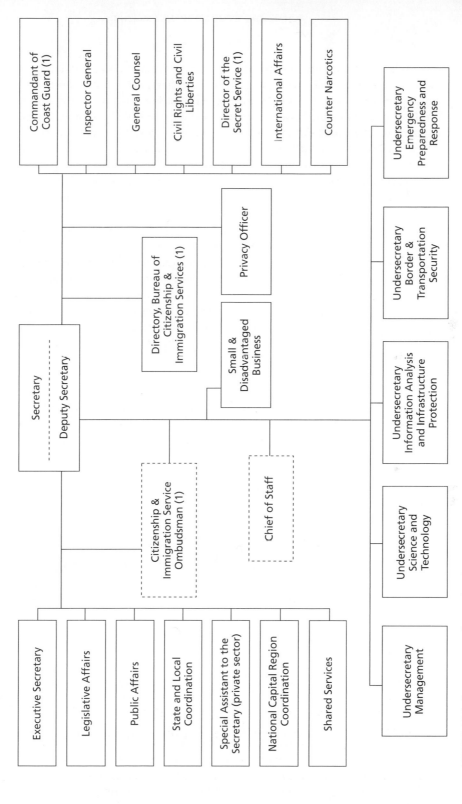

FIGURE 10.3 Department of Homeland Security

SOURCE: U.S. Department of Homeland Security Web site
(http://www.dhs.gov/dhspublic/theme_home1.jsp)

While the advisory system has normally fluctuated between levels 2 and 3 since the system's inception, the advisory level has been raised to level 4 on a few occasions for brief periods of time, especially around major American holidays. While some have questioned the overall effectiveness of the system, the advisory system has reminded Americans to take sensible cautionary actions in the post–September 11 world without unduly disrupting their lifestyle.

In sum, the DHS has moved to develop and implement several new policy actions to address possible threats at home. Yet the department's overall impact on the national security policy and process has remained a source of debate, and several concerns have been raised. One concern has focused on the problems associated with the creation and functioning of the department. With the massive reorganization and its broad set of responsibilities, DHS has had considerable growing pains. Indeed, one analysis has contended that the department has been "hobbled by money problems, turf battles and unsteady support from the White House." As a result, its ability to focus on important security goals has been weakened. Another concern is the degree to which the department is really the focus of policy making, since the Bush administration has made "only limited efforts" to have officials cooperate with DHS. Moreover, the newly created Homeland Security Council, located within the White House, has been critical of the department and has seemingly been its rival as well.[156] Finally, a more general concern is whether this kind of centralized bureaucracy is the best strategy to promote homeland security. As one analysis noted, "Even with full Cabinet status, the secretary of a new Department of Homeland Security will not be able to coordinate the activities and actions of his many cabinet colleagues who have an interest in and share responsibility for protecting the American homeland."[157] In sum, the policy-making role of the Department of Homeland Security on threat questions at this early stage remains unclear.

POLICY COORDINATION
AMONG COMPETING BUREAUCRACIES

For the sake of convenience and clarity, we have described the role of the various executive bureaucracies in the foreign policy process separately. While each department, and groups within departments, may have an impact on policy, the formulation process is also coordinated across the various bureaucracies and policy makers. In the last section of this chapter, we briefly discuss how this coordination is achieved and how "bureaucratic politics" is played out among the foreign policy departments.

The National Security Coordinating System

Beginning in 1966, and initially as a means of placing the Department of State more fully at the center of the foreign policy process, a series of Interdepartmental Regional Groups (IRG) were established to coordinate policy recommendations. Each of these IRGs was headed by the appropriate assistant secretary of state.[158] An IRG, for instance, might consist of representatives from Defense, AID, the National Security Council, the Joint Chiefs of Staff, or whatever departments were appropriate for a particular region or issue. The principal aim in seeking widespread representation was to gain policy advice from various bureaucracies throughout the government. While these groups became a source of bureaucratic coordination, they also became a source of competition. Above the IRGs in the hierarchy, a Senior Interdepartmental Group (SIG), composed of higher-level representatives from the foreign policy bureaucracies and headed by the undersecretary of state, coordinated the activities of the IRGs. The SIGs, in turn, were accountable to the NSC or the various departmental secretaries.

These kinds of working groups were the principal means of carrying the policy process across departments and became the model for subsequent administrations. Although succeeding presidents changed the IRGs to interdepartmental or interagency groups (IGs) or policy coordinating committees (PCC), their use as the principal mechanism for coordinating policy options continued. Even in the extremely hierarchical arrangements of the national security system during the Kissinger years, the use of IGs was not wholly abandoned, although it was altered. Over the years, however, these groups have undergone an important change; they have shifted from dominance by the Department of State toward greater control and direction by the National Security Council and its staff. A description of the interagency process during the four recent administrations (Ronald Reagan, George H. W. Bush, Bill Clinton, and George W. Bush) provides a fuller sense of how these groups facilitate both coordination and competition among the various bureaucracies and how the National Security Council increasingly directs their operation.

The Reagan, Bush, and Clinton Administrations
and Their NSC Systems

The Reagan administration initially followed the same design as had earlier presidents, with a system of SIGs and IGs, but with a clear division of responsibility among the secretary of state, secretary of defense, and the director of central intelligence for different aspects of policy.[159] Specifically, the Reagan administration established four SIGs, which reflected the four major areas of national security issues—foreign policy, defense policy, intelligence policy, and international economic policy—with each headed by a representative from the Department of State, Department of Defense, the CIA, and the Department of Treasury, respectively. Under this arrangement, each SIG created its own IGs for development and review of policy options. These IGs, however, included representatives from other appropriate bureaus and agencies.

By the Reagan administration's second term, several changes emerged. The intelligence SIG was eventually supplanted by the National Security Planning Group (NSPG) in monitoring covert operations. The Crisis Preplanning Group and the Strategic Arms Control Group largely assumed the functions of the SIGs on foreign and defense policy, while the international economic SIG was transferred to the Economic Policy Council.[160] By early 1987, the system was changed once again with the establishment of the Policy Review Group (PRG), a body chaired by the deputy national security advisor and composed of other subcabinet officials from various foreign policy bureaucracies. Along with the NSPG, these groups became the key forums for policy coordination in the last two years of the Reagan administration, meeting over 170 times and coordinating policy on a wide range of activities.[161]

The first Bush administration sought to streamline the policy coordination system across the various bureaucracies and to give even greater control to the national security advisor and his staff in shaping policy. As a result, a relatively simple three-tier hierarchical system of committees was established leading to the National Security Council itself. The most important committee below the NSC for policy coordination was the NSC Principals Committee (NSC/PC).[162] It was the senior interagency group for the consideration of all national security questions and was comprised of key cabinet-level officials with foreign policy responsibilities. The national security advisor chaired this committee and had responsibility for calling its meetings, setting its agenda, and preparing the appropriate policy papers. The second ranking committee in this process was the NSC Deputies Committee (NSC/DC). This committee reviewed the initial work of the interagency groups or the NSC Policy Coordinating Committees (NSC/PCC) and made its recommendations on policy as well. It was composed of subcabinet-level officials from the various foreign policy bureaucracies, and the deputy assistant to the president for national security affairs chaired it. By presidential directive, it had the responsibility to "ensure that all papers to be discussed by the NSC or the NSC/PC fully analyze the issues, fairly and adequately set out the facts, consider a full range of views and options, and satisfactorily assess the prospects, risks, and implications of each." The last set of committees in the policy coordination hierarchy was the NSC Policy Coordinating Committees (NSC/PCC). These committees, comparable to the interagency groups (the IGs) used by other administrations, were the ones that initially developed and prepared the policy options across departments for the administration. The NSC/PCC were both regional, covering all areas of the world, and functional, covering particular issues that were current.

As with the George H. W. Bush administration, the Clinton administration also used a three-tiered set of committees. Two of the three committees had the same names as during the Bush administration, NSC Principals Committee (NSC/PC) and the NSC Deputies Committee (NSC/DC), while the third one was renamed the NSC Interagency Working Groups (NSC/IWGs), a name more closely aligned to that used by earlier presidents for these committees. In function, the three committees varied only slightly from the Bush administration.

For the Principals Committee, the most important difference between the two administrations was its membership.[163] The Clinton administration added the U.S. ambassador to the United Nations and the assistant to the president for economic policy to the usual members on the committee (the secretaries of state and defense, the national security advisor, the director of central intelligence, and the chairman of the Joint Chiefs of Staff). It also invited, as necessary, the secretary of the treasury, the attorney general, and other department heads or agency heads to these meetings. The aim was to provide a more global perspective and to focus beyond political-military issues. As before, though, the national security advisor chaired these committee meetings.

For the NSC Deputies Committee, the Clinton administration expanded its membership from the Bush years and increased its workload, both in policy formulation and implementation. While the deputy national security advisor, undersecretary of state for political affairs, undersecretary of defense for policy, the deputy director of central intelligence, and the vicechairman of the JCS remained on the committee, the deputy assistant for economic policy and the national security advisor to the vice president were added to it. In the policy formulation area, the Deputies Committee now reviewed the work of all the Interagency Working Groups, and apparently had special responsibilities in the area of intelligence activities as well. In addition, this committee was redesignated the Deputies Committee/ CM when it dealt with crisis management issues. In the implementation area, the NSC/DC now had the central responsibility for evaluating the effectiveness of administration initiatives and for considering whether various policy directives "should be revamped or rescinded." Finally, and as had been the practice in the previous administration, the deputy national security advisor chaired the committee, although he was now required to consult with officials from state and defense and the National Economic Council, as appropriate, in operating the committee.

The series of Interagency Working Groups (NSC/IWGs) under the Clinton administration continued to be established by the Deputies Committee. They were either permanent or ad hoc, and, as in the Bush administration, they dealt with regional issues (e.g., an IWG on the Middle East) and functional issues (e.g., an IWG on counterterrorism). In this sense, although the names of these committees changed, their functions remained much like those in the previous administration.

The George W. Bush Administration
and the NSC System

Continuity with past administrations largely characterizes the NSC system under the George W. Bush administration.[164] Much like the George H. W. Bush and Bill Clinton administrations, the new Bush administration adopted a three-tiered national security system. Figure 10.4 shows the structure of the administration's NSC system. Some committee names and membership changes have changed, and a few new wrinkles have been added, but no fundamental structural transformation in the system took place from earlier years. As we shall note, though, some operational changes appear to have occurred after the events of September 11.

For the George W. Bush administration, the NSC Principals Committee (NSC/ PC) continues to consist of the secretary of state, secretary of defense, secretary of the treasury, and the assistant to the president for national security affairs, but it now includes the chief of staff to the president, the national security advisor to the vice president, and the deputy national security advisor. In this sense, President Bush has a larger number of key advisors than previous administrations and has ordered that some regular members in the past (e.g., director of central

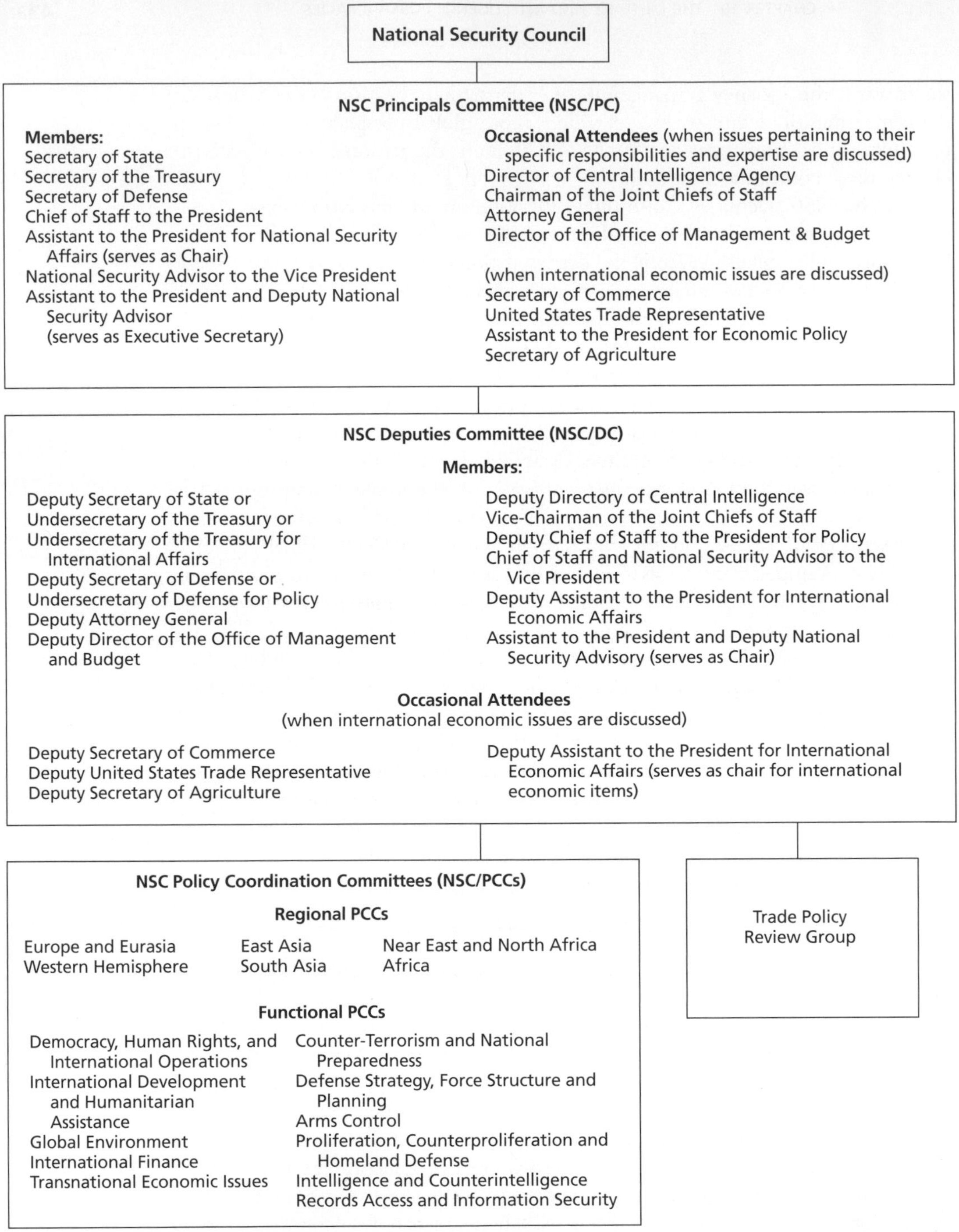

National Security Council

NSC Principals Committee (NSC/PC)

Members:
Secretary of State
Secretary of the Treasury
Secretary of Defense
Chief of Staff to the President
Assistant to the President for National Security
    Affairs (serves as Chair)
National Security Advisor to the Vice President
Assistant to the President and Deputy National
    Security Advisor
    (serves as Executive Secretary)

Occasional Attendees (when issues pertaining to their
        specific responsibilities and expertise are discussed)
Director of Central Intelligence Agency
Chairman of the Joint Chiefs of Staff
Attorney General
Director of the Office of Management & Budget

(when international economic issues are discussed)
Secretary of Commerce
United States Trade Representative
Assistant to the President for Economic Policy
Secretary of Agriculture

NSC Deputies Committee (NSC/DC)

Members:

Deputy Secretary of State or
Undersecretary of the Treasury or
Undersecretary of the Treasury for
    International Affairs
Deputy Secretary of Defense or
Undersecretary of Defense for Policy
Deputy Attorney General
Deputy Director of the Office of Management
    and Budget

Deputy Directory of Central Intelligence
Vice-Chairman of the Joint Chiefs of Staff
Deputy Chief of Staff to the President for Policy
Chief of Staff and National Security Advisor to the
    Vice President
Deputy Assistant to the President for International
    Economic Affairs
Assistant to the President and Deputy National
    Security Advisory (serves as Chair)

Occasional Attendees
(when international economic issues are discussed)

Deputy Secretary of Commerce
Deputy United States Trade Representative
Deputy Secretary of Agriculture

Deputy Assistant to the President for International
    Economic Affairs (serves as chair for international
    economic items)

NSC Policy Coordination Committees (NSC/PCCs)

Regional PCCs

Europe and Eurasia   East Asia   Near East and North Africa
Western Hemisphere   South Asia   Africa

Functional PCCs

Democracy, Human Rights, and   Counter-Terrorism and National
    International Operations   Preparedness
International Development   Defense Strategy, Force Structure and
    and Humanitarian   Planning
    Assistance   Arms Control
Global Environment   Proliferation, Counterproliferation and
International Finance   Homeland Defense
Transnational Economic Issues   Intelligence and Counterintelligence
                                     Records Access and Information Security

Trade Policy
Review Group

FIGURE10.4 National Security Council Policy Coordination Committees
in the George W. Bush Administration

SOURCE: National Security Presidential Directive-1, February 13, 2001.

intelligence agency or the chairman of the JCS) would now be occasional attendees. For example, the secretary of commerce, the USTR, and the assistant to the president for economic policy would now be involved only when international economic issues are discussed.

The NSC Deputies Committee (NSC/DC) continues to serve the same function of overseeing work of the policy coordination committees as in the previous administrations, but its membership is considerably expanded from earlier administrations. Indeed, the membership may differ depending upon the issue under discussion. As Figure 10.4 shows, the deputy secretary of state or the undersecretary of treasury or the undersecretary of treasury for international affairs may participate, but the committee also includes the deputy secretary of defense or undersecretary of defense for policy, the deputy attorney general, deputy director of the office of management and budget, the deputy director of the CIA, vice-chairman of the JCS, chief of staff and national security advisor to the vice president, the deputy chief of staff to the president for policy, the deputy assistant to the president for international economic affairs, and the deputy national security advisor. In addition, other attendees may be invited for international economic issues, as the figure indicates. Consistent with the two previous administrations, the deputy national security advisor chairs this committee, ensuring that the national security staff largely guides these two key committees of the NSC system.

Finally, the NSC Policy Coordination Committees (PCCs) are "the main day-to-day fora for interagency coordination of national security policy. They shall provide policy analysis for consideration by the more senior committees of the NSC system and ensure timely responses to decisions make by the President." There are both regional and functional PCCs. In a structural departure from earlier administrations, there is now an interagency group for trade (the Trade Policy Review Group). Other PCCs, however, may be established by the national security advisor at the direction of the president and in consultation with the secretary of state, secretary of defense, secretary of treasury, and the vice president of the United States. Finally, and importantly, each PCC has an "executive secretary" from the staff of the National Security Council to ensure coordination through that bureaucracy as well and to ensure overall control of the process by the NSC staff.

At least two changes have occurred in the operation of the NSC system in the aftermath of September 11. The most significant, and hardly unexpected, was the increase of the number of NSC and Principals Committee meetings. In the two-month period after September 11 (September 11 to November 13), 42 NSC meetings and 16 meetings of the Principals Committee were held.[165] In this sense, the need for foreign policy management quickened and put increased pressure on the system. The other change has been the creation of the Homeland Security Council in the legislation creating the Department of Homeland Security. Modeled on the National Security Council membership and function, the Homeland Security Council, primarily composed of the president, vice president, secretary of homeland security, the attorney general, and the secretary of defense, may be convened in conjunction with the NSC at the president's discretion, especially on issues of interest to both bureaucracies. This new council thus has added another layer of organizational complexity and management to national security policy.

In all, though, the NSC system, especially through the coordinated work of the Deputies Committee and the Policy Coordination Committees at the levels below the National Security Council and the Principals Committee, effectively manages both foreign policy formulation and foreign policy implementation within the U.S. Government. Furthermore, this system, if competently administered, serves as a ready mechanism for managing conflicts between departments and bureaus.

CONCLUDING COMMENTS

The diplomatic, economic, military, and intelligence bureaucracies that we have discussed over the last two chapters all contribute to the shaping of the foreign policy of the United States. The influence of some has increased, while impact of others has declined in recent years. The National Security Council (and especially the NSC staff and the national security advisor), the Department of Defense, and key economic bureaucracies, such as the Department of Treasury and the U.S. Office of the Trade Representative, have gained influence in the shaping of policy. By contrast, the Department of State and the intelligence community have been beset by various problems and have probably lost influence over past decades. In the post–September 11 world, however, the intelligence community and the newly created Department of Homeland Security will likely regain some of that influence if they can operate efficiently and effectively. Still, the precise contribution of the bureaucracies in an administration is heavily dependent upon how the president chooses to use them and on the individuals within them. Just as the president is dependent upon the bureaucracy for policy advice, the standing of a bureaucracy within the policy process is dependent upon how the president decides to employ its advice.

In the next two chapters, we expand our analysis of the foreign policy-making process by examining those participants outside of the formal governmental structure. Political parties and interest groups are the focus of attention in Chapter 11. Our aim is to assess how America's two major political parties have shaped foreign policy and to determine which interest groups, and under what conditions, play a role in policy making on international issues.

NOTES

1. See Stanley Lieberson, "An Empirical Study of Military-Industrial Linkages," *American Journal of Sociology* 76 (January 1971): 562–584.

2. See, for example, Adam Yarmolinsky, *The Military Establishment: Its Impacts on American Society* (New York: Harper and Row, 1971).

3. See the chapter entitled, "Is There a Military-Industrial Complex Which Prevents Peace?" in Marc Pilisuk, with the assistance of Mehrene Larudee, *International Conflict and Social Policy* (Englewood Cliffs, NJ: Prentice-Hall, Inc., 1972), pp. 108–141.

4.   See "DOD Announces Top Contractors for Fiscal 2002," January 23, 2003, at http://www.defense.link.mil/.

5.   The data in this section are taken from the following: http://www.dod.mil/pubs/almanac, accessed on September 26, 2003; Jim Garamone, "Budget Request Funds War on Terrorism, Transformation," February 3, 2003, at http://www.dod.mil/news/Feb2003/n02032003_200302031.html, accessed September 26, 2003; *National Defense Budget Estimates for FY2003,* Office of the Undersecretary of Defense (Comptroller), March 2002, pp. 5 and 213 available as fy03_greenbook.pdf and at http://www.dtic.mil/comptroller/fy2003budget; and "Military Strengths," a chart in the *Des Moines Sunday Register,* September 28, 2003, 11A.

6.   Taken from "Office of the Secretary of Defense," Web site at http://www.defenselink.mil/odam/omp/pubs/GuideBook/osd.htm, accessed on June 9, 2003.

7.   See Hoopes, *The Limits of Intervention* (New York: David McKay, 1968), pp. 33–34, for a statement of ISA's role during the Kennedy–Johnson period.

8.   See the "International Security Affairs (ISA)" Web site at http://www.defenselink.mil/policy/isa/, accessed on June 9, 2003.

9.   See Henry T. Nash, *American Foreign Policy* (Homewood, IL: Dorsey, 1985), p. 94. By contrast, the Bureau of Politico-Military Affairs in the Department of State might be labeled the "little Defense Department" because of the military considerations in policy examined by this bureau. Further, there tend to be regular personnel exchanges between this bureau and the Pentagon that facilitate this military analysis. The "little Defense Department" was particularly important during the tenure of Secretary Alexander Haig because of the close working relationship between its director, Richard Burt, and Secretary Haig. On the changes in the role of ISA in the policy process, see Geoffrey Piller, "DOD's Office of International Security Affairs: The Brief Ascendancy of an Advisory System," *Political Science Quarterly* 98 (Spring 1983): 59–78.

10.   *U.S. Government Manual 1989/1990,* p. 186.

11.   See Strobe Talbott, *Deadly Gambits* (New York: Vintage Books, 1985), for a discussion of the key role of Assistant Secretary of Defense Richard Perle in arms control policy.

12.   See, for example, Joseph S. Nye, Jr., "The Case for Deep Engagement," *Foreign Affairs* 74 (July/August 1995): 90–102, which he published while at ISA.

13.   Eric Schmitt, "Aide Denies Shaping Data to Justify War," *New York Times,* June 5, 2003.

14.   Amos A. Jordan, William J. Taylor, Jr., and Lawrence J. Korb, *American National Security: Policy and Process,* 4th ed. (Baltimore and London: The Johns Hopkins University Press, 1993), p. 178. On the responsibilities of the JCS, also see Lawrence J. Korb, *The Fall and Rise of the Pentagon: American Defense Policies in the 1970s* (Westport, CT: Greenwood Press, 1979), p. 112; Korb's *The Joint Chiefs of Staff: The First Twenty-Five Years* (Bloomington: Indiana University Press, 1976), p. 7; and *U.S. Government Manual 1995/1996,* July 1, 1995, pp. 180–181.

15.   Ibid.

16.   Jordan, Taylor, and Korb, *American National Security: Policy and Process,* p. 178–180; and Korb, *The Fall and Rise of the Pentagon,* pp. 112–137.

17.   Jordan, Taylor, and Korb, *American National Security: Policy and Process,* p. 178.

18.   Korb, *The Fall and Rise of the Pentagon,* p. 115.

19.   See the discussion in Neil Sheehan, Hedrick Smith, E. W. Kenworthy, and Fox Butterfield, *The Pentagon Papers as Published by New York Times* (New York: Bantam Books, Inc., 1971), pp. 234–270, on the bombing of North Vietnam and on the acceptance of the domino theory. Although the Department of Defense and its advisors did not get all they proposed, its influence in these decisions is still evident.

20.   Jordan, Taylor, and Korb, *American National Security: Policy and Process,* p. 179.

21.   Ibid.

22.   David C. Martin and Michael A. Lerner, "Why the Generals Can't Command," *Newsweek,* February 14, 1983, 22.

23. Lawrence J. Korb, "The Joint Chiefs of Staff: Access and Impact in Foreign Policy," *Policy Studies Journal* 3 (Winter 1974): 171.

24. Ibid., pp. 171–173.

25. Martin and Lerner, "Why the Generals Can't Command," p. 22.

26. "Excerpts from Reagan's Testimony on the Iran-Contra Affair," *New York Times,* February 23, 1990, A18.

27. This discussion of the Goldwater–Nichols Reorganization Act is taken from *Congressional Quarterly Almanac 1986* (Washington, DC: Congressional Quarterly, Inc., 1987), pp. 455–457.

28. Robert Previdi, *Civilian Control versus Military Rule* (New York: Hippocrene, 1988), p. 8, as cited in Douglas Johnson and Steven Metz, "American Civil-Military Relations: A Review of the Recent Literature," in Don M. Snider and Miranda A. Carlton-Carew, eds., *U.S. Civil-Military Relations: In Crisis or Transition?* (Washington, DC: The Center for Strategic & International Studies, 1995), p. 209.

29. Richard Halloran, "Bush Plans to Name Colin Powell to Head Joint Chiefs, Aides Say," *New York Times,* August 10, 1989, 1, 10.

30. Johnson and Metz, "American Civil-Military Relations," p. 210.

31. Eleanor Clift and Thomas M. DeFrank, "Bush's General: Maximum Force," *Newsweek,* September 3, 1990, 36.

32. Richard H. Kohn, "Out of Control: The Crisis in Civil-Military Relations," *National Interest* 35 (Spring 1994): 13–14, as cited in Johnson and Metz, "American Civil-Military Relations," p. 210.

33. Colin L. Powell, John Lehman, William Odom, Samuel Huntington, and Richard H. Kohn, "Exchange on Civil-Military Relations," *National Interest* 36 (Summer 1994): 23, as cited in Johnson and Metz, "American Civil-Military Relations," p. 211.

34. Pat Towell with Matthew Phillips, "Shalikashvili Wins Praise as Joint Chiefs Nominee," *Congressional Quarterly Weekly Report,* August 14, 1993, 2238.

35. Ibid.

36. Dana Priest, *The Mission* (New York: W. W. Norton and Company, 2003), pp. 21–23.

37. Ibid., p. 45.

38. See, ibid., for an extended discussion of these CinCs and their activities in their various regions of responsibility.

39. The reform acts strengthening the secretary's role within the Department of Defense are "Reorganization Plan No. 6 of 1953," 67 Stat. 638–639, and the "Department of Defense Reorganization Act of 1958," P.L. 85-599, 72 Stat. 514-523.

40. See James Schlesinger, "The Role of the Secretary of Defense," in Robert J. Art, Vincent Davis, and Samuel P. Huntington, eds., *Reorganizing America's Defense: Leadership in War and Peace* (Washington, DC: Pergamon-Brassey's, 1985), p. 261; and Laurence E. Lynn, Jr., and Richard I. Smith, "Can the Secretary of Defense Make a Difference?" *International Security* 7 (Summer 1982): 45–69. The former discusses the role of the secretary of defense more generally, while the latter looks at the role of the secretary in the weapons development and acquisition process and the impact of the bureaucracy within the Pentagon in shaping outcomes.

41. Korb, *The Fall and Rise of the Pentagon,* p. 85.

42. Bernard Weinraub, "Browning of the Pentagon," *New York Times Magazine,* January 29, 1978, 44.

43. Zbigniew Brzezinski, *Power and Principle: Memoirs of the National Security Advisor 1977–1981.* (New York: Farrar, Straus & Giroux, 1983), pp. 44–47.

44. Theodore H. White, "Weinberger on the Ramparts," *New York Times Magazine,* February 6, 1983, 18; Alice C. Maroni, *The Fiscal Year 1984 Defense Budget Request: Data Summary* (Washington, DC: Congressional Research Service, February 1, 1983); and Ellen C. Collier, "Arms Control Negotiations at Home: Legislative-Executive Relations," paper presented at the Annual Meeting of the International Studies Association, March 1984, p. 8.

45. The data reported here were calculated from Table IX in Alice C. Maroni, "The Fiscal Year 1989 Defense Budget Request Data

Summary," Congressional Research Service, No. 88-182F. The data are for the National Defense function category that included the Department of Defense and defense-related programs carried out by other agencies. If only the Department of Defense budget is used, the average increase from 1981–1985 is 9.1 percent, while the average decline in 1986–1988 is 2 percent.

46. White, "Weinberger on the Ramparts," p. 18.

47. John M. Broder and Melissa Healy, "Likeable Dick Cheney Can Get Mad When He Has To," *Los Angeles Times,* March 16, 1989, 20.

48. Andrew Rosenthal, "Cheney Steps to Center of the Lineup," *New York Times,* August 24, 1990, A7.

49. See, for example, Pat Towell, "Aspin's Career a Balance of the Highs and Lows," *Congressional Quarterly Weekly Report,* May 27, 1995, 1484.

50. Charles Lane, "Perry's Parry," *The New Republic* 26 (June 27, 1994): 21–25.

51. Elizabeth Drew, *On the Edge: The Clinton Presidency* (New York: Simon & Schuster, 1994), p. 356.

52. Ibid., p. 373.

53. Lane, "Perry's Parry," p. 22.

54. "Remarks as Prepared for Delivery by William J. Perry, Secretary of Defense," John F. Kennedy School of Government, Harvard University, May 13, 1996, via the Internet.

55. Priest, *The Mission,* p. 29.

56. James Risen, "Man in the News: A Pentagon Veteran—Donald Henry Rumsfeld," *New York Times,* December 29, 2000, online at http://www.nytimes.com/2000/12/29/politics/29RUMS.html?pagewanted=all, accessed on March 18, 2001.

57. Priest, *The Mission,* pp. 23–32.

58. Ivo H. Daalder and James M. Lindsay, "Bush's Foreign Policy Revolution," in Fred I. Greenstein, ed., *The George W. Bush Presidency: An Early Assessment* (Baltimore and London: The Johns Hopkins University Press, 2003), p. 116.

59. Bob Woodward, *Bush at War* (New York: Simon & Schuster, 2002), p. 49.

60. *Report of the Joint Inquiry Into the Terrorist Attacks of September 11, 2001* by The House Permanent Select Committee on Intelligence and the Senate Select Committee on Intelligence, July 24, 2003 (hereafter, *Joint Inquiry Into the Terrorist Attacks*), available at http://new.findlaw.com/cnn/docs/911rpt/index.html, accessed on July 24, 2003.

61. *Intelligence: The Acme of Skill* (Washington, DC: Central Intelligence Agency, Public Affairs, n.d.), pp. 12–13.

62. Jeffrey T. Richelson, *The U.S. Intelligence Community,* 4th ed. (Boulder, CO: Westview Press, 1999), pp. 30–33.

63. Ibid., pp. 37.

64. Ibid, pp. 40–47.

65. Victor Marchetti and John D. Marks, *The CIA and the Cult of Intelligence* (New York: Dell, 1974), p. 95, provides a breakdown of spending in the intelligence community for 1974 totaling $6.2 billion. Charles W. Kegley and Eugene R. Wittkopf report that for fiscal 1980 the budget for the intelligence community was thought to be $10 billion, based on *Congressional Quarterly* reports. See their *American Foreign Policy: Pattern and Process* (New York: St. Martin's Press, 1982), p. 373. The quoted passage is from "Reagan Puts Bombing Blame on Democrats: Carter-Era Intelligence Cuts Cited," *Des Moines Register,* September 27, 1984, 13A.

66. "Intelligence Budget Calls For a Record $30 Billion," *Des Moines Sunday Register,* April 8, 1990, 2A; and Robin Wright, "'91 Intelligence Budget Still Targets East Bloc," *Los Angeles Times,* April 8, 1990, A1.

67. A Senate committee first reported the aggregate budget figure. See Tim Weiner, "The Worst-Kept Secret in the Capital," *New York Times,* July 21, 1994, A11. A more detailed breakdown was reported in Tim Weiner, "$28 Billion Spying Budget Is Made Public by Mistake," *New York Times,* November 5, 1994, 54, as cited in Roger Hilsman, "Does the CIA Still Have a Role?" *Foreign Affairs* 74 (September/October 1995): 105.

68. For the fiscal 1998 data, see Mark M. Lowenthal, *Intelligence: From Secrets to Policy,* 2nd ed. (Washington, DC: CQ Press, 2003), p. 164.

69. See Executive Order 12333, "United States Intelligence Activities," December 4, 1981. This executive order can be found in *Code of Federal Regulations* (Washington, DC: Office of the Federal Register, National Archives and Records Service, 1982), pp. 200–216. Richelson, *The U.S. Intelligence Community,* p. 18, notes that it remains in effect.

70. Ibid., p. 201.

71. The interagency membership listing is from *Central Intelligence Agency Factbook* (Washington, DC: Central Intelligence Agency, Public Affairs, July 1982), p. 12. The reference to the National Security Planning draws upon the discussion in the unclassified extract from National Security Decision Directive (NSDD) 286, released on December 12, 1987, by the National Security Council.

72. See the memo from the National Security Council on "National Security Council Organization," dated April 17, 1989.

73. *Presidential Decision Directive 2,* "Organization of the National Security Council," January 20, 1993, p. 3.

74. See *National Security Presidential Directive 1,* The White House, Washington, DC, February 13, 2001, at http://www.fas.org/ irp/offdocs/nspd-1.html, accessed July 15, 2002.

75. Richelson, *The U.S. Intelligence Community,* pp. 316–318.

76. Ibid., pp. 319–321.

77. Ibid., pp. 315–329.

78. Joseph S. Nye, Jr., "Peering into the Future," *Foreign Affairs* 73 (July/August 1994): 83. Nye was chairman of the NIC at the time that he published the article.

79. Marchetti and Marks, *The CIA and the Cult of Intelligence,* pp. 291–296.

80. See Chester L. Cooper, "The CIA and Decisionmaking," *Foreign Affairs* 50 (January 1972): 221–236.

81. John H. Esterline and Robert B. Black, *Inside Foreign Policy: The Department of State Political System and Its Subsystems* (Palo Alto, CA: Mayfield Publishing Company, 1975), p. 35.

82. David E. Rosenbaum, "U.S. Sees Threats to Soviet Economy," *New York Times,* April 21, 1990, 4.

83. Philip Taubman, "CIA Taking Control of Nicaraguan Policy*," Des Moines Register,* April 20, 1984, 1A.

84. Tim Weiner, David Johnston, and Neil A. Lewis, *Betrayal: The Story of Aldrich Ames, An American Spy* (New York: Random House, 1995), p. 287.

85. See Irving Janis, *Victims of Groupthink* (Boston: Houghton Mifflin Company, 1972), pp. 14–49, for a discussion of the decision making on the Bay of Pigs invasion and the crucial involvement of the CIA. Also see Marchetti and Marks, *The CIA and the Cult of Intelligence,* p. 294, for how dissatisfied President Kennedy was over CIA action in the Bay of Pigs and how this might have affected his view of intelligence estimates during the Cuban Missile Crisis.

86. Harry Howe Ransom, *The Intelligence Establishment* (Cambridge, MA: Harvard University Press, 1970), p. 240.

87. Esterline and Black, *Inside Foreign Policy,* p. 35.

88. The note is quoted from Stansfield Turner, *Secrecy and Democracy: The CIA in Transition* (Boston: Houghton Mifflin Company, 1985), p. 113.

89. The "Iran Postmortem" report is discussed in Bob Woodward, *Veil: The Secret Wars of the CIA, 1981–1987* (New York: Pocket Books, 1987), pp. 106–108.

90. Robert F. Ellsworth and Kenneth L. Adelman, "Foolish Intelligence," *Foreign Policy* 36 (Fall 1979): 147–159. President Carter is quoted here at p. 148. Michael Wines, "C.I.A. Faulted on Rating Soviet Economy," *New York Times,* July 23, 1990, A5.

91. Several sources report some of these intelligence failures. See, for example, John Barry, "Failures of Intelligence?" *Newsweek,* May 14, 1990, 20–21; "NBC Nightly News," June 9, 1990; and Wines, "C.I.A. Faulted on Rating Soviet Economy," p. A5. On the Persian Gulf War failures, see "Intelligence Goofs," *Newsweek,* March 18, 1991, 38.

92. Nye, "Peering into the Future," pp. 84–85.

93. The quotations are taken from "9/11 Failures Still Threaten, Report Says," at http://www.msnbc.com/news/943459.asp?cp1=1, accessed on July 24, 2000.

94. The descriptions here are taken from the "Abridged Findings and Conclusions" in the *Joint Inquiry Into the Terrorist Attacks.*

95. The quoted passages are from "In Tenet's Words: 'I Am Responsible' for Review," *New York Times,* July 12, 2003, A5, but a fuller discussion of this matter can be found in David E. Sanger and James Risen, "C.I.A. Chief Takes Blame in Assertion on Iraqi Uranium," *New York Times,* July 12, 2003, A1 and A5.

96. Ibid.

97. Philip Shenon, "Saudi Bombers Got Outside Support, Perry Tells Panel," *New York Times,* July 10, 1996, A4.

98. Allan E. Goodman, "Testimony: Fact-Checking at the CIA," *Foreign Policy* 102 (Spring 1996): 180–182.

99. Quoted in Barry, "Failures of Intelligence?" p. 20. The first two quotations in this paragraph are from this article and at this page.

100. Turner, *Secrecy and Democracy: The CIA in Transition,* pp. 113–127, especially at p. 125. For a more recent assessment of the analytic difficulties of the CIA, see Tim Weiner, "House Panel Says C.I.A. Lacks Expertise to Carry Out Its Duties," *New York Times,* June 19, 1997, A13.

101. Nye, "Peering into the Future," p. 85.

102. Barry, "Failures of Intelligence?" pp. 20–21.

103. See Sanger and Risen, "C.I.A. Chief Takes Blame in Assertion on Iraqi Uranium."

104. Turner, *Secrecy and Democracy: The CIA in Transition,* pp. 273–274.

105. See "Recommendations" in the *Joint Inquiry Into the Terrorist Attacks.*

106. Two books that catalogue Aldrich Ames's activities are David Wise, *Nightmover: How Aldrich Ames Sold the CIA to the KGB for $4.6 Million* (New York: HarperCollins, 1995); and Weiner, Johnston, and Lewis, *Betrayal: The Story of Aldrich Ames, An American Spy.* Information on the case here and in

the subsequent section is taken from these sources.

107. Tim Weiner, "CIA's Chief Says Russians Duped the U.S.," *New York Times,* December 9, 1995, 1, 5.

108. Tim Weiner, "CIA Remains in Darkness on Extent of Spy's Damage," *New York Times,* August 25, 1995, A1, A8.

109. See Weiner, Johnston, and Lewis, *Betrayal: The Story of Aldrich Ames, An American Spy.* Only after an associate reported his apparent extravagant living was an initial inquiry begun. See pp. 144–145. The CIA did not start a full investigation apparently until late 1990. See p. 158.

110. Ibid., pp. 262–269. Also, see Mark T. Kehoe, "Brown Commission Shies Away From Radical Suggestions," *Congressional Quarterly Weekly Report,* March 2, 1996, 567, on the establishment of the commission.

111. See the *Joint Inquiry Into the Terrorist Attacks* and the National Commission on Terrorist Attacks Upon the United States Web site at http://www.9-11Commission.gov for its missions and initial reports. On the testimony by Clinton and Bush administration officials before the commission, see Philip Shenon and Eric Schmitt, "Bush and Clinton Aides Grilled by Panel," *New York Times,* March 24, 2004, A1 and A16; Philip Shenon and Richard W. Stevenson, "Ex-Bush Aide Says Threat of Qaeda Was Not Heeded," *New York Times,* March 25, 2004, A1, A2; and David Johnston and Todd S. Purdum, "Missed Chances in a Long Hunt for bin Laden," *New York Times,* March 25, 2004, A1, A20. Also, see "Fox News Sunday" interview with Governor Kean and Congressman Hamilton, March 28, 2004.

112. See, for example, Hilsman, "Does the CIA Still Have a Role?"

113. Bob Woodward, *Bush at War;* and Douglas Jehl and Dexter Filkins, "U.S. Moved to Undermine Iraqi Military Before War," *New York Times,* August 10, 2003, 1.

114. Pat Holt, *Secret Intelligence and Public Policy* (Washington, DC: CQ Press, 1995), p. 109.

115. John E. Rielly, ed., *American Public Opinion and U.S. Foreign Policy 1995* (Chicago: Chicago Council on Foreign Relations, 1995), p. 37.

116. See Marshall M. Bouton and Benjamin I. Page, eds., *Worldviews 2002: American Public Opinion and Foreign Policy.* (Chicago: The Chicago Council on Foreign Relations, 2002), p. 23.

117. P.L. 253 in *United States Statutes at Large,* Volume 61, Part 1, 80th Cong., 1st sess., p. 498.

118. See Executive Order 12333, "United States Intelligence Activities," p. 215. See Marchetti and Marks, *The CIA and the Cult of Intelligence and the Church Committee Report* for a discussion of types of covert operations.

119. Marchetti and Marks, *The CIA and the Cult of Intelligence,* pp. 281–282.

120. Foreign and Military Intelligence," Book 1, Final Report of the Select Committee to Study Governmental Operations with respect to Intelligence Activities, United States Senate, April 26, 1976, p. 425 (hereafter, the *Church Committee Report,* after chairman of the Committee, Senator Frank Church).

121. Ibid., p. 56.

122. Ibid., pp. 56–57.

123. Ibid., p. 57.

124. Bernard Gwertzman, "Top Reagan Aide Supports the Use of Covert Action," *New York Times,* May 14, 1984, 1, 6.

125. Scowcroft made this statement during his appearance in "President Vs. Congress: War Powers and Covert Action," in the Public Broadcasting Series entitled *The Constitution: That Delicate Balance,* 1984.

126. Woodward, *Bush at War,* at pp. 75–78, where the information and quotations are derived.

127. See "Recommendations" from the *Joint Inquiry Into the Terrorist Attacks*

128. *Church Committee Report,* pp. 49–50.

129. Ibid., pp. 51–52.

130. Ibid., p. 54.

131. Ransom, *The Intelligence Establishment,* p. 162.

132. Gregory F. Treverton, "Intelligence: Welcome to the American Government," in Thomas E. Mann, ed., *A Question of Balance* (Washington, DC: The Brookings Institution, 1990), pp. 72–76.

133. Ibid., pp. 74–75.

134. See P.L. 93–559, 88 Stat. 1804. The quoted passage is from section 32.

135. See *Church Committee Report,* note 68; and *Report to the President by the Commission on CIA Activities Within the United States* (Washington, DC: Government Printing Office, June 1975), note 76, for a complete listing of the recommendations. The latter was named the Rockefeller Commission after its chairman, Vice President Nelson Rockefeller.

136. On this point, see Harry Howe Ransom, "Strategic Intelligence and Intermestic Politics," in Charles W. Kegley and Eugene R. Wittkopf, *Perspectives on American Foreign Policy* (New York: St. Martin's Press, 1983), p. 313. President Ford's Executive Order 11905 can be found in *Weekly Compilation of Presidential Documents* 12 (February 23, 1976): 234–243.

137. "Controversy Over 'Czar' for Intelligence," *U.S. News and World Report,* February 6, 1978, 50–52.

138. "Intelligence Authorization Act for Fiscal Year 1981," P.L. 96–450, 94 Stat. 1981–1982. This section and the following one draw upon earlier work reported in James M. McCormick and Steven S. Smith, "The Iran Arms Sale and the Intelligence Oversight Act of 1980," *PS* 20 (Winter 1987): 29–37.

139. The passage is quoted in Philip Taubman, "Moynihan to Keep Intelligence Post," *New York Times,* April 27, 1984, 7. On the extent to which the intelligence committees were informed, see Philip Taubman, "House Unit Says Report on Mines Arrived Jan. 31," *New York Times,* April 14, 1984, 1 and 6; and his "How Congress Was Informed of Mining of Nicaragua Ports," *New York Times,* April 16, 1984, 1, 4.

140. The following examples draw upon the "Executive Summary" in *Report of the Congressional Committees Investigating the Iran–Contra Affair* (Washington, DC: U.S. Government Printing Office, 1987), pp. 3–21. The quoted phrases are from this report as well.

141. Unclassified extract from National Security Decision Directive (NSDD) 286, and "Text of Letter on Covert Operations," by President Reagan to Senator David

Boren in *New York Times,* August 8, 1987, 5. See also James M. McCormick, "Prior Notification of Covert Actions," *Chicago Tribune,* September 8, 1987, 11.

142. *Congressional Quarterly Almanac 1988* (Washington, DC: Congressional Quarterly, Inc., 1989), pp. 498–499; and *Congressional Quarterly Almanac 1989* (Washington, DC: Congressional Quarterly, Inc., 1990), p. 541.

143. Holt, *Secret Intelligence and Public Policy,* pp. 138–139.

144. Elaine Sciolino, "Conferees Agree to Curb President on Covert Action," *New York Times,* July 27, 1991, 1, 8. The quote is at p. 8.

145. John Deutch and Jeffrey H. Smith, "Smarter Intelligence," *Foreign Policy* (January/February 2002): 64–69. The quoted passages are at p. 68.

146. "U.S. Counterintelligence Effectiveness," Statement by the Press Secretary, the White House, May 3, 1994; and "Fact Sheet: U.S. Counterintelligence Effectiveness," White House/NSC Press Office, July 19, 1994.

147. This summary of the commission's report is drawn from Kehoe, "Brown Commission Shies Away From Radical Suggestions," p. 567.

148. Cassata, "Spy Budget Cleared for Clinton; Plan for New Agency Curbed," *Congressional Quarterly Weekly Report,* December 23, 1995, 3894–3895.

149. The following is drawn from the "Recommendations" in the *Joint Inquiry Into the Terrorist Attacks* report.

150. Hilsman, "Does the CIA Still Have a Role?" The quoted passages are at pp. 110, 112, and 116, respectively.

151. See the Web site for the Department of Homeland Security at http://www.dhs.gov and the section on "DHS Organization—History," which reproduces the executive order creating the Office of Homeland Security.

152. Ibid. See the section under "DHS Organization—Building a Secure Homeland."

153. Ibid.

154. Ibid. The descriptions here are drawn from the discussion of the major divisions and from the discussion of the actions taken in the first 100 days of the Department's operation at this Web site.

155. This system is described in ibid. under the "Threats and Protection" header, and it is where the quoted material is derived.

156. These first two concerns, and the quoted materials, are from John Mintz, "Security Goals Compromised by Problems in Department," *Des Moines Register,* September 8, 2003, 1A and 4A with the quote at p. 1A.

157. Ivo H. Daalder and I. M. Destler, "Advisors, Czars, and Councils," *The National Interest* 68 (Summer 2002): 70.

158. Esterline and Black, *Inside Foreign Policy,* p. 23. On the Kissinger reorganization, see pp. 24–26 of the NSC system mentioned in the next paragraph of Esterline and Black.

159. The following discussion of SIGs and IGs in the Reagan administration is based upon the Statement of the President, "National Security Council Structure," January 12, 1982, reprinted in Robert E. Hunter, *Presidential Control of Foreign Policy: Management or Mishap?* The Washington Papers/91 (New York: Praeger, 1982), pp. 109–115 (additionally, see Hunter's discussion of this system, pp. 96–102, upon which we also relied); and Colin Campbell, *Managing the Presidency: Carter, Reagan, and the Search for Executive Harmony* (Pittsburgh: University of Pittsburgh Press, 1986), p. 43. In the original directive, only the first three SIGs were established. The international economic SIG was added later.

160. Ibid. The reference to the NSPG draws upon the unclassified extract from National Security Decision Directive (NSDD) 286.

161. The discussion of the changes since the Tower Commission Report of 1987 is based upon Paul Schoot Stevens, "The National Security Council: Past and Prologue," *Strategic Review* 17 (Winter 1989): 61.

162. The description of the George H. W. Bush administration's NSC policy coordination process is based upon material provided by the U.S. Army War College, Carlisle Barracks, Pennsylvania, December 1989, and a memo from the National Security Council on "National Security Council Organization," April 17, 1989.

163.   The descriptions of the NSC committees and quotation about their activities during the Clinton administration are taken from *Presidential Decision 2,* January 20, 1993.

164.   This discussion of the George W. Bush administration's NSC system is drawn from *National Security Presidential Directive 1,* February 13, 2001.

165. Karen M. Hult, "The Bush White House in Comparative Perspective," in Fred I. Greenstein, *George W. Bush Presidency: An Early Assessment* (Baltimore and London: The Johns Hopkins University Press, 2003), p. 64.

11

Political Parties, Bipartisanship, and Interest Groups

So let us find inspiration in the great tradition of Harry Truman and Arthur Vandenburg—a tradition that builds bridges of cooperation, not walls of isolation; that opens the arms of Americans to change instead of throwing up our hands in despair; that casts aside partisanship and brings together Republicans and Democrats for the good of the American people and the world.

PRESIDENT WILLIAM CLINTON
MAY 22, 1995

The Armenian lobby enjoyed unprecedented success during the 104th Congress. . . . U.S. aid to Armenia steadily increased. . . . We owe these successes to the tireless efforts of countless Armenian Americans.

ARAM HAMPARIAN, EXECUTIVE DIRECTOR OF THE ARMENIAN
NATIONAL COMMITTEE OF AMERICA, QUOTED IN TONY SMITH,
*FOREIGN ATTACHMENTS: THE POWER OF ETHNIC GROUPS
IN THE MAKING OF AMERICAN FOREIGN POLICY,* P. 70

Beyond the president, Congress, and the bureaucracies, other participants also influence the American foreign policy process. Two additional key participants are political parties and interest groups. While these groups probably have less direct impact upon policy than the other participants discussed so far, they are increasingly viewed as important to the foreign policy process. By political parties we mean those organized groups who pursue their goals by contesting elections and perhaps controlling political offices.[1] These political organizations can influence foreign policy decisions directly by controlling elective offices, but they can also affect the policy content of others who control executive and legislative offices through criticism and debate. By interest groups we mean those portions of the population who are organized and seek political goals that they are unable to provide on their own.[2] These groups seek their political goals through the use of various lobbying techniques, ranging from making campaign contributions to a political candidate to face-to-face discussions with policy makers.

In the first half of this chapter, we examine the contribution of America's two principal political parties to the foreign policy process over the last four decades. We begin by focusing on the concept of bipartisanship in foreign affairs—a notion often invoked by policy makers to dampen partisan divisions over United States foreign policy—and assess its overall success. Next we turn to examine how the Vietnam War, and the events surrounding it, weakened any bipartisanship that may have existed. Finally, we summarize some evidence in the past several decades challenging the notion that bipartisanship ever existed and which instead points to the consistency in partisan differences in foreign affairs. At this juncture, too, we assess the impact of the events of September 11 in restoring some bipartisanship. In the second half of the chapter, we discuss several traditional foreign policy interest groups, identify some newer ones that have emerged in the foreign policy arena, and assess the relative impact of these various groups on the decision-making process. To illustrate the increased importance of foreign policy interest groups generally, we focus on two types, economic and ethnic ones, which often have been viewed as particularly important in shaping U.S. foreign policy.

POLITICAL PARTIES
AND THE BIPARTISAN TRADITION

America's two political parties historically do not differ in their programmatic or ideological positions on many domestic and foreign issues. Both the Democratic and Republican parties are more often seen as pragmatic organizations that adopt policy positions on such issues as taxation, social security policy, and health care to attract as many adherents as possible. While this description of the two major parties can be overstated and tends to apply more to party followers than to party leaders, it generally represents an accurate portrait of U.S. political parties, especially when compared to their European counterparts.[3]

This depiction of America's two major parties, moreover, has been applied particularly to the foreign policy arena. Despite the fact that the Republican Party more often controlled the White House, and the Democratic Party Congress, since World War II, bipartisanship has frequently been used to describe the nature of America's approach to foreign affairs. The origins of bipartisanship usually are attributed to the circumstances that the United States faced in the late 1940s and early 1950s. Because the international environment was so threatening during that period, a united approach seemed to be required for U.S. national security. In the words of one prominent politician of the time, "partisan politics . . . stopped at the water's edge."[4] In this approach, the United States' national interest would necessarily supplant any partisan interest in foreign policy, and bipartisan cooperation between Congress and the president would supplant both institutional and partisan differences as well.

The exact meaning of bipartisanship, however, was not always clear, but it seemed to require at least two different, albeit complementary, kinds of cooperation between the legislative and executive branches.[5] One kind focused on achieving "unity in foreign affairs," and referred to the degree to which "policies [are] supported by majorities within each political party" in Congress. The other kind referred to a set of "practices and procedures designed to bring about the desired unity."[6] Put differently, Congress and the president would develop procedures in which each would participate in and consult with one another in the formulation of foreign policy and, in turn, a majority of congressional members from both parties would support the policy developed. These two kinds of cooperation implied that bipartisanship would involve collaboration in both the *process* of foreign policy making and its *outcome*.

The Cold War Years and Bipartisanship

The beginning of this bipartisan effort is usually attributed to the foreign policy cooperation that developed between Democratic President Harry Truman and the Republican chairman of the Senate Foreign Relations Committee, Senator Arthur Vandenberg of Michigan, in the immediate post–World War II years. After Senator Vandenberg had altered his isolationist stance and after President Truman committed himself to global involvement for the United States, the two leaders consciously sought to build a bipartisan foreign policy against Communist expansionism. To a large extent, they were successful in doing so. Indeed, the major foreign policy initiatives of the late 1940s were accomplished with substantial support across political parties. The passage of the Bretton Woods agreement, the United Nations Charter, the Greek-Turkish aid program, and the Marshall Plan, among others, garnered support from both parties and passed Congress with over 83 percent support, on average.[7]

The acceptance of the Cold War consensus by the major political parties and the public at large seemingly continued this bipartisan tradition in foreign policy through the Eisenhower and Kennedy administrations and into the Johnson one as well. Despite some party divisions over the attacks by Senator Joseph McCarthy upon "Communists" within the United States government, the "loss" of China, and the Korean war, the essential foreign policy unity of the two parties re-mained.[8] Even with the so-called missile gap of the late 1950s that was eventually carried into the 1960 presidential campaign, the parties continued to display markedly similar foreign policy orientations. Both parties in their 1956 party plat-forms expressed a desire for a bipartisan foreign policy, and the Republicans expressed this sentiment again in 1960.[9]

Both Democrats and Republicans came to stand for a similar posture toward world affairs: a strong national defense, an active global involvement by the United States, and staunch anticommunism. To be sure, some divisions existed within the two parties. The Republicans had to contend with a wing that still cherished iso-lationism, and the Democrats had to contend with a wing that was initially sus-picious of the confrontational approach toward the Soviet Union. Further, the Democrats had to live with popular perceptions that portrayed them as the party associated with war (but also with prosperity), while the Republicans probably enjoyed the label as the party associated with peace (but not the one associating them with recession).[10] Democratic presidents—such as Franklin Delano Roo-sevelt with his role in leading the United States into World War II and Harry Tru-man with the outbreak of the Korean War—often convey the former perception, while Republican presidents—such as Herbert Hoover in the interwar years and Dwight Eisenhower after the Korean War—convey the latter.

Despite these different party factions and popular labels, the members of the two parties tended to stand for the same general principles in foreign policy. As political scientist Herbert McClosky and his associates report from their 1957–1958 survey data on party leaders and followers, the foreign policy differ-ences between the parties were indeed small. In fact, the average difference between Democratic and Republican leaders was smaller for foreign policy than for any of the four domestic policy areas that McClosky examined. Democratic and Republican followers demonstrated the same pattern generally.[11]

This bipartisanship was also reflected in the policy "planks" that each party placed into its national platforms during the Cold War years. In a systematic analy-sis of the platforms of the Democrats and the Republicans from 1944 to 1964, political scientist Gerald Pomper reports that 47 percent of the party pledges on foreign policy were essentially the same in each and only 6 percent were in con-flict.[12] Defense policy pledges were also quite similar: Seventy-three percent were the same and only 2 percent were in conflict. Such a level of bipartisanship on for-eign policy was second only to civil rights among eight different policy categories analyzed, while the level of bipartisanship on defense policy was tied for third position with labor and agricultural issues. Finally, the percentages of conflicting pledges across the parties were equally low in comparison with the other policy categories.

The important consequence of this bipartisanship tradition is that separate party influence, as such, seemingly did not have a strong effect on the general strategies of American foreign policy. Instead, policy influence was mainly con-fined to the executive branch because the president could generally count on con-gressional and public support across political parties. Recall the high level of presidential success in foreign policy that we discussed in Chapter 7.

THE LIMITS OF BIPARTISANSHIP
THROUGH THE VIETNAM ERA

Although bipartisanship was indeed the preeminent way to describe the roles of the two political parties during the Cold War years and beyond, some analysts now (and even some at the time) have argued that the degree of partisan unity on foreign affairs was often overstated. I. M. Destler, Anthony Lake, and Leslie Gelb best capture this alternate view in describing the first 15 years of the Cold War:

> These were said to be the halcyon days of bipartisanship or nonpartisanship, of Democrats and Republicans putting national interests above party interests. But such a description has always been more myth than reality. Conservatives and liberals were at one another's throat constantly. There was never a time when Truman was not besieged. . . . [Adlai E.] Stevenson tried to make foreign policy a key issue in the 1956 [presidential] campaign, and Mr. Kennedy succeeded in doing so in 1960.[13]

Destler, Lake, and Gelb do acknowledge, however, that part of the reason for the apparent unity in policy is explained by the fact that politicians would primarily "rally around the President's flag in East–West confrontations." But on "second-order issues," the parties "would squabble" regularly.[14]

Two decades earlier, a prominent foreign policy analyst, Cecil Crabb, reached a similar conclusion in characterizing the magnitude of bipartisanship from the late 1940s to the late 1950s.[15] In reviewing several cases of foreign policy and bipartisanship in that period, Crabb concluded that "there have been relatively few genuinely bipartisan undertakings in American postwar relations." While a bipartisan approach may provide stability and continuity in policy, he noted, it may also weaken the level of executive leadership, reduce the vigor of opposition party debate, and even weaken the party system. Such disadvantages, of course, could ultimately be harmful to the quality of United States foreign policy. In short, the characterization of the period as a bipartisan one was not wholly accurate, nor was the attempt to achieve such a policy approach necessarily a wise one.

Partisan/Ideological Differences
and Foreign Policy Issues

A closer examination of several foreign policy issues during those years lends credence to the more limited view of bipartisanship. On foreign aid, military aid, defense expenditures, and trade issues, for example, a rather continuous degree of partisan division has been evident, even at the height of presumed bipartisan cooperation. Often, too, the Democrats were split on these issues between their Northern wing (traditionally more liberal in orientation) and their Southern wing (traditionally more conservative in orientation). Still, even when one of these wings joined forces temporarily with the Republicans, there were sufficient fluctuations between issues to limit the degree of bipartisanship and to produce partisan and ideological divisions.

On foreign economic assistance, for instance, Northern Democrats and Republicans in the 1950s joined together ideologically to support these programs, while Southern Democrats opposed them. In the 1960s through the early 1970s, Northern Democrats generally continued their support and Southern Democrats their opposition. Republicans, on the other hand, fluctuated from opposition in the early 1960s to support late in that decade and into the 1970s.[16]

On the issue of military assistance, in the Senate, Northern Democrats generally supported the increase or maintenance of the same levels of funding until the early 1960s. By contrast, Southern Democrats fluctuated in their support of military aid during the height of the Cold War, but they became more supportive during the Vietnam period. Republicans increasingly came to support such assistance over the course of the postwar period, albeit starting with some initial reluctance in the early 1950s. In the House, the voting trends on military assistance tended to be much more irregular across party lines, but the general direction for the parties was about the same as in the Senate.

On defense expenditures, too, partisan differences existed. Northern Democrats in the Senate, but less so in the House, supported increasing, or at least maintaining, defense expenditures in the 1950s, but Northern Democrats in both houses began to oppose such expenditures in the 1960s and 1970s. Republicans, on the other hand, opposed such expenditures in the 1950s more than Democrats, but they tended to be much more supportive from 1960 onward when compared to the Democrats. Southern Democrats exhibited less variation in their behavior and continued to support defense expenditures during these years.

On trade policy, some partisan differences in congressional behavior existed. Democrats generally were more supportive of a free-trading system in the 1950s, while the Republicans were generally more protectionist in their orientation. By the middle of the 1960s, however, these trends had reversed, with Democrats becoming more protectionist, and the Republicans becoming more free-trade oriented.

The upshot of these analyses suggests that party influence—even at the height of bipartisanship—had an impact on specific details of foreign policy. To the extent that bipartisan foreign policy occurred, it necessarily had to operate within the confines of party differences. In this sense, partisan politics assisted in shaping U.S. foreign policy behavior to a greater extent than some might wish to acknowledge. Nevertheless, as political scientist Barry Hughes and others have reminded us, the position and party of the president still played an important role in these congressional voting results.[17]

The Effects of Vietnam

Although Destler, Gelb, and Lake acknowledge that some bipartisanship (or more accurately, "majorityship") existed from the 1940s to the 1960s, they go on to argue that "Vietnam changed all this."[18] As more Americans were drafted and sent abroad following the escalation of the Vietnam War in 1965, and as the conflict became a regular feature on the evening news, President Johnson found himself facing a domestic political problem every bit as challenging as the war itself. The

effects of this war were profound on domestic harmony and on any great sem-
blance of cooperation across party lines. As Destler, Gelb, and Lake note, "The
conceptual basis of American foreign policy was now shaken, and the politics of
foreign policy became more complicated."

Zbigniew Brzezinski has aptly summarized the effect of Vietnam on any
domestic unity in foreign policy in yet another way:

> Our foreign policy became increasingly the object of contestation, of sharp
> cleavage, and even of some reversal of traditional political commitments. The
> Democratic Party, the party of internationalism, became increasingly prone
> to the appeal of neo-isolationism. And the Republican Party, the party of iso-
> lationism, became increasingly prone to the appeal of militant intervention-
> ism. And both parties increasingly found their center of gravity shifting to the
> extreme, thereby further polarizing our public opinion.[19]

These changes in bipartisanship became evident in the support patterns for the
Vietnam War within Congress. President Lyndon Johnson now had to rely upon
Republicans and conservative (largely Southern) Democrats for much of his support on Southeast Asian policy.[20] Opposition now began to come from liberals
within his party and from a few Republicans. Party and ideological lines began
to be drawn; strong support across party lines on a major foreign policy initiative
was beginning to erode. As contentious as this issue was, Congress, controlled by
Democratic majorities in the House and the Senate, was never successful in defeating Presidents Johnson or Nixon (through 1972) on a major funding bill for the
Vietnam War.[21] In this sense, the essence of both party loyalty and bipartisanship
remained, although both forces were drawn taut by the Vietnam involvement.

Toward the end of the Vietnam War, bipartisanship began to wear even thin-
ner. With a Republican president in the White House and a Congress controlled
by the Democrats, the consequence was the series of foreign policy reforms discussed in Chapter 8. While both parties supported a number of these reforms,
Democrats, and particularly liberal Democrats, were generally more favorable to
placing limits on the foreign policy powers of the executive than were the Republicans. Moreover, the major foreign policy reforms enacted by Congress occurred
when Republican presidents were in office and the Democrats controlled both
the Senate and the House.

In yet another barometer of changing foreign policy bipartisanship in the Vietnam period, we find increasing evidence of foreign policy partisanship, especially
when compared to the Cold War years. The party platforms for 1968, 1972, and
1976 showed a marked decrease in bipartisanship.[22] Only 24 percent of the foreign
policy pledges for these platforms were the same for Republicans and Democrats,
while only 11 percent of the defense policy pledges were bipartisan. (Recall that
the bipartisan pledges were about twice to three times those figures during the
Cold War.) The two parties seemed to be moving in different directions in that the
preponderance of pledges on foreign and defense policy were unique to each party.
At the same time, the degree of foreign policy conflict on pledges remained low (at
about 6 percent) for each policy area. In short, then, while bipartisanship was
declining, outright partisan conflict had still not emerged.

By the 1980s, however, the level of partisan division on foreign policy increased even more. Key foreign policy issues like Central America, the Middle East, and national defense policy elicited clashes along party and ideological lines.[23] Congressional voting on covert aid to Nicaraguan rebels, for example, often saw Democrats pitted against the Republicans in Congress. On key defense votes, such as the development of the MX missile, the B-1 bomber, and the Strategic Defense Initiative ("Star Wars"), the pattern was much the same.[24] In this sense, there has been clear movement away from the bipartisan tradition of the past, especially on crucial defense and foreign policy issues.

BIPARTISANSHIP AND CONGRESSIONAL FOREIGN POLICY VOTING

Indeed, recent research raises some questions about the extent to which this tradition ever actually operated in terms of one aspect of bipartisanship, policy outcome. Recall that one component of bipartisanship implied unified policy outcome across the two branches and the parties. That is, a majority of congressional members of both parties supported the president's position on foreign policy. Research by McCormick and Wittkopf suggests that such bipartisanship, when defined by congressional voting on foreign policy issues, was less frequent than the popular view.[25] In several analyses of congressional foreign policy voting from the late 1940s to the late 1980s, they have argued that partisan and ideological conflict was more often the norm in foreign policy making than was any bipartisan harmony. In the analyses of over 2,400 congressional foreign policy votes on which the president took a position, they found that bipartisan policy unity was as often fantasy as fact.

Figure 11.1 portrays the results obtained by McCormick and Wittkopf for the extent of bipartisan voting in the House and Senate from 1947 to 1988 for eight different American administrations. With few exceptions, bipartisan voting has been more infrequent than conventional wisdom suggests. Only during the Eisenhower administration did bipartisan support (defined as the majority of both parties supporting the president) exist across the House and Senate on more than 50 percent of the foreign policy votes. While bipartisan support was greater in the Senate than in the House across these administrations, the level of bipartisanship was especially low in the latter chamber. If the Eisenhower administration were excluded, no more than 50 percent of the votes in any other administration obtained bipartisan support in the House. These results hardly support the view that bipartisanship was the norm for any extended period in the post–World War II years.

By contrast, Figure 11.2 illustrates the substantial degree of partisan divisions in these administrations since World War II. While the partisan gaps are greater in the House than in the Senate across these administrations, the divisions between the parties are still quite substantial. On average, the difference between parties in

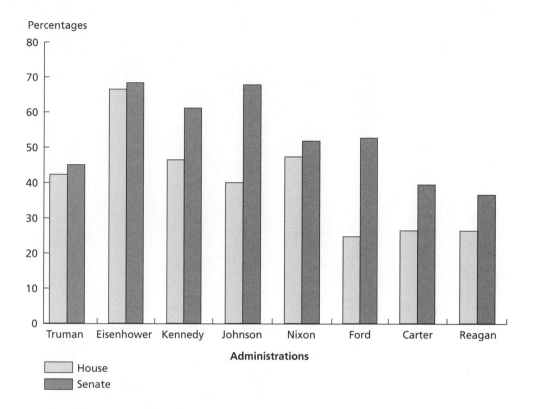

FIGURE 11.1 Bipartisan Foreign Policy Voting in Congress, 1947–1988

Note: Each bar represents the proportion of foreign policy votes on which a majority of both parties supported the president's position.

SOURCE: James M. McCormick and Eugene R. Wittkopf, "Bipartisanship, Partisanship, and Ideology in Congressional-Executive Foreign Relations, 1947–1988," *The Journal of Politics* 52 (November 1990): 1085. Reprinted by permission of Blackwell Publishing, Ltd.

each chamber is about 20 percentage points, with only the Eisenhower administration (in both the House and the Senate) and the Johnson administration (in the Senate) obtaining a noticeably smaller gap. These partisan gaps held across four different foreign policy issues (foreign aid, foreign relations, national security, and trade), and the partisan differences are pronounced across all of them. In short, these results suggest that congressional voting on foreign policy issues has always been more partisan and less bipartisan than often portrayed.

When the Vietnam War was factored into these analyses, it did not change the overall conclusions. While partisan divisions increased somewhat in the post-Vietnam period, the impact of the war could generally not be separated from the effects of other factors. Only on national security voting did the pre- and post-Vietnam periods show some marked differences. Overall, though, the Vietnam War appeared not to be "a watershed in postwar American bipartisanship."[26]

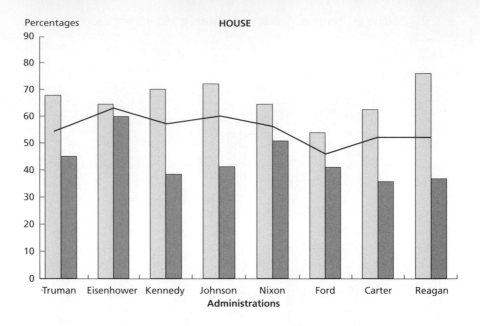

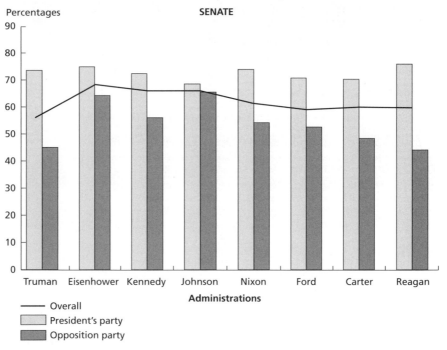

FIGURE 11.2 Partisan Differences in Congressional Voting on Foreign Policy Issues

Note: Each bar represents for each party the average precentage of support by members of Congress for the president's position on foreign policy votes. The overall line measures the average level of support for the president regardless of party.

SOURCE: James M. McCormick and Eugene R. Wittkopf, "Bipartisanship, Partisanship, and Ideology in Congressional-Executive Foreign Relations, 1947–1988," *The Journal of Politics* 52 (November 1990): 1090. Reprinted by permission of Blackwell Publishing, Ltd.

Only in combination with other changes at home and in Congress did Vietnam produce an increase in partisan and ideological divisions.

While these results thus appear to raise doubts about the degree of bipartisanship, at least as measured through formal congressional voting, some caution needs to be exercised in interpreting the figures and pushing them beyond what they can demonstrate about bipartisanship in American foreign policy generally. These analyses, for instance, do not consider the other component of bipartisanship—the process side or the degree of informal consultations between the branches. That is, collaborative arrangements may have been developed and used between the branches, but these arrangements are not (and cannot) be reflected in the formal voting analyses. Further, these analyses do not weigh the importance of particular issues to the president, even though these are issues on which he has indicated a position. Thus, bipartisan outcomes may have operated on highly selective issues salient to the president and the Congress, but that bipartisan cooperation may be imbedded in this larger set of votes on which the president still stated a position. Despite these necessary cautions, the congressional voting analyses do alert us against applying too quickly and too easily the "bipartisan" label to American foreign policy making during the Cold War years and after.

PARTISAN DIVISIONS TODAY: FROM RONALD REAGAN TO GEORGE W. BUSH

Although the debate continues over whether bipartisanship ever existed and over how much it has declined, partisan acrimony on foreign policy issues persists. The party differences in the foreign policy arena became so substantial during the first term of the Reagan administration that he felt compelled to undertake at least two important steps in an effort to rebuild bipartisan support. First, he appointed bipartisan presidential commissions to garner support for the modernization of America's strategic nuclear arsenal and for his Central American policy.[27] The task of both commissions was to diffuse the partisan bickering over these issues and to build support across party lines. Second, President Reagan also felt compelled to deliver a major foreign policy address in which he called for a return to an earlier era of executive-legislative cooperation:

> We must restore bipartisan consensus in support of U.S. foreign policy. We must restore America's honorable tradition of partisan politics stopping at the water's edge, Republicans and Democrats standing united in patriotism and speaking with one voice.[28]

Despite this appeal, party differences in Reagan's second term actually accelerated on foreign policy, fueled largely by the controversy surrounding the Iran–Contra affair.

When President George H. W. Bush took office, partisan accord was so low that he felt it necessary to appeal for bipartisanship in foreign policy in his inaugural address. Two key passages summarize his view:

> We need a new engagement . . . between the Executive and the Congress. . . . There's grown a certain divisiveness. . . . And our great parties have too often been far apart and untrusting of each other.
>
> It's been this way since Vietnam. That war cleaves us still. . . . A new breeze is blowing—and the old bipartisanship must be made new again.[29]

Despite some initial efforts by both Republicans and Democrats and an important initial bipartisan Contra aid package early in 1989, Bush still faced partisan divisions over his foreign policy actions. Spirited debates occurred over defense expenditures in the post–Cold War era, the amount of assistance to the newly independent Eastern Europe, and the response to the Chinese crackdown in Tiananmen Square. The fractious argument in January 1991 over whether to continue with sanctions against Saddam Hussein's Iraq after his seizure of Kuwait or to go to war against Iraq sustained this partisan and ideological debate.

There were important exceptions to partisan discord (e.g., over the American intervention and the seizure of Manuel Noriega of Panama in 1989 and the initial bipartisan support over Iraq's seizure of Kuwait), but the level of bipartisanship in the Bush administration generally remained low. In fact, only one in five foreign policy votes in the House and less than one in three votes in the Senate received bipartisan support. Partisan divisions remained as wide as during the Reagan administration, with gaps of 34 percent and 35 percent between Republicans and Democrats in the House and Senate, respectively.[30]

President Bill Clinton, too, made an appeal for bipartisan support, although his appeal was directed toward staving off the American impulse toward isolationism, seemingly revived with the end of the Cold War: "The new isolationists both on the left and the right would radically revise the fundamentals of our foreign policy that have earned bipartisan support since the end of World War II." Invoking the name of the father of bipartisanship, Senator Arthur Vandenberg, Clinton noted that America's past foreign policy "successes would not have been possible without a strong, bipartisan commitment to American's [sic] leadership." "Today," he continued, "it is Vandenburg's [sic] spirit that should drive our foreign policy and our politics."[31]

Still, the bipartisan decline and the partisan gaps continued unabated for the Clinton administration. During its first term, the Clinton administration enjoyed bipartisan support only on about one in four foreign policy votes in the House of Representatives, and only about one in three in the Senate on which the president took a position. (This level of support was roughly in line with the relatively low level of bipartisan support received by the Bush and Reagan administrations.) Instead, partisan and ideological differences were quite pronounced across several key foreign policy areas. On the use of American forces abroad, whether in Somalia, Bosnia, or Haiti, partisan differences were often sharply drawn in Congress, with Republicans less supportive of the use of force than Democrats. On defense issues, both partisan and ideological differences arose during the Clinton administration, with conservatives and liberals of both parties divided on spending on defense. Trade, too, produced sharp partisan differences, with the Clinton administration ultimately relying on Republican support to gain approval of the North American Free Trade agreement (NAFTA).

During its second term in office, the Clinton administration faced a Congress that was as equally as challenging on foreign policy, and the administration suffered major foreign policy delays or setbacks at the hand of that institution, still controlled by the Republican opposition. In the economic area, for example, Congress took more than one year to approve an appropriation to refinance the International Monetary Fund to assist with the bailout of several countries affected by the Asian financial crisis of 1997–1998, and it did so only after obtaining a series of financial conditions desired by the Republicans. Significantly, too, Congress refused to approve fast-track trading authority for the Clinton administration, forestalling efforts to complete trading pacts around the world. In the security area, whether on supporting the air war against Kosovo in 1999 or considering the Comprehensive Test Ban Treaty, the Congress was often sharply divided or opposed to presidential action. Over Kosovo, for example, the Senate largely divided on party lines to support the NATO operation there by a 58–41 margin, while the House actually rejected a resolution over U.S. involvement in the war by a tie vote of 213 to 213. On the Comprehensive Test Ban Treaty, the Senate registered a stinging defeat to the Clinton administration by supporting the treaty largely on a party line vote (51–48). Such a vote total was 16 votes short of the needed 67 to win approval.[32] In all, partisan and ideological divisions continued to dominate the foreign policy process in the late 1990s.

By contrast, the George W. Bush administration came to office with a narrow Republican-controlled Congress, and the administration initially enjoyed foreign policy support across party lines. Propelled by September 11, bipartisan foreign policy support accelerated, especially on security questions. As noted in Chapter 6, the administration was able to pass a series of anti-terrorism measures by wide margins and with bipartisan support. Within a little more than one year of September 11, members of the House and the Senate—across partisan lines— approved a resolution authorizing the president to use force against Saddam Hussein's Iraq by wide margins. Indeed, one analysis, written during this time period, contended that the Congress had now moved back from its activism after the end of the Cold War and was once again more deferential to presidential wishes. Although some lawmakers may have wished to adopt a different position either for policy or party reasons, the "political reality" demanded that they support the president in a time of national threat. In this sense, it had now become difficult for members of Congress—of either party—to criticize a popular president confronting a foreign policy crisis.[33] In this sense, bipartisanship appeared to have been restored through the effect of September 11.

Yet, such bipartisan support can be short-lived, as President George W. Bush began to learn less than two years after September 11. By summer 2003, as the reconstruction of Iraq began to prove more challenging, both in blood and treas-ury, Bush's approval rating declined to 50 percent in one poll in September 2003, and his level of support for whether the Iraqi War was worthwhile fighting reached a similar level.[34]

Members of Congress, across party lines and along the ideological spectrum, also began to criticize foreign policy generally, and the war on terrorism specifi-cally. On the Republican side, Senator Richard Lugar of Indiana, the chairman of the Senate Foreign Relations Committee and a longtime internationalist, called upon the president to explain more fully the length and cost of American involve-ment in Iraq. As he noted in the opening statement at a committee hearing in summer 2003, "we are intensely interested in the Administration's effort to secure contributions from other nations that will reduce long-term U.S. financial bur-dens and broaden the interests of the international community in a successful outcome in Iraq."[35] Another moderate Republican, Senator Chuck Hagel of Nebraska, also faulted the administration over its failure to develop a better plan for a postwar Iraq. On the other side of the political aisle, a leading liberal Demo-crat, Senator Edward Kennedy, was even harsher over the Bush administration's going to war against Iraq, charging that "there was no imminent threat. This [pol-icy] was made up in Texas, announced in January to the Republican leadership that war was going to take place and was going to be good politically. This whole thing was a fraud."[36] Several of the candidates seeking the presidential nomination also harshly criticized the administration's foreign policy. For example, Senator John Kerry questioned the administration's policy in Iraq, especially its postwar policy; former Vermont governor Howard Dean made opposition to the initiation of the Iraqi War the centerpiece of his campaign; and Congressman Richard Gephardt likewise criticized the direction of Bush administration's foreign policy. In all, such statements seemed to ensure that partisan and ideological differences on foreign affairs were once again central to the debate over policy making even after the events of September 11.

PARTISAN POLITICS AND THE FUTURE

With the exception of the brief period immediately following September 11 in which both parties joined together on foreign policy, bipartisanship has rarely been the norm in recent years and remains unlikely for the foreseeable future. Instead, the more likely prospect is that partisan divisions on foreign policy will continue to be a part of the American political landscape. Several reasons make this projection likely.

First, divided government at the national level over the last several decades supports a continuation and intensification of partisan conflicts, not a diminu-tion of their levels. Republicans won six of the last nine presidential elections between 1968 and 2000, and Democrats won control of both chambers of Con-gress in 18 of the last 27 congressional elections between 1950 and 2002. During a majority of time, then, one party often controlled the White House and the other party Congress. Even when President George W. Bush's Republican party controlled both houses of Congress, the margins have been so thin that it was hardly a working majority; indeed, in early 2001, when one senator left the Republican party and became an Independent, control of the Senate switched to the Democrats until the November 2002 election. In a setting of divided government (or narrow majority control), partisanship appears more likely and bipartisanship less likely.

Second, partisan and ideological cleavages have also deepened between the major political parties over the past several decades, eroding further the prospect for bipartisan accommodation. Conservative Republicans are now replacing conservative Democrats in the South; conservative Democrats are switching parties; and ideological preferences and party affiliations are now more closely aligned. Furthermore, moderates are fewer in both parties, as contentious issues increasingly divide them. Put differently, Democrats are more likely to be liberal Democrats on domestic and foreign policy issues, and Republicans are more likely to be conservative Republicans across these two kinds of issues. Without the cross-pressures between ideology and party within parties, bipartisanship on foreign policy remains elusive.

Third, the proliferation of issues, now increasingly recognized as foreign policy ones, portends more, not fewer, partisan divisions as well. For example, as economic issues are increasingly viewed as having foreign and domestic policy implications, and as Americans are affected differentially by policy choices on such issues, partisan debate will intensify. Similarly, even if scientific agreement can be reached on the dimensions of such ecological challenges as acid rain, nuclear waste disposal, and global warming, common political actions to address these global environmental concerns will remain elusive, and they will continue to be ripe for partisan discord.

Fourth, some security issues, and particularly the threat now posed by international terrorism, may yield more temporary consensus politics across party lines—as the immediate aftermath of the September 11 attacks demonstrated—but even those issues, in the context of divided government and polarized political parties, eventually prove divisive in a relatively short time. Indeed, discord rather quickly set in over how to deal with a postwar Iraq and how best to deal with the continuing terrorist threat represented by al-Qaeda and other similar groups. Other issues with important security components—immigration, drug trafficking, weapons of mass destruction, and territorial, ethnic, and religious conflicts—remain on the agenda, and such issues do not easily evoke a common domestic response. For instance, the major political parties are hardly in agreement over how to address immigration and border problems and the potential security threat that such problems might pose. Or alternately, Republicans and Democrats are not united over how to address the dangers posed by North Korea and its commitment to develop nuclear weapons. These and other security concerns (and issues often involving more than just security concerns) then not only fail to evoke a common response, but they are increasingly politicized.

In sum, the influence of partisan politics on the direction of U.S. foreign policy has become more identifiable over the past several decades. While the Cold War may have produced some level of bipartisanship, the post-Vietnam and post–Cold War year eroded this sense of unity. Although the September 11 attacks may have temporarily restored some bipartisanship, the partisan differences have risen anew. And they are likely to intensify in the future.

INTEREST GROUPS
AND THE FOREIGN POLICY PROCESS

Another participant in foreign affairs whose role has increased in importance is that of interest groups. The number of interest groups participating in the American political process in Washington is astounding, estimated at about 11,000 firms or groups and 17,000 individuals with an annual spending of $3 billion.[37] The interest groups concerned either with foreign policy exclusively, or with foreign and domestic policy in combination, are less than those totals, but their overall magnitude is still conveyed by them. These foreign policy interest groups range from the oldest—the economic interest groups—to the newest—foreign lobbying groups. Within and between these two types of organizations, we can identify several other categories of foreign policy interest groups: labor unions, agricultural organizations, religious groups, ethnic groups, veterans organizations, single-issue interests, academic think tanks, and ideological groups, among others.

Interest groups primarily target Congress with their influence efforts. They seek to influence members of Congress and policy making through the use of professional lobbyists (e.g., lawyers or public relations firms) or their own staff personnel located or assigned to Washington. Yet a considerable portion of interest-group activities may also focus on influencing key foreign policy bureaucracies. The Department of Defense and the Department of State, for example, are important targets for these various pressure groups.

Sometimes, too, these governmental bureaucracies (and others discussed over the last two chapters) actually lobby the U.S. Congress as well. In fact, a recent count listed 141 government bureaucracies, agencies, and commissions involved in lobbying efforts, ranging from the Executive Office of the President, the Department of Agriculture, the Department of Commerce, the Department of State, and Department of Defense to the Agency for International Development, the CIA, and the Federal Trade Commission.[38] The political clout of these governmental interest groups should not be underestimated, as Dana Priest notes in her analysis of the American military:

> Each branch of the military also has a Capitol Hill staff of its own, the talent of which rival that of the renowned law and lobbying firms on Washington's K Street. If one of the services opposes an administration policy or direction, it has the networks and political savvy to thwart the White House in Con-

gress—without fingerprints, of course, since lobbying by government agencies is forbidden by law.[39]

In all, foreign policy lobbying is not done solely from outside the government, although most of it is.

Types of Foreign Policy Interest Groups

In order to give some sense of the magnitude of nongovernmental interest groups (although without pretending to provide an exhaustive list) and some of their foreign policy concerns, we identify several examples of the different types of foreign policy interest groups that are operating today.

Business Groups Economic interest groups probably comprise the largest number of foreign policy groups. Several umbrella economic organizations lobby for business interests. For example, the National Association of Manufacturers, the U.S. Chamber of Commerce (and its global affiliates), the Committee on Economic Development, and the Business Roundtable, among others, would fit into this category.[40] Beyond these umbrella groups, particular manufacturing, industrial, and commodity interests usually engage in separate lobbying activities. The American Bankers Association, the American Petroleum Institute, the American Textile Manufacturers Institute, the American Footwear Manufacturers Association, the National Cotton Council, and the National Coal Association are all examples of such lobbying groups. In addition, virtually all major corporations actively lobby for their particular foreign policy interests. The major defense contractors (such as General Dynamics, Lockheed Martin, Boeing, United Technologies, and General Electric), for instance, lobby Congress and the Department of Defense in particular. In short, virtually every major corporation on the Fortune 500 list has some kind of representation in Washington, and a large percentage of them are involved in foreign policy lobbying, too. All of these business lobbies generally share similar foreign policy goals: They seek to increase foreign trade, to expand their own exports, and, in a number of instances, to promote a strong national defense policy.

Labor Unions A second important economic interest group is the American labor movement. This movement actively lobbies Congress and the executive branch on foreign policy issues. Its main interests are policy decisions that would affect the job security of its workers or would increase the amount of foreign imports. The labor movement recently has worked to protect American workers from importation of cheaper goods and the export (or outsourcing) of jobs by American multinational firms that seek cheaper labor markets abroad. As might be expected, such policy positions are often directly opposed to those of the business groups on both foreign and domestic policy questions.

The most prominent labor unions that have extensive lobbying efforts are the American Federation of Labor and Congress of Industrial Organizations (the

AFL-CIO), the United Automobile Workers of America (UAW), and the International Brotherhood of Teamsters. In addition, within the AFL-CIO umbrella organization, there are 86 national and international unions "across virtually every industry in the United States."[41] In the early 1990s, during the debate over the North American Free Trade Agreement (NAFTA), the AFL-CIO weighed in heavily in opposition to the pact, fearing the loss of jobs to cheaper labor in Mexico. Opposition to NAFTA, most-favored-nation trading status for China, and other free trade measures have always been important lobbying targets for the labor union movement. More recently, the AFL-CIO has focused on stopping the expansion of NAFTA into Latin America and the expansion of coverage by the World Trade Organization (WTO). Over the years, then, unions and other interest groups have fought to pass restrictions in trade legislation to protect American jobs at home.

Although labor unions, like the major industrial concerns, are primarily interested in economic issues, they also have adopted positions on other foreign policy questions. Under the longtime leadership of George Meany, the AFL-CIO was particularly known for its staunch anti-Communist stances and for its effort to assist the global trade union movement, which would foster these positions.[42] Lane Kirkland, Meany's successor as president of the AFL-CIO, continued that policy. The concern of the AFL-CIO and its president, John Sweeney, has now turned more domestic and has sought to rejuvenate labor unions at home among American ethnic groups and the young.[43]

Nonetheless, labor unions have been involved in a broad array of foreign policy issues from time to time. The National Endowment for Democracy (NED) program initiated during the Reagan administration afforded the AFL-CIO a way to become more involved in the foreign policy process. As a result of legislation in the 1980s, the NED provided the AFL-CIO with funds to promote democracy in foreign countries. Such funds were to be used to set up seminars for foreign labor leaders, bring them to the United States, and assist them in promoting free and democratic institutions within their own countries.[44] The American Institute of Free Labor Development (AIFLD), a joint enterprise with American business, was also a mechanism for promoting union development in poor countries and in affecting foreign policy. The AIFLD received considerable funding from the U.S. government's foreign assistance program and provided covert assistance to friendly groups within developing countries, too.[45] It has also been criticized to this day by those on the left for its actions.

Agricultural Groups Agricultural interests also attempt to influence the foreign policy process. The principal lobbying groups in this area are the American Farm Bureau Federation, the National Farmers Union, and the National Farmers Organization,[46] but other such groups are also numerous in Washington. By one assessment, "20–25 percent of all lobbyists in Washington, D.C. represent interest groups involved in the food production process."[47] While these organizations vary in the degree to which they believe that the federal government should intervene in the market economy, they all support efforts to increase the exports of farm products. Although these interest groups are primarily concerned with issues directly affecting agriculture, they also take stands on a variety of other foreign policy issues that may indirectly impact farmers and producers. The American Farm Bureau Federation, for example, routinely lobbies on numerous foreign policy issues. In recent years, that organization has lobbied Congress opposing the Kyoto Treaty on greenhouse emissions, urging limits on the authority of the World Trade Organization, favoring passage of fast-track negotiating authority for the executive branch, supporting reductions in capital gains and estate taxes for individuals, and promoting regulatory reform for businesses, among other issues.[48]

Religious Organizations Yet another set of readily identifiable interest groups seeking to affect foreign policy are religious organizations. The most prominent among these groups are the National Council of Churches (various Protestant churches), the American Friends Service Committee (Quakers), and the National Conference of Catholic Bishops. Major religious groups, including the Methodists, the Unitarians, the Presbyterians, and the Baptists, have also been involved in foreign policy lobbying.[49] In addition, numerous affiliates of these different religious movements have engaged in lobbying efforts. Several faith-based non-governmental organizations—World Vision for evangelical Protestants, World Council of Churches for mainline Protestant religions, and Catholic Relief Services for Roman Catholics—are also important religious lobbies. By one estimate, there are about 100 different religious lobbies in Washington, DC, alone.[50]

"Peace and justice" and "social concern" committees have been established by various religions as a better means of informing and involving their memberships in both foreign and domestic policy matters. Indirectly, too, these efforts assist the members of these religious faiths in petitioning their representatives, if they choose to do so. The American Friends Service Committee (AFSC), for example, has long been involved in group discussions of current international issues, in aiding the various conflicting parties in the Middle East and elsewhere, for instance, and in offering suggestions for a resolution of the conflict between the Palestinians and the Israelis.[51] Similarly, the May 1983 pastoral letter by the National Conference of Catholic Bishops on the possession and use of nuclear weapons, *The Challenge of Peace,* signaled a major illustration of foreign policy activism by that organization.[52] Various religious groups were also active in opposition to the Reagan administration's policy in El Salvador and Nicaragua, largely led by members of the Catholic Church.[53] In the 1980s, too, the Christian Coalition, led by Pat Robertson, was an important addition to these religious lobbying efforts. More recently, in the 1990s, religious lobbies have become involved in lobbying on behalf of humanitarian interventions to address gross human rights violations in ethnic and religious conflicts in Bosnia, Haiti, Rwanda, and Kosovo.

In the months prior to the war with Iraq, the major religious organizations lined up in opposition and in support to the United States initiating military action against that country. In September 2002, for instance, the President of the United States Conference of Catholic Bishops wrote a letter to President Bush on behalf of that organization raising "serious questions about the moral legitimacy of any preemptive, unilateral use of military force to overthrow the government of Iraq."[54] Similarly, the Mennonite Central Committee, the United Church of

Christ, the United Methodists, and the Quakers, among others, also spoke out against going to war against Iraq. The President of the Ethics and Religious Liberty Commission of the Southern Baptist Convention, some evangelical Christian leaders, and Union of American Hebrew Congregations, however, lined up in support of going to war against Iraq.[55]

Ethnic Groups   Ethnic groups are another gathering of important interests active in the foreign policy arena. Traditionally, the most active American ethnic groups have been those of Jewish, Irish, and East European heritage. Greeks, Hispanics, and African-Americans have also sought to influence American foreign policy.[56] With the end of the Cold War, ethnics with Central and Eastern European roots (e.g., Armenian-Americans, Czech-Americans, Slovak-Americans, Hungarian-Americans, among others) have either revived or initiated their foreign policy activitism.[57]

For all of these ethnic groups, the dominant theme of their participation in foreign affairs focuses usually on American policy toward the particular country or region of their ancestors' origin, rather than on general foreign policy questions. On policy issues related to Israel, Ireland, Cyprus, Central America, South Africa, and Central and Eastern Europe, these groups have been most active and have made their voices heard. Ethnic groups, as a whole, have often been identified as an especially important source of American foreign policy, and we shall have more to say about their influence later in this chapter.

Veterans Groups   Veterans groups or associations are also active in trying to influence the foreign policy of the United States. Such organizations as the Veterans of Foreign Wars, the American Legion, and the American Veterans of World War II are the best known of these groups.[58] Near the end of the Vietnam War, the Vietnam Veterans Against the War also entered the political arena, seeking at first to end American involvement and, later, to petition for better treatment of returning Vietnam veterans. Veterans from the Persian Gulf War of 1991 raised their collective voice in calling for the American government to seek the origin of the "Gulf War syndrome," which has afflicted scores of military personnel returning from that war. Veterans from the Iraq War of 2003, including the number of reservists and National Guard forces that were activated, are also seeking additional government support for the sacrifices that they made in that conflict and its aftermath. One tangible indication of how effective veterans groups have been over the years is that Congress established a separate cabinet department in 1988 to serve their interests.

Ideological Groups   Ideological groups have long been involved in American politics. Although these groups are often identified with questions of domestic politics, some are also active on foreign policy issues. The most prominent ideological groups are the Americans for Democratic Action (ADA), the principal liberal interest group in Washington politics, and the American Conservative Union (ACU), the principal conservative interest group in the nation's capital. Both of these groups evaluate members of Congress on foreign and domestic policy from their particular perspectives and issue yearly voting "scores" for all senators and representatives. These groups also actively work to make known their positions on major foreign policy issues.

Many other ideological groups from both ends of the political spectrum participate in foreign affairs issues. Over the years, those with a conservative viewpoint included the American Security Council, the John Birch Society, and the National Conservative Political Action Committee (NCPAC), while those with a liberal viewpoint included the Coalition for a New Foreign and Military Policy, the Women's International League for Peace and Freedom, the World Peace Through Law Association, the World Federalists, and the World Policy Institute.[59] In the post–September 11 environment, the American Civil Liberties Union (ACLU), an organization promoting the protection of individual rights of Americans, has been particularly involved in questioning and challenging provisions of the USA PATRIOT Act passed by Congress in the immediate aftermath of the attacks on the World Trade Center and the Pentagon. Its concerns focus on some restrictions on civil liberties that were incorporated in the Act as means of combating and investigating potential terrorists.

Think Tanks Yet another category that might not be immediately identified as interest groups are the numerous "think tanks" that are located primarily in Washington, DC.[60] These are organizations funded by individuals, corporations, and foundations that focus on analyzing a particular problem or array of problems to offer policy advice. These organizations share their results with the congressional and executive branches through testimony on Capitol Hill, through the publication of scholarly books and articles, and through opinion pieces appearing in several key elite newspapers, such as the *Christian Science Monitor, Los Angeles Times, New York Times, Wall Street Journal,* or *Washington Post.* In these various ways, they seek to influence policy and have been relatively successful: "More so than in any other country," one analysis reported, American think tanks "have played an influential role in foreign policy making," largely owing to the open nature of the American political system.[61]

The number of think tank groups is quite large and diverse, even if we were to consider only those devoted exclusively to foreign policy issues. These groups may be categorized in a variety of ways: ideologically (e.g., as liberal, moderate, or conservative in orientation) or chronologically (as the "Old Guard," think tanks, the "Cold War" contemporaries, and the new "partisan institutes").[62] While space precludes an exhaustive survey of these think tanks, a brief word or two about the major ones will illustrate the range and policy orientations of these organizations.

The best-known conservative think tanks in Washington are the Heritage Foundation and the Cato Institute. The Heritage Foundation analyzes both domestic and foreign policy issues from a relatively hard-line conservative position. Its views are disseminated through a quarterly magazine entitled *Policy Review* and through a myriad of reports on current topics. The Heritage Foundation gained prominence particularly during the Reagan administration, but it remains an important and influential political force in Washington to this day. Depending upon the administration in power, the Heritage Foundation is likely to be the site of an important foreign or domestic policy speech by a governmental official. As the Bush administration was being attacked for his handling of postwar Iraq, Vice President Dick Cheney used the venue of the Heritage Foundation to issue a ringing defense of White House policy (just as National Security Advisor Condoleezza Rice had used a speech at a Midwest think tank, the Chicago Council on Foreign Relations, for a similar purpose a fewer days earlier).[63]

The Cato Institute was established in 1977 and "is named for *Cato's Letters,* a series of libertarian pamphlets that helped lay the philosophical foundation for the American Revolution."[64] The Institute's libertarian orientation translates into policy recommendations that promote a more isolationist or noninterventionist approach on the part of the United States in global affairs. On a regular basis, scholars and analysts affiliated with the Cato Institute investigate a host of research questions on foreign and domestic policy issues, and disseminate their views through books, policy analyses papers, "op-ed" pieces, and testimony on Capitol Hill, among other ways.

Somewhat in the middle politically are the American Enterprise Institute for Public Policy Research (AEI) and the Center for Strategic and International Studies (CSIS). AEI's goal is "dedicated to preserving and strengthening the foundations of freedom—limited government, private enterprise, vital cultural and political institutions, and a strong foreign policy and national defense—through scholarly research, open debate, and publications."[65] This think tank began as a strong conservative voice on foreign policy issues (and has retained that characteristic on most foreign policy matters), but it has also begun to broaden its political perspectives in recent years. It currently houses 50 resident scholars/fellows and has 100 or more adjunct scholars in the United States and abroad. Like the other think tanks, it produces a broad array of books and articles and publishes its policy journal, *The American Enterprise,* as mechanisms to get its message out.

CSIS began as an institute affiliated with Georgetown University and, while generally a conservative institute, it, too, has moved toward more moderation in its outlook. Since 1987, it has operated independently and has attracted many distinguished individuals to its staff over the years, including Zbigniew Brzezinski and Henry Kissinger. Like AEI and most other think tanks, CSIS publishes a foreign policy journal, *The Washington Quarterly,* holds periodic seminars, and publishes various foreign policy materials. Unlike the other think tanks mentioned so far, CSIS devotes its work solely to foreign policy matters, nationally and internationally.

The best-known liberal-leaning think tank is the Brookings Institution. Brookings has several divisions, with one devoted exclusively to foreign policy studies. Its policy recommendations are usually moderate or liberal in orientation, and it sometimes has been referred to as the "Democratic government in exile," since officials from Democratic administrations have often staffed it. Its seminars, publications—including a wide array of foreign policy books annually—and conferences are highly regarded among those of all political stripes. The *Brookings Review,* until it ceased publication in 2004, long provided a discussion of topical domestic and foreign policy issues and was a ready vehicle for gaining an understanding of the thinking of Brookings scholars (and others) on current issues.

Along with the other think tanks, policy recommendations by Brookings fellows or associates are often relied upon for policy ideas and policy critiques on Capitol Hill and in the executive branch. For example, within days of the George W. Bush administration's issuance of its *National Security Strategy of the United States of America* in September 2002, a group of leading Brookings foreign policy scholars held a briefing critiquing the policy directive, issued a written analysis of it shortly thereafter, and provided a more exhaustive assessment of Bush policy a few months later.[66] In this way, the Brookings Institution was in a good position to impact the debate on the administration's foreign policy approach.

Finally, two other think tanks—two of the oldest—deserve brief mention. The Council on Foreign Relations arose after World War I, with an expressed anti-isolationist sentiment. Because membership was restricted to those elected to participate, it became a rather exclusive group that reviewed and commented on foreign policy issues.[67] It has remained so to this day. Over the years, too, the council has sponsored numerous studies and book projects on foreign policy matters, continues to publish numerous books each year, and reviews published works throughout the foreign policy and international relations field. Perhaps its most important vehicle for exercising influence is its flagship journal, *Foreign Affairs*. Without question the leading journal in the field, *Foreign Affairs* has published several articles (e.g., George Kennan on containment in 1947, Richard Nixon on China in 1967) that foreshadowed the change in direction of American foreign policy or that allowed policy makers to justify past actions or explain future direction. For instance, Sandy Berger, outgoing Clinton national security advisor, summarized Clinton foreign policy at the end of 2000 and Condoleezza Rice, incoming national security advisor, outlined some foreign policy priorities for a future George W. Bush administration. In this sense, while the journal is theoretically open to a wide array of contributors, policy makers and former policy makers are often afforded a ready venue in this influential outlet. For an academic publication, *Foreign Affairs* has an extraordinarily large circulation, and it is widely read and quoted in official Washington.

The Carnegie Endowment of International Peace was established prior to World War I in 1910, originally with a large gift from philanthropist Andrew Carnegie, who was interested in how to achieve and promote world peace. Over the years, the Carnegie Endowment has maintained that focus although evolving in various ways over the past century. Today, its mission is directed toward "advancing cooperation among nations and promoting active international engagement by the United States." It seeks to promote these goals "through research, publishing, convening, and on occasion, creating institutions and international networks." In the past decade or so, for instance, the Carnegie Endowment has developed comprehensive studies of the new global environment after the Cold War, generated an assessment of the executive branch in this new environment, and opened up the Carnegie Moscow Center to study that part of the world. More recently, the endowment has focused upon the phenomenon of globalization and its impact on world affairs. While books, policy analyses, and presentations are its principal ways of sharing its foreign policy view, the endowment has now been the publisher of *Foreign Policy* magazine for over three decades. Much like its counterpart, *Foreign Affairs,* the journal seeks to give voice to a wide array of foreign policy views, including academics, policy analysts, and public officials.[68]

Single-Issue Groups The single-issue interest group represents somewhat of a residual category for different kinds of groups that seek to influence foreign policy because of members' deeply held views on a particular policy question. These groups range widely, from the United Nations Association of the United States, which seeks to enhance support for the UN, to the Union of Concerned Scientists and the Arms Control Association, which back efforts to achieve arms limitations, to the Friends of the Earth or Greenpeace, which support efforts to preserve the global environment.[69] Moreover, these single-issue groups probably dwarf in size any other categories that we might identify, since they can form, lobby, and disband rather quickly. They also may be an amalgam of other interest groups that join together to lobby on a new issue on the political agenda at a particular moment in time.

Perhaps the leading illustration of a single-issue foreign policy group in the postwar period was the anti–Vietnam War movement of the 1960s and early 1970s. This group (really a coalition of groups such as the National Mobilization to End the War, the Moratorium Movement, the War Registers League, and even the radical wing of the Students for a Democratic Society, the Weathermen) was highly successful in rallying support among the American public and, eventually, in altering the course of American policy in Southeast Asia. At the height of the detente period in the early 1970s, too, other single-issue groups arose. Supporters and opponents of detente with the Soviet Union vigorously lobbied for their point of view with Congress and the executive with a more mixed record of success.

In the late 1970s and early 1980s, the most prominent single-issue foreign policy groups were those supporting and opposing the development of more nuclear weapons. The Committee on the Present Danger, composed primarily of conservative ex-government officials, was most active in opposition to the ratification of the SALT II treaty signed by President Jimmy Carter. The nuclear freeze movement—a broadly based coalition of individuals from various walks of life—that arose in opposition to the nuclear arms buildup by the Reagan administration called for the enactment of a mutual and verifiable freeze on the production and development of all nuclear weapons.[70]

By the mid-1980s, the largest set of single-issue groups united around the question of American policy in Central America. A decade-long debate developed over whether to provide or withhold aid to the Nicaraguan Contras in their fight against the Sandinista government. One study identified about 100 interest groups that were involved in lobbying Congress and the president on that issue.[71] Some were formed exclusively to address Central America; others had a larger policy agenda but were still very involved in this issue.

In the 1990s, the issue of whether Congress should give its approval to the North American Free Trade Agreement (NAFTA)—establishing a free trade zone among the United States, Mexico, and Canada—sparked significant interest group activity. Several different groups participated in this debate from across the political spectrum.[72] U.S.A.-NAFTA was the umbrella organization for over 2000 business groups supporting the agreement, while Citizen's Trade Campaign was the umbrella organization for a variety of opposition groups, including Ralph Nader's Public Citizen and other liberal groups. Labor unions and agricultural, environmental, and ideological groups lined up on opposite sides of this debate.[73]

In the early years of the twenty-first century, single-issue groups arose over the increasing globalization of the international economy and over support and opposition to the war with Iraq. Several antiglobalization groups are internationally based groups (e.g., Third World Network, the International Forum on Globalization, and Focus on the Global South), but one prominent one, Global Exchange, maintains its headquarters in California. Through publications, reports, seminars, and teach-ins, these groups seek to point out the dangers that globalization poses and seek to influence the political process through such educational techniques. In addition, the groups develop local initiatives to lobby against the impacts of globalization, such as the existence of sweatshops and child labor violations.[74]

The war against Iraq in 2003 also generated a number of individuals and groups that voiced their opposition in various cities around the country. These groups, although drawn from different areas and often with an array of other interests, came together and demonstrated as a single coalition in Washington against the administration's policy. The one-year anniversary of the U.S. attack on Iraq (March 2004) also generated a whole series of demonstrations by anti-war groups around the country.

A group of foreign policy and international relations scholars with differing political perspectives did likewise. In September 2002, this group of academics took out an advertisement in the *New York Times* charging that "war with Iraq is *not* in America's national interest."[75] What was particularly interesting about the group was that signatories were comprised of both foreign policy "realists," who often support the use of force, and nonrealists, who do not. Yet this coalition of academics, usually possessing different foreign policy perspectives, temporarily joined forces seeking to influence American policy on this particular foreign policy issue.

Foreign Lobbies Foreign lobbies has been the newest recognized lobby group on foreign policy and their presence in Washington has grown significantly over the past three decades. In the 1970s about 75 countries had representation in Washington. By the end of the century, about 140 nations from every corner of the world, both large and small, were represented by lobbyists in Washington.[76] In the main, the lobbyists for these nations are often American citizens who have been hired to explain their policies and to try to persuade Congress to give them more favorable treatment. Prominent examples are the lobbying efforts undertaken by South Africa, El Salvador, Saudi Arabia, and other Third World nations at various times. Saudi Arabia, for instance, was particularly active in its lobbying efforts on the AWACS aircraft sale in 1981 and enlisted the support of several large American corporations to back its position.[77]

Perhaps the best-known (and the most often maligned) foreign lobby in the late 1980s and early 1990s was Japan. Over the years, Japan hired numerous former members of Congress (e.g., James Jones [D-Oklahoma] and Michael Barnes [D-Maryland]) and former administrative officials (e.g., Eliot Richardson, former attorney general during the Nixon administration, and Stuart Eizenstat, former domestic policy aide to President Carter) to serve as its lobbyists and to attempt to influence Congress and the executive branch on American-Japanese relations, especially trade policy. In addition, Japan hired some of the best-known public relations firms in Washington to get its message out. Both of these tactics made its lobbying effort formidable, and often successful.

But Japan had also done more than this. It has provided research money for several Washington think tanks, such as Brookings Institution, AEI, and the Center for Strategic and International Studies, to support various studies, conferences, and academic chairs. While no direct Japanese benefit is specified from such think tank support, it does at least raise the question of whether independent analysis can be undertaken with such arrangements.[78] All of these efforts allow Japan access in Washington, and they make its lobbying effort powerful, although "the Japan lobby rarely wins battles on its own."

In the early 1990s, the republics of the former Soviet Union and the People's Republic of China were rapidly hiring Washington law and lobbying firms to promote their interests in the nation's capital. By one assessment, Azerbaijan, Belarus, Kazakhstan, Kirghizstan, Latvia, Moldova, Russia, Ukraine, and Uzbekistan have hired one or more firms to represent them. In fact, Russia and Russian firms had contracted with nine different law and consulting companies within two years of the collapse of the Soviet Union.[79] China also has developed a very large set of representatives to argue its case, especially on trade matters. High-priced and high-powered lawyers and former American government officials representing U.S. business concerns are opening doors to Chinese officials, while other firms and individuals are representing Chinese businesses in the United States. Representatives include former members of Congress (e.g., Howard Baker and Gary Hart) and former officials in the executive branch (e.g., Carla Hills, Lawrence Eagleburger, and Alexander Haig), among others.[80] Their access to Chinese and American officials on behalf of the two countries' companies made for a very potent political force for maintaining most-favored-nation (MFN) trade status and eventually achieving "permanent normal trading relations" for China in 2000. These efforts, too, expanded American investment in, and trade with, China.

In all, these kinds of activities by Japan, Russia, China, and the myriad number of other foreign countries, reflect the internationalization of lobbying efforts that has taken place today, and how lobbying, and even foreign lobbying, has become a normal part of the American foreign policy process.

THE IMPACT OF INTEREST GROUPS

How successful are these interest groups in affecting foreign policy? Unlike the president, Congress, and the foreign affairs bureaucracies that have direct control over policy, interest groups have at best only an indirect effect. By definition, interest groups do not control policy; rather, they seek to influence it. In this con-

Table 11.1 Interest Group Activity over Most-Favored-Nation (MFN) Status for China

Groups that supported MFN	Groups that opposed MFN
National Association of Manufacturers	Public Citizen
Business Coalition for U.S.-China Trade	United Auto Workers
Business Roundtable	International Brotherhood of Teamsters
U.S. Chamber of Commerce	AFL-CIO
National Economic Council	Union of Needletrades; Industrial & Textile Employees
	American Conservative Union
	Christian Coalition

SOURCES: Warren P. Strobel and Nancy E. Roman, "Clinton to Seek MFN Renewal for China," *The Washington Times,* June 2, 1998; Susan Crabtree, "Inside the War Room Clinton's Team Puts Blitz on Fence-Sitters," *Roll Call,* March 20, 2000; Robert Kagan, "Clinton's China Two-Step," *The Washington Post,* January 17, 2000; Gary Bauer, "Don't Reward China," *The Washington Times,* June 4, 1999; Juliet Eilperin, "'Normal Trade Relations' Finds Favor Over MFN," *The Washington Post,* July 21, 1998; Morton M. Kondracke, "Levin's 'Bridge' Could be Key to China Trade," *Roll Call,* April 13, 2000; Bob Deans, "Despite Lopsided Trade Picture, Clinton in Dogfight to Pass China Trade Bill," *Cox News Service,* May 12, 2000; Susan Crabtree. "Wu Feels PNTR Pinch," *Roll Call,* September 21, 2000; Bill Pascoe, "Gore, Gephardt and Global Warming." *The Washington Times,* December 3, 1997; Nancy E. Roman, "Normal Trade for Beijing Survives; House Beats Repeal of Renamed MFN," *The Washington Times,* July 23, 1998.

nection, most analysts suggest that, on the whole, these foreign policy groups do not do very well at that task. Several reasons are given for this view.[81] First of all, American foreign policy tends to be made more in the executive branch than in the congressional branch, as we noted in Chapter 7. Access by interest groups to the executive branch is more difficult than is access to Congress, with its varied committee and subcommittee structures. While interest groups do lobby the foreign affairs bureaucracies, their efforts may actually end up serving the bureaucracies' interests more than the lobbyist's.[82] Second, foreign policy issues and decisions are usually quite remote from the lives of Americans, and rallying support or opposition by interest groups poses a significant challenge.[83] Third, important foreign policy decisions are often made under crisis conditions—short decision time, high threat, or surprise in the executive branch. Under such conditions, foreign policy making is likely to be even more elitist than normal—more confined to a few members of the executive branch and more restricted in the amount of congressional participation. In such situations, avenues of influence for interest groups are further limited. Fourth—and perhaps most pivotal—with the magnitude of interest groups operating, it is likely that "countervailing" groups will arise to balance off the impact of a given interest group and, therefore, allow the policy makers more freedom of action.[84] Competing interest groups on creating NAFTA or competing interest groups seeking to open trade with China give members of Congress or the executive branch officials some latitude in making their own decisions on foreign policy questions (see Table 11.1).

Despite such difficulties, interest groups still do impact policy on some key issues and under particular circumstances. The principal areas appear to be issues involving American long-range policy toward the international system and on budget issues related to defense and foreign economic policy.[85] The former issues might be labeled "strategic" policy questions because they "specif[y] the goals and tactics of defense and foreign policy." Policy guidelines for actions directed toward a particular region (e.g., East Asia), country (e.g., Ukraine), or issue (e.g., nuclear proliferation) would qualify as strategic policies. The latter issues might be labeled as "structural" policy questions because they focus on "procuring, deploying, and organizing military personnel and material . . . [and deciding] which countries will receive aid, what rules will govern immigration. . . ."[86] Policy guidelines on the number of bases, the size and composition of the defense budget, and the distribution of foreign assistance would qualify as structural issues. The president often takes the lead on both policy questions (and especially strategic ones), but congressional approval and fine-tuning of actions in both areas are almost always necessary. Since Congress allows more avenues of access by interest groups, they are likely to be more successful on these two kinds of issues. Finally, and importantly, there is no easy or permanent demarcation among these types of issues, including crisis issues. Indeed, interest groups may even weigh in on "crisis" issues, especially if they are extended over time. Consider, for example, U.S. antiterrorist actions. While the president may be given latitude to respond to terrorist attacks, over time antiterrorism policy may be transformed into a strategic or even a structural issue. Creating new administrative structures and providing new funding allow more participants, including interest groups, to impact policy directions, including affected interest groups. In this sense, active interest groups may play a part across a broad array of foreign policy issues.

Two types of interest groups appear to be particularly influential on foreign policy, especially within Congress, and have been recognized as such during the Cold War and even as the Cold War ended.[87] One is those economic groups that can be loosely identified as the "military-industrial complex," the other is ethnic groups. The impact of the former set of groups is based upon the extensive access and involvement by numerous corporations over economic and defense issues that so often arise in Congress. The impact of the latter set of groups is based upon the interest that many Americans have in U.S. policy toward the country of their origin or toward a country with which they identify, e.g., Israel.[88] Let us examine both of these types of interest groups in a little more detail to give some sense of their relative influence today.

Economic Interest Groups

Our earlier discussion highlights the extraordinary number of economic interest groups seeking to influence foreign policy. These groups come from within the society, and now come from foreign countries as well. For an industrial capitalist economy, such as the United States, the existence of these groups should not be surprising. Yet, for several decades now, the close ties between these groups and the government have raised concerns over whether this linkage so dominates the foreign policy process that American society and American democracy suffer as a result. The most often cited constellation of economic interest groups affecting, or perhaps even dominating, American foreign policy is labeled "the military-industrial complex (MIC)." The origins of this label, and the theory underpinning it, deserve mention before we assess the degree of influence of the MIC on foreign policy.

The Theory of the Military-Industrial Complex (MIC)

First introduced into the American political lexicon by President Dwight Eisenhower, a decorated World War II general, as he was leaving office, the "military-industrial complex" refers to the presumed symbiotic relationship between the major industrial firms in the United States and the American defense establishment.[89] According to this theory, these industries become dependent upon the Department of Defense for military defense contracts and often apply pressure for a policy of strong military preparedness or even global military involvement as a means of continuing their economic well-being. More broadly, the phrase "military-industrial complex" has also been used to describe the informal ties that have developed among the top corporate sectors of American society and the political-military sectors of the American government.[90]

The first assumption underlying the military-industrial complex theory is that there is a unified elite within American society that dominates all important national and foreign policy decisions. This elite is held together by a set of interlocking structural relationships and by psychological and social constraints among the occupants of the key institutions.[91] In other words, the elites share similar educational and social backgrounds and frequently interact with one another.

The second assumption implicit in this theory is that this single elite's domination of policy making produces a distinct kind of American foreign policy, consistent with its interests. Such a policy emphasizes high military spending, interventionism abroad, and the protection of private property.[92] By pursuing these policies, the private interests of the military-industrial complex are safeguarded, especially in a world of ideological tension that existed during the Cold War.

Are these assumptions accurate? Does this political elite really exist? And is it successful in shaping policy consistent with the predictions of the theory of the MIC? With the end of the Cold War in the early 1990s and then the terrorist attacks of 2001, how will the MIC's influence (to the extent that it exists) change? Definitive answers to these questions are not easy to obtain, even though numerous researchers have sought to address them over the years. In our review of the available evidence, we believe that more of a case can be made for identifying the existence of a policy elite than for supporting the foreign policy consequences that are presumed to follow from the influence of that elite.

Evidence of a Single, Interlocking Elite Analyses identifying the similar backgrounds of personnel in governmental offices and documenting the interactions between the military and the governmental sectors provide substantial support to the first assumption of the MIC theory. One of the earliest studies in this area reported that from 1944 to 1960, 60 percent of some 234 officials, mainly in the foreign affairs bureaucracies (Department of Defense, Department of State, the Central Intelligence Agency, etc.) came from important business, investment, and law firms. A relatively small number of these individuals (84) held more than

63 percent of the positions. Thus, according to this research, a few key individuals dominated the foreign policy bureaucracies and circulated in and out of the government from the mid-1940s to 1960.[93]

More recently, political scientist Thomas Dye documented the background of key foreign policy officials throughout much of the post–World War II era and reached a similar conclusion about the extensive business ties of these policy makers.[94] Various secretaries of defense, for example, have had extensive links to large American corporations. Charles E. Wilson (1953–1957) was the president and a member of the board of directors for General Motors; Thomas Gates (1960–1961) was chairman of the board and chief executive officer of Morgan Guaranty Trust and also served on the boards of directors of General Electric, Bethlehem Steel, Scott Paper Company, and Insurance Company of America, among others; Robert S. McNamara (1961–1967) was president and a member of the board of directors of the Ford Motor Company; and Caspar Weinberger (1981–1987) was a vice president and a corporate director for Bechtel Corporation, a major global contractor, and served on the board of directors of such companies as Pepsico and Quaker Oats.

The same pattern has held true for secretaries of state. John Foster Dulles (1953–1959) was a partner of Sullivan and Cromwell, a prominent Wall Street law firm, and was on the boards of directors for the Bank of New York, Fifth Avenue Bank, the American Cotton Oil Company, and the United Railroad of St. Louis, among others; Dean Rusk (1961–1968) was a former president of the Rockefeller Foundation; and William P. Rogers (1969–1973) was a senior partner in Royal, Koegal, Rogers, and Wall, another prominent Wall Street law firm. Alexander Haig (1981–1982), for instance, not only served as military attaché to Henry Kissinger and as supreme allied commander of NATO, but he also served as an executive with United Technologies—a leading defense contractor. Before his appointment as secretary of state, George Shultz (1982–1989) was a high-ranking official with the Bechtel Corporation, and also had served on the boards of directors for the Borg-Warner Corporation, General Motors, and Stein, Roe, and Farnham, a Chicago-based investment advisory firm. James Baker (1989–1992) came from a background of the law and wealth (his father owned the Texas Commerce Bank).

The pattern continues for more recent administrations, too. Although Dye characterized the Clinton administration's top posts as largely "filled by lawyers, lobbyists, politicians, and bureaucrats,"[95] elements of a political and economic elite existed in that administration. While Clinton's own beginnings were modest, he was quickly taken under the wing of Senator J. William Fulbright, the influential chairman of the Senate Foreign Relations Committee, during his undergraduate days at Georgetown University in Washington, DC. Fulbright's support and encouragement aided Clinton in obtaining a prestigious Rhodes scholarship to Oxford and afforded him the opportunity to develop contacts with many future leaders there.[96] His secretaries of state, Warren Christopher and Madeleine Albright, for instance, had served in the Carter administration, and Christopher came from a prestigious law firm in California. His national security advisors—Anthony Lake and Samuel Berger—also had served in the Carter administration. And continuing the political pattern, his defense secretaries—Les Aspin, William Perry, and William Cohen—

had extensive ties to Washington with Aspin and Cohen serving for many years in Congress and Perry previously working in Congress.

Several key appointees came with prominent business credentials, too. Clinton's first chief of staff, and later a counselor to the president, Thomas McLarty, was an executive with a major natural gas company in Arkansas, and his secretary of energy, Hazel O'Leary, was an executive of a Minnesota utility company. Both of Clinton's secretaries of treasury had pronounced business ties: Lloyd Bentsen was a longtime U.S. senator from Texas who chaired the Finance Committee, but he also had extensive wealth and business holdings in Texas; and Robert Rubin was a Wall Street financier prior to assuming the position as deputy secretary of treasury and then the secretary position itself.[97]

Officials in the George W. Bush administration continue to reflect the appointment of political and business elite to key policy-making positions.[98] By one assessment, 11 of 18 cabinet-level appointments by the Bush administration gained Washington experience in earlier Republican administrations, including such key foreign policy officials as Vice President Richard Cheney, Secretary of State Colin Powell, Secretary of Defense Donald Rumsfeld, and National Security Advisor Condoleezza Rice. Similarly, individuals with extensive business ties also populate the key policy-making positions in the Bush administration. Indeed, previous business experience was the most popular prior occupation among these elites by one analysis. Vice President Cheney, for example, was president of Halliburton, a large oil company; Paul O'Neill, Bush's first treasury secretary, served as president of International Paper and as a key executive of Alcoa; Secretary of Defense Rumsfeld was president of G. D. Searle, a leading drug company; and Secretary of Commerce Donald Evans previously worked as an executive of an oil company, among others.

Evidence for DOD/Defense Contractor Links While this kind of study seems to identify some linkage between the business and political community and to suggest a circulating set of policy makers, other evidence provides support for the linkage between the military and major defense contractors, the other key component of this interlocking elite argument. In an analysis of the late 1980s and early 1990s, for example, the "revolving door" phenomenon between DOD personnel and defense contractors continued to operate as it had in the past.[99] In fiscal year 1987, 328 senior DOD officials and 3,199 DOD military officers who left government service went to work for defense contractors, and in fiscal year 1993, 145 senior DOD officials and 1,164 DOD military officers who left government service took positions with defense contractors.[100] While the 1987 totals and the 1993 totals represent only about 13 and 4 percent, respectively, of those who left government service among those ranks, the top military retirees—over half of the generals and admirals in 1988 and a quarter of the generals and admirals in 1994—took jobs with defense contractors. In other words, the highest-ranking military officers continued to find ready positions with the defense industry. Importantly, as this analysis noted, "the true number of crossovers is understated because the methodology for identifying the revolving-door population only captures persons whose employment with a defense contractor required a security clearance."[101]

This symbiotic relationship between the DOD officials and defense contractors gains even more credence in light of the various criminal charges that have been brought against lobbyists for defense contractors and in light of the large number of revelations about cost overruns and overcharging by defense contractors themselves. Several lobbyists have been charged and convicted of bribing DOD procurement officers to obtain lucrative contracts, for example, and major defense contractors (e.g., General Electric and the Electric Boat division of General Dynamics) have been accused of dramatic cost overruns. Still others have been accused of charging exorbitant prices for commonplace supplies to the military. By one analysis, "the military paid $511 for light bulbs that cost ninety cents, $640 for toilet seats that cost $12, $7600 for coffee makers, and $900 for a plastic cap to place under the leg of a navigator's stool" in an airplane.[102]

On balance, these analyses provide considerable evidence for the linkage among the business, military, and political community in American society. What they cannot answer directly, however, is whether these common backgrounds and ties produced policy primarily meeting the interests of these elites. Presumably, shared backgrounds would lead policy makers to take into account these economic groups in any foreign policy decisions or, at the very least, to allow ready access to key economic groups in order to make their case. Yet, more direct evidence on the second assumption of the MIC theory—the policy consequences of elite dominance—is needed to draw any firm conclusions about the role of the military industrial complex in foreign policy. Several studies have been undertaken to evaluate just such policy implications of the MIC theory.

Unfortunately, the evidence on the policy implications of the MIC theory is disparate, often focusing on various policy components and then attempting to draw larger inferences from those results. Further, these policy studies have more often pointed to differing conclusions about the MIC's effect than have the studies identifying close elite ties. On the one hand, some case analyses of particular foreign policy decisions provide strong support for the MIC theory, and the evidence on the awarding of military contracts to a select number of defense contractors does as well. On the other hand, other analyses of defense contracting raise doubts about the grip that the MIC has on American society and economy, and extensive studies of defense spending (and its effect) raise more general doubts about the theory's accuracy. On balance, these various studies point to a more mixed policy influence of the MIC than its proponents contend. To provide a flavor of the differing findings on the policy effects of the military-industrial complex, let us summarize some of the evidence over recent decades.

Analyses Supporting the Influence of the MIC   First, several case analyses of American foreign policy, ranging from the Marshall Plan of 1948 to the decision not to intervene in Indochina in 1954, to the decision to cut back the bombing in Vietnam in 1968, provide some support for the MIC. Berkowitz, Bock, and Fuccillo contend that "it would be difficult to point to a single decision that directly contravenes the interests of the business elite within the presidential court."[103] While they quickly add that the business elite may not have been successful on every decision, "when major issues are at stake, or when its interests are clearly and incontrovertibly involved, . . . the business elite proceeds with absolute unity of purpose and action."[104] Thus, they contend that the business elite view of foreign policy making provides the best explanation for America's actions abroad.

Second, the pattern of defense contracting is often used to demonstrate the policy influence of the military-industrial complex. The prime military contractors often turn out to be among the largest industrial corporations, and they are often the same ones year in and year out. In an analysis of the largest defense contractors for fiscal year 2002, for instance, we found that 10 of the top 50 and 14 of the top 100 defense contractors were also ranked among the 100 largest corporations in America, based on the Fortune 500 list (Table 11.2).[105] In fact these totals represent somewhat of a decline from our earlier analyses: For fiscal year 1982, fiscal year 1988, and fiscal year 1995, this same comparison found 40, 35, and 23, respectively, of the 100 largest corporations among the top 100 defense contractors in those years. At the same time, it is worth keeping in mind that the spending concentration remained high, with the top ten defense contractors in fiscal year 2002 obtaining 39 percent of the total contracts and the top twenty-five contractors getting 48 percent of the total DOD contracts.

Political scientist James Kurth has pointed out, moreover, that other evidence of concentration and continuity in defense contracting are available. That is, the

Table 11.2 Top 100 Defense Contractors and Their Corporate Sales Rank for FY2002

Company	Rank of Prime Contract Awards FY02	Corporate Sales Rank FY02
Lockheed Martin Corp.	1	56
The Boeing Company	2	15
Northrop Grumman Corp.	3	99
Raytheon Company	4	*
General Dynamics	5	*
United Technologies Corp.	6	49
Science Applications International	7	*
TRW Inc.	8	*
Health Net Inc.	9	*
L3 Communications Holding Inc.	10	*
General Electric Company Inc.	11	5
United Defense Industries Inc.	12	*
Dyncorp	13	*
Humana Inc.	14	*
Honeywell International Inc.	15	*
B A E Systems PLC	16	*
Bechtel Group Inc.	17	*
ITT Industries Inc.	18	*
Textron Inc.	19	*
Computer Sciences Corp.	21	*
Triwest Healthcare Alliance Co.	20	*
URS Corporation	22	*

(continued)

Table 11.2 *(continued)*

Company	Rank of Prime Contract Awards FY02	Corporate Sales Rank FY02
Booz Allen & Hamilton Inc.	23	*
GM GDLS Defense Group LLC, JOI	24	*
Alliant Techsystems	25	*
Boeing Sikorsky Comanche Team	26	*
Cardinal Health	27	19
North American Airlines	28	*
Oshkosh Truck Corp.	29	*
Exxon Mobil Corp.	30	3
N.V. Koninklijke Nederlandsche	31	*
Veritas Capital Management LLC	32	*
Washington Group International	33	*
Dell Computer Corporation	34	36
The Titan Corporation	35	*
Jacobs Engineering Group Inc.	36	*
Halliburton Company (Inc.)	37	*
The Mitre Corporation	38	*
The Aerospace Corp.	39	*
Electronic Data Systems Corp.	40	*
Stewart and Stevenson Services I	41	*
Johnson Controls Inc.	42	*
Longbow Limited Liability Comp.	43	*
Worldcom Inc.	44	*
Javelin Joint Venture	45	*
Government of Canada	46	*
FedEx Corp.	47	83
Harris Corporation	48	*
International Business Machines	49	8
Johns Hopkins University	50	*
Rockwell Collins Inc.	51	*
Massachusetts Institute of Tec	52	*
Goodrich Corporation	53	*
Veridian Corporation	54	*
Sierra Health Services Inc.	55	*
The Renco Group Inc.	56	*
Anteon International Corporation	57	*
Amerisource Bergen Corp.	58	24
AT&T Corp.	59	22
Engineered Support Systems Inc.	60	*
GTSI Corporation	61	*
Battelle Memorial Institute	62	*
CACI International Inc.	63	*

Company	Rank of Prime Contract Awards FY02	Corporate Sales Rank FY02
United States Dept. of Energy	64	*
Chugach Alaska Corp.	65	*
Arinc Inc.	66	*
Motorola Inc.	67	*
B P PLC	68	*
Rolls-Royce PLC	69	*
Hensel Phelps Construction	70	*
A M E C PLC	71	*
Federal Prison Industries Inc.	72	*
Valero Energy Corp.	73	55
CH2M Hill Companies LTD	74	*
The Parsons Corporation	75	*
General Atomic Technologies Inc.	76	*
Sumitomo Heavy Industries Ltd.	77	*
TYCO International Ltd.	78	*
The Proctor & Gamble Company	79	31
Kuwait Petroleum Corporation	80	*
Foster Wheeler LTD	81	*
Mantech International Corp.	82	*
Wallenius Holdings Inc.	83	*
United Industrial Corp.	84	*
Cubic Corporation	85	*
Caltex Trading and Transport Company	86	*
Leo Burnett USA Inc.	87	*
Philipp Holzmann Ag	88	*
A P Moller Gruppen	89	*
The Shaw Group Inc.	90	*
National Oil Distribution Company	91	*
Parker Hannifin Corporation	92	*
NCED	93	*
Charles Stark Draper Laboratory	94	*
Pepco Holdings Inc.	95	*
Great Lakes Dredge & Dock Corp.	96	*
The Bahrain Petroleum Company	97	*
Day & Zimmerman Group Inc.	98	*
Bearingpoint Inc.	99	*
LG-Caltex Oil Corporation	100	*

*Indicates companies that were not ranked in the top 100 companies in corporate sales.

SOURCES: Defense contract rankings were taken from *100 Companies Receiving the Largest Dollar Volume of Prime Contract Awards—Fiscal Year 2002* at http://www.dior.whs.mil/peidhome/procstat/p01/fy2002/top100.htm, while the corporate sales rankings for 2002 were taken from "The 500 Largest U.S. Corporations," *Fortune*, April 14, 2003, pp. F-1 to F-20.

defense contractors have largely remained the same over the last four decades—mainly the aircraft industries, and more recently the electronics industries; they have maintained their same ties with particular military branches (e.g., Boeing and Rockwell International with Air Force contracts and Grumman primarily with the Navy); and they have maintained the same "product specialties"—particular kinds of weapons systems for each manufacturer.[106] The merger of Lockheed and Martin Marietta and the consolidation of control by Boeing in the aircraft industry—all major defense contractors—only reinforces the degree of concentration in these areas. Such continuity provides additional evidence on how and why certain defense systems are purchased, and why some manufacturers are advantaged over others as well. Indeed, a recent analysis of keeping the Osprey aircraft under consideration for so long was due in part to the effective lobbying by the principal contractors—Bell Helicopter Textron and Boeing.

Analyses Challenging the Influence of the MIC Other studies, however, raise doubts about the success of the military-industrial complex to shape and influence foreign policy, especially on defense spending. First, until the dramatic increase in military expenditures during the Reagan administration, defense spending, measured either as a percentage of the gross national product or as a percentage of the national budget, had actually declined over time. For the former measure, defense spending dropped below the 6 percent level, and, for the latter measure, defense spending fell to less than 25 percent. While defense expenditures edged up during the Reagan years to about 6.6 as a percent of the GNP for 1986 and constituted 28 percent of the federal budget (fiscal year 1987), both measures dropped significantly during the Bush and Clinton administrations. In the mid-1990s, defense expenditures were just over 4 percent of gross domestic product (GDP) and just under 19 percent of the federal budget.[107] Even with projected increases in defense spending to fight the war on terrorism in the twenty-first century by the George W. Bush administration, the aggregate clout of the military-industrial complex on shaping defense spending has hardly been as pronounced as some imply. Defense outlays for 2004 are projected to be about 3.5 percent of GDP and 18 percent of the federal budget.

Second, political scientist Bruce Russett, long a student of American defense expenditures, has cast doubt on the explanation for high defense budgets as attributable to the military-industrial complex only. Most assuredly, the military-industrial complex contributes to continued defense spending, but other factors in combination (such as domestic bureaucratic politics, technological momentum, and international actions) better explain the overall defense levels. Russett is quick to acknowledge, however, that domestic factors tend to have somewhat greater weight in this explanation than do international factors alone.[108] Furthermore, Hartley and Russett found "strong evidence . . . that public opinion . . . influence[d] government policy" on military spending from 1965 to 1990, although they acknowledged that the "exigencies of the arms race and the budget deficit were equally or more influential."[109]

Third, have American industries really been as dependent on defense spending for their prosperity as some imply or as the analyses focusing only on defense contractors suggest? In the aggregate, as reported in a classic study by sociologist Stanley Lieberson, few of the 100 largest industrial corporations in 1968 depended on military contracts for the bulk of their sales; in fact, 78 of the top 100 had less than 10 percent of their sales from military contracts, and only five corporations made more than 50 percent of their sales by military contracts.[110] In addition, Lieberson demonstrated that corporate income over time has been less dependent on military spending by the federal government than on nonmilitary spending. Finally, he shows that defense spending cutbacks would seriously harm only certain sectors of the economy (aircraft, ordinance, research and development, electronics, and nonferrous metals) rather than the economy as a whole. In short, while Lieberson does not deny the existence of the military-industrial complex, his evidence suggests that its dominance is less than others might contend.

Fourth, political scientist Steve Chan has carefully surveyed and analyzed myriad studies on the relationship between the economy and military spending.[111] These studies, too, produce mixed and inconsistent results on the positive or negative effect of military spending overall. On the one hand, several studies suggest that military spending actually serves both as an "economic prop" and as a "political prop" within the American setting. It is an economic prop because it provides jobs and cushions economic downturns, and it is a political prop because it changes according "to the rhythms of electoral cycles."[112] On the other hand, several alternative studies failed to find—or found limited—effects of defense spending on economic growth within the American economy. More generally, as Chan noted, "there is no direct, simple link between defense spending and macroeconomic performance."[113]

In sum, these various studies over the past several decades suggest two conclusions with important ramifications for the theory of the MIC: Neither the dependence of the American economy on high defense spending nor its substantial negative effects across the entire American economy is easily demonstrable. Instead, the military-industrial complex is a convergence of defense-oriented organizations that are constantly pursuing their interests. It has hardly been as successful as the common view that is advanced; defense spending has not been as dramatic as sometimes implied and its negative effect on the American economy may be less than is often assumed. Further, the MIC has met public resistance and interest-group opposition and continues to face such challenges to this day.

Such assertions are not likely to end the debate over the relative influence of the military-industrial complex in policy making. This amalgam of interests may continue to be viewed as a powerful foreign policy interest group, especially in the post–September 11 world. In fact, the real test of these interest groups' influence may be yet to come. Can these interest groups continue to affect policy and achieve their goals in the new threatening international environment, or will they continue to meet resistance even under such circumstances? If they can succeed, then perhaps the argument about the relative impact of the MIC will become clear. If they cannot, those who took a more differentiated view of the power of this interest group may be more accurate.

What should not be lost in this discussion of the military-industrial complex is the continuing size and impact of these concentrations of interests. No matter what one's judgment is about the degree of control of the MIC, it is fair to conclude that the military-industrial sector seems to occupy a potentially important position in the shaping of foreign policy decisions, especially when compared to other interest groups. Moreover, the use of many high-tech weapons in the 1991 Persian Gulf War or 2003 Iraq War (e.g., bombs sent down air shafts into Iraqi storage facilities and the remarkable accuracy of cruise missiles attacking Baghdad), the rise of terrorist activity against Americans and American installations in the 1990s and 2000s (whether in New York or Washington, or in Saudi Arabia), and the increased American military presence around the world (whether Afghanistan or Iraq) may well have provided a resurgence in political clout for the military-industrial complex on Capitol Hill and with the executive branch.

Ethnic Groups

The second major type of interest group that has enjoyed some success in influencing American foreign policy is comprised of ethnic groups. The leading ethnic lobbies in recent decades are probably the Jewish and Greek communities, two relative newcomers to the American political process. The Jewish lobby has been able to obtain a remarkable level of economic and military assistance for Israel over the postwar years (at $3 billion per year) and has been able to assist in steering American policy toward supporting that state since 1948. Only in the past two decades or so has this strong support for Israel begun to wane a bit. In a more limited way, the Greek lobby has also enjoyed some success, especially in the middle 1970s.[114] It was able to garner sufficient congressional support to impose an American arms embargo on Turkey during the middle 1970s, despite active opposition by the executive branch.

By contrast, the influence of the older ethnic lobbies—those Americans of Irish and Eastern European heritage—has generally declined over the past 50 years. The Irish lobby enjoyed its greatest success prior to World War II, while the East Europeans seemed most influential in the early Cold War years.[115] A new variant of the latter lobby, however, appears to be undergoing some resurgence recently. The Central and East European Coalition, formed in 1993, comprises 16 American ethnic associations representing Armenian-Americans, Ukrainian-Americans, Czech-Americans, Slovak-Americans, Polish-Americans, Hungarian-Americans, Latvian-Americans, and a host of others. Members of this coalition seek to steer American policy toward the more rapid expansion of NATO, provide more aid to the former Soviet republics and the nations of Eastern Europe, and place less emphasis on the "Russian-centered path" in American foreign policy. Although these ethnics constitute only 8.5 percent of the total American population, they are concentrated in several Midwestern states—with significant electoral votes in any hotly contested national election. As a result, both political parties have been wooing these ethnics heavily, changing national security legislation in response to their demands in the mid-1990s or supporting the effort at NATO and European Union expansion for these newly independent nations more recently.[116]

Two newer American ethnic groups—Hispanics and African-Americans—are beginning to exercise some influence in the foreign policy process as well. TransAfrica, an organization to promote the interests of African-Americans, especially in Africa and the Caribbean, was formed only in 1977, but it has already had a noticeable effect on American foreign policy.[117] This group lobbied to keep economic sanctions on Rhodesia in the late 1970s in an effort to complete that country's movement toward majority rule and the creation of the nation of Zimbabwe. In conjunction with the "Free South Africa Movement," TransAfrica played an important role in prodding the Reagan administration to apply economic sanctions in 1985 and then pushing Congress to override the Reagan veto of the Anti-Apartheid Act of 1986, a bill imposing more extensive sanctions than the 1985 measure. This organization and its leader, Randall Robinson, were pivotal in keeping the Haitian issue on the foreign policy agenda during 1993 and 1994 and in pushing the Clinton administration for stronger action against the military rulers in that country. In particular, the hunger strike by Robinson had an important symbolic effect on American policy makers at a time when Clinton policy toward the restoration of democracy in Haiti appeared to be faltering. More recently, TransAfrica lobbied against the African Growth and Opportunity Act, but it failed to defeat the bill's passage in Congress. That piece of legislation, which called for more trade with Africa and more duty free access to the American market from African countries, actually sparked involvement by a series of other groups promoting African issues, including Africare, the African American Institute, and key members of the Congressional Black Caucus.[118]

With the increasingly large percentage of Hispanics located in the South and Southwest, this ethnic group mainly focuses its attention on American policy toward Central and South America and toward such issues as immigration and refugees. So far, however, the Cuban American National Foundation (CANF) is the best-known and most successful of the Hispanic lobbying groups. Its strong anti-Castro message has impacted both political parties over the past several decades. While this lobby has generally been more influential on Republican administrations than Democratic ones, the Clinton administration heard its voice in the 1990s—whether in halting appointments to the State Department, challenging efforts to cut funding for Radio Marti (the anti-Castro station in south Florida), or responding to Cuba's shoot-down of two unarmed "Brothers to the Rescue" planes over international waters. The George W. Bush administration, too has been sensitive to the wishes of this lobby and its electoral clout, especially in Florida. In late 2003, the administration announced the formation of a set of advisors to plan for a post-Castro era.

In general, this lobby has been instrumental in keeping sanctions on Cuba over more than four decades and proved instrumental in getting Congress to pass, and President Clinton to sign, the 1996 Helms–Burton Act. That legislation imposed tougher economic sanctions against Cuba and companies that deal with the Castro regime and actually incorporated previous sanctions into American law (rather than having them imposed by executive order). Yet, with the death of CANF's founder, Jorge Mas Canosa in 1997, with increased divisions between younger and older Cuban-Americans, and with the rise of other lobbying groups that are more favorable to improving ties with Cuba (e.g., American for Humanitarian Trade with Cuba and USA*Engage), some evidence suggests that CANF is losing some of its clout. Still, one member of Congress many years ago indirectly verified the foundation's importance and influence by claiming that the lobby "uses difficult, difficult tactics whenever you disagree with them."[119]

Another sizable Hispanic group, the Mexican-American community, has been less successful and less prominent than CANF. Until its recent activism over anti-immigration legislation and NAFTA, this community had neither the same interest nor the same effect on national policy, either toward Mexico, Central America, or elsewhere, especially when compared to the Cuban-American community. Indeed, according to one analysis, on many issues regarding Central America, Mexican-American attitudes were not much different than those of the rest of the American public. Put differently, "Mexican-American policy preferences on major issues such as immigration and border control also differ from those of the Mexican government." Overall, and excluding Cuban-Americans, one analysis concludes that "the Hispanic community exerts almost no systematic influence on US.–Latin American relations or, for that matter, on U.S. foreign policy in general."[120]

Still, why have some of these ethnic groups been so successful and others less so? How can only some six million Jewish-Americans, just over one million Greek-Americans, or slightly more than one million Cuban-Americans excise influence in a nation of over 280 million citizens?[121] While we suggested some of the possible reasons earlier, a brief examination of perhaps the most successful ethnic lobby, the Jewish lobby, is particularly instructive in gaining some insight in how interest group influence can occur. Its ability to offer voting support in key states, campaign contributions to potential office-holders, and its organizational skills on key issues give this lobby considerable political clout.[122]

The Jewish Lobby: Sources of Its Influence   First of all, the Jewish lobby appears to be very well organized and directs its energies primarily toward foreign policy issues related to a single state, Israel. By one estimate, more than 75 organizations exist that support Israel, and most are Jewish. Furthermore, these groups have two umbrella organizations to coordinate and guide their activities, the Conference of Presidents of Major American Jewish Organizations and the American-Israel Public Affairs Committee (AIPAC).[123]

AIPAC, in particular, is pivotal in lobbying by the Jewish community. It now has a membership of about 60,000–65,000 offices in 10 different American cities, including Washington, DC, and a staff of 130. Moreover, it has experienced considerable growth even since the mid-1980s.[124] It has a well-organized operation to facilitate maximum legislative and executive impact. "Action Alerts" are sent to key leaders throughout the country to stimulate response over some strategic issues, and members are directly linked through the Internet.[125] These mechanisms enable members to learn about key issues under discussion in Congress, access sample letters for writing campaigns, and learn the names and addresses of members of Congress to contact. Indeed, AIPAC's activism has been pronounced, claiming to have passed "more than 100 pro-Israel legislative initiatives a year."[126] In fact, the lobby's comprehensive organizational structure appears crucial to its overall effort, in the estimate of one close observer: "The multitiered structural pyramid that links individual Jews in local communities across the country to centralized national foreign policy leadership groups in Washington and New York is the primary organizational factor that can explain the ability of the pro-Israel movement to mobilize rapidly and in a coordinated fashion on a national scale when important foreign policy issues arise."[127] Indeed, the potency of AIPAC has been recognized by the *New York Times:* "The most important organization affecting America's relationship with Israel."[128]

Second, AIPAC has particularly good access to Capitol Hill, although perhaps less access to the executive branch. It "is the envy of other lobbies for its easy access to the highest levels of government."[129] Through its frequent contacts with members of Congress and congressional staff—"more than 200 meetings," as the AIPAC Web site says—AIPAC has been able to garner remarkable levels of support for some pro-Israeli legislation and has been able to stop legislation viewed as harmful to Israel.[130]

Indeed, the lobby has achieved significant legislative victories over the years. For instance, the lobby was able to gain seventy-six co-sponsors in the Senate for the Jackson–Vanik Amendment to the Trade Act of 1974. This legislation prohibited the granting of most-favored-nation (MFN) status to any state that did not have a free emigration policy (see Chapter 8). It was clearly directed at the Soviet Union and its policy on restricting Jewish emigration. A few years later, an identical number of senators co-authored a letter to President Ford urging him to stand behind Israel in any search for peace in the Middle East.[131] Most important, the lobby continues to assure high levels of American foreign assistance year-in and year-out.

Yet, AIPAC has also been able to alter or stop legislation that it did not support. Over the years, for instance, arms sales to Arab countries have been difficult to obtain in Congress. When such sales were approved, they often required modification, consistent with AIPAC's concerns. In 1987, for example, the Reagan administration had to change the composition of a proposed arms sale to Saudi Arabia to satisfy objections raised by Israel's supporters in the Senate. In 1988, Saudi Arabia completed a $30 billion arms deal with Britain, rather than incur the potential problems within Congress. At about the same time, a prospective arms deal with Kuwait was altered to address concerns raised by AIPAC.[132] More significant, and less measureable, the lobby has usually been able to stop legislation that might be harmful to Israel before it advances. Finally, and perhaps most indicative of the strong support that the Jewish lobby can generate, one study from the early 1970s found that Senate support for Israel averaged 84 percent and that such support existed across party lines.[133] While this level of support may not be sustained over time, it is indicative of the high level of residual congressional support for Israel.

Yet a third reason for the success of the Jewish lobby is tied to the degree of sympathy for Israel among the American public, for differing reasons. The American public is often sympathetic toward Israel for moral and ethical reasons. It represents a people who have suffered greatly through history and who are believed to deserve a homeland of their own. American support is also tied to political motivation. Israel represents a democratic and Western-oriented state in a region of the world that does not seem to have many such examples. Further, while the Democratic Party has traditionally been a strong supporter of Israel, the Republican Party lately—and especially among religious conservatives, has adopted a pro-Israel position.[134] In short, this latent public sympathy and support for Israel allows Jewish interest groups to obtain considerable overt support within Congress.

Equally important is the support for Israel that can be generated for domestic electoral reasons. Although the Jewish community is quite a small percentage of the nation's population (less than 3 percent), it is concentrated in some key states, especially along the East Coast and in California, Illinois, and Ohio.[135] As a consequence, its support can be pivotal in those areas in the success of any potential congressional or presidential candidate. Furthermore, while AIPAC does not make direct contributions to political campaigns, it has "close communications with the eighty-plus PACs [political action committees] that favor the Israeli cause. Its interlocking connections and directors with these PACs provide readily available funds when necessary."[136] Moreover, AIPAC's funding and support (or opposition) were crucial in key House and Senate campaigns in the 1980s and continue to be so today.[137] For example, this lobby was apparently instrumental in the defeat of incumbent Senators Jepsen (R-Iowa) and Percy (R-Illinois), who failed to support its position on some key votes. Finally, because the Jewish population has traditionally been quite active politically, there is even more incentive for potential presidents, senators, and representatives to be sympathetic to its view on the question of Israel. More recently, in the period from 1997 to 2001, "the 46 members of AIPAC's board together gave well in excess of $3 million to politicians."

A fourth reason deals with the relative weakness of the pro-Arab lobby, the counterpart of the pro-Israeli lobby. While the National Association of Arab Americans (NAAA) has increased its visibility and its activism since the Arab oil embargo of 1973–1974, it remains much less potent than the supporters of Israel.[138] The American-Arab Anti-Discrimination Committee, a more recent Arab lobby, has faced similar difficulties. As its leader, former Senator James Abourezk, once indicated, his committee faces a formidable task of obtaining money and organization: "To have influence in Congress you have to have money for candidates or control a lot of votes. We're trying to build a grass-roots network; it's difficult for us to raise money."[139] Furthermore, these Arab lobbies have to contend with the impression they are more anti-Israel than pro-Arab. It is a charge they deny, but one that continues to plague them. In addition, the Arab lobby is often divided. After all, it represents a variety of different Arab states with differing political traditions in each and with considerable rivalries among one another. For these reasons, the pro-Arab lobbies do not yet serve as a good countervailing group to the influence of the Jewish lobby.

The Jewish Lobby: Questions about Its Influence Although the Jewish lobby is usually identified as the most successful ethnic organization, its overall influence still remains a hotly debated issue. Especially with the changing events in the Middle East over the past three decades, new questions have been raised about its impact. To some observers, the lobby remains far from omnipotent over American policy toward Israel or the Middle East in general, as illustrated by several setbacks and conflicts with Congress and the president and within its own organization.

Prior to the late 1970s and the Camp David Accords on the Middle East, the Jewish lobby had generally been able to forestall the supplying of military supplies to the Arab states and had been able to gain large military assistance for Israel from the American Congress. By 1978, however, success in these areas began to wane a bit, as the United States sought to pursue a more even-handed policy. The Jewish lobby was unable to stop the supply of United States fighter aircraft to Saudi Arabia and Egypt, despite strong lobbying efforts. More significantly, perhaps, the sale of AWACS and other technologically advanced aircraft equipment to Saudi Arabia in October 1981 was approved by Congress, despite strong AIPAC lobbying. Indeed, this defeat actually motivated the organization to double its efforts for the future, but it also suggested its limitations.[140]

American presidents and their administrations have challenged and criticized the Israeli government, despite possible opposition from the Jewish lobby. One former Carter administration aide put it this way: "The president can take a position that Israel opposes if the American people as a whole are behind him. . . . Then the Jewish community will support him also. That happened with Ike [President Eisenhower] and the Sinai and it is still true."[141] Indeed, Presidents Carter and Reagan publicly opposed the expansion of Israeli settlements in the occupied territories and called for Israeli support of "land for peace" in the region as well. Reagan, too, pursued his own extensive lobbying effort to counteract AIPAC's over the sale of arms to Saudi Arabia in 1981. In 1990, President George H. W. Bush held up $10 billion loan guarantees to the Israeli government over the settlement issues for a time, despite considerable political pressure to do otherwise. President Clinton and his administration did not alter their position in Middle East peace negotiations, despite the victory of Benjamin Netanyahu in the 1996 Israeli election. Similarly, President George W. Bush called for the creation of an independent Palestinian state in 2003—the first time for an American president to do so—and opposed Israeli settlements in the West Bank.

Finally, internal discord within the American Jewish community has also weakened the unity of its lobbying effort. After the massacres at the Palestinian camps of Shabra and Shatilla outside Beirut in September 1982, and the repressive response of the Israeli government to the intifada—the Palestinian uprisings in Israeli-occupied territories on the West Bank and the Gaza Strip beginning in 1987—fissures developed within the Jewish community and undoubtedly weakened the overall impact of this group in the American policy process.[142] As the peace process between Israel, its Arab neighbors, and the Palestinians evolved in the 1990s, additional divisions developed within the American Jewish community. In 1993, for example, the officers of AIPAC fired its longtime pragmatic director and moved the group's policy position toward a more hard-line stance on making concessions in peace negotiations in the Middle East. In effect, it moved AIPAC's position away from the Israeli Labor government of Yitzhak Rabin and closer to the opposition forces within Israel. This action divided the American Jewish community and AIPAC's relations with the Israel government at that time, and it hurt AIPAC's ties with some members of Congress.[143] In 1995, too, Israeli Prime Minister Rabin publicly criticized the American Jewish community for lobbying against policies of the Israeli government: "Never before have we witnessed an attempt by U.S. Jews to pressure Congress against the policies of a legitimate, democratically elected government."[144] These fissures remained in the late 1990s and early 2000s with the election of two hard-line Israeli prime ministers and will likely continue due to internal disputes within the American Jewish community.[145] That is, the Jewish community remained divided over American policy toward Israel and the Middle East—whether over supporting the peace process with the Palestinians, the actions of the Israeli government, or the prosecution of the war against Iraq.

Although evidence cited suggest that the Jewish lobby does not always succeed and may have some incipient organizational fissures, it also shows how an ethnic group may enter the foreign policy process, and, more specifically, how a well-organized and committed interest group can sometimes alter the direction of American foreign policy. Increasingly, interest groups, like political parties, are exercising an independent effect on U.S. foreign policy making.

CONCLUDING COMMENTS

Both political parties and interest groups are playing a more important role in foreign policy making today. Despite the American tradition of bipartisanship in foreign affairs, partisan differences have always been a characteristic of policy making. In recent decades, moreover, partisan (and ideological) differences on foreign policy questions have actually intensified and are likely to remain part of the American political landscape, especially as the United States confronts the dramatic changes of the twenty-first century. Interest groups, too, have become more pervasive in the foreign policy process. Both a greater number and a wider array of interest groups now participate in foreign affairs activities. While economic and ethnic groups remain particularly effective, foreign interests are increasingly seeking to influence policy as well.

In the next chapter, we complete our analysis of the policy-making process by examining the role of the media and public opinion in the foreign policy process. These two forces usually generate different reactions among casual observers. Because the media have grown so dramatically and intrude on so many aspects of American life, their influence, even on foreign affairs, is often taken for granted. The public, on the other hand, is at such a distance from where foreign policy decisions are made that considerable skepticism and questions often accompany a discussion of its role. In the next chapter, in examining the role of the media and public opinion, we seek to identify more fully their relative impact on the making of American foreign policy.

NOTES

1. On the various definitions of political parties, see Frank J. Sorauf, *Party Politics in America* (Boston: Little, Brown and Company, 1984), pp. 6–28.

2. L. Harmon Ziegler and G. Wayne Peak, *Interest Groups in American Society,* 2nd ed. (Englewood Cliffs, NJ: Prentice-Hall, Inc., 1972), p. 3.

3. Herbert McClosky, Paul J. Hoffmann, and Rosemary O'Hara, "Issue Conflict and Consensus among Party Leaders and Followers," *American Political Science Review* 14 (June 1960): 408–427.

4. The quote is taken from a speech by Senator Arthur H. Vandenberg to the Cleveland Foreign Affairs Forum. See John Felton, "The Man Who Showed Politicians the Water's Edge," *Congressional Quarterly Weekly Report,* February 18, 1989, 336.

5. For a history of bipartisanship and its various meanings, see Ellen C. Collier, ed., *Bipartisanship and the Making of Foreign Policy: A Historical Survey* (Boulder, CO: Westview Press, 1991).

6. Cecil V. Crabb, Jr., *Bipartisan Foreign Policy* (Evanston, IL: Row, Peterson and Company, 1957), p. 5.

7. Robert Dahl, *Congress and Foreign Policy* (New York: Harcourt, Brace and Company, 1950), p. 229.

8. See the Republican party platform of 1952, which strongly attacks the Democrats, reprinted in Donald Bruce Johnson and Kirk H. Porter, *National Party Platforms, 1840–1972* (Urbana: University of Illinois Press, 1973), pp. 497–500.

9. See the 1956 party platforms in ibid., pp. 524 and 556; and the 1960 Republican platform, p. 606.

10. These trends had shifted by the 1980s (and perhaps beyond), with the Democrats more associated with peace and the Republicans with prosperity. Public opinion data on these questions of war and peace and prosperity and recession from 1951–1984 are summarized in George Gallup, "GOP Edges Democrats in Poll on Prosperity Helm," *Des Moines Sunday Register,* April 29, 1984, 4A.

11. See McClosky, Hoffman, and O'Hara, "Issue Conflict and Consensus Among Party Leaders and Followers," Table I, p. 410. At the same time, they do argue against the view that the two parties "hold the same views" on foreign policy (p. 417). Some differences are detectable.

12. Gerald Pomper, *Elections in America: Control and Influence in Democratic Politics* (New York: Dodd, Mead & Company, 1965), p. 194.

13. I. M. Destler, Leslie H. Gelb, and Anthony Lake, *Our Own Worst Enemy: The Unmaking of American Foreign Policy* (New York: Simon & Schuster, 1984), p. 17.

14. Ibid., pp. 60–61.

15. Crabb, *Bipartisan Foreign Policy,* p. 256.

16. This discussion and the following on military assistance, defense, and trade policy are drawn from the data and discussion in Barry Hughes, *The Domestic Context of American Foreign Policy* (San Francisco: W. H. Freeman and Company, 1975), pp. 130–144. On foreign aid voting, also see Barbara Hinckley, *Stability and Change in Congress,* 3rd ed. (New York: Harper and Row, 1983), p. 272.

17. Ibid. and Hughes, *The Domestic Context of American Foreign Policy.* Also see Aage R. Clausen, *How Congressmen Decide: A Policy Focus* (New York: St. Martin's Press, 1973), pp. 192–212.

18. Destler, Gelb, and Lake, *Our Own Worst Enemy,* p. 61.

19. Zbigniew Brzezinski, "The Three Requirements for a Bipartisan Foreign Policy," in *The Washington Quarterly White Paper* (Washington, DC: Center for Strategic and International Studies, Georgetown University), pp. 14–15.

20. Leslie H. Gelb with Richard K. Betts, *The Irony of Vietnam: The System Worked* (Washington, DC: The Brookings Institution, 1979), p. 216.

21. "Congress Took 94 Roll-Call Votes on War 1966–1972," *Congress and the Nation, 1969–1972,* vol. III (Washington, DC: Congressional Quarterly Service, 1973), p. 944.

22. The figures were computed for these years by the author from the data provided in Pomper, *Elections in America;* and Gerald M. Pomper with Susan S. Lederman, *Elections in America: Control and Influence in Democratic Politics,* 2nd ed. (New York: Longman, 1980), p. 169. The former volume covered 1944–1964 party platforms, while the latter covered 1944–1976 ones.

23. One recent alternative explanation suggests that personal ideology more than any other factor (including party) may explain congressional voting in the post-Vietnam period. See, for example, Robert A. Bernstein and William W. Anthony, "The ABM Issue in the Senate, 1968–1970: The Importance of Ideology," *The American Political Science Review,* 65 (September 1974): 1198–1206; Wayne Moyer, "House Voting on Defense: An Ideological Explanation," in Bruce M. Russett and Alfred Stepan, eds., *Military Force and American Society* (New York: Harper and Row, 1973), pp. 106–141; and James M. McCormick and Michael Black, "Ideology and Senate Voting on the Panama Canal Treaties," *Legislative Studies Quarterly* 8 (February 1983): 45–63.

24. See, for example, "House Votes to Aid El Salvador, Denies Nicaragua's Rebels," *Des Moines Register,* May 25, 1984, 1A and 20A; and "House Curb's MX, Votes $284 Billion to Military," *Des Moines Register,* June 1, 1984, 1A, 12A. For a systematic analysis of partisan differences in congressional voting on the MX, B-1, and SDI in the 1970s and 1980s, see James M. Lindsay, "Parochialism, Policy, and Constituency Constraints: Congressional Voting on Strategic Weapons, Systems," *American Journal of Political Science* 34 (November 1990): 936–960.

25. The following sections draw upon these pieces of research by James M. McCormick and Eugene R. Wittkopf: "Bush and Bipartisanship: The Past as Prologue?" *Washington Quarterly* 13 (Winter 1990): 5–16; "Bipartisanship, Partisanship, and Ideology in Congressional-Executive Foreign Policy Relations, 1947–1988," *Journal of Politics* 52 (November 1990): 1077–1100; and "At the Water's Edge: The Effects of Party, Ideology and Issues on Congressional Foreign Policy Voting, 1947–1988," *American Politics Quarterly* 20 (January 1992): 26–53.

26. McCormick and Wittkopf, "Bipartisanship, Partisanship, and Ideology in Congressional-Executive Foreign Policy Relations, 1947–1988," p. 1097. For an alternate view on the impact of Vietnam, see James Meernik, "Presidential Support in Congress: Conflict and Consensus on Foreign and Defense Policy," *Journal of Politics* 55 (August 1993): 569–587.

27. See the statement by the president, "President's Commission on Strategic Forces," *Weekly Compilation of Presidential Documents* 19 (January 10, 1983): 3; and see "Summary of Kissinger Commission Report," *Congressional Quarterly Weekly Report,* January 14, 1984, 64–66, on these commissions.

28. "Excerpts From President Reagan's Speech on Foreign Policy and Congress," *New York Times,* April 7, 1984, 5.

29. These passages are taken from the inaugural address by President Bush, January 20, 1989.

30. The data and discussion on the Bush and Clinton administrations are based upon the work by the author with Eugene R. Wittkopf and David M. Danna. See our "Politics and Bipartisanship at the Water's Edge: A Note on Bush and Clinton," *Polity* 30 (Fall 1997): 133–149. The figures are taken from that work.

31. "Remarks by the President to the Nixon Center for Peace and Freedom Policy Conference," Washington, DC, March 1, 1995, obtained via the Internet.

32. James M. McCormick, "Clinton and Foreign Policy: Some Legacies for a New Century," in Steven E. Schier, ed., *The Postmodern Presidency* (Pittsburgh: University of Pittsburgh Press, 2000), pp. 71–73.

33. James M. Lindsay, "From Deference to Activism and Back Again: Congress and the Politics of American Foreign Policy," in Eugene R. Wittkopf and James M. McCormick, eds., *The Domestic Sources of American Foreign Policy,* 4th ed. (Lanham, MD: Rowman & Littlefield Publishers, Inc., 2004), pp. 183–195.

34. Richard Benedetto, "Poll: Bush Trails Clark, Kerry," *Des Moines Register,* September 23, 2003, pp. 1A, 9A. The poll results are on p. 9A.

35.   Chairman Richard Lugar, "Opening Statement for Hearing on Iraq Reconstruction," U.S. Senate Foreign Relations Committee, June 4, 2003.

36.   Sean Loughlin, "Kennedy Stands by Criticism of Bush on Iraq," at http://www.cnn.com/2003/ALLPOLITICS/09/19/kennedy.iraq/index.htm, September 19, 2003, accessed on September 29, 2003.

37.   J. Valerie Steel, ed., Washington *Representatives 1999,* 23rd ed. (Washington, DC: Columbia Books, Inc., 1999), pp. 3–4. Also see the publisher's statement for this book at amazon.com summarizing the number of organizations and individuals involved in lobbying in Washington.

38.   The count was done by the author from ibid., pp. 645–652. It should be noted that not all of these government groups necessarily are engaged in foreign policy lobbying efforts, although many are.

39.   Dana Priest, *The Mission* (New York: W. W. Norton and Company, 2003), p. 36.

40.   Norman J. Ornstein and Shirley Elder, *Interest Groups, Lobbying and Policymaking* (Washington, DC: Congressional Quarterly Press, 1978), pp. 35–39; and Immanuel Ness, *Encyclopedia of Interest Groups and Lobbyists in the United States,* vols. 1 and 2. (Armonk, NY: Sharpe Reference, 2000). The discussion also draws upon the list of organizations in Thomas L. Brewer, *American Foreign Policy: A Contemporary Introduction* (Englewood Cliffs, NJ: Prentice-Hall, Inc., 1980), p. 85; and upon Hughes, *The Domestic Context of American Foreign Policy,* pp. 157–171, for the foreign policy goals of business, labor, and farm groups.

41.   Ness, *Encyclopedia of Interest Groups and Lobbyists in the United States,* p. 359, for the quote and p. 351 for other information in this paragraph. Also see Ornstein and Elder, *Interest Groups, Lobbying, and Policymaking,* p. 24.

42.   For an overview of the foreign policy of the labor movement, and especially the AFL-CIO, see Carl Gershman, *The Foreign Policy of American Labor, The Washington Papers,* vol. 3, no. 29 (Beverly Hills: Sage Publications, 1975).

43.   "It's Hip to Be Union," *Newsweek,* July 8, 1996, 44–45.

44.   "Program to Promote Democracy Passed . . . After Deleting Funds for Two Parties," *Congressional Quarterly Almanac 1983* (Washington, DC: Congressional Quarterly, Inc., 1984), pp. 148–149.

45.   See Pat M. Holt, *Secret Intelligence and Public Policy* (Washington, DC: CQ Press, 1995), p. 146. On criticism of the AIFLD, a quick search of the Internet will reveal numerous sources doing so.

46.   Hughes, *The Domestic Context of American Foreign Policy,* pp. 168–171.

47.   Ness, *Encyclopedia of Interest Groups and Lobbyists in the United States* p. 209.

48.   See the Web site for the American Farm Bureau Federation at http://www.fb.com for a listing of the lobbying efforts by this organization in Congress.

49.   *The Washington Lobby,* 4th ed. (Washington, DC: Congressional Quarterly, Inc., 1982), pp. 150–151, includes a list of the religious groups active over U.S. policy toward El Salvador.

50.   See Steel, *Washington Representatives 1999* for the listing of religious organizations. For a good recent source on religious organizations involved in U.S. foreign policy, see Elliott Abrams, ed., *The Influence of Faith: Religious Groups and U.S. Foreign Policy* (Lanham, MD: Rowman & Littlefield Publishers, Inc., 2001).

51.   See, for instance, any of the myriad publications from the American Friends Service Committee. See its plan for addressing the Middle East conflict from several decades ago entitled *Search for Peace in the Middle East,* rev. ed. (Greenwich, CT: Fawcett Publications, Inc., 1970).

52.   See *The Challenge of Peace: God's Promise and Our Response* (Washington, DC: United States Catholic Conference, May 3, 1983).

53.   *The Washington Lobby,* pp. 152–153.

54.   See the letter by Bishop Wilton Gregory, President of the United States Conference of Catholic Bishops to President George W. Bush, dated September 13, 2002.

55.   For some evidence on the positions of the major religions on war with Iraq, see "Statement from Religious Leaders About Iraq," at http://www.salsa.net/peace, accessed on October 10, 2003. For those

who expressed support for the war, see Laurie Goodstein, "Threats and Responses: The Religious Leaders; Evangelical Figures Oppose Religious Leaders' Broad Antiwar Sentiment," *New York Times,* October 5, 2002, A10.

56. For an excellent overview of the key American ethnic groups and their role in foreign policy, see Charles McC. Mathias, Jr., "Ethnic Groups and Foreign Policy," *Foreign Affairs* 59 (Summer 1981): 975–998. Also see Abdul Aziz Said, *Ethnicity and U.S. Foreign Policy,* rev. ed. (New York: Praeger, 1981); and Tony Smith, *Foreign Attachments: The Power of Ethnic Groups in the Making of American Foreign Policy* (Cambridge, MA: Harvard University Press, 2000).

57. Dick Kirschten, "Ethnics Resurging," *National Journal,* February 25, 1995, 484–486.

58. Hughes, *The Domestic Context of American Foreign Policy,* pp. 171–174.

59. For a discussion of the development of the conservative movement and its foreign policy goals, see Richard A. Viguerie, *The New Right: We're Ready to Lead* (Falls Church, VA: The Viguerie Company, 1981); for a listing of other liberal and conservative interest groups as well as other types, see Brewer, *American Foreign Policy,* pp. 85–86; and for a listing of recent ratings of members of Congress for some of these groups, see J. Michael Sharp, ed., *Directory of Congressional Voting Scores and Interest Group Ratings,* vols. 1 and 2 (Washington, DC: Congressional Quarterly, Inc., 1997). Also see this source for the discussion of ADA and ACU upon which we draw (pp. ix–x).

60. This section draws upon the following sources: Arthur C. Close, Gregory C. Bologna, and Curtis W. McCormick, eds., *Washington Representatives 1990* (Washington, DC: Columbia Books, Inc., 1990), pp. 480, 513, 517, 518, 520; the 1988–1989 *Annual Report of the American Enterprise Institute for Public Policy Research* (Washington, DC: American Enterprise Institute, 1989); Howard J. Wiarda, *Foreign Policy Without Illusion* (Glenview, IL: Scott, Foresman/Little, Brown Higher Education, 1990), pp. 162–168; and many of the Web sites of the think tanks discussed.

61. Richard Higgott and Diane Stone, "The Limits of Influence: Foreign Policy Think Tanks in Britain and the USA," *Review of International Studies* 20 (January 1994): 32.

62. Ibid., pp. 15–34.

63. Dana Milbank and Walter Pincus, "Cheney Blunt in his Defense of Iraq Policy," *Des Moines Register,* October 11, 2003, p. 4A.

64. The information on the Cato Institute is taken from http://www.cato.org, accessed on June 6, 2003.

65. The information on AEI comes from its Web site at http://www.aei.org, accessed on June 11, 2003.

66. Shortly after the issuance of the national security strategy statement, for example, Ivo Daalder, James M. Lindsay, and James M. Steinberg held a briefing at Brooking, and that briefing was formalized into "The Bush National Security Strategy: An Evaluation," October 2002, online. Available: http://www.brookings.edu/comm/policybriefs/pb109.htm. A little while later, Ivo H. Daalder, James M. Lindsay, and James B. Steinberg published their analysis in "Hard Choices: National Security and the War on Terrorism," *Current History* 101 (December): 409–413. Finally, a few months later, Ivo Daalder and James M. Lindsay did a further analysis of Bush's foreign policy in their "The Bush Revolution: The Remaking of America's Foreign Policy," revised version of paper prepared for presentation at The George W. Bush Presidency: An Early Assessment Conference, Princeton University, April 25–26, online. Available: http://www.wws.princeton.edu/bushconf/DaalderLindsayPaper.pdf.

67. Higgott and Stone, "The Limits of Influence: Foreign Policy Think Tanks in Britain and the USA," pp. 18–19.

68. The information here is taken from the Carnegie Endowment for International Peace's Web site at http://www.ceip.org, accessed on October 12, 2003.

69. For a compilation of different categories of foreign policy interest groups (partly upon which we draw in our discussion), see Brewer, *American Foreign Policy: A Contemporary Introduction,* pp. 85–86.

70. Indeed, the freeze movement was very broadly based, in terms of both the kinds of groups and the individuals who participated in it. See Fox Butterfield, "Anatomy of the Nuclear Protest," *New York Times Magazine,* July 11, 1982, 14–17ff, for a discussion of the nature of this movement. For other assessments of the nuclear freeze, see Pam Solo, *From Protest to Policy: The Origins and Future of the Freeze Movement* (Cambridge, MA: Ballinger Publishing, 1988); and Douglas C. Waller, *Congress and the Nuclear Freeze: An Inside Look at the Politics of a Mass Movement* (Amherst: University of Massachusetts Press, 1987).

71. See Cynthia J. Arnson and Philip Brenner, "The Limits of Lobbying: Interest Groups, Congress and Aid to the Contras," paper prepared for presentation at a conference on Public Opinion and Policy Toward Central America, Princeton University, May 4–5, 1990.

72. See Box 12.2 in Stephen D. Cohen, Joel R. Paul, and Robert A. Blecker, *Fundamentals of U.S. Foreign Policy* (Boulder, CO: Westview Press, 1996), pp. 254–255.

73. See Keith Bradsher, "Last Call to Arms on the Trade Pact," *New York Times,* August 23, 1993, D1 and D3; Elizabeth Kolbert, "A Trade Pact Byproduct: $10 Million in TV Ads," *New York Times,* November 13, 1993, 10; and Peter T. Kilborn, "Little Voices Roar in the Chorus of Trade-Pact Foes," *New York Times,* November 13, 1993, 10.

74. A description of these antiglobalization groups is in Manfred B. Steger, *Globalism* (Lanham, MD: Rowman & Littlefield Publishers, Inc., 2002), pp. 111–112. Steger also provides discussion of the protest activities by these antiglobalization groups at pp. 117–134.

75. See the advertisement entitled "War with Iraq is *Not* in America's National Interest," *New York Times,* September 26, 2002. Emphasis in original.

76. The total was compiled from the listing in Steel, *Washington Representatives 1999.*

77. "How U.S. Firms Lobbied for AWACS on Saudi Orders," *Des Moines Sunday Register,* March 14, 1982, 1C.

78. The section on Japanese lobbying is based on John B. Judis, "The Japanese Megaphone," *The New Republic,* January 22, 1990, 20–25. The quoted passages are at pp. 22 and 24. For a more comprehensive and critical treatment of the lobbying efforts by Japan, see Pat Choate, *Agents of Influence* (New York: Alfred A. Knopf, 1990).

79. See the listing of countries and firms in Dick Kirschten, "Greetings, Comrades!" *National Journal,* October 2, 1993, 2191.

80. Peter H. Stone, "China Connections," *National Journal,* March 26, 1994, 708–712.

81. The most succinct argument for this limited influence of interest groups is in Hughes, *The Domestic Context of American Foreign Policy,* pp. 198–202, from which part of this argument is drawn. Also see, however, Bernard Cohen, *The Public's Impact on Foreign Policy* (Boston: Little, Brown and Company, 1973); and Robert H. Trice, "Domestic Interest Groups and the Arab-Israeli Conflict: A Behavioral Analysis," in Abdul Aziz Said, *Ethnicity and U.S. Foreign Policy,* pp. 128–129, on the problem of gaining access to Congress and the executive on some types of issues.

82. See Cohen, *The Public's Impact on Foreign Policy,* pp. 100–103, and his discussion of how interest groups can be used by the executive branch.

83. On this point, see Eric M. Uslaner, "All Politics Are Global: Interest Groups and the Making of Foreign Policy," in Allan J. Cigler and Burdett A. Loomis, *Interest Group Politics,* 4th ed. (Washington, DC: CQ Press, 1995), p. 370.

84. Brewer, *American Foreign Policy: A Contemporary Introduction,* p. 89.

85. On those points, see Hughes, *The Domestic Context of American Foreign Policy,* pp. 200–201, especially Table 7.1.

86. James M. Lindsay and Randall B. Ripley, "How Congress Influences Foreign and Defense Policy," in Randall B. Ripley and James M. Lindsay, eds., *Congress Resurgent: Foreign and Defense Policy on Capitol Hill* (Ann Arbor: The University of Michigan Press, 1993), p. 19.

87. Samuel Huntington especially notes "the displacement of national interests by commercial and ethnic interests" in recent years. See his "The Erosion of American National Interests," in Wittkopf and

McCormick, *The Domestic Sources of American Foreign Policy: Insights and Evidence,* pp. 55–65. The quote is at p. 64. Also Cohen, *The Public's Impact on Foreign Policy,* p. 96, asserts that economic and ethnic groups appear most prominently, although his analysis is based primarily on interviews with the executive branch.

88. For some reasons for the strength of ethnic influence, see Mathias, "Ethnic Groups and Foreign Policy," pp. 980–981 and 996.

89. See Dwight D. Eisenhower, "The Military-Industrial Complex," in Richard Gillam, ed*., Power in Postwar America* (Boston: Little, Brown, 1971), p. 158.

90. See C. Wright Mills, *The Power Elite* (New York: Oxford University Press, 1956); and Gabriel Kolko, *The Roots of American Foreign Policy* (Boston: Beacon Press, 1969).

91. For a good summary presentation of this argument, see Marc Pilisuk, with the assistance of Mehrene Larudee, *International Conflict and Social Policy* (Englewood Cliffs, NJ: Prentice-Hall, Inc., 1972), pp. 108–141.

92. Ibid., pp. 113–132, especially p. 129.

93. Kolko, *The Roots of American Foreign Policy,* pp. 17–23.

94. The following data on the key foreign officials are from Thomas R. Dye, *Who's Running America? Institutional Leadership in the United States* (Englewood Cliffs, NJ: Prentice-Hall, Inc., 1976), pp. 56–58; and from *Who's Running America? The Bush Era,* 5th ed. (Englewood Cliffs, NJ: Prentice-Hall, Inc., 1990), pp. 89–105. The dates of service for some individuals have been corrected from what Dye reports. For a complete description of the background of Reagan administration appointees, see the national security section of Ronald Brownstein and Nina Easton, *Reagan's Ruling Class* (Washington, DC: The Presidential Accountability Group, 1982).

95. Thomas R. Dye, *Who's Running America? The Clinton Years,* 6th ed. (Englewood Cliffs, NJ: Prentice-Hall, 1995), p. 84.

96. Ibid., p. 70–71.

97. Ibid., pp. 84, 87, 89–91.

98. The leadership data on the George W. Bush administration is taken from Thomas R. Dye, *Who's Running America? The Bush Restoration,* 7th ed. (Upper Saddle River, NJ: Prentice-Hall, 2002), pp. 77–81. In particular, see Table 4–2 and Table 4–3.

99. See William Proxmire, "The Community of Interests in Our Defense Contract Spending," in Richard Gilliam, ed., *Power in Postwar America.*

100. These data are taken from, and in one instance recalculated from, Mark J. Eitelberg and Roger D. Little, "Influential Elites and the American Military After the Cold War," in Don M. Snider and Miranda A. Carlton-Carew, eds., *U.S. Civil-Military Relations: In Crisis or Transition?* (Washington, DC: The Center for Strategic and International Studies, 1995), pp. 47 and p. 48 (Table 3.1).

101. Ibid., p. 47.

102. Michael Parenti, *Democracy for the Few,* 5th ed. (New York: St. Martin's Press, 1988), p. 88.

103. Morton Berkowitz, P. G. Bock, and Vincent J. Fuccillo, *The Politics of American Foreign Policy* (Englewood Cliffs, NJ: Prentice-Hall, Inc., 1977), p. 289.

104. Ibid.

105. Defense contract rankings were taken from *100 Companies Receiving the Largest Dollar Volume of Prime Contract Awards—Fiscal Year 2002* at http://www.dior.whs.mil/peidhome/procstat/p01/fy2002/top100.htm, while the corporate sales rankings for 2002 were taken from "The 500 Largest U.S. Corporations," *Fortune,* April 14, 2003, F-1 to F-20. The statistics for fiscal year 1982, fiscal year 1988, and fiscal year 1995 are taken from earlier editions of this book.

106. For the information on the continuity and concentration in defense contracting, see James R. Kurth, "The Military-Industrial Complex Revisited," in Joseph Kruzel, ed., *1989–1990 American Defense Annual* (Lexington, MA: Lexington Books, 1989), pp. 195–215, especially pp. 196–199. The "product specialties" notion is his at p. 198. On the Osprey aircraft, see Christopher M. Jones, "Roles, Politics, and the Survival of the V-22 Osprey," in Wittkopf and McCormick, *The Domestic Sources of American Foreign Policy,* 4th ed., pp. 383–401.

107. The data in this paragraph come from U.S. Bureau of the Census, *Statistical Abstract of the United States: 2003,* 123rd ed. (Wash-

ington, DC, 1995), p. 342; and U.S. Arms Control and Disarmament Agency, *World Military Expenditures and Arms Transfers 1985* (Washington, DC: U.S. Government Printing Office, April 1985), p. 99.

108. Bruce Russett, *The Prisoners of Insecurity* (San Francisco: W. H. Freeman and Company, 1983), pp. 77–96.

109. Thomas Hartley and Bruce Russett, "Public Opinion and the Common Defense: Who Governs Military Spending in the United States?" *American Political Science Review* 86 (December 1992): 905–915. The quote is at pp. 911–912. This study is cited in Steve Chan, "Grasping the Peace Dividend: Some Propositions on the Conversion of Swords into Plowshares," *Mershon International Studies Review* 39 (April 1995): 58, and which directed me to it.

110. Stanley Lieberson, "An Empirical Study of Military-Industrial Linkages," *American Journal of Sociology* 76 (January 1971), especially pp. 568–572 and 575–581.

111. Chan, "Grasping the Peace Dividend: Some Propositions on the Conversion of Swords into Plowshares," pp. 53–95. The quoted phrases are Chan's.

112. Ibid., p. 62. As Chan discusses, there are empirical studies on both sides of these contentions, but he specifically challenges the notion that there is evidence for "a powerful military-industrial complex" to sustain high military expenditures (p. 63).

113. Ibid., p. 68. Chan's conclusion here is drawn from a study by Stephen J. Majeski, "Defense Spending, Fiscal Policy, and Economic Performance," in Alex Mintz, ed., *The Political Economy of Military Spending in the United States* (London: Routledge, 1992), pp. 217–237. Majeski's general conclusion is at p. 231. Other studies showing different results are included in the Chan analysis, but most of the evidence seems to point in the direction of the findings reported here.

114. For a study that judges the Greek lobby second behind the Jewish lobby in influence, see Mathias, "Ethnic Groups and Foreign Policy," p. 990. Also see, Morton Kondracke, "The Greek Lobby," *The New Republic,* April 29, 1978, 14–16. For two studies that raise doubts about the importance of the Greek lobby over the Turkish

arms embargo issue, see Clifford Hackett, "Ethnic Politics in Congress: The Turkish Embargo Experience"; and Sallie M. Hicks and Theodore A. Couloumbis, "The 'Greek Lobby': Illusion or Reality?" in Abdul Aziz Said, ed., *Ethnicity and U.S. Foreign Policy,* pp. 33–96.

115. Mathias, "Ethnic Groups and Foreign Policy," pp. 982–987.

116. Kirschten, "Ethnics Resurging," pp. 484–486, with the quoted passage at p. 486.

117. Robert W. Walters, "African-American Influence on U.S. Foreign Policy Toward South Africa," in Mohammed E. Ahrari, ed., *Ethnic Groups and U.S. Foreign Policy* (New York: Greenwood Press, 1987), pp. 65–82.

118. See the Association of Concerned African Scholars Briefing Paper at http://www.prairienet.org/acas/agoabm.htm, accessed on March 30, 2000, for information about these other lobbying groups on this piece of legislation.

119. Dick Kirschten, "From the K Street Corridor," *National Journal,* July 17, 1993, 1815 and Philip Brenner, Patrick J. Haney, and Walter Vanderbush, "Intermestic Interests and U.S. Policy toward Cuba," in W. Hopf and McCormick, *The Domestic Sources of American Foreign Policy: Insights and Evidence,* 4th ed., pp. 72–73.

120. See Damian J. Fernandez, "From Little Havana to Washington, DC: Cuban-Americans and U.S. Foreign Policy"; and Rodolfo de la Garza, "U.S. Foreign Policy and the Mexican-American Political Agenda," in Mohammed E. Ahrari, ed., *Ethnic Groups and U.S. Foreign Policy* (New York: Greenwood Press, 1987), pp. 115–134 and 101–114, respectively. For the last two quotations, see Rodolfo de la Garza, "Introduction," and Peter Hakim and Carlos A. Rosales, "The Latino Foreign Policy Lobby," in Rodolfo de la Garza and Harry P. Pachon, eds., *Latinos and U.S. Foreign Policy* (Lanham, MD: Rowman & Littlefield Publishers, Inc., 2000), pp. 9 and 133, respectively.

121. Estimates for these groups vary, of course. These data are taken from tables in U.S. Bureau of the Census, *Statistical Abstract of the United States: 2002,* 122nd ed. (Washington, DC, 2002), at pp. 28, 56, and 862.

122. Tony Smith, *Foreign Attachments: The Power of Ethnic Groups in the Making of American Foreign Policy,* pp. 85–129 for his discussion of these three means of gaining influence by ethnic groups.

123. See Trice, "Domestic Interest Groups and the Arab-Israeli Conflict: A Behavioral Analysis," pp. 121 and 122. Also see Patrick Smyth, "The Hawkish Factions of Jewish Lobby May Be Out of Step with Members," *The Irish Times,* April 12, 2002, 11.

124. Paul Findley, *Deliberate Deceptions: Facing the Facts about U.S.-Israeli Relationship* (New York: Lawrence Hill Books, 1995), p. 95; Peter Beinart and Hanna Rosin, "Aipac Unpacked," *The New Republic* (September 20 and 27, 1993), p. 22; Hedrick Smith, *The Power Game* (New York: Ballantine Books, 1988), p. 216; and information on AIPAC from the Web site: http://www.aipac.org/.

125. George W. Ball and Douglas B. Ball, *The Passionate Attachment* (New York: W. W. Norton and Company, 1992), p. 209.

126. See http://www.aipac.org.

127. Trice, "Domestic Interest Groups and the Arab-Israeli Conflict: A Behavioral Analysis," p. 126.

128. See the AIPAC Web site (http://www.aipac.org), where this quotation is prominently displayed.

129. Findley, *Deliberate Deception,* p. 95.

130. See http://www.aipac.org.

131. *The Middle East: U.S. Policy, Israel, Oil and the Arabs,* 3rd ed. (Washington, DC: Congressional Quarterly, Inc., 1977), p. 96.

132. Harry Anderson, "Forced into British Arms," *Newsweek,* July 25, 1988, 47, and Smyth, "The Hawkish Factions of Jewish Lobby May Be Out of Step with Members," p. 11.

133. Robert H. Trice, "Congress and the Arab-Israeli Conflict: Support for Israel in the U.S. Senate, 1970–1973," *Political Science Quarterly* 92 (Fall 1977): 443–463.

134. Some of these reasons are discussed and indirectly tested in ibid. See the comments by Ron Brownstein on "CNN Live Today 10:00," April 15, 2002 at http://web.lexis-nexis.com/universe/document?_m=f30a/2da473b58abc980/cc9fcd72

ace&docuum=18wchp=dGLbV/2-2SKVA&ind5=2fe2793839d2.

135. Trice, "Congress and the Arab–Israeli Conflict: Support for Israel in the U.S. Senate, 1970–1973," p. 457 and Smith, *Foreign Attachments: The Power of Ethnic Groups in the Making of American Foreign Policy,* p. 99 for key states.

136. Ball and Ball, *The Passionate Attachment,* p. 209.

137. Smith, *The Power Game,* pp. 228–229, and Smyth, "The Hawkish Factions of Jewish Lobby May Be Out of Step with Members," p. 11 for the quote at the end of the paragraph.

138. *The Middle East: U.S. Policy, Israel, Oil and the Arabs,* pp. 102–108.

139. Christopher Madison, "Arab-American Lobby Fights Rearguard Battle to Influence U.S. Mideast Policy," *National Journal,* August 31, 1985, 1936.

140. Ball and Ball, *The Passionate Attachment,* pp. 213–215; and Smith, *The Power Game,* pp. 218–221.

141. Quoted in Charlotte Saikowski, "America's Israeli Aid Budget Grows," *Christian Science Monitor,* November 30, 1983, 5. The reference is to President Eisenhower's decision to stand firm against Israel after it invaded the Sinai Peninsula and to demand its immediate withdrawal, despite a pending election.

142. For a discussion of some of the dilemmas that the Jewish community faces in its advocacy of American policy in the Middle East, see Stephen S. Rosenfeld, "Dateline Washington: Anti-Semitism and U.S. Foreign Policy," *Foreign Policy* 47 (Summer 1982): 172–183.

143. Beinart and Rosin, "Aipac Unpacked," pp. 20–23.

144. Alison Mitchell, "Rabin Rebukes Jews in U.S. Who Lobbied Against Pact," *New York Times,* September 30, 1995, 1.

145. Tony Smith, *Foreign Attachments: The Power of Ethnic Groups in the Making of American Foreign Policy,* pp. 110–115, and Smyth, "The Hawkish Factions of the Jewish Lobby May Be Out of Step with Members," p. 11.

12

The Media,
Public Opinion,
and the Foreign
Policy Process

The news media have less influence over American foreign
and military policy than many observers believe to be the case.
Claims that this influence is growing do not hold up under scrutiny.

WARREN P. STROBEL, *LATE-BREAKING FOREIGN POLICY:*
THE NEWS MEDIA'S INFLUENCE ON PEACE OPERATIONS, P. 211

Public opinion may constrain policy, but policymakers
need not always be constrained by public attitudes.

RICHARD SOBEL, *THE IMPACT OF PUBLIC OPINION*
ON U.S. FOREIGN POLICY, P. 240

The final two participants in the American foreign policy process that we shall discuss are the media and the public at large. Both the media and the public can and do affect the shape of U.S. foreign policy, albeit more indirectly than the other participants that we have described so far. The foreign policy issues that the media cover, and how they cover those issues, can affect the foreign policy process. The public's general views on foreign policy may be transmitted periodically through national polls, often conducted by the media, through contacts with their elected congressional officials at "town meetings," through visits with executive branch officials as they travel across the country, and through new electronic media as well. Furthermore, elections at both the congressional and presidential levels are two periodic ways for the public to convey its sentiments on the direction of foreign as well as domestic policy. In all of these ways, the media and the public can share in the shaping of foreign policy.

In this chapter, we discuss the role and impact of these participants in the foreign policy process in some detail. In the earlier sections, we consider the expansion of the media in American political life and the different roles that analysts have suggested the media play in the foreign policy process. That is, are the media a separate actor and critic in the process (much like an interest group), or are they an accomplice of the government (often championing official policy positions)? Alternately, are the media some combination of these two roles? Further, how do the media affect the public and their views? In the later sections of the chapter, we consider the public's role in the foreign policy process and seek to answer several compelling questions about public opinion and foreign policy. Is the public largely uninformed about foreign policy? Are its views fickle and changeable, guided primarily by the wishes of the political leadership? Alternately, are the public's views more stable and consistent on foreign policy issues than some would suggest? Does, in fact, the public shape the directions of foreign policy at least over the long term, if not on every decision that occurs?

THE PERVASIVENESS OF THE MEDIA

We need to begin the discussion of the media in the foreign policy process by considering the media's magnitude (and growth) over the past few years and their place in American society. In general, media outlets of all kinds increasingly bombard Americans, with the electronic media more pervasive than the print media. A caricature of this growth is the presumed "CNN-ization of the world," a reference to the highly successful Turner Broadcasting/Time Warner/AOL station that claims to be the "network of record" for breaking news events at home and around the world. Yet, the electronic explosion goes beyond CNN to include the growth in radio stations, changes in programming (such as the growth of talk radio and television news interview and magazine programs), and the rapid expansion of cable stations and cable systems seeking to rival CNN nationwide and worldwide (e.g., Fox News Channel, MSNBC, CNBC, C-SPAN, and Sky

TV). More recently, the development of the Internet and the World Wide Web and cellular phones have added other avenues of instantaneous global communications. A few simple statistics will illustrate the kind of media transformation that has taken place over the past several decades.[1]

The Growth in Differing Media Outlets

In 1997, for example, 98 million Americans had access to radios, compared to 62 million just three decades earlier. During roughly the same time span, the number of radio stations grew by more than 60 percent, from 6,519 (1970) to 10,577 (2000). Television usage increased even more dramatically during that same time period, with 101 million sets in use in 2000 compared to 59 million sets in 1970. The number of television stations, however, increased at an even faster rate than the number of radio stations, growing from 862 to 1,663, an increase of 93 percent. Tied to this increase in television stations was the growth of cable television systems, spreading from 2,490 available systems in 1970 to 10,243 systems in 2000, an increase of 300 percent in 30 years.

By contrast, the print media has actually been contracting and consolidating. As of 2001, 1,468 daily newspapers were being published, a decline of 16 percent since 1970.[2] Fewer and fewer companies (e.g., Gannett, Knight-Ridder, Times-Mirror, *New York Times,* and *Washington Post*) have gained an increasingly large foothold throughout the nation, by purchasing regional newspapers and nationalizing their circulations. *The New York Times* publishes regional editions that are readily available with your morning coffee in most major markets throughout the country; the *Wall Street Journal,* long available across the nation, has intensified its circulation effort on a national basis; the *Washington Post* publishes a national weekly edition with an established readership as well; and *USA Today* has emerged as a prime mass-circulation daily over the past three decades. Further, the Gannett chain (and publishers of *USA Today*), Times-Mirror, and the *New York Times* company now own newspapers (and television stations) across the country. Yet, these efforts at consolidation and increased national availability have not enhanced newspaper circulation or readership. Circulation, in fact, has declined from about 62.1 million readers in 1970 to 55.6 million readers in 2001.

In addition to the traditional electronic and print media, newer electronic entries have propelled the worldwide communications explosion as well. The facsimile, or more popularly the fax machine, was instrumental in continuing the democracy movement in China in the late 1980s and has revolutionized communications to virtually every corner of the globe. The impact of computer technology has been even more profound via the Internet and the World Wide Web. Although instantaneous communications through electronic mail (e-mail) is commonplace for all ages over the past decade, the impact of e-mail in transforming global politics is indeed revolutionary. The newest, and in some sense the largest, entrant in this communication explosion is the cell phone. They are now ubiquitous—in cars, offices, and homes—with 751 cell phone systems in 1990 and 2,587 in 2001 and 5.3 million subscribers in 1990 and 128.4 million in 2001. In short, then, the fax machine, the Internet, the World Wide Web, and the cell phone have accelerated the pervasiveness of electronic communication worldwide as never before in human history.

Old News versus New News

The emergence of these different communications and media outlets (e.g., talk radio, cable TV, the Internet), or "new news" sources, has seemingly altered reliance on the traditional media outlets (e.g., network news and national newspapers), or the "old news" sources.[3] One indicator of this change is the precipitous drop in the viewership of the nightly network news broadcasts over the past three decades. In 2002, only 32 percent of Americans regularly watched the nightly network news, compared to 42 percent in 1996 and 60 percent in 1993. In the 1970s, this figure was about 80 percent. Furthermore, among young viewers (those under thirty), only about 20 percent watched the nightly news broadcasts on a regular basis in 2002.[4] The cable news audience has increased with about 33 percent of the public regularly watching one of these channels (e.g., CNN and Fox). Still, the young audience (under 30) only views that source at a slightly higher rate (about 23 percent) than the network nightly news broadcasts. In all, the "old news" sources continue to have an important role in shaping the agenda and in stimulating discussion on the "new news" forums—talk radio or cyberspace—but clearly those latter sources are challenging traditional ones for viewership and listeners.[5] In this sense, both traditional and new media sources continue to have a crucial role in political and social life.

The ultimate impact of this communication explosion on foreign policy is difficult to estimate. On the one hand, foreign policy coverage by the media is hardly immune to these dramatic changes in the communication arena. Indeed, these revolutionary changes are often viewed as having enhanced the American public's access to foreign affairs and, in turn, as having contributed to an enlarged role for the media in the foreign policy arena. Dramatic events worldwide bring dramatic and continuous coverage by the various media outlets. The use of "imbedded reporters" during the Iraq War in March and April of 2003 illustrated how global events could be brought into the lives of Americans in real time—something hardly seen or experienced before. On the other hand, since coverage of foreign affairs by the American news media in a continuous fashion remains relatively small, with late 1980s estimates of foreign policy coverage at about 11 to 16 percent in the print and national television networks[6] (and at only 2.6 percent in one study of ten leading newspapers),[7] the implications of these changes for foreign policy should not be exaggerated. Still, what events in the foreign policy arena are covered—and how they are covered—may have an important impact on the public debate over foreign policy. Moreover, some more recent evidence exists that "soft news" sources, even with limited foreign policy coverage, can be important in affecting the public at large.[8] In this rapidly changing environment, then, the role of the media in the foreign policy process remains a topic of continued interest and discussion.

THE ROLE OF THE MEDIA
IN THE FOREIGN POLICY PROCESS

More precise assessments of the media's role in American foreign policy immediately provoke a torrent of commentary and controversy. For purposes of our discussion, we can divide these assessments into three different categories.[9] One set of analyses focuses upon the media as largely a separate actor in the foreign policy process, sometimes seeking to advance their own views among the American people. Another set sees the media as largely an accomplice of the government policy and more often supportive, than critical, of official action. Yet, a third role portrays the media and the government in a "mutually exploitative" relationship in which each gains from the other. While all of these roles are often intermingled in discussions of the media and foreign policy, this last role appears to best represent the current relationship between the media and foreign policy makers. Before we discuss that third role, however, we first outline the two most frequently identified roles for the media in the foreign policy process and discuss some criticisms that question the accuracy of each one.

The Media as Actor

The argument is that in this role, the media in fact shape the foreign policy agenda for policy makers and the public. Since policy makers and the public depend upon the media for information about global events (and especially television, for instantaneous communication from around the world),[10] the media are a powerful force for determining the issues considered. Put somewhat differently, what the media decide to portray (or not portray) may have a powerful influence on the direction of American foreign policy. By extension, the media as a whole may exercise an independent effect on the foreign policy process. While evidence exists for this argument, other analysts caution against pushing this interpretation too far. Let us consider both kinds of evidence on this media role.

The Vietnam War The emergence of this "media as actor" role usually dates from the Vietnam War. The media (and particularly television) provided vivid pictures of that conflict to the American public and policy makers, virtually on a nightly basis. The media portrayals of that war produced a lasting set of images for the American public and policy makers: The magnitude of killings and destruction on both sides often became nightly staples of the coverage; interviews with battlefield military officers and spokespersons often conveyed the difficulties of the war (including a particularly vivid interview in which a military officer declared that American forces had "to destroy the town to save it");[11] and protests against the war at home became standard fare as well. These portrayals were often at odds with the upbeat assessments by American and South Vietnamese officials, who tended to laud the progress being made in the war. In short, the media often put policy makers on the defensive to explain their positions and to defend their policies. In this way, the media ultimately had a powerful effect on the direction of policy in the Vietnam War.

The so-called Tet offensive, countrywide attacks across South Vietnam by Viet Cong and North Vietnamese forces beginning in late January 1968, in particular illustrates the impact of the media on the conduct of the war and American foreign policy. Although these attacks ultimately proved to be a military failure, the amount of physical destruction, the number of casualties, and the widespread nature of the attacks, as portrayed by the media, conveyed another message. Indeed, the image created by the media implied a massive defeat for South Vietnamese and American forces. Despite efforts to explain the events in other ways, the media impression produced a "profound impact on American perceptions of the war at all levels," as one analyst noted, with a sharp decline in public optimism. In short, "the dramatic impact of the television coverage of the carnage, set against the official statements of optimism, had its effects."[12] (Years later, a detailed study documented the impact of the press coverage on this crucial foreign policy episode and the misleading way in which the Tet offensive was portrayed by the media.[13]) Indeed, in the immediate aftermath of this offensive, President Lyndon Johnson announced on March 31, 1968, that he would not be a candidate for president that fall. In short, the Tet offensive remains one of those events often described to convey the power of the media in affecting policy.

The Iran Hostage Crisis   In the late 1970s and early 1980s, the Iran hostage crisis, in which 52 Americans were held for 444 days in the U.S. embassy in Tehran, is another example used to portray the media's foreign policy role. In the first days of the hostage taking, the ABC television network initiated a nightly program, *America Held Hostage,* to outline the developments during the crisis. Each night, the title was augmented with the appropriate day (e.g., *America Held Hostage, Day 25*).[14] As the crisis wore on, seemingly without resolution, the impact of these nightly episodes became clear: The American government appeared powerless to do much to intervene, and the ineptitude of the Carter administration became firmly planted in the minds of many Americans. Furthermore, with these continued portrayals, the impression created was that little else mattered on the world stage during those days. While the point is not to debate whether ABC and other media outlets were seeking this outcome, what is important is the fact that the media played a forceful role in conveying and creating a particular foreign policy image.

Ethiopia and Somalia   In the 1980s and 1990s, the media's portrayal of the death and starvation in Ethiopia and Somalia further demonstrates their power in the foreign policy arena. In the former case, journalist Peter Boyer summarized the media's impact in a 1984 NBC report on the widening Ethiopian famine:

> It was a jarring piece, movingly narrated by BBC correspondent Michael Buerk. "The faces of death in Africa," [Anchor Tom] Brokaw called it.
>
> The impact was immediate and overwhelming. The phones started ringing at NBC and at the Connecticut headquarters of Save the Children. . . . The next night, NBC aired another BBC report and, again, the response was stag-

gering. CBS and ABC a week later aired more reports on the famine—with even more response, more reports. The story had exploded.[15]

In 1991 and 1992, the media prodded the Bush administration to take more vigorous actions about the starvation and suffering in Somalia. Former Secretary of State Lawrence Eagleburger described the impact of television on policy making over Somalia in this way:

> I will tell you quite frankly television had a great deal to do with President Bush's decision to go in the first place, and, I will tell you equally frankly, I was one of those two or three that was strongly recommending he do it, and it was very much because of the television pictures of these starving kids, substantial pressures from the Congress that comes from the same source, and my honest belief that we could do this. . . .[16]

Once again, the media's riveting portrayal of the suffering in that country ultimately led to the dispatch of American military forces to help with the distribution of food and needed supplies. Indeed, "among the most vivid scenes from that operation was the look of startled Navy seals in war paint hitting the beaches which had already been secured by television news crews to record the landing."[17] Such a scene was a dramatic and stark illustration of the power of the media in setting the foreign policy agenda and even in arranging a foreign policy action.

After the 2003 Iraq War By the fall of 2003, the Bush administration and its supporters laid a severe charge against the national news media for its portrayal of the attacks upon Americans in Iraq, the instability within the country, and the difficulty faced in the reconstruction efforts. The claim was that the media was highlighting the attacks upon the American military in Iraq and the problems of reconstructing that country and not telling the full story about what was happening in that country. In doing so, the media was contributing to a decline in support for the administration's policy at home and abroad. Put differently, the media were neither conveying the political and social achievements in much of the country nor the overall stability of life within Iraq. In an effort to combat this national media imagery, President Bush met with reporters from regional media within the country to convey his views on the situation in Iraq, and several administration officials (e.g., Condoleezza Rice, Secretary of State Colin Powell, Secretary of Defense Donald Rumsfeld) were dispatched on speaking engagements around the country to get the message out about the "real" conditions in Iraq. In addition, some of these same administration officials went to Iraq itself to seek to portray the story more favorably from that venue. In all, though, these actions were taken to combat what was seen as the media serving as an actor by seemingly setting the agenda on the question of Iraq.

On occasion, too, *individual* members of the media can play an even more direct role in the foreign policy process—a role that media analyst Doris Graber has called "media diplomacy."[18] Four examples will suffice to illustrate this aspect of the media's foreign policy role.

The Missile Crisis   ABC television reporter John Scali is often given considerable credit for aiding in the peaceful resolution of the nuclear standoff between the United States and the Soviet Union during October 1962—the Cuban Missile Crisis. Scali was approached by a Soviet official and asked to transmit a proposal to the U.S. government for ending the crisis, a proposal that ultimately bore a resemblance to the final outcome.[19] Another American might have served as the channel for such information, but the fact that Scali, as a journalist, had contacts with Soviet officials reveals how members of the media may participate in the process.

Sadat and Begin   A second illustration of the role that individuals in the media can play involved the visit by Egypt's Anwar Sadat to Israel in November 1977.[20] During a CBS evening news broadcast anchored by Walter Cronkite a month or so earlier, Anwar Sadat and Israeli Prime Minister Menachem Begin were simultaneously interviewed from their home countries. During the course of the interview, Cronkite encouraged Begin to issue an invitation to Sadat to visit Israel. Begin did so, and Sadat's pathbreaking trip to Jerusalem was initiated. In a small but important way, a member of the media became an actor in the foreign policy process.

The Persian Gulf War   Yet another illustration occurred during the Persian Gulf War of 1991. Peter Arnett was a reporter for CNN who went to Baghdad, Iraq, prior to the outbreak of the war and stayed on during the conflict.[21] His actions gained him both notoriety and political attacks in the United States for his continued reporting from Iraq. As virtually the only Western source in Baghdad once the war broke out, Arnett became a lightning rod for critics of the media and foreign policy for seemingly taking at face value the Iraqi explanations of events during the war. He was also criticized by many "when he engaged Iraqi president Saddam Hussein in a long television interview," since this appeared to offer a ready "propaganda forum" for Hussein against his adversaries.[22]

The Iraq War of 2003   During the war itself during March and April of 2003, the media was deeply involved in portraying the conflict, since they had been "imbedded" into numerous units by the military. (Indeed, many of the reporters had actually taken some combat training before taking part in the military units that advanced on Baghdad from Kuwait.) In this sense, the media were real-time participants and actors in shaping this foreign policy agenda and action. They were under particular restrictions (e.g., reporters were prohibited from identifying their exact locations during combat), but they were still in a position to convey a wartime situation to the American public and policy makers as never before. In addition, a few reporters stayed in Baghdad or went into Iraq during the fighting outside of these officially sanctioned imbedded reporters and also provided other important images and commentaries on the actions during that war. Finally, of course, during the reconstruction of Iraq, the degree of independent reporting on the situation there led the Bush administration to go on its "media offensive" as we noted above.

Other Interpretations of the Role of the Media Despite these examples and evidence that seem to support this first role, several analysts doubt the accuracy of describing the media as a foreign policy actor. Instead, they point to other explanations for the changing media coverage of foreign policy events. One leading media analyst, for example, disputes the accuracy of an "oppositional media" that presumably developed over Vietnam, and the Tet offensive in particular.[23] While acknowledging that television references to Tet do reveal that the media coverage was more critical of policy after this offensive than before, this analyst contends that the reason was not that the media had changed its role, but rather that the domestic consensus on this foreign policy issue had evaporated, bringing more and more criticism of government policy.[24] As a result, the members of the media, relying on their norm of objective journalism, gave more and more coverage to this emerging controversy. Furthermore, as this analyst endeavors to show, the media continued to convey official government statements about the Vietnam War, provided about the same ratio of comments about antiwar supporters and supporters of the government after Tet, and offered little explicit independent commentary on the war.[25] Thus, this analyst challenges whether the media really was an actor in this case:

> The case of Vietnam suggests that whether the media tend to be supporting or critical of government policies depends on the degree of consensus those policies enjoy, particularly within the political establishment. . . . News content may not mirror the facts, but the media, as institutions, do reflect the prevailing pattern of political debate: when consensus is strong, they tend to stay within the limits of the political discussion it defines; when it begins to break down, coverage becomes increasingly critical and diverse in the viewpoints it represents, and increasingly difficult for officials to control.[26]

Contrary to the earlier argument, others would question that the media shaped the coverage of the Iran hostage crisis. Instead, they would point to the actions of the Carter administration itself for producing the significant media emphasis on this event.[27] Since President Carter proceeded to treat this issue as the most important problem facing the country and thus refused to leave Washington to campaign until it was resolved (the so-called Rose Garden strategy), the media necessarily provided more and more attention to the hostage crisis. While this argument surely has some attraction as an alternate explanation, it fails to explain the sustained coverage in Tehran by American media outlets.

Similarly, critics also would contend that the media have not always succeeded in shaping the foreign policy agenda. At least three cases suggest that significant media coverage does not always produce a foreign policy response by the United States. Consider the cases of Cambodia (Kampuchea), Bosnia, and Rwanda. Despite the "killing fields" in Cambodia in the late 1970s, and the media coverage of the 2 million who were being massacred by the Pol Pot regime there, American foreign policy changed very little toward that country or region during those years. Instead, due to the aftermath of the Vietnam War experience, the United States took a less assertive stance toward that country. Similarly, despite dramatic television pictures from Bosnia revealing the killings in the markets of Sarajevo, the haunting figures of men held in prisoner of war camps, and wholesale killings and rapes in the name of ethnic cleansing, American policy makers were slow to change policy directions in the early 1990s. Once again, fear of a Vietnam-style quagmire prevailed for several years. Indeed, it was not until mid-1995 that the Clinton administration took a more determined stance. Finally, the ethnic slaughter of Tutsis in Rwanda in 1994 and its vivid portrayal by the media brought only a limited response by U.S. policy makers. In this instance, too, the media had limited success in setting the foreign policy agenda. In contrast, and to make the point more fully about the limited effect of the media, consider instances when the United States acted without being prodded by television coverage. In humanitarian disasters, whether in Africa (e.g., Sierra Leone or Liberia) or Southeast Asia (e.g., East Timor), American assistance often arrives before, or simultaneously with, the media.

Finally, the importance of media diplomacy should not be pushed too far. Despite the earlier examples, it is difficult to conclude that any of these media members ultimately shaped foreign policy. We now know, for example, that "back-channel" communications over resolving the Cuban Missile Crises were already under way between American and Soviet officials before John Scali became involved. Similarly, while Walter Cronkite may have aided the peace process in the Middle East, the Israeli and Egyptian officials ultimately had to take the bold steps to adjust their long-standing policies toward one another. Furthermore, despite the criticism of Peter Arnett's reporting in Iraq, no evidence exists that his actions changed American policy in any significant way during the Persian Gulf War. Similarly, the Bush administration has actually reaffirmed its commitment to see through the reconstruction of Iraq, despite sustained media criticism and questioning from domestic and international critics. In sum, the role of the media as an actor appears overstated—or even inaccurate—to some critics.

The Liberal Media? Another aspect of this first role for the media focuses upon the ideological characteristics of the members themselves and the possible bias that they bring to their reporting. The American public often views the media as being elitist, as possessing a liberal political bias, and as trying to foist such views on policy. Several studies provide some support for these assertions. First, the media as a group is largely elitist in demographic characteristics and do not reflect the characteristics of the American public as a whole. In a survey of members of both print and television media, one major study reported that the media elite largely came from the northeast and north-central part of the country with urban and ethnic roots, were highly educated and from "mostly well off, highly educated members of the upper middle class," and had primarily "secular roots," with only half religious believers and less than 10 percent church attenders.[28] Moreover, these demographic characteristics differed little between members of the print and electronic media surveyed. Second, members of the media were largely liberal in orientation, with 54 percent describing themselves as left of center and 17 percent as right of center. Another study of only the Washington press corps at about the same time found that 42 percent were liberal in orientation and 19 percent conservative.[29] Third, the partisan orientation of media members tended to be skewed in one direction as well. More than four-fifths of those surveyed supported Democratic presidential candidates Johnson, Humphrey, McGovern, and Carter in the elections immediately prior to the survey.[30]

More recent surveys in the mid-1980s, mid-1990s, and 2000 largely support this earlier media portrait. In 1985, the *Los Angeles Times* surveyed more than 2,700 print journalists and found that 56 percent had a liberal orientation, while only 18 percent had a conservative orientation. In 1996, in a survey of the heads of Washington bureaus for various media outlets and congressional correspondents, the Freedom Forum and the Roper Center found about the same breakdown—61 percent of these members of the media characterized themselves as "liberal" or "moderate to liberal," while only 9 percent viewed themselves as "conservative" or "moderate to conservative." Further, 89 percent of those surveyed said that they had voted for Clinton in 1992, while only 7 percent had voted for Bush.[31] Finally, in a 2000 study of 3,400 journalists they were found to be "less likely to get married and have children, less likely to do volunteer community service, less likely to own homes, and less likely to go to church than others who live in the communities where they work."[32]

The important question is whether these personal characteristics mattered in what was reported or how it was reported. Many members of the media would argue that their journalistic training directs them to be fair and not to allow their personal beliefs and background affect their work. Thus, their social-political background or political leanings would not significantly alter their reporting on domestic or foreign policy matters. Moreover, some of these liberal members of the media work for conservative organizations whose principal goals are increasing their share of the market among American viewers and listeners and enhancing the corporations' profits. In such an environment, the reporters will be directed to follow a "good story," despite their political leanings, and will likely do so.

Others disagree strongly over claims that members of the media will not allow their personal views to intrude in their reporting. Indeed, one prominent political scientist and media analyst calls this argument "absurd." Instead, he argues that this liberal bias comes into play "more in the setting of the agenda than in the reporting of particular facts. What they choose to cover, what they think is important is the liberal agenda."[33] Bernard Goldberg, former CBS reporter and author of a major book on the media, also disagrees with this argument. As he puts it, "Liberal bias is the result of how they [media] see the world." This, in turn, affects the way that they report the news.[34]

In this sense, we are back to where we started this discussion: That is, the media are important in setting the foreign policy agenda, as a recent study by Soroka has demonstrated empirically for recent decades.[35] This analysis also suggests that the media effects on the public's attention to foreign policy goes beyond cataloguing the kinds of real-world events happening at the time. In this sense, how much the media set the agenda and how much they influence policy remain hotly debated questions. Longtime media analyst Bernard Cohen, writing more than four decades ago about the press and foreign policy, still provides an apt summary of this first role of the media:

[T]he press is significantly more than a purveyor of information and opinion. It may not be successful much of the time in telling people what to think, but it is stunningly successful in telling its readers what to think *about*.[36]

The Media as Accomplice

A second role for the media might be stated most strongly as one wholly at variance with the first: The media, knowingly or not, act as an accomplice of the government. Put differently, they become the "handmaidens" of the government in the portrayal of news and information.[37] At least three kinds of evidence support this view. First, the media are ultimately dependent upon the government for information and for providing sources of information on many foreign policy questions that arise. Second, the media elite and the political elite often share similar values and beliefs about foreign policy. As such, the media will give credence to the policy maker's positions on foreign policy. Third, government officials often seek to utilize the media for promotion of particular policies, and, increasingly, they are trained to do so.[38] In this environment, and in contrast to the first media role we discussed, members of the media have a difficult time being an independent actor in the process.

Media Dependency The American interventions in Grenada (1983) and Panama (1989) as well as the Persian Gulf War (1990–1991) and the Iraq War (2003) illustrate the problems that the media have in playing an independent role and reveal how dependent they may become on the government for information. During the American intervention in Grenada in October 1983, and with the memory of the media's role in Vietnam in mind, the Reagan administration decided to exclude the media from joining the invading forces and sent home members who had reached the island nation on their own.[39] In this instance, information about American actions was tightly channeled so as to control the situation, leaving the media largely to report the official positions.

After this episode, a commission was established to arrange a new relationship between the media and the government (in this case, the Pentagon) over future American engagements abroad. This new system created a "pool": reporters representing both print and electronic media would accompany future military actions.[40] The intervention in Panama in December 1989 was the first test of this arrangement. On the one hand, this procedure largely failed in the view of the media, since they remained under close scrutiny and control of Pentagon officials in Panama and were kept away from combat areas for long periods. On the other hand, the military and the government largely succeeded in conveying the media picture that they wanted.

The Persian Gulf crisis and war of 1990–1991 produced even greater governmental efforts to control and shape the information that emanated from that area of the world. Indeed, the Pentagon outlined detailed "ground rules" for reporting from the region.[41] Sizes of American or coalition units and their military components could not be disclosed, future operational plans were also forbidden, and exact locations of forces in Saudi Arabia, for example, could not be revealed.

News "pool" operations were once again established, and "they became the essential mode of operation."[42] The daily military briefings on the Persian Gulf operations, generally carried live on CNN worldwide, were the primary sources of information for the many news organizations present in Saudi Arabia. Once again, the efforts to shape the story in a way that the government wanted proved to be largely successful.

The Iraq War of 2003 extended this governmental involvement in media reporting. Once again, the Pentagon provided media summaries of battlefield actions on a daily basis from the Department of Defense's Central Command headquarters located in Qatar during the war or from the Pentagon in Washington. In addition, and as we have discussed above, the military took the relationship between the military and the media a step further in this conflict by utilizing "imbedded" reporters with units involved in fighting in Iraq. With video phones and satellite capabilities, these reporters could send back real-time images to the American public and others portraying the battlefield activities. These reporters, though, were under severe strictures about the nature of their reporting, even as they continued to try to do their work. That is, they could not identify their precise location, and they were restricted in the kind of media shots that they could show for security reasons, though their reporting was presumably conveying the story that the military wanted told. (Note how this discussion, too, illustrates the difficulties of separating out the first media role from the second.) Finally, President George W. Bush's surprise visit to the American troops in Baghdad on Thanksgiving Day, 2003, stunned much of the media, and those selected media that accompanied him were under strict orders about the reporting that they could do before the president left Iraq to return home.

Close Personal and Working Relationships While these illustrations are recent instances of the ability of the government to utilize the media in a way favorable to it, other mechanisms are available and have operated for some time. Often, members of the media and public officials form close personal and working relationships and can thus use one another to get a particular message across to the public and other policy makers. The leaking of information to particular reporters is the obvious and most direct way to achieve this end. Just as "sources" for the media develop in the government, foreign policy officials may use their media "contacts" to make their case to the American people. Some of these reporters, in either print or electronic media, become "Washington insiders," with easy contact and access to policy makers (although not always complying with the wishes of government officials).

While a pure example of such reporters is difficult to identify (since few media people would accept this characterization), the late James Reston, longtime columnist for the *New York Times,* fits this portrait, in part. A first-rate reporter and columnist on foreign and domestic issues, he was also closely tied with and highly trusted by Washington officials—"the quintessential Washington insider," in one commentator's judgment. In fact, in that analyst's view, he was too close to key officials: "Officials used him to test out new ideas on the public or to drop leaks for which they did not want to be held accountable. Because of his high position at the *Times* and his personal integrity, he was trusted both by those who provided the news and by those who read it."[43] Further, on at least one important occasion, Reston was willing to withhold a story after a presidential phone call. The story involved the emplacement of Soviet missiles in Cuba in 1962, at a time when the crisis had yet to become public. Yet, the Reston example is hardly a pure case because he also demonstrated journalistic independence at times, in particular with his support for the *Times*'s publication of the *Pentagon Papers* in 1971. Moreover, he seemingly always judged the relationship between politicians and the press as a conflictual one.[44]

At a more general level, media representatives and public officials often have worked closely with one another to gain information and have relied on and trusted one another. The extent of this cooperation abroad is considerable, since the American embassy or consulate is the primary source of information for many reporters. This collaboration may extend to a reporter reading American embassy cable traffic on a regular basis in an African country, another reporter holding back information about secret negotiations over Afghanistan at the request of an American ambassador, or a Washington columnist allegedly utilizing information from a White House source to affect the foreign policy debate on Iraq.[45] At the very least, though, the collaboration often involves a regular and sustained exchange of information.

Government Use of the Media Increasingly, the government has sought to establish ground rules for dealing with the media, not just in times of interventions or wars as the Grenada, Persian Gulf, or Iraq cases suggest, but on a more ongoing basis. A former assistant secretary of state for Inter-American Affairs made the point bluntly about the need by government officials to shape the message emanating from the media: "We are not taught about the press as an instrument of foreign policy execution, and that is crucial. . . . You have to use the press, and when I say 'use,' I don't mean cynically, in the sense of hoodwinking. I mean use it in the sense that it's an instrument that is there for you."[46] As a result, in recent years, the Department of State has developed an extensive series of guidelines for dealing with the media and offered stern warnings about what to say and not say.[47] In short, governmental officials now receive both formal and informal training in managing media relations.

Much as with the role of the media as actor, critics would caution about relying too fully on this second role to summarize the relationship between the media and foreign policy makers. First, while acknowledging that members of the media are dependent upon the "golden triangle" (White House, Pentagon, and State Department) for gathering news (and hence the official government position often gets considerable attention), a "professional norm" exists that "discourages taking sides by looking to report different sides of a debate."[48] As we noted earlier, too, as the policy debate among officials emerges—whether between the Pentagon or State or between the White House and Congress—the media are able to play a more expansive role than just conveying the officially stated government position. Moreover, "when official conflict is sustained, the news gates tend to open to grass-roots groups, interest groups, opinion polls, and broader social participation."[49] In this way, the media are increasingly successful in being more than an accomplice of the government.

Second, members of the media are fully aware of the effort by government officials to engage in *spinning*—the strategy of officials to convey a particular image or interpretation of foreign policy events and to try to get the media to convey that view.[50] As a result, members of the media would likely take precautions to guard against conveying only the official interpretation. Furthermore, as foreign policy issues become interestingly contentious and partisan, members of the media will seek out alternate sources in order to get their interpretation of events.

The Media and the Government: Mutually Exploitative?

As the criticism of the media as accomplice illustrates, an increasing tension has developed in the relationship between the media and the foreign policy community, suggesting a third possible relationship between these two organizations today. This third possibility actually strikes a middle ground between the two roles discussed so far. Neither the "media as actor" nor the "media as accomplice" best characterizes the relationship; instead, an intermediate role exists in which the media and the government seek to take advantage of the relationship with the other. One analyst has aptly described this role as a "mutually exploitative" relationship between the media and foreign policy makers:

> Both organizations [the United States foreign policy community and the media] promote their own version of reality around the world; the foreign policy apparatus does so to serve its own policy interests; the media do so because that is what they do. Both are adept at supporting, manipulating, or attacking the other. The relationship is sometimes competitive and sometimes cooperative, but that is only incidental to its central driving force: self-interest.[51]

In particular, recent foreign policy and media activities, most notably in connection with the Persian Gulf War and the Iraq War, gave credence to this characterization of the relationship. In analyzing interview data from foreign and defense officials during the Gulf War and other interview data with journalists and officials regarding Soviet-American relations somewhat earlier, "the mutual exploitation theme quickly emerged," according to one media analyst. For large percentages of the policy officials, the media sources were often the only or "the fastest source of information."[52] Conversely, "the policymakers saw nothing unusual about using the media as a communications instrument to address other national leaders and populations."[53] The Iraq War appears to support this mutual exploitation theme, too. While the media were eager to take advantage of the use of "imbedded" reporters to cover the war more fully, the military and policy makers saw this arrangement as a way to maintain some stake in the reporting that would be done. Similarly, after the ground war was over in Iraq, the coverage of the reconstruction efforts—and the differences over that coverage between policy makers and the media—again illustrated the efforts by both participants to shape the coverage.

The success of the media versus the policy makers in this relationship varies by issue.[54] On issues dealing with the environment, human rights, and human-interest stories generally, sometimes called "low politics" issues, the media are more effective in impacting the policy process. Human rights violations of ethnic minorities and the struggle for freedom and independence by indigenous groups are often easily portrayed through the medium of television. The media can use compelling visual images to try to get such an issue on the foreign policy agenda. On issues dealing with arms control or the accuracy of weapons systems, sometimes called "high politics" issues, policy makers may have an advantage. Consider the media's difficulty of trying to convey the debate for and against arms control agreements without official arguments, or strategies against international terrorism without reliance on the military. As a longtime foreign policy journalist noted recently: "Media technology is rarely as powerful in the hands of journalists as it is in the hands of political figures who can summon the talent to exploit the new invention."[55] In sum, then, both media and the foreign policy community may well feed off the skills of one another as both seek to promote their interests. In many ways, "mutually exploitative" may be a more accurate way to think about the relationship between these two organizations, rather than simply trying to characterize the media as always an independent actor or as always a government accomplice in the foreign policy process.

THE MEDIA'S IMPACT ON THE PUBLIC

The final topic to consider in their relationship is the media's effects upon the views and opinions of the public. While our next section will focus more directly on the nature of the public's view of foreign policy and its foreign policy role, the media obviously have some impact on the public's perceptions prior to those opinions. In a real sense, of course, the public is greatly subject to the kind and extent of information that the media provide it. As political scientists Benjamin Page and Robert Shapiro note: "Many events—especially distant happenings in foreign affairs—do not directly and immediately affect ordinary citizens, and therefore, do not speak for themselves." Instead, such events must be reported and "*interpreted*."[56] In this sense, the media matters, but how much and to what degree?

In a study covering a 15-year period (1969–1983), Page and Shapiro have begun to sort out the media's role by assessing the impact of several different providers of news on television, such as "the president, members of his administration and fellow partisans, members of the opposing party, interest groups, . . . experts, network commentators or reporters . . . foreign nations or individuals, unfriendly states," and several others on the changes in the public's view of foreign and domestic policies.[57] From their analyses, two important findings emerged. First, the public's views were relatively stable over time (only about 50 percent of the time over the years did they change), even in the context of a variety of different interpreters of television news. (We shall discuss more fully the stability of public opinion on foreign policy in the next section.) Second, when opinion change did occur in the short term, news commentators—more than any of the other providers of news—produced the most change of the public's opinion. In this sense, the media, and especially news commentators, mattered in affecting the public's view more than presidents, policy experts, and foreign nations.

In a more recent study, Stuart Soroka also examines the effect of media content on foreign policy opinion. After systematically examining the foreign and domestic policy contents in the *New York Times* and the *Times* of London between 1981 and 2002 on the British and American public, Soroka concludes that there is a "remarkably powerful effect of media content on the salience of foreign affairs for the public."[58] That is, foreign affairs coverage raises the salience of these issues for the public. On the face of it, such a finding is hardly unexpected or exceptional in light of what we have been discussing. What he also demonstrates, however, is important: There is a media effect in addition to the impact of the occurrence of the foreign policy events themselves. In turn, such issue salience affects how the public evaluates governments and political leaders. In this sense, media reporting of foreign affairs—beyond the events themselves—can be crucial to the nature of public opinion within a country. To be sure, Soroka acknowledges that more work needs to be done to understand fully the relationship among media content, foreign policy events, and public opinion, but his analysis, like the work of Shapiro and Page, helps to specify this relationship.

Finally, though, Shapiro and Page add some important cautions about the relationship between the media and foreign opinion that ought to be kept in mind throughout this discussion. They note, for example, that "gradual social and economic trends, and world and national events—which have some unmediated impact" combine with those reported through the mass media to affect opinion change.[59] In addition, while foreign policy views by the public are often interpreted through the media by elites, "people seem to have reacted directly to events themselves, sometimes going against elite interpretations."[60] In this sense, the evidence is quite strong that the public is not made up of mindless robots wholly swayed by the latest media pictures and portrayals, but that opinion change among the public comes from many sources and not exclusively from the media.[61]

PUBLIC OPINION AND FOREIGN POLICY: ALTERNATE VIEWS

With an understanding of the role of the media, we now turn to examine more directly the public's role in the foreign policy process. We divide our discussion and analysis into two differing perspectives about public opinion and foreign policy and evaluate the evidence for each of them. We conclude by judging which perspective seems more appropriate for the current period.

According to the first perspective about foreign policy opinion, the public is uninterested, ill informed, and subject to considerable leadership from the top on foreign policy matters. In the strongest form of this position, public opinion is less a shaper of U.S. foreign policy and more likely to be shaped by it. As a consequence, public opinion plays little or no role in shaping American foreign policy. According to the second perspective, the public plays a somewhat larger, albeit still limited, role in the foreign policy process. While the public may not be fully informed on foreign policy and may lack sustained interest in such matters, its views are more structured and consistent over time than many have previously contended. As such, the public can affect foreign policy making, especially over the long haul. In the course of this discussion, too, we evaluate how much impact public opinion has on policy making—indirectly through presidential and congressional elections and directly through current policy actions—as a way to gain some insight into the utility of these two alternate perspectives.

FOREIGN POLICY OPINION: UNINFORMED AND MOODISH

Except for very rare occurrences, public opinion has limited impact on the foreign policy process. In this view, only during wars or international crises is the public sufficiently concerned about foreign policy to affect it directly. The principal reason for this limited impact is the public's lack of interest in, and knowledge about, foreign affairs. Even when specific foreign policy views of the public are expressed, they often prove susceptible to short-term shifts—produced, for example, by presidential leadership, the wording of questions in public opinion polls, or rapidly changing international events. In this context, public opinion serves as a relatively weak restraint on policy makers.

Public Interest and Knowledge of Foreign Affairs

Low levels of public understanding of and concern about foreign policy issues have existed since America's sustained global involvement began after World War II. In a 1947 study of Cincinnati, Ohio, for instance, only 30 percent of the public were able to explain in a simple way what the United Nations did. In an analysis two years later, the public was equally uninformed. By this assessment, only 25 percent of the public was judged to possess reasonably developed opinions, 45 percent had only limited knowledge of world affairs, and 30 percent was classified as uninformed.[62]

Public opinion data from more recent decades are not much different. According to studies by Free and Cantril, only 26 percent of the American population were well informed on foreign policy issues during the 1960s, another 35 percent were moderately informed on foreign affairs, and 39 percent were simply uninformed. Somewhat indicative of this low level of knowledge was the public's information on the North Atlantic Treaty Organization (NATO), the center of America's containment efforts during the Cold War. According to this analysis, 28 percent of the public had never heard of NATO, only 58 percent knew that the

United States belonged to that organization, and only 38 percent indicated that the Soviet Union was not a member of NATO.[63]

Throughout the past three decades—until the events of September 11, 2001—the level of interest in foreign affairs had not changed appreciably—even in the context of a more educated electorate. Based upon the seven quadrennial surveys of the American public on foreign policy issues conducted by the Chicago Council on Foreign Relations from 1974 to 1998, local community news received the highest level of interest (between 55 percent and 65 percent over the years), while news about other countries was much lower (about 31 percent on average).[64] News about America's relations with other countries, however, ranked a bit higher, ranging from 44 percent to 53 percent across the surveys. Interestingly, news about U.S. relations with other countries stimulated more interest than simply news about other countries, but it still trailed interest in local community affairs. Figure 12.1 shows a comparison of interest in different types of news across these surveys.

After September 11, however, the public's interest in news about U.S. relations with other countries jumped to 62 percent, about the same level of interest in news about the local community and interest in news about other countries rose to 42 percent. Also see Figure 12.1 for the 2002 data. In this sense, September 11 had a profound effect on the level of interest about foreign affairs. Indeed, the 2002 Chicago Council survey points to this change as one of its key findings: "Public interest in world news is the strongest it has been in the last three decades of Council surveys."[65] Whether this interest in foreign affairs continues remains somewhat doubtful in light of past patterns, but it is a useful indicator of how significant and important the events of September 11 were to the American people.

While interest in foreign affairs may have increased lately, it is hard to argue that the level of knowledge about foreign affairs has also increased. In fact, the Chicago Council surveys over the years generally conclude that only about 20 to 25 percent of the American public is fully informed on foreign policy matters and constitutes what has been called the "attentive public." The results for 1990 were a little higher, with 29 percent of the public surveyed characterized as "high attentives," although the criteria for attentiveness are less demanding in this survey than in earlier ones.[66] Furthermore, as the 1998 survey noted, the "'don't know' responses among the public are not uncommon, especially on specific foreign policy issues requiring more detailed information" and the level of this kind of response has remained about the same over the years.

We can demonstrate the paucity of knowledge among the public on foreign affairs more concretely by considering the accuracy of the public's information about different kinds of foreign policy activities and about the high level of "don't know" or "no opinion" to foreign policy questions over recent decades. One example involves funding the Nicaraguan Contras in their battle against the Sandinista regime, an issue that dominated the foreign policy landscape during the Reagan administration. Yet, during a substantial portion of the 1980s, a majority of the public did not know, with certainty, which side the United States was backing: the Contra rebels or the Sandinista government. Based upon a series of public opinion surveys by ABC/*Washington Post* from 1983 to 1987, it was not until a

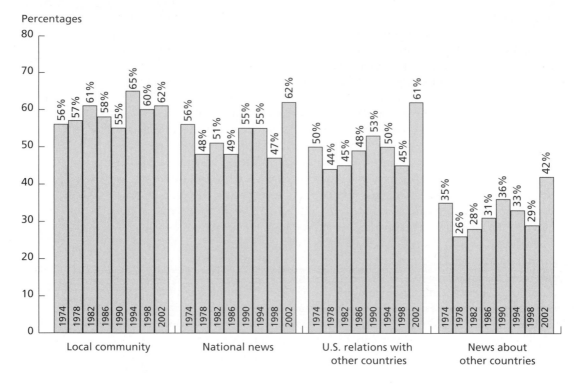

FIGURE 12.1 Percent of the American Public Very Interested in Various Types of News, 1974–2002

SOURCE: Marshall M. Bouton and Benjamin I. Page, eds., *Worldviews 2002: American Public Opinion & Foreign Policy* (Chicago: The Chicago Council on Foreign Relations, 2002), Figure 1–6, p. 13. Adapted with permission.

June 1985 poll that a majority of the public correctly noted that the United States government was supporting the Contras. Even at that late date in American involvement, one-third of the public still had "no opinion" when asked which side the United States was backing in Nicaragua. Indeed, throughout 1983, 1984, and part of 1985, "no opinion" was generally the most popular response when asked this kind of question.[67]

A second example deals with the amount of foreign aid that the United States transfers to other countries. While foreign aid is hardly a new item on the foreign policy agenda (foreign aid has been a staple of American foreign policy since the end of World War II), the public has a low level of knowledge about how much the United States actually provides to other countries. In a 2002 survey by The Chicago Council on Foreign Relations, the public's median estimate of the amount of the federal budget spent on American foreign aid was 25 percent. In reality, it is about 1 percent and has been at that level for a long time. Only 2 percent of the public correctly estimated this level.[68] In fairness to the American public (and perhaps the reason for the confusion in responding to this question), the United States has always been the leading donor or second leading donor (after Japan) in terms of total dollar amount of foreign assistance. Yet this inability on the part of the American public to differentiate between the total amount of aid versus relative amount of effort still suggests some limitation on the level of knowledge about foreign aid.

More recent examples illustrate the same degree of limited knowledge among the public, even for international events currently in the news.[69] In February 1999, when Kosovo and its ethnic conflicts had been in the news for some time and only one month prior to American military action there, a Gallup poll asked a sample of Americans "to choose which of four geographic locations best described Kosovo." Forty-two percent of the public correctly choose the Balkans, 26 percent placed the province in the former Soviet Union, 8 percent placed it in Africa or Southeast Asia, and 24 percent responded "don't know." For another ongoing dispute, the public was even less informed. When asked by Gallup in late 1999 the country that East Timor was having a dispute with, two-thirds of the American public did not have an answer, and only 20 percent (i.e., the "attentive public") answered correctly (Indonesia).

While these disputes might be regarded as off the radar screen for most Americans, the public also displays limited knowledge when asked about key foreign policymakers at home and abroad. In February 2003, for example, 37 percent of the public had "no opinion" when asked the name of the current secretary of state. Only 6 percent of the public could identify the prime minister of Canada, and 92 percent of the public had "no opinion." Similarly, 57 percent of the public had "no opinion" when asked to name the president of Russia and 46 percent responded in a similar way when asked the name of the prime minister of England—at a time when the United States and Britain were on the verge of going to war against Iraq.[70]

Foreign Policy as an Important Issue

Despite the low level of knowledge and interest in international affairs over past decades, the public still has viewed foreign policy as an important issue facing the country. During portions of the last six decades, for example, foreign policy has been identified as the most important issue facing the nation, but during the past thirty years or so, economic or domestic concerns (e.g., crime, unemployment, inflation) had generally been regarded as the principal issue identified by the American people. After September 11, though, terrorism quickly became identified as the key issue, with 36 percent of the public listing that issue as one of the two or three biggest problems, but, by 2003, the economy once again matched that issue as most important.[71]

During the height of the Cold War and throughout America's involvement in Vietnam, for instance, national security issues usually were cited by 40 to 60 percent of the public as the most important problem.[72] In the early to middle 1980s, foreign policy issues (e.g., such as fear of war or international tensions) were occasionally listed as "the most important problem facing this country today" in the periodic polls taken by the Gallup organization.

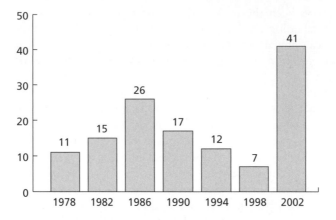

FIGURE 12.2 The Relative Percentage of Foreign Policy Problems as a Percentage Mentions of Problems Facing the Country by the American Public, 1978–2002

SOURCE: Marshall M. Bouton and Benjamin I. Page, eds., *Worldviews 2002: American Public Opinion & Foreign Policy* (Chicago: The Chicago Council on Foreign Relations, 2002), Figure 1–3, p. 11. Adapted with permission.

By contrast, in the immediate post-Vietnam years (e.g., 1973 through 1980) and in much of the 1980s and early 1990s, however, domestic issues, and particularly domestic economic issues, generally outstripped any foreign policy issue as the most important concern of the public.[73] By one estimate, economic concerns from about 1975 through 1985 often captured "over 60 percent of the public. The level of [economic] concern rarely dropped below an absolute majority and typically fell below the 50 percent mark only when energy concerns periodically peaked at 10 percent or higher."[74]

During the early to mid-1990s, economic and social issues typically were identified as the most important problems, too. General concerns about the economy, issues of crime and violence, and, somewhat less so, health care ranked at or near the top of the list. Foreign policy issues or issues tied to international affairs received very few mentions in the identification of the most important problems during those years.[75]

Figure 12.2 graphically portrays the extent to which the public identified foreign policy related problems "as a percentage of the total mentions of problems facing the country." Since 1978 through 1998, foreign policy problems as a percentage of the total ranged from 7 percent in 1998 to a high of 26 percent in 1986, but the average foreign policy percentage mentions over those years was only 13 percent. In the wake of September 11, foreign policy problems constituted 41 percent of the mentions—a very dramatic increase from the low in 1998 of 7 percent or even the previous high of 26 percent in 1986.[76] A May 2003 survey, however, reveals that the economy and economic issues have returned to the top spot, although concerns about terrorism remain.[77]

Still, if foreign policy has now captured a portion of the public's attention, why has the public not been more informed and more influential in shaping policy? Part of the explanation rests in the two earlier items we discussed: the low level of sustained interest in foreign policy over the years (albeit not immediately after September 11) and the low level of knowledge of foreign policy generally. Because the public's foreign policy concern has largely been episodic and tied to particular international events, and because the public's knowledge of, foreign policy questions has remained relatively low, its ability to influence policy has remained relatively weak.

Presidential Leadership

Another important factor in why the public has not been more influential is related to the American public's susceptibility to presidential leadership. According to evidence provided by political scientist John Mueller, the president has often been the most admired person in the country.[78] As a consequence, because the public is not well informed on foreign policy issues, a tendency has developed to defer to the president's judgment on such matters. Several examples illustrate this phenomenon.

When President Lyndon Johnson changed his war policy during the Vietnam conflict, the public generally was willing to shift to support that policy—even if it were a reversal of its earlier expressed position. Prior to the bombing of oil depots around Hanoi and Haiphong, a majority of the public opposed such bombing. After the bombing policy was begun by the Johnson administration, however, 85 percent supported it. A similar shift, dictated by a presidential initiative, occurred later in that war. Before President Johnson initiated a bombing halt in 1968, 51 percent of the public supported the continuation of bombing. After President Johnson announced his decision for a partial bombing halt, a majority (64 percent) of the public favored this new policy option.[79] In both instances, then, the American public was very susceptible to presidential leadership.

A similar example occurred during President Nixon's handling of the war in Southeast Asia. Just prior to the American invasion of Cambodia in 1970, a Harris Poll was conducted that asked whether the public supported the commitment of the American forces to that country. Only 7 percent favored such a policy. Yet, after President Nixon went on national television to explain his decision to send American troops into Cambodia, another Harris Poll indicated that 50 percent of the American public supported the policy.[80] In other words, in a matter of three weeks, public opinion turned around rather dramatically, with only the president's speech as the important intervening event.

In the post-Vietnam and post–Cold War periods, such ready acceptance of presidential leadership might seem more difficult to obtain, but, in fact, it continued. Prior to the seizure of American hostages in Iran in November 1979, President Jimmy Carter's approval rating was only 32 percent. By the end of December, his approval rating had jumped up to 61 percent. Furthermore, President Carter initially got high marks from the public over his handling of the

Iranian situation, with 82 percent of the American people applauding his actions.[81] While this "rallying around the president" can be short-lived, as President Carter was to find out, it nevertheless allowed the executive considerable latitude to take foreign policy initiatives without suffering any immediate domestic repercussions.

President Reagan also influenced public opinion on foreign policy issues by exercising presidential leadership. Although he met resistance on several foreign policy issues—placing American forces in Lebanon in 1982, backing the Contras in Central America, and opposing the nuclear freeze issue—he was still able, by his actions, to increase support from the American public for his policy positions. After the terrorist bombing of the marine headquarters in Beirut, Lebanon in October 1983, and the loss of 241 Americans, the level of the public's approval of U.S. troops stationed in that country increased from 36 percent in late September 1983 to 48 percent by late October 1983. Similarly, President Reagan's decision to send U.S. troops to Grenada won quick approval from the American public, with 55 percent supporting this action and 31 percent opposing it. Both of these levels of support for the president were accompanied by an increase in overall approval of his handling of the presidency.[82]

President George H. W. Bush was also able to use his foreign policy actions to gain additional public support. In the first two years of his term, President Bush generally enjoyed strong support for his foreign policy actions. Yet his decisions to intervene in Panama in December 1989 to topple and seize Manuel Noriega, as well as to respond with military forces to Iraqi President Saddam Hussein's intervention in Kuwait in August 1990, won him even greater approval. After the U.S. assault on Panama, President Bush's approval rating went up to 80 percent in January 1990, and after his decision on August 8, 1990, to send American forces to support Saudi Arabia against Saddam Hussein, his approval rating shot up again, reaching 77 percent in mid-August 1990.[83] After Congress gave its approval to use force in the Gulf against the Iraqis in January 1991, and as first the air war and then the ground war began, President Bush's popularity shot up once again. Indeed, his popularity reached about 90 percent by the time of the cease-fire in March 1991.[84] Dramatic and decisive foreign policy actions have often tended to rally support for the president, and thus President Bush was no exception.

President Clinton, too, experienced the same phenomenon of "rallying around the flag" by the American people over his Haitian actions during the fall of 1994. As the military government in Haiti was steadfast in its resistance to restoring the democratically elected government, the Clinton administration increasingly hinted that military action would be required and gained UN authorization to do so if necessary. Yet the American public was skeptical of such action, with only a little more than one-third supporting this option.[85] Overall approval "of the way Bill Clinton is handling the situation in Haiti" was equally low (27 percent) in early September 1994, and was only slightly higher (35 percent) on September 14, 1994, the day before President Clinton's nationwide address pledging to use American force to remove the military regime. After that speech, however, the poll results demonstrated the potency of presidential leadership. Clinton's approval for handling Haiti shot up to 53 percent and was still at 48 percent at the end of the month of September.[86]

After September 11, 2001, however, President George W. Bush experienced the greatest "rally effect" of any president in polling history. President Bush's approval rating soared from 51 percent just before September 11, 2001, to 86 percent approval shortly after that day. The "rally effect" of 35 points was the largest ever found by the Gallup polling organization. Within a matter of days, Bush's approval rating had reached 90 percent, a level at or surpassing his father's approval during the Gulf War.[87] Furthermore, during the four months after September 11, the President's average approval rating was 84 percent. By September 11, 2002, Bush's public support was still at 70 percent. By one analysis, this average level of public support for Bush during his first 18 months was 72 percent—the highest average of American president since Vietnam ant the third highest among post–World War II presidents.

While this long "rally effect" was unusual, Bush's support did eventually decline in 2003 prior to the Iraq War, then increased when the war broke out, and declined again as the reconstruction effort in Iraq proved challenging by the summer and fall of 2003. By the end of 2003, President Bush's level of support was at about 50 percent or just slightly above that level—virtually the same as pre–September 11.[88] In sum, then, the potency of the presidency as a shaper of foreign policy opinion continues, and it serves as an important restraint on the effectiveness of overall public sentiment in directing foreign policy making. Yet, the presidency is not all encompassing, as we shall show later in this chapter.

Gauging Public Opinion

Other difficulties also seemingly diminish the effectiveness of public opinion. Because the public's views are not always well developed or firmly held, question wording and even the terms used in public opinion polls can alter the public's view from survey to survey. As Rosenberg, Verba, and Converse hypothesized, the concepts used to describe American involvement in Vietnam could influence the level of public support or opposition to that war. If negative terms were used (such as "defeat" or "Communist takeover"), the public would likely be more defensive and hawkish in its response. If other negative terms were used ("the increase in killings" or "the continued costs of the war"), the public might respond in a more dovish or conciliatory manner.[89]

A study of the various public opinion polls regarding aid to the Nicaraguan Contras in the 1980s confirmed the effects of question wording. When the public was asked about funding these opposition forces and specific references were made to "President Reagan," to "the Contras," or to the "Marxist government" in Nicaragua, the level of support for Contra aid was generally higher among the American public than when such references were left out. By contrast, when references to the amount of money involved in supporting the Contras was mentioned, or when the question format was more "balanced" in treating the competing parties involved in the conflict, the level of public support was lower than in polls without such characteristics. While the overall effect of question wording on support or opposition to Contra aid was relatively modest, it did have a discernible effect.[90]

Similarly, the number of options presented to a respondent can also be important in affecting the result. One analysis of public attitudes on the SALT treaty in the 1970s illustrated how different question wording produced different policy implications. Two sets of polls (a Harris Poll and an NBC-AP Poll) asked only the questions of support or opposition to the SALT treaty; another set of polls (Roper) provided information on the treaty and provided more options. The latter found only about 40 percent support for SALT, while the former found between 67 and 77 percent approval.[91] The explanation for such disparity in the results was tied to the kind of options and information provided to the respondents. While question wording is always a possible source of error in gauging public opinion, it is a particularly crucial one when the public's views are not well developed or deeply held.

Survey results about American involvement in Bosnia in the 1990s also demonstrated the role of question wording and the number of options in affecting opinion results. After the December 1995 signing of the Dayton Accords, which supported the placing of a NATO implementation force (IFOR) in Bosnia (a force that would include about 20,000 American military personnel), the American public disapproved of the presence of U.S. troops in that country by a 54 percent to a 41 percent margin. Moreover, Gallup reported a greater degree of intensity among those who disapproved ("43% strongly disapprove") than among those who approved ("only 24% strongly approve"). Yet, when a more detailed question about this deployment was asked using three options and including a reference to the president in each, the results differed: Thirty-six percent continued to disapprove and opposed Clinton's actions, 33 percent opted for supporting the deployment and the president's decision, and 27 percent contended that the United States should not deploy troops, but the president's decision as commander in chief should be supported. By this breakdown, and in the words of one assessment, "60% of the public can be counted as at least weak supporters of U.S. involvement in Bosnia."[92] Such results contrast sharply with those when only the approve/disapprove dimensions were used, and when no explicit reference to the president was made.

In 2002 survey results asking the public whether they favor or oppose U.S. military action against Iraq, different options and different wording cues produced differing results. When the general question was asked (favor or oppose such action), 57 percent of the public favored military action against Iraq, and 38 percent opposed it. When the question wording was changed to ask the public's support or opposition "if the United Nations supports invading Iraq," the results were 79 percent favorable and only 19 percent opposed. Alternately, when the same question was asked with a different conditionality ("if the United States has to invade alone"), 59 percent of the public opposed U.S. military action, and 38 percent favored it—virtually a reversal of the answer given when the question was asked without any qualifiers.[93] While these differing responses by the public might be viewed as reflecting a sophisticated and informed public (as we will discuss in the next section), the differing results for differing question wording allow policy makers to select the polling results nearest to their intended policy actions and thus to be less constrained by the public's views.

In sum, in an environment of limited foreign policy knowledge and a variety of options, one may get different responses to the questions asked. Such results once again raise doubts about how much credence officials give to competing results and thus may erode the impact of public opinion on foreign policy.

Public Opinion and Fluctuating Moods

Gabriel Almond, an early pioneer in the analysis of public attitudes on foreign policy, has aptly summarized the portrait of American public opinion that we have sketched so far. The American public view is essentially a "mood" toward foreign affairs that lacks "intellectual structure and factual content." This mood is largely "superficial and fluctuating," "permissive," and subject to the elite leadership influence "if they [the policy makers] demonstrate unity and resolution."[94]

With these fluctuating and permissive moods, the role of public opinion as a shaper of foreign policy is surely diminished. While the public can exercise some impact during periods of crises or war, in general it is more apt to follow the direction of the leadership. Similarly, while the fluctuation in moods may not be as great as it once was, as Almond later acknowledged, public opinion is still largely unstable and unstructured. Consequently, and as Almond put it, public opinion "cannot be viewed as standing in the way of foreign policy decisions by American governmental leaders."[95]

The influential American journalist and student of public opinion Walter Lippmann took an equally dim view of the role of public opinion and foreign policy, but he saw it as far more dangerous than did Almond. As one analyst put it, Lippmann saw "the mass public as not merely uninterested and uninformed, but as a powerful force that was so out of synch with reality as to constitute a massive and potentially fatal threat to effective government and policies."[96] As Lippmann himself wrote, "The people have impressed a critical veto upon the judgments of informed and responsible officials. They have compelled the government, which usually knew what would have been wiser, or was necessary, or what was more expedient, to be late with too little, or too long with too much, too pacifist in peace and too bellicose in war. . . ."[97]

Some evidence by other scholars seems to allay Lippmann's fears.[98] One scholar, for example, found, as the earlier discussion implied, that the public's views were not consistent or "constrained." That is, an individual's views in one area did not correlate well with views in another. In other words, the American mass public seems to lack any underlying structures, at least with the 1950s and 1960s data. As a result, mass opinion, with such disparate and changeable views across individuals, could hardly serve as a restraining force on policy makers. A whole series of scholars, too, have questioned whether public opinion really affects foreign policy. Whether these analysts studied Congress or the executive, only the most tenuous link (or none at all) existed between opinion and policy. In short, in the perception of these early scholars, little compelling evidence could be summoned to suggest that public opinion mattered much in the conduct of foreign policy.

FOREIGN POLICY OPINION:
STRUCTURED AND STABLE

Recent research reaches a less pessimistic conclusion about public opinion and its role in the foreign policy process. In this view, even in the context of a relatively uninformed mass public and one that is susceptible to elite or presidential leadership, foreign policy attitudes of the American public are not as irrelevant to policy making as others might suggest. At least two interrelated reasons are offered to support this view: (1) the public's attitudes are more structured and stable than has often been assumed; (2) the public mood is more identifiable and less shiftable and potentially more constraining on policy makers' actions than is sometimes suggested.

The Structure of Foreign Policy Opinions

How is it possible that opinions can be structured and stable if, as we demonstrated earlier, knowledge and interest in foreign affairs are so relatively low among the American public? Political scientists Jon Hurwitz and Mark Peffley have begun to untangle this apparent anomaly. They have argued that individuals utilize information shortcuts to make political judgments and to relate preferences toward specific foreign policy issues from general attitudes. Thus, paradoxically, ordinary citizens can hold coherent attitude structures, even though they lack detailed knowledge about foreign policy. As they write:

> Individuals organize information because such organization helps to simplify the world. Thus, a paucity of information does not *impede* structure and consistency; on the contrary, it *motivates* the development and employment of structure. Thus, we see individuals as attempting to cope with an extraordinarily confusing world (with limited resources to pay information costs) by structuring views about specific foreign policies according to their more general and abstract beliefs.[99]

Research by political scientists Benjamin Page, Robert Shapiro, and Eugene Wittkopf has begun to demonstrate more fully the accuracy of this position. In extensive analyses of public opinion surveys from the 1930s to the 1980s, Shapiro and Page demonstrated that public opinion has changed relatively slowly over time. "When it has changed, it has done so by responding in rational ways to international and domestic events. . . ." In their view, public opinion does not tend to be "volatile or fluctuate wildly." Instead, they conclude that "collective opinion tends to be rather stable; it sometimes changes abruptly, but usually by only small amounts; and it rarely fluctuates."[100] In short, the public is markedly "rational" and stable in its foreign policy beliefs.

Through comprehensive analyses of Chicago Council on Foreign Relations surveys, Wittkopf determined the structure of American foreign policy opinion and demonstrated its stability over the past three decades.[101] His analyses reveal that the American people have not only been divided over *whether* the United States should be involved in foreign affairs (the traditional isolationism/internationalist dimension) but they also have been divided over *how* it should be involved (the cooperative/militant dimension). These divisions over America's foreign policy role, moreover, have remained remarkably consistent among the public over the years.

More specifically, the American public is divided along two continua: a continuum of *cooperative internationalism* and a continuum of *militant internationalism*. Where Americans fall on those continua are based upon attitudes and opinions "about how broad or narrow the range of U.S. foreign policy goals should be; about the particular countries in which the United States has vital interests; and about the use of force to protect others."[102] The intersection of those two continua produces four distinct belief systems and best describes the structure of American foreign policy opinion today. Figure 12.3 visually displays the structure of the belief systems across the four quadrants for the surveys from 1974 through 1994. (Wittkopf has also done the same kind of analysis for the 1998 Chicago Council data with generally the same kind of results as reported for these earlier surveys, but those results are not yet published.[103])

Wittkopf labeled the four segments of the public holding these belief systems as *internationalists, isolationists, accommodationists,* and *hard-liners*.[104] Internationalists are those individuals who support both cooperative and militant approaches to global affairs and are largely reflective of American attitudes prior to the Vietnam War. Both the unilateral use of American force and cooperative efforts through the United Nations would find support among this segment of the public. In the Persian Gulf War, for example, internationalists likely supported both UN efforts to resolve the conflict over Kuwait, and then the use of American and coalition forces to expel Iraq from Kuwait. In Bosnia, too, this segment would support American efforts at diplomatic resolution (e.g., through the Dayton Accords), but it would also back the deployment of American forces as part of a peacekeeping force.

Isolationists are those individuals who tend to reject both cooperative internationalism and militant internationalism and would favor a reduced role for the United States in global affairs. In the Gulf War, they would not have supported the use of force toward Iraq or even believed that a vital interest was at stake over the seizure of Kuwait. In Bosnia, isolationists would neither support American involvement nor would they believe that an American interest was at stake in that ethnic conflict.

Accommodationists are those individuals who favor cooperative internationalism but oppose militant internationalism. They would likely have supported the use of economic sanctions against Iraq over Kuwait, but they would not have supported the use of force. The same distinction toward American action in Bosnia would arise: support for the use of sanctions against Serbia and Bosnia, opposition to the use of force by the United States there.

Finally, and in contrast to accommodationists, hard-liners are those individuals who favor militant internationalism and oppose cooperative internationalism In the case of the Gulf War, hard-liners would likely have wanted to use force earlier against Iraq than would the other segments of the public and would prefer that option over the use of diplomacy. They would have preferred the same option in the case of Bosnia as well.

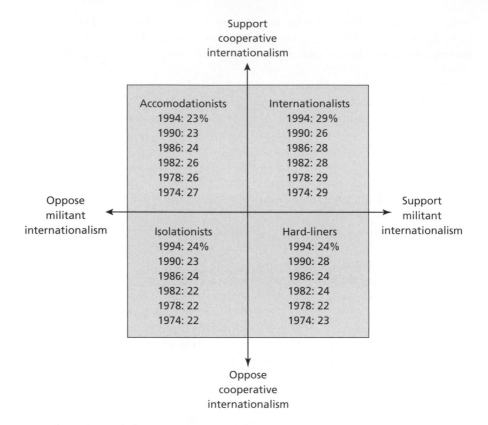

FIGURE 12.3 The Distribution of the Mass Public
among the Four Types of Foreign Policy Beliefs, 1974–1994

SOURCES: The source for the diagram and the data for the years 1974–1986 are from Eugene
R. Wittkopf, *Faces of Internationalist: Public Opinion and American Foreign Policy*, p. 26.
Copyright © 1990, Duke University Press. Reprinted by permission of the publisher. The more
recent data are drawn from Eugene R. Wittkopf, "Faces of Internationalism in a Transitional
Environment," *Journal of Conflict Resolution* 38 (September 1994); 383; and personal
communication with Eugene R. Wittkopf.

By Wittkopf's assessment, these segments are almost evenly divided among the
public.[105] As a result, the restraints upon American policy makers come from a
variety of directions. Internationalists, for example, constitute about 28 percent of
the public; isolationists about 23 percent; accommodationists 25 percent; and
hard-liners 24 percent.[106] These percentages, moreover, have remained remarkably stable from the initial survey in 1974 through the 1994 one, as Figure 12.3
also shows.

These underlying belief systems among the public are important for understanding the role of public opinion and foreign policy for several reasons. First,
they are highly predictive of what policy these segments of the public will support. Over 80 percent of internationalists and over 60 percent of accommoda-

tionists are supporters of U.S. participation in peacekeeping operations, while isolationists and hard-liners oppose such actions. Similarly, internationalists and accommodationists are strong supporters of continuing or increasing aid to Russia, while, once again, hard-liners and isolationists strongly oppose it. In contemplating another kind of action in Europe—the use of American troops to defend that region—internationalists and hard-liners are the strongest proponents of such action, while accommodationists and isolationists are the weakest. Similarly, an overwhelming majority of both internationalists and hard-liners are strongly supportive of coming to the aid of Japan if it were invaded, but only a minority of accommodationists and isolationists are. Indeed, these two coalitions are evident across a wide array of issues that have been examined.[107]

Second, the different foreign policy belief systems are closely tied to a number of other sociopolitical characteristics of the American public. As such, these foreign policy divisions are deeply ingrained within the American political landscape. In particular, the political ideology of an individual and his or her level of education are good predictors where that individual falls among these belief systems.[108] Political "liberals," for instance, tend to be accommodationists, political "conservatives" tend to be hard-liners, and political "moderates" tend to be internationalists. College-educated individuals tend to be both internationalists and accommodationists, those with a high school education tend to be both internationalists and hard-liners, and those with less than a high school education tend to be hard-liners. As Wittkopf's analysis of the 1994 survey reveals, however, those respondents who "describe themselves as either very conservative or very liberal both reveal strong isolationist tendencies—the only political groups that do."[109]

The patterns of these belief systems are less clear-cut by region and party. The East is, by and large, composed of those individuals who are accommodationists; the Midwest and West fluctuate among three belief systems—the accommodationist, internationalist, and hard-liner categories—during the four earlier surveys; and the South varies between the hard-liner and internationalist camp over these analyses. Most interestingly, though, these belief systems are not closely tied to partisanship. While there was some tendency for those possessing hard-line or internationalist belief systems to be Republicans and those possessing accommodationist and internationalist belief systems to be Democrats, the differences among these belief systems were sufficiently blurred across the parties to make accurate predictions quite difficult.

Third, because these divisions exist within the public and have been consistent over time, the leadership is now more constrained than some might argue. Foreign policy decision makers must now gauge which groups will support or oppose particular foreign policy actions and must calculate the acceptable limits of their foreign policy actions. In any earlier era, if previous research findings were accurate portrayals of the public, the president, for example, did not have to make such calculations; instead, he could rather routinely count on public support. With these persistent divisions, though, that possibility is less assured. In this sense, this kind of structure and consistency in belief, far from freeing the foreign policy leaders to pursue their own course, may actually constrain the actions of various administrations.

Unfortunately, the 2002 Chicago Council survey results are not susceptible to the same analysis since the appropriate questions were not contained in that survey instrument.[110] Yet there is reason to believe that the same underlying processes are still at work—at least as the events of September 11 recede somewhat. Public support for a vigorous U.S. response to these events cut all four belief systems—except perhaps isolationists—in the days after September 11. More recently, and especially in light of the aftermath of the Iraq War, divisions between the so-called unilateralists and multilateralists over the proper direction for the American foreign policy incorporate the competing public belief systems outlined above. Support for the unilateralist position appears to be drawn from hard-liners and internationalists, while support for multilateralists appears to be drawn from accommodationists and to a lesser extent from internationalists. In this sense, the public divisions over the direction of American foreign policy seem to be continuing in the post–September 11 and the post-Iraq world.

AN ALTERNATIVE VIEW
OF THE PUBLIC MOOD

If we can take this initial conclusion about the public's restraints on policy makers one step further, we can begin to suggest a somewhat larger role for the "public mood" in the policy process as well. Two political scientists, Bernard Cohen and V. O. Key, writing shortly after Almond's initial work on the public "mood" and foreign policy, suggest as much with their concepts of "climate of opinion" and the "context of public opinion."

Bernard Cohen introduced the concept of "climate of opinion" to summarize the public's view on foreign policy actions. This notion refers to the foreign policy decision-making environment which, "by creating in the policymaker an impression of a public attitude or attitudes, or by becoming part of the environment and cultural milieu that help to shape his own thinking, may consciously affect his official behavior."[111] A few years later, V. O. Key expanded upon this notion by introducing what he called the "context of public opinion." This notion suggests how the public's overall views can affect governmental action, including the foreign policy arena. Key's description of this concept and how it operates is worth quoting at some length:

> That context is not a rigid matrix that fixes a precise form for government action. Nor is it unchangeable. It consists of opinion irregularly distributed among the people and of varying intensity, of attitudes of differing convertibility into votes, and of sentiments not always readily capable of appraisal. Yet that context, as it is perceived by those responsible for action, conditions many of the acts of those who must make what we may call "opinion-related decisions." The opinion context may affect the substance of action, the form of action, or the manner of action.[112]

These alternate views of the "public mood" suggest that the foreign policy opinions of the American people form a part of the political milieu—even in the foreign policy realm. In this way, foreign policy opinion might be thought of as setting the broad outlines of "acceptable" policy without necessarily dictating the day-to-day policy choices of decision makers. Thus, gauging the public mood, and acting within the constraints of that mood, becomes an important task for successful policy makers. A brief survey of the recent public moods or climates of opinion, gleaned from several sources, will illustrate their relationship to, and impact on, American foreign policy. Keep in mind, however, that policy makers will also try to alter or adjust that public mood to their liking, much as Almond and others have suggested.

The Cold War Mood During the height of the Soviet-American Cold War period, for instance, the public expressed strong support for an active American role in global affairs. The level of support for global involvement was also quite predictive of public commitments to the Marshall Plan, NATO, and a willingness to stop communism through military action. In fact, after examining a number of public opinion polls for the late 1940s through the early 1960s, political scientist William Caspary concluded that the American public demonstrated a "*strong* and *stable* 'permissive mood' toward international involvements."[113] Further, another analyst saw the Cold War period as one in which "policymakers became imprisoned by popular anticommunism even though, in most cases, the policymakers were too sophisticated really to share the popular perspective."[114] Thus the values of the postwar consensus (see Chapters 2 and 3) were firmly embedded in the public and policy makers alike and largely shaped the policy choices.

The "Vietnam Syndrome" The "searing effects" of the Vietnam War on the beliefs of the American public toward international affairs have been widely analyzed.[115] In the immediate post-Vietnam period, for instance, there was a decided turn inward on several important dimensions of foreign and military involvement. In late 1974, roughly one-third of the American public favored a cutback in the defense budget, and over 50 percent believed that "we should build up our own defenses and let the world take care of itself."[116] In addition, there was considerable public aversion to sending U.S. troops to support friendly nations that were attacked or even to sending military and economic aid to such states. Only in the case of an attack upon Canada did a majority of the public (77 percent) support American military involvement. Attacks upon Western Europe or upon Israel gained support from only 39 percent of the public in the case of the former region and only 27 percent in the case of the latter state. Support for using military and economic aid to help friendly countries that were attacked was equally low. Only 37 percent of the public supported the American government's using these tactics. Finally, the American public also favored a cutback in military aid and opposed CIA political operations, presumably because each of these areas further involved the United States abroad.

While the public mood tended to reject an active military and political involvement in international affairs in the immediate post-Vietnam period, this view should not imply an abandonment of an "active role" for the United States in world affairs. In fact, 66 percent of the public still supported a continued global role for the United States, but this global role was to take a different form than that prescribed by the Cold War consensus. When asked to rank the importance of a variety of different goals for the United States, the public placed greatest importance on such aims as keeping the peace and promoting and defending America's security. Next, however, the public indicated that the United States should concentrate on a large number of domestic and global economic problems—such as securing adequate energy supplies, protecting American jobs, and solving global food, inflation, and energy problems. Most important, perhaps, the traditional goals of the Cold War period, such as containing communism, defending allies, and helping to spread democracy and capitalism abroad, were ranked relatively low by the public. In the words of one analyst at that time: "The cold war sense of urgent threat is gone from America's political consciousness."[117]

This mood, moreover, did seem to have a dampening effect on the actions of both the Ford and Carter administrations. The ability to use force and to intervene globally was sharply reduced. The Ford administration, for example, was unable to win any public (or congressional) support for last-minute aid to South Vietnam and Cambodia prior to their collapse in 1975. Nor was President Ford about to muster support for vigorous action on behalf of the National Front for the Liberation of Angola in their struggle with the Soviet-backed Popular Movement for the Liberation of Angola. An exception, however, was the popular response to the swift military action ordered by President Ford over the seizure of the American merchant vessel the *Mayaguez* by Cambodia in May 1975.

In the context of this foreign policy mood, the appeal of a Jimmy Carter presidential candidacy is quite understandable. With Carter's call for an emphasis upon global issues, downplaying of the East–West dispute, and calling for universal human rights, his candidacy was well within the limits of the public mood in the middle 1970s. In essence, the popular mood, summarized under the heading of the "Vietnam syndrome," was in place among the American public and was generally respected by the political leadership.

The "Self-Interest" Mood[118]   The public mood changed somewhat, however, by the late 1970s, especially as the relationship between the United States and the Soviet Union began to deteriorate during the second and third years of the Carter administration. Moreover, there was an increased perception of threat from the Soviet Union among the American public. By one analysis, concern with the power of the Soviet Union had replaced Vietnam as the "central preoccupation of American foreign policy."[119] As a result, the public mood began to move away, albeit slowly, from the limits of the "Vietnam syndrome."

In this context, the public was now more willing to increase defense expenditures, support American military actions abroad, and tolerate CIA activities in other nations.[120] Thirty-two percent of the public now said that the United States spent too little on defense (as compared to 13 percent in 1974) and only 16 percent said that the United States spent too much (as compared to 32 percent in 1974). A majority of the public now supported sending troops if Panama closed access to the Canal or if the Soviets invaded Western Europe. Furthermore, a plurality (48 percent of the public) favored the use of American troops if West Berlin were attacked, and 42 percent favored a U.S. response to a Soviet invasion of Japan. The public was now also more supportive of allowing the CIA to work inside other countries to support American interests. In 1978, 59 percent of the public supported such actions, compared to only 43 percent in 1974. While this interventionist sentiment still had its limits, it had increased from the 1974 period.[121]

At the same time, there was a certain amount of ambivalence about any rekindling of past crusading efforts on the part of the United States. Although some Cold War goals (such as protecting allies and containing communism) had increased in importance as foreign policy preferences from their 1974 levels, the domestic and foreign economic concerns remained most important for the American public (such as "keeping up the value of the dollar," "securing adequate supplies of energy," and "protecting the jobs of American workers").[122]

This ambivalence was especially demonstrated in the mixed reaction to the Soviet Union. Although 56 percent of the public believed that the United States was "falling behind the Soviet Union in power and influence," the public remained committed to greater cooperation in joint energy efforts, joint scholarly exchanges, and pursuing arms limitations.[123] In short, sentiment for maintaining detente seemed still in place, especially among the attentive public.[124]

In sum, then, by the late 1970s, the public mood was for a more "self-interested" and nationalistic foreign policy than in 1974, but one that continued to maintain elements of economic and political cooperation with other nations. Furthermore, the public continued to be "wary of direct involvement that characterized United States policy in the 1960s," but they still remained determined to defend important commitments in the world.[125] In this context, the success of the Reagan candidacy is explainable, especially as President Jimmy Carter was increasingly perceived as incapable of dealing effectively with foreign policy matters.

The Public Mood in the 1980s   The public mood in the 1980s changed little from that of the late 1970s. Yet the Reagan administration adopted some policies that were at variance with the public mood. In this situation, it is important to evaluate the ultimate effect of the public mood.

The foreign policy goals, as expressed by the public in two national polls conducted in late 1982 and late 1986, remained essentially the same as in 1978.[126] Global and domestic economic concerns continued to have the highest priority, while containing communism and defending allies retained their somewhat lower ranking. At the same time, the public expressed a slight increase in the level of support for interventionism than they did in the late 1970s. For instance, the public supported sending U.S. troops to Western Europe and Japan if they were attacked. No other country or region received over 45 percent approval for such action, but one-third of the public favored using U.S. troops "if the Arabs cut off oil shipments to the U.S. or if Arab forces invade Israel."[127] The public thus seemed to be selective in choosing between vital and secondary interests that were necessary to protect. There was, for example, substantial opposition to sending American troops into El Salvador if the leftists were succeeding or into Taiwan if China invaded.[128]

On the question of the Soviet Union in 1982 and 1986, the public remained ambivalent, much as they had in 1978. While the Soviet Union ranked the lowest or second lowest of any nation (after Iran) when the public was asked to rank states on a "thermometer scale," the public remained committed to seeking better ties with the USSR: Seventy-seven percent (in 1982) and 82 percent (in 1986) favored arms control agreements, 64 percent in 1982 favored undertaking joint energy projects with the Soviets, and 70 percent (in 1982) and 76 percent (in 1986) favored the resumption of cultural and educational exchanges.[129]

As previously indicated, such a public mood generally clashed with the priorities of the Reagan administration, especially during its first term.[130] While President Reagan brought back some of the rhetoric and policies of the Cold War consensus, the public mood opposed several of these foreign policy priorities. The Reagan administration wanted to increase defense spending and engage in a defense buildup; the public was now content to keep the budget as it was and to seek arms control agreements instead. The Reagan administration wanted to engage in a more confrontational policy toward the Soviet Union; the public wanted to seek more cooperative exchanges with that nation. The Reagan administration wanted to increase military assistance; the public continued to oppose such aid by a wide margin.

Such disagreements between the public mood and public policy undoubtedly put some strain on what the Reagan administration could do in its foreign policy. In this sense, these disagreements contributed to a political climate that ultimately facilitated accommodation with the Soviet Union, on the one hand, and served as a restraint on the extent of the policy course pursued toward Nicaragua, on the other.

The Public Mood in the 1990s With the repercussions from the dramatic events during 1989 through 1991—the fall of the Berlin Wall, the emergence of democracy in Eastern Europe, the unification of Germany, the Iraqi invasion of Kuwait, and the collapse of the Soviet Union—the public mood evolved to one described as "pragmatic internationalism" and later as "guarded engagement."[131] While about two-thirds of citizens remained committed to an active role for the United States in global affairs, the public continued to be more concerned about domestic economic and social problems than foreign policy ones and appeared less willing to intervene in the affairs of other states. While the American public did not reject global leadership, it sought a greater sharing of that responsibility with multilateral organizations and wanted the United States to be more selective in the actions it took abroad.

Perhaps a better indicator of the public's mood toward international affairs during this period was where individuals believed that American interests lay. Interestingly, Russia held an important place after the Cold War, although the public still viewed that country with an admixture of friendliness and wariness. Russia was viewed as more friendly and in a more favorable light than in the past.

Indeed, it was tied for sixth place at 54 degrees (with Israel and Brazil) out of 23 countries on a "thermometer" ranking of friendliness ranging from 0 to 100 degrees in 1994, although it fell to 49 degrees by the time of the 1998 survey. In this sense, Russia was surpassed only by Canada, Great Britain, Italy, Germany, Mexico, and France in terms of friendliness.[132] Even as the public expressed these views, however, a substantial majority of the American public (81 percent in 1994) believed "that the military power of Russia represents either a critical or an important possible threat to the vital interests of the United States in the next 10 years."[133]

In other ways, though, the post–Cold War era evoked some different priorities among the public. In 1994, the public ranked Japan, Saudi Arabia, Kuwait, and Mexico as vital interests. While Japan remained an important ally in a region of increasing problems, its economic competitiveness also continued to be a concern.[134] Saudi Arabia and Kuwait ranked as vital interests owing to their vast supply of oil, their proximity to troublesome states in the Middle East—Iran and Iraq—and questions about their domestic political stability. Mexico also emerged as a vital interest for the United States. Not only does that country border on the United States, but, with the North American Free Trade Agreement now in effect, the fortunes of the two countries were linked as never before. By mid-decade, too, China emerged as one of the vital interests of the United States. Almost three-fifths of the public viewed China's emergence as a world power as a "critical" threat to the United States, and two-thirds of the public believed that China's role in 10 years would be greater than it was in 1994.[135] By the end of the decade, Great Britain, Germany, Russia, Japan, Israel, and China, among a few others, were viewed as being in the vital interest of the United States, with Europe generally more crucial than Asia.

Despite identifying some new states as vital foreign policy interests, several traditional security concerns continued, and the public remained cautious about American interventions abroad. Indeed, on defense spending, the public's views stabilized with general support for increasing or maintaining spending in this area.[136] The same held for views toward the NATO commitment. In addition, the public continued its commitment to multilateral engagements in efforts abroad and look warily on the use of force. In fact, in the 1998 Chicago Council survey, when the public was asked to consider a series of hypothetical cases where American forces might be used, in no instance did a majority of the public favor such an option. Interestingly, and importantly, though, a majority of the public expressed support for a range of options to address international terrorism, from pursuing diplomatic means to closing terrorist camps to using military air strikes against such facilities. Moreover, a majority of Americans supported "assassination of individual terrorist leaders" to combat international terrorism. In short, the public remained cautious and selective about where it would support the use of American military force abroad, but, and perhaps foreshadowing the post–September 11 period, supported vigorous actions against international terrorism.

In sum, the overall portrait of the public mood during the immediate post–Cold War period suggested a continued, but limited, role for the United States in foreign affairs, with new actors and issues replacing the long-dominant

Cold War focus. The rise of a more powerful China, both economically and militarily, or the ethnic conflicts rife in Bosnia, Somalia, and Rwanda, for example, were now the kind of concerns dominating the foreign policy agenda. At the same time, new threats (e.g., the spread of nuclear weapons, terrorism, and drug trafficking) as well as the expanding global economic competition, continued to share the attention and priorities of the American public.

The Post–September 11 Mood[137] After September 11, public attitudes seemed to have shifted in several significant ways from the post–Cold War mood to one that has been described as "refocused internationalism." That internationalism now "refocused on containing and defeating the international threat." It took on several different dimensions from only a few years earlier, but it also maintained some continuity as well.

First of all, the public's commitment to internationalism was at a higher level than was evidenced in recent decades. Seventy-one percent of the public were now committed to an "active role in world affairs" for the United States. Second, international terrorism now ranked as the "biggest problem facing the country," and the public was now willing to support a variety of actions to combat this threat. Third, the public continued to place a "very high priority" on domestic economic issues and on particular "regional conflicts, the global environment, and world hunger." In this sense, while the security issues became more important than economic and social issues, the latter were not abandoned in addressing the new international threat environment.

An important change in public attitudes in this new environment was the increased level of public support for the use of American military power. Very large majorities of the public (about 80 to 90 percent) now favored military air strikes and the use of ground troops against terrorist camps. Majorities of the public, too, favored the use of American troops to aid friendly countries fighting terrorism (e.g., the Philippines) and countries faced with radical Islamic uprisings (e.g., Pakistan). In addition, there were now strong majorities among the American public that favored the United States taking part in a variety of peacekeeping operations around the world. Furthermore, the American public generally favored the maintenance of military bases in a wide array of countries around the world, and a sizeable minority (44 percent) now favored increasing defense expenditures—a notable increase from the pre–September 11 view.

While the American public was now more willing to support a more activist and militant approach to the international system, the public also supported some limitations on American actions abroad. For instance, the public remained committed to a multilateral approach to dealing with global issues and largely opposed (62 percent of the public) the United States acting as the "world policeman." Instead, most Americans (roughly about two-thirds of the public) supported a multilateral approach to international crises, including actions toward Iraq. Moreover, when several different scenarios about American interventions to address security challenges were proposed to the public, support for these scenarios were systematically higher when multilateral efforts were mentioned.

The American public also remained supportive of international institutions, international agreements, and diplomatic measures in the post–September 11 environment. For example, the public continued to be supportive of regional (e.g., NATO, European Union) and international (e.g., the United Nations, the World Trade Organization) institutions. The public also backed several important international initiatives over the past decades that the United States has not embraced: a complete ban on the testing of nuclear weapons, a ban on the use of land mines, the creation of the International Criminal Court, and the Kyoto Treaty to combat global warming. Finally, and importantly, even as the public supported more militant efforts to combat terrorism, it offered strong support for diplomatic efforts to address this problem.

Toward the global economy, the public's attitudes changed only slightly after September 11. The American people were now slightly less threatened by competition from other countries (e.g., Japan) and regions (e.g., the European Union), but they continued to view globalization warily. The same ambivalence permeated public attitudes toward immigration, free trade, and foreign aid. The American public couched support for free trade, for example, with calls for aiding displaced workers or for foreign assistance when it was linked to humanitarian purposes.

Finally, the focus of American vital interests abroad has increasingly turned to traditional allies and friends, such as European nations, but it has also been directed toward those countries that are tied to addressing international terrorism, such as Afghanistan, Saudi Arabia, Pakistan, Iran, and Egypt. While the former trend has begun to emerge in the post–Cold War years, the latter is obviously a manifestation of the impact of September 11. Another important impact of September 11 was increased public attention to the Israeli-Palestinian and the India–Pakistan conflicts.

In all, then, the public mood after September 11 revealed elements of continuity and change. The public was now more supportive of a militant approach to international affairs—with a clear focus on international terrorism—but it remained committed to multilateral and diplomatic solutions to international issues as well.

Some Evidence of Stability and Consistency in Public Opinion

Although the public mood can change over time and seems to do so in reasonable and predictable ways, several researchers have found that American foreign policy opinion remains equally "coherent," "consistent," and "stable" when considering several salient issues. As we discussed earlier, Shapiro and Page are leading proponents of this view of public opinion, and their work is worth citing in some detail.

In an important analysis, for example, these scholars report that, "the proportions of Americans thinking the United States should sell arms varied markedly from one country to another" from 1975 to 1985, yet they also contend that this variation always occurred in a coherent way.[138] While some countries (e.g., England and West Germany) received more support from the public for such sales than other countries (e.g., Greece, Turkey, and Iran), the patterns were markedly the same or consistent across the years. A similar consistency occurred regarding aid to El Salvador during the early to mid-1980s. The public consistently supported sending military advisors and assisting with training for the Salvadorian troops, but just as consistently opposed the introduction of American troops, over a series of surveys. Support and opposition for foreign aid generally, the building of the MX missile in the 1980s, free trade, and other foreign policy issues exhibit the same stability over differing time periods. Thus Shapiro and Page conclude: "Stability is the rule for foreign as well as domestic issues. When opinion changes do occur, many do so quite gradually. . . ."[139] In addition, they add that the public—even in the face of new information and new global conditions—"are regular, predictable, and generally sensible" in their opinions."[140]

In another context, political scientist Bruce Jentleson also illustrates the consistency and stability of public opinion on a highly salient issue—the use of American military force abroad. In a detailed analysis of public opinion polls on nine different uses of American force in the 1980s and early 1990s (including the Persian Gulf War of 1990 and 1991), Jentleson finds that public support or opposition is closely tied to the *"principal policy objective"* for using force. In instances of *"foreign policy restraint"*—the use of force to stop "aggressive actions against the United States or its interests"—public support is generally always higher than for instances of seeking *"internal political change"*—the use of force to support a friendly government in power or trying to overthrow an unfriendly regime. While those findings in themselves are of interest, the important implication for public opinion and foreign policy is that the public is not always swayed by presidential leadership and that the public is not "as boorish, overreactive, and generally the bane of those who would pursue an effective foreign policy." Instead, as Jentleson says, the public is "pretty prudent" and, we might add, pretty consistent in its foreign policy beliefs.[141]

Two other studies largely support Jentleson's main conclusion about the stability of public opinion. One study extends Jentleson's analysis back in time to include the entire Cold War period and also introduces a number of other factors that may account for his earlier results. Contrary to Jentleson's position that the consistency in public support or opposition was only a recent phenomenon, Oneal and his colleagues find that "Jentleson . . . is correct in believing that the American people discriminate among foreign policy objectives in evaluating the use of force" and have done so throughout the Cold War years.[142] Put differently, the "pretty prudent" public is not a recent phenomenon.

Another study by Andrew Kohut and Robert Toth focused exclusively on the early to mid-1990s, including the Gulf War, Somalia, and Bosnia, and generally found that public opinion on the use of force was consistent as well. In particular, they report that the American public was willing to use force in only two situations: "[I]f it feels America's vital interests are at stake, and if American military force can provide humanitarian assistance without becoming engaged in a protracted conflict."[143] Once again, their analysis suggests that the policy objective is crucial (albeit a bit broader than what Jentleson found) in affecting the level of support and that the public does not blindly follow its leaders in any use of force (e.g., the expansion of the American involvement in Somalia in 1993). At the same time, they do point out that the ability of leaders (e.g., President George H. W. Bush over the Persian Gulf) to explain their objectives to the American people was important in gaining support.[144] On balance, and in line with a more optimistic view of public opinion, support for the use of force was arrayed in consistent ways in these episodes.

A final example of the public's stability and consistency in its foreign policy opinion, even in the face of changing international events, is its continuous support for multilateralism in the use of force and in addressing global problems. As Page and Barabas report, the public has had a long history of supporting the United Nations at a much higher percentage than American policy makers since the inception of the quadrennial surveys conducted by the Chicago Council on Foreign Relations in 1974 and right through to the one in 1998. What is interesting to note, however, is the continued support for multilateralism after September 11 in which 71 percent of the public preferred that the United States "share in efforts to solve international problems together with other countries." In addition, the majority of the public (65 percent in 2002) also supported invading Iraq "with UN approval and the support of its allies."[145] This kind of consistency remained despite sustained discussions of the United States acting alone if necessary.

THE IMPACT OF PUBLIC OPINION ON FOREIGN POLICY

One of the most difficult analytic tasks is to assess the overall effect of public opinion on foreign policy. Even if public opinion can be characterized as structured and stable, as we have suggested, a fundamental question remains: How much difference does public opinion really make in the foreign policy process? Are congressional and presidential elections mechanisms of popular control on foreign policy issues? Is Congress or the president really constrained in policy choices by what the public thinks? Some recent analyses provide partial answers to these questions, but the questions also remain important subjects of debate.

Foreign Policy Opinion and Presidential Elections

One way for public opinion to register an impact on foreign policy is through the electoral process, and especially through presidential elections every four years. In this way, the electorate can use their votes to punish political candidates with unpopular foreign policy views and reward those with whom they agree. Yet numerous analyses have raised doubts about whether presidential elections are really referenda on foreign policy.

First, for example, presidential elections are rarely fought on foreign policy issues. Instead, domestic issues, and especially domestic economic issues, have dominated American presidential campaigns in the post–World War II years. By most assessments, only in the 1952 and 1972 presidential elections was foreign policy a central campaign issue between the candidates. Both of these elections, however, occurred in very special circumstances—during U.S. involvement in two highly unpopular wars, Korea and Vietnam.

Second, even when foreign policy might be an issue in a presidential election, the stances of the candidates are not sufficiently different from one another for the public to distinguish between them. In the 1968 presidential campaign, for example, the Vietnam War was an issue, but the two candidates, Richard Nixon and Hubert Humphrey, were not perceived to be markedly different from one another in their positions on the war.[146] As a result, foreign policy did not turn out to be decisive in how the public voted in that campaign.

Third, even if the public viewed foreign policy as salient, its overall effect on the election outcome is viewed as quite small. In a classic analysis on this point, Warren Miller reports that the decline in support for the Republican candidate from the 1956 to the 1960 election based upon their respective foreign policy stances was minuscule—one half of 1 percent. Instead of the Republicans having a 2.5 percent vote advantage because of their foreign policy position in 1956, the advantage fell to 2 percent in the 1960 election.[147] Two decades later, in the 1980 contest between Jimmy Carter and Ronald Reagan, a similar small effect was reported. Despite the popular impression that the impact of the Iran hostage situation would severely hurt Carter's reelection prospects, a careful analysis of voting behavior in that election found otherwise. Ronald Reagan's issue position on foreign and domestic matters produced only about a 1 percent difference in the vote outcome. Instead, the voters' decisions were more fully related to the overall dissatisfaction with President Carter's performance in office and with doubts "about his competence as a political leader."[148]

Left unanswered by these and similar analyses, however, is whether even these small differences between the candidates in the aggregate did not affect the outcome in particular states, and hence the electoral votes of one presidential candidate over another. Especially in a close national election, such as the 1960 election between Kennedy and Nixon, in which less than one percentage point separated the candidates, foreign policy opinion may have mattered. More recently, of course, the 2000 presidential election results, especially in some key states such as Florida, foreign policy stances may have mattered. Put more precisely, in close state votes during presidential elections, a swing of even a few percentage points could dramatically affect the national electoral vote count. To date, however, detailed state studies of presidential elections are not available to answer such questions.

Also left unanswered by these analyses is whether the activities in the foreign policy arena by incumbents contribute to creating an image of competence or incompetence that can also affect the outcome of elections. While specific foreign policy opinion may not be a central factor in voting decisions, presidential actions can convey a general impression of effectiveness in the global arena. On the face of it, this description seems to fit what happened in 1980, when President Carter's inability to manage foreign affairs probably hurt him at the polling booth with the public. In this (albeit indirect) way, foreign policy mattered. Conversely, President Clinton seemingly sought to be "Peacemaker in Chief" with his actions in Haiti, Bosnia, and Northern Ireland. By taking these actions, according to one analysis, the "president hopes to do well with voters by doing good on the international stage."[149] Similarly, the presidential election of 2004 surely revolved in part on the ability of the candidates to deal with global security in the face of international terrorism.[150] At the same time, too much emphasis by an incumbent president on foreign affairs may also have an effect electorally. In 1992, the perceived excessive attention by President Bush on foreign affairs, and his perceived inattention to domestic policy, proved costly among voters.

Finally, at least two recent studies have begun to reconceptualize the relationship between foreign policy opinion and presidential elections. One analysis suggests that when candidate differences are large and foreign policy issues are salient, the public's views do affect the election outcomes. These conditions existed not only in 1952 and 1972, as has been noted, but they also were prevalent in the 1964, 1980, and 1984 presidential elections.[151] In such circumstances, public opinion on foreign policy matters probably made a difference in the election outcomes. Voters could see differences between the candidates, and these differences influenced voting decisions.

Another analysis by Miroslav Nincic argues that foreign policy matters, both directly and indirectly in presidential elections. Directly, foreign policy matters because about 10 percent of the public identified "foreign affairs" as the most important issue in their voting decisions in two recent elections (1988 and 2000). Indirectly, as suggested earlier, a candidate's stance on foreign affairs "can create an impression of leadership, decisiveness, and forcefulness" to the American people. In this way, the public's view of a candidate or his/her party may well be impacted.[152]

Foreign Policy Opinion and Congressional Elections

To an even greater degree than presidential elections, congressional elections are rarely depicted as referenda on foreign policy questions. Elections for the House of Representatives, in particular, are hardly ever fought on foreign policy questions. Foreign policy questions in U.S. Senate races are only occasionally salient. In both instances, the foreign policy positions of candidates are likely to be marginal to their campaigns.

Still, foreign policy may play a role in these elections in some negative and positive ways. On the one hand, if an incumbent is perceived as too involved in foreign affairs or spends too much time on foreign policy matters, he or she could be subject to electoral punishment by the public for neglecting the "folks back home." On the other hand, congressional candidates are often sure to be on the "right" side of particular issues related to foreign affairs in order to foreclose electoral punishment. Candidates from districts or states with substantial military spending are unlikely to oppose such activities; candidates with large Jewish constituencies are likely to be very supportive of Israel; and candidates from south Florida districts, for example, are likely to be strongly opposed to any compromise policy with Cuba's Fidel Castro. It is perhaps no accident that a Democratic congressman and later senator from New Jersey in the 1990s was a leading proponent of a tougher policy toward Cuba, especially with a large Hispanic population in that state. On occasion then, a congressional candidate's foreign policy position may have considerable substantive impact, especially on a vocal and politically active minority within a member's district or state.

On occasion, too, foreign policy issues may take on an important *symbolic* importance in congressional races, even if their substantive importance is less clear. An illustration from a special congressional election in Oklahoma in May 1994 makes this point, but the congressional elections in November 2002 also offer some support for this position.[153] The Democratic candidate in the 1994 race allowed as how he did not object to placing American troops under a UN commander in a peacekeeping operation. While it is unclear how important or salient this issue really was to Oklahoma congressional voters (although large percentages, when asked, said they opposed this position), the Republican candidate seized upon his opponent's stance to portray him as out of touch with Oklahomans. Indeed, the Republican candidate used a mailing to district voters outlining his opponent's position on the potential UN action and was able to spark interest and concern among some voters who responded. Based upon polling data, he was able to target a particularly sensitive group (in this case, young Republicans) to stimulate its support over this foreign policy issue. In this way, a congressional candidate was able to have a foreign policy issue assume much greater importance than its substance implied, and he was able to paint his opponent as too closely tied to Washington and the Clinton administration, and not sufficiently tied to Oklahoma voters. In this sense, foreign policy opinion may matter to congressional candidates, although in a slightly different, and more irregular way than we might expect.

In the 2002 congressional elections, security matters were at least partially on the minds of the American voters,[154] and President Bush sought to take advantage of this sentiment by campaigning in key congressional districts and key states to seek to maintain his party's control of the U.S. House of Representatives and to regain control of the U.S. Senate. In fact, he succeeded in doing so. Part of the explanation for this success by some analysts was his campaigning on national security issues in closely contested states and districts.

Foreign Policy Opinion and Policy Choices

If it is difficult to argue that elections are regular referenda on foreign policy opinion, it is perhaps even more difficult to sustain the view that foreign policy opinion matters for particular policy choices. Only in rare instances, when the public has been mobilized, for example, by the president with a nationwide television address or by some interest groups over an upcoming vote in Congress, does public opinion seem to matter over an immediate foreign policy decision facing the country. In this sense, the effect of public opinion on individual policy decisions appears to be sporadic and exceptional.

Over the last three decades, we have witnessed examples of just these kinds of sporadic events, although the public's success level in controlling the outcomes has been mixed. In the late 1970s, public opinion, as expressed in various polls, was strongly opposed to the treaties calling for the transference of the Panama Canal back to the country of Panama by the year 2000. As a result, President Carter had a very difficult time gaining Senate approval. Despite his initial opposition to any changes in the treaties, he had to accept several understandings and amendments to make them more acceptable at home. Further, President Carter was forced to lobby hard for their passage with members of the U.S. Senate. Only then was he able to squeak out the required two-thirds majority, 68–32. While public opinion did not ultimately stop these treaties, it affected the nature of the debate and their final provisions.

President Reagan had a similar experience over the issue of aid to the Nicaraguan Contras. He went on nationwide television several times to appeal for public support for his position. In this case, though, he was not always successful in obtaining increased support for the Contras. Indeed, in the aggregate, public opinion remained opposed, and Congress generally gave him much less than he wanted. In this particular case, then, public opinion, more than in the Panama Canal debate, ultimately contributed to a change in policy course by the Reagan administration and later by the Bush administration.

More recently, two studies examining a series of cases over several decades came to differing conclusions about the overall effect of public opinion on foreign policy. In an examination of American policy toward Vietnam in the 1960s and 1970s, toward Nicaragua in the 1980s, and toward the Gulf War and Bosnia in the 1990s, Richard Sobel concluded that "public opinion has constrained the U.S. foreign policy decision-making process over the last generation."[155] That effect has often been manifested more in policy restraint (i.e., eliminating policy option for decision makers) than in policy setting (i.e., prescribing the precise policy options). Furthermore, Sobel argues that public opinion is now playing an "increasing role . . . in foreign policymaking."

Douglas Foyle examines a longer time frame and more cases than Sobel, extending from Truman through Clinton.[156] He offers a more cautious conclusion than Sobel, although public opinion may still contribute to the policy process. He concludes that "the public's influence can be generally described as no-impact or constraint during crises and elite efforts to lead public opinion on longer-term decisions." Ultimately, though, the impact of public opinion is a function of the policy makers' belief system and the particular policy context. That is, how receptive policy makers are to public opinion and how the decision setting allows the public to affect policy. Among recent presidents, for example, President Clinton was receptive to public opinion and that opinion in turn affected his policy response to Somalia and Bosnia, while President Reagan tended to reject the importance of looking toward public opinion or responding to it.

Other systematic studies provide some promising results on the relative effectiveness of public opinion in shaping specific foreign policy decisions. These studies have analyzed long-term trends in the relationship for particular issues (e.g., defense spending and arms control), and assessed the receptivity of foreign policy makers to public opinion. On balance, the results suggest that public opinion (or the public mood) does serve as a guide to policy direction in the foreign policy area, although not as a guide to every individual foreign policy decision.

Political scientists Benjamin Page and Robert Shapiro, to whom we referred earlier, provide important results on the long-term trends in this relationship. In their massive analysis of the directional changes in public opinion and public policy over five decades (1935 to 1979), they sought to answer a central question: When public opinion moved in one direction on an issue, did public policy follow that direction? What they found was that policy changes generally *did* follow the direction of opinion in both the domestic and foreign affairs arenas in the period of their analysis. For the foreign policy arena, in particular, they report that policy and opinion were congruent in 62 percent of the foreign policy cases examined. Further, policy really did seem to follow opinion, rather than the other way around. As they conclude, "it is reasonable in most of these cases to infer that opinion change was a *cause* of policy change, or at least a proximate or intervening factor leading to government action, if not the ultimate cause."[157] Nonetheless, they also indicate that their analysis could not and did not answer how much opinion was affected by the efforts of politicians and interest groups. While normatively optimistic about the effect of public opinion on policy formation, they caution that all the intervening linkages between opinion and policy are yet to be fully explored.

Examining the impact of public opinion and arms control, political scientist Thomas Graham has begun to specify these linkages. In particular, he identifies the importance of four factors for public opinion to affect foreign policy making at the executive and congressional level.[158] First, the magnitude of public opinion on a foreign policy issue must be substantial. He estimates that "public opinion must reach at least consensus levels (60 percent and higher) before it begins to have a discernible effect on decision making."[159] Second, public opinion can be most effective when it aids in getting an issue on the decision-making agenda (e.g., public support for arms control talks) and during the ratification process (e.g., support or opposition to arms control treaties). Third, the effectiveness of public opinion is also contingent on political elites evaluating and understanding the public's view. While modern polling techniques aid this process, the level of understanding of the public's view by post–World War II administrations varies considerably. In Graham's view, this level of understanding by the executive, not the public, poses a formidable barrier for policy impact. Fourth, the president or the political elites must be effective in translating the public's views into "articulate themes" that will reinforce or elicit public support. While these factors pose problems for the impact of public opinion, Graham still contends "that public opinion has had a significant impact on decision making for several decades, and it can be documented as far back as Franklin D. Roosevelt."[160]

Finally, analyses by political scientist Philip Powlick demonstrate the new attention that foreign policy makers in Washington are giving to public opinion.[161] While National Security Council staffers and State Department officials generally have retained a skeptical view about the public's knowledge and sophistication in assessing foreign policy, they are quite receptive to incorporating public opinion into the foreign policy process: "Among the foreign policy officials interviewed for this study," Powlick reports, "the notion that public support of policy is a sine qua non—and that it must therefore be a major factor in policy decisions—is so widespread as to suggest the existence of a 'norm' within the bureaucratic subculture."[162] Furthermore, this result stands in sharp contract to analyses of more than three decades earlier when public opinion seemed to matter little to these policy makers.[163] These officials, however, often rely upon Congress, the news media, interest groups, and other elites to gauge "public opinion," rather than "unmediated opinion" (e.g., public opinion polls) only. Thus while the amount of unmediated opinion transmitted to the policy makers appears to be greater than in earlier decades, and public opinion appears to be more important as well, the level of "filtered" opinion remains an obstacle for sustained public impact. As a result, foreign policy makers can "justify their policy decisions as having been made after taking public opinion into account, whether or not such decisions necessarily reflect the opinions of the mass public."[164]

CONCLUDING COMMENTS

Both the media and the foreign policy opinions of the American people play a part in the foreign policy making process in the United States. Some characterize the media as playing a separate role, both an actor and critic, others see the role as more of an accomplice of governmental policy, and still others view the media and governmental officials as vying with one another to serve their own purposes in the foreign policy arena. The latter role appears to best describe the relationship. Furthermore, we found that the media has an important impact on how the public views global affairs but that public also exercises an independent assessment of foreign policy actions.

While public opinion matters in shaping foreign policy, the magnitude of the impact of those opinions remains a source of debate. One view sees those opinions as "moodish," relatively shiftable, and subject to leadership from the top; another view sees them as structured, relatively stable, and setting some limits on executive (or even congressional) action. Additionally, the debate over the public's impact on foreign policy, extends to other questions as well. Differing views exist on the overall influence of public opinion on specific foreign policy decisions and general policies adopted by the government. Even the impact of foreign policy opinion on presidential and congressional elections remains unclear. In short, then, while the precise impact of public opinion on foreign policy may still be debated, the fact remains that political leaders, or prospective ones, cannot (and do not) wholly ignore the public's views—even on seemingly distant foreign policy issues.

NOTES

1. The data on the media reported here are taken from, and percentages calculated from, the U.S. Bureau of the Census, *Statistical Abstract of the United States: 2002,* 122nd ed. (Washington, DC, 2002), various pages.

2. Ibid.; and David D. Newsom, *The Public Dimension of Foreign Policy* (Bloomington and Indianapolis: Indiana University Press, 1996), pp. 45, 240, note 3.

3. The title of the section and initial information draws from "Old News Ain't Beat Yet," *The Economist,* May 18, 1996, 32.

4. These data are from ibid. and from *Americans Lack Background to Follow International News: Public's News Habits Little Changed by Sept. 11* (Washington, D.C.: The Pew Research Center for the People and the Press, 2002), pp. 1–4.

5. Ibid.

6. Doris A. Graber, *Mass Media and American Politics,* 3rd ed. (Washington, DC: CQ Press, 1989), p. 328.

7. Michael Emery, "An Endangered Species: The International Newshole," *Gannett Center Journal* 3 (Fall 1989): 151–164.

8. Matthew A. Baum, "Sex, Lies, and War: How Soft News Brings Foreign Policy to the Inattentive Public," *American Political Science Review* 96 (March 2002): 91–109.

9. For an early analysis of different roles of the press in the foreign policy process, see Bernard Cohen, *The Press and Foreign Policy* (Princeton, NJ: Princeton University Press, 1963), pp. 4–5; and for a more recent one, see John T. Rourke, Ralph G. Carter, and Mark A. Boyer, *Making American Foreign Policy* (Guilford, CT: The Dushkin Publishing Group, Inc., 1994), pp. 338–354. Another study that identifies the first two roles and analyzes them for the *New York Times* can be found in Nicholas O. Berry, *Foreign Policy and the Press* (Westport, CT: Greenwood Press, 1990). Also see, Bill Kovach, "Do the News Media Make Foreign Policy?" *Foreign Policy* 102 (Spring 1996): 169–179. All of these studies aided our thinking about these roles.

10. It is not an accident that the Communications Center at the Department of State in Washington always has a television set available (and usually on), even as cables from American posts around the world are being sorted and distributed to the appropriate bureau, office, or desk within the department.

11. Quoted in Leslie H. Gelb with Richard K. Betts, *The Irony of Vietnam: The System Worked* (Washington, DC: The Brookings Institution, 1979), p. 171.

12. Both quotes are from Timothy J. Lomperis, *The War Everyone Lost—and Won* (Washington, DC: CQ Press, 1993), p. 78.

13. See Peter Braestrup, *Big Story: How the American Press and Television Reported and Interpreted the Crisis of Tet 1968,* 2 vols. (Boulder, CO: Westview Press, 1977), as cited in ibid.

14. Interestingly, this program evolved into the late-night ABC program *Nightline* at the end of the crisis. This program continues to

this day as a weeknight news and analysis forum.

15. Quoted in Newsom, *The Public Dimension of Foreign Policy,* pp. 47–48.

16. Quoted in Stephen Hess, *International News & Foreign Correspondents* (Washington, DC: The Brookings Institution, 1996), pp. 1–2. The passage originally came from the CNN program *Reliable Sources,* October 6, 1994.

17. W. Lance Bennett, "The News about Foreign Policy," in W. Lance Bennett and David L. Paletz, eds., *Taken by Storm: The Media, Public Opinion, and U.S. Foreign Policy in the Gulf War* (Chicago and London: The University of Chicago Press, 1994), p. 12.

18. Doris A. Graber, *Mass Media and American Politics,* 5th ed. (Washington, DC: CQ Press, 1997), p. 349.

19. Robert F. Kennedy, *Thirteen Days* (New York: W. W. Norton and Company, 1969), pp. 90–91. While Soviet withdrawal of missiles for an American pledge not to invade Cuba was the proposal, the ultimate settlement also involved the American withdrawal of missiles from Turkey.

20. See Graber, *Mass Media and American Politics,* 5th ed., pp. 349–350, for a discussion of this episode.

21. See Peter Arnett's detailed description of his time in Baghdad in his *Live From the Battlefield* (New York: Simon & Schuster, 1994). Arnett's flight jacket from the war was put on display at CNN headquarters in Atlanta after his return to the United States.

22. Graber, *Mass Media and American Politics,* 5th ed., p. 351.

23. Daniel C. Hallin, *We Keep America on Top of the World: Television and the Public Sphere* (London and New York: Routledge, 1994), pp. 40–57.

24. Ibid., at pp. 44–48 and pp. 52–53.

25. Ibid., at pp. 48–50, 51, and 50, respectively.

26. Ibid., p. 55. For a similar conclusion on how the media "index" news coverage "to the intensity and duration of official conflicts," see W. Lance Bennett, "The Media and the Foreign Policy Process," in David A. Deese, ed., *The New Politics of American For-*

eign Policy (New York: St. Martin's Press, 1994), pp. 168–188, especially at pp. 179–181.

27. I am grateful to James M. Lindsay for bringing this argument to my attention.

28. S. Robert Lichter, Stanley Rothman, and Linda S. Lichter, *The Media Elite* (Bethesda, MD: Adler & Adler, 1986), pp. 21–23. The quoted passages are at p. 23.

29. The first study reported is from ibid., p. 28, while the second is from a study by Stephen Hess of the Brookings Institution and quoted in ibid., p. 40.

30. Ibid., p. 30.

31. The studies and the data in this paragraph are taken from James K. Glassman, "The Press: Obvious Bias . . ." *The Washington Post,* May 7, 1996, A19.

32. Survey cited in Bernard Goldberg, *Bias: A CBS Insider Exposes How the Media Distort the News* (Washington, DC: Regnery Publishing, Inc., 2002), p. 126.

33. The media argument is taken from "The Press: Obvious Bias . . . ," as is the quotation, which is from Larry Sabato.

34. Goldberg, *Bias: A CBS Insider Exposes How the Media Distort the News,* p. 221.

35. Stuart N. Soroka, "Media, Public Opinion, and Foreign Policy," *Harvard International Journal of Press/Politics* 9 (Winter 2003): 27–48.

36. Cohen, *The Press and Foreign Policy,* p. 13. Emphasis in original.

37. The term is from Patrick O'Heffernan, "A Mutual Exploitation Model of Media Influence in U.S. Foreign Policy," in W. Lance Bennett and David L. Paletz, eds., *Taken by Storm: The Media, Public Opinion, and U.S. Foreign Policy in the Gulf War,* p. 231, in which he summarizes Bernard Cohen's conclusion of his 1963 book.

38. See, for example, David D. Pearce, *Wary Partners: Diplomats and the Media* (Washington, DC: Congressional Quarterly, Inc., 1995).

39. Newsom, *The Public Dimension of Foreign Policy,* p. 86. For a scathing account of the press' deference during the Reagan administration, see Mark Hertsgaard, *On Bended Knee: The Press and the Reagan Presidency* (New York: Farrar, Straus & Giroux, 1988).

40. Johanna Neuman, *Lights, Camera, War* (New York: St. Martin's Press, 1996), pp. 207–208. The "pool" term is quoted from Neuman at p. 207.

41. These are outlined in Pete Williams, "Ground Rules and Guidelines for Desert Shield," in Hedrick Smith, ed., *The Media and the Gulf War* (Washington, DC: Seven Locks Press, 1992), pp. 4–12.

42. Hedrick Smith, "Preface," in Hedrick Smith, ed., *The Media and the Gulf War,* p. xviii.

43. R. W. Apple, Jr., "James Reston, a Journalist Nonpareil, Dies at 86," *New York Times,* December 7, 1995, B19. The commentator quoted was Ronald Steel.

44. Ibid.

45. The first two examples are from Pearce, *Wary Partners: Diplomats and the Media,* pp. 1–3.

46. Ambassador Alexander Watson was quoted in ibid., p. 10.

47. See the various appendices in ibid., pp. 169–186.

48. Bennett, "The Media and the Foreign Policy Process," p. 179.

49. Ibid.

50. On the problems for the media in this connection, see ibid., pp. 180–181.

51. O'Heffernan, "A Mutual Exploitation Model of Media Influence in U.S. Foreign Policy," pp. 232–233.

52. Ibid., p. 236.

53. Ibid., p. 237.

54. The discussion of issues draws upon ibid., p. 240.

55. Journalist Johanna Neuman is quoted in Kovach, "Do the News Media Make Foreign Policy?" p. 171. The comment is originally from Neuman, *Lights, Camera, War,* p. 8.

56. Benjamin I. Page and Robert Y. Shapiro, *The Rational Public: Fifty Trends in Americans' Policy Preferences* (Chicago and London: The University of Chicago Press, 1992), p. 321. Emphasis in original.

57. Ibid., p. 342. The discussion of the findings is drawn from pp. 341–347.

58. Soroka, "Media, Public Opinion, and Foreign Policy," p. 43.

59. Page and Shapiro, *The Rational Public,* p. 353.

60. Ibid., p. 354.

61. Ibid.

62. These data are from Gabriel A. Almond, *The American People and Foreign Policy* (New York: Praeger, 1960), p. 82.

63. These data are from Lloyd A. Free and Hadley Cantril, *The Political Beliefs of Americans: A Study of Public Opinion* (New York: Clarion Books, 1968), pp. 60–61.

64. See John E. Rielly, ed., *American Public Opinion and U.S. Foreign Policy 1987* (Chicago: The Chicago Council on Foreign Relations, 1987), p. 8; John E. Rielly, ed., *American Public Opinion and U.S. Foreign Policy 1991* (Chicago: The Chicago Council on Foreign Relations, 1991), p. 9; John E. Rielly, ed., *American Public Opinion and U.S. Foreign Policy 1995* (Chicago: The Chicago Council on Foreign Relations, 1995), p. 9; and John E. Rielly, ed., *American Public Opinion and U.S. Foreign Policy 1999* (Chicago: The Chicago Council on Foreign Relations, 1999), p. 6. The data for the period from 1974 through 2002 are summarized in Marshall M. Bouton and Benjamin I. Page, eds., *Worldviews 2002: American Public Opinion & Foreign Policy* (Chicago: The Chicago Council on Foreign Relations, 2002), p. 13.

65. Ibid., p. 5.

66. Rielly, *American Public Opinion and U.S. Foreign Policy 1987,* p. 9; and John E. Rielly, ed., *American Public Opinion and U.S. Foreign Policy 1983* (Chicago: The Chicago Council on Foreign Relations, 1983), p. 9. The results for 1990 can be found at p. 9 in Rielly, *American Public Opinion and U.S. Foreign Policy 1991.* The 1995 survey did not indicate the size of the attentive public for the 1994 data. Given the modest changes overall in the latest survey, the percentage estimate from the early ones still appears to hold. The quotation from the 1998 survey can be found in Rielly, *American Public Opinion and U.S. Foreign Policy, 1999,* p. 9.

67. Richard Sobel, "Public Opinion about United States Intervention in El Salvador and Nicaragua," *Public Opinion Quarterly* 53 (Spring 1989): 120. Also see Richard Sobel, "Public Opinion about U.S. Intervention in Nicaragua: A Polling Addendum," in Richard Sobel, ed., *Public Opinion in U.S.*

Foreign Policy: The Controversy Over Contra Aid (Lanham, MD: Rowman & Littlefield Publishers, Inc., 1993), pp. 59–70.

68. Bouton and Page, *Worldviews 2002: American Public Opinion & Foreign Policy,* pp. 43–44.

69. On the events and the public's knowledge about them, see Mark Gillespie, "New Poll Shows Support for Peacekeeping in Kosovo," Poll Analyses: The Gallup Organization, February 22, 1999, online. Available: http://www.gallup.com/poll/releases/pr990222.asp; and Frank Newport, "East Timor Has Yet to Register Strongly on Americans' Consciousness," Poll Analyses: The Gallup Organization, October 4, 1999, online. Available: http://www.gallup.com/poll/releases/pr991004.asp.

70. See Darren K. Carlson, "Can Americans Name Key Foreign Leaders?" Gallup Poll Tuesday Briefing, March 4, 2003, online. Available: http://www.gallup.com/poll/tb/goverpubli/20030304b.asp.

71. See Bouton and Page, *Worldviews 2002: American Public Opinion & Foreign Policy,* pp. 10–11 for the top problem about one year after September 11. For the return of the economy as a top issue see Frank Newport, "Americans Clear That Economy Is Most Important Problem Facing Country," Poll Analyses: The Gallup Organization, May 12, 2003, online. Available: http://www.gallup.com/poll/releases/pr030512.asp.

72. On this point, see John E. Rielly, "American Opinion: Continuity, Not Reaganism," *Foreign Policy* 50 (Spring 1983): 88; and Bruce Russett and Donald R. Deluca, "'Don't Tread on Me': Public Opinion and Foreign Policy in the Eighties," *Political Science Quarterly* 96 (Fall 1981): 393–395.

73. See various years of *The Gallup Poll: Public Opinion* (New York: Random House, Annual); John E. Rielly, ed., *American Public Opinion and U.S. Foreign Policy 1975* (Chicago: The Chicago Council on Foreign Relations, 1975); John E. Rielly, *American Public Opinion and U.S. Foreign Policy, 1979;* Rielly, *American Public Opinion and U.S. Foreign Policy, 1983;* (Chicago: Chicago Council on Foreign Relations, 1979) Rielly; *American Public Opinion and U.S. Foreign Policy, 1987;* and Tom W. Smith, "The Polls: America's Most Important Problems, Part I:

National and International," *Public Opinion Quarterly* 49 (Summer 1985): 264–274.

74. Ibid., p. 266.

75. George Gallup, Jr., *The Gallup Poll: Public Opinion 1993* (Wilmington, DE: Scholarly Resources, Inc., 1994), pp. 168–169; George Gallup, Jr., *The Gallup Poll: Public Opinion 1994* (Wilmington, DE: Scholarly Resources, Inc., 1995), p. 28; and George Gallup, Jr., *The Gallup Poll: Public Opinion 1995* (Wilmington, DE: Scholarly Resources, Inc., 1996), pp. 13–14.

76. See Bouton and Page, *Worldviews 2002: American Public Opinion & Foreign Policy,* p. 11.

77. Newport, "Americans Clear That Economy Is Most Important Problem Facing Country."

78. John E. Mueller, *War, Presidents and Public Opinion* (New York: John Wiley and Sons, 1973), ch. 8.

79. Ibid., pp. 70–74.

80. Milton J. Rosenberg, Sidney Verba, and Philip E. Converse, *Vietnam and the Silent Majority* (New York: Harper and Row, 1970), pp. 26–28.

81. See "Opinion Roundup," *Public Opinion* (February/March 1980), pp. 27 and 29.

82. These *New York Times*/CBS News Poll results are reported in David Shribman, "Poll Shows Support for Presence of U.S. Troops in Lebanon and Grenada," *New York Times,* October 29, 1983, 9.

83. These data are taken from Michael Oreskes, "Support for Bush Declines in Poll," *New York Times,* July 11, 1990, A8; and Andrew H. Malcolm, "Opponents to U.S. Move Have Poverty in Common," *New York Times,* September 8, 1990, 6.

84. On the patterns in Presidents Bush's popularity, see Robin Toner, "Did Someone Say 'Domestic Policy'?" *New York Times,* March 3, 1991, 1E and 2E. A CNN (Cable News Network) poll and a *Newsweek* poll placed President Bush's popularity at about 90 percent at the immediate end of the Persian Gulf War. See Ann McDaniel and Evan Thomas with Howard Fineman, "The Rewards of Leadership," *Newsweek,* March 11, 1991, 30.

85. Andrew Kohut and Robert C. Toth, "Arms and the People," *Foreign Affairs* 73 (November/December 1994): 60.

86. Gallup, *The Gallup Poll: Public Opinion 1994,* pp. 141, 145, 148.

87. On these data and trends, see Shoon Kathleen Murray and Christopher Spinosa, "The Post-9/11 Shift in Public Opinion: How Long Will It Last?" in Eugene R. Wittkopf and James M. McCormick, eds., *The Domestic Sources of American Foreign Policy: Insights and Evidence,* 4th ed. (Lanham, MD: Rowman & Littlefield Publishers, Inc., 2004), pp. 97–115; Frank Newport, "Terrorism Fades as Nation's Most Important Problem," January 14, 2002, online. Available: http://www.gallup.com/poll/releases/pr020114.asp.; and Gallup Tuesday Briefing, "Rallying behind the Country's Leaders and Institutions," September 25, 2001, online. Available: TuesdayBriefing@Gallup.com.

88. For the changing trends, see Lydia Saad, "Iraq War Triggers Major Rally Effect," March 25, 2003, online. Available: http://www.gallup.com/poll/releases/pr0300325.asp. Lydia Saad, "Bush's Job Rating Still Above 60%," July 2, 2003, online. Available: http://www.gallup.com/poll/releases/pr030702.asp. For a poll near the end of 2003, see "State of the Nation," The Gallup Organization, November 25, 2003, online. Available: http://www.gallup.com/poll/stateNation/.

89. Rosenberg, Verba, and Converse, *Vietnam and the Silent Majority,* pp. 24–25. The authors do not actually use poll data to make this point about question wording; instead, they rely upon these hypothetical examples to demonstrate the underlying argument.

90. Brad Lockerbie and Stephen A. Borrelli, "Question Wording and Public Support for Contra Aid, 1983–1986," *Public Opinion Quarterly* 54 (Summer 1990): 195–208.

91. David W. Moore, "The Public Is Uncertain," *Foreign Policy* 35 (Summer 1979): 68–70.

92. Gallup, *The Gallup Poll: Public Opinion 1995,* pp. 192–195. The quoted materials are from p. 195. For the approve/disapprove question, the public could respond along a continuum from strongly approve or approve to disapprove or strongly disapprove. See p. 192.

93. For the alternate responses and level of public support for each, see Lydia Saad and Frank Newport, "Americans' View: U.S.

Should Not Go It Alone in Iraq," Poll Analyses: The Gallup Organization, September 24, 2002, online. Available: http://www.gallup.com/poll/releases/pr020924.asp.

94. Gabriel A. Almond, *The American People and Foreign Policy* (New York: Frederick A. Praeger, 1960), pp. 53, 69, 88. Harcourt, Brace, and Company, Inc., published the original edition of this book in 1950.

95. Ibid., p. xxii, from the new introduction to the 1960 edition.

96. Ole R. Holsti, "Public Opinion and Foreign Policy: Challenges to the Almond-Lippmann Consensus," *International Studies Quarterly* 36 (December 1992): 442.

97. Quoted in ibid.

98. Ibid., pp. 443–444. The studies referred to in this paragraph from Holsti are Philip E. Converse, "The Nature of Belief Systems in Mass Publics," in David E. Apter, ed., *Ideology and Discontent* (New York: Free Press, 1964), pp. 206–261; Bernard C. Cohen, *The Public's Impact on Foreign Policy* (Boston: Little, Brown, 1973); and Warren E. Miller and Donald E. Stokes, "Constituency Influence in Congress," *American Political Science Review* 57 (March 1963): 45–56.

99. Jon Hurwitz and Mark Peffley, "How Are Foreign Policy Attitudes Structured? A Hierarchical Model," *American Political Science Review* 81 (December 1987): 1114. Emphasis in original.

100. Robert Y. Shapiro and Benjamin I. Page, "Foreign Policy and the Rational Public," *Journal of Conflict Resolution* 32 (June 1988): 211, 243. A more complete statement of their views can be found in their *The Rational Public.*

101. Eugene R. Wittkopf, *Faces of Internationalism: Public Opinion and American Foreign Policy* (Durham, NC: Duke University Press, 1990), pp. 25–33. Analyses of the more recent Chicago Council surveys by Wittkopf may be found in Eugene R. Wittkopf, "Faces of Internationalism in a Transitional Environment," *Journal of Conflict Resolution* 38 (September 1994): 376–401, for the 1990 survey; and Eugene R. Wittkopf, "What Americans Really Think About Foreign Policy," *The Washington Quarterly* 19 (Summer 1996): 91–106.

102. These are the items used for the analysis of the 1994 survey in ibid., p. 94. Slightly different ones were used for analyzing the 1990 survey; see Wittkopf, "Faces of Internationalism in a Transitional Environment," p. 381. For the 1974 through 1986 surveys, these underlying attitudes were largely tapped by questions about the use of American force abroad, communism, and American-Soviet relations. See *Faces of Internationalism: Public Opinion and American Foreign Policy,* p. 25. The end of the Cold War necessitated the use of different items, since the attitudes toward communism and American-Soviet relations were no longer appropriate.

103. Personal communication with Eugene R. Wittkopf, September 19, 2003.

104. Wittkopf, *Faces of Internationalism,* pp. 25–30. The application of Wittkopf's typology to the Persian Gulf War was aided by a personal communication with him.

105. The analytic technique of factor analysis contributes to the more even distribution among the four quadrants, although differences exist among the groupings.

106. Wittkopf, *Faces of Internationalism,* p. 26; Wittkopf, "Faces of Internationalism in a Transitional Environment," pp. 376–401, for the 1990 results; and personal communication with Eugene R. Wittkopf for the 1994 data. The numbers are rough averages within each quadrant across the surveys.

107. These examples are drawn from Wittkopf, "What Americans Really Think About Foreign Policy," pp. 95–99; and Wittkopf, *Faces of Internationalism,* pp. 27–32, especially the table at p. 28 and the discussion at p. 30.

108. Ibid., pp. 44–49.

109. Wittkopf, "What Americans Really Think About Foreign Policy," p. 103. His 1994 analysis of the other sociodemographic characteristics of the public for these belief systems (reported at pp. 103–104) generally support the results from his earlier work.

110. Personal Communication with Eugene R. Wittkopf on September 19, 2003. Thanks to him for the insight into the current distribution of opinion summarized in this paragraph.

111. Bernard Cohen, *The Political Process and Foreign Policy: The Making of the Japanese Peace Settlement* (Princeton, NJ: Princeton University Press, 1957), p. 29. We should note, however, that Cohen is relatively skeptical about the impact of public opinion overall. See note 36.

112. V. O. Key, Jr. *Public Opinion and American Democracy.* (New York: Alfred A. Knopf, 1961), p. 423.

113. William R. Caspary, "The 'Mood Theory': A Study of Public Opinion and Foreign Policy," *The American Political Science Review* 54 (June 1970): 546. Emphasis in original.

114. Bruce Russett, "The Americans' Retreat from World Power," *Political Science Quarterly* 90 (Spring 1975): 9.

115. The phrase is from ibid., p. 8. For other judgments of the Vietnam War and its impact on the foreign policy beliefs of the American public and its leaders, see, for instance, Eugene R. Wittkopf and Michael A. Maggiotto, "Elites and Masses: A Comparative Analysis of Attitudes Toward America's World Role," *The Journal of Politics* 45 (May 1983): 303–334; and Ole R. Holsti and James N. Rosenau, "Vietnam, Consensus, and the Belief Systems of American Leaders," *World Politics* 32 (October 1979): 1–56.

116. Rielly, *American Public Opinion and U.S. Foreign Policy 1975,* p. 12. The rest of the data in this section are from this report. The national sample survey was conducted in December 1974, by Harris and Associates for the Chicago Council on Foreign Relations.

117. Russett, "The Americans' Retreat from World Power," p. 8.

118. The title is from John E. Rielly, "The American Mood: A Policy of Self-Interest," *Foreign Policy* 34 (Spring 1979): 74–86.

119. John E. Rielly, ed., *American Public Opinion and U.S. Foreign Policy 1979,* p. 4.

120. The data cited here are from ibid.

121. A Harris survey in early 1980 showed majority public support for use of U.S. troops if the Soviets attacked the Persian Gulf area, Iran, or Pakistan. See "Use of U.S. Troops to Defend Invaded Countries Endorsed," *Houston Post,* February 26, 1980, 3C.

122. Rielly, *American Public Opinion and U.S. Foreign Policy 1979,* p. 12.

123. Ibid., p. 15.

124. Ibid., p. 12.

125. Ibid., p. 7. Also Rielly, "The American Mood: A Foreign Policy of Self-Interest."

126. Rielly, *American Public Opinion and U.S. Foreign Policy 1983,* p. 4.

127. Ibid., p. 6; and Rielly, *American Public Opinion and U.S. Foreign Policy 1987,* p. 32.

128. Rielly, *American Public Opinion and U.S. Foreign Policy 1983,* pp. 6, 31; and Rielly, *American Public Opinion and U.S. Foreign Policy 1987,* p. 32.

129. These results are taken from Rielly, *American Public Opinion and U.S. Foreign Policy 1983,* p. 32; and Rielly, *American Public Opinion and U.S. Foreign Policy 1987,* p. 31.

130. See the tables in Rielly, *American Public Opinion and U.S. Foreign Policy 1983,* p. 35; and Rielly, *American Public Opinion and U.S. Foreign Policy 1987,* p. 35, which compare the public's views with those of the Reagan administration. Also, see p. 29 of the latter report for a discussion of public attitudes on military expenditures.

131. The summary of this mood is based upon John E. Rielly, "The Public Mood at Mid-Decade," *Foreign Policy* 98 (Spring 1995): 76–93; Rielly, *American Public Opinion and U.S. Foreign Policy 1995;* and John E. Rielly, , *American Public Opinion and U.S. Foreign Policy 1999.* The title of the moods come from these reports.

132. See Figures III-3 in Rielly, *American Public Opinion and U.S. Foreign Policy 1995,* p. 22, and the discussion on p. 21. For the 1998 data, see Rielly, *American Public Opinion and U.S. Foreign Policy, 1999,* p. 28 and Figure 5–1.

133. Rielly, *American Public Opinion and U.S. Foreign Policy, 1995,* p. 21. Also see the tables on the public's views toward Russia on pp. 24–25.

134. Ibid., p. 23.

135. Ibid., pp. 23, 25; and Rielly, *American Public Opinion and U.S. Foreign Policy, 1999,* pp. 12–14 for the 1998 ("end of the decade") data.

136. Rielly, "Public Opinion: The Pulse of the '90s," pp. 83, 86, 89; and Rielly, *American Public Opinion and U.S. Foreign Policy 1995,* p. 34.

137. The discussion of the public mood after September 11 is drawn from the data and analysis in Bouton and Page, *Worldviews 2002: American Public Opinion & Foreign Policy.* The quoted passages throughout this discussion are from this sources as well.

138. Robert Y. Shapiro and Benjamin I. Page, "Foreign Policy and Public Opinion," in David A. Deese, ed., *The New Politics of American Foreign Policy* (New York: St. Martin's Press, 1994), pp. 216–235. The quote is from p. 218.

139. Ibid., p. 223.

140. Ibid., p. 226.

141. Bruce W. Jentleson, "The Pretty Prudent Public: Post Post-Vietnam American Opinion on the Use of Military Force," *International Studies Quarterly* 36 (March 1992): 49–74. The quoted passages are from pp. 50 and 71, respectively. Emphasis in the original.

142. John R. Oneal, Brad Lian, and James H. Joyner, "Are the American People 'Pretty Prudent'? Public Responses to U.S. Uses of Force, 1950–1988," *International Studies Quarterly* 40 (June 1996): 261–280. The quoted passage is at p. 273.

143. Kohut and Toth, "Arms and the People," p. 47.

144. Ibid., p. 50.

145. See Benjamin I. Page and Jason Barabas, "Foreign Policy Gaps Between Citizens and Leaders," *International Studies Quarterly* 44 (September 2000): 339–364, and especially at p. 358; Rielly, *American Public Opinion and U.S. Foreign Policy 1995* and Rielly, *American Public Opinion and U.S. Foreign Policy 1999,* for discussion of multilateral support more recently. For the post–September 11 support for multilateralism, see Bouton and Page, *Worldviews 2002: American Public Opinion & Foreign Policy,* p. 27, for both quotations and for some data.

146. See John H. Aldrich, John L. Sullivan, and Eugene Borgida, "Foreign Affairs and Issue Voting: Do Presidential Candidates 'Waltz Before a Blind Audience'?" *American Political Science Review* 83 (March 1989): 136.

147. Warren E. Miller, "Voting and Foreign Policy," in James N. Rosenau, ed., *Domestic Sources of Foreign Policy* (New York: The Free Press, 1967), p. 226. Also, see John Spanier and Eric M. Uslaner, *American Foreign Policy Making and the Domestic Dilemmas* (Pacific Grove, CA: Brooks/Cole Publishing Company, 1989), p. 216.

148. Gregory B. Markus, "Political Attitudes During an Election Year: A Report on the 1980 NES Panel Study," *American Political Science Review* 76 (September 1982): 558. This point is also discussed in Spanier and Uslaner, *American Foreign Policy Making and the Democratic Dilemmas,* p. 216, from which we draw.

149. R. W. Apple, Jr., "Clinton's Peace Strategy," *New York Times,* December 2, 1995, 1.

150. The Democratic candidates for the 2004 nominations started early in the campaign cycle focusing on foreign policy issues, especially the situation in Iraq. In turn, the Republican National Committee starting airing campaign advertisement defending the Bush administration's antiterrorism policy. Such an early focus on foreign policy insured its centrality in the 2004 election.

151. See the chart in Aldrich, Sullivan, and Borgida, "Foreign Affairs and Issue Voting: Do Presidential Candidates 'Waltz Before a Blind Audience'?" p. 136.

152. Miroslav Nincic, "Elections and Foreign Policy," in Eugene R. Wittkopf and James M. McCormick, eds., *The Domestic Sources of American Foreign Policy: Insights and Evidence,* 4th ed. (Lanham, MD: Rowman & Littlefield Publishers, Inc., 2004), pp. 117–127. The quoted passage is at p. 119.

153. The discussion in this paragraph draws upon the description and analysis of the Oklahoma case provided in Jeremy Rosner, "The Know-Nothings Know Something," *Foreign Policy* 101 (Winter 1995–1996): 116–127.

154. While an admixture of issues were in the public's minds at the midterm congressional elections, concerns about terrorism, war, and international issues were mentioned slightly more frequently than economic issues. See Lydia Saad, "Americans Troubled by Issues, Upbeat About Leaders This Election Day," Poll Analyses: The Gallup Orga-

nization, online. Available: http://www.gallup.com/poll/releases/pr021105.asp.

155. Richard Sobel, *The Impact of Public Opinion on U.S. Foreign Policy: Constraining the Colossus* (New York: Oxford University Press, 2001). The quoted passages are at p. 240 and p. 234, respectively.

156. Douglas C. Foyle, *Counting the Public In: Presidents, Public Opinion, and Foreign Policy* (New York: Oxford University Press, 1999). The quoted passage is from p. 259.

157. Benjamin I. Page and Robert Y. Shapiro, "Effects of Public Opinion on Policy," *American Political Science Review* 77 (March 1983): 186. Emphasis in original. The discussion in this paragraph is drawn from this article. For a more recent summary of their work on foreign policy, see Benjamin I. Page and Robert Y. Shapiro, *The Rational Public,* pp. 172–320.

158. Thomas Graham, "Public Opinion and U.S. Foreign Policy Decision Making," in David A. Deese, ed., *The New Politics of*

American Foreign Policy (New York: St. Martin's Press, 1994), pp. 190–215.

159. Ibid., p. 196. These four factors are discussed at pp. 195–199, from which we draw.

160. Ibid., p. 195.

161. Philip J. Powlick, "The Attitudinal Bases for Responsiveness to Public Opinion among American Foreign Policy Officials," *Journal of Conflict Resolution* 35 (December 1991): 611–641; and Philip J. Powlick, "The Sources of Public Opinion for American Foreign Policy Officials," *International Studies Quarterly* 39 (December 1995): 427–451.

162. Powlick, "The Attitudinal Bases for Responsiveness to Public Opinion among American Foreign Policy Officials," p. 634.

163. See Bernard C. Cohen, *The Public's Impact on Foreign Policy*.

164. Powlick, "The Sources of Public Opinion for American Foreign Policy Officials," p. 447.

PART III

Conclusion

In Part I of this book, we suggested how the formulation of American foreign policy has been marked by a considerable degree of value consensus prior to the Vietnam War and to a substantial amount of value shifts from one administration to the next ever since, including the post–September 11 period. In Part II, a central message was how the various political institutions—the executive, the Congress, and the bureaucracies, for example—have become increasingly competitive in the shaping of American foreign policy. Indeed, the impetus for foreign policy change gained even more momentum with the collapse of the Berlin Wall, the unraveling of communism in Eastern Europe, and the collapse of the Soviet Union in the early 1990s. The events of September 11 restored dominance to some foreign policy bureaucracies and stimulated change and reform in others. But crucial questions remain for American foreign policy: Can a coherent foreign policy be developed without the emergence of a new foreign policy value consensus? Will the terrorist threats and the legacy of September 11 continue to shape the future direction of foreign policy? What should be the values and beliefs to guide American foreign policy in the new millennium and in a changed international context? Put more generally, what should be the shape of America's role and its rationale?

The concluding chapter examines both the prospects for a new consensus in U.S. foreign policy making and some alternate approaches that might be pursued.

As we move into the new millennium, the need for such a consensus appears to be greater than ever before, but the task of building and sustaining one remains formidable as well. Several approaches have been offered over the years both to incorporate the antiterrorist policy of the past few years and to alter the direction of that policy as well. A summary of the different approaches will increase awareness of the various options available and will facilitate discussion and debate on the values and beliefs in American foreign policy in the years ahead.

13

American Foreign Policy Values and the Future

[I]n a world where borders are becoming more porous than ever
to everything from drugs to infectious diseases to terrorism, we are forced
to work with other countries behind their borders and inside ours. . . .
We are not only bound to lead, but bound to cooperate.

JOSEPH S. NYE, JR.
THE PARADOX OF AMERICAN POWER

In exercising our leadership, we will respect the values, judgment,
and interests of our friends and partners. Still, we will be prepared to act
apart when our interests and unique responsibilities require.

NATIONAL SECURITY STRATEGY OF THE UNITED STATES OF AMERICA
SEPTEMBER 2002

As we move through the first decade of the twenty-first century, a consensus among the American people on the role of the United States in world affairs remains elusive. While the events of September 11, 2001, seemingly produced a temporary degree of foreign policy unity among the American people and its leaders, the post–September 11 period has produced a cacophony of voices that have criticized the direction of policy pursued by the Bush administration. Yet if American policy is to be coherent and consistent, policy makers and the public need to begin to identify the values and beliefs to guide American diplomacy and, if possible, to pursue a series of policies consistent with those principles. The constant shifts in policy emphasis from one administration to the next neither serves America's long-term interests nor provides much guidance to policy makers in the executive or legislative branches of government. These constant policy shifts, too, raise legitimate concerns over whether any consensus can or should be pursued. Efforts to build a consensus are difficult and time-consuming, and any consensus may be incomplete or even dangerous in today's world, characterized as it is by increasingly complex and interrelated problems within and between states.

In this last chapter, we discuss the issue of a new foreign policy consensus. We begin by identifying more fully the extent of underlying value conflicts among the leaders of American foreign policy in recent years. Then we turn to evaluating the problems of, and prospects for, developing a new foreign policy consensus at this juncture of the twenty-first century. In an effort to stimulate discussion on this important topic, too, we provide a brief sketch of the several alternate approaches that have been proposed for shaping the future role of the United States in the post–September 11 world.

A NATION DIVIDED

An abundance of evidence exists at both the mass and elite levels on the degree of value conflict over the direction of foreign policy. As we have noted, the United States has witnessed discernible shifts in its foreign policy approach with the coming of each new administration over the past three decades. From the rejection of the values of the Cold War consensus, to the power politics of the Nixon–Kissinger period and the idealism of the Carter years, to the revival of containment of the Reagan years and the modified realism of the Bush administration, and, more recently, to the liberal internationalism of the Clinton administration and the unilateralism of the George W. Bush administration, the American approach to foreign policy has gone through substantial modification almost every four years. While some would argue that significant underlying stability in American foreign policy goals and objectives has largely characterized policy over much of the past 50 years, that view fails to account fully for the changes in emphasis from one administration to the next.[1] That view also fails to capture the pervasive divisions in value orientation among the leadership (the foreign policy elites) and the American people, beginning in the post-Vietnam era, and now continuing in the post–Cold War and post–September 11 years.

VALUE DIFFERENCES WITHIN ELITES

Political scientists Ole Holsti and James Rosenau's recent analyses provide compelling evidence of divisions among foreign policy leaders or elites that started after the Vietnam War and continue to the present. Employing the fourfold analytic categories (isolationists, hard-liners, accommodationists, and internationalists) that Wittkopf developed to assess public opinion (see Chapter 12), Holsti and Rosenau's evaluation of four foreign policy leadership opinion surveys from 1984 through 1996 found significant elite divisions across those four categories. Moreover, the divisions were reasonably constant from one survey to the next, with the elites perhaps more divided recently.[2] (Table 13.1 shows the percentages of the foreign policy leaders in each of the four belief systems across the four surveys.) Accommodationists and internationalists turn out to be the two largest components of those surveyed, with the former constituting 48 percent in 1996 and the latter 29 percent. Hard-liners and isolationists, by contrast, form much smaller components of the foreign policy leadership with 13 percent and 10 percent, respectively.[3]

Consistent with the earlier analyses of the public, Holsti and Rosenau report that "partisan, ideological and, to a less degree, occupational differences" account for these differing belief systems."[4] On a partisan level, they found that hard-liners were Republicans, and accommodationists were Democrats among the 1996 respondents. "To a less dramatic extent," they report, "internationalists and isolationists preferred the GOP to the Democratic Party." On an ideological level, the hard-liners tended to be conservatives, the accommodationists were liberals, and the internationalists and isolationists "tended to tilt toward the conservative end of the ideological self-identification scale."[5]

In a related set of analyses, Ole Holsti has demonstrated that partisan differences among elites have existed across a whole series of specific foreign policy issues, beginning with a 1976 survey and continuing through five other quadrennial surveys from 1980 through 1996. Indeed, his data "offer only modest evidence that the end of the Cold War has resurrected a foreign policy consensus among opinion leaders." Instead, "partisan cleavages are evident on a great many issues," although "trade stands out as an exception."[6] On that issue, liberal Democrats and conservative Republicans come together to oppose trade liberalization, albeit for different reasons. That issue aside, though, partisan differences divide elites on foreign policy—and have for a considerable time.

A 2002 leadership survey by The Chicago Council on Foreign Relations suggests the continuation of divisions among an array of foreign policy leadership (or elite) groups (composed of knowledgeable Americans from government, business, labor, communications, education, religious groups, and foreign policy interest

Table 13.1 The Distribution of American Leaders among Four Categories of Foreign Policy Beliefs, 1984–1996 (Percentages)

	Cooperative Internationalism			
	Oppose		**Support**	
Militant Internationalism	*Hardliners*		*Internationalists*	
	1984	17	1984	25
Support	1988	16	1988	25
	1992	9	1992	33
	1996	13	1996	29
	Isolationists		*Accommodationists*	
	1984	7	1984	51
Oppose	1988	8	1988	52
	1992	5	1992	53
	1996	10	1996	48

Note: Percentages for each year may not add up to 100 due to rounding.

SOURCE: Ole R. Holsti and James N. Rosenau, "The Political Foundations of Elites' Domestic and Foreign Policy Beliefs," in Eugene R. Wittkopf and James M. McCormick, eds., *The Domestic Sources of American Foreign Policy: Insights and Evidence,* 3rd. ed. (Lanham, MD: Rowman & Littlefield Publishers, Inc., 1999), Table 3.1, p. 37. Reprinted by permission.

groups).[7] Although the same comprehensive analyses have not been completed on this leadership survey as in the studies cited above, the Council's report points to clear divisions among several specific leadership groups within and outside the government on recent important foreign policy issues. Consider four specific conclusions from the Council's leadership survey:

> Groups of leaders outside the government agree with the public that the United States should not take action alone if it does not have the support of its allies, but the majorities in all three policy-making bodies (House, Senate, and the administration) support the United States acting alone.

> Although majorities of the public and leaders overall support committing 1,000 troops to a rapid deployment force that the UN Security Council can call up in short notice, most respondents in the administration and the Senate oppose this idea.

> Large majorities of the public and leaders as a whole believe the United States should participate in the Kyoto agreement to reduce global warming. But majorities of leaders in business, in the Senate, and especially in the Bush administration indicate that the United States should not participate in the agreement.

Large majorities of the public and leaders believe that the United States should accept the international agreement to establish an International Criminal Court (ICC) . . . none of the groups within the national government support it.[8]

In all, then, these issue examples reveal that differences within the foreign policy elite continue and complicate the shaping of American foreign policy, much as Holsti and Rosenau demonstrated through their analysis of the four belief systems held by America's leaders.

VALUE DIFFERENCES
BETWEEN ELITES AND MASSES

This lack of consensus within elites (and also among the mass public, as we indicated in Chapter 12) is complicated in yet another way: the failure of both elites and masses to share the four belief systems to the same degree. That is, despite the fact that attitudes of elites and masses are similarly structured into comparable belief systems, some of the different belief systems are not held in the same proportion by the foreign policy elites and the public. For instance, the American leadership tends to be much more internationalist (in both the militant and cooperative varieties) than is the mass public. By contrast, the mass public tends to favor more hard-line (supporting a more militant internationalism) and isolationist policies than do the elites.[9] Such disparities between elites and masses reduce the effectiveness of making foreign policy with widespread support.

Elite/mass issue differences are also more directly portrayed in some data from the 2002 Chicago Council survey. Table 13.2 compares responses to several foreign policy questions of a general public survey and a leadership survey (the same groups described above).[10] These surveys were conducted in May through July of 2002.

Attitudes toward the world and toward specific policy questions differ significantly between the public and their leaders. The public, for instance, is less committed to an active world role than are leaders, but it is more committed to strengthening the United Nations than are the foreign policy elites. The difference between the public and the leaders on these two questions are wide, at 23 and 30 percentage points, respectively. The leaders (or elites) are more willing to increase aid to other countries generally and to several countries specifically than are the public as a whole.[11] On these particular questions, the gaps between the leaders and the public are even wider, ranging from 30 percent to 45 percent. The leaders are also much more willing to use force and to share intelligence information on terrorism than the public is. For instance, a majority of the public now favor using American troops if Arab forces attacked Israel, but the majority of the leaders support using troops across several different scenarios. A majority of the public (60 percent) supports sharing intelligence information on matters dealing

Table 13.2 Policy Differences between the Leaders and the Public—2002 (Percentages)

	Public	Leaders	Gap (leaders minus public)
Diplomatic and involvement abroad			
Take an active part in world affairs	74	97	+23
Strengthening the United Nations a very important goal	58	28	−30
Foreign aid			
Favor expanding aid to other countries	14	59	+45
Increase aid to Palestinians	13	43	+30
Increase aid to Afghanistan	23	67	+44
Increase aid to Africa	37	75	+38
Use of force/protecting the homeland			
Favor use of U.S. troops if North Korea invaded South Korea	39	83	+44
Favor use of U.S. troops if Arab Forces invade Israel	52	79	+27
Favor use of U.S. troops if a Chinese invasion of Taiwan	35	54	+19
Favor sharing intelligence information against terrorism	60	94	+34
Trade/immigration			
View protecting jobs as a very important goal	85	35	−50
View immigration and refugees as critical threat to United States	60	14	−40

Note: Percentages are of those holding an opinion.

SOURCE: Constructed from discussion, tables, and questions in Marshall M. Bouton and Benjamin I. Page, eds., *Worldviews 2002: American Public Opinion & Foreign Policy* (Chicago: The Chicago Council on Foreign Relations, 2002), pp. 69–72.

with terrorism, but the leadership (94 percent) overwhelmingly does so. As with the other issues, then the gap for taking such actions is markedly wide between the groups surveyed.

On two other important issues, trade and immigration/refugees concerns, the public and the leadership are likewise divided—and by a considerable margin. Eighty-five percent of public (as opposed to 35 percent of the leaders) view protecting American jobs as a very important goal of U.S. foreign policy. By contrast, the public (60 percent) sees immigration and refugees as a critical threat to the United States, while the leadership (14 percent) is much less concerned about both issues. Finally, across all the questions asked in these two surveys, the Chicago Council reports, the public and the leaders are generally divided. Indeed, on almost two-thirds (62 percent) of the questions asked, the public and the leaders disagreed by at least 10 percentage points.[12] In this sense, even as the shape of public opinion has changed in recent years, the gap between elites and masses on several foreign policy questions remains. As the Chicago Council report concludes, these results "are sobering" and have important implications. Indeed, one implication is that "leaders need to do a better job either educating the public or following their preferences."[13]

In sum, then, major analyses of post-Vietnam, post–Cold War, and post–September 11 opinions portray the same picture of America's leadership: a foreign policy elite divided over how the United States ought to act in the world. Further, the divisions between the elite and the masses on a number of important foreign policy questions remain as well. Whether the danger posed by international terrorism will stimulate the development of a new foreign policy consensus remains an open question, but, given the significant divisions over the last three decades, the challenge remains a formidable one.

A NEW FOREIGN POLICY CONSENSUS?

Indeed, the shifts in policy from one president to another and the divisions that have developed both among and between American leaders and the public seem to point to the need to develop a new foreign policy consensus. In a more dangerous international system, too, the need for a consensus appears greater than ever. Such a consensus could engender widespread support among the American people and lend coherence and direction to U.S. policy. While calls for a new foreign policy consensus are hardly new, dating since immediately after the Vietnam War, they accelerated in the post–Cold War period and have now been heard once again after the events of September 11.

Calls for a New Consensus

Sprinkled throughout the writings of foreign policy scholars and practitioners in the 1970s, for example, were calls for new approaches to replace the Cold War consensus in guiding American foreign policy.[14] Prior to his becoming national security advisor in the Carter administration, for example, Zbigniew Brzezinski argued that the Vietnam experience had shattered the WASP foreign policy elite and that Henry Kissinger's global design failed to replace the lost elite. Thus, he contended, there was a "need for national leadership that was capable of defining politically and morally compelling directions to which the public might then positively respond."[15]

In the 1980s and 1990s, the debate continued. One scholar lamented that a foreign policy consensus had not emerged and that the United States was experiencing a foreign policy "crack-up."[16] As American leaders and the public became increasingly divided into those concerned with the "security culture" and those concerned with the "equity culture," foreign policy faltered badly in this scholar's judgment. Thus, a new foreign policy coalition was still needed to replace the working coalition of the Cold War years. A little while later, with the demise of communism in Eastern Europe and the collapse of the Soviet Union, calls for a new consensus, or at least new approaches, were once again widespread.[17]

In the immediate aftermath of the events of September 11, the prospects for a new consensus were quickly discussed and debated. In a provocative essay, James Steinberg, director of the foreign policy program at the Brookings Institution, asked whether counterterrorism was "a new organizing principle for American national security?"[18] At the time of his assessment, the umbrella concept appeared to have the potential to gain new friends for the United States, unite old friends, and aid the United States in setting new priorities for the future. To do so, Steinberg cautioned, the strategy needed to be sustained, adjusted to meet changing circumstances, and required international support and international institutions. At roughly the same time, Jessica Matthews, president of another Washington think tank, Carnegie Endowment for International Peace, questioned whether September 11 was "a transforming event" for American foreign policy.[19] In her assessment, "it does not . . . restore the strategic clarity and unitary purpose that have been missing in foreign policy since the end of the Cold War." While Matthews acknowledged that the events of that day affected some American relations abroad (e.g., ties with Russia and China), structural and ideological differences continue with those nations, and new (Central Asia) and old (Europe) issues remained as well. In this sense, September 11 may have altered the attention of the United States, but it did not reshape the global political landscape and some traditional issues that were extant. Furthermore, the George W. Bush administration sought to advance a new consensus with its National Security Strategy statement of 2002 "against terrorists and tyrants." In light of the criticism that it has received (see Chapter 6) and subsequent events, it is hard to argue that it has galvanized the American public (or the global community) into a new universal foreign policy approach. In this sense, it is difficult to claim that a new foreign consensus has emerged. This remains a formidable challenge for American foreign policy.

But are there any real prospects that a new consensus will come about in the near future? At least three crucial questions remain over forming a new consensus. First, should it be developed? Will a new consensus be necessary or functional for American policy? Second, can it be developed? That is, in the context of a divided leadership and a divided public, how is a new consensus going to be forged? Third, and most important, perhaps, what values should constitute this new consensus?

Some have long doubted that a foreign policy consensus can be constructed and believe that any short-term consensus that might emerge may be detrimental to sound foreign policy. One view, for example, is that the foreign policy interests of the United States today are too diverse to be summarized under a single rubric, as anticommunism did during the height of the Cold War or presumably antiterrorism more recently. Domestic interests are now often perceived to be closely linked to foreign policy (e.g., trade policy and domestic employment), so that foreign policy action might only reinforce existing domestic policy divisions rather than pursuing the wider "national interest."[20] Further, "while a consensus may make a country easier to govern, it does not necessarily make for good policy."[21] As a result, foreign policy may have to be made piecemeal—on a case-by-case basis—and in the same manner as domestic policy, by building coalitions as issues come to the fore.

Another approach—less demanding than an overarching consensus, but more than a case-by-case approach to policy—would be to identify and obtain agreement on dealing with key issues or key nations in the world.[22] For instance, a consensus might be built on the need to address terrorism or drug trafficking, regardless of policy differences in other issue areas. Similarly, it might be possible to gain some consensus among the American public and its leadership on how to conduct relations with specific countries or regions (e.g., Russia, China, or the Middle East). In short, this intermediate approach to consensus building would be less demanding and, in this sense, more achievable.

If a consensus were to emerge, however, dangers might accompany it. If a premature consensus develops—i.e., one that is not firmly embedded in the elites and the public at large—it might simply be a set of simple moral slogans that would not reflect the complexity of policy needed for today's world.[23] For instance, both the Carter and Reagan administrations might have been accused of employing such a strategy, with the resultant consequence that neither's effort sufficed as a satisfactory consensus for the public as a whole. A consistent complaint about both the George H. W. Bush and Clinton administrations was that they tended to make their foreign policy decisions more with an eye on the public opinion polls at home and less with an eye to the long-term interests of the United States. Some view the attempt by the George W. Bush administration to employ antiterrorism as an umbrella concept for responding to all global affairs questions as a premature consensus, too.

A premature consensus could easily turn out to be a target for those opposed to a particular approach. The actions of the Bill Clinton and the George W. Bush administrations over Somalia and Iraq, respectively, illustrate this argument. Emboldened by some initial success in providing humanitarian relief to Somalia in early 1993, the Clinton administration moved to expand its efforts into "nation building," activities to restore a working government by attempting to defeat a particularly troublesome clan and capture its leader in mid-1993. Such efforts quickly failed, American lives were lost, and opposition forces within Congress and the public turned against these expanded American actions. Similarly, encouraged by public and international approval for its response to al-Qaeda and the Taliban after the events of September 11, the Bush administration next turned to deal with Iraq. As the administration became increasingly insistent on initiating war against Iraq over the perceived threat posed by its weapons of mass destruction, international (and some domestic) support wavered. Although the administration enjoyed initial success in the Iraq War during March and April 2003, the reconstruction efforts faltered as Iraqi insurgency and opposition arose. Both domestic and international support for the antiterrorism campaign waned, and calls for new approaches quickly arose.

A related and more critical danger for any consensus has been aptly summarized by Gelb and Betts.[24] "Doctrine and consensus," they note, "are the midwives to necessity and the enemy of dissent and choice." Because the military containment belief system had been so firmly interwoven into the American policy process in the 1950s and 1960s, America's Vietnam policy became almost a certainty. Once the policy of preemption against Iraq was invoked in the post–September 11 years, some feared that military actions against other states would likely follow. That is, once beliefs become so dominant in the policy process, movement away from them becomes extraordinarily difficult.

Still, Gelb and Betts acknowledge that some doctrinal consensus is necessary in foreign policy making ("It lends coherence and direction to policy; it puts particular challenges in perspective; it enables the bureaucracy to handle routine problems without constant and enervating debates; it translates values into objectives. . . ."), but they call for one "with escape hatches."[25] A more pragmatic consensus that will be adaptive to changing circumstances is the key in their view. Given America's past, however, that task may be more difficult than it sounds. Gelb and Betts note that while Americans often pride themselves on pragmatism in domestic affairs, they have been much more prone to adopt ideological postures in foreign affairs. In their view, a new consensus must necessarily avoid this tendency.

Developing a New Consensus

Can a workable foreign policy consensus emerge that takes into account these possible dangers? The answer, of course, is still very much open to question, but one proponent argues: "There is no sensible alternative but to try."[26] At a minimum, the following requirements would seem to be necessary.

Political leadership will undoubtedly be the first requisite. This leadership, however, must not be one that yearns for some past glory; instead, it must accept the changed global reality—a world increasingly divided—and be willing to evoke change by pursuing a more differentiated foreign policy. The second requisite is that the leadership must be willing to educate the public continuously on foreign policy. A third, and crucial, requisite for this new consensus is that the public evaluate its beliefs and values on what the United States should stand for in the world, the extent to which domestic values should shape American policy, and the degree to which various political, economic, and military instruments are acceptable for implementing foreign policy.

None of these requisites will be easy to achieve. Political leaders often opt for domestically attractive foreign policy stances, and they find educating the public on foreign policy issues difficult. Similarly, the public has too often shown little interest in or knowledge about foreign affairs; traditional beliefs remain appealing. A coherent foreign policy, however, requires that the leadership and the public make such an effort. The leadership task is especially difficult today because the elite–mass value divisions are ideologically based and because these divisions are within generations rather than across them. Thus, simple appeals to only one segment of the American public will not suffice; instead, the leadership must be much more creative in identifying values and policies that will appeal across groups. Furthermore, with pressing international political problems—whether it be terrorism, the potential spread of nuclear weapons, the continuing global debt crisis, or the effects of global warming—American political leadership probably does not have the luxury of waiting until dramatic international events help to forge a new value consensus, as the events of the late 1940s and early 1950s assisted in forging the Cold War consensus.[27] The dramatic events of September 11 have the potential for this effect, but it is difficult to argue that a foreign policy consensus has yet fully crystallized among the American public or its elites.

Alternate Approaches to Building a Consensus

What, then, might be some of these overarching values that the political leadership could use to mold any new consensus? Several alternate approaches have been proposed recently, and they largely conform to the four different segments within the elites and the public that we discussed earlier. For simplicity's sake, let us group them under four general headings: (1) a neo-isolationist approach to American foreign policy; (2) a more self-interested and unilateral approach to American involvement; (3) an approach emphasizing more completely democratic and ethical ideals in American foreign policy; and (4) an approach emphasizing greater international cooperation in American foreign policy. While we cannot do full justice to any of them in this short space, and some of the approaches are not as mutually exclusive as the four groupings suggest, we can give some sense of the range of options that are being suggested.

Neo-Isolationism The first alternative might be labeled a *neo-isolationism* approach. In the immediate aftermath of the Vietnam War, for example, several calls arose for neo-isolationism as the most promising path for American foreign policy. With the end of the Cold War and after September 11, this general theme emerged once again. This approach is closely akin to the isolationist segment in the mass and elite opinion analyses that we reported earlier.

As the Cold War was winding down, for instance, a former government official perhaps best portrayed the view of those who yearned for a reduced or detached role for the United States in world affairs.[28] His proposed approach called for less of a conscious American policy abroad and more a policy responding to the changing international circumstances. Because he viewed the emerging international system as more fragmented and regionalized, the United States should move toward greater "strategic independence" by seeking "to quarantine regional violence and compartmentalize regional instability." The best approach to achieve this outcome would not be "by active intervention" but by encouraging "regional balances of power, whether bipolar or multipolar."[29]

In this kind of an international system, the national security strategy of the United States would involve protecting only limited key values: "the lives and domestic property of citizens, the integrity of national territory, and the autonomy of political processes."[30] Promoting and protecting values beyond these will lose their relevance. Efforts to reshape the international system, for example, or to expand human rights globally would no longer be core United States values. On balance, the United States will be able to do nothing less because, in this view, the nation must "adjust to a world beyond order and control."[31]

After the end of the Cold War, Eric Nordlinger echoed this approach and called for a new national strategy based on "isolationism reconfigured."[32] The proposed strategy called for "an exceptionally narrow security perimeter, beyond which political-military activism is limited to a bare minimum."[33] In other words, the United States would work to protect key concerns, but it would take a very limited role in world affairs.

Nordlinger pointed to at least five reasons or assumptions for promoting this nonengagement approach. First, the United States "enjoys a privileged position in being strategically immune"[34] from external threats, reducing the need for an expansive American role. Second, the intention of potential challengers cannot be determined with much confidence, and as a result, the United States should not pursue a more assertive international posture. Third, a strategy of nonengagement is at least as effective as a strategy of engagement for the United States "in warding off any and all unacceptable actions against the narrow core perimeter—be they economic competition and pressures, minor probes, deterrent challenges, coercive threats or outright attacks."[35] Fourth, the "challenger's intentions" in the international arena today are assumed to be largely benign, furthering support for nonengagement over engagement. Fifth, and finally, there are "ubiquitous possibilities of strategic mismanagement"[36] with a more complex approach than a national strategy based on limited engagement. In other words, the likelihood of policy-making mistakes increases with greater global involvement.

Furthermore, Nordlinger argues that this strategy had other advantages. It would better allow the United States to promote its "extrasecurity values"—such as promoting its liberal ideals and its domestic welfare—than would a strategy of "strategic internationalism."[37] This national strategy, too, is also more compatible with the various competing political cultures prevalent in American society.[38]

While the events of September 11 seriously challenged how "strategically immune" the United States was and questioned whether the challenger's intentions were "benign," arguments still emerged encouraging a more isolationist posture for the United States. Ted Galen Carpenter, for example, argues for "a global role based on America's strategic independence combined with a policy of selective engagement that emphasized economic, diplomatic, and cultural interaction rather than promiscuous military intervention."[39] This strategic approach would be based on three key principles: the United States should "encourage multiple centers of power" in global affairs to move the international system toward multipolarity (and hence reduce American prominence); the United States should reduce its military engagements around the world while maintaining other forms of ties; and the United States should focus on the "big issues" that truly affect the nation rather than the whole array of issues that currently command attention and involvement.

While Carpenter argues that this approach should have been embraced prior to September 11, it is even more imperative now. "As we confront a fanatical adversary," he noted, "we cannot afford the distraction of maintaining obsolete and irrelevant security commitment around the globe." Instead, the United States "must clear the decks for war against its terrorist adversaries, . . . jettisoning unnecessary commitments and exploiting the advantages of a multipolar world."[40] While this approach is surely not wholly isolationist, it represents a much narrower foreign policy approach for the post–September 11 world than the United States adopted.

A New Unilateralism Others suggest a different approach for the United States in the post–Cold War and post–September 11 world—an approach based on greater American unilateralism in foreign policy. In this approach, the United States would remain engaged in the world, albeit in a more selective, self-interested way than it operated during the Cold War. Some variants of unilateralism would be pursued by design, others by sheer happenstance of American power. Either of these variants would be particularly appealing to those who identify with the hard-liner/internationalist segments of the American public and its leaders.

Soon after the end of the Cold War, for instance, William Kristol and Robert Kagan advanced a particularly strong variant of the unilateral approach for the United States.[41] They called for the United States to pursue a "benevolent global hegemony,"[42] an approach in which American power and influence would be largely generous and unselfish in leading and promoting global order. A principal aim of this approach would be to preserve American predominance around the world through "strengthening America's security, supporting its friends, advancing its interests, and standing up for its principles."[43] As they saw it, "American hegemony is the only reliable defense against a breakdown of peace and international order." To sustain and promote this global role, the United States must also pursue a policy of "military supremacy and moral confidence" by enhancing defense spending, increasing citizen awareness of America's international role, and pursuing actions abroad "based on the understanding that its moral goals and its fundamental national interests are almost always in harmony."[44] In light of the events of September 11 and the challenges that those actions posed for the United States, this approach continues to have appeal for many, including members of the George W. Bush administration.

Political scientist Robert Lieber echoed these same sentiments about American primacy at about the time that the Bush administration assumed office.[45] His view was that American primacy would likely continue because there was no real challenger to American power and because American leadership was the "necessary catalyst" for effective global action, including "international collaboration." That is, Russia, China, Germany, or the European Union were not in a position to replace or challenge American preeminence. Furthermore, action by the United States was crucial for international actions to be carried out. Yet, Lieber also noted that (at the time of his analysis) no identifiable external threat existed and that made gaining domestic support for foreign policy making more difficult. In light of September 11, of course, that factor has changed and domestic attention and support for foreign policy making have been enhanced. In this sense, the ability of the United States to exercise primacy in foreign affairs appears even more likely.

Richard N. Haass, head of the Policy Planning Staff of the Department of State for a time in the George W. Bush administration and later president of the Council on Foreign Relations, also proposed the continuation of American leadership for what he labeled "the post–post–Cold War years" (the period after September 11), but his design sought to do so in a less hegemonic and singular way than some other variants of unilateralism.[46] Instead, Haass proposed the use of the "doctrine of integration" as the organizing strategy in this new era. Under his design, "the principal aim of American foreign policy is to integrate other countries and organizations into arrangements that will sustain a world consistent with U.S. interests and values, and thereby promote peace, prosperity, and justice as widely as possible." The United States would largely take the lead in developing this global integration "by persuading more and more governments and . . . peoples to sign on to certain key ideas as how the world would operate for our mutual benefit." This integration would occur in relations on traditional security concerns with Russia or China, for instance, but it would also be developed to address new transnational issues such as global terrorism.

The ultimate aim of this approach would be to move "from a balance of power to a pooling of power" across a series of issues and relationships. While all the "tools of statecraft" would be used by the United States to accomplish this end, Haass emphasized "certain truths" in implementing this approach. First, American leadership would be crucial. Second, the United States would work with a variety of nations, "not shackled by the memories of past animosities." In working through coalitions to accomplish its ends, the United States would create them as needed. Some would be through international institutions, and others would be created outside of them. Third, American willingness to work with others would be conditioned on getting good results, not on going "along simply to get along." Finally, and importantly, the United States "can and will act alone when necessary."

Each of these first two approaches has problems and shortcomings as organizing schema for U.S. foreign policy. While we cannot delineate them in detail here, some indication of these potential difficulties merits brief mention. On the one hand, the neo-isolationist proposals inevitably bump up against a public (and most leaders) that remains largely internationalist in focus, albeit less so in the political-military area than in the economic and social area. On the other hand, too much unilateral involvement and a sustained hegemonic role must confront a public consistently committed to multilateral effort to address global problems and less willing to be the "world policeman" that this approach might connote. Finally, too stark an emphasis on realist principles—acting only on narrow national interests to create global stability and order—without a reliance on guiding moral principles runs two possible risks: increasing public cynicism about the short-term motivations of politicians, and affronting the ethical impulses toward foreign affairs still prevalent among the American people.

A Democratic Imperative A third alternative, first suggested almost two decades ago by George Quester, would involve a return to America's traditional emphasis upon its domestic values in dealing with the world and would likely tap the ethical impulses in the American public.[47] Under this alternative, the United States would place greater reliance upon the principles of political democracy (e.g., "free contested elections with a free press") as the basis of our policy toward other nations. This alternative should be particularly appealing to those who identify with the internationalist/accommodationist segments of the American public and its leaders. That is, the United States would stand for its principles in the world, but the government would promote them cooperatively with other states and organizations in the international system.

According to Quester's original formulation, the consensus that really was lost by the Vietnam War more than three decades ago was a sense of confidence in America's values and its sense of worth to the rest of the world. As a result, Americans subsequently applied a double standard in approaching the international system. While we were willing to apply the standards of political democracy in conducting foreign relations with Western Europe and Canada, for instance, we were unwilling to apply those same standards in dealing with states of the developing world.

This movement away from the "democratic ideal" had serious consequences for the United States in the immediate post-Vietnam years. For many Americans the United States no longer served as a model to the world. Instead, other states, without democratic values, assumed that position. Further, as those nations have moved away from traditional American beliefs, the "altruistic impulses" within the United States—its social and economic concern for other nations—declined. In fact, an isolationist sentiment has gained some credibility. In order to arrest such trends, a return to democratic values as a basis of policy was crucial in Quester's view.

This democratic impulse gained renewed currency with the demise of communism in Eastern Europe and the Soviet Union. Democracy has the advantage of being an approach in which the United States supports "the good guys in the world, a Wilsonian foreign policy."[48] Such a policy has another attraction as well. By perfecting democratic institutions at home and then seeking to promote them abroad, "democracy promotion would forge a sense of community that would make both the internal and international purpose of the United States not just a 'government policy' but a source of national identity."[49]

Both the Bill Clinton and the George W. Bush administrations invoked this democratic ideal as part of its foreign policy. For instance, the Clinton administration's emphasis on the "enlargement of democracy" around the world, coupled with its emphasis on free trade, sought to capture elements of these Wilsonian and democratic traditions.[50] The key assumption of the Clinton administration, that "democracies do not fight one another," translated into building a more peaceful world by building a more democratic one. The Bush administration's goal of reconstructing Iraq into a domestic society that would serve as a model for nations in the Middle East also reflects this alternative. In fact, in a major foreign policy address during his visit to Great Britain in November 2003, President Bush identified "the global expansion of democracy" as a key pillar of American security. "We cannot rely exclusively on military power to assure our long-term security," he noted. "Lasting peace is gained as justice and democracy advance."[51] A short time earlier, President Bush also embraced the promotion of democracy and individual liberties as core aims of the United States. "The resolve we show" in this area, Bush contended, "will shape the next stage of world democratic movement."[52]

The emphasis upon democracy as the organizing scheme for foreign policy making, the emphasis upon promoting American values abroad, and the efforts to transform the global community to a more pacific one resonate well with the American public. Despite this appeal, however, this approach faces serious challenges. How does one go about building democracies? Does the United States have "the will and the wallet" to undertake such a task? Even if the democratic peace proposition is valid,[53] the transition from nondemocracies to democracies is destabilizing for the global community. That is, as states go through this process of democratization, the road is rocky for the nation itself and for global community. Consider the myriad set of difficulties in postwar Iraq or in the post-Taliban Afghanistan. In short, while the end condition of movement to a democratic world may be pacific, the process of building a democratic order and the movement toward "mature democracies" may not be.[54]

A New Internationalism   A fourth approach would focus upon building a more multilateral approach into American foreign policy and would represent a rather dramatic break from the essentially bipolar arrangement of the Cold War or the unilateral/unipolar impulse of the United States more recently. The approach should be particularly appealing to those who identify with the accommodationist segment of the American public and its leaders and want to work cooperatively with the world community.

Much as some unilateralists recognized the need for the United States to lead in global affairs, Ivo H. Daalder and James M. Lindsay have emphasized the need to move beyond that approach to incorporate a greater degree of multilateralism into American foreign policy during the present era of globalization.[55] While they acknowledge that the unilateralists (or "Americanists" as they call them) are correct in recognizing that "power remains the coin of the realm in international politics," that "the wise application of American primacy can further U.S. values and interests," and that the United States differs from past hegemons "in not seeking to expand its power through territorial gains," American primacy and power are not sufficient. "Some crucial problems do defy unilateral solution," as they contend, whether those problems are global warming, international terrorism, or a whole range of other issues tied to the effects of globalization. As such, international "cooperation can extend the life of American primacy" and manage some of the positive and negative effects of globalization. "By creating international regimes and organizations," Daalder and Lindsay argue, "Washington can imbed its interests and values in institutions that will shape and constrain countries for decades, regardless of the vicissitudes of American power." In this sense, it is in the U.S. national interest to create a global order "based on democracy, human rights, and free enterprise. By doing so, the United States enhances its own liberty, security, and prosperity."[56]

To achieve this end, Daalder and Lindsay outline four basic components or strategies of American foreign policy in this "age of global politics." Although the initial component calls for sustained American economic and military strength, the other three focus on international institutions and American involvement with them. The first calls on the United States "to extend and adapt proven international institutions and arrangements" such as NATO or global trading organizations; the second directs the United States to "enforce compliance with existing international agreements and strengthen the ability of institutions to monitor and compel compliance"; and the third proposes that the United States "take the lead in creating effective international institutions and arrangements to handle new challenges, especially those arising from the downside of globalization." As these latter three components make clear, the United States cannot go it alone in global politics, and international institutions and international agreements are essential to American foreign policy in this era. According to Daalder and Lindsay, the United States "has no other choice" in global politics but to try "to create a world community that shares American values,"[57] and it should do so by working with other nations and with international institutions.

Joseph S. Nye, Jr. would largely agree with Daalder and Lindsay and the title of his post–September 11 book aptly implies the direction that American foreign policy should take: *The Paradox of American Power: Why the World's Only Superpower Can't Go It Alone.*[58] The essential challenge for the United States in the post–September 11 world, Nye contends, is to "define our national interest to include global interests."[59] To do so, the United States will need to pursue interests and values that will have broad appeal and will need to build a global community that is compatible and supportive of such values. A unilateral approach is not sufficient to achieve those ends; instead, an approach that weds unilateralism and multilateralism, albeit with an emphasis on the latter, is his essential prescription for the future.

A unilateral or hegemonic approach is not sufficient, Nye contends, for at least two central reasons. First, that approach underestimates the degree to which the United States can manage the forces of globalization alone. That is, while globalization has the potential to knit together the international system for the benefit of all, as some aspects of trade and investment suggest, globalization also has a dark side, as the events of September 11 surely demonstrated. Despite its substantial power, the United States needs the help and assistance of others to manage both the positive and negative aspects of globalization. A unilateral strategy is also not sufficient for another reason: it has the potential of damaging America's "soft power" in global politics. That is, it has the ability to create envy or rivalry from other states, especially if the United States is viewed as bullying in global affairs.[60] In this case, an important asset of American influence over the years—the attractiveness of its culture, values, and society (or its soft power)—would erode.

Instead, Nye outlines a "grand strategy" that the United States should pursue.[61] It has a number of commonalities with what Daalder and Lindsay describe, but it goes beyond their approach by specifying more fully the values that the United States needs to pursue in a multilateral context and the conditions that should shape American actions. First, Nye acknowledges that protecting vital interests are at the core of his approach and that these interests can and should be defended unilaterally. Yet, as Nye notes, "survival is the necessary condition of foreign policy, but it is not all there is to foreign policy." The national interest also includes the values that the people believe "are so important to our identity or sense of who we are that people are willing to pay a price to promote them."[62]

Second, Nye argues that the United States must work to create three "global public goods." In particular, the United States should work to maintain "regional balances of power" as a way to reduce the incentive for states or groups to try to change international borders. The United States must continue its efforts to promote "an open international economic system," since it serves both the interests of the United States and the rest of the world. The third global public good is keeping open the global commons. This task involves such concerns as freedom of the seas, but today, it also involves addressing "global climate change, preservation of endangered species, and the uses of outer space, as well as the virtual commons of cyberspace."[63] By protecting the global commons, the United States would be in a good position to manage the impact of globalization and would also enhance its soft power in the rest of the world.

Third, Nye argues that the United States should promote human rights and democracy as part of this global approach. While these values should constitute part of America's foreign policy, the United States also needs to integrate them into larger foreign policy considerations. Moreover, Nye sets out "rules of prudence" for when humanitarian interventions should be undertaken in the defense of human rights. Standing for and promoting these values globally will enhance America's soft power. Similarly, the United States would be in a position to enhance its soft power by promoting democracy, but "the role of force is usually less central" to doing so "and the process [of democratization] is of a longer-term nature."[64]

CONCLUDING COMMENTS

Which approach or combination of these approaches (if any) will emerge as the basis of a new foreign policy consensus after September 11 and for the twenty-first century? A greater emphasis on domestic values? A movement toward greater unilateralism? The development of greater international cooperation? A revival of isolationism? We obviously cannot say with any certainty, because the public and elite debate continues. Nevertheless, these contrasting approaches continue to highlight the fact that one important component of the historical American debate has largely been resolved, while the other continues. Most of these approaches generally agree upon the need for continued American engagement in world affairs, albeit in sharply different degrees, but the extent to which and the nature of what domestic moral values should act as an overarching guide to policy actions remains a source of debate. In this sense, the debate over a key value that was closely associated with America's past has changed dramatically, largely away from isolationism to some global participation, but the debate over the other continues.

Such a values debate, however, does not have to be debilitating for American foreign policy. Instead, it can strengthen the unity and resolve of the nation to address its common foreign policy concerns, even as American society seeks to resolve what values it wants to promote in the global arena. The role of values in foreign policy deliberations has perhaps never been more pronounced. As two analysts recently noted, "the rise of ethics in foreign policy" has become increasingly crucial, and, in their estimate, we are in a new era:

> We have passed from an era in which ideals were flatly opposed to self-interests into an era in which tension remains between the two, but the stark juxtaposition of the past has largely subsided. Now ideals and self-interests are generally considered necessary ingredients of the national interest.[65]

NOTES

1. See Eugene R. Wittkopf, Charles W. Kegley, and James M. Scott, *American Foreign Policy: Pattern and Process,* 6th ed. (Belmont, CA: Wadsworth, 2003), pp. 14–15 for an argument along these lines.

2. Ole R. Holsti and James N. Rosenau, "The Political Foundations of Elites' Domestic and Foreign-Policy Beliefs," in Eugene R. Wittkopf and James M. McCormick, eds., *The Domestic Sources of American Foreign Policy: Insights and Evidence,* 3rd ed. (Lanham, MD: Rowman & Littlefield Publishers, Inc., 1999), pp. 33–50.

3. Ibid., p. 37.

4. Ibid., p. 42.

5. Ibid., p. 46.

6. Ole R. Holsti, "Public Opinion and Foreign Policy," in Robert J. Lieber, ed., *Eagle Rules? Foreign Policy and American Primacy in the Twenty-first Century* (Upper Saddle River, NJ: Prentice Hall, Inc., 2002), pp. 16–46. The quoted passages are at p. 39. Other post-Vietnam analyses of elite beliefs by Wittkopf have largely confirmed and more fully specified the foreign policy divisions that Holsti and Rosenau initially suggested. (See Eugene R. Wittkopf, *Faces of Internationalism: Public Opinion and American Foreign Policy* [Durham, NC: Duke University Press, 1990], pp. 107–133.)

7. Marshall M. Bouton and Benjamin I. Page, eds., *Worldviews 2002: American Public Opinion & Foreign Policy* (Chicago: The Chicago Council on Foreign Relations, 2002), pp. 63–72. Here is how Bouton and Page describe the components of the leadership survey: "Administration officials in the State, Treasury, Commerce, and other departments, and agencies dealing with foreign policy; members of the House and Senate or their senior staff with committee responsibilities in foreign affairs, senior business executives from Fortune 1000 firms who deal with international matters; university administrators and academics who teach in the area of international relations; presidents of major organizations or large interest groups active in foreign affairs; presidents of the largest labor unions; religious leaders; and journalists and editorial staff who handle international news" (p. 63).

8. Ibid., pp. 66–68.

9. See Eugene R. Wittkopf and Michael A. Maggiotto, "Elites and Masses: A Comparative Analysis of Attitudes Toward America's World Role," *The Journal of Politics* 45 (May 1983), especially pp. 312–323; Eugene R. Wittkopf, "Elites and Masses: Constancy and Change in Public Attitudes Toward America's World Role," a paper delivered at the annual meeting of the Southern Political Science Association, Birmingham, Alabama, November 1983; and Wittkopf, *Faces of Internationalism,* pp. 134–165.

10. See Bouton and Page, *Worldviews 2002: American Public Opinion & Foreign Policy,* pp. 66–73.

11. See ibid. at pp. 69–72. The data discussed here are summarized in Table 13.2.

12. Bouton and Page, *Worldviews 2002: American Public Opinion & Foreign Policy,* pp. 68–69.

13. Ibid., p. 69.

14. For some Vietnam-era calls for a new consensus, see, for example, Lincoln P. Bloomfield, "Foreign Policy for Disillu-

sioned Liberals," *Foreign Policy* 9 (Winter 1972–73): 55–68; Thomas L. Hughes, "The Flight From Foreign Policy," *Foreign Policy* 10 (Spring 1973): 141–156; and Philip Windsor, "America's Moral Confusion: Separating the Should from the Good," *Foreign Policy* 13 (Winter 1973–74): 139–153. A survey of *Foreign Affairs,* the other leading journal on foreign policy, produced a number of commentaries on this breakdown of the old consensus and a need for another set of unifying values purposes. Interested readers should see, for example, John V. Lindsay, "For a New Policy Balance," *Foreign Affairs* 50 (October 1971): 1–14; Kingman Brewster, Jr., "Reflections on Our National Purpose," *Foreign Affairs* 50 (April 1972): 399–415; Zbigniew Brzezinski, "U.S. Foreign Policy: The Search for Focus," *Foreign Affairs* 51 (July 1973): 708–727; and Max Lerner, "America Agonistes," *Foreign Affairs* 52 (January 1974): 287–300.

15. Zbigniew Brzezinski, "America in a Hostile World," *Foreign Policy* 23 (Summer 1976): 89.

16. Thomas L. Hughes, "The Crack-Up: The Price of Collective Irresponsibility," *Foreign Policy* 40 (Fall 1980): 33–60. Actually Hughes argues that the two "cultures" have always existed in the postwar period, even during the time of presumed consensus before Vietnam. At that time, however, there had been a "workable dissensus" (p. 52). This point raises the larger issue of the extent to which the Cold War consensus was a true consensus. Admittedly, the systematic empirical evidence for the present "dissensus" among the leadership and the public is more readily available than that for the consensus of the immediate postwar years.

17. See, for example, Graham Allison and Gregory F. Treverton, eds., *Rethinking America's Security: Beyond Cold War to New World Order* (New York: W. W. Norton and Company, 1992); Terry L. Deibel, "Strategies Before Containment: Patterns for the Future," *International Security* 16 (Spring 1992): 79–108; John Lewis Gaddis, *The United States and the End of the Cold War: Implications, Reconsiderations, and Provocations* (New York: Oxford University Press, 1992); Zalmay Khalilzad, "Losing the Moment? The United States and the World After the Cold War," *The Washington Quarterly* 18 (Spring 1995); 87–107; Richard A. Melanson, *American Foreign Policy Since the Vietnam War: The Search for Consensus from Nixon to Clinton,* 2nd ed. (Armonk, NY: M. E. Sharpe, 1996); and Andrew Rosenthal, "Farewell, Red Menace," *New York Times,* September 1, 1991, 1 and 14, among many others.

18. James Steinberg, "Counterterrorism," *Brookings Review* 20 (Summer 2002): 4–7.

19. Jessica T. Matthews, "September 11, One Year Later: A World of Change," *Policy Brief,* special edition 18 (Washington, DC: Carnegie Endowment for International Peace, 2002).

20. On how American foreign policy has become captive of domestic interests at the expense of the "national interest," see Samuel P. Huntington, "The Erosion of American National Interests," in Eugene R. Wittkopf and James M. McCormick, eds., *The Domestic Sources of American Foreign Policy: Insights and Evidence.* 4th ed. (Lanham, MD: Rowman & Littlefield Publishers, Inc., Inc., 2004), pp. 55–65.

21. See James Chace, "Is a Foreign Policy Consensus Possible?" *Foreign Affairs* 57 (Fall 1978): 16 for the view advanced at the beginning of this paragraph. For Chace's later view, including this quotation, see James Chace, "The Dangers of a Foreign Policy Consensus," *World Policy Journal* 13 (Winter 1996–1997): 97.

22. I am indebted to Professor Ole Holsti of Duke University for suggesting this point about consensus on issues.

23. Chace, "Is a Foreign Policy Consensus Possible?" p. 15. Actually, Chace quotes from Stanley Hoffmann's *Primacy or World Order* (New York: McGraw-Hill, 1978) to make this point.

24. Leslie H. Gelb with Richard K. Betts, *The Irony of Vietnam: The System Worked* (Washington, DC: The Brookings Institution, 1979), pp. 365–369.

25. Ibid., pp. 365, 366.

26. Hughes, "The Crack-Up: The Price of Collective Irresponsibility," p. 59.

27. For the classic statement of the impact of international events on domestic images, see Karl W. Deutsch, "External Influences on the Internal Behavior of States," in

R. Barry Farrell, ed., *Approaches to Comparative and International Politics* (Evanston, IL: Northwestern University Press, 1966), pp. 5–26.

28. Earl C. Ravenel, "The Case for Adjustment," *Foreign Policy* 81 (Winter 1990–1991): 3–19.

29. Ibid., pp. 3, 4, 6, 8.

30. Ibid., p. 15, is the source of the quotation. The discussion of changed defense needs follows at pp. 16–17.

31. Ibid., p. 19.

32. Eric A. Nordlinger, *Isolationism Reconfigured: American Foreign Policy for a New Century* (Princeton, NJ: Princeton University Press, 1995).

33. Ibid., p. 31.

34. Ibid., p. 41.

35. Ibid., p. 43.

36. Ibid.

37. Ibid., p. 181.

38. Ibid., pp. 263–278.

39. Ted Galen Carpenter, *Peace and Freedom: Foreign Policy for a Constitutional Republic* (Washington, DC: Cato Institute, 2002), pp. 1–11, with the quoted passage at p. 11.

40. Both quotations in this paragraph are from ibid., p. 12.

41. William Kristol and Robert Kagan, "Toward A Neo-Reaganite Foreign Policy," *Foreign Affairs* 75 (July/August 1996): 18–32.

42. Ibid., p. 20.

43. Ibid., p. 23.

44. Ibid., pp. 23, 27.

45. Robert J. Lieber, "Foreign Policy and American Primacy," in Robert J. Lieber, *Eagle Rules? Foreign Policy and American Primacy in the Twenty-first Century,* pp. 1–15. The quoted passages are at p. 5.

46. Richard N. Haaas, "Defining U.S. Foreign Policy in a Post-Post–Cold War World," The 2002 Arthur Ross Lecture, Remarks to the Foreign Policy Association, New York, April 22, 2002, online. Available: http://www.state.gov/s/p/rem/9632.htm. As Haas acknowledges, the "post-post–Cold War world" is how Secretary of State Colin Powell liked to refer to the present environment.

47. This section relies upon Quester, "Consensus Lost," *Foreign Policy* 40 (Fall 1980): 18–32. The quoted phrases are at pp. 22, 29, and 31. A more complete analysis of his views is presented in George Quester, *American Foreign Policy: The Lost Consensus* (New York: Praeger, 1982).

48. The comment was by the late congressman Les Aspin (D-Wisconsin), and he is quoted in Norman J. Ornstein and Mark Schmitt, "Dateline Campaign '92: Post-Cold War Politics," *Foreign Policy* 79 (Summer 1990): 184.

49. Ibid., p. 185.

50. The discussion in this and the next paragraph draws from my "Assessing Clinton's Foreign Policy at Midterm," *Current History* 94 (November 1995): 373.

51. George W. Bush, "President Bush Discusses Iraq Policy at Whitehall Palace in London," remarks by the President at Whitehall Palace, London, England, November 19, 2003, online. Available: http://www.whitehouse.gov/news/releases/2003/11/20031119–1.html.

52. George W. Bush, "President Bush Discusses Freedom in Iraq and Middle East," remarks by the President at the 20th Anniversary of the National Endowment for Democracy, United States Chamber of Commerce, Washington, DC, November 6, 2003, online. Available: http://www.whitehouse.gov/news/releases/2003/11/20031106–2.html.

53. Bruce M. Russett, *Grasping the Democratic Peace: Principles for a Post-Cold War World* (Princeton, NJ: Princeton University Press, 1993), p. 21; and Zeev Maoz and Bruce Russett, "Normative and Structural Causes of Democratic Peace, 1946–1986," *American Political Science Review* 87 (September 1993): 624–638. Also see David A. Lake, "Powerful Pacifists: Democratic States and War," *American Political Science Review* 86 (March 1992): 24–37.

54. Edward D. Mansfield and Jack Snyder, "Democratization and War," *Foreign Affairs* 74 (May/June 1995): 79–97.

55. Ivo H. Daalder and James M. Lindsay, "The Globalization of Politics: American Foreign Policy for a New Century," *Brookings Review* 21 (Winter 2003): 12–17.

56. Ibid., pp. 16 and 17 for the quotations in this paragraph.

57. Ibid., p. 17 for quotations in this paragraph.

58. Joseph S. Nye, Jr., *The Paradox of American Power: Why the World's Superpower Can't Go It Alone.* (New York: Oxford University Press, 2002).

59. Ibid., p. xiv.

60. See, for example, ibid. at pp. xvi, 137–138, and 140.

61. Ibid., pp. 141–153.

62. The two quotations are from ibid. at p. 139.

63. The previous quotations in this paragraph are from ibid., pp. 144–145.

64. The previous quotations in this paragraph are from ibid., pp. 152–153.

65. Leslie H. Gelb and Justine A. Rosenthal, "The Rise of Ethics in Foreign Policy: Reaching a Values Consensus," *Foreign Affairs* 82 (May/June 2003): 2–7. The first quote is from the title of the article at p. 2 and the second is from p. 7.

A Selected Bibliography

Abrams, Elliott, ed. *The Influence of Faith: Religious Groups and U.S. Foreign Policy.* Lanham, MD: Rowman & Littlefield Publishers, Inc., 2001.

Acheson, Dean. *Present at the Creation.* New York: W. W. Norton and Company, 1969.

Adler, David Gray. "The Constitution and Presidential Warmaking: The Enduring Debate." *Political Science Quarterly* 103 (Spring 1988): 1–36.

"African-Caribbean Initiative Lower Tariffs, Quotas on Some Foreign-Made Apparel," *Congressional Quarterly Almanac 2000.* Washington, DC: Congressional Quarterly, Inc., 2001

Aldrich, John H., John L. Sullivan, and Eugene Borgida. "Foreign Affairs and Issue Voting: Do Presidential Candidates 'Waltz Before a Blind Audience'?" *American Political Science Review* 83 (March 1989): 123–141.

Allison, Graham. *Essence of Decision: Explaining the Cuban Missile Crisis.* Boston: Little, Brown and Company, 1971.

———, and Philip Zelikow. *Essence of Decision: Explaining the Cuban Missile Crisis.* 2nd ed. New York: Longman, 1999.

———, and Gregory F. Treverton, eds. *Rethinking America's Security: Beyond Cold War to New World Order.* New York: W. W. Norton and Company, 1992.

Almond, Gabriel A. *The American People and Foreign Policy.* New York: Praeger, 1960.

———, and Sidney Verba. *The Civic Culture.* Boston: Little, Brown and Company, 1963.

Alperovitz, Gar. *Atomic Diplomacy: Hiroshima and Potsdam.* New York: Random House, 1965.

Ambrose, Stephen E. *Rise to Globalism: American Foreign Policy 1938–1976.* New York: Penguin Books, 1976.

American Lack Background to Follow International News: Public's News Habits Little Changed by Sept. 11. Washington, DC: The Pew Research Center for the People and the Press, 2002.

Anderson, Curt. "Bush Seeks More Powers, Money for National Safety," *Des Moines Register* (July 17, 2002): 1A.

Arnett, Peter. *Live From the Battlefield*. New York: Simon & Schuster, 1994.

Aron, Raymond. "Ideology in Search of a Policy." In *America and the World 1981,* William P. Bundy, ed. New York: Pergamon Press, 1982.

Bailey, Thomas A. *A Diplomatic History of the American People*. New York: F. S. Crofts & Co., 1942.

———. *The Man on the Street: The Impact of American Public Opinion on Foreign Policy*. New York: Macmillan, Inc., 1948.

Baker, James A., III, with Thomas M. DeFrank. *The Politics of Diplomacy: Revolution, War and Peace, 1989–1992*. New York: G. P. Putnam's Sons, 1995.

Ball, George W., and Douglas B. Ball. *The Passionate Attachment*. New York: W. W. Norton and Company, 1992.

Balz, Dan. "Kerry Raps Bush Policy on Postwar Iraq." *The Washington Post* (July 11, 2003): A1, A6.

Baum, Matthew A. "Sex, Lies, and War: How Soft News Brings Foreign Policy to the Inattentive Public," *American Political Science Review* 96 (March 2002): 91–109.

Bay, Christian. *The Structure of Freedom*. New York: Atheneum Publishers, 1965.

Beaumont, Thomas. "Gephardt Takes Aim at Bush." *Des Moines Register* (July 14, 2003): 1B.

Benedetto, Richard. "Poll: Bush Trails Clark, Kerry." *Des Moines Register* (September 23, 2003): 1A, 9A.

Bennet, Douglas J., Jr. "Congress in Foreign Policy: Who Needs It?" *Foreign Affairs* 57 (Fall 1978): 40–50.

Bennett, W. Lance. "The Media and the Foreign Policy Process." In *The New Politics of American Foreign Policy,* David A. Deese, ed. New York: St. Martin's Press, 1994.

———, and David L. Paletz, eds. *Taken by Storm: The Media, Public Opinion, and U.S. Foreign Policy in the Gulf War*. Chicago and London: The University of Chicago Press, 1994.

Beres, Louis Rene. *People, States, and World Order*. Itasca, IL: F. E. Peacock Publishers, Inc., 1981.

Berger, Samuel R. "A Foreign Policy for a Global Age." *Foreign Affairs* 79 (November/December 2000): 22–39.

Berkowitz, Bruce. "Information Age Intelligence." *Foreign Policy* 103 (Summer 1996): 35–50.

Berkowitz, Morton, P. G. Bock, and Vincent Fuccillo, eds. *The Politics of American Foreign Policy*. Englewood Cliffs, NJ: Prentice-Hall, Inc., 1977.

Bernstein, Robert A., and William W. Anthony. "The ABM Issue in the Senate, 1968–1970: The Importance of Ideology." *American Political Science Review* 68 (September 1974): 1198–1206.

Berry, Nicholas O., ed. *U.S. Foreign Policy Documents, 1933–1945: From Withdrawal to World Leadership*. Brunswick, OH: King's Court Communications, Inc., 1978.

———. *Foreign Policy and the Press*. Westport, CT: Greenwood Press, 1990.

Betts, Richard K. "Misadventure Revisited." In *A Reader in American Foreign Policy,* James M. McCormick, ed. Itasca, IL: F. E. Peacock Publishers, Inc., 1986.

Blechman, Barry M., and Stephen S. Kaplan. *Force Without War*. Washington, DC: The Brookings Institution, 1978.

Blight, James G., and David A. Welch. *On the Brink: Americans and Soviets Reexamine the Cuban Missile Crisis*. 2nd ed. New York: The Noonday Press, 1990.

Bliss, Howard, and M. Glen Johnson. *Beyond the Water's Edge: America's Foreign Policies*. Philadelphia: J. B. Lippincott Co., 1975.

———. *Consensus at the Crossroads: Dialogues in American Foreign Policy*. New York: Dodd, Mead & Co., Inc., 1972.

Bloomfield, Lincoln P. "Foreign Policy for Disillusioned Liberals?" *Foreign Policy* 9 (Winter 1972–73): 55–68.

———. "From Ideology to Program to Policy." *Journal of Policy Analysis and Management* 2 (Fall 1982): 1–12.

————. *In Search of American Foreign Policy.* New York: Oxford University Press, 1974.

Bond, Jon R., and Richard Fleisher. *The President in the Legislative Arena.* Chicago: The University of Chicago Press, 1990.

Boorstin, Daniel J. *America and the Image of Europe: Reflections on American Thought.* New York: Meridian Books, 1960.

Bouton, Marshall M., and Benjamin I. Page. *Worldviews 2002: American Public Opinion & Foreign Policy.* Chicago: The Chicago Council on Foreign Relations, 2002.

Braestrup, Peter. *Big Story: How the American Press and Television Reported and Interpreted the Crisis of Tet 1968.* 2 vols. Boulder, CO: Westview Press, 1977.

Brewer, Thomas L. *American Foreign Policy: A Contemporary Introduction.* Englewood Cliffs, NJ: Prentice-Hall, Inc., 1980.

Brewster, Kingman, Jr. "Reflection on our National Purpose." *Foreign Affairs* 50 (April 1972): 339–415.

Brown, Seyom. *The Faces of Power: Constancy and Change in United States Foreign Policy From Truman to Reagan.* New York: Columbia University Press, 1983.

Browne, Marjorie Ann. *Executive Agreements and the Congress.* Issue Brief Number IB75035. Washington, DC: The Library of Congress, 1981.

Brownstein, Ronald, and Nina Easton. *Reagan's Ruling Class.* Washington, DC: The Presidential Accountability Group, 1982.

Brzezinski, Zbigniew. "America in a Hostile World." *Foreign Policy* 23 (Summer 1976): 65–96.

————. "How The Cold War Was Played." *Foreign Affairs* 51(October 1972): 181–204.

————. *Power and Principle: Memoirs of the National Security Advisor, 1977–1981.* New York: Farrar, Straus & Giroux, 1983.

————. "U.S. Foreign Policy: The Search for Focus." *Foreign Affairs* 51 (July 1973): 708–727.

Buckley, William F., Jr. "Human Rights and Foreign Policy." *Foreign Affairs* 58 (Spring 1980): 775–796.

Bull, Hedley. "A View From Abroad: Consistency Under Pressure." In *America and the World 1978,* William P. Bundy, ed. New York: Pergamon Press, 1979.

Bundy, William P. "A Portentous Year." In *America and the World 1983,* William P. Bundy, ed. New York: Pergamon Press,1984.

Burgin, Eileen. "Congress and Foreign Policy: The Misperceptions." In *Congress Reconsidered,* Lawrence C. Dodd and Bruce I. Oppenheimer, eds. Washington, DC: CQ Press,1993.

Bush, George W. "A Distinctly American Internationalism." Delivered at the Ronald Reagan Presidential Library. November 19, 1999, online. Available: http://www.georgewbush.com/speeches/foreignpolicy/foreignpolicy.asp.

————. "Address to a Joint Session of Congress and the American People." September 20, 2001, online. Available: http://www.whitehouse.gov/news/releases/2001/09/20010920–8.html.

————."President Bush Discusses Iraq Freedom in Iraq and Middle East." Remarks by the President at the 20th Anniversary of the National Endowment for Democracy, United States Chamber of Commerce, Washington, DC, November 6, 2003, online. Available: http://www.whitehouse.gov/news/releases/2003/11/20031106–2.html.

————. "President Bush Discusses Iraq Policy at Whitehall Palace in London." Remarks by the President at Whitehall Palace, London, England, November 19, 2003, online. Available: http://www.whitehouse.gov/news/releases/2003/11/20031119–1.html.

————. "President's Remarks at the United Nations General Assembly." September 12, 2002, online. Available: http://www.whitehouse.gov/news/releases/2002/09/2002/09.

————. "President Says Saddam Hussein Must Leave Iraq Within 48 Hours." March 17, 2003, online. Available: http://www.whitehouse.gov/news/releases/2003/03/20030317–7.html.

Cameron, Maxwell A., and Brian W. Tomlin. *The Making of NAFTA: How the Deal Was Done.* Ithaca, NY, and London: Cornell University Press, 2000.

Campbell, Colin. *Managing the Presidency: Carter, Reagan, and the Search for Executive Harmony.* Pittsburgh: University of Pittsburgh Press, 1986.

Campbell, John Franklin. "The Disorganization of State." In *Problems of American Foreign Policy.* 2nd ed., Martin B. Hickman, ed. Beverly Hills: Glencoe Press, 1975.

Carleton, David, and Michael Stohl. "The Foreign Policy of Human Rights: Rhetoric and Reality from Jimmy Carter to Ronald Reagan." *Human Rights Quarterly* 9 (May 1985): 205–229.

Carpenter, Ted Galen. *Peace and Freedom: Foreign Policy for a Constitutional Republic.* Washington, DC: Cato Institute, 2002.

Carroll, Holbert N. *The House of Representatives and Foreign Affairs.* Pittsburgh: University of Pittsburgh Press, 1958.

Carter, Jimmy. *Keeping Faith.* New York: Bantam Books, 1982.

Carter, Ralph G. *Contemporary Cases in U.S. Foreign Policy: From Terrorism to Trade.* Washington, DC: CQ Press, 2002.

———, and James M. Scott. "Funding the IMF: Congress versus the White House." In *Contemporary Cases in U.S. Foreign Policy: From Terrorism to Trade,* Ralph G. Carter, ed. Washington, DC: CQ Press, 2002.

Caspary, William R. "The 'Mood Theory': A Study of Public Opinion and Foreign Policy." *American Political Science Review* 54 (June 1970): 536–547.

Chace, James. "The Dangers of a Foreign Policy Consensus." *World Policy Journal* 13 (Winter 1996–1997): 97–99.

———. "Is a Foreign Policy Consensus Possible?" *Foreign Affairs* 57 (Fall 1978): 1–16.

The Challenge of Peace: God's Promise and Our Response. Washington, DC: The United States Catholic Conference, May 3, 1983.

Chan, Steve. "Grasping the Peace Dividend: Some Propositions on the Conversion of Swords into Plowshares." *Mershon International Studies Review* 39 (April 1995): 53–95.

The Chicago Council on Foreign Relations. "A World Transformed: Foreign Policy Attitudes of the U.S. Public after September 11th." September 4, 2002, online. Available: http://www.world-views.org/key_findings/us_911_report.htm.

Christopher, Warren. "Ceasefire Between the Branches: A Compact in Foreign Affairs." *Foreign Affairs* 60 (Summer 1982): 989–1005.

Choate, Pat. *Agents of Influence.* New York: Alfred A. Knopf, 1990.

———, and Bruce Stokes. *Democratizing U.S. Trade Policy.* New York: Council on Foreign Relations, Inc., 2001

Clarke, Duncan L. *Politics of Arms Control: The Role and Effectiveness of the U.S. Arms Control and Disarmament Agency.* New York: The Free Press, 1979.

———. "Why State Can't Lead." *Foreign Policy* 66 (Spring 1987): 128–142.

Clausen, Aage R. *How Congressmen Decide: A Policy Focus.* New York: St. Martin's Press, 1973.

Clausewitz, Carl von. *On War.* Ed. and trans. by Michael Howard and Peter Paret. Princeton, NJ: Princeton University Press, 1976.

Clinton, David. "Tocqueville's Challenge." *The Washington Quarterly* 11 (Winter 1988): 173–189.

Cohen, Bernard. *The Political Process and Foreign Policy: The Making of the Japanese Settlement.* Princeton, NJ: Princeton University Press, 1957.

———. *The Press and Foreign Policy.* Princeton, NJ: Princeton University Press, 1963.

———. *The Public's Impact on Foreign Policy.* Boston: Little, Brown and Company, 1973.

Cohen, Stephen D. *The Making of United States International Economic Policy.* 3rd ed. New York: Praeger, 1988.

————. *The Making of United States International Economic Policy.* 4th ed. Westport, CT: Praeger, 1994.

————. *The Making of United States International Economic Policy.* 5th ed. Westport, CT: Praeger, 2000.

————, Joel R. Paul, and Robert A. Blecker. *Fundamentals of U.S. Foreign Trade Policy.* Boulder, CO: Westview Press, 1996.

Coles, Harry L. *The War of 1812.* Chicago: The University of Chicago Press, 1965.

Collier, Ellen C. "Foreign Policy by Reporting Requirement." *The Washington Quarterly* 11 (Winter 1988): 75–84.

Committee on Foreign Relations, United States Senate. *Treaties and Other International Agreements: The Role of the United States Senate.* A Study Prepared for the Committee on Foreign Relations, United States Senate, by the Congressional Research Service. Washington, DC: U.S. Government Printing Office, January 2001.

Congress and the Nation 1945–1964. Washington, DC: Congressional Quarterly Service, 1965.

Congressional Quarterly's Guide to Congress. 3rd ed. Washington, DC: Congressional Quarterly, Inc., 1982.

Cooke, Jacob E., ed. *The Federalist.* Middletown, CT: Wesleyan University Press, 1961.

Cooper, Chester L. "The CIA and Decisionmaking." *Foreign Affairs* 50 (January 1972): 221–236.

Cooper, Joseph, and Patricia A. Hurley. "The Legislative Veto: A Policy Analysis." *Congress & the Presidency* 10 (Spring 1983): 1–24.

Corwin, Edward S. *The President: Office and Powers 1787–1957.* New York: New York University Press, 1957.

Crabb, Cecil V., Jr. *Bipartisan Foreign Policy.* Evanston, IL: Row, Peterson and Company, 1957.

————. *The Elephants and the Grass: A Study of Nonalignment.* New York: Frederick A. Praeger, 1965.

————. *Policymakers and Critics: Conflicting Theories of American Foreign Policy.* New York: Frederick A. Praeger, Inc., 1976.

————, and Pat M. Holt. *Invitation to Struggle: Congress, the President, and Foreign Policy.* Washington, DC: Congressional Quarterly Press, 1980.

Craig, Gordon A., and Alexander L. George. *Force and Statecraft.* 3rd ed. New York and Oxford: Oxford University Press, 1995.

Cumings, Bruce. *The Origins of the Korean War. Volume II: The Roaring of the Cataract, 1947–1950.* Princeton, NJ: Princeton University Press, 1990.

Daalder, Ivo H., and I. M. Destler. "A New NSC for a New Administration," *Brookings Policy Brief #68,* online. Available: http://www.brook.edu.dyb-docroot/comm/policybriefs/pb068/pb68.htm.

————. "Advisors, Czars, and Councils," *The National Interest* 68 (Summer 2002): 66–78.

————. "How National Security Advisers See Their Role," In *The Domestic Sources of American Foreign Policy: Insights and Evidence.* 4th ed., Eugene R. Wittkopf and James M. McCormick, eds. Lanham, MD: Rowman & Littlefield Publishers, Inc., 2004.

————, and James M. Lindsay. "Bush's Foreign Policy Revolution." In *The George W. Bush Presidency: An Early Assessment,* Fred I. Greenstein, ed. Baltimore and London: The Johns Hopkins University Press, 2003.

————. "The Bush Revolution: The Remaking of America's Foreign Policy." Revised version of paper prepared for presentation at The George W. Bush Presidency: An Early Assessment Conference, Princeton University, April 25–26, 2003, online. Available http://www.wws.princeton.edu/bushconf/DaalderLindsayPaper.pdf.

————. "The Globalization of Politics: American Foreign Policy for a New Century." *Brookings Review* 21 (Winter 2003): 12–17.

————, James M. Lindsay, and James B. Steinberg. "Hard Choices: National

Security and the War on Terrorism." *Current History* 101 (December 2002): 409–413.

———. "The Bush National Security Strategy: An Evaluation." October 2002, online. Available: http://www.brook-ings.edu/comm/policybriefs/pb109.htm.

Dahl, Robert A. *Congress and Foreign Policy.* New York: Harcourt, Brace and Company, 1950.

———. *Modern Political Analysis.* 2nd ed. Englewood Cliffs, NJ: Prentice-Hall, Inc., 1970.

Dallek, Robert. *The American Style of Foreign Policy.* New York: Alfred A. Knopf, 1983.

Deering, Christopher J. "Decision Making in the Armed Services Committees." In *Congress Resurgent: Foreign and Defense Policy on Capitol Hill,* Randall B. Ripley and James M. Lindsay, eds. Ann Arbor: The University of Michigan Press, 1993.

Deibel, Terry L. "Strategies Before Containment: Patterns for the Future." *International Security* 16 (Spring 1992): 79–108.

De la Garza, Rodolfo O. "U.S. Foreign Policy and the Mexican-American Political Agenda." In *Ethnic Groups and U.S. Foreign Policy,* Mohammed E. Ahrari, ed. New York: Greenwood Press, 1987.

———, and Harry P. Pachon. *Latinos and U.S. Foreign Policy.* Lanham, MD: Rowman & Littlefield Publishers, Inc., 2000.

De Long, Bradford, Christopher De Long, and Sherman Robinson. "The Case for Mexico's Rescue." *Foreign Affairs* 75 (May/June 1996): 8–14.

DeParle, Jason. "The Man Inside Bill Clinton's Foreign Policy." *New York Times Magazine,* August 20, 1995, 32–39, 46, 55, 57.

Destler, I. M. *American Trade Politics.* Washington, DC: Institute of International Economics and New York: The Twentieth Century Fund, 1992.

———. "Dateline Washington: Congress as Boss?" *Foreign Policy* 42 (Spring 1981): 167–180.

———. "National Security Advice to U.S. Presidents: Some Lessons from Thirty Years." *World Politics* 24 (January 1977): 143–176.

———. "National Security Management: What Presidents Have Wrought." *Political Science Quarterly* 95 (Winter 1980–1981): 573–588.

———. *Presidents, Bureaucrats, and Foreign Policy.* Princeton, NJ: Princeton University Press, 1974.

———, Leslie H. Gelb, and Anthony Lake. *Our Own Worst Enemy: The Unmaking of American Foreign Policy.* New York: Simon & Schuster, 1984.

De Tocqueville, Alexis. *Democracy in America.* Ed. and abridged by Richard D. Heffner. New York: New American Library, 1956.

Deutch, John, and Jeffrey H. Smith. "Smarter Intelligence." *Foreign Policy* (January/February 2002): 64–69.

Deutsch, Karl W. "External Influence on the Internal Behavior of States." In *Approaches to Comparative and Inter-national Politics,* R. Barry Farrell, ed. Evanston, IL: Northwestern University Press, 1966.

Devine, Donald J. *The Political Culture of the United States.* Boston: Little, Brown and Company, 1972.

De Young, Karen, and Steven Mufson. "A Leaner and Less Visible NSC Reorganization Will Emphasize Defense, Global Economics." *The Washington Post* (February 10, 2001): 1.

Donovan, John C. *The Cold Warriors: A Policy-Making Elite.* Lexington, MA: D. C. Heath and Company, 1974.

Dorrien, Gary, "Axis of One." *Christian Century* 120 (March 8, 2003): 30–35.

Drew, Elizabeth. "A Reporter At Large: Brzezinski." *The New Yorker* (May 1, 1978): 90–130.

———. *On the Edge: The Clinton Presidency.* New York: Simon & Schuster, 1994.

Dye, Thomas R. *Who's Running America? The Bush Era.* Englewood Cliffs, NJ: Prentice-Hall, Inc., 1990.

————. *Who's Running America? The Clinton Years.* 6th ed. Englewood Cliffs, NJ: Prentice Hall, Inc., 1995.

————. *Who's Running America? Institutional Leadership in the United States.* Englewood Cliffs, NJ: Prentice-Hall, Inc., 1976.

————. *Who's Running America? The Bush Restoration.* 7th ed. Upper Saddle River, NJ: Prentice-Hall, 2002.

Easton, David. *The Political System.* New York: Alfred A.Knopf, Inc., 1953.

Eisenhower, Dwight D. "The Military-Industrial Complex." In *Power in Postwar America,* Richard Gillam, ed. Boston: Little, Brown and Company, 1971.

Emery, Michael. "An Endangered Species: The International Newshole." *Gannett Center Journal* 3 (Fall 1989): 151–164.

Esterline, John H., and Robert B. Black. *Inside Foreign Policy: The Department of State Political System and Its Subsystem.* Palo Alto, CA: Mayfield Publishing Company, 1975.

Etzold, Thomas H. "The Far East in American Strategy, 1948–1951." In *Aspects of Sino American Relations Since 1784,* Thomas H. Etzold, ed. New York: New Viewpoints, 1978.

Executive Legislative Consultation on Foreign Policy. *Strengthening Foreign Policy Information Sources for Congress.* Washington, DC: Government Printing Office, February 1982.

Falk, Richard A. "What's Wrong with Henry Kissinger's Foreign Policy." *Alternatives* 1 (March 1975): 79–100.

Fenno, Richard F., Jr. *Congressmen in Committees.* Boston: Little, Brown and Company, 1973.

Fernandez, Damian J. "From Little Havana to Washington, D.C.: Cuban-Americans and U.S. Foreign Policy." In *Ethnic Groups and U.S. Foreign Policy,* Mohammed E. Ahrari, ed. New York: Greenwood Press, 1987.

Ferrell, Robert H. *American Diplomacy: A History.* 3rd ed. New York: W. W. Norton and Company, 1975.

————. *American Diplomacy: The Twentieth Century.* New York: W. W. Norton and Company, 1988.

Findley, Paul. *Deliberate Deceptions: Facing the Facts about U.S.-Israeli Relationship.* New York: Lawrence Hill Books, 1995.

Fisher, Louis. *The President and Congress: Power and Policy.* New York: Free Press, 1972.

————. *Presidential War Power.* Lawrence: University Press of Kansas, 1995.

Fleisher, Richard. "Economic Benefit, Ideology, and Senate Voting on the B-1 Bomber." *American Politics Quarterly* 13 (April 1985): 200–211.

————, and Jon R. Bond. "Are There Two Presidencies? Yes, But Only for Republicans." *The Journal of Politics* 50 (August 1988): 747–767.

Fleming, D. F. *The Cold War and Its Origins, 1917–1960.* New York: Doubleday & Co., Inc., 1961.

Foyle, Douglas C. *Counting the Public In: Presidents, Public Opinion, and Foreign Policy.* New York: Oxford University Press, 1999.

Franck, Thomas M., and Edward Weisband. *Foreign Policy by Congress.* New York: Oxford University Press, 1979.

Frankel, Glenn. "Poll: Opposition to U.S. Policy Grows in Europe." *The Washington Post* (September 4, 2003): A15

Free, Lloyd A., and Hadley Cantril, *The Political Beliefs of Americans: A Study of Public Opinion.* New York: Clarion Book, 1968.

Freedman, Lawrence. *The Evolution of Nuclear Strategy.* New York: St. Martin's Press, 1981.

Frye, Alton. *Humanitarian Intervention: Crafting a Workable Doctrine.* New York: Council on Foreign Relations, Inc., 2000.

Fulbright, J. William. *The Arrogance of Power.* New York: Vintage Books, 1966.

Furlong, William L. "Negotiations and Ratification of the Panama Canal Treaties." In *Congress, The Presidency, and American Foreign Policy,* John Spanier and

Joseph Nogee, eds. New York: Pergamon Press, 1981.

Gaddis, John Lewis. "A Grand Strategy." *Foreign Policy* (November/December 2002): 50–57.

———. "Containment: A Reassessment." *Foreign Affairs* 55 (July 1977): 873–887.

———. *The Soviet Union and the United States: An Interpretative History.* New York: John Wiley and Sons, 1978.

———. *Strategies of Containment.* New York: Oxford University Press, 1982.

———. *The United States and the End of the Cold War: Implications, Reconsiderations, and Provocations.* New York: Oxford University Press, 1992.

———. *The United States and the Origins of the Cold War 1941–1947.* New York and London: Columbia University Press, 1972.

———. "Was the Truman Doctrine a Real Turning Point?" *Foreign Affairs* 52 (January 1974): 386–402.

Garnham, David. "Foreign Service Elitism and U.S. Foreign Affairs." *Public Administration Review* 35 (January/February 1975): 44–51.

———. "State Department Rigidity: Testing a Psychological Hypothesis." *International Studies Quarterly* 18 (March 1974): 31–39.

Gelb, Leslie H., with Richard K. Betts. *The Irony of Vietnam: The System Worked.* Washington, DC: The Brookings Institution, 1979.

———, and Justine A. Rosenthal, "The Rise of Ethics in Foreign Policy: Reaching a Values Consensus." *Foreign Affairs* 82 (May/June 2003): 2–7.

Gershman, Carl. *The Foreign Policy of American Labor. The Washington Papers,* 3, no. 29. Beverly Hills: Sage Publications, 1975.

Gibson, Martha Liebler. "Managing Conflict: The Role of the Legislative Veto in American Foreign Policy." *Polity* 26 (Spring 1994): 441–472.

———. *Weapons of Influence: The Legislative Veto, American Foreign Policy, and the Irony of Reform.* Boulder, CO: Westview Press, 1992.

Glennon, Michael. *Constitutional Diplomacy.* Princeton, NJ: Princeton University Press, 1990.

———. "The Good Friday Accords: Legislative Veto by Another Name?" *The American Journal of International Law* 83 (September 1989): 544–546.

Goldberg, Bernard. *Bias: A CBS Insider Exposes How the Media Distort the News.* Washington, DC: Regnery Publishing, Inc., 2002.

Goldstein, Judith, and Robert O. Keohane, eds. *Ideas and Foreign Policy: Beliefs, Institutions, and Political Change.* Ithaca, NY, and London: Cornell University Press, 1993.

Goncharov, Sergei N., John W. Lewis, and Xue Litai. *Uncertain Partners: Stalin, Mao, and the Korean War.* Stanford, CA: Stanford University Press, 1993.

Goodman, Allan E. "Testimony: Fact-Checking at the CIA." *Foreign Policy* 102 (Spring 1996): 180–182.

Goodstein, Laurie. "Threats and Responses: The Religious Leaders; Evangelical Figures Oppose Religious Leaders' Broad Antiwar Sentiment." *New York Times* (October 5, 2002): A10.

Graber, Doris A. *Mass Media and American Politics.* 5th ed. Washington, DC: CQ Press, 1997.

Graham, Thomas. "Public Opinion and U.S. Foreign Policy Decision Making." In *The New Politics of American Foreign Policy,* David A. Deese, ed. New York: St. Martin's Press, 1994.

Greenstein, Fred I. "The Changing Leadership of George W. Bush: A Pre- and Post-9/11 Comparison." In *The Domestic Sources of American Foreign Policy: Insights and Evidence.* 4th ed., Eugene R. Wittkopf and James M. McCormick, eds. Lanham, MD: Rowman & Littlefield Publishers, Inc., 2004.

———. *The George W. Bush Presidency: An Early Assessment.* Baltimore and London: The Johns Hopkins University Press, 2003.

Grier, Peter, and Amelia Nemcomb, "US, China Find a New Middle Way." *Christian Science Monitor* (December 11, 2003): 1.

Grimmett, Richard F. *War Powers Resolution: After Twenty Eight Years.* Washington, DC: Congressional Research Service, November 30, 2001.

———. *IB81050: War Powers Resolution: Presidential Compliance.* Washington, DC: Congressional Research Service, June 12, 2002, and September 16, 2003.

Grosser, Alfred. *French Foreign Policy Under DeGaulle.* Boston: Little, Brown and Company, 1965.

Gulick, Edward V. *Europe's Classical Balance of Power.* Ithaca, NY: Cornell University Press, 1955.

Haaas, Richard N. "Defining U.S. Foreign Policy in a Post-Post–Cold War World." The 2002 Arthur Ross Lecture to the Foreign Policy Association, New York, New York, April 22, 2002, online. Available: http://www.state.gov/s/p/rem/9632.htm.

Hackett, Clifford. "Ethnic Politics in Congress: The Turkish Embargo Experience." In *Ethnicity and U.S. Foreign Policy,* Abdul Aziz Said, ed. New York: Praeger, 1981.

Haig, Alexander. Opening Statement at Confirmation Hearings. Washington, DC: Bureau of Public Affairs, Department of State, January 9, 1981.

———. A Strategic Approach to American Foreign Policy. Washington, DC: Bureau of Public Affairs, Department of State, August 11, 1981.

Hakim, Peter and Carlos A. Rosales. "The Latino Foreign Policy Lobby." In *Latinos and U.S. Foreign Policy,* Rodolfo de la Garza and Harry P. Pachon, eds. Lanham, MD: Rowman & Littlefield Publishers, Inc., 2000.

Hallin, Daniel C. *We Keep America on Top of the World: Television Journalism and the Public Sphere.* New York: Routledge, 1994.

Halperin, Morton H., with the assistance of Priscilla Clapp and Arnold Kanter. *Bureaucratic Politics and Foreign Policy.* Washington, DC: The Brookings Institution, 1974.

Hamilton, Lee. "The Role of the U.S. Congress in American Foreign Policy." *Elliott School Special Lectures Series,* The George Washington University, 1999–2000.

———, and Michael H. Van Dusen. "Making the Separation of Powers Work." *Foreign Affairs* 57 (Fall 1978): 17–39.

Haney, Patrick J., and Walt Vanderbush, "The Helms-Burton Act: Congress and Cuba Policy." In *Contemporary Cases in U.S. Foreign Policy: From Terrorism to Trade,* Ralph G. Carter, ed. Washington, DC: CQ Press, 2002.

Hansen, Roger D., Albert Fishlow, Robert Paarlberg, and John P. Lewis. *U.S. Foreign Policy and the Third World Agenda 1982.* New York: Praeger, 1982.

Hart, Albert Bushnell. *The Monroe Doctrine: An Interpretation.* Boston: Little, Brown and Company, 1916.

Hartley, Thomas, and Bruce Russett. "Public Opinion and the Common Defense: Who Governs Military Spending in the United States?" *American Political Science Review* 86 (December 1992): 905–915.

Hendrickson, Ryan. *The Clinton Wars: The Constitution, Congress and War Powers,* Nashville: Vanderbilt University Press, 2002.

Henkin, Louis. "Foreign Affairs and the Constitution." *Foreign Affairs* 66 (Winter 1987–1988): 284–310.

———. *Foreign Affairs and the Constitution.* Mincola, NY: The Foundation Press, Inc. 1972.

Herring, George C. *America's Longest War: The United States and Vietnam 1950–1975.* 2nd ed. New York: Alfred A. Knopf, 1986.

———. *LBJ and Vietnam: A Different Kind of War.* Austin: University of Texas Press, 1994.

Hersman, Rebecca K. C. *Friends and Foes.* Washington, DC: The Brookings Institution, 2000.

Hertsgaard, Mark. *On Bended Knee: The Press and the Reagan Presidency.* New York: Farrar, Straus & Giroux, 1988.

Hess, Stephen. *International News & Foreign Correspondents.* Washington, DC: The Brookings Institution, 1996.

Hicks, Sallie M., and Theodore A. Couloumbis. "The 'Greek Lobby': Illusion or Reality?" In *Ethnicity and U.S. Foreign Policy,* Abdul Aziz Said, ed. New York: Praeger, 1981.

Higgott, Richard, and Diane Stone. "The Limits of Influence: Foreign Policy Think Tanks in Britain and the USA." *Review of International Studies* 20 (January 1994): 15–34.

Hilsman, Roger. *To Move a Nation.* Garden City, NY: Doubleday Publishing, 1964.

———. "Does the CIA Still Have a Role?" *Foreign Affairs* 74 (September/October 1995): 104–116.

Hinckley, Barbara. *Less Than Meets the Eye.* Chicago and London: The University of Chicago Press, 1994.

———. *Stability and Change in Congress.* 3rd ed. New York: Harper and Row, 1983.

Hoffmann, Stanley. "Carter's Soviet Problem." *The New Republic* 79 (July 29, 1978): 20–23.

———. *Gulliver's Troubles, or the Setting of American Foreign Policy.* New York: McGraw Hill, 1968.

———. *Primacy or World Order.* New York: McGraw-Hill, 1978.

———. "Requiem." *Foreign Policy* 42 (Spring 1981): 3–26.

———. "A View From at Home: The Perils of Incoherence." In *America and the World 1978,* William P. Bundy, ed. New York: Pergamon Press, 1979.

Holloway, David. "Gorbachev's New Thinking." In *America and the World 1988/89,* William P. Bundy, ed. New York: Council on Foreign Relations, 1989.

Holmes, Jennifer S. "The Colombian Drug Trade: National Security and Congressional Politics." In *Contemporary Cases in U.S. Foreign Policy: From Terrorism to Trade,* Ralph G. Carter, ed. Washington, DC: CQ Press, 2002.

Holsti, Ole R. "The Belief System and National Images: A Case Study." *The Journal of Conflict Resolution* 6 (September 1962): 244–252.

———. "Public Opinion and Foreign Policy." In *Eagle Rules? Foreign Policy and American Primacy in the Twenty-first Century,* Robert J. Lieber, ed. Upper Saddle River, NJ: Prentice Hall, Inc., 2002.

———. "Public Opinion and Foreign Policy: Challenges to the Almond-Lippmann Consensus." *International Studies Quarterly* 36 (December 1992): 439–466.

———. "The Three-Headed Eagle: The United States and System Change." *International Studies Quarterly* 23 (September 1979): 339–359.

———, and James N. Rosenau. *American Leadership in World Affairs.* Boston: Allen & Unwin, 1984.

———. "The Political Foundations of Elites' Domestic and Foreign-Policy Beliefs." In *The Domestic Sources of American Foreign Policy: Insights and Evidence.* 3rd ed., Eugene R. Wittkopf and James M. McCormick, eds. Lanham, MD: Rowman & Littlefield Publishers, Inc., 1999.

———. "America's Foreign Policy Agenda: The Post-Vietnam Beliefs of American Leaders." In *Challenges to America: United States Foreign Policy in the 1980s,* Charles W. Kegley, Jr., and Patrick J. McGowan, eds. Beverly Hills: Sage Publications, 1979.

———. "Does Where You Stand Depend on When You Were Born? The Impact of Generation on Post-Vietnam Foreign Policy Beliefs." *Public Opinion Quarterly* 44 (Spring 1980): 1–22.

———. "A Leadership Divided: The Foreign Policy Beliefs of American Leaders, 1976- 1980." In *Perspectives on American Foreign Policy,* Charles W. Kegley, Jr., and Eugene R. Wittkopf, eds. New York: St. Martin's Press, 1983.

———. "The Structure of Foreign Policy Attitudes Among Leaders." *Journal of Politics* 52 (February 1990): 94–125.

———. "The Structure of Foreign Policy Beliefs Among American Opinion Leaders After the Cold War." *Millennium* 22 (Summer 1993): 235–278.

———. "Vietnam, Consensus, and the Belief Systems of American Leaders." *World Politics* 32 (October 1979): 1–56.

———, Richard A. Brody, and Robert C. North. "The Management of International Crisis: Affect and Action in American-Soviet Relations." In *Theory and Research on the Cause of War*, Dean G. Pruitt and Richard C. Snyder, eds. Englewood Cliffs, NJ: Prentice-Hall, Inc., 1969.

Holt, Pat. *Secret Intelligence and Public Policy*. Washington, DC: CQ Press, 1995.

Hoopes, Townsend. *The Limits of Intervention*. New York: David McKay, 1968.

Hopkins, Raymond F., and Donald J. Puchala. *Global Food Interdependence: Challenge to American Foreign Policy*. New York: Columbia University Press, 1980.

Hormat, Robert D. "The World Economy Under Stress." In *America and the World 1985*, William G. Hyland, ed. New York: Pergamon Press, 1986.

Hsiao, Gene T., ed. *Sino-American Detente and Its Policy Implications*. New York: Praeger Publishers, Inc., 1974.

Hughes, Barry B. *The Domestic Context of American Foreign Policy*. San Francisco: Freeman, 1978.

Hughes, Thomas L. "The Crack-Up: The Price of Collective Irresponsibility." *Foreign Policy* 40 (Fall 1980): 33–60.

———. "The Flight From Foreign Policy." *Foreign Policy* 10 (Spring 1973): 141–156.

Hult, Karen M. "The Bush White House in Comparative Perspective." In *The George W. Bush Presidency: An Early Assessment*, Fred I. Greenstein, ed. Baltimore and London: The Johns Hopkins University Press, 2003.

Hunt, Michael H. *Ideology and U.S. Foreign Policy*. New Haven, CT: Yale University Press, 1987.

Hunter, Robert E. *Presidential Control of Foreign Policy: Management or Mishap?* The Washington Papers/91. New York: Praeger, 1982.

Huntington, Samuel P. "The Erosion of American National Interests." In *The Domestic Sources of American Foreign Policy: Insights and Evidence*. 4th ed., Eugene R. Wittkopf and James M.

McCormick, eds. Lanham, MD: Rowman & Littlefield Publishers, Inc., 2004.

Hurwitz, Jon, and Mark Peffley. "How Are Foreign Policy Attitudes Structured? A Hierarchical Model." *American Political Science Review* 81 (December 1987): 1099–1120.

Hyland, William G. "U.S.-Soviet Relations: The Long Road Back." In *America and the World 1981*, William P. Bundy, ed. New York: Pergamon Press, 1982.

"In Tenet's Words: 'I Am Responsible' for Review." *New York Times* (July 12, 2003): A5.

Isaacson, Walter. *Kissinger: A Biography*. New York: Simon & Schuster, 1992.

Janis, Irving. *Victims of Groupthink*. Boston: Houghton Mifflin Company, 1972.

Jensen, Kenneth M., ed. *Origins of the Cold War: The Novikov, Kennan, and Roberts' 'Long Telegrams' of 1946*. Washington, DC: United States Institute of Peace, 1991.

Jensen, Lloyd. *Explaining Foreign Policy*. Englewood Cliffs, NJ: Prentice-Hall, Inc., 1982.

Jentleson, Bruce W. "American Diplomacy: Around the World and Along Pennsylvania Avenue." In *A Question of Balance*, Thomas E. Mann, ed. Washington, DC: The Brookings Institution, 1990.

———. "The Pretty Prudent Public: Post Post-Vietnam American Opinion on the Use of Military Force." *International Studies Quarterly* 36 (March 1992): 49–74.

———. *With Friends Like These*. New York and London: W. W. Norton and Company, 1994.

Jervis, Robert. "The Impact of the Korean War on the Cold War." *The Journal of Conflict Resolution* 24 (December 1980): 563–592.

Joffe, Josef. "The Foreign Policy of the German Federal Republic." In *Foreign Policy in World Politics*. 5th ed., Roy C. Macridis, ed. Englewood Cliffs, NJ: Prentice-Hall, Inc., 1976.

Johnson, Loch, and James M. McCormick. "Foreign Policy by Executive Fiat." *Foreign Policy* 28 (Fall 1977): 117–138.

———. "The Making of International Agreements: A Reappraisal of Congressional Involvement." *The Journal of Politics* 40 (May 1978): 468–478.

Jones, Christopher M. "American Prewar Technology Sales to Iraq: A Bureaucratic Politics Explanation." In *The Domestic Sources of American Foreign Policy: Insights and Evidence.* 2nd ed., Eugene R. Wittkopf, ed. New York: St. Martin's Press, 1994.

———. "Roles, Politics, and the Survival of the V-22 Osprey." In *The Domestic Sources of American Foreign Policy: Insights and Evidence.* 4th ed., Eugene R. Wittkopf and James M. McCormick, eds. Lanham, MD: Rowman & Littlefield Publishers, Inc., 2004.

Jones, Joseph M. *The Fifteen Weeks.* Chicago: Harcourt, Brace and World, Inc., 1955.

Jordan, Amos A., William J. Taylor, Jr., and associates. *American National Security: Policy and Process.* Baltimore: The Johns Hopkins University Press, 1981.

———, and Lawrence J. Korb. *American National Security: Policy and Process.* 4th ed. Baltimore: The Johns Hopkins University Press, 1993.

Kahler, Miles. "The United States and Western Europe: The Diplomatic Consequences of Mr. Reagan." In *Eagle Defiant: United States Foreign Policy in the 1980s,* Kenneth A. Oye, Robert J. Lieber, and Donald Rothchild, eds. Boston: Little, Brown and Company, 1983.

Kaiser, Fred. "Congressional Control of Executive Actions in the Aftermath of the Chadha Decision." *Administrative Law Review* 36 (Summer 1984): 239–274.

———. "Oversight of Foreign Policy: The U.S. House Committee on International Relations." *Legislative Studies Quarterly* 2 (August 1977): 233–254.

———. "Structural and Policy Change: The House Committee on International Relations." *Policy Studies* Journal 5 (Summer 1977): 443–451.

Kaiser, Karl. "Germany's Unification." In *America and the World 1990/1991,* William P. Bundy, ed. New York: Council on Foreign Relations, Inc., 1991.

Karnow, Stanley. *Vietnam: A History.* New York: The Viking Press, 1983.

Katzmann, Robert A. "War Powers: Toward a New Accommodation," In *A Question of Balance,* Thomas E. Mann, ed. Washington, DC: The Brookings Institution, 1990.

Kaufman, Natalie Hevener. *Human Rights Treaties and the Senate.* Chapel Hill and London: The University of North Carolina Press, 1990.

Kavass, Ivor I., and Mark A. Michael. *United States Treaties and Other International Agreements Cumulative Index 1776–1949.* Buffalo, NY: William S. Hein and Company, Inc., 1975.

Kegley, Charles W. "The Bush Administration and the Future of American Foreign Policy: Pragmatism or Procrastination?" *Presidential Studies Quarterly* 19 (Fall 1989): 717–731.

———, ed. *Controversies in International Relations Theory.* New York: St. Martin's Press, 1995.

———, and Eugene R. Wittkopf. *American Foreign Policy: Pattern and Process.* 5th ed. New York: St. Martin's Press, 1991.

———. "Beyond Consensus: The Domestic Context of American Foreign Policy." *International Journal* 38 (Winter 1982–1983): 77–106.

Kellerman, Barbara, and Ryan J. Barilleaux. *The President as World Leader.* New York: St. Martin's Press, 1991.

Kennan, George. *American Diplomacy 1900–1950.* New York: Mentor Books, 1951.

———. "Containment Then and Now." *Foreign Affairs* 65 (Spring 1987): 885–890.

———. "Is Detente Worth Saving?" *Saturday Review* (March 6, 1976): 12–17.

———. *Memoirs 1925–1950.* Boston: Little, Brown and Company, Inc., 1967.

———. "The Sources of Soviet Conduct." *Foreign Affairs* 65 (Spring 1987): 852–868.

Kennedy, Robert F. *Thirteen Days.* New York: Signet Books, 1969.

Kihl, Young Whan. "Nuclear Issues in U.S.-Korea Relations: An Uncertain Security Future." *International Journal of Korean Studies* 7 (Spring/Summer 2003): 79–97.

———. *Politics and Policies in Divided Korea: Regimes in Contest.* Boulder, CO: Westview Press, 1984.

Kirkpatrick, Jeane J. "Dictatorships and Double Standards." *Commentary* 68 (November 1979): 34–45.

Kissinger, Henry A. *American Foreign Policy.* 3rd ed. New York: W. W. Norton and Company, 1977.

———. *Diplomacy.* New York: Simon & Schuster, 1994.

———. "Domestic Structure and Foreign Policy." In *International Politics and Foreign Policy.* Rev. ed., James N. Rosenau, ed. New York: Free Press, 1969.

———. *A World Restored: Metternich, Castlereagh and Problems of Peace 1812–1822.* Boston: Houghton Mifflin Company, 1957.

Knight, Andrew. "Ronald Reagan's Watershed Year?" In *America and the World 1982,* William P. Bundy, ed. New York: Pergamon Press, 1983.

Koh, Harold Hongju. *The National Security Constitution.* New Haven, CT: Yale University Press, 1992.

Kohut, Andrew, and Robert C. Toth. "Arms and the People." *Foreign Affairs* 73 (November/December 1994): 47–61.

Kolko, Gabriel. *The Roots of American Foreign Policy.* Boston: Beacon Press, 1969.

Kolodziej, Edward A. *French International Policy Under DeGaulle and Pompidou.* Ithaca, NY: Cornell University Press, 1974.

———. "Revolt and Revisionism in the Gaullist Global Vision: An Analysis of French Strategic Policy." *The Journal of Politics* 33 (May 1971): 448–477.

Kondracke, Morton. "The Greek Lobby." *The New Republic* (April 29, 1978): 14–16.

Korb, Lawrence J. *The Fall and Rise of the Pentagon: American Defense Policies in the 1970s.* Westport, CT: Greenwood Press, 1979.

———. "The Joint Chiefs of Staff: Access and Impact in Foreign Policy." *Policy Studies Journal* 3 (Winter 1974): 170–173.

———. *The Joint Chiefs of Staff: The First Twenty-Five Years.* Bloomington: Indiana University Press, 1976.

Korbel, Josef. *Detente in Europe: Real or Imaginary?* Princeton, NJ: Princeton University Press, 1972.

Korn, Jessica. *The Power of Separation.* Princeton, NJ: Princeton University Press, 1996.

Kovach, Bill. "Do the New Media Make Foreign Policy?" *Foreign Policy* 102 (Spring 1996): 169–179.

Krasner, Stephen D. "The Tokyo Round: Particularistic Interests and Prospects for Stability in the Global Trading System." *International Studies Quarterly* 23 (December 1979): 491–531.

Kristol, William, and Robert Kagan. "Toward a Neo-Reaganite Foreign Policy." *Foreign Affairs* 75 (July/August 1996):18–32.

Kull, Steven. "What the Public Knows That Washington Doesn't," *Foreign Policy* 101 (Winter 1995–1996): 102–115.

Kurth, James R. "The Military-Industrial Complex Revisited." In *1989–1990 American Defense Annual,* Joseph Kruzel, ed. Lexington, MA: Lexington Books, 1989.

Lacey, Marc, and Raymond Bonner. "A Mad Scramble by Donors for Plum Ambassadorships." *New York Times* (March 17, 2001), online. Available: http://www.nytimes.com/2001/03/17/worlld/18AMBA.html.

Ladd, Everett C., Jr. "Traditional Values Regnant." *Public Opinion* 1 (March/April 1978): 45–49.

LaFeber, Walter. *America, Russia, and the Cold War 1945–1975.* New York: John Wiley and Sons, 1976.

———. *The American Age: United States Foreign Policy at Home and Abroad since 1750.* New York: W. W. Norton and Company, 1989.

———. *Inevitable Revolutions: The United States in Central America.* New York: W. W. Norton and Company, 1984.

Lake, David A. "Powerful Pacifists: Democratic States and War." *American Political Science Review* 86 (March 1992): 24–37.

Lane, Charles. "Perry's Parry." *The New Republic* 26 (June 27, 1994): 21–25.

Lasswell, Harold D. *Politics: Who Gets What, When, and How.* New York: Whittlesey, 1936.

"Lawmakers Hand Clinton Big Victory in Granting China Permanent Trade Status," *Congressional Quarterly Almanac 2000.* Washington, DC: Congressional Quarterly, Inc., 2001.

Lawson, Ruth C. *International Regional Organizations: Constitutional Foundations.* New York: Praeger, 1962.

Leffler, Melvyn P., and David S. Painter, eds. *Origins of the Cold War: An International History.* London and New York: Routledge, 1994.

Legg, Keith R. "Congress as Trojan Horse? The Turkish Embargo Problem, 1974–1978." In *Congress, the Presidency, and American Foreign Policy,* John Spanier and Joseph Nogee, eds. New York: Pergamon Press, 1981.

Legum, Colin. "The African Crisis." In *America and the World 1978,* William P. Bundy, ed. New York: Pergamon Press, 1979.

LeLoup, Lance T., and Steven A. Shull. "Congress Versus the Executive: The 'Two Presidencies' Reconsidered." *Social Science Quarterly* 59 (March 1979): 704–719.

Lerche, Charles O., Jr., and Abdul A. Said. *Concepts of International Politics.* 3rd ed. Englewood Cliffs, NJ: Prentice-Hall, Inc., 1979.

Lerner, Max. "America Agonistes." *Foreign Affairs* 52 (January 1974): 287–300.

Levgold, Robert. "The Revolution in Soviet Foreign Policy." In *America and the World 1988/89,* William P. Bundy, ed. New York: Council on Foreign Relations, 1989.

Lichter, S. Robert, Stanley Rothman, and Linda S. Lichter, *The Media Elite.* Bethesda, MD: Adler & Adler, 1986.

Lieber, Robert J., ed. *Eagle Rules? Foreign Policy and American Primacy in the Twenty-first Century.* Upper Saddle River, NJ: Prentice Hall, Inc., 2002.

———. "Foreign Policy and American Primacy." In *Eagle Rules? Foreign Policy and American Primacy in the Twenty-first Century,* Robert J. Lieber, ed. Upper Saddle River, NJ: Prentice Hall, Inc., 2002.

Lieberson, Stanley. "An Empirical Study of Military-Industrial Linkages." *American Journal of Sociology* 76 (January 1971): 562–584.

Lieberthal, Kenneth. "A New China Strategy." *Foreign Affairs* 74 (November/December 1995): 35–49.

Lindsay, James M. "Congress and Defense Policy: 1961 to 1986." *Armed Forces and Society* 13 (Spring 1987): 371–401.

———. "Congress and Foreign Policy: Avenues of Influences." In *The Domestic Sources of American Foreign Policy: Insights and Evidence.* 2nd ed., Eugene R. Wittkopf, ed. New York: St. Martin's Press, 1994.

———. *Congress and the Politics of U.S. Foreign Policy.* Baltimore and London: The Johns Hopkins University, 1994.

———. "Parochialism, Policy, and Constituency Constraints: Congressional Voting on Strategic Weapons Systems." *American Journal of Political Science* 34 (November 1990): 936–960.

———, and Wayne M. Steger. "The 'Two Presidencies' in Future Research: Moving Beyond Roll-Call Analysis." *Congress & The Presidency* 20 (Autumn 1993): 103–117.

Lindsay, John V. "For a New Policy Balance." *Foreign Affairs* 50 (October 1971): 1–14.

Lipset, Seymour Martin. *The First New Nation.* Garden City, NY: Anchor Books, 1967.

Locke, John. *The Second Treatise of Government.* Oxford: Basil Blackwell 1966.

Lockerbie, Brad, and Stephen A. Borrelli. "Question Wording and Public Support for Contra Aid, 1983–1986." *Public Opinion Quarterly* 54 (Summer 1990): 195–208.

Lomperis, Timothy J. *The War Everyone Lost—and Won*. Washington, DC: CQ Press, 1984.

Lowenthal, Mark M. *Intelligence: From Secrets to Policy*. Washington DC: CQ Press, 2003.

Lugar, Richard. "Opening Statement for Hearing on Iraq Reconstruction." U.S. Senate Foreign Relations Committee (June 4, 2003).

Lynn, Laurence E., Jr., and Richard I. Smith. "Can the Secretary of Defense Make a Difference?" *International Security* 7 (Summer 1982): 45–69.

Maggiotto, Michael, and Eugene R. Wittkopf. "American Public Attitudes Toward Foreign Policy." *International Studies Quarterly* 25 (December 1981): 601–632.

Maier, Charles S., ed. *The Origins of the Cold War and Contemporary Europe*. New York: New Viewpoints, 1978.

Majeski, Stephen J. "Defense Spending, Fiscal Policy, and Economic Performance." In *The Political Economy of Military Spending in the United States,* Alex Mintz, ed. London: Routledge, 1992.

Mandelbaum, Michael. "Foreign Policy as Social Work." *Foreign Affairs* 75 (January/February 1996): 16–32.

———. *The Nuclear Question: The United States and Nuclear Weapons 1946–1976*. Cambridge: Cambridge University Press, 1979.

Mansfield, Edward, and Jack Snyder. "Democratization and War." *Foreign Affairs* 74 (May/June 1995): 79–97.

Maoz, Zeev, and Bruce Russett. "Normative and Structural Causes of Democratic Peace, 1946–1986." *American Political Science Review* 87 (September 1993): 624–638.

Marantz, Paul. "Prelude to Detente: Doctrinal Change Under Khrushchev." *International Studies Quarterly* 19 (December 1975): 501–528.

Marchetti, Victor, and John D. Marks. *The CIA and the Cult of Intelligence*. New York: Dell, 1974.

Mark, Eduard. "The Questions of Containment: A Reply to John Lewis Gaddis." *Foreign Affairs* 56 (January 1978): 430–441.

Markus, Gregory B. "Political Attitudes During an Election Year: A Report on the 1980 NES Panel Study." *American Political Science Review* 76 (September 1982): 538–560.

Mathias, Charles McC., Jr. "Ethnic Groups and Foreign Policy." *Foreign Affairs* 59 (Summer 1981): 975–998.

Matthews, Jessica T. "September 11, One Year Later: A World of Change." *Policy Brief*. Special Edition 18. Washington, DC: Carnegie Endowment for International Peace, 2002.

May, Ernest R. *"Lessons" of the Past: The Use and Misuse of History in American Foreign Policy*. New York: Oxford University Press, 1973.

Mayer, Kenneth R., and Kevin Price. "Unilateral Presidential Powers: Significant Executive Orders, 1949–99," *Presidential Studies Quarterly* 32 (June 2002): 367–386.

Mayne, Richard. *The Recovery of Europe 1945–1973*. Garden City, NY: Anchor, 1973.

Maynes, Charles W. "America Without the Cold War," *Foreign Policy* 78 (Spring 1990): 3–25.

———. "Who Pays for Foreign Policy?" *Foreign Policy* 15 (Summer 1974): 152–168.

McCain, John. "Imagery or Purpose? The Choice in November." *Foreign Policy* 103 (Summer 1996): 20–34.

McClosky, Herbert, Paul J. Hoffmann, and Rosemary O'Hara. "Issue Conflict and Consensus Among Party Leaders and Followers." *American Political Science Review* 14 (June 1960): 408–427.

McCormick, James M. "Assessing Clinton's Foreign Policy at Midterm." *Current History* 94 (November 1995): 370–374.

———. "The Changing Role of the House Foreign Affairs Committee in the 1970s and 1980s." *Congress & The Presidency* 12 (Spring 1985): 1–20.

———. "Clinton and Foreign Policy: Some Legacies for a New Century." In *The Postmodern Presidency,* Steven E. Schier, ed. Pittsburgh: University of Pittsburgh Press, 2000.

———. "Congressional Voting on the Nuclear Freeze Resolutions." *American Politics Quarterly* 13 (January 1985): 122–136.

———. "Decision Making in the Foreign Affairs and Foreign Relations Committees." In *Congress Resurgent: Foreign and Defense Policy on Capitol Hill,* Randall B. Ripley and James M. Lindsay, eds. Ann Arbor: The University of Michigan Press, 1993.

———. "Human Rights and the Clinton Administration: American Policy at the Dawn of a New Century." In *Universal Human Rights?* Robert G. Patman, ed. New York: St. Martin's Press, 2000.

———. "The NIEO and the Distribution of American Assistance." *The Western Political Quarterly* 37 (March 1984): 100–119.

———, ed. *A Reader in American Foreign Policy.* Itasca, IL: F. E. Peacock Publishers, Inc., 1986.

———, and Michael Black. "Ideology and Voting on the Panama Canal Treaties." *Legislative Studies Quarterly* 8 (February 1983): 45–63.

———, and Neil Mitchell. "Human Rights and Foreign Assistance: An Update." *Social Science Quarterly* 70 (December 1989): 969–979.

———, and Steven S. Smith. "The Iran Arms Sale and the Intelligence Oversight Act of 1980." *PS* 20 (Winter 1987): 29–37.

———, and Eugene R. Wittkopf. "At the Water's Edge: The Effects of Party, Ideology, and Issues on Congressional Foreign Policy Voting, 1947–1988." *American Politics Quarterly* 20 (January 1992): 26–53.

———. "Bipartisanship, Partisanship, and Ideology in Congressional-Executive Foreign Policy Relations, 1947–1988."

The Journal of Politics 52 (November 1990): 1077–1100.

———, Eugene R. Wittkopf, and David M. Danna. "Politics and Bipartisanship at the Water's Edge: A Note on Bush and Clinton." *Polity* 30 (Fall 1997): 133–149.

McElroy, Robert W. *Morality and American Foreign Policy: The Role of Ethics in International Affairs.* Princeton, NJ: Princeton University Press, 1992.

Mee, Charles L., Jr., *Meeting at Potsdam.* New York: M. Evan & Co., Inc., 1975.

Meernik, James. "Presidential Support in Congress: Conflict and Consensus on Foreign and Defense Policy." *Journal of Politics* 55 (August 1993): 569–587.

Melanson, Richard A. *American Foreign Policy Since the Vietnam War: The Search for Consensus from Nixon to Clinton.* 2nd ed. Armonk, NY: M. E. Sharpe, 1996.

Merrill, John. *Korea: The Peninsular Origins of the War.* Newark: University of Delaware, 1989.

The Middle East: U.S. Policy, Israel, Oil and the Arabs. 3rd ed. Washington, DC: Congressional Quarterly, Inc., 1977.

Milbank, Dana. "The 'Bush Doctrine' Experiences Shining Moments." *The Washington Post* (December 21, 2003): A26.

———, and Walter Pincus. "Cheney Blunt in his Defense of Iraq Policy." *Des Moines Register* (October 11, 2003): 4A

Miller, Hunter, ed. *Treaties and Other International Acts of the United States of America.* Vol. 2. Washington, DC: U.S. Government Printing Office, 1931.

Miller, Robert Hopkins. *Inside an Embassy: The Political Role of Diplomats Abroad.* Washington, DC: Congressional Quarterly, Inc., 1992.

Miller, Warren E., and Donald E. Stokes. "Constituency Influence in Congress." *American Political Science Review* 57 (March 1963): 45–56.

Mills, C. Wright. *The Power Elite.* New York: Oxford University Press, 1956.

———. "The Structure of Power in American Society." In *Power in Postwar America,* Richard Gillam, ed. Boston: Little, Brown and Company, 1971.

Mintz, John. "Security Goals Compromised by Problems in Department,." *Des Moines Register* (September 8, 2003): 1A, 4A.

Molineu, Harold. "Human Rights: Administrative Impact of a Symbolic Policy." In *The Analysis of Policy Impact,* John G. Grumm and Stephen L. Wasby, eds. Lexington, MA: Lexington Books, D. C. Heath and Company, 1981.

Moore, David W. "The Public Is Uncertain." *Foreign Policy* 35 (Summer 1979): 68–73.

Morgenthau, Hans J. "The Mainsprings of American Foreign Policy." In *A Reader in American Foreign Policy,* James M. McCormick, ed. Itasca, IL: F. E. Peacock, Inc., 1986.

———. *Politics Among Nations: The Struggle for Power and Peace.* New York: Alfred A. Knopf, 1973.

Moyer, Wayne. "House Voting on Defense: An Ideological Explanation." In *Military Force and American Society,* Bruce M. Russett and Alfred Stepan, eds. New York: Harper and Row, 1973.

———, and Timothy E. Josling. *Agricultural Policy Reform: Politics and Process in the EC and the USA.* New York: Harvester/ Wheatsheaf, 1990.

Mueller, John E. *War, Presidents and Public Opinion.* New York: John Wiley and Sons, 1973.

Murray, Shoon Kathleen, and Christopher Spinosa. "The Post-9/11 Shift in Public Opinion: How Long Will It Last?" In *The Domestic Sources of American Foreign Policy: Insights and Evidence.* 4th ed., Eugene R. Wittkopf and James M. McCormick, eds. Lanham, MD: Rowman & Littlefield Publishers, Inc., 2004.

Nash, Henry T. *American Foreign Policy: Changing Perspectives on National Security.* Homewood, IL: The Dorsey Press, 1978.

The National Security Strategy of the United States of America. September 17, 2002, online. Available: http://www. whitehouse.gov/usc/nss.html.

Nelson, Michael. ed. *Congressional Quarterly's Guide to the Presidency.* Washington, DC: Congressional Quarterly, Inc., 1989.

Ness, Immanuel. *Encyclopedia of Interest Groups and Lobbyists in the United States.* Vols. 1 and 2. Armonk, NY: Sharpe Reference, 2000.

Neuman, Johanna. *Lights, Camera, War.* New York: St. Martin's Press, 1996.

Newhouse, John. "Profiles (James Baker)." *The New Yorker* (May 7, 1990): 50–82.

Newsom, David C. *The Public Dimension of Foreign Policy.* Bloomington and Indianapolis: Indiana University Press, 1996.

Nincic, Miroslav. "Elections and Foreign Policy." In *The Domestic Sources of American Foreign Policy: Insights and Evidence.* 4th ed., Eugene R. Wittkopf and James M. McCormick, eds. Lanham, MD: Rowman & Littlefield Publishers, Inc., 2004.

Nivola, Pietro S. "Trade Policy: Refereeing the Playing Field." In *A Question of Balance,* Thomas E. Mann, ed. Washington, DC: The Brookings Institution, 1990.

Nixon, Richard M. "Asia After Viet Nam." *Foreign Affairs* 46 (October 1967): 111–125.

———. *U.S. Policy for the 1970s: A New Strategy for Peace: A Report to the Congress.* Washington, DC: Government Printing Office, February 12, 1970.

Nordlinger, Eric A. *Isolationism Reconfigured: American Foreign Policy for a New Century.* Princeton, NJ: Princeton University Press, 1995.

North, Robert C. *The Foreign Relations of China.* 2nd ed. Encino and Belmont, CA: Dickenson Publishing Company, Inc., 1974.

Nye, Joseph S., Jr. "The Case for Deep Engagement." *Foreign Affairs* 74 (July/ August 1995): 90–102.

———. *Nuclear Ethics.* New York: The Free Press, 1986.

———. *The Paradox of American Power: Why the World's Only Superpower Can't Go It Alone.* New York: Oxford University Press, 2002.

————. "Peering into the Future." *Foreign Affairs* 73 (July/August 1994): 82–93.

Nye, Russel B. *This Almost Chosen People.* East Lansing: Michigan State University Press, 1966.

Oldfield, Duane M., and Aaron Wildavsky. "Reconsidering the Two Presidencies." *Society* 26 (July/August 1989): 54–59.

Ogley, Roderick, ed. *The Theory and Practice of Neutrality in the Twentieth Century.* New York: Barnes & Noble, Inc., 1970.

O'Halloran, Sharyn. "Congress and Foreign Trade Policy." In *Congress Resurgent: Foreign and Defense Policy on Capitol Hill,* Randall B. Ripley and James M. Lindsay, eds. Ann Arbor: The University of Michigan Press, 1993.

O'Heffernan, Patrick. "A Mutual Exploitation Model of Media Influence in U.S. Foreign Policy." In *Taken by Storm: The Media, Public Opinion, and U.S. Foreign Policy in the Gulf War,* W. Lance Bennett and David L.Paletz, eds. Chicago and London: The University of Chicago Press, 1994.

Oneal, James R., Brad Lian, and James H. Joyner. "Are the American People 'Pretty Prudent'? Public Responses to U.S. Uses of Force, 1950–1988." *International Studies Quarterly* 40 (June 1996): 261–280.

Origins and Development of Congress. Washington, DC: Congressional Quarterly, Inc., 1976.

Organski, A. F. K. *World Politics.* New York: Alfred A. Knopf, Inc., 1968.

Ornstein, Norman J., and Shirley Elder. *Interest Groups, Lobbying and Policymaking.* Washington, DC: Congressional Quarterly Press, 1978.

————, and David W. Rohde. "Shifting Forces, Changing Rules, and Political Outcomes: The Impact of Congressional Change on Four House Committees." In *New Perspectives on the House of Representatives,* Robert L. Peabody and Nelson W. Polsby, eds. Chicago: Rand McNally, 1977.

————, and Mark Schmitt. "Dateline Campaign '92: Post-Cold War Politics." *Foreign Policy* 79 (Summer 1990): 169–186.

Osgood, Robert E. *Ideals and Self-Interest in America's Foreign Relations.* Chicago: The University of Chicago Press, 1953.

————. "The Revitalization of Containment." In *America and the World 1981,* William Bundy, ed. New York: Pergamon Books, 1982.

Page, Benjamin I., and Robert Y. Shapiro. "Effects of Public Opinion on Policy." *American Political Science Review* 77 (March 1983): 175–190.

————. *The Rational Public: Fifty Years of Trends in Americans' Policy Preferences.* Chicago: The University of Chicago Press, 1992.

————, and Jason Barabas. "Foreign Policy Gaps Between Citizens and Leaders." *International Studies Quarterly* 44 (September 2000): 339–364

"Pakistan Waivers," *CQ Weekly* (December 22, 2001): 3040.

Park, Richard L. "India's Foreign Policy." In *Foreign Policy in World Politics.* 5th ed., Roy C. Macridis, ed. Englewood Cliffs, NJ: Prentice-Hall, Inc., 1976.

Pastor, Robert. *Congress and the Politics of U.S. Foreign Economic Policy 1929–1976.* Berkeley: University of California Press, 1980.

Payne, James L. *The American Threat.* College Station, TX: Lytton Publishing Company, 1981.

Pearce, David C. *Wary Partners: Diplomats and the Media.* Washington, DC: Congressional Quarterly, Inc., 1995.

Percy, Charles H. "The Partisan Gap." *Foreign Policy* 45 (Winter 1981–1982): 3–15.

Perkins, Dexter. *The American Approach to Foreign Policy.* Cambridge, MA: Harvard University Press, 1962.

————. *The Evolution of American Foreign Policy.* 2nd ed. New York: Oxford University Press, 1966.

————. *Hands-Off: A History of the Monroe Doctrine.* Boston: Little, Brown and Company, 1941.

Perlez, Jane. "Washington Memo: Divergent Voices Heard in Bush Foreign Policy." *New York Times* (March 12, 2001), online. Available: http://

www.nytimes.com/201/03/12/world/12DIPL.html.

———, "With Berger in Catbird Seat, Albright's Star Dims." *New York Times* (December 14, 1999): A14.

Pew Global Project Attitudes. *Views of a Changing World June 2003.* Washington, DC: The Pew Research Center for the People & The Press, 2003.

Pierre, Andrew J. *The Global Politics of Arms Sales.* Princeton, NJ: Princeton University Press, 1982.

Pilisuk, Marc, with the assistance of Mehrene Larudee. *International Conflict and Social Policy.* Englewood Cliffs, NJ: Prentice-Hall, Inc., 1972.

Pomper, Gerald. *Elections in America: Control and Influence in Democratic Politics.* New York: Dodd, Mead & Company, 1968.

———, with Susan S. Lederman. *Elections in America: Control and Influence in Democratic Politics.* 2nd ed. New York: Longman, 1980.

Pomper, Miles A. "International Relations: Rep. Henry J. Hyde of Illinois." *CQ Weekly* (January 6, 2001): 17.

———. "Powell Calls on Hill to Remedy State Department Underfunding." *CQ Weekly* (March 10, 2001): 547–548.

Powlick, Philip J. "The Attitudinal Bases for Responsiveness to Public Opinion Among American Foreign Policy Officials." *Journal of Conflict Resolution* 35 (December 1991): 611–641.

———. "The Sources of Public Opinion for American Foreign Policy Officials." *International Studies Quarterly* 39 (December 1995): 427–451.

Preston, Thomas, and Margaret G. Hermann. "Presidential Leadership Style and the Foreign Policy Advisory Process." In *The Domestic Sources of American Foreign Policy: Insights and Evidence.* 4th ed., Eugene R. Wittkopf and James M. McCormick, eds. Lanham, MD: Rowman & Littlefield Publishers, Inc., 2004.

Priest, Dana. *The Mission.* New York: W. W. Norton and Company, 2003.

Pringle, Robert. "Creeping Irrelevance at Foggy Bottom." *Foreign Policy* 29 (Winter 1977–1978): 128–139.

Proxmire, William. "The Community of Interests in Our Defense Contract Spending." In *Power in Postwar America,* Richard Gillam, ed. Boston: Little, Brown and Company, 1971.

Purdom, Todd S., and Patrick E. Tyler. "Top Republicans Break with Bush on Iraq Strategy." *New York Times* (August 16, 2002): 1.

Quester, George. *American Foreign Policy: The Lost Consensus.* New York: Praeger, 1982.

Ransom, Harry Howe. *The Intelligence Establishment.* Cambridge, MA: Harvard University Press, 1970.

Ravenal, Earl C. "The Case for Adjustment." *Foreign Policy* 81 (Winter 1990–1991): 3–19.

———, et al. "Who Pays for Foreign Policy? A Debate on Consensus." *Foreign Policy* 18 (Spring 1975): 80–122.

Ray, James Lee. *Global Politics.* 2nd ed. Boston: Houghton Mifflin Company, 1983.

Report of the Congressional Committees Investigating the Iran-Contra Affair. Washington, DC: U.S. Government Printing Office, November 1987.

Report of the Joint Inquiry Into the Terrorist Attacks of September 11, 2001. The House Permanent Select Committee on Intelligence and the Senate Select Committee on Intelligence, July 24, 2003, online. Available: http://new.findlaw.com/cnn/docs/911rpt/index.html.

Report to the President by the Commission on CIA Activities Within the United States. Washington, DC: U.S. Government Printing Office, June 1975.

Report of the President's Special Review Board (Tower Commission Report). Washington, DC: U.S. Government Printing Office, February 26, 1987.

Rice, Condoleezza. "Promoting the National Interest." *Foreign Affairs* 79 (January/February 2000): 45–62.

Richelson, Jeffrey T. *The U.S. Intelligence Community.* 3rd ed. Boulder, CO: Westview Press, 1995.

———. *The U.S. Intelligence Community* 4th ed. Boulder CO: Westview Press, 1999.

Rielly, John E. "The American Mood: A Foreign Policy of Self Interest." *Foreign Policy* 34 (Spring 1979): 74–86.

———. "American Opinion: Continuity, Not Reaganism." *Foreign Policy* 50 (Spring 1983): 86–104.

———. "America's State of Mind." *Foreign Policy* 66 (Spring 1987): 39–56.

———. "The Public Mood at Mid-Decade." *Foreign Policy* 96 (Spring 1995): 76–93.

———. "Public Opinion: The Pulse of the '90s." *Foreign Policy* 82 (Spring 1991): 79–96.

———, ed. *American Public Opinion and U.S. Foreign Policy 1975.* Chicago: Chicago Council on Foreign Relations, 1975.

———, ed. *American Public Opinion and U.S. Foreign Policy 1979.* Chicago: Chicago Council on Foreign Relations, 1979.

———, ed. *American Public Opinion and U.S. Foreign Policy 1983.* Chicago: Chicago Council on Foreign Relations, 1983.

———, ed. *American Public Opinion and U.S. Foreign Policy 1987.* Chicago: Chicago Council on Foreign Relations, 1987.

———, ed. *American Public Opinion and U.S. Foreign Policy 1991.* Chicago: Chicago Council on Foreign Relations, 1991.

———, ed. *American Public Opinion and U.S. Foreign Policy 1995.* Chicago: Chicago Council on Foreign Relations, 1995.

———, ed. *American Public Opinion and U.S. Foreign Policy 1999.* Chicago: Chicago Council on Foreign Relations, 1999.

Ripley, Randall B. *Congress: Process and Policy.* 2nd ed. New York: W. W. Norton and Company, 1978.

———, and James M. Lindsay, eds. *Congress Resurgent: Foreign and Defense Policy on Capitol Hill.* Ann Arbor: The University of Michigan Press, 1993.

Risen, James. "Man in the News: A Pentagon Veteran—Donald Henry Rumsfeld." *New York Times* (December 29, 2000), online. Available: http://www.nytimes.com/2000/12/29/politics/29RUMS.html?pagewanted=all.

Rizopoulous, Nicholas, ed. *Sea-Changes: American Foreign Policy in a World Transformed.* New York: Council on Foreign Relations Press, 1990.

Robinson, James A. *Congress and Foreign Policy-Making.* Rev. ed. Homewood, IL: The Dorsey Press, 1967.

Rockman, Bert A. "America's Departments of State: Irregular and Regular Syndromes of Policymaking." *American Political Science Review* 75 (December 1981): 911–927.

Rokeach, Milton. *Beliefs, Attitudes and Values.* San Francisco: Jossey-Bass, Inc., 1953.

Rosenberg, Milton J., Sidney Verba, and Philip E. Converse. *Vietnam and the Silent Majority.* New York: Harper and Row, 1970.

Rosenfeld, Stephen S. "Dateline Washington: Anti-Semitism and U.S. Foreign Policy." *Foreign Policy* 47 (Summer 1982): 172–183.

Rosner, Jeremy D. "The Know-Nothings Know Something." *Foreign Policy* 101 (Winter 1995–1996): 116–129.

———. *The New Tug-of-War: Congress, the Executive Branch, and National Security.* Washington, DC: A Carnegie Endowment Book, 1995.

Russett, Bruce. "The Americans' Retreat from World Power." *Political Science Quarterly* 90 (Spring 1975): 1–22.

———. "Defense Expenditures and National Well-being." *American Political Science Review* 76 (December 1982): 767–777.

———. *Grasping the Democratic Peace: Principles for a Post-Cold War World.* Princeton, NJ: Princeton University Press, 1993.

———. *The Prisoners of Insecurity.* San Francisco: W. H. Freeman and Company, 1983.

—, and Donald R. Deluca. "'Don't Tread on Me': Public Opinion and Foreign Policy in the Eighties." *Political Science Quarterly* 96 (Fall 1981): 381–399.

————, and Elizabeth C. Hanson. *Interest and Ideology: The Foreign Policy Beliefs of American Businessmen.* San Francisco: W. H. Freeman, 1975.

————, Harvey Starr, and David Kinsella. *World Politics: The Menu for Choice.* 6th ed. Boston: Bedford/St. Martin's Press, 2000.

Sagan, Scott. *The Limits of Safety: Organizations, Accidents, and Nuclear Weapons.* Princeton, NJ: Princeton University Press, 1993.

Said, Abdul Aziz. *Ethnicity and U.S. Foreign Policy.* Rev. ed. New York: Praeger, 1981.

Salisbury, Harrison E. *War Between China and Russia.* New York: W. W. Norton and Company, 1969.

Sanger, David E., and James Risen. "C.I.A. Chief Takes Blame in Assertion on Iraqi Uranium." *New York Times* (July 12, 2003): A1, A5.

————, and Judith Miller. "Libya to Give Up Arms Programs, Bush Announces." *New York Times* (December 20, 2003): A1, A8.

Schier, Steven E. *The Postmodern Presidency.* Pittsburgh: University of Pittsburgh Press, 2000.

Schlesinger, Arthur, Jr. "Congress and the Making of American Foreign Policy." *Foreign Affairs* 51 (October 1972): 78–113.

————. "Foreign Policy and the American Character." *Foreign Affairs* 62 (Fall 1983): 1–16.

————. "Human Rights and the American Tradition." *Foreign Affairs* 57 (Winter 1978–1979): 503–526.

————. *The Imperial Presidency.* Boston: Houghton Mifflin Company, 1973.

Schlesinger, James. "The Role of the Secretary of Defense." In *Reorganizing America's Defense: Leadership in War and Peace,* Robert J. Art, Vincent Davis, and Samuel P. Huntington, eds. Washington, DC: Pergamon-Brassey's, 1985.

Schmitt, Eric. "Aide Denies Shaping Data to Justify War." *New York Times* (June 5, 2003): 20.

Schoultz, Lars. "Politics, Economics, and U.S. Participation in Multilateral Development Banks." *International Organization* 36 (Summer 1982): 537–574.

Scott, Andrew M. "The Department of State: Formal Organization and Informal Culture." *International Studies Quarterly* 13 (March 1969): 1–18.

————. "The Problem of the State Department." In *Problems of American Foreign Policy.* 2nd ed., Martin B. Hickman, ed. Beverly Hills: Glencoe Press, 1975.

Scott, James M. "Trade and Trade-Offs: The Clinton Administration and The 'Big Emerging Markets' Strategy." *Futures Research Quarterly* 13 (Summer 1997): 37–66.

Scott, Len, and Steve Smith. "Political Scientists, Policy-Makers, and the Cuban Missile Crisis." *International Affairs* 70 (October 1994): 659–684.

Scudder, Evarts Seelye. *The Monroe Doctrine and World Peace.* Port Washington, NY: Kennikat Press, 1972.

Search for Peace in the Middle East. Rev. ed. Greenwich, CT: Fawcett Publications, Inc., 1970.

Sewell, John W. *The United States and World Development Agenda 1980.* New York: Praeger, 1980.

————, and John A. Mathieson. "North-South Relations." In *Setting National Priorities Agenda for the 1980s,* Joseph A. Pechman, ed. Washington, DC: The Brookings Institution, 1980.

Shapiro, Robert Y., and Benjamin I. Page. "Foreign Policy and the Rational Public." *Journal of Conflict Resolution* 32 (June 1988): 211–247.

————. "Foreign Policy and Public Opinion." In *The New Politics of American Foreign Policy,* David A. Deese, ed. New York: St. Martin's Press, 1994.

Sheehan, Neil, Hedrick Smith, E. W. Kenworthy, and Fox Butterfield. *The Pentagon Papers as Published by New York Times.* New York: Bantam Books, Inc., 1971.

Shull, Steven A., ed. *The Two Presidencies: A Quarter Century Assessment.* Chicago: Nelson/Hall Publishers, 1991.

Sigelman, Lee. "A Reassessment of the Two Presidencies Thesis." *The Journal of Politics* 41 (November 1979): 1195–1205.

Sigler, John H. "Descent From Olympus: The Search for a New Consensus." *International Journal* 38 (Winter 1982–1983): 18–38.

Sigmund, Paul E. "Latin America: Change or Continuity?" In *America and the World 1981,* William P. Bundy, ed. New York: Pergamon Press, 1982.

Silverstein, Gordon. *Imbalance of Powers: Constitutional Interpretation and the Making of American Foreign Policy.* New York: Oxford University Press, 1997.

———. "Judicial Enhancement of Executive Power." In *The President, The Congress, and the Making of Foreign Policy,* Paul E. Peterson, ed. Norman and London: University of Oklahoma Press, 1994.

Smith, Hedrick. *The Media and the Gulf War.* Washington, DC: Seven Locks, 1992.

———. *The Power Game: How Washington Works.* New York: Ballantine Books, 1988.

Smith, Jean Edward. *The Constitution and American Foreign Policy.* St. Paul, MN: West Publishing Company, 1989.

Smith, Tom W. "The Polls: America's Most Important Problems, Part I: National and International." *Public Opinion Quarterly* 49 (Summer 1985): 264–274.

Smith, Tony. *Foreign Attachments: The Power of Ethnic Groups in the Making of American Foreign Policy.* Cambridge, MA: Harvard University Press, 2000.

Snider, Don M., and Miranda A. Carlton-Carew, eds. *U. S. Civil-Military Relations: In Crisis or Transitions?* Washington, DC: The Center for Strategic & International Studies, 1995.

Sobel, Richard. "Public Opinion About United States Intervention in El Salvador and Nicaragua." *Public Opinion Quarterly* 53 (Spring 1989): 114–128.

———, ed. *Public Opinion in U.S. Foreign Policy: The Controversy Over Contra Aid.* Lanham, MD: Rowman & Littlefield Publishers, Inc., 1993.

———. *The Impact of Public Opinion on U.S. Foreign Policy: Constraining the Colossus.* New York: Oxford University Press, 1999.

Solo, Pam. *From Protest to Policy: The Origins and Future of the Freeze Movement.* Cambridge, MA: Ballinger Publishing, 1988.

Soroka, Stuart N. "Media, Public Opinion, and Foreign Policy." *Harvard International Journal of Press/Politics* 9 (Winter 2003): 27–48.

Spanier, John. *American Foreign Policy Since World War II.* 9th ed. New York: Holt, Rinehart and Winston, 1982.

———. *The Truman-MacArthur Controversy and the Korean War.* New York: W. W. Norton and Company, 1965.

———, and Eric M. Uslaner. *American Foreign Policy Making and the Democratic Dilemmas.* 5th ed. New York: Holt, Rinehart and Winston, 1989.

Spero, Joan Edelman. *The Politics of International Economic Relations.* 2nd ed. New York: St. Martin's Press, 1981.

Steel, J. Valerie, ed. *Washington Representatives 1999.* Washington, DC: Columbia Books, Inc., 1999.

Steger, Manfred B. *Globalism.* Lanham, MD: Rowman & Littlefield Publishers, Inc., 2002.

Steinberg, James. "Counterterrorism." *Brookings Review* 20 (Summer 2002): 4–7.

Steinbrunner, John D. "Nuclear Decapitation." *Foreign Policy* 45 (Winter 1981–1982): 1628.

Stiglitz, Joseph E. *Globalization and Its Discontents.* New York: W. W. Norton and Company, 2002.

Stillman, Edmund, and William Pfaff. *Power and Impotence: The Failure of America's Foreign Policy.* New York: Vintage Books, 1966.

Stockton, Paul. "Beyond Micromanagement: Congressional Budgeting for a

Post-Cold War Military." *Political Science Quarterly* 110 (Summer 1995): 233–259.

———. "Congress and U.S. Military Policy Beyond the Cold War." In *Congress Resurgent: Foreign and Defense Policy on Capitol Hill,* Randall B. Ripley and James M. Lindsay, eds. Ann Arbor: The University of Michigan Press, 1993.

Stoessinger, John G. *Crusaders and Pragmatists.* 2nd ed. New York: W. W. Norton and Company, 1985.

———. *Henry Kissinger: The Anguish of Power.* New York: W. W. Norton and Company, 1976.

———. *Nations in Darkness: China, Russia, and America.* 3rd ed. New York: Random House, 1978.

———. *Why Nations Go To War.* 5th ed. New York: St. Martin's Press, 1990.

Stokes, Bruce, and Pat Choate. *Democratizing U.S. Trade Policy.* New York: Council on Foreign Relations, Inc., 2001.

Story, Dale. "Trade Politics in the Third World: A Case Study of the Mexican GATT Decision." *International Organization* 36 (Autumn 1982): 767–794.

Strobel, Warren P. *Late-Breaking Foreign Policy.* Washington, DC: United States Institute of Peace Press, 1997.

Stubbing, Richard A., with Richard A. Mendel. *The Defense Game: An Insider Explores the Astonishing Realities of America's Defense Establishment.* New York: Harper and Row, 1986.

Sundquist, James L. *The Decline and Resurgence of Congress.* Washington, DC: The Brookings Institution, 1981.

Talbott, Strobe. "Buildup and Breakdown." In *America and the World 1983,* William P. Bundy, ed. New York: Pergamon Press,1984.

———. *Deadly Gambits: The Reagan Administration and the Stalemate in Nuclear Arms Control.* New York: Vintage Books, 1985.

———. "Globalization and Diplomacy: The View From Foggy Bottom," In *The Domestic Sources of American Foreign Policy: Insights and Evidence.* 4th ed., Eugene R. Wittkopf and James M.

McCormick, eds. Lanham, MD: Rowman & Littlefield Publishers, Inc., 2004.

Tananbaum, Duane. *The Bricker Amendment Controversy: A Test of Eisenhower's Political Leadership.* Ithaca, NY, and London: Cornell University Press, 1988.

Terhune, Kenneth W. "From National Character to National Behavior: A Reformulation." *Journal of Conflict Resolution* 14 (June 1970): 203–264.

Towell, Pat. "Armed Services: Rep. Bob Stump of Arizona," *CQ Weekly* (January 6, 2001): 14

———. "Armed Services: Missile Defense Skeptic." *CQ Weekly* (May 26, 2001): 1221.

Tower, John G. "Congress Versus the President: The Formulation and Implementation of American Foreign Policy." *Foreign Affairs* 60 (Winter 1981–1982): 229–246.

Treaties and Other International Agreements: The Role of the United States, Washington, DC: U.S. Government Printing Office, January 2001.

Treverton, Gregory F. "Intelligence: Welcome to the American Government." In *A Question of Balance,* Thomas E. Mann, ed. Washington, DC: The Brookings Institution, 1990.

Trice, Robert H. "Congress and the Arab-Israeli Conflict: Support for Israel in the U.S. Senate, 1970–1973." *Political Science Quarterly* 92 (Fall 1977): 443–463.

———. "Domestic Interest Groups and the Arab-Israeli Conflict: A Behavioral Analysis." In *Ethnicity and U.S. Foreign Policy.* Rev. ed., Abdul Aziz Said, ed. New York: Praeger, 1981.

Trout, B. Thomas. "Rhetoric Revisited: Political Legitimation and the Cold War." *International Studies Quarterly* 19 (September 1975): 251–284.

Truman, Harry S. *Year of Decision.* New York: Doubleday & Co., Inc., 1955.

Tucker, Robert. "America in Decline: The Foreign Policy of 'Maturity.'" In *America and the World 1979,* William P. Bundy, ed. New York: Pergamon Press, 1980.

———, and David C. Hendrickson. "Thomas Jefferson and American Foreign Policy." *Foreign Affairs* 69 (Spring 1990): 135–156.

Turner, Stansfield. *Secrecy and Democracy: The CIA in Transition*. Boston: Houghton Mifflin Company, 1985.

United States Department of State. *State 2000: A New Model for Managing Foreign Affairs*. Washington, DC: U.S. Department of State, January 1993.

U.S. Bureau of the Census. *Statistical Abstract of the United States: 2002*. Washington, DC, 2002.

U.S. Department of State. "Operation Enduring Freedom Overview." October 1, 2001, online. Available: http://www.state.gov/s/ct/rls/fs/2001/5194.htm.

———, Office of the Historian. "The United States and the Global Coalition Against Terrorism, September–December 2001: A Chronology." December 31, 2001, online. Available: http://www.state.gov/r/pa/ho/pubs/fs/5889.htm.

U.S. Embassy Islamabad. "Fact Sheet: Coalition Contributions to the War on Terrorism." May 25, 2002, online. Available: http://usembassy.state.gov/posts/pk1/wwwh02052502.html.

Uslaner, Eric. "All Politics Are Global: Interest Groups and the Making of Foreign Policy." In *Interest Group Politics*, Allan J. Cigler and Burdett A. Loomis, eds. Washington, DC: CQ Press, 1995.

Varg, Paul A. *Foreign Policies of the Founding Fathers*. East Lansing: Michigan State University, 1963.

Viguerie, Richard A. *The New Right: We're Ready to Lead*. Falls Church, VA: The Viguerie Company, 1981.

Waller, Douglas C. *Congress and the Nuclear Freeze: An Inside Look at the Politics of a Mass Movement*. Amherst: University of Massachusetts Press, 1987.

Walt, Stephen M. "Two Cheers for Clinton's Foreign Policy." *Foreign Affairs* 79 (March/April 2000): 63–79.

Walters, Robert W. "African-American Influence on U.S. Foreign Policy Toward South Africa." In *Ethnic Groups and U.S. Foreign Policy*, Mohammed E. Ahrari, ed. New York: Greenwood Press, 1987.

The Washington Lobby. 4th ed. Washington, DC: Congressional Quarterly, Inc., 1982.

Weiner, Tim, David Johnston, and Neil A. Lewis. *Betrayal: The Story of Aldrich Ames, An American Spy*. New York: Random House, 1995.

Westphal, Albert C. V. *The House Committee on Foreign Affairs*. New York: Columbia University Press, 1942.

Whalen, Charles W., Jr. *The House and Foreign Policy: The Irony of Congressional Reform*. Chapel Hill: The University of North Carolina Press, 1982.

Whiting, Allen S. *China Crosses the Yalu*. Stanford, CA: Stanford University Press, 1960.

Wiarda, Howard J. *Foreign Policy Without Illusion*. Glenview, IL: Scott, Foresman/Little, Brown Higher Education, 1990.

Wildavsky, Aaron. "The Two Presidencies." *Transaction* 3 (December 1966): 7–14.

Willetts, Peter. *The Non-Aligned Movement: The Origins of a Third World Alliance*. London: Frances Pinter, Ltd., 1979.

Willrich, Mason, and John B. Rhinelander, eds. *SALT: The Moscow Agreements and Beyond*. New York: The Free Press, 1974.

Windsor, Philip. "America's Moral Confusions: Separating the Should from the Good." *Foreign Policy* 13 (Winter 1973–1974): 139–153.

Winham, Gilbert. "Developing Theories of Foreign Policy Making: A Case Study for Foreign Aid." *The Journal of Politics* 32 (February 1970): 41–70.

Wise, David. *Nightmover: How Aldrich Ames Sold the CIA to the KGB for $4.6 Million*. New York: HarperCollins, 1995.

Wiseman, Henry, and Alastair M. Taylor. *From Rhodesia to Zimbabwe: The Politics of Transition*. New York: Pergamon Press, 1981.

Wittkopf, Eugene R. "Elites and Masses: Constancy and Change in Public

Attitudes Toward America's World Role." Paper delivered at the Annual Meeting of the Southern Political Science Association, Birmingham, Alabama, November 3–5, 1983.

———. *Faces of Internationalism: Public Opinion and American Foreign Policy.* Durham, NC: Duke University Press, 1990.

———. "Faces of Internationalism in a Transitional Environment." *Journal of Conflict Resolution* 38 (September 1994): 376–401.

———. "Public Attitudes Toward American Foreign Policy in the Post-Vietnam Decade." Paper delivered at the Annual Meeting of the International Studies Association, March 27–31, 1984.

———. "What Americans Really Think About Foreign Policy." *The Washington Quarterly* 19 (Summer 1996): 91–106.

———. Charles W. Kegley, Jr., and James M. Scott. *American Foreign Policy: Pattern and Process.* 6th ed. Belmont, CA: Wadsworth, 2003.

———. and Michael A. Maggiotto. "Elites and Masses. A Comparative Analysis of Attitudes Toward America's World Role." *The Journal of Politics* 45 (May 1983): 303–334.

———. and James M. McCormick. "The Cold War Consensus: Did It Exist?" *Polity* 22 (Summer 1990): 627–653.

———. "The Domestic Politics of Contra Aid: Pubic Opinion, Congress, and the President." In *Public Opinion in U.S. Foreign Policy: The Controversy over Contra Aid,* Richard Sobel, ed. Lanham, MD: Rowman & Littlefield Publishers, Inc., 1993.

———. *The Domestic Sources of American Foreign Policy: Insights and Evidence.* 3rd ed. Lanham, MD: Rowman & Littlefield Publishers, Inc., 1999.

———. *The Domestic Sources of American Foreign Policy: Insights and Evidence.* 4th ed. Lanham, MD: Rowman & Littlefield Publishers, Inc., 2004.

Woodward, Bob. *Bush at War.* New York: Simon & Schuster, 2002.

———. *Veil: The Secret Wars of the CIA, 1981–1987.* New York: Pocket Books, 1987.

Wormuth, Francis D. "Presidential Wars: The Convenience of 'Precedent.'" In *Problems of American Foreign Policy.* 2nd ed. Martin B. Hickman, ed. Beverly Hills: Glencoe Press, 1975.

Yankelovich, Daniel. "Farewell to 'President Knows Best.'" In *America and the World 1978,* William P. Bundy, ed. New York: Pergamon Press, 1979.

Yarmolinsky, Adam. *The Military Establishment: Its Impact on American Society.* New York: Harper and Row, 1971.

Yergin, Daniel. *Shattered Peace. The Origins of the Cold War and the National Security State.* Boston: Houghton Mifflin Company, 1977.

Zagoria, Donald S. *The Sino-Soviet Conflict 1956–1961.* Princeton, NJ: Princeton University Press, 1962.

Zakaria, Fareed. *From Wealth to Power: The Unusual Origins of America's World Role.* Princeton, NJ: Princeton University Press, 1998.

Zelikow, Philip D. "The United States and the Use of Force: A Historical Summary." In *Democracy, Strategy, and Vietnam,* George K. Osborn, Asa A. Clark IV, Daniel J. Kaufman, and Douglas E. Lute, eds. Lexington, MA: D. C. Heath and Company, 1987.

Ziegler, L. Harmon, and G. Wayne Peak. *Interest Groups in American Society.* 2nd ed. Englewood Cliffs, NJ: Prentice-Hall, Inc., 1972.

Name Index

Subject Index